**VOICES
OF A
NATION**

VOICES OF A NATION

A HISTORY OF MEDIA IN THE UNITED STATES

Jean Folkerts
Mount Vernon College

Dwight L. Teeter, Jr.
University of Wisconsin, Milwaukee

MACMILLAN PUBLISHING COMPANY

NEW YORK

FOR
LEROY TOWNS
AND
TISH TEETER

Freedom to agree with prevailing opinions is no test of freedom. It is when hated opinions are uttered that the existence — or absence — of freedom will be found. It should be kept in mind that freedom to move about without government permission and to speak or write one's mind — including criticizing government or government officials — is not the usual condition, either in world history or in late twentieth century geopolitics. Philosopher Eric Hoffer has taken issue with Rousseau's eighteenth century dictum: "Man is born free, and everywhere he is in chains." The mid-twentieth century gave Hoffer the perspective to suggest that mankind is born in chains, and that freedom is our most precious achievement. For those who would be free, there is a hard duty to sometimes take a chance, to stand on principle, to take the risk of speaking out.

Copyright © 1989 by Macmillan Publishing Company, a division of Macmillan, Inc.

Printed in the United States of America

All rights reserved. No part of this book may be reproduced or transmitted in any form or by any means, electronic or mechanical, including photocopying, recording, or any information storage and retrieval system, without permission in writing from the Publisher.

Macmillan Publishing Company
866 Third Avenue, New York, New York 10022

Collier Macmillan Canada, Inc.

Library of Congress Cataloging-in-Publication Data

Folkerts, Jean.
   Voices of a nation.

   Includes index.
   1. Mass media—United States—History.
I. Teeter, Dwight L. II. Title.
P92.U5F58 1989   302.2'3   88-9231
ISBN 0-02-419030-6

Photo facing the title page is reproduced courtesy of the Library of Congress Collection.

PREFACE

Voices of a Nation was written for professors and students studying mass media history of the United States, for journalists interested in the history of their profession, and for others who want to know more about how the media have become integrated into the political, economic, and social systems of the United States. *Voices* is divided into four chronological parts, with short introductory essays for each part, designed to explore thematically the developments of each time period.

Numerous research articles and monographs written by scholars who have mined voluminous files of newspapers, conducted surveys and completed meticulous content analyses form the bibliographic base that enabled us to write an analytical synthesis of the history of U.S. media. We express our gratitude to those authors, who often receive little student or public recognition, and hope that *Voices* will stimulate further appreciation of their work.

This book addresses the media as a complex societal and cultural institution—a product of many voices. It views these voices within a social, political, and economic framework and considers the impact of owners, audiences, journalists, technology, and government. Within this framework, the voices of blacks, women, immigrants, and other minorities speak convincingly, as do the voices of media corporations that produce metropolitan dailies, mass circulation magazines, and television news and entertainment.

Significant themes are examined within contemporary political and historical contexts. *Voices* examines the use of varying technologies by diverse groups and emphasizes cultural aspects of technological innovation. Media are analyzed as business institutions from colonial days when groups of printers first formed networks to share supplies and contacts, to the late twentieth century when media organizations began to issue shares on the stock exchange. Within that context the development of advertising achieves significance. *Voices* analyzes the relationship of the media to government, recognizing that while government has, particularly in times of crisis, imposed censorship, media often have sought, and won, cooperation, and have devised mutually powerful roles with government through regulation. As journalists and journalism professors, the authors believe that freedom of speech and press must be fought for by each successive generation and cannot be permanently achieved.

Throughout this analysis individuals also retain distinction. Particular owners are discussed as examples of specific developments, journalists and public relations practitioners are treated as significant contributors to a process of information, and audiences are seen as changing factors in the interplay of various media. Throughout, the authors hope to convey the excitement of the role of media in a modernizing society, the conflicts between traditional values and commercial development, the exuberance with which editors confronted the diversity of city life, and the seriousness with which Native Americans, suffragists, blacks, immigrants, and agrarian radicals fought for increased recognition.

Both authors thank their teachers and their students, whose insights made this book possible. Neither the teachers nor the students, however, should be held accountable for any shortcomings in this book. Errors of commission or omission may be ascribed solely to Jean Folkerts and Dwight Teeter.

Many colleagues and friends contributed to the writing of this book, either by reviewing portions of the manuscript or by sharing their knowledge, their time, and their support. Among those are Owen V. Johnson, Indiana University; James L. Baughman, University of Wisconsin-Madison; Donald Shaw, University of North Carolina at Chapel Hill; Jeffery A. Smith, University of Iowa; Judith Paterson, the University of Maryland; Terry Hynes, University of California at Fullerton; Patrick S. Washburn, Ohio University; Robert Hudson, Michigan State University; Mary Minners, Mount Vernon College; Michele Berg, Topeka, Kansas; Carolyn Grote, Berkeley, California; Stephen Lacy, Michigan State University; and Anthony Scinta,

PREFACE

Alexandria, Virginia. A special thanks goes to Owen V. Johnson, who provided bibliographic information and a critical review, generously sharing his superb scholarship in a most helpful way.

Jean Folkerts also would like to acknowledge Rita Napier, Professor of History at the University of Kansas, for her challenging but supportive stance as a dissertation adviser and mentor. Other colleagues who have been particularly helpful over the years include Del Brinkman and Norman Yetman at the University of Kansas; the late Jack Backer; Roberta Applegate and Robert Bontrager of Kansas State University; and Robert Heywood of Washburn University. Elaine Prostak Berland, Webster College, also provided insightful critiques on the 1920s, as well as a deep and abiding faith that this project would succeed. Folkerts thanks her husband, Leroy Towns, for his love and for sharing his ability as an editor, and her parents, Betty and Leonard Folkerts. She also thanks her children, Sean Lange and Jenny Towns.

Dwight Teeter thanks his wife, Tish, for her support and editorial help. He acknowledges a special debt to his one-time graduate adviser, his coauthor, and all-time friend, Professor Emeritus Harold L. Nelson of the University of Wisconsin-Madison. Another historian's voice that has remained with Teeter through the years is that of the late Professor Merrill Jensen of the University of Wisconsin-Madison. Thanks also go to Susan Teeter, who provided editorial help, and to a splendid historian who is also a law professor, David A. Anderson of the University of Texas at Austin. Other colleagues who have helped Teeter include Hillier Krieghbaum; William E. Ames, Don R. Pember, Roger A. Simpson, and Gerald Baldasty at the University of Washington; and Professors John D. Stevens, University of Michigan; Dean MaryAnn Yodelis Smith, University of Minnesota; and Bill F. Chamberlin, University of Florida.

The authors also thank Lucy Cocke, Anne Emery, Ruth Duvall and Valerie St. Pierre of Eckles Library at Mount Vernon College. Other library staffs also have contributed, including those of the periodical reading room, the photo and copyright divisions of the Library of Congress; Professor Roy Mersky, law librarian at the University of Texas at Austin; Professor William C. Roselle, Librarian, University of Wisconsin-Milwaukee; and George A. Talbot, Myrna Williamson, and Christine I. Schelshorn of the iconography collections of the State Historical Society of Wisconsin. Generous help also was received from the public relations department of the *Chicago*

PREFACE

Tribune through the good offices of Jeffrey D. Bierig, from Gloria Gilbert of the *Washington Post,* and from Terry Everette at WJLA-TV. Also helpful in the photography effort were John Klein of the *Milwaukee Journal*'s picture desk and Howard Fibich, deputy managing editor for news of that paper. Mount Vernon College provided two summer research grants for Jean Folkerts which substantially contributed to the completion of the manuscript. And finally, the authors would like to thank Julie Levin Alexander of the Macmillan Publishing Company for fulfilling her role as editor with grace and competence.

J. F.
D. L. T., Jr.

Contents

Preface   v

PART 1   Early America   1

CHAPTER 1
CROSSING THE ATLANTIC   3

The Printing Revolution   5
Printing in England   8
Colonial Beginnings   11
Colonial Newspapers   15
Birthed in Boston   17
Conclusion   25

CHAPTER 2
COMMERCIAL AND POLITICAL DEVELOPMENT   29

Commercial Development   31
Political Development   40
After Zenger   45
Conclusion   45

CHAPTER 3
TIMES THAT TRIED MEN'S SOULS   49

Colonial Resistance to Economic Policy   50
Economic Resistance Turns Political   52
News of Congress and of War   57

Newspapers for a Continent 68
Conclusion 75

CHAPTER 4
FROM REVOLUTION TO CONSTITUTION 79

Constitutional Politics 82
A Printer for the Times 87
The Developing Daily 90
Delivering the News 92
Newspapers as Commercial Ventures 93
Conclusion 95

PART 2 Expansion and Conflict 99

CHAPTER 5
A NEW NATION 101

A Partisan Press 104
Alien and Sedition Acts of 1798 110
Jeffersonian Democracy 115
The Election of 1824 121
Magazines and Some Questions about Audience 123
Conclusion 124

CHAPTER 6
PENNY PAPERS IN THE METROPOLIS 129

Characteristics of the Penny Press 131
The New York Leaders 134
Reasons for Development 144
Conclusion 149

CHAPTER 7
WESTWARD HO! 153

The Movement Westward 154
Transportation and Communication 157
Covering the Mexican War 163
Newspapers on the Frontier 163
Conclusion 175

CHAPTER 8
SECTIONAL CONFLICT AND ABOLITIONIST AGITATION 179

New Developments in the Penny Press 181
Abolitionist Press 187

The Black Press 195
Slavery's Defenders 198
Conclusion 199

CHAPTER 9
COVERING THE CIVIL WAR: CORRESPONDENTS AND CENSORSHIP 203

Press in the North 205
The Confederate Press 208
Correspondents 210
Censorship in the North 213
Censorship in the South 215
Photography and Pictorial Illustration 217
Conclusion 220

PART 3 Modernization and Reform 225

CHAPTER 10
GROWTH AND REUNIFICATION 229

Reconstruction 230
Manufacturing and Advertising 234
Newspapers after the Civil War 237
The Associated Press 244
Editors of the Times 245
Conclusion 251

CHAPTER 11
THE PRESS AND MODERNIZATION 255

New Styles and Greater Numbers 259
Sensation at Its Height 265
Covering the Spanish-American War 274
Information as a Goal 278
Reporters and Editors 281
Conclusion 284

CHAPTER 12
REFORM IS MY RELIGION 289

The Suffragist Press 291
Black Press after the Civil War 295
Agrarian Press 297
Ethnic Press 303
Conclusion 305

CHAPTER 13
THE MUCK AT OUR FEET 309

Quality Monthlies 310
General Interest and Women's Magazines 318
Muckraking 322
Conclusion 332

CHAPTER 14
THE GREAT WAR 337

General Characteristics 339
World War I 344
Media Reaction to the War 355
On the Front 362
The Black Press during and after the War 363
Conclusion 366

PART 4 Media in a Modern World 371

CHAPTER 15
THE ROARING TWENTIES: THE MYTHICAL DECADE 373

Tabloids 375
The 1920s Newspaper 376
Development of Public Relations 379
Advertising 381
Radio 387
Going to the Movies 393
Conclusion 397

CHAPTER 16
DEPRESSION AND DISILLUSION 403

The Newspaper Industry 406
Reporters and Editors 406
Development of Interpretation 409
Electronic Media 415
The President and the Press 422
Individuals, Innovation, and Criticism 425
Conclusion 438

CHAPTER 17
WAR AND PROSPERITY 443

Covering the War 445
Depictions of War 450

Censorship 454
Commission on Freedom of the Press 464
The Campaign for International Freedom of the Press 466
Prosperity at War's End 467
Conclusion 468

CHAPTER 18
TECHNOLOGICAL ADVANCEMENT AMIDST A COLD WAR 473

Television Technology Comes of Age 477
The Press and Government 487
Criticism and Alternatives 494
Conclusion 496

CHAPTER 19
AFFLUENCE AND ACTIVISM 499

Changes in the Newsroom 502
Financial Status and Corporate Development 503
Covering Vietnam 512
Covering the Civil Rights Movement 517
The Language of Participant Journalism 520
Magazines 525
Conclusion 526

CHAPTER 20
TROUBLES IN PARADISE 531

"Watergate" and the News Media 534
Efforts to Restore Credibility 538
Corporate and Public Ownership 540
Deregulation 548
Changing News Agenda 549
Magazines 551
UPI's Continuing Troubles 553
Conclusion 555
Index 559

This reproduction of an engraving by Philip Galle from Jan Van Der Straet's *Nova Reperta* depicts a sixteenth-century book printing shop. (Library of Congress Collection)

PART 1

EARLY

AMERICA

When John Campbell began his handwritten newspaper in Boston in 1700, he began an enterprise that during the colonial period developed into an institution characterized by a network of printers scattered throughout the colonies and by a complex relationship between printers, government, and the socioeconomic system.

The technology for such an enterprise was developed in the fifteenth century when Gutenberg invented movable type, paving the way for a transition from an oral and scribal culture to a culture distinguished by print, shared information, and facts that could be validated. Newspapers, first developed on the continent of Europe and then in England, became common carriers of information and created bonds of shared knowledge between the mother country and the Atlantic colonies.

From the beginning, the press was intricately connected to government. Licensing systems developed in England that precluded criticism of government as "seditious libel" were transported to the New World. Some printers, reluctant in the early years to become involved in local controversial politics, focused on foreign news. But as the colonies grew stronger and more independent, printers spoke more freely on political issues and began to champion freedom of the press as a philosophical tenet.

Government and the press also were interrelated by the economics of distribution and the importance of postal legislation. The earliest newspapers were started by postmasters, who had free access to the mails. Later editors helped start postal systems in order to expand their distribution. Distribution of newspapers outside the major urban centers occurred primarily along major trade routes.

At least by the 1750s, politicians of opposing sides confronted the issues of civil liberties, including freedom of the press. Libertarians argued the necessity of protecting printers not only from government, but from popular majorities as well.

The development of the press was not tied solely to governmental interaction, but also was part of an entrepreneurial enterprise. Printers, who often were shopkeepers and booksellers before they were publishers, established ties through family and friendship networks. These ties were important in the distribution of supplies, as well as of newspapers, and also because family or professional ties often could earn printers government printing contracts. More importantly, the existence of a network of printers with shared values suggests that one should examine how those shared values are reflected in the press.

Editors recruited their audiences, or subscribers, from the colonial elite and from the merchants needing information from abroad. The small urban populations of early colonial days supported few newspapers. As these newspapers expanded and became involved with the ideology of revolution and espoused republican values, the audience broadened to include more shopkeepers and artisans.

By the time the Constitution was ratified in 1788, the newspaper press had established itself as a profitable enterprise with an expanding audience and as an institution intricately connected with the new government it had participated in forming.

CHAPTER · 1

CROSSING THE ATLANTIC

Methinks we see already that happy time when we shall surpass the Asiaticians in civility, the Jews in religion, the Greeks in philosophy, the Egyptians in geometry, the Phoenicians in arithmetic, and the Chaldeans in astrology. O happy Virginia.—Written by a student at the 1699 May Day exercises at the College of William and Mary.

Virginians were similar to other American colonists in boldly believing that their society would surpass those that had gone before, but the student orator at the May Day exercises at the College of William and Mary also noted a debt to the past. The press of the new colonies, like the other institutions of their societies, did not spring virginally from the colonial earth in the late seventeenth century, but traced its origins to European cultural, societal, and technological developments.

Although printing techniques developed in Egypt as early as 1700 B.C., it was a European printing revolution in the fifteenth century that paved the way for a shift from an oral and scribal transmission of culture to a printed culture. This technological revolution resulted in the appearance of new relationships among elites, new occupational groups, new trade networks and new markets for printed matter. The ability to produce many simultaneous copies of a printed work increased the accuracy, speed, and penetration with which ideas could be communicated. Printing therefore affected nonelite groups—persons who before lacked the materials from which to learn to read, and elites—those literate individuals who still had scant access to the rare and carefully hand-copied books available in the society. Such technological change altered the conditions under which printed matter could be produced, as well as the audiences available for consuming it.[1] The development of newspapers in the various countries of Europe during the seventeenth and eighteenth centuries, often despite strict governmental controls, extended the printing revolution. Historian Ian Steele described newspapers as "the most powerful and extensive public communications innovation . . . within the English Atlantic empire between 1675 and 1740." These papers made news available to a wide audience and reduced the distortions of information created by passing stories on by word-of-mouth.[2]

Newspapers in England multiplied during the Civil War of the 1640s and again in the early 1680s, when no licensing act was in effect. After 1701, provincial and colonial newspapers developed to compete with and supplement the London press. By 1739, thirteen newspapers were being published in English America. Relying heavily on news transported from England, these newspapers carried news of the empire to which the colonies belonged and enabled colonists to remain informed about world events that affected their economic, social, and political lives. Publishing English and continental news, as well as some intercolonial information, the newspapers helped to build a sense of community among the heterogeneous and often intolerant colonial population and provided "a vernacular—a common language in both words and pictures"—to allow colonists to express and share political interests.[3] By the mid-1730s, Boston, a major colonial harbor, was second only to London in the number of newspapers produced, with local and regional markets large enough to support a newspaper enterprise. Boston's harbor, with access to news from London, made the city a natural center of newspaper development. Colonial newspapers imitated each other and English newspapers, cautiously avoided political criticism, and

Chapter 1 **Crossing the Atlantic**

cultivated little local identity during the early years. Although the press sometimes profited by government printing contracts, various factions of colonial governments tolerated little criticism, and ventures into local politics brought harassment to colonial editors.

THE PRINTING REVOLUTION

Although a variety of printing techniques, including some forms of movable type, were developed in Egypt and other areas of the Mediterranean as early as 1700 B.C., it was Marco Polo, an Italian adventurer, who in A.D. 1295 first brought word to Europe about printing techniques developed by the Chinese. In South America, the Aztecs hung colored paper banners in the main public square of the capital to spread the news. Although these developments were significant in expanding communication within cultures, it was not until the fifteenth century and the invention of movable type in Germany that printing underwent a revolution.

In a print shop in Mainz, Germany, Johann Gutenberg invented movable type. Although today Gutenberg is given credit for his innovation, at the time he might have been classified as the first victim of a capitalistic venture in publishing. Gutenberg, who had used woodcuts for printing pictures, planned to carve letters from wood and create movable letters. Woodcuts employed ridges that formed the lines of the picture, which then were coated with ink and laid flat on parchment to produce a rough print.

Needing money to accomplish this task, Gutenberg borrowed it from a merchant who saw value in the printer's idea. With the money Gutenberg hired a skilled worker who suggested that wood would produce blurry letters and that metal might be a better medium with which to work. Once a metal mold had been made, the letter could be cast from metal as many times as required. Gutenberg and his worker, Peter Schoeffer, produced a copy of the Bible by 1455, but just as it was ready for sale his financier demanded that Gutenberg repay his loan. Since he could not, the merchant commandeered

The type of press used by Gutenberg. (Library of Congress Collection)

Chapter 1 **Crossing the Atlantic**

his printing press and his metalworker. Gutenberg borrowed money from a friend and built another press, but it took most of his profit to pay back his original loan and he never again achieved financial independence.[4] However, Gutenberg's invention achieved much more notoriety than he did, and Peter Schoeffer established an important printing business in Mainz.

Prior to Gutenberg's invention, European cultures were primarily oral cultures, or scribal cultures.[5] For centuries, monks in monasteries or lay copyists, primarily in university towns, reproduced manuscripts for distribution among a select group of elites. Hand copying each manuscript required inordinate amounts of time and created possibilities for shifts and changes within the manuscript. Because manuscripts were rare and expensive, even members of the educated classes often relied on teachers reading aloud from a single book, rather than reading their own copies. This situation changed dramatically after 1450, when early printed editions ranged from 200 to 1,000 copies and printers' workshops began to appear in every important city in Europe.

The printing revolution affected social relationships, as formerly isolated priests and printers began to work with university professors, and as both groups had contact with metalworkers and mechanics. Careful and competent printer-merchants began to achieve prestigious positions in the cities. Such printers worked hard to remain on good terms with officials, as well as to secure supplies and labor. The printer's shop became a meeting place and educational center within the European town. Soon printers began searching for new markets for their products, printing handbills, circulars and sales catalogs advertising their products, which they sent to neighboring countries.

The ability to reproduce a scientific, technical, or religious manuscript in exact form and in many copies enabled the scholarly community to begin to eliminate errors that had persisted through generations as books were copied and recopied. Further, the scholar no longer was required to be a traveler, moving from book collection to book collection, but could remain at home. Rather than intensively studying a single text, the scholar was able to compare texts. More importantly, the ability to preserve information by circulating copies of a text gradually led to increased "democratization" of knowledge, or the decentralization of information, and ultimately became the basis for enlightenment and national thought.[6] What once might have remained local, such as a slight change in church liturgy or social thought, now was dispersed regionally, nationally, and internationally.[7] The best village storytellers were no longer those who manufactured or remembered the tales of yore, but the literate men who passed on orally what they had read. Thus the "popular culture" of medieval romances became commonly available to villagers long before it was widely available in published form in the nineteenth century.[8]

PART 1   EARLY AMERICA

PRINTING IN ENGLAND

William Caxton, the first printer in England, set up a press at Westminster about 1476, on which he published nearly 100 books. Caxton enjoyed royal patronage and worked in a time when the press had not yet become controversial. Printing, however, soon became a dangerous occupation in England, when Henry VIII, who assumed the throne in 1509, struggled with the pope to determine who would control the destiny of England. Although news accounts of single events appeared in parts of Europe during the late 1400s and early 1500s, the king closely controlled publication in England and it was not until the seventeenth century that such accounts were published in England.

As a young man, Henry VIII was content to remain subordinate to the Catholic Church and to the pope, who held supremacy not only in religious affairs but also in political life. When Henry first challenged the church by requesting a divorce from his first wife, Catherine of Aragon, he asserted the power of state—national government—over the power of the pope. The average Englishman, who no doubt sympathized with the wife overthrown by the upstart mistress Anne Boleyn, nevertheless supported the overthrow of papal domination that governed England according to Italian, Spanish, and Imperial standards. Thus, popular support swung with the king.

The Reformation Parliament (1529–1536) through legislation destroyed the monasteries that remained loyal to the pope and established Henry VIII as the supreme head of England. Henry, however, did not reject many of the tenets of Catholicism and continued persecuting Protestants. To maintain his control, Henry imposed prior restraint, a system of prepublication censorship that has had many imitators over the years. When publications eluded the network of censors, Henry's government punished those responsible for "seditious libel." Such punishment could be both deadly and unutterably cruel. In 1529, Henry published a list of prohibited books, and on Christmas Day of 1534, he ordered printers to secure royal permission to operate.

Henry VIII's orders reinforced the concept of sedition, already present in English law, and introduced the concept of prior restraint—two important concepts that remain controversial in today's legal world. Starting in 1542, the kings' advisors, the Privy Council, arrested individuals for sedition, or criticism of the government, prevented some individuals from publishing, and required, in essence, permission or a license to operate.

Despite these controls, printing gained a foothold in England. One-third of the books published in sixteenth-century England were printed outside the official channels.[9] With the overthrow of papal domination, clerical lands were seized and sold to noblemen. Many of these gentlemen's sons replaced the abbots who had studied at Oxford and Cambridge, thus promoting an educated commercial class as well as the study and questioning of religious dogma. The Bible, printed in English, circulated freely in parish churches. Parishioners were able to read for themselves and no longer relied as intensely on clerical interpretation. Thus, under Henry VIII England established national independence and freedom of religious inquiry. These two concepts would color the colonists' view of English domination of their colonial world.

When Queen Mary succeeded Henry VIII, subjugated England to Spain through marriage, and attempted to reinstate papal authority, conflict reigned supreme. The queen in 1557 formalized the licensing procedure by establishing the Stationers Company, an organization of printers and dealers in books, in an attempt to stop the growth of protestantism. Only select printers were allowed to belong to the Stationers, and therefore to print, and the company controlled its own members, ordering searches and seizures of unauthorized works.

Throughout the sixteenth century, licensing and prior restraint were common. Under Queen Elizabeth all new works had to be submitted before publication for clearance by the queen or another authority. During the early years of her reign, Queen Elizabeth allowed both religions to flourish, but when the pope excommunicated her in 1570 and invaded Ireland with his own troops, Catholics were hanged for treason and Puritans persecuted. Illegal printers forfeited books, binders were fined a substantial amount of up to a day's pay per book, and convicted printers served three months in jail and were banned from future printing. The Court of the Star Chamber in 1570 arrested defendants on whim or mere suspicion. Defendants were examined in private, giving the government the right to arrest secretly, confine, and try a printer. If a defendant refused to talk before the Star Chamber, guilt was assumed and the person imprisoned and punished.

Nevertheless, Elizabeth was a popular queen, and she allowed the use of the printing press to expand. Music and literature were printed and disseminated, and the Bible and Anglican Prayer Book circulated freely. Much of the English population, however, resented her attempt to make Anglicanism a state religion and resisted the curbs on their religious freedom.

NEWSPAPERS IN ENGLAND

The development of the newspaper in English was opposed by James I and Charles I, who ruled England from 1603 to 1649. The first weekly news sheet, *The Corrant out of Italy, Germany, &c,* was published in English in Amsterdam in 1620, but James I soon gained a Dutch ban on exports of English-language newspapers. He reminded his subjects of existing controls on the press and imprisoned English publishers for attempting to print without governmental approval. Despite the threat of the Star Chamber, broadsheet ballads printed

> **THE POWER OF TRUTH**
>
> And though all the winds of doctrine were let loose to play upon the earth, so truth be in the field, we do injuriously by licensing and prohibiting to misdoubt her strength. Let her and falsehood grapple; who ever knew truth put to the worse, in a free and open encounter?
>
> SOURCE. Milton's *Areopagitica*

news of crimes, catastrophes, and scandals. Cautiously printing no local news, Nathaniel Butter and his associates issued news books from 1621 to 1642. *The Continuation of Our Weekly News* appeared at least twenty-three times. Circulation probably averaged about 250 to 500 copies.[10]

During the early 1640s, at the beginning of the English Civil War, newspapers flourished in London until Parliament began to exert greater control later in the decade. By 1644, about 6,000 copies of a dozen newspapers in London circulated to the city's residents, and John Milton, a Puritan, took advantage of the short-lived open political climate to write *Areopagitica,* a plea for a free press. "Give me the liberty to know, to utter, and to argue freely according to conscience, above all liberties," he wrote. Milton addressed his plea to Parliament, and argued that licensing of the press restricted the dissemination of truth. Milton's argument, far from truly liberal, was made within the context of his Protestant religion. He did not tolerate freedom of expression for Catholic or atheistic ideas. In 1651, serving as secretary to the commonwealth's Council of State, Milton was an official licenser for the Puritans.[11]

Two years after the restoration of the monarchy in 1660, Parliament passed a licensing act that allowed only twenty master printers in the kingdom, concentrated them in London, and put them under the control of the secretaries of state. Based on the theory that freedom to print was dangerous to the king and a threat to "faith, loyalty and morality," the act limited both the right and the ability to print.[12] When the licensing act lapsed in 1679, Charles II controlled the press through executive order, and James II managed to get Parliament to revive the act in 1685. Nevertheless, following the Glorious Revolution of 1688–1689, licensing was unpopular and regarded as ineffective. In 1695, due less to a public outcry for freedom of the press than to Parliament's belief that the existing system did not work sufficiently to control the press, the licensing act was not renewed. Ultimately, increased volume of printing made controls more difficult. Ministers, responding to William III's attempt to involve both Whigs and Tories in the ministries, found it difficult to know what to censor. From 1693 to 1712, Parliament made a number of attempts to redesign and enact a licensing bill, but in 1712, the economic provisions of the first Stamp Act superseded other attempts at legislation.

Although printers could sometimes evade the provisions of the Stamp Act, the taxes became oppressive enough that newspapers had difficulty surviving without subsidies by government or party.[13]

The lapsing of the licensing act in 1695 left controls by the king in place, but still signaled an open door for the proliferation of newspapers. By 1704, London had nine newspapers, including a daily, issuing twenty-seven editions each week. Between 1695 and 1712, London newspapers established new markets in the countryside, and London printers migrated to provincial and colonial towns to publish their own newspapers.[14]

COLONIAL BEGINNINGS

The American colonies grew from tiny settlements of political, religious, and economic dissenters in the early 1600s to an extensive network of intricately governed colonies, which by 1700 supplied much of Britain's raw materials and served as an extensive colonial market for the mother country. By 1704, the time of the first continuously printed newspaper in the colonies, Boston had a population of more than 7,000. Philadelphia and New York were home for about 4,000 colonists each, and the southern towns of Newport and Charleston had populations of between 1,100 and 1,600.[15] Although printing arrived in Latin America as early as 1534 and in the North American colonies as early as 1638, another sixty years passed before newspapers were considered as tools of communication.[16]

The development of newspapers in the colonies followed the cessation of the English licensing act in 1695, coincided with development of provincial newspapers in England, and used the existing technology that had been brought to the new world to print religious and political documents. In the colonies the newspapers were closely tied to the postal system, with postal services clearly predating the first colonial newspapers. Although the development of postal systems simplified news collection and distribution, printers and editors still struggled to find a literate audience that would support the newspapers either through subscription or by providing advertising. Although government suppression may have slowed newspaper development, lack of economic incentive to produce a sheet probably was more significant.[17]

PATTERNS OF SETTLEMENT

Colonists immigrated to the New World for economic, religious, and political reasons, creating a diverse population in the American colonies. Small landowners, second sons of aristocratic English families who could not inherit land in England, and the politically and religiously disenfranchised crossed the Atlantic, hoping for new beginnings. Under James I, Puritans, who did not approve of the Anglican hierarchy of priests and bishops; separatists, who wanted to "separate" from the Anglican Church; and Quakers, who believed religion was a matter of individual conscience, all looked to the New World as a place where they could practice their individual religions. During the years of Puritan rule from 1649 to 1660, many royalists left England. After the restoration of the crown it was the Puritans who left. And, in 1745, after an attempt to restore the Stuarts to the throne, many Scots left the British Isles to settle in America.

Despite the mass migration from England between 1607 and 1642 of 58,000 Englishmen to America, the colonies remained heterogeneous. By the end of the colonial period the colonies were inhabited by 500,000 slaves, 15,000 Huguenots (French Protestants), and 100,000 Germans and the Scotch Irish. By 1643, eighteen different languages were spoken in New York alone.[18]

Such heterogeneity did not, however, contribute necessarily to freedom and tolerance in the New World. Rather, groups of colonists settled separately, creating their own religious and political rules within the constraints of British control.

The Massachusetts Bay Colony, settled in 1630, was the home of dissident Puritans. In the colony only the most rigid of Puritan church members gained full political rights, and dissidents moved to Rhode Island under Roger Williams' tolerant leadership. The early settlements in New England were composed primarily of Puritans from the villages of southeast England. In the new country they established New England townships with solid institutions governing the villages:

> They were indeed the very men to found solid institutions in the wilderness, because in their old homes they had combined self-help and economic individualism with residence in large village groups, where agriculture, crafts, and trade had flourished together.[19]

It was into this colony that the first printing press was brought in 1638. Jose Glover, a Puritan parson, arranged to bring a press to North America, but he did not survive the Atlantic crossing. His press, type, and paper arrived and were operated at Harvard College by Glover's assistant. In 1649 Samuel Green and his sons, Samuel, Jr., and Bartholomew, took over the printing shop and operated it until 1692.

The press was used to extend the religious influence of the Puritan fathers. About 1638, "The Freeman's Oath," the formal contract required by citizens of the Massachusetts Bay Colony, and the *Bay Psalm Book* were put into

Pilgrims signing the compact on board the Mayflower, November 11, 1620. From a Gauthier engraving, 1857. (Library of Congress Collection)

circulation. Almanacs, laws, and official documents for Harvard College also were products of the press. But colonial leaders were little different from the English kings and feared that diversity of opinion might disrupt the colony. Therefore, in 1665, a court restricted printing to Cambridge and required that all print work be reviewed by licensers. Until 1674, no printing was allowed outside of Cambridge.[20]

Massachusetts was the rule, rather than the exception, in colonial society. Virginia, populated by royalist Anglicans, and given to commercial development rather than religious purity, rejected the printing press perhaps even more than New England Puritans. In 1671, the royal governor of Virginia, William Berkeley, thanked God that there were no uncontrolled presses or free schools in his colony,

> for learning has brought disobedience, and heresy, and sects into the world, and printing has divulged them, and libels against the best government. God keep us from both.[21]

COLONIAL DEVELOPMENT

Although Queen Elizabeth initiated colonial settlement in America by sending Sir Walter Raleigh and 120 colonists to Roanoke in 1587, it was not until the reign of James I (1603–1625) and Charles I (1625–1649) that colonial America flourished.

From 1620 to 1640, during the years of Puritan persecution in England, religious groups and investment companies secured charters from the Crown and established seven colonies, including the Massachusetts Bay Colony, Connecticut, Maryland, Rhode Island, and Virginia. Charles I gladly agreed to the charters, assuming that exporting religious dissenters would assure Anglican conformity at home. After the Restoration in England in 1660, Charles II and Parliament took a new economic and political interest in the North American colonies. New colonists secured land grants and charters, organizing New York, New Jersey, Carolina, Pennsylvania and Delaware. The new colonial proprietors promised cheap land, religious freedom, low taxes and representative government to encourage a high level of immigration and rapid distribution of land.

Determined to maintain its status as the mother country and to make the colonies dependent on it, England created trade restrictions and established royal governments. England valued the colonies as producers of agricultural goods to be exported to the mother country and as a market for manufactured goods. Between 1700 and 1750, colonial imports from England more than quadrupled, and during a similar period colonial exports to England multiplied seven times.[22] In the late 1600s and early 1700s, a series of navigation acts restricted the colonies' abilities to trade with countries other than those that constituted the British Empire. Colonists were dependent on England for their money supply, and when the economy contracted in the mother country, colonists became debtors to the merchants of London.

The political structure of the colonies changed as the economic structure expanded. Royal governments replaced charters and proprietary agreements, beginning in 1624 with Virginia and ending with Georgia in 1752. The king appointed royal governors, who shared powers with a popularly elected house and with a royally appointed council.[23] By 1763, the popularly elected houses had assumed considerable control over militia, local government, public works, Indian affairs, and expenditures. As early as 1721, newspapers were not licensed, and in 1729, the Massachusetts Assembly refused to grant the governor permission to institute licensing.

During the years from 1680 to 1720, New England was forced by English law and by popular demand to change its political and religious ways. In 1681, Charlestown colonists appealed to the Puritan leaders of the Massachusetts Bay Colony for religious freedom. The Puritan leaders responded that they had left England, not to pursue toleration, but to establish Puritanism as the Religion for Posterity.[24] By 1700, Massachusetts' original charter had been revoked and the colony operated under royal governorship. The Anglican Church, predominant in the southern colonies as well as in England, was gaining what Puritans considered to be dangerous ground, and the aging Increase Mather and his son, Cotton Mather, urged harmony among different branches of Puritanism in an attempt to strengthen the failing church.

COLONIAL NEWSPAPERS

The first exchange of news in the American colonies depended on word-of-mouth transactions or letters from ship captains from abroad, from official proclamations carried through a colonial postal service reserved primarily for the governmental and religious elite, and from formal town meetings and less formal tavern or coffee-house conversations. The first newspapers appeared in Boston, the site of one of the earliest postal services and where the largest literate population of the colonies lived. The content of the newspapers was diverse, including correspondence from travelers, reprints of political pamphlets, official proclamations, accounts of sermons and speeches, essays, poetry, fiction, economic data on commercial transactions, and agricultural advice. In colonial days, newspapers represented only one source of communication. Other forms included public speaking, sermons and other traditional styles of oral communication.[25]

COMMUNICATION AND TRANSPORTATION

Written communication was heavily tied to transportation. News could be collected only as fast as the ships crossed the ocean or the postrider galloped from New York to Boston. Although a variety of attempts were made during the colonial period to link the colonies and to create communication links with the mother country, the colonies remained relatively isolated. Initiatives to link colonial cities began in 1673, when the New York governor wanted to insure that he would receive news from England, even in the winter months when ships sailed infrequently. His attempts were short-lived, and it was 1692 before the first postal service in the colonies began, privately run under a charter from the king. New York and Massachusetts passed postal acts and initiated service between New York, Massachusetts, and New Hampshire. The postriders also tied together the smaller ports of Massachusetts with the commercial center of Boston.

The first legislative assembly in America met in James Town, Virginia, August, 1619. Reproduction of engraving in Goodrich's History of the United States of America, *1828. (Library of Congress Collection)*

Other colonies soon joined New York and Massachusetts. In 1693, Pennsylvania passed a postal act. Although Maryland and Virginia passed postal legislation, the legislatures, fearful of military problems occurring in the North, opposed expanding communication routes with the northern colonies. Further, the navigable rivers of Virginia that kept planters in close touch with information from across the Atlantic provided barriers to postriders from the North. Virginians opposed the expensive construction of ferries that would promote land transportation to the North. In 1711, about ten years after John Campbell began the first newspaper, Parliament placed the postal service under government control, but Maryland, Virginia, and the Carolinas remained without service. These colonies finally instituted postal services in the late 1720s and 1730s. The connection between postal services and printers went both ways. The earliest newspapers were begun by postmasters, but later, particularly in the southern colonies, printers helped start the postal services that enabled them to mail their newspapers free of charge to other printers and to subscribers.

BIRTHED IN BOSTON

The first newspaper appeared in Boston, the colonies' largest town, which had a population between 7,000 and 12,000. Colonial towns—urban centers—had the largest concentration of literate elites, who had both the skill to read the papers and the money to buy them. Towns imported European ideas and tastes, and produced intellectual, cultural and artistic achievements.

By mid-century fourteen newspapers circulated in colonial America. Massachusetts, New York, and Pennsylvania, where populations were more concentrated, where the postal service operated under fair circumstances, and where towns, rather than farms, dominated the landscape, boasted the most newspapers. Between 1730 and 1750, newspapers appeared in the southern colonies of Maryland, Virginia, and South Carolina. The growth of newspapers accompanied a rapid expansion in population from 251,000 in 1700 to 1,171,000 in 1750.

THE *BOSTON NEWS-LETTER*

As early as 1700, John Campbell—postmaster of the growing town of Boston—was sending handwritten news letters to governors of the New England colonies ringing Massachusetts. From this laborious effort to summarize English news grew colonial America's first successful newspaper, the *Boston News-Letter*. Campbell enjoyed special privileges as Boston's postmaster. As such, he gleaned a substantial amount of news from postriders and others who came by the post office, and he could send and receive mail and newspapers at reduced expense. He published with prior permission from government, focusing on foreign news. Although he operated to make a profit, his limited audience of about 300 brought him little subscription money for his effort despite occasional government subsidies.

After several years of scratching out his newsletters by hand, Campbell must have regarded the creaking wooden-framed press that he used to print the edition on April 24, 1704, as a great luxury. The publication was tiny by twentieth-century standards—$6\frac{1}{4} \times 10\frac{1}{2}$ inches—smaller than a piece of typing paper, but comparable to its English predecessors.

Issued from the primary colonial commercial center, Boston, the newspaper represented conformity rather than conflict. Campbell avoided the local politics that had caused quick demise of Benjamin Harris' 1690 attempt to publish *Publick Occurrences, Both Foreign and Domestick* and obtained approval of news before publishing. Set in bold-face type, just under the newspaper's nameplate, was the prominent statement, "Published by Authority." Campbell strived to give his readers a continuing account of news from abroad, but his news often was published from six to thirteen months after its occurrence. Although Campbell often received London accounts more quickly than he published them, he hesitated to leave out information and lacked the finances to print enough pages to include all the news.

The first issue brought the colonists news from England, but also indicated a growing interest in the relationship between colonies. It contained an extract about James VIII of Scotland from the *London Flying Post,* an account of the queen's speech to Parliament, a few articles from Boston, four paragraphs of marine intelligence from New York, Philadelphia and New London, and a sole advertisement — for Campbell's newspaper.[26]

Campbell's ad brought no immediate revenue:

> This News Letter is to be continued Weekly; and all Persons who have any Houses, Lands, Farmes, Ships, Vessels, Goods, Wares or Merchandizes, &c., to be Sold or Lett; or Servants Runaway; or Goods Stoll or Lost, may have the same Inserted at a Reasonable Rate; from Twelve Pence to Five Shillings. . . .
>
>   All Persons in Town and Country may have said News Letter Weekly upon reasonable terms, agreeing with John Campbell Post Master for the same."[27]

John Campbell edited the *Boston News-Letter* for eighteen of its seventy-two years, but never managed to make money from the effort. At the end of the first year he wrote that his paper

> was propounded to be Printed for one year for a tryal . . . to see Income by the Sale thereof at a moderate price would be sufficient to defray the necessary Charge expended in the procuring and printing of same, which Charge is considerable beyond what most conceive it to be, besides the trouble and fatigue attending it."[28]

Campbell listed some of his expenses, which included gathering information along the continent's edge, with post riders and ships having to cover ". . . almost 500 miles from E. to W. from N. Hampshire to Pensilvania." He also paid correspondents who lived in other seaports "for sending intelligence." Campbell lamented time, as well as money, spent. He complained of

"Waiting on Masters, Merchants, and others when Ships & Vessels arrive to have from them what Intelligence they can give," and of "Waiting on His Excellency [the Governor] or [his] Secretary for approbation of what is Collected."

Campbell's occasional appeals to the government for subsidies to supplement his paper's finances further indicated the economic insecurity of the proposition. Despite the subsidies, the *News-Letter* suspended publication from March of 1709 until January of 1710.[29]

Although Campbell endeavored to be noncontroversial and to please the officials of Massachusetts Bay Colony, he was unsuccessful. Even his abject apologies for one tiny error—putting a comma in the wrong place in a story—did not save his political hide. In 1719, Campbell lost his job as postmaster to William Brooker.

Campbell continued to publish his *News-Letter* after losing his postmastership, keeping the paper going until 1722. He and Brooker, with his own newspaper, overtly competed for subscribers, primarily on the basis of who could provide the latest news. Bartholomew Green, who printed the paper for Campbell during much of the *News-Letter*'s existence, took over the paper in 1722.[30] Once Campbell lost his postmastership, the motto under the *News-Letter*'s nameplate—"Published by Authority"—also disappeared.

THE *BOSTON GAZETTE*

The new postmaster, William Brooker, began a newspaper in December of 1719. The *Boston Gazette,* not unlike Campbell's sheet, carried the "Published by Authority" label, indicating it was a semiofficial government organ. The *Gazette* continued as a postmaster's organ for many years after Brooker. Brooker's *Gazette,* like Campbell's *News-Letter,* focused on foreign news, but unlike Campbell's paper, strived to have the "latest" rather than a continuing account of news.[31]

Brooker's primary distinction may have been hiring the smoldering firebrand of a printer, James Franklin. Relatively ignored by historians because of the eminence of his younger brother Benjamin, James Franklin nevertheless is a notable if feisty figure in the history of American journalism.

Brooker was not a printer; he was "hiring out" his printing to James Franklin. Franklin had assimilated unusual skills for a young printer: a native of Boston, he was a printer's apprentice in England during his teens.[32] Returning to Boston with a used press after his apprenticeship, Franklin printed the *Gazette* for Brooker from 1719 until 1720, when Samuel Kneeland took over as postmaster and as editor of the *Boston Gazette*.

Benjamin Franklin greets visitors to his bookshop in Philadelphia. (Library of Congress Collection)

THE *NEW ENGLAND COURANT*

After losing his printing job with Brooker, James Franklin turned to printing controversial materials such as Daniel Defoe's pamphlet, "News from the Moon," a criticism of suppression of information in England. The pamphlet appeared while a Boston pamphleteer was resisting the threat of prosecution for publishing a pamphlet on colonial currency problems. A few months after a grand jury refused to indict the pamphleteer, on August 7, 1721, James Franklin published the first issue of the *New England Courant.* The newspaper appeared at the end of a summer distinguished by a raging smallpox epidemic; half the population of Boston was infected and one person in seven died.

The *Courant* represented several major departures from the Boston newspapers that preceded it. The newspaper began what may have been the first journalistic crusade on these shores. The editors noted from the beginning that the paper would be controversial, attacking the Congregational clergy and actively opposing inoculation for smallpox.[33] The *Courant* introduced items of wit and humor, reprinting the popular English essays of Addison and Steele, as well as supplying local humor and news. Further, and significantly, it was the first Boston newspaper to start without benefit of postmaster support. For his efforts, James Franklin served time in jail for seditious libel, a warning to future printers of colonial America.[34]

James Franklin Begins a Crusade

Franklin began his *New England Courant* in 1721 during an economic depression in a small community in competition with five other printers. In the long run, repression turned out to be more of a problem for James Franklin than finances. In 1721, criticism of government could lead a writer or printer to jail. Government authorities sought, and at times exercised, the even more stringent power of prior censorship.

In 1719, for example, the Anglican minister Reverend John Checkley challenged the Puritan-controlled government and society of that colony. The governor exercised prior restraint by ordering Checkley not to publish anti-Calvinist writing. The Massachusetts legislature then passed a statute requiring anyone who was suspected to be "disaffected" with the king to swear an oath of loyalty. When Checkley refused to take the oath, he was fined six pounds and ordered by the court to be on "good behavior."[35]

The dissenting minister, Checkley, found an ally in the iconoclastic printer, James Franklin. Both were ready to challenge the Puritan clergy, led by father Increase Mather and son Cotton Mather. The treatment of smallpox represented a challenge to an existing leadership, rather than an effort to investigate or publish facts to resolve a controversy:

Defiance was the soul of the *Courant,* the spirited cry of newcomers bumping against an old elite, of artisans mocking the more respectable classes, of provincials picking up the language of London coffee houses, and of eighteenth-century men recovering the nerve to mock and amuse in the face of the grave.[36]

Cotton Mather had learned of experiments in inoculating healthy persons to prevent them from contracting smallpox and urged that this strange-sounding new procedure be used to halt the epidemic. Many Bostonians, however, including all but one physician, countered that inoculation — using blood from persons who had survived the 'pox — would surely add to deaths from the disease.[37]

Checkley, who wrote most of the material for the first issues, confronted the Puritan advocates of inoculation, saying they were men

Who like faithful Shepherds take care of their Flocks,
By teaching and practicing what's Orthodox,
Pray hard against Sickness, yet preach up the POX![38]

Reverend Thomas Walter, the grandson of Increase Mather, who strongly favored inoculation, responded to the *Courant*'s first issue with a single-sheet labeled the *Little-Compton Scourge:* or, the *Anti-Courant.* The third issue of the *Courant* accused Reverend Walter of drunkenness and other improprieties. Franklin, uncomfortable with such attacks, removed Checkley as the "editor" of the *Courant,* but did not abandon the controversy. The *Courant* continued to publish anti-inoculation pieces, with the supporters of the Mathers using the *Boston Gazette* to return journalistic salvos.

Echoing — or mimicking — the journalistic disputes in England which had led to the dubbing of a political faction there "The Hell-Fire Club," Franklin and his supporters of the *Courant*'s side were also given that label. And the Reverend Increase Mather asserted in the *Boston Gazette* that James Franklin was indeed perdition-bound:

I can well remember when the Civil Government would have taken an effectual Course to suppress such a Cursed Libel! which if it be not done I am afraid that some Awful Judgment will come upon this Land, and that the Wrath of GOD will arise, and there will be no Remedy. I cannot but pity the poor Franklin, who, tho' but a Young Man, it may be Speedily he must appear before the Judgment Seat of God, and what answer will he give for printing things so vile and abominable?[39]

Franklin Adopts Satirical Tone

After several issues, James Franklin's *Courant* turned away from a virtually exclusive concern with the inoculation controversy and adopted the satirical tone of contemporary British newspapers. James Franklin wrote an essay in letter form, attributing it to "Ichabod Henroost," not at all unlike a "Nathaniel Henroost" piece published earlier in the *Spectator* of London.[40]

James Franklin's journalistic rambunctiousness came at a time of dispute about the governor's licensing power. During the 1720s a standard section of a governor's set of formal instructions from the king involved establishing licensing. When the Massachusetts governor turned to the legislature for approval of the licensing power, the House of Representatives, struggling to secure dominance over the governor, refused to cooperate. As a by-product of the struggle, printers gained some limited freedom.[41]

That freedom was tenuous at best, however, and in 1722, Franklin slyly suggested in the *Courant* that the Massachusetts General Court was not trying hard enough to keep pirates from preying on colonial shipping. Franklin satirically wrote that a ship was being prepared to pursue the pirates "'sometime this month, wind and weather permitting.'"[42]

Benjamin Franklin: Interim Editor

This reflection on government resulted in a month's imprisonment for James Franklin. While in jail, he continued to run the newspaper with a highly able substitute editor, his younger brother Benjamin. Benjamin Franklin, almost ten years younger than James Franklin, had been apprenticed to his brother's printing house for five years, since the age of twelve. With his brother in jail, the seventeen-year-old got to see first hand the dangers of confronting an autocratic political structure head-on.

Indeed, a committee of the General Court was named to study the offensive publication called the *New England Courant*. Early in 1723, the committee reported that the tendency of the paper was to mock religion, profanely abuse scriptures, and affront government. The committee forbade James Franklin to print any unapproved publication and released him on good behavior and sufficient bond. Franklin went into hiding after refusing to obey and was arrested when he reappeared. However, a grand jury refused to indict him. Meanwhile, James released his brother Ben from his indenture, but asked Ben to sign a secret agreement, still binding the younger brother.[43]

So in 1723, if only as a "front man" for his brother, seventeen-year-old Benjamin Franklin began publishing the *Courant*. The younger Franklin's cleverness could not be contained by the drab life of an apprentice printer;

> **SILENCE DOGOOD SPEAKS**
>
> I DOUBT not but moderate Drinking has been improv'd for the Diffusion of Knowledge among the ingenious part of man-kind, who want the Talent of a ready Utterance, in order to discover the Conceptions of their Minds in as entertaining and intelligible Manner. 'Tis true, drinking does not improve our Faculties, but it enables us to USE them; and therefore I conclude, that much Study and Experience, and a little Liquor, are of absolute Necessity or some Tempers, in order to make them accomplish'd Orators.

since March of 1722, he had been writing essays under the pen name of "Silence Dogood."

Through fourteen essays the young Franklin had gently satirized the foibles of human nature.[44] He modeled the essays after those he read in London's *Spectator*. Silence Dogood purported to be a talkative and philosophical widow, who, in more high-flown moments, styled herself an "Enemy to Vice, and Friend to Virtue, . . ." as well as a "mortal Enemy to arbitrary Government & Unlimited Power."[45] According to Ben Franklin, it took his brother James six months to discover the identity of the letters.

The young man's far-wiser-than-his-years tone colored Benjamin Franklin's introductory prospectus for his *Courant*:

> The main design of this Weekly Paper will be to entertain the Town with the most comical and diverting Incidents of Human Life, which in so large a Place as Boston, will not fail of a universal Exemplification: Nor shall we be wanting [lacking] to fill up these Papers with a grateful Interspersion of more serious Morals, which may be drawn from the most ludecrous and odd Part of Life.[46]

The secret indenture papers had no force, and within months, Benjamin Franklin quarreled with his brother, leaving Boston to seek freedom and his fortune.

James Franklin continued his *New-England Courant*, still sassy, but economically unsuccessful. He ended the *Courant* in 1726 and moved to Newport, Rhode Island, to become a government printer. In 1732, he established the *Rhode-Island Gazette*, which lasted only a year, evidently not proving profitable. His health failed, and he died in 1735 after a long illness. His widow, Anne Smith Franklin—whom he had married in 1724—then ran the printing house successfully, including printing the laws of Rhode Island in 1745. Journalism historian Isaiah Thomas wrote that Anne Franklin "was aided in her printing by her two daughters, and afterward by her son when he gained a competant age." The daughters, "sensible and amiable women," were termed "correct and quick compositors at the [type] case."[47] His son, James Franklin Jr., became his mother's partner and, after an apprenticeship in Philadelphia with his Uncle Ben, established the *Newport Mercury*, a newspaper that endured into the twentieth century.[48]

CONCLUSION

A printing revolution in the fifteenth century paved the way for a transition from a primarily oral or scribal culture to a printed culture. The ability to print simultaneous copies of a work enabled more accurate transmission of information and encouraged the sharing of identical information. In moving the copying of books from the monasteries and universities to the print shops, literate elites and printers developed new relationships. Printing developed in England despite strict controls on presses and printers, and newspapers flourished particularly during periods when licensing acts were not in effect.

Despite the heterogeneity of the colonial population, intolerance rather than diversity characterized the early use of the printing press, which first was used to print official proclamations and religious pamphlets. Colonial newspapers appeared at about the same time English provincial papers began developing. The early newspapers lacked a substantial economic base, focused heavily on foreign news, and cautiously approached the types of local controversy that could bring printers into conflict with licensing acts or governmental authority. James Franklin, in publishing the *New England Courant*, demonstrated the difficulty of writing about local controversy. Nevertheless, his newspaper represented a departure from the earlier *News-Letter* and *Gazette* by introducing controversy, wit and humor, and coverage of local events.

NOTES

1. For a detailed discussion of this thesis and the impact of the printing revolution on the Renaissance and the Reformation, see Elizabeth L. Eisenstein, *The Printing Revolution in Early Modern Europe* (Cambridge: Cambridge University Press, 1983). For further exploration of the relationship between elites and non-elites see David Hall, "The World of Print and Collective Mentality," in John Higham and Paul K. Conkin, eds., *New Directions in American Intellectual History* (Baltimore: John Hopkins University Press, 1980), pp. 166–180.
2. Ian K. Steele, *The English Atlantic, 1675–1740: An Exploration of Communication and Community* (New York: Oxford University Press, 1986), p. 133. For comparison of development in various European countries, see Anthony Smith, *The Newspaper: An International History* (London: Thames and Hudson Ltd., 1979).

3. For comments on "conscious interdependence," see Jerome E. Reich, *Colonial America* (Englewood Cliffs, N.J.: Prentice-Hall, 1984) p. 224; Thomas C. Leonard, *The Power of the Press* (Oxford: Oxford University Press, 1986), p. 4, and David Paul Nord, unpublished manuscript, "The American People."

4. S.H. Steinberg, *Five Hundred Years of Printing* (New York: Criterion Books, 1959), pp. 21–22.

5. For discussions of history of literacy, with particular attention to development of theories of oral traditions and definitions of literacy, see Carolyn Marvin, "Constructed and Reconstructed Discourse: Inscription and Talk in the History of Literacy," *Communication Research* 11:4 (October, 1984): pp. 563–594 and Harvey J. Graff, "The Legacies of Literacy," *Journal of Communication* 32 (Winter, 1982), pp. 12–26.

6. The Enlightenment was an eighteenth-century philosophical movement concerned with criticism of existing institutions and doctrines, usually from a rationalist point of view. Rationalism is based on a theory that reason, rather than spiritual revelation or authority, is the valid basis for action.

7. Eisenstein, *Printing Revolution*, p. 80.

8. Eisenstein, *Printing Revolution*, p. 94.

9. Hall, "Collective Mentality," p. 167.

10. Steele, *The English Atlantic*, pp. 133–4.

11. Jeffrey A. Smith, *Printers and Press Freedom: The ideology of Early American Journalism* (New York: Oxford Univ. Press, 1988), p. 34.

12. Jeremy Black, *The English Press in the Eighteenth Century* (Philadelphia: University of Pennsylvania Press, 1987), p. 2.

13. Black, *English Press,* pp. 9–11; Smith, *Printers and Press Freedom,* p. 21.

14. Steele, *The English Atlantic,* pp. 136–138.

15. In colonial times, Charles Town was the proper description for the South Carolina capital.

16. For further investigation of the early entry of the printing press and the publishing of news events in Latin America, see Al Hester, "Newspapers and Newspaper Prototypes in Spanish America, 1541–1750," *Journalism History* 6:3 (Autumn 1979), pp. 73–77, 88. See also Felix Gutierrez and Ernesto Ballesteros, "The 1541 Earthquake: Dawn of Latin American Journalism," *Journalism History* 6:3 (Autumn 1979), pp. 78–83.

17. For expansion of the economic argument, see Steele, *The English Atlantic,* pp. 132–167. See also Chapter Seven, "The Posts."

18. For details of political, economic and religious emigration see Reich, *Colonial America.*

19. G.M. Trevelyan, *A Shortened History of England* (Hammondsworth, Middlesex, England: Penguin Books, 1942), p. 318. (The *Shortened History* is an abridged version of *History of England,* originally published by Longmans, Green & Co. Ltd.)

20. For a more positive view of the Puritans, see Samuel Eliot Morrison, *Builders of the Bay Colony* (Boston: Northeastern University Press, 1981).

Chapter 1 **Crossing the Atlantic**

21. William Waller Henning, *The Statutes at Large Being a Collection of All the Laws of Virginia (1619–1792)* (Richmond: 1809–23) vol. 2, p. 517, cited in Leonard W. Levy, *Emergence of a Free Press* (New York: Oxford, 1985), p. 18.
22. Robert McCluer Calhoon, *Revolutionary America: An Interpretive Overview* (New York: Harcourt Brace Jovanovich, Inc., 1963) p. 6.
23. Policy varied slightly from colony to colony. For example, the charter colonies of Rhode Island and Connecticut elected their own councils, lower houses, and governors.
24. Perry Miller, "The Puritan State and Puritan Society," in *The American Past: Conflicting Interpretations of the Great Issues,* ed. Sidney Fine and Gerald Brown, vol. 1, 4th ed. (New York: The Macmillan Co., 1976), p. 11.
25. John Pauly, "Reflections on Writing a History of News as a Form of Mass Culture," University of Wisconsin-Milwaukee: Center for Twentieth Century Studies, Fall 1985, Working Paper No. 6, p. 5.
26. Isaiah Thomas, *The History of Printing in America,* ed. Marcus A. McCorison from the 2nd edition (New York: Weathervane Books, 1970), p. 215.
27. Cited in Thomas, *History of Printing,* pp. 215–216.
28. *Boston News-Letter,* April 2–9, 1705.
29. Jo Anne Smith, "John Campbell," in Perry J. Ashley, ed., *Dictionary of Literary Biography,* vol 43: *American Newspaper Journalists, 1690–1872* (Detroit: Gale Research, 1985), p. 95.
31. Steele, *English Atlantic,* p. 155.
32. Jeffery A. Smith, "James Franklin," *DLB,* vol. 43, p. 212.
33. *New England Courant,* August 14–21, 1721, cited in Bleyer, *Main Currents,* p. 53.
34. The formal charge against Franklin was breach of legislative privilege. Legislators had the ability to charge printers in such a manner, thereby punishing them for offensive, or seditious, writings. For an analysis of colonial use of legislative privilege against the press, see Jeffery A. Smith, "A Reappraisal of Legislative Privilege and American Colonial Journalism," *Journalism Quarterly* (Spring, 1984), 61:1, pp. 97–103, 141.
35. Clyde A. Duniway, *The Development of Freedom of the Press in Massachusetts* (New York: Longmans, Green, 1906), pp. 84–86, cited in Levy, *Free Press,* p. 29. See also Edmund F. Slafter, *John Checkley; or, the Evolution of Religious Tolerance in Massachusetts Bay,* 2 vols. (Boston: Prince Society, 1891).
36. Leonard, *Power of the Press,* pp. 26–27.
37. Smith, "James Franklin," *DLB,* vol. 43, pp. 214–215.
38. Smith, "James Franklin," *DLB,* vol. 43, p. 213.
39. Thomas, *History of Printing,* p. 236; see also Bleyer, *Main Currents,* p. 54. The date assigned here was January 24, 1721, based on an Old Style calendar. More current calendars would refer to it as 1722.
40. Bleyer, *Main Currents,* p. 55.
41. Levy, *Free Press,* p. 30.
42. Levy, *Free Press,* p. 30.

43. *New-England Courant,* February 4–11, 1723, quoted in Bleyer, *Main Currents,* p. 59. See also Michael J. Kirkhorn, "Benjamin Franklin," *DLB,* vol. 43, p. 197.
44. Kirkhorn, "Benjamin Franklin," *DLB,* vol. 43, p. 196.
45. Kirkhorn, "Benjamin Franklin," *DLB,* vol. 43, p. 196.
46. *New-England Courant,* February 4–11, 1723.
47. Thomas, *History of Printing,* p. 315.
48. Thomas, *History of Printing,* pp. 315–316; Kirkhorn, *DLB,* vol. 43, p. 217.

CHAPTER 2

COMMERCIAL AND POLITICAL DEVELOPMENT

The North American colonial press experienced substantial growth in the seventy-two years from the first appearance of the *Boston News-Letter* to the Declaration of Independence, as printers throughout the colonies created a professional network and laid an institutional base for a press with common characteristics. Only three colonial newspapers existed in 1720; by 1760 that number had grown to twenty-two.[1]

Printers most commonly were of the artisan class and often doubled as postmasters and shopkeepers, usually printing a newspaper only after their businesses were established. The newspapers carried advertising, were designed to make a profit, and acted as promotional tools for the printer's various enterprises such as bookseller, coffee-house operator, and small merchant. For a portion of their income, printers relied on contacts with London booksellers.[2] Connections to government provided another source of income, either through positions as postmasters or official printers or through subsidized printing of official documents. Printers were related to each other, sometimes by family ties and often by apprenticeships and partnership agreements.

Print, whether in the form of newspapers or books, was a scarce commodity, particularly in the small towns and in the country, and literate audiences hungered for printed products. Newspaper delivery remained restricted by transportation, and deliveries were common only along major trade routes. Recalling life in late eighteenth-century Connecticut, Boston editor Joseph Buckingham noted that when a printer arrived in Windham, Connecticut, in 1793 and began to publish a weekly paper, the event marked "a memorable epoch in our village history."[3]

Publisher-author Samuel Goodrich said people read carefully, with deliberation and reverence, the few printed works available:

> Books and newspapers—which are now [1850] diffused even among the country towns, so as to be in the hands of all, young and old— were then scarce, and were read respectfully, and as if they were grave matters, demanding thought and attention. . . . Even the young approached a book with reverence, and a newspaper with awe. How the world has changed![4]

During the seventy-two years a few printers and editors challenged English authority and cautiously ventured into local politics, printing exposes on the fifty presses available in the colonies. Although printers such as John Peter Zenger, who gave men like James Alexander the opportunity to speak anonymously through their newspapers, faced the brunt of English repression, these printers also became popular heroes.

Scholars have long debated whether the colonial press was courageous in its criticism of government. Stephen Botein maintained that most printers pursued a strategy of neutrality in politics. Although printers often argued that their pages were "open to all," they sometimes discouraged the more radical contributions of political factions, or offered to print pamphlets advancing the ideas rather than include them in their newspapers. Botein argued that such a practice decreased the range of discussion rather than intensifying it. Botein further claimed that faced with limited audiences for their products, printers were reluctant to alienate possible customers by restricting themselves to one political group. In addition, some ambiguity in political orientation also enabled official printers to tread carefully through troubled colonial legislative factions and disputes between the assemblies and governors. Jeffery Smith maintained that some printers, following the dictates of impartiality, often published ideas they disagreed with, and that non-partisanship was a form of radical Whig Republicanism. During the latter half of the eighteenth century as the colonists became increasingly dissatisfied with English rule, printers fought first against commercial restrictions such as the stamp act, and then for political control.[5]

COMMERCIAL DEVELOPMENT

ARTISANS AND NEWSPAPERS

The social and economic status of printers varied among colonies and from one printer to another, depending on background, training, and whether a printer was able to move into the merchant or landed class. The first newspapers were printed by members of either the artisan or professional class. The status of an artisan fell somewhere below that of the large landowners, wealthy merchants, and professional class, and somewhat above that of the landless laborers and indentured servants. Those printers who also were minor governmental officials probably fell into the lower ranks of the professional class, although it is difficult to know for sure. Class structure was fairly fluid until the middle of the eighteenth century, and although lawyers and clergy, for example, were not considered professionals in the latter part of the sixteenth century, those individuals rose in status over time. Printers who completed their apprenticeships in London probably gained status more quickly than those trained in colonial shops.

Artisans were scarce in colonial America because the development of a trade did not offer the same social mobility as did ownership of land, but such scarcity assured artisans of higher pay than their counterparts in England. Printers often were supported by men of higher standing, who wrote for and helped finance the papers. Printers were hard pressed to find equipment for their task because England, determined not to let the colonies compete in manufacturing, prohibited many exports of machinery.[6]

Printers learned their trade by the standard method of apprenticeship. An apprentice agreed to work for a set number of years, to serve his masters faithfully and not to marry while learning his craft. At the end of the set time, the apprentice became a journeyman, and perhaps later, a master craftsman. Women were not admitted to the apprenticeship system, but many women learned printing in the shops of their fathers or husbands, and fourteen women printers were active in the colonies before the start of the Revolution. Most took over established businesses when their husbands died, but at least one woman printer, Mary Crouch, moved her family, type, and presses to another community 1,000 miles away and began a new printing business.[7]

Most printers also were small merchants, and some grew to prominence within their communities. William and Andrew Bradford, Benjamin Franklin, and William Parks, as well as other printers, operated extensive bookselling operations, often dealing directly with London book dealers. They sold other imports, as well, through their shops, and because currency in the colonies was scarce, often traded paper and other similar items for goods and services. The newspaper and book trades were intricately intertwined. Newspapers advertised books available, and book sales supplemented printers' incomes.

THE BOSTON NETWORK

Boston, which continued as the newspaper center for the first half of the eighteenth century, was home to an important group of printers and booksellers who shared contacts, supplies, and geographic location. These printers, whose businesses were clustered south of Dock Square or close to the shops of King Street and Cornhill, shipped books and paper along trade routes to various New England states. Jeremy Condy, Boston bookseller in the 1760s, kept account books indicating that cash was used sparingly in trade and that consignment, trading of goods and services, and selling on credit were far more common modes of trade. For example, Condy sold paper to Boston publishers Benjamin Edes and John Gill in return for printing and advertising.

Condy's ledgers suggested that books and paper traveled longer distances as commercial commodities than did most colonial goods. Although he had customers in more than 134 towns in Connecticut, Rhode Island, Massachusetts, and New Hampshire, each town usually had only two or three customers. These towns were on major trade routes—along the coast, the rivers, or stage routes. Newspapers and booksellers' catalogs traveled along these routes as well. What is strikingly apparent in the account books is that no books traveled to towns not located on the trade routes, indicating a line of "cultural demarcation" created by the routes.[8]

Another type of important network involved close family ties; such a network could help family printers acquire government printing contracts or other profitable printing jobs. In Boston, members of the Green family established what some historians have referred to as a printing dynasty.[9] Timothy Green, Jr., who with Samuel Kneeland started *The New England Journal* in 1727, was the great-grandson of Samuel Green, a Massachusetts printer who earned his reputation as printer of an Indian Bible. Timothy Green's grandfather was a Boston bookseller, and his father was the official printer for Connecticut. He also was related to Bartholomew Green, who printed the *Boston News-Letter* for John Campbell beginning in 1704. In 1742, the Kneeland and Green partnership combined two papers under the name, *The Boston Gazette and Weekly Journal*.[10] Under different management, this newspaper later became an important voice in revolutionary America.

Competing with the Green network was Campbell's *Boston News-Letter*, which lasted until 1776, the last Tory voice in Boston. Margaret Draper, the *News-Letter*'s last printer, vacated the town with the British at the beginning of the War for Independence. As Boston declined in importance and Philadelphia ascended, both in population and commercial importance, the newspaper center also shifted to that city.

PHILADELPHIA COMPETITION

In the 1720s and 1730s several printers operated in Philadelphia, and at least two newspapers successfully competed. Andrew Bradford, Samuel Keimer, and Benjamin Franklin all established printing houses and all, at one time or another, published newspapers. Although Bradford and Franklin succeeded, Keimer soon sold out to Franklin. Andrew Bradford's adopted son, William, also successfully entered the newspaper business in competition with Andrew's widow, and with Franklin.

The Bradfords

Andrew Bradford, who learned printing in the shop of his father, William Bradford, in New York, moved to Philadelphia about 1712, and in 1719 began printing the first newspaper in Pennsylvania, *The American Mercury*. Until 1723, he was the only printer in Pennsylvania, and he became postmaster of Philadelphia in 1732.

In 1741, Andrew Bradford published *The American Magazine, or a Monthly View of the Political State of the British Colonies*. Its publication date — February 13, 1741 — established it as the first magazine in the British North American Colonies, but only by three days. Competition came from Benjamin Franklin's *General Magazine, and Historical Chronicle, for all the British Plantations in North America*. These two publications were short-lived, with Bradford's magazine lasting only three months and Franklin's only six.[11]

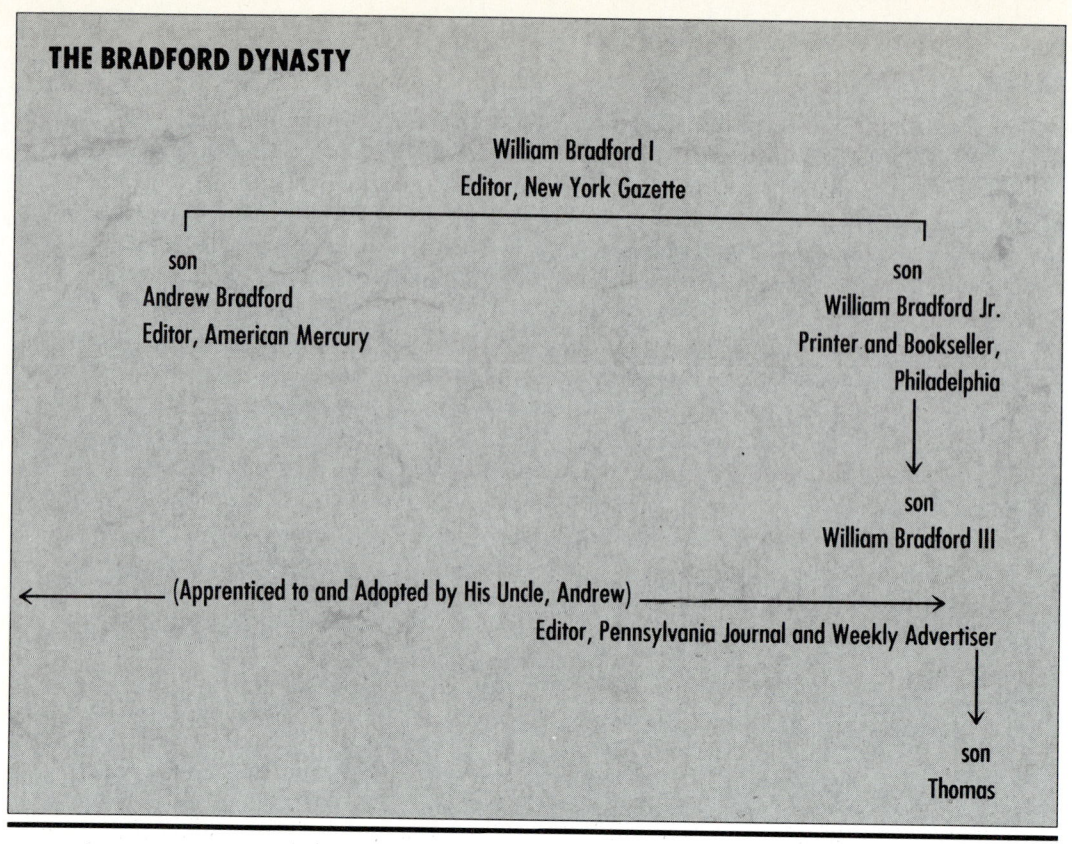

Andrew Bradford's brother, William Bradford, Jr., also was a printer and bookseller in Philadelphia, but is little remembered today. He was the father of William Bradford III, who was born in New York City in 1719. At age fourteen, William III was apprenticed to his childless Uncle Andrew, who adopted him. Andrew and William Bradford III were partners in Philadelphia in 1739–1740, but young William sailed to London in 1741 to visit a great aunt who had inherited the substantial Sowle printing house in London, where his grandfather had learned printing.[12]

William Bradford III, who earned the title of colonel for his military activity during the French and Indian Wars, began publishing the *Pennsylvania Journal and Weekly Advertiser* in December 1742. The *Journal*, with new type brought from England, quickly became one of the best appearing papers in the colonies. In 1752, Bradford opened the London Coffee-House at Front and Market streets, which became a major commercial center in Philadelphia. William Bradford III, with his major ties to the London printing houses and booksellers, made bookselling a substantial portion of his business, dealing with London bookdealer John Oswald, who sponsored popular dissenting authors, both in religion and in politics.[13]

In 1762, William Bradford III's son, Thomas Bradford, joined his father in the printing house and subsequently became a partner. Thomas assumed total responsibility for the newspaper in 1778, after his father suffered business losses during the War for Independence, especially during the British occupation of Philadelphia in 1777–1778. Thomas converted the *Journal* to a daily and the paper continued until 1814.

Benjamin Franklin

Benjamin Franklin, who had escaped his brother's iron hand by moving to Philadelphia, had gone by way of New York, where he hoped to find work with William Bradford. Bradford sent him to Philadelphia with an introduction to his son, Andrew Bradford.

Franklin found work with printer Samuel Keimer, and soon became involved in a scheme with Pennsylvania Governor William Keith to establish a printing house in Philadelphia. Promised letters of credit from Governor Keith, Franklin went to London in 1724 to buy printing equipment. The nineteen-year-old soon discovered the letters of credit had not been written, and he worked for a time at a London printing establishment.[14] He returned to the Philadelphia shop of Samuel Keimer, but left in 1728 after a squabble with the older man. After entering the printing business with a friend, Franklin attracted considerable business through a group of friends who formed a debating society called the Junto.

Upon hearing a rumor that Franklin intended to start a newspaper, Samuel Keimer rushed into print with *The Universal Instructor in all Arts and Sciences; and Pennsylvania Gazette.* The grandiose title competed with William Bradford's *American Weekly Mercury*, which Franklin and his friends, in an attempt to outwit Keimer, helped make popular by submitting satirical essays, the "*Busy-Body Papers.*" After nine months of publication Keimer sold his paper to Franklin and his friend.

In 1729, the twenty-four-year-old Franklin became sole owner of his printing house and the newspaper he titled *The Pennsylvania Gazette*. This paper, "Carrying the Freshest Advices Foreign and Domestick," was only the most visible part of a growing business. Franklin not only published advertisements, he also peddled a variety of goods and services from his printing house. He offered stationery, paper, ink, and pens, did bookbinding, and sold books, dried fish, cheese, and chocolate.

Ben Franklin practiced the common colonial printing strategy of cautious neutrality, writing in "An Apology for Printers," published in the *Pennsylvania Gazette* on June 10, 1731, that

> Printers are educated in the Belief, that when Men differ in Opinion, both Sides ought equally to have the Advantage of being heard by the

> **Franklin Leaves Boston**
>
> At length a fresh Difference arising between by Brother and me, I took upon me to assert my Freedom. It was not fair in me to take this Advantage, and this I therefore reckon one of the first Errata in my life; But the Unfairness of it weighed little with me, when under the Impressions of Resentment for the Blows his Passion too often urg'd him to bestow upon me. Tho' he was otherwise not an ill-natur'd Man Perhaps I was too saucy and provoking.
>
> SOURCE. Benjamin Franklin's Autobiography.

> Publick; and that when Truth and Error have fair Play, the former is always an overmatch for the latter: Hence they chearfully serve all contending Writers that pay them well, without regarding on which side they are of the Question in Dispute.[15]

Franklin further argued that printing both sides of an issue was necessary to making a living:

> That hence arises the peculiar Unhappiness of that Business, which other Callings are no way liable to; they who follow Printing being scarce able to do any thing in their way of getting Living, which shall not probably give Offence to some, and perhaps to many; whereas the Smith, the Shoemaker, the Carpenter, or the Man of any other Trade, may work indifferently for People of all Persuasions, without offending any of them and the Merchant may buy and sell with jews, Turks, Hereticks and Infidels of all sorts, and get Money by every one of them, without giving Offense to the most orthodox, of any sort, or suffering the least Censure or Ill will on the Account from any Man whatever.

Franklin's arguments in his "Apology" contended that a practical approach helped bring in money.[16] His comments were couched in the romantic notations of John Milton's *Areopagitica*: That if all opinions could be heard, given a free and open encounter, truth would "overmatch" error.

Although Andrew Bradford's newspaper and printing house successfully continued, Benjamin Franklin's enterprising spirit and ready wit constituted formidable opposition. His *Pennsylvania Gazette* became the most successful newspaper of the colonial years. In 1732, Franklin first published *Poor Richard's Almanack*, a money-maker — and advertisement for his printing house — for years to come. It combined predictions for the ensuing year, humor, and a seemingly endless fund of self-improvement advice:

Poor Richard, 1733.

AN Almanack

For the Year of Chrift

1733,

Being the Firft after LEAP YEAR:

And makes fince the Creation	Years
By the Account of the Eastern *Greeks*	7241
By the Latin Church, when ☉ ent. ♈	6932
By the Computation of *W. W.*	5742
By the *Roman* Chronology	5682
By the *Jewish* Rabbies	5494

Wherein is contained

The Lunations, Eclipfes, Judgment of the Weather, Spring Tides, Planets Motions & mutual Afpects, Sun and Moon's Rifing and Setting, Length of Days, Time of High Water, Fairs, Courts, and obfervable Days.

Fitted to the Latitude of Forty Degrees, and a Meridian of Five Hours Weft from *London*, but may without fenfible Error, serve all the adjacent Places, even from *Newfoundland* to *South-Carolina*.

By *RICHARD SAUNDERS*, Philom.

PHILADELPHIA:
Printed and fold by *B. FRANKLIN*, at the New Printing-Office near the Market.

Poor Richard's Almanack, *1733. (Library of Congress Collection)*

> In Things of moment, on they self depend,
> Nor trust too far they Servant or thy Friend:
> With private views, thy Friend may promise fair,
> And servants very seldom prove sincere.
>
> . . .
>
> He that would be beforehand in the World, must be beforehand with his Business: It is not only ill Management, but discovers a slothful Disposition, to do that in the Afternoon, which should have been done in the morning.

SOUTHERN COLONIES

Benjamin Franklin's influence extended throughout many of the colonies. Lewis Timothy, a French Protestant immigrant, French teacher, and printer, was sponsored by Franklin in his position of official printer to South Carolina and editor of the *South Carolina Gazette*. The first printers in South Carolina had arrived there in 1731 or 1732 and apparently published a few issues of a *South Carolina Weekly Journal* and the *South Carolina Gazette*, but the two died during the next year. Franklin established a partnership with Timothy, signing a six-year contract that provided for Timothy's elder son Peter to take over in case of the elder Timothy's death. The *Gazette* resumed publication in February 1734. Timothy was a commercial success, operating a shop as well as the newspaper and functioning as official printer. In 1736 he gained a grant for 600 acres of valuable Charleston property. When he died in December 1738, Elizabeth Timothy, his wife, continued to operate the newspaper successfully. Benjamin Franklin commented that

> she not only sent me as clear a state as she could find of the transactions past, but continued to account with the greatest regularity and exactitude every quarter afterwards, and managed the business with such success that she not only brought up reputably a family of children but at the expiration of the term was able to purchase of me the printing house and establish her son in it.[17]

Elizabeth Timothy turned the shop over to her son in 1746. She and her husband evidently had been quite successful, for in her will she left her son and three daughters a silver watch, two houses, two slaves, and clothing in addition to money that would accrue from selling another house, three slaves, and furniture.[18]

Meanwhile, William Parks in 1727 began the *Maryland Gazette*. Isaiah

Old Bruton Parish Church in Williamsburg, Virginia, was completed in 1715. (Library of Congress Collection)

Thomas said Parks's salary consisted of 2,000 pounds in produce, which coincides with other interpretations that goods, rather than cash, often provided the means of exchange between a printer and his clients. As the official printer of the Laws of Maryland, he not only continued to maintain his Maryland printing shop, but moved to Virginia in 1731, for a time serving as official printer to both colonies. In 1736 he started the first newspaper in Virginia, the *Virginia Gazette*.[19]

    The Williamsburg printing office, established nearly a century after printing began in New England, was a major source of information for Virginians during the last four colonial decades. The shop, positioned along Duke of Gloucester Street, the main street of the Virginia capital, served as a printing office, book shop, and post office from the 1740s onward. Religious protest and the development of a well-educated clergy that promoted printing in New England did not exist in Virginia, and colonists were content to read the products of English writers and relied primarily on direct imports from Lon-

PART 1   EARLY AMERICA

don.[20] Parks imported Bibles, prayer books, and schoolbooks from England. By the time Parks died in 1750, his inventory had expanded greatly and bookselling assumed a greater portion of his business.

In addition to bookselling, Parks contributed to Williamsburg's economy by establishing a paper mill with the assistance of Benjamin Franklin. When the intercolonial postal service reached Williamsburg in 1738, Parks's shop also became the post office, and Parks published a variety of the colony's laws as the official printer for Virginia.[21]

Also active in the middle colonies was another descendant of Samuel Green, the colonial Massachusetts printer. Jonas Green, brother of Timothy Green of Boston, who published the *New England Journal*, apprenticed with his father in Connecticut and then joined his brother's firm of Kneeland and Green. He worked for several years in Philadelphia for the Franklin and the Bradford printing houses. In the late 1730s Green was offered "liberal encouragement" financially to become Maryland's public printer. He moved to Annapolis and opened a printing house there in 1740. When he died at age forty, he left nine children, including three sons who all became printers.[22]

POLITICAL DEVELOPMENT

Until the passing of the Stamp Act of 1765, many colonial newspapers avoided highly controversial local politics and extensive criticism of English policy. Nevertheless, during the 1740s and 1750s newspapers became indispensable tools for campaigning for office and for pressuring those who were considering controversial bills. The newspapers were powerful enough that local elites feared the "unthinking multitude" and attacked what they saw as irresponsible attempts to inflame the public mind.[23]

James Franklin's attempt to write about local controversy led him to jail, although it did not silence him, and then to a more lucrative government post. Another exception to the generally cautious printing establishment was John Peter Zenger, who printed the views of attorney James Alexander in his newspaper, *The New York Journal*. Because Zenger's case created no legal precedent, because the reasoning of the defense was not enacted into law until about sixty years later, and because the framers of the Constitution did not address freedom of speech and press in the initial document, historians have long debated the significance of the printer's triumph over New York Governor William Cosby. The late eighteenth-century New York politician Gouverneur Morris probably overestimated the impact of the trial when he termed its outcome "the germ of American freedom, the morning star of that liberty which subsequently revolutionized America." Nevertheless, accounts of the

Zenger trial were widely reprinted and circulated, emphasizing basic tenets of eighteenth-century liberalism, and marking an important milestone in colonial religious and political freedom.

BRADFORD AS FORERUNNER

William Bradford I, who began his colonial printing career in 1692 in Pennsylvania, quickly learned that criticism of government was detrimental to prosperity. Bradford took the first printing press to Philadelphia under the protective sponsorship of the colony's proprietor, William Penn. The arrangement quickly dissolved after Bradford offended the Quaker establishment by publishing a dissident speech.

The 1692 trial of Bradford for printing a seditious pamphlet posed the questions of law, fact, and truth, the same issues that arose more than forty years later in the trial of John Peter Zenger. Although Bradford did not succeed as well as did Zenger's attorney, Andrew Hamilton, in persuading a jury of his innocence, charges against him were dropped. Isaiah Thomas claimed it was not Bradford's eloquent defense, but a juror's inadvertent destruction of evidence, that freed the printer. As the jurors viewed a frame of hand-set type, one of the jurors bumped it with his cane, and "the types fell from the frame . . . formed a confused heap, and prevented further investigations."[24]

Whether or not the yarn retold by Isaiah Thomas about the scattered type may be believed, it is known that Bradford argued fiercely in his own defense. In a sedition trial under English law—which also applied in colonial Pennsylvania—the judge determined the law, and the jury determined the fact. This meant that if a judge decided that a publication or utterance was "Malitious [sic] and Seditious," then a crime had been committed. That was the law of the matter. The jury was to determine only the fact of publication; if the material bore a printer's imprint or had been seized in his shop, the printer would be found guilty of a crime and punished.[25]

For the first time in an American seditious libel prosecution, William Bradford contended that jury members "are to find also, whether this be a seditious paper or not, and whether it does tend to the weakening of the hands of the magistrates." When Justice Jennings told the jury that they were "only to try, whether William Bradford printed it or not," Bradford retorted, "This is wrong, for the jury are judges in law as well as the matter of fact."[26] Nevertheless, William Bradford soon left for New York, where, as government's printer and editor for the *New York Gazette*, he happily celebrated Zenger's misfortunes rather than support the printer who faced charges similar to those Bradford contended with. Bradford wrote in 1734 that all men should be responsible for their words: "'Tis the abuse not the use of the press that is criminal and ought to be punished."[27]

THE NEW YORK JOURNAL

John Peter Zenger was born in Germany and immigrated to America in 1710 with his family. His father died en route, and in 1711 — when he was fourteen — Zenger was apprenticed to printer William Bradford I in New York.

After printing in New York for more than seven years, Zenger was asked late in 1733 to begin publishing a newspaper in support of a political faction. The heart of this faction was made up of well-to-do New York merchants and landowners whose position and income were jeopardized by a newly appointed governor, William Cosby. Bradford's newspaper did not allow them to carry on their crusade in its pages.

The political setting was labyrinthine. The crown-appointed governor had died, which left Rip Van Dam in control for thirteen months as the acting governor. Van Dam, evidently following what he saw as the standard political practice in New York, collected a large amount of money by assessing fees as his salary. But the crown's appointee, Sir William Cosby, arrived in 1732 and soon demanded half of the fees Van Dam had collected.

When Van Dam refused to hand over that money, Governor Cosby resolved to take him to court. Using his power as governor, Cosby re-constituted the colony's Supreme Court into a Court of Equity. That form of court had the virtue, in Governor Cosby's eyes, of sitting without a jury. It was clear to Cosby that a local jury would not allow him, as the new governor and an outsider, to win his action. When the chief justice ruled that it was illegal for the governor to create such a court, the governor replaced him.

Governor Cosby's high-handed behavior infuriated a number of politicians, and led to the forming of a "Popular Party" to oppose him. One member of the party, attorney James Alexander, was particularly threatened by the governor. Cosby owed Alexander money and refused to pay it back, and attempted to discredit him in London. Alexander, seeing no alternative method for exposing the governor, subsidized and became chief contributor to the *New York Journal*, begun November 5, 1733, by printer John Peter Zenger.[28]

Alexander represented a political faction that not only opposed Governor Cosby in a narrow political sense, but who also advanced the ideas of eighteenth-century English and American thought that government should not exercise arbitrary power. Alexander quoted liberally from the writings of the British political writers John Trenchard and Thomas Gordon, who, beginning in 1720, wrote widely on resistance to arbitrary power and on the need for freedom to oppose government violations of the public trust.[29] Cato's letters by Trenchard and Gordon were an important source of libertarian thought in eighteenth-century England and America. James Alexander recast these arguments — emphasizing the need for freedom of expression — for use in

New York.³⁰ The anonymity of James Alexander's work placed Zenger in a vulnerable position. When Governor Cosby decided to silence the offending newspaper, Zenger was arrested and imprisoned under a warrant signed by New York's governor and Council "for printing and publishing several seditious libels."³¹ The arrest procedure used was regarded as high-handed by many, and the new chief justice could not persuade a grand jury to indict Zenger. The governor then asked his Council to convince the Assembly to order the burning of certain issues of Zenger's *Journal*. New York City's Court of Quarter Sessions was approached with a similar proposal, and it too refused to act.³² Governor Cosby and the Council then ordered the mayor and magistrates of New York City to see to the "burning by the common hangman, or whipper, near the pillory, the libelous papers." Because city officials refused to obey the order, "the papers were therefore burnt by the order of the governor, not by the hangman or whipper, who were officers of the corporation (of New York City) . . ."³³

In the midst of these irregular procedures, Zenger sat in jail for nine months. He was, however, a mere scapegoat. Although the attorney general arrested him by issuing an "information" November 17, 1734, Governor Cosby simultaneously offered fifty pounds to anyone who discovered the authors of the "seditious libel."³⁴ Zenger was not allowed to communicate with anyone except his wife, Anna, who continued Zenger's printing operation until he was released. Although the printer often has been considered a hero, he might also be described as a German immigrant used by rich and powerful individuals in an attempt to bolster their own "flagging social and economic power."³⁵ Like Franklin, Zenger showed how printers could receive public support.

THE ZENGER TRIAL: THE PRELIMINARIES

On August 4, 1735, Attorney General Richard Bradley opened Zenger's case, levying the charges of seditious libel. Zenger's lead attorney, the author of most of the newspaper copy Zenger printed, James Alexander, was disbarred. But meanwhile Alexander drafted a brief for the defense and contacted Andrew Hamilton of Philadelphia, a friend of Benjamin Franklin and believed to be the most able trial lawyer in the colonies. (Some speculate, indeed, that Hamilton's expertise helped give rise to the advice still offered, "Get yourself a Philadelphia lawyer.")³⁶

The sixty-five-year-old Hamilton rose among the spectators at the trial and, following strategy planned by Alexander, began Zenger's defense most remarkably. Attorney General Bradley already had stated the law of libel as then understood: juries would decide only the fact of publication; judges would decide the law, or whether the material was libelous. But Hamilton simply stipulated that Zenger had printed the publications under question, saying that he did not think it proper "to deny the publication of a complaint which I think is the right of every free-born subject to make . . . "[37]

Attorney General Bradley then declared that the jury must find Zenger guilty "for supposing they [the statements] were true, the law says that they are not the less libelous for that; nay indeed the law says their being true is an aggravation of the crime." Hamilton replied that "bare printing and publishing" a paper should not make it a libel, but that the words themselves "must be libelous, that is, false, scandalous, and seditious or else we are not guilty."

The prosecution clearly had the law of the times on its side, but Hamilton spoke with great ingenuity and force, arguing that truthful publications should not be punishable. Perhaps because of his youth and inexperience, coupled with the older lawyer's towering reputation, Chief Justice DeLancey did not stop Hamilton's eloquent plea, despite the fact the law was on the side of the court. Hamilton appealed to the jury as citizens of New York, as honest and lawful men. He maintained the accusations printed in Zenger's newspaper were known widely to be true, noting that "therefore in your justice lies our safety." He said that although in the Court of the Star Chamber men suffered for speaking truth, "the practice of informations for libels is a sword in the hands of a wicked king." Quickly chided by Attorney General Bradley, Hamilton altered his statement, claiming "we are governed by the best of kings," and pleading pardon for his zeal. But he also pleaded his own health, telling the court, "And you see I labor under the weight of many years, and am borne down by great infirmities of body." But even though he called himself old and weak, he asserted that he would go "to the utmost part of the land to help quench the flame of prosecutions upon informations." He concluded his arguments to the jury:

> the question before the court and you, gentlemen of the jury, is not of small nor private concern, it is not the cause of a poor printer, nor of New York alone, which you are now trying. No! It may in its consequence affect every freeman that lives under a British government on the Main of America. It is the best cause. It is the cause of liberty; and I make no doubt but your upright conduct this day will not only entitle you to the love and esteem of your fellow citizens; but every man who prefers freedom to a life of slavery will bless and honor you as men who have baffled the attempt of tyranny, and, by an impartial and uncorrupt verdict, have laid a noble foundation for securing to ourselves, our posterity, and our neighbors that to which nature and the laws of our country have given us as a right—the liberty both of exposing and opposing arbitrary power (in these parts of the world, at least) by speaking and writing truth.

At the end of the trial, happy crowds carried Andrew Hamilton, who had won a "not guilty" verdict for Zenger, to the Black Horse Tavern to celebrate a people's victory, but printer Zenger remained in jail until the next day.[38]

AFTER ZENGER

Unwilling to confront popular opinion by striking down the jury verdict, the chief justice and Governor Cosby let the decision stand. Although decisions of juries do not create legal precedent as would a judicial decision, post-Zenger seditious libel situations generally admitted truth as a defense. In 1742, when Thomas Fleet of the *Boston Evening-Post* suggested that Sir Robert Walpole would be taken into custody, he escaped prosecution by obtaining affidavits that a naval officer had so advised him.[39]

William Parks of the *Virginia Gazette* escaped in a similar way. Around 1740, after accusing a member of Virginia's House of Burgesses of stealing sheep, Parks escaped prosecution by producing court records, proving his accusations true. Looking back from the vantage point of 1810, Isaiah Thomas wrote that after the incident the member of the house withdrew from public life "and never more ventured to obtrude himself into a conspicuous situation, or to trouble printers with prosecutions for libels." Thomas concluded "Thus, it is obvious that a free press is, of all things, the best check and restraint on wicked men and arbitrary magistrates."[40]

CONCLUSION

From the beginning of the North American newspaper to the years preceding the War for Independence, active artisans and members of the professional class established print shops in connection with bookselling operations, stationery sales, and newspaper production. Printers trained in apprenticeships, both in the colonies and in London or the English provinces. Their incomes depended on the success not only of their newspapers, but of their operations as a whole, including appointments to positions of postmaster and payment for printing official documents. The printing trade first developed in the cities, such as Boston, Philadelphia, New York, and then Annapolis and Williamsburg. Distribution of newspapers and books followed the major trade routes. Attempts at magazines were short-lived.

Editors focused primarily on business dealings and continued to print foreign news, as well as intercolonial news, and they became involved to some degree in controversial local politics. John Peter Zenger, printing for James Alexander, gained popular support and was able to thwart government interference, although at a high personal cost. Although his trial and acquittal did not necessarily establish legal precedents, it aired the controversy of seditious libel issues that presented significant dilemmas for printers of the time.

NOTES

1. Stephen Botein, "'Meer Mechanics' and an Open Press: The Business and Political Strategies of Colonial American Printers," *Perspectives in American History* 9 (1975), pp. 140–150.
2. Botein, in "Meer Mechanics," discusses the income printers made from book sales and newspaper production.
3. Joseph T. Buckingham, *Personal Memoirs and Recollections of Editorial Life*, 2 vols. (Boston, 1852), 1:15–16, 21, 8, cited in William L. Joyce, David D. Hall, Richard D. Brown and John B. Hench, eds. *Printing and Society in Early America* (Worcester, Mass.: American Antiquarian Society, 1983), p. 2.
4. Samuel Goodrich, *Recollections of a Lifetime*, 2 vols. (New York, 1857), 2:284, cited in Joyce, et al., eds. *Printing and Society*, p. 21.
5. For an alternative view to that of Stephen Botein, see Jeffery A. Smith, "Impartiality and Revolutionary Ideology: Editorial Politics of the *South Carolina Gazette*, 1732–1775," *Journal of Southern History*, XLIX (November 1983), pp. 511–26. Smith argues that for thirty years before the 1765 passage of the Stamp Act the *Gazette* delivered controversy and "expanded the opportunity for public debate" (p. 23). For expansion of Smith's thesis, see his book, *Printers and Press Freedom: The Ideology of Early American Journalism* (New York: Oxford University Press, 1988). Leonard Levy, in *Legacy of Suppression: Freedom of Speech and Press in Early American History* (Cambridge, Mass.: Belknap Press of Harvard University Press, 1960), argues that printers had failed to oppose the restrictions of seditious libel until the violent sentiment of patriots created an issue impossible to avoid.
6. Jerome R. Reich, *Colonial America* (Englewood Cliffs, N.J.: Prentice-Hall, 1984), p. 154.
7. Susan Henry, "Exception to the Female Model: Colonial Printer Mary Crouch," *Journalism Quarterly* 62:4 (Winter 1985), pp. 725–733, 749.
8. For a full account of Condy's business see Joyce, et al., eds. *Printing and Society*, pp. 104–117.
9. Botein, "Meer Mechanics," p. 153.
10. Isaiah Thomas, *The History of Printing in America*, ed. Marcus A. McCorison from the 2nd edition (New York: Weathervane Books, 1970), p. 102.
11. Frank Luther Mott, *A History of American Magazines, 1741–1850* (Cambridge, Mass.: Harvard University Press, 1930), p. 24.
12. Thomas, *History of Printing*, pp. 374–375; Elsie Hebert, "William Bradford III,"

in Perry J. Ashley, ed., *Dictionary of Literary Biography*, vol. 43 (Detroit: Gale Research, 1985) pp. 73–74.

13. Stephen Botein, "The Anglo-American Book Trade before 1776: Personnel and Strategies," in Joyce, et al., eds. *Printing and Society*, p. 57.

14. *The Autobiography of Benjamin Franklin*, Gordon S. Haight, ed. (New York: Walter J. Black, 1941), p. 62; Michael J. Kirkhorn, "Benjamin Franklin," *DLB*, vol. 43, p. 197.

15. Franklin's argument was directed specifically at religious topics. His comment about writers who paid printers well may have referred to the publishing of pamphlets or to the fact that printers were paid to include polemics in their newspapers.

16. Leonard Levy, *Emergence of a Free Press* (New York: Oxford University Press, 1985), pp. 119–120.

17. Elizabeth Cook, *Literary Influences in Colonial Newspapers* (New York, 1912), p. 6, cited in Ira L. Baker, "Elizabeth Timothy: America's First Woman Editor," *Journalism Quarterly*, 54:2 (Summer 1977), p. 282.

18. Baker, "Elizabeth Timothy," p. 285. See also Jeffery A. Smith, "Impartiality and and Revolutionary Ideology: Editorial Policies of the *South-Carolina Gazette*, 1732–1775," *Journal of Southern History* 49 (November, 1983), pp. 511–26.

19. Thomas, *History of Printing*, pp. 530, 552–553. See also Lawrence C. Wroth, *William C. Parks: Printer and Journalist of England and Colonial America* (Richmond, Va, 1926) and Wroth, *The Colonial Printer*, 2nd ed. (Portland, Me, 1939).

20. Joyce, et al., eds. *Printing and Society*, p. 139.

21. Joyce, et al., eds. *Printing and Society*, pp. 135–153.

22. Thomas, *History of Printing*, p. 297.

23. Gary Nash, *The Urban Crucible* (Cambridge, Mass.: Harvard University Press, 1986), pp. 123–127.

24. Thomas, *History of Printing*, pp. 354–355.

25. Thomas, *History of Printing* p. 344. See Norman Rosenberg, *Protecting the Best Men: An Interpretive History of the Law of Libel* (Chapel Hill: University of North Carolina Press, 1986), p. 35.

26. Thomas, *History of Printing*, p. 350, evidently citing, as did Rosenberg, at p. 283, *New England's Spirit of Persecution Transmitted to Pennsylvania [sic] . . . in the Trial of Peter Boss, George Keith, Thomas Budd, and William Bradford . . .* (Philadelphia, 1693).

27. *New York Gazette*, No. 432, January 28–February 4, 1734, cited in Stanley Katz's introduction to James Alexander's *A Brief Narrative of the Case and Trial of John Peter Zenger* (Cambridge, Mass.: Harvard University Press, 2nd ed., 1971), p. 13.

28. For a thorough description of the background of the Zenger case, see Cathy Covert, "'Passion is Ye Prevailing Motive': the Feud Behind the Zenger Case," *Journalism Quarterly* (Spring 1973):50:1, pp. 3–10.

29. Levy, *Free Press*, pp. 109–112; Arthur M. Schlesinger, *Prelude to Independence: The Newspaper War on Britain, 1764–1776* (New York: Knopf, 1958), p. 137.

30. Paul Finkelman, "The Zenger Case: Prototype of a Political Trial," in Michael R. Belknap, ed., *American Political Trials* (Westport, Conn.: Greenwood Press, 1981). For interpretation that operating principle in Zenger case was truth, rather than freedom of expression, see David Paul Nord, "The Authority of Truth: Religion and the John Peter Zenger Case," *Journalism Quarterly* (Summer 1985) 62:2, pp. 227–235.
31. Thomas, *History of Printing*, p. 487.
32. Katz, *John Peter Zenger*, pp. 41–42, 45; Levy, *Emergence of a Free Press*, p. 40.
33. Thomas, *History of Printing* p. 488.
34. New York *Weekly Journal*, November 18–25, 1734; Bleyer, *Main Currents*, p. 65 f.
35. Catherine L. Covert, "Journalism History and Women's Experience: A Problem in Conceptual Change," *Journalism History* 9:1 (Spring 1981), p. 4.
36. Vincent Buranelli, *The Trial of Peter Zenger* (New York: NYU Press, 1957), p. 49.
37. All quotations from Andrew Hamilton's defense are cited in Katz, *John Peter Zenger*, pp. 62–101.
38. Covert, "Journalism History and Women's Experience," p. 4.
39. *Boston Evening Post*, Mar. 8, 15, 1742; Levy, pp. 32–33.
40. Thomas, *History of Printing*, p. 553.

CHAPTER 3

TIMES THAT TRIED MEN'S SOULS

During the early revolutionary period, from the end of the French and Indian War in 1763 until the Declaration of Independence in 1776, printing flourished in the colonies. The number of master printers grew from forty-seven to eighty-two, and newspapers doubled from twenty-one in 1763 to forty-two in 1775.[1] Less able to import stationery and books from London during the period of colonial resistance to English economic policy, printers developed new strategies for making money, for relating to government entities, and for interacting with public opinion. Different strategies often served varied purposes. Printers produced political pamphlets as money-making enterprises as well as documents of political discussion, and disseminated an increased amount of political news along the trade routes already established during the mid-part of the century.

As political events encouraged colonial resistance to English policy, editorial strategies included exposing the injustices of the old system under English rule and associating English authority with criminal action. The logical arguments of John Dickinson's "Letters From a Farmer in Pennsylvania" appealed to an audience familiar with formal argument and formal documents, and the horrible tales propagated by the *Journal of Occurrences* made use of exaggeration and outright fabrication as political weapons. Thomas Paine's *Common Sense* also appealed to a wide audience.[2] From the time of the Stamp Act of 1765 until the end of the War for Independence in

1783, printers abandoned neutrality as a profitable position and, pressured by the violence of public opinion and wise enough to exploit a profitable position, ultimately joined sides. Colonial support for Loyalist printers was limited, however, as free press ideology supported colonists in revolt against oppression. Patriots were not likely to have their presses freely support what they regarded as an outside power.[3]

COLONIAL RESISTANCE TO ECONOMIC POLICY

THE FRENCH AND INDIAN WAR

Called the Seven Years' War in England, the French and Indian War represented the culmination of many years of struggle between England and France over colonial territory in Canada and along the Mississippi River, particularly in the Ohio Valley. The English had long coveted the French fur trade in the region. In 1748, when some Indian tribes agreed to sell furs to the English, and not to the French, fighting broke out throughout the region.

In an attempt to unify colonial resources, Benjamin Franklin drew up the Albany Plan of Union in 1754, enabling the colonies to act as a unit under a president-general appointed by the king. However, neither the colonists nor the British were ready for unification. The British, fearing a united colonial government, and the colonists, fearing British unified control, both rejected Franklin's plan. Although recalcitrant colonial assemblies only reluctantly granted provisions for the British war, after major losses, the British defeated the French and signed the Treaty of Paris in 1763. France surrendered all lands east of the Mississippi to England and Louisiana to Spain; Spain relinquished control of Florida to the English.

The war left England overextended and burdened by debt, and left colonists weary of English war. England's victories, however, freed colonists from fear of border wars and encouraged their recalcitrance. The war also assisted economic development in the colonies, as colonial manufactures developed to meet military needs. By the end of the French and Indian War, the shipbuilding industry of New England was thriving and the number of forges and furnaces surpassed those in England.

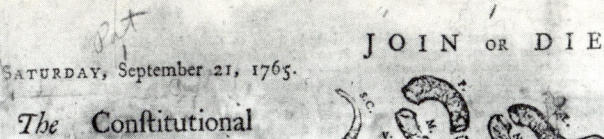

Masthead of the Constitutional Courant, *September 21, 1765. The "Join or Die" emblem indicated the necessity of unity among colonists. (Library of Congress Collection)*

The economic well-being of the colonies, combined with ill-considered British tax measures instituted after the war to provide unchallenged trade advantages for England, encouraged cohesive colonial resistance to English policy. The Sugar Act of 1764 taxed refined sugar, wool, wine and coffee imports and—perhaps an underrated irritant to hard-drinking colonials—prohibited importation of French wines and foreign rum. The Currency Act of the same year, extending a policy already in existence in the northern colonies, forbade Virginia from issuing paper money as legal tender.

Leading Massachusetts dissidents who organized the "Popular Party," and the wealthy Massachusetts legislator James Otis, Jr., issued a pamphlet in July 1764 to list grievances against the royal governor and King George III. The pamphlet, "The Rights of the British Colonies Asserted and Proved," had little effect beyond the colonies, but served as a vehicle to advance what would become a familiar marching slogan: "No taxation without representation." The pamphlet contended that legislatures were bound by God and nature to (1) govern by stated laws; (2) assure that laws be designed with the good of the people as the only ultimate goal; and (3) tax only by consent.[4]

THE STAMP ACT

The Stamp Act of 1765 infuriated influential persons because it put a ten-pound fee on admittance to the bar (higher than the fee in London) and taxed legal documents, business papers, and newspapers.

The colonial press, which had much to lose economically, protested vigorously. On October 31, 1765, the day before the Stamp Act went into effect, the *Pennsylvania Journal*'s front page was laid out like a tombstone with the newspaper's nameplate displayed before a large representation of a skull and crossbones, and picks and shovels. The motto for the issue was "EXPIRING: In Hopes of a Resurrection to Life Again." The lower right-hand corner where the stamps were to be placed carried another skull and crossbones illustration, with the legend, "An Emblem of the Effects of the STAMP. O! the fatal STAMP!"[5]

Some papers sailed defiantly along, publishing without stamps. Setting such a pattern were the *New London Gazette* and the *Connecticut Gazette*, with issues for November 1, 1765, which appeared without stamps.[6] In New York, John Holt's *New York Gazette or Weekly Post-Boy*, used the motto: "The United Voice of all His Majesty's free and loyal subjects in America—LIBERTY, PROPERTY AND no STAMPS."[7]

Colonial mobs assailed printers who accepted the stamp tax or who tried to avoid it by not publishing. Across a number of colonies, the Sons of Liberty organized resistance. In August 1765, horns and whistles sounded, calling Boston's rum-inspired mob from the taverns to the streets, terrorizing stamp master Andrew Oliver by hanging him in effigy from the Liberty Tree, then destroying a building erected for the stamp master and cutting down and beheading the effigy.[8] Oliver promised to resign his office, but the mob then proceeded to the home of Oliver's father-in-law, Governor Thomas Hutchinson, and burned it. Governor Hutchinson later referred to one of the leaders, Sam Adams, as "the Grand Incendiary of the Province."[9]

John Holt of the *New York Gazette and Weekly Post Boy* was threatened with violence to his person and his property if he stopped publishing his newspaper to avoid the stamp issue. In November 1765, a North Carolina mob compelled Andrew Steuart to print "at Hazard of Life" if he refused. James Johnston of Georgia, however, resisted popular demand to continue printing, and closed his shop from mid-November 1765 to the end of May 1766, when the news reached the colonies that Parliament yielded to political pressure and repealed the Stamp Act.

The reaction by and toward colonial printers carried a strong message: the former neutrality that had seemed to be the wisest course no longer was acceptable. Those printers who tried to maintain an impartial stance soon found that their audience labeled them Tories.

Economic Resistance Turns Political

EDES AND GILL AND THE *BOSTON GAZETTE*

Benjamin Edes and John Gill, who jointly published the *Boston Gazette* from 1755 until 1775, belonged to a group of young colonial printers. The *Gazette* conducted partisan crusades before the Stamp Act made such activity popular, and became strongly patriot during the Revolutionary period. Edes was a member of Boston's "Loyall Nine," the group that clandestinely stirred up the Sons of Liberty to occasional mob work and which often met at the Green Dragon tavern adjoining the *Gazette* office.

Sam Adams, patriot and rabble-rouser. (State Historical Society of Wisconsin)

Edes and Gill opposed British taxes and began advocating boycotts of British imports in the fall of 1767. They worked closely with James Otis, who received an advance copy of John Dickinson's "Letters from a Farmer in Pennsylvania." Dickinson hoped, correctly, that Boston's propaganda factories could rouse the public, making Massachusetts once again, "first to kindle the Sacred Flame."[10] Edes, Gill and the "Loyal Nine" did not disappoint Dickinson, and printed the Whig's opposition letters in serial form.

The *Gazette* gained greater notoriety with its coverage of the Boston Massacre, when several Bostonians were killed after a scuffle with British soldiers in 1770. The *Gazette* printed small Paul Revere woodcuts of four coffins that represented four victims killed by British soldiers. Recording the incident for the *Gazette* was political agitator Sam Adams, who displayed outrage when the British officer and six of his men escaped heavy punishment when tried for murder. Despite the fact that John Adams and another Caucus Club intellectual, Josiah Quincy, bravely defended the British soldiers, Sam Adams wrote angrily under the pen name of "Vindex the Avenger" when five were released and two ordered to have their hands branded.

Edes participated directly in planning the 1773 Boston Tea Party.[11] Not only did the *Gazette* print a protest asking the return of the tea to Britain, but also organized armed guards to prevent the tea from being landed. On the night of the Tea Party in Boston, some men drank punch mixed by son Peter Edes at Edes's home in Brattle Street, and then regrouped at the *Gazette* office to disguise themselves by painting their faces and putting on feathered headdresses. It took three hours for the tea to be dumped from 342 chests, destroying 15,000 pounds of East India Company property.[12]

John Gill retired from the newspaper when it suspended business for two months in 1775 during the British occupation of Boston. Edes reinstated the paper in Boston and continued it there until the late 1790s; former partner John Gill had opened his own paper, *The Constitutional Journal*, which he ran until 1787. The *Gazette*'s success caused Massachusetts Governor Hutchinson to grumble, "The misfortune is that seven eights of the people read none but this infamous paper, and so are never undeceived."

"LETTERS FROM A FARMER"

The twelve "Letters from a Farmer in Pennsylvania," published serially in colonial newspapers in 1767 and 1768, actually were a series of essays written by Philadelphia politician John Dickinson. The specific point of the letters was to persuade an already wary audience that the British taxation of tea, paper and other goods represented a conspiracy against the colonists—an attempt

> **LETTERS FROM A FARMER**
>
> I hope, my dear countrymen, that you will in every colony be upon your guard against those who may at any time endeavor to stir you up, under pretences of patriotism, to any measures disrespectful to our sovereign and our mother-country. Hot, rash, disorderly proceedings injure the reputation of a people as to wisdom, valour, and virtue, without procuring them the least benefit. I pray GOD that he may be pleased to inspire you and your posterity to the latest ages with that spirit, of which I have an idea, but find a difficulty to express: To express in the best manner I can, I mean a spirit that shall so guide you, that it will be impossible to determine whether an *American's* character is most distinguishable for his loyalty to his sovereign, his duty to his mother-country, his love of freedom, or his affection for his native soil.
>
> SOURCE. John Dickinson, Letter III of "Letters From a Farmer in Pennsylvania."

to impose external measures on the colonies and to deprive them of liberty. Dickinson opposed the kind of rabble-rousing Sam Adams deliberately encouraged, and appealed to the rational side of the Whig businessman.

JOURNAL OF OCCURRENCES

While the Farmer from Pennsylvania appealed to reason, the widely circulated diary called the *Journal of Occurrences* disseminated news of imaginary and embellished grievances, a parade of loathsome incidents designed to agitate sentiment against the British. The *Journal*, published during 1768 and 1769, carried highly colored accounts of the actions of British troops, who were in Boston during 1768 and 1769 to maintain control during the aftermath of riots protesting revenue provisions.[13]

The *Journal* format was a series of articles, written in diary form and sprinkled with editorial comment. The diary, while focusing extensively on Massachusetts with vitriolic attacks on the royal governor, appeared in whole or in part in at least fourteen colonial newspapers and in several periodicals in England.[14]

The authors of the *Journal* have never been identified. Boston royal officials, however, believed it was the work of Sam Adams and his friends. Historians have suggested that possible authors include Henry Knox, who was running a bookstore in Boston; Benjamin Edes, copublisher with John Gill of the *Boston Gazette*; William Greenleaf, an employee of Edes and Gill's printing house; Isaiah Thomas, then working as a printer in Boston; and Sam Adams's cousin (and later the second President of the United States) John Adams.[15]

The *Journal* celebrated the 1766 repeal of the Stamp Act, but claimed Bostonians had little else to celebrate. In the *Journal*'s opinion, the Townshend Duties (taxes on paper, glass and other items) were intolerable. Further, the *Journal* objected to customs commissioners' attempts to stop smuggling and to the quartering of British troops in the city of Boston.

The Massachusetts royal governor was incensed by the *Journal*, claiming that "Nine-tenths of what you read in the *Journal of Occurrences* in Boston is either absolutely false or grossly misrepresented."[16] He wrote that the diary was calculated "to raise a general clamor against his Majesty's government in England and throughout America," and that the *Journal* was a collection of "impudent, virulent, and seditious lies."[17]

John Holt's *New York Journal* published the first installment of the *Journal of Occurrences* September 28, 1769. It reported that British ships—men of war and transports—had arrived at Nantasket Harbor from Halifax, Nova Scotia, and that the ships carried about 900 soldiers.[18] The item also needled British authorities by commenting that inland settlements were left unprotected when troops were moved to Boston.

Once troops landed in Boston in September 1768, the *Journal* described the quartering of troops in the town, repeatedly claiming that British officers often were whipped or executed for desertion and that blacks usually were chosen to administer the whippings.

The most pervasive, theme, however, involved tales of soldiers mistreating Boston citizens. Most of these so-called incidents were reported without attribution:

> A Physician of the Town walking the Streets the other evening was jostled by an Officer, when a Scuffle ensued, he was afterwards met by the same Officer in Company with another, both as yet unknown, who repeated his Blows, and as is supposed gave him a Stroke with a Pistol, which so wounded him as to endanger his life.[19]

Other frightening tales included that of a British captain who was said to have attempted "to excite an insurrection."[20] The *Journal* claimed women were no longer safe but were treated rudely by the soldiers, being "taken hold of" or nearly abducted. An old woman's resistance and screams were all that prevented her from being raped.[21]

Chapter 3 **Times That Tried Men's Souls**

NEWS OF CONGRESS AND OF WAR

CONGRESSIONAL PROCEEDINGS SECRET

In mid-October 1774, young William Bradford, Jr., of Philadelphia wrote to his Princeton college classmate, James Madison of Virginia. Bradford wanted to tell his friend about the impressive men assembled in Philadelphia as the Continental Congress. But Bradford had difficulty learning what was going on in Carpenters' Hall where Congress met. "Their proceedings," Bradford told Madison, "are a profound secret & the doors open to no one; so that were you here as you wish your curiosity would be but poorly gratified . . ."

Young Bradford was in a better position than most Philadelphians to learn what was happening behind the closed doors of the First Continental Congress. His father, Colonel William Bradford, and his older brother, Thomas, were official printers for what young William called "a great concourse of gentlemen from all parts of the continent." His unsatisfied curiosity reflected the effectiveness of Congress's resolve that "the doors be kept shut during the time of business, and that the members consider themselves under the strongest obligations of honour, to keep the proceedings secret, untill [sic] a majority shall direct them to be made public."[22]

Because most of the colonial legislatures met in secret and released information only after it had been edited carefully, printers were familiar with secret proceedings. Although legislatures and Congress agreed that the public needed to have information, they were unwilling to allow their own dissension to be covered in the press. Congress, organized to protest British imperial policies and not a regularly constituted legislature, was eager for publicity. But this publicity consisted of carefully edited proclamations and petitions to the British Parliament, to the king, and to the inhabitants of Canada and America. As Bradford wrote to Madison, the deliberations of the body remained secret.

America's printers in 1774 and 1775 did not protest as Congress continued to meet in secret throughout the War for Independence (1775–1783) and during the early national years. Congressional delegates denounced breaches of secrecy, and on one such occasion, fired Thomas Paine for leaking secrets from his post as secretary to a congressional committee.[23]

NEWS OF WAR SPREADS THROUGH COLONIES

The news of the "Shots Heard Round the World"—the outbreak of fighting between British soldiers and American colonists at the Massachusetts villages

Carpenter's Hall in Philadelphia, meeting place of the First Continental Congress. (Library of Congress Collection)

Chapter 3 **Times That Tried Men's Souls**

of Lexington and Concord—circulated through the colonies in contradictory and confusing driblets.[24] Colonial printers relied on reports from postriders, travelers, and coasting ships and had few resources to check the accuracy of the reports they received. The problem of reliability continued throughout the War for Independence, and one acid observer, dubious of the accuracy of newspaper accounts, wrote in 1783:

> The four winds (the initials of which make the word NEWS) are not so capricious, or so liable to change, as our public intelligencers; we have on Monday a whisper;—On Tuesday a rumour;—on Wednesday a conjecture;—on Thursday, a probable;—on Friday, a positive;—and on Saturday, a premature.[25]

The fighting began on the morning of April 19, 1775, and Philadelphia, the city where the Second Continental Congress met in May to react to the fighting, received no news until five days later. At that time the *Pennsylvania Packet* had this inconclusive statement:

> We have no papers from Boston by yesterday's post.—The report is, that as the printers were moving their types out of the town the packages were stopped and broken open by the soldiery, and the letters scattered or thrown into disorder, so that no paper could be got ready for the post.[26]

Actual news of the fighting arrived with the postrider from Trenton, New Jersey, at 5 P.M. on April 24.[27]

A week later, the *Pennsylvania Packet* published accounts of the hostilities, presenting bits of information in roughly the order they were received. One item bore the unwieldy title of "Accounts from Rhode-Island, respecting the late transaction in Massachusetts-Bay, being the substance of several letters arrived at New York, dated April 21, seven o'clock, A.M. 1775."

The "First Account" said that the British troops had taken boats from Boston to Watertown, Massachusetts, "where they had fired upon the minute men, then proceeded to Concord, examined the magazines there, destroyed about 50 barrels of flour, and spiked up four pieces of cannon—." This account added that about three or four hundred men had killed about forty British soldiers, and had taken another forty prisoners.

The "Second account" from Rhode Island said that the colony's governor had called the Assembly to meet because of the attack on "our brethren of the Massachusetts." The third version of the firing near Boston said that "the action was at Lexington, about twelve miles from Boston, to which place about 1200 of the King's Troops had advanced upon 30 minute men . . . then fired and killed 7. . . ."

Meanwhile, news came from other colonies. A message dated April 23 from Hartford, Connecticut, said "that we have undoubted intelligence of hostilities being begun at Boston by the regular troops. . . ." The letter from Connecticut added that the Redcoats

> went to the house where Mr. [John] Hancock lodged, who with Samuel Adams, luckily got out of their way by secret and speedy intelligence from Paul Revere, who is now missing . . . when they searched the house for Mr. Hancock and Adams, and not finding them there, killed the woman of the house and all the children and set fire to the house; from thence they proceeded on their way to Concord, firing at, and killing hogs, geese, cattle, and every thing that came in their way, and burning houses.

This version added that the British soldiers "destroyed one hundred barrels of flour at Concord and took possession of the Court-House . . ."[28]

DECLARATION OF INDEPENDENCE

Nearly a year after the outbreak in Lexington and Concord, in May 1776, the Continental Congress took a bold—and treasonable step—and recognized the revolutionary assemblies as legal governments. A few weeks later, news reached Philadelphia that the Virginia Convention had passed resolutions calling for a declaration that the colonies were free and independent states. And on June 7, 1776, Virginia Delegate to Congress Richard Henry Lee submitted the resolution that led toward formal independence:

> RESOLVED, That these United Colonies are, and of right ought to be, free and independent States, that they are absolved from all allegiance to the British Crown, and that all political connection between them and the State of Great Britain is, and ought to be totally dissolved.
>
> That it is expedient forthwith to take the most effectual measures for forming Alliances.
>
> That a plan of confederation be prepared and transmitted to the respective Colonies for their consideration and approbation.[29]

On June 11, a committee was appointed to draft a declaration of independence: Thomas Jefferson of Virginia, John Adams of Massachusetts, Roger Sherman of Connecticut, and Robert R. Livingston of New York.[30]

THE OLD EPHRATA PRINTING PRESS.

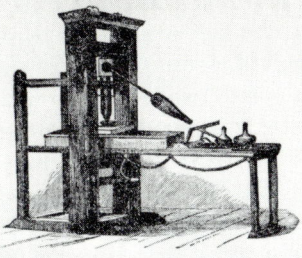 

The Old Ephrata Printing Press, on which the Declaration of Independence was printed, and the Original House, No. 702 Market Street, in which it was actually written by THOS. JEFFERSON.

The Ephrata Press on which the Declaration of Independence was printed in 1776. (Library of Congress Collection)

Although the Declaration of Independence was presented to the Continental Congress July 2, news of the document did not reach some colonies until several weeks later. On July 4, the Declaration of Independence was concurred in by the Congress, and a copy was sent to each of the legislatures of the states. It was signed by the delegates August 2. The Bradfords' *Pennsylvania Journal* and David Hall's *Pennsylvania Gazette* both announced on July 3, 1776, that "the CONTINENTAL CONGRESS declared the UNITED COLONIES FREE and INDEPENDENT STATES." The first publication of the Declaration of Independence was in the newspaper of Benjamin Towne, a "Sunshine Patriot," who got the news printed first because *The Pennsylvania Evening Post* was triweekly. The Declaration was printed by John Dunlap in the *Pennsylvania Packet* July 6. *The Freeman's Journal* in Portsmouth, New Hampshire, printed the Declaration July 20. News reached the Southern Colonies by August 2.[31]

THE IMPACT OF PUBLIC OPINION

James Rivington: Tory Target

Those printers who remained loyal to England suffered the wrath of public opinion. New York Loyalist James Rivington, a prosperous bookseller in London, quickly discovered that public opinion would not tolerate opposition viewpoints. When he arrived in Philadelphia in 1760, he opened bookstore partnerships in Philadelphia, New York, and Boston. In 1773, Rivington began a newspaper in New York, grandly named *Rivington's New York Gazette* or the *Connecticut, Hudson's River, New-Jersey, and Quebec Weekly Advertiser*.

At first, Rivington was noted for publishing a neutral newspaper. Lurking in New York, however, was Rivington's nemesis to be, one of the most feared mob leaders of the Revolutionary era, Isaac (King) Sears.

In 1774, Sears, a member of the quasi-secret Sons of Liberty, led a New York City mob through a duplication of the much more famous Boston Tea Party. In response, New York Lieutenant Governor Cadwallader Colden declared that destroying tea in the New York Harbor and other violence by the mob had upset the "principal inhabitants" of New York City. Colden suggested that the mob had gone too far and declared mob-leader Sears and his lieutenants "in disgrace."[32]

Rivington's *New-York Gazetteer* sided with the "principal inhabitants" of New York City. The August 18, 1774, issue included a letter bearing the printed greeting, "To I- - -c S- - -s, Esq.," and was signed, "A Merchant of New York." In the letter, Rivington described Sears as possibly insane, and at least a "political cracker, sent abroad to alarm and terrify, sure to do mischief to the cause he means to support . . ."[33]

Sears responded, wanting "to know without delay my abuser, or [I] shall Consider you the Author and do myself Justice." Rivington retorted in the *Gazetteer* that he would not "deliver up any author, without his permission, and I am ready to defend the freedom of the press when attacked in my person."[34]

The outraged Sears accused Rivington of "Sculking behind your press, and pleading its Liberty. . . ." He continued, "A press in Such hands as yours, instead of being beneficial to Society, may be Justly considered a nuesance [sic], tending to both publick and private Mischief — Free only to do evil, restrained from doing good. . . ."[35]

Although the quarrel subsided, an April 1775 dispute with another merchant, Ralph Thurman, provoked Sears to violence. After Sears accused Thurman of selling supplies to British troops, Thurman retorted in a broadside published by Rivington that perhaps it was Sears who sent ships to supply the Redcoats in Boston.

Sears, urging his supporters to arm themselves, was arrested and taken before the mayor of New York. But just as Sears was being taken to jail, a mob rescued him and carried him through the streets like a conquering hero.

Rivington threw aside caution, mocking a mob that hanged him in effigy. He denounced the mob as dregs of the city and published a parody of a Sears speech to a mob.

Three days later, on April 23, 1775, when news of the fighting at Lexington and Concord reached New York, the Sears-led mob broke into New York's City Hall and took arms and ammunition. Sears, in glory and with the mob at his back, took the keys to the customs house, closing the Port of New York.

On May 10, 1775, Sears led the mob to Rivington's printing house, breaking into his shop and destroying frames of type and copies of a pamphlet. One jump ahead of the mob, Rivington fled to a British ship in New York Harbor.

When he returned to New York from the ship, he was taken into custody for a short time, but eventually was allowed to resume printing. New York's Provincial Congress noted on June 6, 1775, that Rivington had published a handbill begging for pardon, and passed a resolution that the printer be allowed to return to his type case without being harmed.

Mob leaders, however, do not always follow the dictates of authority. Sears, who had moved to Connecticut, returned to New York in November 1775. Again leading a mob, he smashed Rivington's printing house, ruining his presses. Rivington again escaped, but fled this time to England. He returned in late 1777, while British troops controlled the city. Reestablishing his newspaper, he called it the *New-York Royal Gazette*. The sheet became synonymous with Toryism throughout the war, and was known in revolutionist strongholds as "the lying gazette."

At the end of 1783, after the war's end, Rivington begged forgiveness and asked the Continental Army to allow him to remain in New York. The army said yes, but Sears said no. On the last day of 1783 Sears and two companions visited Rivington and ordered him to cease publishing. Rivington's last issue was December 31, 1783, although he continued as a bookseller and stationer in New York for some years. Imprisoned for debt in 1797, the most famous of the Loyalist printers died, ironically, on July 4, 1802—Independence Day.[36]

Although mobs sometimes attacked patriots as well as Tories, patriot printers more successfully elicited support through official channels. Samuel Loudon, a patriot who started his *New-York Packet* early in 1776, advertised publication of a Tory response to Thomas Paine's *Common Sense*. A mob subsequently broke into Loudon's printing house, dragged him out of bed, and carried the pamphlets outside for burning. Loudon protested to New York's Committee of Safety, claiming seventy-five pounds in damages and contending that he was a patriot and entitled to freedom of the press. The Committee of Safety clearly believed Loudon, and soon was paying him 200 pounds per year for carrying its news in his *Loudon's Packet*.[37]

POLITICAL PAMPHLETS

Newspapers and pamphlets served as important vehicles of public opinion during the Revolutionary Period. Historian Bernard Bailyn concluded that "much of the most important and characteristic writing of the American Revolution" appeared in pamphlet form. Arthur Schlesinger, on the other hand, emphasized the contribution of newspapers, saying that of the "many ways of kneading men's minds, none . . . equaled the newspapers."[38] Political pamphlets served as a source of income for printers deprived of income from importing stationery and books from England. In Philadelphia alone, 25 percent of printing income was derived from printing political pamphlets.[39]

Newspapers and pamphlets often contained pieces of the other in reprint form. Series of newspaper articles frequently were republished as pamphlets, and pamphlets were excerpted or run as a series of articles by newspapers. Occasionally, a newspaper writer would be countered by a pamphleteer who disagreed with him. Newspaper contributors likewise dissected arguments presented in pamphlets.

During the War for Independence, men occasionally debated the relative merits of pamphlets and newspapers. Dr. Benjamin Rush of Philadelphia took credit for inspiring Thomas Paine to write *Common Sense*, a startling publishing sensation. As Rush put it, he influenced Paine to do something "beyond the

Despite Thomas Paine's eloquent words at the time of the revolution, he died a ridiculed man, as this drawing, published in 1800, indicates. The social change that Paine advocated was not popular in post-revolutionary times. (Library of Congress Collection)

ordinary short and cold address of newspaper publication."[40] Paine originally planned to serialize *Common Sense* in the newspapers, much in the same fashion that John Dickinson published his influential "Farmer's Letters" in 1767–1768.[41]

Thomas Paine, however, feared that his work might not be "generally inserted" in the newspapers, so he turned his manuscript over to Philadelphia printer Robert bell. From Bell's shop, *Common Sense* was widely printed and reprinted; Paine asserted that more than a quarter-million copies of *Common Sense* were sold in the three months after it was first issued.[42]

An enthusiastic reader of *Common Sense*, however, regretted that it had not been published first as a series of newspaper essays. The Reverend John Witherspoon, president of Princeton, wrote that "Common Sense had been read by many, yet the news papers are read by many more."[43]

Although pamphleteers and the men who wrote for newspapers did not earn salaries or wages, they sometimes received gratuities or public offices if they needed money. More often, however, writers were men in public life with positions to state who postured, rather than hid, behind fancy pseudonyms. Much of the time, the authors of pseudonymous writings quickly were identified by their readers, as was John Dickinson, alias the "Pennsylvania Farmer."

Thomas Paine and *Common Sense*

Thomas Paine, a former corset maker, was paid little for his contributions to Robert Aitken's struggling *Pennsylvania Magazine*. Paine, who had worked for Aitken since arriving in Philadelphia, received fifty pounds a year in Pennsylvania currency, twenty pounds less than Aitken's journeyman printer John McCulloch.[44] Paine left Aitken's shop in December 1775 on less than cordial terms. Aitken possibly felt that Paine's "seditious writing," which ultimately was published as *Common Sense*, was too hot to handle.

The Continental Congress, fearful that the British would use rivers originating in Canadian territory as routes to cut off the northern colonies from the middle colonies, planned a military expedition in the fall of 1775. If the colonies could control the Canadian lands, they could present a solid front against the British.

The Canadian expedition was disastrous. The few men who survived illness, brutal terrain, and the arduous march into the bitter Canadian winter, were soundly defeated as they attempted to take Quebec. The expedition's leader was killed, and the second in command, Colonel Benedict Arnold, was wounded.[45]

Despite the low spirits of those hoping for independence, Thomas Paine gave the cause of resistance and independence great encouragement by publishing anonymously, *Common Sense*, on January 9, 1776. In an essay published

> **PAINE DESCRIBES THE CRISIS**
>
> These are the times that try men's souls. The summer soldier and the sunshine patriot will in this crisis, shrink from the service of his country; but he that stands it NOW, deserves the love and thanks of man and woman. Tyranny, like hell, is not easily conquered; yet we have this consolation with us, that the harder the conflict, the more glorious the triumph. What we obtain too cheap, we esteem too lightly; 'tis dearness only that gives everything its value. Heaven knows how to put a proper price upon its goods; and it would be strange indeed, if so celestial an article as FREEDOM should not be highly rated.
>
> SOURCE. Thomas Paine, The Crisis, No. 1.

in the *Pennsylvania Journal* late in 1775, Paine had predicted that "The Almighty will finally separate America from Britain."[46] But *Common Sense* went much further, for it directly attacked King George III. Paine wrote, "Government, like dress, is the badge of lost innocence; the palaces of kings are built upon the ruins of the bowers of paradise."[47] Writing at a time when the king was the strongest remaining link between England and America, Paine dared to call George III a "hardened, sullen temperate Pharoah" and a "wretch who was able to sleep with the blood of Bunker Hill upon his soul."[48]

Common Sense quickly became the center of a rancorous debate in the newspapers. The success of the pamphlet, wrote historian Harry Stout, was that it was not limited by the constraints of classical style. Paine, repudiating the "language and form of classical discourse," established "a new style that anticipated the wave of nineteenth century literature" intended for people generally, rather than for an elite audience.[49] Indeed, the revolutionary elite did not regard Paine as particularly influential.

Printer Robert Bell, first publisher of *Common Sense*, was ready to make money from loyalists and patriots alike. He assembled the conservatives' first angry attempts at rebutting *Common Sense* into a pamphlet called *Large Additions to Common Sense*. Writing in the *Pennsylvania Packet*, Anglican minister William Smith, who strongly opposed independence, derided Paine's suggestion that the colonies could expect help from foreign nations. Recalling old English prejudices, Smith asked what assistance American Protestants might expect from "Popish Princes." He labeled Paine guilty of "Common Nonsense."[50] By late spring of 1776, Thomas Paine's *Common Sense* was an unprecedented best-seller in America. The pamphlet was to go through twenty-five separate editions by year's end, and reached hundreds of thousands of avid readers at a time when the colonies' total population was little more than 2.5 million.

As Paine biographer Eric Foner wrote, *Common Sense* attacked the British king and constitution at a time when most Americans believed they had or could have full rights of Englishmen and were sprinkling their protests with the language of conciliation. Paine, wrote Foner,

> articulated the deepest meaning of the struggle with Britain. . . . The success of *Common Sense* reflected the perfect conjunction of a man and his time, a writer and his audience, and it announced the emergence of Paine as the outstanding political pamphleteer of the Age of Revolution.

NEWSPAPERS FOR A CONTINENT

NETWORK OF PRINTERS

The vigorous political dialogues in the newspapers of Colonial America in 1775 and 1776—the words that reflected and fueled the early days of the War for Independence—were important up and down the seaboard of North America. The printers of North America during the late eighteenth century were publishers for a continent. Their newspapers, broadsides, printed sermons, and pamphlets traveled by postrider's saddlebag, by stage, and by sailing ships to all of the thirteen colonies and beyond.[51] Men wrote freely about politics, and once printed, their opinions on matters affecting the developing revolution could be read throughout America. As Merrill Jensen noted, the printers "made constant use of scissors so that the same news item or political essay often appears in the newspapers all the way from New Hampshire to Georgia, sometimes with acknowledgment and sometimes not."[52]

Although Philadelphia's able bookbinder and printer, Robert Aitken, never published a newspaper, a record book kept in his ship suggests much about the distances over which printers maintained business contacts and exchanged information. Between 1775 and 1784, Aitken did business with printers up and down the Atlantic coast of the new nation, sending them paper and supplies, books, pamphlets, and, occasionally, type. In return, Aitken received either money or merchandise such as books and pamphlets which he, in turn, could sell from his Philadelphia shop.[53]

As a Philadelphian, of course, the bulk of Aitken's business was done with residents of that city. His shop record book is dotted with frequent entries for Philadelphia printers Robert Bell, William and Thomas Bradford, John Dunlap, and James Humphreys, Jr., and the German printers Henry Miller, Melchior Steinter, and Charles Cist. In the mid-1770s, Aitken had extensive dealings with Francis Bailey, printing some seventy miles to the west, in

Lancaster. (Bailey later moved to Philadelphia, establishing one of the city's major newspapers, the *Freeman's Journal,* in 1782.) Additionally, Aitken had business with printers Robert Wells of Charleston, South Carolina; Sheppard Kollock of Burlington, Vermont; Isaac Collins of Trenton, New Jersey.; Benjamin Edes of Boston, and John Holt and Samuel Loudon of New York City.[54]

In addition to doing business with printers, Aitken also traded with many other stationers, booksellers, and bookbinders, both in Philadelphia and in surrounding areas, including James Leishman in distant Burlington, Vermont.

THE SIGNIFICANCE OF CIRCULATIONS

In the absence of authoritative information on newspaper circulations—as provided for twentieth-century newspapers by the Audit Bureau of Circulations—historians have made do with publishers' own circulation claims. Annual or semiannual subscriptions were the usual method used to provide a newspaper with some working capital, and subscription lists usually are the best source of circulation information. With a yearly subscription, a printer might take half "in advance" at the time a person agreed to take the newspaper. The second half of the subscription price would then be due and payable in six months.[55]

In 1719, the *Boston News-Letter*, then New England's only newspaper, struggled along with fewer than three hundred subscribers.[56] By 1754, when four competing weekly newspapers were published in Boston, each apparently had an average circulation of about six hundred copies. And Isaiah Thomas, publisher of *The Massachusetts Spy* in Boston and Worcester and author of the first major history of American journalism, wrote that a subscription list of about six hundred was needed for a weekly newspaper to make ends meet.[57]

Beyond these figures, there is a never-never land made up of claims of biased or self-serving witnesses. James Rivington claimed a weekly circulation of 3,600 for his Tory *New-York Gazetteer* in 1775. The *Boston Gazette* listed its weekly circulation as 2,000 the same year, while Isaiah Thomas's rival *Massachusetts Spy* said that its circulation was 3,500.[58]

It is more than possible that publishers padded their circulation figures to impress their readers. Historians also have to contend with the puffs of uncritical biographers. Robert Hurd Kany guessed that the circulation of the *Pennsylvania Gazette* during the partnership of David Hall, Sr., and Benjamin Franklin was between 8,000 and 9,000 copies, far higher than the 1,600 to 1,700-copy circulation estimated for the *Gazette* by Lawrence C. Wroth.[59] Kany's estimate also differs from that by a thorough student of the finances of Benjamin Franklin's printing house. George Moranda noted that Kany's estimate was based on Frankin's statement that only one of every five copies of the *Gazette* was paid for. If that five-to-one ratio is taken seriously, the *Gazette's*

Front page of the December 23, 1773 issue of The Massachusetts Spy. *(Library of Congress Collection)*

circulation would have been about 750 during the 1740s; Moranda found settlement of 137 *Gazette* subscription accounts over a seventeen-year period covered by Franklin's account books.[60]

Such circulation numbers games, however, do little to measure the importance of the newspapers of the American Revolution. The tiny newspapers, often running only four pages, were read for every single word, even through they often published more advertising than news. These printed sheets were popular diversions in the taverns, coffee houses, shops, and inns where people read newspapers, or heard them read aloud.

The *Pennsylvania Journal*

The circulation pattern of a major late-eighteenth-century newspaper is well described in Col. William Bradford's "List of Subscribers on the 25th of April et. postea to the Pennsylvania Journal."[61] William and Thomas Bradford's *Pennsylvania Journal*'s circulation book counted only 167 subscribers in Philadelphia in 1767 and only 220 by mid-1775. But the *Journal* reached the rich and powerful men of Philadelphia, the heads of political factions, and the major merchants. These leaders were tied closely together by business and religious connections, and quite often, by family or marital ties.[62] The 1767 Philadelphia circulation of the *Journal* was almost a "Who's Who" of the city. Subscribers included William Allen, the Tory Chief Justice of colonial Pennsylvania; Robert Morris, a rising merchant; Benjamin Chew, a wealthy Quaker politician; and Joseph Galloway, political boss of what was called the anti-proprietary faction. Also included in the list were a few "new men," people, such as Daniel Roberdeau, without old-line ties who would become important in the revolutionary struggle. But by and large, the *Journal*'s Philadelphia circulation in 1767 echoed the names of powerful old families or men connected to them, such as Joseph Shippen, Jr., or James Biddle.[63]

Bradford's ledger in 1776 reflects some societal changes taking place after the outbreak of the War for Independence. The fighting at Lexington and Concord, Massachusetts, in the spring of 1775 — coupled with the revolutionists' overthrow of the colonial government of Pennsylvania in 1776 — added greatly to the number of subscribers Bradford crossed off or recorded as having moved away. Committed Tories wisely moved to places such as New York City, still under British control, where Redcoat troops could protect them.

The *Pennsylvania Journal*'s circulation in early 1776 was about 2,400. Of that, less than one-tenth — or 230 — subscribers actually lived in Philadelphia. A larger number (roughly 400) lived in the "hinterland" of Pennsylvania, the regions outside of Philadelphia.

Once out of Pennsylvania, the paths traveled by the *Journal* were many and varied. Papers left at Captain Long's in Philadelphia were destined for "sundrey places." One such place was the printing shop of John Hunter Holt, a young printer who tried to begin a printing business in Virginia, but whose press was stolen by Virginia Governor Lord Dunmore's British and carried off in a British warship.[64]

Despite all the difficulties attending the complicated business of getting papers to subscribers who lived far from Philadelphia, about 90 percent of the *Journal*'s circulation was outside of the city. But even more important than the number of the newspaper's subscribers were positions of influence held by many of the persons reached by the *Journal*. Its circulation, both in Philadelphia and in outlying areas, included many men who were important political leaders or newspaper publishers. Eight newspapers listed in Bradford's circulation book as being sent to "Connecticutt" were addressed to this group: "The Post Master in Hartford, Thomas Green Printer Do. Timothy Green Printer New London, Parker & Company Printers O' New Haven, Silas Deane, Esq'r. [an important merchant and politician] and Alexander and James Robertson Printers, Norwich,"[65] One of the two copies of the *Journal* sent to Westmoreland County, Virginia, was addressed to Richard Henry Lee, one of the most powerful politicians of the American Revolution. For the *Pennsylvania Journal* and for the emerging nation's other newspapers, circulation patterns including printers, postmasters, and important politicians insured maximum impact for newspapers.

COLONIAL PRINTING HISTORY

Isaiah Thomas: Printer and Historian

Much of what is known about early American printers—except for the body of published work that has survived them—is known because of the first historian of American publishing, Isaiah Thomas. Author of the often-quoted *History of Printing in America*, first published in 1810, Thomas also founded what is today a great research library, The American Antiquarian Society of Worcester, Massachusetts.

The youngest of five children, he was apprenticed to Boston printer Zechariah Fowle in 1756, some four years after Thomas's father had died. The apprentice printer was just six years old, and he served Fowle until he was twenty-one.[66]

After a quarrel with Fowle in 1765, Thomas left for Nova Scotia, and after working in several colonies as a printer, in 1770 he returned to Boston and to Zechariah Fowle's printing house. This time he used Fowle's equipment to begin publishing a smaller-than-usual newspaper, to be published triweekly in competition with four other newspapers in Boston, all weeklies.

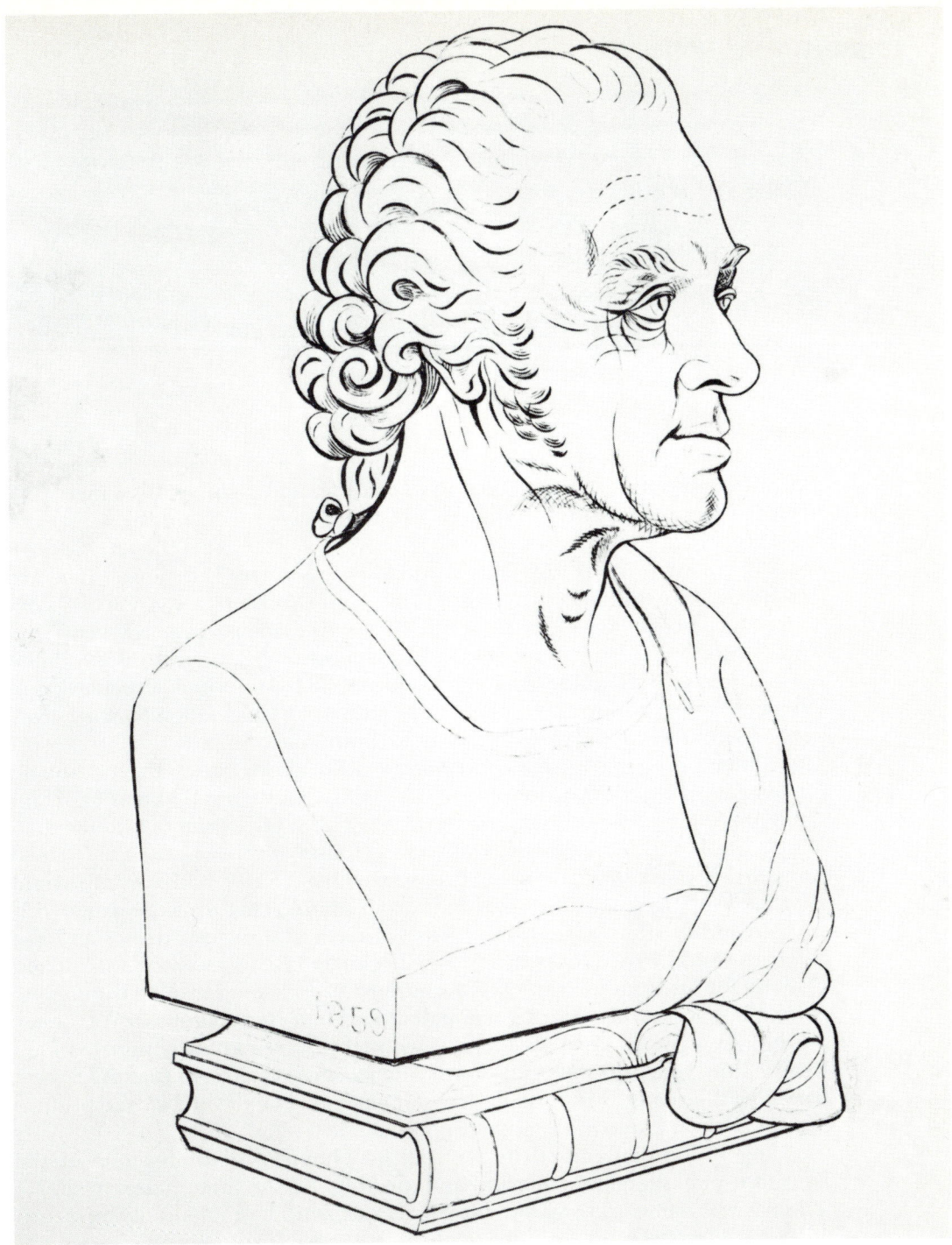

Depiction of Isaiah Thomas, early journalism historian, taken from the marble bust by B.H. Kinney. The bust is owned by the American Antiquarian Society. (State Historical Society of Wisconsin)

> **COLONIAL SENSATIONALISM**
>
> Americans! Forever bear in mind the BATTLE OF LEXINGTON!—where British troops, unmolested and unprovoked, wantonly and in a most inhuman manner, fired upon and killed a number of our countrymen, then robbed, ransacked, and burnt their houses! nor could the tears of defenseless women, some of whom were in the pains of childbirth, the cries of helpless babes, nor the prayers of old age, confined to beds of sickness, appease their thirst for blood—or divert them from their DESIGN OF MURDER and ROBBERY!
>
> SOURCE. Isaiah Thomas, Massachusetts Spy, May 3, 1775.

On August 7, 1770, Thomas's *Massachusetts Spy* began regular publication. After three months, Thomas bought out Fowle, and changed his paper from quarter-sheet to half-sheet and its publication frequency from three times to twice weekly.[67]

Like many printers, Thomas headed his paper with the motto "Open to all Parties, but Influenced by None," but soon moved to the Patriot side. When he bought Fowle's equipment, he secured loans from colonists who were protesting British measures. John Hancock had financial responsibility for the press, and rather wild-eyed radicals such as Joseph Greenleaf and Thomas Young became frequent contributors. Thomas felt sufficiently cornered to consider moving as far away as Bermuda.

Thomas and one of his contributors, who wrote under the pen name Mucius Scaaevola, were ordered to appear before Governor Thomas Hutchinson, but Thomas refused three times to attend. The Governor's Council then faced a legal dilemma: Thomas could not be found in contempt of the Council and jailed because he never actually appeared before that body. After several alternative approaches were tried to indict Thomas, charges were dropped.[68]

Meanwhile, Thomas wrote, it was apparent that British troops and the colonials would soon attack each other. Tories and British soldiers threatened Thomas for his antiestablishment *Massachusetts Spy*. Seeing trouble coming, he packed up most of his printing equipment and sent it in wagons to Worcester during the night of April 16, 1775. Two nights later, Thomas signaled Paul Revere, who rode through the countryside to warn Americans that the British troops were leaving Boston to destroy military stores collected by the protesting colonials at Concord, eighteen miles away.

This dislocation caused by war led to Thomas's becoming one of the foremost publishers in America and making his fortune. Late in 1775, Thomas was named postmaster for Worcester, and, by the end of the war in 1783, he had overcome his debts and was prospering with his newspaper and with a profitable almanac, book bindery, and bookstore.[69] Thomas, who was to become something of an early nineteenth-century publishing conglomerate, by 1801 had a fortune estimated at $150,000, one of the largest in the nation.

CONCLUSION

During the French and Indian Wars American colonists gained economic independence through the development of manufacturing, but soon faced new forms of taxation by England, which strived to make colonialism pay through increased trade advantages to the mother country. The first major reaction by the press was to the Stamp Act of 1765, which taxed paper and posed a definite economic hardship on colonial printers and lawyers.

Public opinion dictated that the common stance of impartiality would no longer benefit printers, and in some cases the public demanded the printers publish without stamps, threatening those who halted publication. Nevertheless, public opinion did not, in those early days of protest, demand a revolution.

During the ten years before the Declaration of Independence in 1776, printers grew more partisan, and some writers, such as John Dickinson, the authors of the *Journal of Occurrences*, Edes and Gill of the *Boston Gazette*, and Sam Adams appealed to various audiences and pleaded for rational, as well as violent, responses to British control.

Meanwhile, the Continental Congress and colonial legislatures conducted secret proceedings, releasing information to selected public printers. News of the first shots fired in the War for Independence traveled from colony to colony, as printers established a network of selling newspapers and stationery products along the Atlantic coast. Printers, cut off from trade items from England, began to publish political pamphlets. These pamphlets conveyed political views, but also were a major source of income for many printers. Newspapers thrived during the years just prior to the War for Independence, and circulations of about 600 were judged to be satisfactory to sustain a profitable newspaper.

NOTES

1. Stephen Botein, "'Meer Mechanics' and an Open Press: The Business and Political Strategies of Colonial American Printers," *Perspectives in American History* 9 (1975), pp. 140–150.
2. Thomas C. Leonard, in *The Power of the Press* (Oxford: Oxford University Press: 1986), pp. 35–53, develops fully the argument that colonial printers exposed the injustice of the old system, particularly in regard to associating English rule to criminal behavior. For a discussion of how elite ideology interacted with popular

tions and the Ideological Origins of the American Revolution," *William and Mary Quarterly* 34 (1977).

3. See Richard Buel, Jr., "Freedom of the Press in Revolutionary America: The Evolution of Libertarianism, 1760–1820," *The Press and The American Revolution* (Worcester: American Antiquarian Society, 1980), p. 81.

4. Merrill Jensen, ed., "Introduction" to *Tracts of the American Revolution, 1763–1776* (Indianapolis: Bobbs-Merrill, 1967), pp. xxii, 26–27. For good summary of various historical explanations of causes of the American Revolution, see Gordon S. Wood, "Rhetoric and Reality in the American Revolution," *The William and Mary Quarterly* 23 (January 1964), pp. 3–32. Wood argues that the revolution occurred because of internal colonial social strains that caused elites to express a sense of tyranny beyond the reality of the restrictions Britain imposed.

5. *Pennsylvania Journal and Weekly Advertiser*, No. 1195, October 31, 1765.

6. Arthur M. Schlesinger, *Prelude to Independence: The Newspaper War on Britain, 1764–1776*, (New York: Knopf, 1958) p. 77.

7. *New York Gazette or Weekly Post-Boy*, November 7, 1765.

8. Cass Canfield, *Sam Adam's Revolution* (New York: Harper & Row, 1976) p. 11.

9. W.V. Wells, *Life and Public Services of Samuel Adams*, 3 vols. (Boston: 1866), vol. 1, p. 237, cited in Willard G. Bleyer, *Main Currents in the History of American Journalism* (Boston: Houghton-Mifflin Co., 1927), p. 82.

10. Warren-Adams Letters, December 5, 1767, W.C. Ford, ed., *Collections of the Massachusetts Historical Society*, XLII-LXXIII, (1917–25), vol. 1, p. 3.

11. Rosemarian V. Staudacher, "Samuel Adams," in Perry J. Ashley, ed., *Dictionary of Literary Biography*, (Detroit: Gale Research, 1985) vol. 43, p. 8.

12. Staudacher, p. 8; Schlesinger, *Prelude*, pp. 179–181.

13. See John C. Miller, *Origins of the American Revolution*, rev. ed. (Palo Alto, Calif.: Stanford University Press, 1959), p. 260; and Edward Channing, *History of the United States, vol. 3: The American Revolution, 1761–1878* (New York: The Macmillan Co., 1930) pp. 95–96, 99.

14. Arthur M. Schlesinger, *Prelude*, Appendix D, pp. 312–313.

15. See O.M. Dickerson, *Boston Under Military Rule, 1768–1769* (Boston: Chapman & Grimes, 1936) p. ix. Schlesinger, in the "Review of Boston Under Military Rule," *New England Quarterly*, vol. 10 (1938), p. 387, and in *Prelude to Independence*, p. 312, argued that neither Isaiah Thomas or John Adams should be listed as possible authors of the *Journal*. Schlesinger said Thomas was then employed as a printer in Charleston, S.C., and Adams had said in June 1771 that he had not "written a line in a newspaper" for the preceding two years. That would cover much of the period during which the *Journal of Occurrences* appeared.

16. Philip Davidson, *Propaganda and the American Revolution* (Chapel Hill: University of North Carolina Press, 1941), p. 237.

17. Dickerson, *Boston Under Military Rule*, p. ix.

18. *New York Journal*, October 13, 1768.

19. *New York Journal* October 13, 1768.

20. *New York Journal*, November 10, 17, 1768 and May 4, June 1, 1769.

21. *New York Journal*, Supplement, June 8, 1769.
22. October 17, 1774, in William T. Hutchinson, et al., eds. *The Madison Papers* (Chicago: 1962) vol. 1, p. 126. See also *Journals of the Continental Congress*, vol. 1, p. 126.
23. Worthington C. Ford, et al., eds., *Journals of the Continental Congress 1774–1789* 3 vols., Washington, D.C., 1904–1937, vol. 13, January 6–16, 1779, pp. 30–37.
24. Frank Luther Mott, "Newspaper Coverage of Lexington and Concord," in Edwin H. Ford and Edwin Emery, *Highlights in the History of the American Press* (Minneapolis, 1954) pp. 86–99.
25. *Pennsylvania Packet*, Philadelphia, August 9, 1783, "On the Advantage and Amusement derived from the reading of News-papers," reprinted from the *Edinburgh Evening Post*.
26. *Pennsylvania Packet*, April 24, 1775.
27. J. Thomas Scharf and Thompon Westcott, *History of Philadelphia*, 3 vols., (Philadelphia, 1884), vol. 1, p. 299.
28. *Pennsylvania Packet*, May 1, 1775.
29. *Journals of the Continental Congress*, vol. 5, p. 425.
30. Carl L. Becker, *The Declaration of Independence* (New York: Vintage, 1959), pp. 135–137.
31. Schlesinger, *Prelude to Independence*, p. 283.
32. Cadwallader Colden to Governor William Tryon, September 7, 1774, Colden Letter Books vol. 2, 1765–1775, New York Historical Society Collections vol. 10 (New York, 1878), p. 361.
33. *New-York Gazetteer*, August 18, 1774.
34. *New-York Gazetteer*, August 18, 1774.
35. *New-York Gazette*, September 2, 1774.
36. Dwight L. Teeter, "'King' Sears, the Mob, and Freedom of the Press in New York, 1765–76," *Journalism Quarterly* 41:4 (Autumn 1964), pp. 539–544; Michael Sewell, "James Rivington," in *DLB*, vol. 43, pp. 398–401.
37. Teeter, "King Sears," pp. 543–544.
38. Bernard Bailyn, *Pamphlets of the American Revolution, 1750–1765* (Cambridge, Mass.: Harvard University Press, 1965), p. 1; Schlesinger, *Prelude*, pp. 45–46.
39. Botein, "Meer Mechanics," p. 216.
40. Benjamin Rush to James Cheetham, in Lyman H. Butterfield, ed., *The Letters of Benjamin Rush*, vol. 2 (Princeton, N.J.: Princeton University Press: 1951), p. 1007.
41. Jensen, *Tracts of the Revolution* p. 1.
42. "The Forester," Thomas Paine, in *Pennsylvania Gazette*, April 10, 1776; cited in Schlesinger, *Prelude*, p. 253.
43. Schlesinger, *Prelude*, quoting "Aristides" (Dr. John Witherspoon) from *Pennsylvania Packet*, May 13, 1776.
44. Arnold K. King, *Thomas Paine in America* (unpublished Ph.D. diss., University of Chicago, 1945;) Robert Aitken, Waste Book, Library Company of Philadelphia, November 19, 1775 entry, p. 284.

45. Page Smith, *John Adams*, (Westport, Conn.: Greenwood Press, 1969), vol. 1, p. 239.
46. Philip S. Foner, ed., *The Complete Writings of Thomas Paine* (2 vols., New York: Citadel Press, 1945), vol. 1, p. 4.
47. Foner, *Complete Writings of Paine*, p. 25.
48. King, *Thomas Paine*, p. 98.
49. Stout, "Religion, Communications and the Ideological Origins of the American Revolution," pp. 536–537.
50. *Packet*, March 25, 1776.
51. William Bradford's "List of Subscribers on the 25th of April et. postea to the Pennsylvania Journal," Bradford Papers, Historical Society of Pennsylvania.
52. Merrill Jensen, *The New Nation*, (New York: Alfred A. Knopf, 1958) p. 430; see also Carl Bridenbaugh, "Press and Book in Philadelphia," *Pennsylvania Magazine of History and Biography*, vol. 65 (January 1941), p. 7.
53. Robert Aitken's "Waste Book," manuscript, Library Company of Philadelphia.
54. Aitken's "Waste Book."
55. *Pennsylvania Journal*, Philadelphia, January 25, 1775.
56. Schlesinger, *Prelude*, p. 303.
57. Isaiah Thomas, *The History of Printing in America*, ed. Marcus A. McCorison from the 2nd ed., (New York: Weathervane Books, 1970), pp. 8, 17.
58. Schlesinger, *Prelude*, pp. 303, 304.
59. Lawrence C. Wroth, *The Colonial Printer*, 2d. ed. (Portland, Me.: Southworth-Anthoensen Press, 1938) pp. 38–39. See also Robert Hurd Kany, *David Hall: Printing Partner of Benjamin Franklin*, Ph.D. thesis, Pennsylvania State University, 1963.
60. George Moranda, *The Finances of Benjamin Franklin's Printing House*, M.A. thesis, School of Journalism and Mass Communication, University of Wisconsin-Madison, 1964, pp. 100–101.
61. Bradford papers, Historical Society of Pennsylvania.
62. William S. Hanna, *Benjamin Franklin and Pennsylvania Politics* (Palo Alto, Calif.: Stanford University Press 1964) pp 3–4.
63. Hanna, *Franklin and Politics*, pp. 3–4.
64. Jeffery A. Smith, "Public Opinion and the Press Clause," *Journalism History*, 14:1, (Spring 1987), p. 13.
65. Bradford's List of Subscribers.
66. Isaiah Thomas, *Three Autobiographical Fragments* (Worcester, Mass.: American Antiquarian Society: 1962) published on 150th anniversary of the founding of the society, p. 19.
67. Terry Hynes, "Isaiah Thomas," in *DLB*, vol. 43, p. 439.
68. Thomas, *History of Printing*, pp. 167–168.
69. Hynes, "Isaiah Thomas," *DLB*, vol. 43, p. 444.

CHAPTER 4

FROM REVOLUTION TO CONSTITUTION

By 1787, the new nation had survived a dozen years of cataclysmic change. After the fighting at Lexington and Concord in April 1775, thirteen colonies declared themselves an independent nation, and fought and won that independence. A series of military losses plagued patriots after the Declaration of Independence, and in 1776 and 1777 the two largest cities in the colonies, New York and Philadelphia, were evacuated. The Continental Congress fled Philadelphia twice in those years, hardly inspiring confidence in revolution.

In late 1777, while the fighting flared and died down, Congress approved the Articles of Confederation, and the new nation signed the Treaties of Amity and Commerce with France early in 1778. By 1779, all states except Maryland accepted the Articles of Confederation; when Maryland finally signed in March of 1781 the articles took full effect.

The articles had been in operation only six years when the Constitutional Convention convened in Philadelphia in May 1787 to refine the governing plan dictated by the articles. Discussions were held behind closed doors, and the press had access only to what delegates were willing to release. Congressional delegates, once in Philadelphia, devised a new constitution rather than revising the articles.

In June 1788, after a ten-month ratification struggle, nine states

This replica of a Currier and Ives print shows General Washington parting in 1783 with officers who had served him during the Revolution. At Francis's Tavern, Broad Street, N.Y., Washington spoke: "With a heart full of love and gratitude, I now take leave of you. I most devoutly wish that your latter days may be as prosperous and happy, as your former ones have been glorious and honorable." (Library of Congress Collection)

adopted the second Constitution of the United States, a document still in full force today. On June 25, Virginia became the tenth state to ratify, although the slim margin of eighty-nine to seventy-five indicated the reservations Virginians held, particularly about the lack of a Bill of Rights. James Madison, however, urged Virginians to ratify the Constitution without attaching strings, pledging himself to obtain the necessary amendments once the document went into effect. Madison's assurances, wrote historian Irving Brant, "did not win the antis, but swung the doubtful and brought victory."[1]

Historians' analyses of the press during this post-Revolutionary War period have focused primarily on the debates over whether a bill of rights would be included in the Constitution. Most of the discussion has been an attempt to determine whether colonial printers had freedom in practice, whether they were free from laws of seditious libel, and whether the framers of the Constitution possessed a clearly developed theory of freedom of the press. Although colonial printers labored first under licensing restrictions and then under the possibility of indictments for seditious libel, toward the end of the period they also experienced considerable freedom to criticize government. During the Revolution, popular opinion certainly acted as more of a restraint than did legislation. In light of the possible restrictions by government and by the majority of the populace, historian Jeffery Smith argued that although public demands were responsible for the First Amendment, political theorists also saw the need to protect the press from the public.[2]

Experiments with triweeklies and dailies emerged during the post-Revolutionary period. Lower costs of production in the cities enabled editors there to produce dailies for less than twice the cost of a frontier weekly. Because the country was highly concerned with the need to establish new political and economic ties with other countries, until 1812 newspapers continued to focus more on European news than on local matters.[3]

Newspapers benefited from extremely low postal rates during the early years of the Republic much as they had under the colonial postal system. When the Constitution was ratified, about seventy-five post offices and twenty-four-hundred miles of roads served three million people. Temporary postal acts of 1790 and 1791 extended colonial arrangements, postponing changes in postal rates until Congress had time to reconsider the postal system. Debate over the temporary acts focused on the importance of the circulation of information and the need to avoid setting postal rates that would act as taxes on information. Furthermore, representatives considered the varied impact of postal rates on urban and small-town newspapers.[4]

The advertising function of the newspapers increased, with the country's first successful daily, *The Pennsylvania Packet and Daily Advertiser*, printing one hundred advertisements in ten of the sixteen columns in its first issue in 1784.[5]

CONSTITUTIONAL POLITICS

ARTICLES OF CONFEDERATION

Drafts of confederation articles had been around for more than twenty years, dating to Benjamin Franklin's 1754 Plan of Union from the Albany Congress, called in an effort to create treaties with the Iroquois during the French and Indian War. Although the colonies and Britain rejected that plan, Franklin in 1775 submitted another plan of confederation to the Continental Congress. The major author of the final articles, was, however, John Dickinson of Pennsylvania, a brilliant lawyer who first urged reconciliation with Britain, but, when he saw that independence was inevitable, wrote a plan to put the colonies "in a league of Friendship with each other."[6]

Congress adopted the Articles of Confederation November 15, 1778, creating a unicameral legislature. The number of delegates from each state varied, but each state had only one vote. Congress possessed sole authority to declare war and conduct foreign relations, supervise Indian affairs, regulate weights and measures, and create post offices. Both Congress and the states could coin money. Most significantly, in reaction to English economic policies, Congress could not tax or regulate commerce. No executive or judicial branches existed.

Submission to the states—with nine states required for adoption—proved to be a lengthy process. Finally, on March 1, 1781, after Maryland's adoption, Congress announced that the Articles of Confederation were in effect. Although the Dickinson-drafted Articles asserted the primacy of Congressional power over the states, the states still retained a strong measure of ultimate control.[7] Politicians who wanted more centralization of power, and those who believed the Articles were insufficient to govern an expanding new nation, continued to agitate for change, but the Articles were difficult to amend, requiring unanimous state agreement on each change.

The next six years were difficult ones for the new country. In an attempt to recover from the loss of traditional trade patterns with Britain and the empire, the colonies devised new patterns of trade with France, Holland, Sweden, and China. Farmers in western Massachusetts rebelled because the state raised taxes despite economic hard times, and required further that taxes be paid in hard cash. Daniel Shays led a group of farmers to seize control of the county courts to prevent foreclosures. In 1787, as the states voted to send delegates to a constitutional convention in Philadelphia, the Massachusetts militia was putting down the rebellion. Other issues included lack of a consistent money supply and uneven actions by state government, some of whom issued paper money and others who did not.

THE PRESS AND THE CONSTITUTIONAL CONVENTION

The impact of the press or of public opinion on the Constitutional Convention, which met in Philadelphia from May 25 until September 17, 1787, was indirect at best: the convention met behind closed doors. In fact, General Washington complained to delegates when he found a copy of agenda proposals lying on the floor: "I must entreat gentlemen to be more careful, lest our transactions get into the newspapers and disturb public repose by premature speculations."[8] Despite such secrecy, the press supported the new Constitution. Of the approximately 100 newspapers being printed in the states in 1787, only a dozen opposed ratification of the Constitution.[9]

The new Constitution was a controversial document. Two major issues were at stake: (1) the level of power granted to the national government versus that reserved for states; and (2) the lack of a bill of rights. Opponents persuasively argued that the new Constitution would create a despotic government; supporters exaggerated the financial and political ills under the Articles of Confederation. Nevertheless, without the opposition—the voices of the Anti-Federalists—it is likely that the nation's new Constitution would have lacked a bill of rights guaranteeing freedom of speech, religion, press, assembly, and the right to petition government.

THE FEDERALIST ARGUMENT

The supporters of the Constitution—the Federalists—argued for a strong national government. They maintained that a bill of rights was unnecessary because powers not specifically given to the national government would be preserved by the states. State bills of rights, therefore, were the key to maintaining freedom of speech, press, and assembly. The Federalists knew they faced serious opposition when three delegates to the Constitutional

> **PLEA FOR STRONG FEDERAL GOVERNMENT**
>
> Nothing is more certain than the indispensable necessity of government; and it is equally undeniable that whenever and however it is instituted, the people must cede to it some of their natural rights, in order to vest it with requisite powers. It is well worthy of consideration, therefore, whether it would conduce more to the interest of the people of America that they should, to all general purposes, be one nation, under one federal government, than that they should divide themselves into separate confederacies and give to the head of each the same kind of powers which they are advised to place in one national government.
>
> SOURCE. John Jay, Federalist Papers, No. 2.

Convention—George Mason and Edmund Randolph of Virginia and Elbridge Gerry of Massachusetts—would not sign the document.

To counteract Anti-Federalist rhetoric, Alexander Hamilton, John Jay, and James Madison, in a series of articles signed "Publius," eloquently argued the Federalist position and sought ratification of the new Constitution. Widely reprinted in newspapers throughout the new states, the articles appeared from late October 1787 into April 1788. These "Federalist Papers" may be more important as historical documents than they were as methods of getting the Constitution ratified. New York, the principle target audience of the "Federalist Papers," ratified the Constitution only after the nine states needed for ratification had already done so.[10] The eighty-five papers, written by three tired, busy men, reflect the multiplicity of authorship and are sometimes redundant and disjointed. But they all followed Hamilton's outline as set forth in the first number, arguing that the creation of a new constitution was necessary to preserve a republican government, liberty and property.

Hamilton, a handsome, ambitious man born out of wedlock in the West Indies, would have preferred a stronger constitution than the one proposed, but fought for its adoption over the weaker Articles of Confederation. Hamilton's approach and personality sparked controversy; some historians disparaged his contempt for common men and women and John Adams referred to him as the "bastard brat of a Scotch pedlar." Hamilton was, however, "a natural journalist and pamphleteer. . . . His perspicacity, penetration, powers of condensation and clarity of expression were those of a premier editorial writer."[11]

James Madison, often called the father of the Constitution and of the Bill of Rights, tried to ease Anti-Federalist fears of a consolidated national government, arguing that the state governments would remain "constituent and essential parts of the federal government."[12]

> **AN ANTI-FEDERALIST WARNING**
>
> Friends, Countrymen and Fellow Citizens: Permit one of yourselves to put you in mind of certain liberties and privileges secured to you by the constitution of this commonwealth, and to beg your serious attention to his uninterested opinion upon the plan of federal government submitted to your consideration, before you surrender these great and valuable privileges up forever.
>
> SOURCE: "Centinel," October 5, 1787, Independent Gazetteer.

THE ANTI-FEDERALIST ARGUMENT

Anti-Federalists argued for inclusion of a bill of rights both because the lack of such provision appealed strongly to popular sentiment and strengthened their cause against ratification, but also because they genuinely lamented the lack of a bill of rights. Anti-Federalist leader John Smilie of Pennsylvania expressed the fear that "an aristocratical Govt. cannot bear the Liberty of the Press."[13] There is some indication that memory of Zenger's trial sparked argument that judges, if unchecked by a bill of rights provision, might harm the press without being held in check by a jury.[14]

A series of Anti-Federalist essays labeled "Centinel," and Virginian Richard Henry Lee's "Letters from a Federal Farmer" argued that unless specific guarantees of freedom of the press were added, government under the national constitution would supersede rights previously taken for granted and could destroy press freedom.

These popular appeals helped secure the Federalist promise to accept a bill of rights in the form of amendments, a promise that encouraged reluctant states, such as Virginia, to ratify the Constitution.[15]

THE FIRST AMENDMENT

In June 1788, nine states adopted the Constitution. Many of the legislators who arrived in New York for the first session of Congress came with specific plans to introduce amendments to the Constitution. James Madison, who initially opposed a bill of rights, responded to Thomas Jefferson's concerns about the lack of protection against government intrusion. Although Madison argued that public opinion, as it had expressed itself during the revolution, determined civil rights more than did legislation, he also recognized the value

James Madison, from a painting by Gilbert Stuart. (State Historical Society of Wisconsin)

of Jefferson's argument. "The political truths declared in that solemn manner acquire by degrees the character of fundamental maxims of free Government," he wrote, "and as they become incorporated with the national sentiment, counteract the impulses of interest and passion."[16] Madison drafted the document that the states, in December 1791 ratified with little recorded debate as the Bill of Rights.[17] The First Amendment as passed guarantees that Congress cannot infringe on specific freedoms, but it makes no reference to what the states might do.[18] Further, the First Amendment addresses a variety of rights, including, but not exclusively protecting, freedom of the press:

> Congress shall make no law respecting an establishment of religion, or prohibiting the free exercise thereof; or abridging the freedom of speech, or of the press; or the right of the public peaceably to assemble, and to petition the government for a redress of grievances.

The remaining nine amendments include protections for the right to carry arms, to trial by jury, to be secure from unreasonable searches and excessive bail, and to reserve rights to the states that are not specifically granted to the federal government.

A PRINTER FOR THE TIMES

The story of Eleazer Oswald, a violent man with a hot temper and a tendency to shout "Freedom of the Press" when it best suited his own interest, demonstrates not only the importance of a continuing network of printers often based on family relationships, and the power of public opinion in post-Revolutionary America, but also the continued threat of seditious libel prosecutions. Persecutions for what Oswald printed made him a likely candidate for supporting the side that demanded a bill of rights. In addition, he was an entrepreneur, operating a paper mill with William Goddard.

Born in Falmouth, England, in 1755, Oswald sailed to New York in 1770. He apprenticed himself to printer John Holt of *The New York Journal, or General Advertiser*, and later married Holt's daughter Elizabeth.[19]

After a stint in the Army in 1775, Oswald joined William Goddard in Baltimore as a printer. Goddard, a former employee of Oswald's father-in-law, John Holt, and Oswald apparently became friends while organizing the postal system in New York. Oswald had been contemplating joining Goddard in business for some time.[20]

Goddard and Oswald operated a paper mill at Elk-Ridge Landing near Baltimore, leaving the *Maryland Journal* in the capable hands of Goddard's sister, Mary Katherine Goddard. Soon after the Oswald-Goddard alliance was formed, the *Maryland Journal* printed the first installment of Major General Charles Lee's "Some Queries Political and Millitary." The "Queries" sharply attacked Washington, and were suspect because Lee had been court-martialed for his role in the Battle of Monmouth in June 1778. Philadelphia editors had refused to print the letters, evidently fearing that criticism of the popular Washington would bring out the mob.[21]

On July 8, 1779, two days after the paper containing the "Queries" appeared, a mob of thirty men led by several Continental officers broke into William Goddard's home. Goddard and Oswald fled on horseback twenty-five miles to the state capital at Annapolis, where they asked for protection and demanded impeachment of Baltimore magistrates who had refused to protect them.[22] The matter subsided after a hearing before the Council of Maryland, although the newspaper fired a parting shot on a printer's right to publish:

> Restraints on the Press in any Cases, except Libels and Treason, narrow and debase the liberal Sentiments of the Soul, and curb the rising efforts of Genius: It is a Mockery of the Understanding to call that Country free, where this Restraint is tolerated, approved of, and supported.[23]

After his unpleasant sojourn in Baltimore, Oswald moved to Philadelphia in 1781 to make his fortune. He established a printing house and took over the Bradfords' famous London Coffee House, an excellent center for gathering information from merchants and travelers. Oswald began publishing the *Independent Gazetteer* on April 13, 1782. The first issue of Oswald's paper contained the printer's vow that his newspaper was "independent of Party, upon Principles of Public Utility."[24] But these aims required more restraint than Oswald had to offer. Oswald's hot-headed publishing led to several threatened libel suits during the first few months of the *Gazetteer*'s existence, and he soon ended up in court for criticizing Pennsylvania Chief Justice McKean's handling of the trial of a soldier who thrashed an election inspector for demanding a certificate that proved he signed a loyalty oath. Oswald's account of the high fine brought him before the chief justice, an appearance Oswald duly recorded in his newspaper.[25]

Chief Justice McKean submitted charges to a grand jury three times, seeking an indictment of Oswald. And three times, the grand jury refused to indict the printer. On January 7, 1783, the grand jurors presented a written statement to the chief justice, denouncing his actions in bringing repeated charges against Oswald.

Meanwhile, Oswald expanded his printing business, acquiring the *New York Journal and State Gazette* at the death of his father-in-law, John Holt, in 1784. Elizabeth Holt, Oswald's mother-in-law, managed the paper during

Political cartoons appeared in American publications as early as 1798. (Library of Congress Collection)

1784 and 1785, but Oswald took charge the next year. His name appeared in the nameplate until January 26, 1787, when Thomas Greenleaf bought an interest.[26]

During the struggle over ratification of the Constitution, Oswald's *Independent Gazetteer* printed twenty-four articles signed by "Centinel." Oswald also carried letters for the Anti-Federalists from New York to Virginia during the spring of 1787, at a time when the Constitution's opponents charged that Federalists sabotaged the mails to disrupt antiratification efforts.[27]

An attempt to muzzle Oswald and his Anti-Federalist *Gazetteer* in 1788 (*Respublica v. Oswald*) is still recognized as an important contempt-of-court case. The attack on Oswald came through the Pennsylvania Supreme Court and his old foe, Chief Justice Thomas KcKean. On July 14, 1788, while publishing "Centinel's" articles, Oswald was ordered to appear before the Supreme Court and was jailed for contempt. Chief Justice McKean sentenced Oswald to pay a ten pound fine and to spend a month in prison. As Oswald was taken away to jail, his backers gave him three cheers.[28]

From his jail cell, Oswald lashed out against McKean, using the *Pennsylvania Packet* to denounce the chief justice's use of the contempt power as "UNPRECEDENTED, ILLEGAL & UNCONSTITUTIONAL, & WICKED & ARBITRARY . . . tending to pull down FREEDOM OF THE PRESS; to abolish the immortal TRIAL BY JURY. . . ."[29] Once out of jail, Oswald pleaded unsuccessfully for McKean's impeachment. Failing that, Oswald threatened to beat the judge, and was again arrested, but was released after promising to be a good citizen.[30]

In 1792, Oswald traveled to England to settle affairs connected with the death of one of his wife's relatives, but the revolution in France attracted him to the continent. Oswald wrote in 1793, "the anxiety I felt for the Success of the [French] Revolution, determined me to defer my Return to America and to come to France and offer my Services. . . ."[31] Oswald returned to the United States in 1794, wearing a French uniform and a tricolored ribbon in his hat. He died on September 30, 1795, at the age of forty, after contracting yellow fever. Given the tempestuous outlines of his life, it was no wonder that his old antagonist, McKean, called him "such a seditious turbulent man."[32]

THE DEVELOPING DAILY

The first abortive attempt at a daily in the United States in 1783 preceded a seven-year period of experimentation with semiweeklies and triweeklies, which began competing with weekly newspapers. By 1790, thirteen dailies were published in Philadelphia, Charleston, New York City, and Baltimore. Seven survived at the turn of the decade.[33] As commerce grew in the cities, and the postal service capable of delivering them expanded, dailies became viable economic enterprises.

By 1800, urban publishers, because of lower costs of production, were able to produce a six-day-a-week newspaper at only about twice the cost of a country weekly. Because local journals focused on foreign affairs much as did the dailies, subscribers could obtain information more quickly from urban dailies than they could the country journals, which took most of their news from the same publications.

BENJAMIN TOWNE

A pudgy man remembered as a turncoat during the War for Independence published the first daily newspaper in North America, *The Pennsylvania Evening Post*. The scruffy little sheet, converted to a daily from a triweekly, lasted only seventeen months after its first issue on May 30, 1783. The *Post*, appearing up to six times a week, seems to have been a product of a printer's desperation rather than a forerunner of successful dailies that later thrived in the rising, rapidly expanding cities of the new nation. Many years before newsboys sold papers on the streets, it was said that Towne had to peddle the last issue of his paper on Philadelphia's streets in 1784, crying "All the news for two coppers."

JOHN DUNLAP

John Dunlap was a successful Philadelphia printer and entrepreneur similar to Benjamin Franklin and Isaiah Thomas. Franklin, Thomas, and Dunlap all moved successfully into society first as printers, then as booksellers and bookbinders, and all three grew wealthy from their printing and merchant enterprise.

Like Franklin and Thomas, Dunlap began life in poverty and was apprenticed to a printer early in life. Born in County Strabane, Ireland, in 1747, he was apprenticed at the age of ten to his Uncle William in Philadelphia. By the age of seventeen, he took charge of the printing house, for his printer-uncle had gone to England to study to become an Anglican priest. When John Dunlap was nineteen, his uncle began selling the shop to him in installments; Dunlap was so strapped financially he slept on a blanket under the shop's counter. After five years of running a printing house producing handbills, pamphlets, and sermons, Dunlap started the weekly *Pennsylvania Packet, or The General Advertiser*.

From its beginning late in 1771 until it became a daily on September 21, 1784, the *Packet* represented a remarkable success story. John Dunlap associated with some of Philadelphia's most prominent individuals as a member of the First Troop of the Philadelphia Light-Horse — nicknamed the Silk-Stocking Cavalry — and proved himself to be a good soldier at the battles of Princeton and Trenton in 1776–1777.

In 1776, Dunlap secured printing contracts from Congress. He also printed for Pennsylvania's Council of Safety, the quasi-official body that took over in the months when colonial structures lapsed and a new government was established under the Pennsylvania Constitution of 1776.

Not all of Dunlap's business dealings were above reproach. Dunlap printed loyalty oaths that the Council of Safety required of suspicious individuals. If Tories — for political reasons — or Quakers — for religious reasons — refused to sign the oaths, the Council confiscated their property. Dunlap, who also printed paper money for Pennsylvania, then used such rapidly depreciating money to buy lands of persons who would not take the oath. He purchased much of the estate of Pennsylvania Tory Joseph Galloway, who fled the Revolution.

Although Dunlap left Philadelphia in September 1777, when the British occupied the city, and did not return until the following June, he industriously stayed in the middle of the public-printing business. Moving his shop to Lancaster, Dunlap increasingly took over congressional printing from his rival Robert Aitken, who abandoned his printing operation during the British occupation. Dunlap did most of the congressional printing from 1779 until 1783. In addition, Dunlap appears to have received more revenue from printing for Pennsylvania's Assembly in 1778 and 1779 than did any other printer.[34]

Dunlap, with his young partner, David C. Claypoole, continued to run a flourishing printing business in Philadelphia from 1780 to 1784. During most of that period, Claypoole's name appeared alone on *The Pennsylvania Packet*, with Dunlap's name reappearing on September 21, 1784, just as the newspaper became a daily.

During his printing career Dunlap amassed a fortune, buying sizable parcels of real estate. In 1788, Governor Edmund Randolph of Virginia, who rented one of Dunlap's better properties, also signed the documents for Dunlap to purchase 131,000 acres of land in what is now Kentucky. When he died in 1812, his estate was estimated at more than $300,000.[35]

DELIVERING THE NEWS

"For the first quarter of a century under the Constitution," wrote historian Richard Kielbowicz, "the commitment to promote the circulation of news through the mails stood virtually unchallenged." Federalists, who appointed partisans to many postmasterships during the early years of the republic, supported low postal rates because they believed circulation of information would promote a strong central government by fostering nationalism and party cohesion. Republicans, or Anti-Federalists, hoped to use the mails to circulate information about Federalist abuses of power.

From colonial days onward, printers were allowed to exchange newspapers free through the mails, a mechanism which dictated the major exchanges of news until the telegraph and the press associations assumed that function in the mid-1800s. Under the provisions of the 1792 postal act, Congress set postal rates far under the letter rate, but representatives argued about the advantages of a set rate versus one based on the distance mail would travel. Those arguing for a flat rate insisted on the importance of wide circulation of information so that "the whole body of the citizens will be enabled to see and guard against any evil that may threaten them."[36] Other congressman argued that publishers should bear some of the transportation costs which increased with distance and that flat rates would enable urban publishers to compete unfairly with their rural colleagues.

After much discussion, Congress passed the Post Office Act of 1792, which established two rates for newspapers. Newspapers sent up to one hundred miles paid one cent postage, and those mailed further were charged one and one-half cents. Similar provisions were incorporated into the 1794 postal law, although one change allowed newspapers to circulate within a state for one cent.

Although magazines were excluded from the 1792 postal act, the 1794

Paul Revere's engraving in Royal American Magazine, *1774, depicted the British forcing tea down the throats of Americans. (Library of Congress Collection)*

law provided they could be sent "where the mode of conveyance and the size of the mails will admit of it."[37] Postal rates were much higher than those for newspapers, with subscribers paying in postage as much as 20 to 40 percent of the subscription price. Postmasters in later years took advantage of the interpretative clause in the postal act to encourage certain publications at the expense of others.

NEWSPAPERS AS COMMERCIAL VENTURES

By 1800, twenty of the twenty-four dailies published indicated their commercial interest by carrying *Advertiser* in their name plates. That percentage would decline during the next twelve years, as newspapers focused increasingly on partisan politics and relied less on advertising for income. Nevertheless, the value of advertising as income was well recognized by colonial editors. John

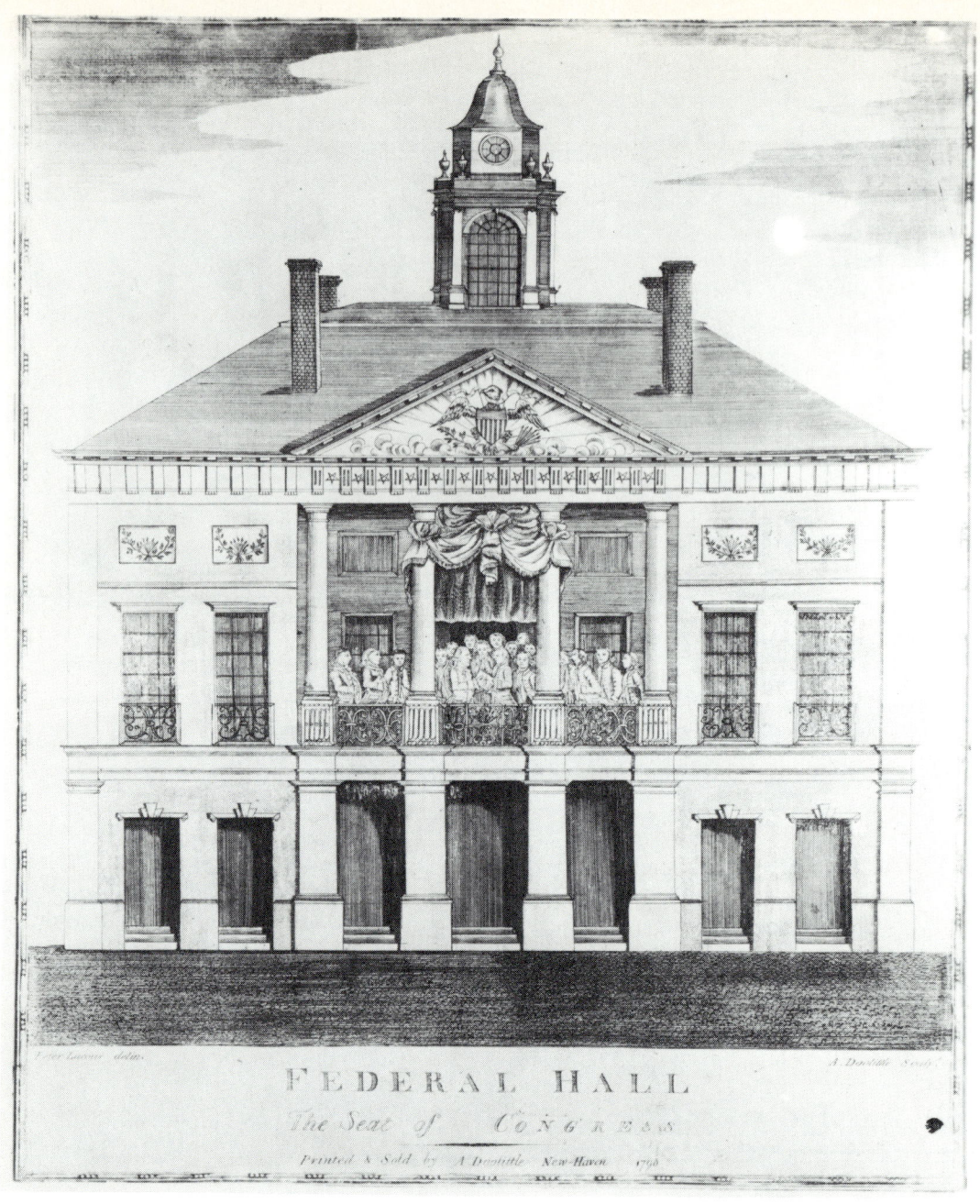

Federal Hall, the seat of Congress in 1790. (Library of Congress Collection)

Peter Zenger's *New York Weekly Journal* in 1743 carried more than a page of advertising, and after 1760 newspapers regularly carried as much as 50 percent advertising.[38] The gentlemen who subscribed to the newspapers also advertised in them, using the papers as "common carriers," or as vehicles through which to exchange commercial information as well as political and social content. Those who advertised regularly used the same copy over a period of a year, and display advertising consisted only of a heading printed in larger type than regular text. Not until after 1800 did publishers seriously debate problems associated with advertising mass-produced products, such as patent medicines. In 1805, when a young girl died after taking a patent medicine, the *New York Evening Post* temporarily banned advertisements for quack nostrums.[39]

CONCLUSION

Although 1776 and the Declaration of Independence often are regarded as milestones of independence for the colonies, twelve years passed before the Constitution was ratified by the various states as statesmen struggled with the political and economic dilemmas of building a new country. Not only did new governmental structures need to be put into functioning order, but also new patterns of trade had to be developed with countries outside the British Empire.

During the course of debate over the Constitution, representatives weighed the merits of central authority versus the independence of states, and pondered the value of a bill of rights. While printers and editors supported passage of the Constitution even without a bill of rights, they argued vociferously in their newspapers for press freedom. Men of conscience such as James Madison and Thomas Jefferson ultimately supported the argument for freedom of expression and for other civil liberties, and Madison helped write the Bill of Rights, which was added to the Constitution in 1791. In addition, Congress, through extension of colonial postal acts, protected and fostered the distribution of newspapers throughout the states.

As the new nation developed political and economic structures to deal with a new age, editors also viewed new opportunities. As commerce expanded, the economic situation benefited developing dailies, and the volume of advertising grew to support expanded news delivery.

NOTES

1. Irving Brant, *The Bill of Rights* (Indianapolis: Bobbs-Merrill, 1965), p. 41.
2. Jeffery A. Smith, "Public Opinion and the Press Clause," *Journalism History* 14:1

(Spring 1987), pp. 8–17. For excellent review of the debates regarding degrees of freedom the colonial press experienced, see the Introduction to Smith, *Printers and Press Freedom: The Ideology of Early American Journalism* (New York: Oxford University Press, 1988). Smith argues persuasively that colonial publishers practiced aggressive journalism for decades before the Revolution and suggests that a libertarian press ideology, based on experience and radical Whig and Enlightenment thought, was forged prior to passage of the First Amendment.

3. Allan R. Pred, *Urban Growth and the Circulation of Information: The United States System of Cities, 1790–1840* (Cambridge, Mass.: Harvard University Press, 1973), p. 22.
4. Richard B. Kielbowicz, "The Press, Post Office, and Flow of News in Early Republic," *Journal of the Early Republic* 3 (Fall 1983), pp. 257–259.
5. Alfred McClung Lee, *The Daily Newspaper in America* (New York: The Macmillan Co., 1937), p. 57.
6. Worthington, C. Ford, et al. eds., *Journals of the Continental Congress, 1774–1789*, 34 vols. (Washington D.C.: U.S. Government Printing Office, 1904–1937) vol. 5, pp. 546–547.
7. Merrill Jensen, preface to *The New Nation: A History of the United States During the Confederation, 1781–1789* (New York: Knopf, 1958), pp. xii–xiii.
8. Cited in Francis X. Clines, "Celebrating a Constitution or Violating Its Spirit?" *The New York Times*, Sunday, November 3, 1985, p. 4E.
9. Robert E. Rutland, "Newspaper Opposition to the Constitution, 1787–1788," Historical Research Panel, Association for Education in Journalism, Eugene, Ore. August 27, 1959, p. 2.
10. Alexander Hamilton, John Jay, James Madison, *The Federalist,* ed. by Edward Meade Earle (New York: Modern Library, 1937), p. x.
11. Claude G. Bowers, *Jefferson and Hamilton* (Boston: Houghton-Mifflin, 1925), p. 26.
12. Federalist No. 45.
13. John Bach McMaster and Frederick Stone, *Pennsylvania and the Constitution* (Lancaster, Pa, 1888), p. 770, cited in Jackson Turner Main, *The Antifederalists: Critics of the Constitution* (Chapel Hill: University of North Carolina Press, 1961), p. 160.
14. *Independent Gazetteer*, Philadelphia, November 16, 1787, reprinted in *New York Journal*, November 1, 1787.
15. Main, *The Antifederalists*, p. 255.
16. James Madison to Thomas Jefferson, October 17, 1788, in *The Papers of Thomas Jefferson*, 14: 19, 20, cited in Jeffery A. Smith, "Public Opinion and the Press Clause," *Journalism History* 14:1 (Spring 1987) p. 15.
17. For a discussion of how Madison's document was altered in the debate, see David A. Anderson, "The Origins of the Press Clause," *UCLA Law Review* (February 1983), pp. 455–541. See also Jeffery A. Smith, "Prior Restraint: Original Intentions and Modern Interpretations," *William and Mary Law Review* (April 1987).
18. In 1925, the Supreme Court of the United States in *Gitlow v. New York* applied the press clause of the First Amendment to the states.

19. The best account of Oswald's life is in "Eleazer Oswald, Lieutenant-Colonel in the Revolution, Printer in Baltimore and Philadelphia, Soldier of Fortune in the French Revolution," in Joseph Towne Wheeler, *The Maryland Press, 1777–1790* (Baltimore: The Maryland Historical Society, 1938), pp. 19–36.
20. Oswald to John Lamb, Philadelphia, October 15, 1778, Lamb Papers, Box II, New-York Historical Society.
21. For complete text of the "Queries," see John Richard Alden, *General Charles Lee: Traitor or Patriot?* (Baton Rouge: LSU Press, 1951), pp. 279–281.
22. Alden, *General Charles Lee*, p. 282.
23. *Maryland Journal*, August 3, 1779, cited in Ward L. Miner, *William Goddard, Newspaperman* (Durham, N.C.: Duke University Press, 1962), p. 179.
24. *Independent Gazetteer*, April 13, 1782.
25. *Independent Gazetteer*, October 1, 1782.
26. Wheeler, *The Maryland Press*, p. 34.
27. Wheeler, *The Maryland Press*, p. 31; Main, *The Antifederalists*, pp. 226, 249–250.
28. Rutland, "Newspaper Opposition to the Constitution," p. 9, and Thomas Richard Meehan, "The Pennsylvania Supreme Court in the Law and Politics of the Commonwealth 1776–1790," (Madison, Wisc. unpublished Ph.D. disser., University of Wisconsin, 1964), pp. 491–492.
29. *Pennsylvania Packet*, July 26, 1788.
30. *Independent Gazetteer*, November 3, 1788.
31. Eleazer Oswald to the National Convention, Paris, September 1, 1783, *Pennsylvania Magazine of History and Biography*, vol. 4, 1880, p. 252.
32. Thomas McKean to William Augustus Atlee, Philadelphia, September 17, 1788, William Augustus Atlee Papers, Library of Congress.
33. Lee, *Daily Newspaper in America*, p. 43.
34. Dwight Teeter, "A Legacy of Expression: Philadelphia Newspapers and Congress During the War for Independence, 1775–1783," (Madison, Wisc: unpublished University of Wisconsin Ph.D. disser., 1966); "John Dunlap: The Political Economy of a Printer's Success," *Journalism Quarterly* (Spring 1965) 52:3–8, 55; "John Dunlap," in Perry J. Ashley, ed., *Dictionary of Literary Biography*. (Detroit, Gale Research Press) vol. 43: 174–179.
35. Benjamin Rush, *The Autobiography of Benjamin Rush*, George W. Corner, ed. (Princeton, N.J.: Princeton University Press, 1948), pp. 319–320.
36. *Annals of Congress*, 2d Cong., 1st sess., 284–286, cited in Kielbowicz, "Press, Post Office, and Flow of News," p. 258.
37. Richard Peters, ed., *Statutes at Large of the United States of America, 1789–1873*, 17 vols. (Boston, 1850–1873), vol. 1, pp. 70, 178, cited in Kielbowicz, "Press, Post Office, and Flow of News," p. 268.
38. Lee, *Daily Newspaper in America*, pp. 32, 59–60.
39. Lee, *Daily Newspaper in America*, pp. 314–316.

The traditional view of Thomas Jefferson dismounting from his horse to attend his inauguration as President in Washington, the new capital, in 1801. (Library of Congress Collection)

P A R T 2

EXPANSION
AND
CONFLICT

The beginning of the nineteenth century in the new nation was characterized primarily by a local press in keeping with a society marked by regional differences and filled with debate over the value of national, centralized power versus local control. The issue was political and ideological in that politicians of the period feared the authoritarianism of centralized power. The struggle over competing theories of political control had a major impact on the press of the nation, particularly during the period of the Alien and Sedition Acts. The partisan press vociferously argued the competing views as political parties developed their own cohesive ideologies.

The debate was cultural as well as political. Early debates over postal law indicated that legislators recognized the effects of communication on modernization and either argued for a free flow of information that would bind the nation together, or for preserving local media voices.

Born into the midst of a nation in transition from a local society to an urbanized nation-state was the penny press, which separated financing from party loyalty and relied on advertising in a growing manufacturing economy. The penny press, developed first in the 1830s in the commercial center of the nation, New York, soon circulated in weekly form to distant communities. Editors used new technologies to expand circulation, attract broad audiences and gather news quickly.

While the penny press was able to attract diverse socio-economic audiences, it was not an accurate model for press activity throughout the nation. Most newspapers remained local and partisan until the end of the Civil War, and many newspapers retained partisan characteristics well into the twentieth century. Native Americans and blacks utilized older technology to develop newspapers designed to build community among geographically disparate groups. Bible societies, utilizing new technologies as early as 1820, also spanned geographic boundaries. Again representing the tensions between traditional and modern society, many prominent Federalists, experiencing loss of power when Jefferson was elected president in 1800, turned to privately organized voluntary associations to counter the spirit of the Enlightenment and to preserve religious tenets of the past. The abolitionist movement also gained momentum from cheap publishing derived from new technology.

Until the mid-1840s communication was tied specifically to transportation, which determined how fast news could be collected and distributed. The telegraph, introduced in the mid-1840s, eliminated geographical barriers, producing a new environment for the press of the last half of the century.

In 1861, legislative and social structures could no longer ameliorate the conflicts of the nation, and on April 12 the Palmetto Guard of South Carolina fired on Fort Sumter. The press scrambled to cover the various activities of the war and, utilizing technology in new ways, developed varied methods of covering the news and debated once more its relationship to government and the social structure of which it was a part.

control. Although the Federalists passed the Alien and Sedition Acts to restrict freedom of information, financial support of the press from various factions probably stimulated diversity of political views. If one accepts that assumption, one could argue that press partisanship actually helped broaden the freedom of the press. Federalists and Republicans regarded the press as essential to spreading their doctrines and thus used newspapers as a means of building political cohesion and a sense of nationalism. In such an atmosphere editors were not always printer-entrepreneurs, but often produced political newspapers without the familiar accompaniment of bookshop and job printing.

In 1817, John Calhoun recognized the importance of newspapers and of the distribution of information when he entreated Congress to "bind the republic together with a perfect system of roads and canals. Let us conquer space. . . . It is thus that a citizen of the West will read the news of Boston still moist from the press. The mail and the press are the nerves of the body politic."[6]

FEDERALIST NEWSPAPERS

John Fenno and the *Gazette of the United States*

On April 15, 1789—fifteen days before George Washington took the oath of office on Federal Hall's balcony in the City of New York—the *Gazette of the United States* published its inaugural issue. The newspaper boldly supported the Federalist cause and President Washington and walked the administration's line. When the national government moved from New York to Philadelphia in November 1790, Fenno's newspaper moved, too.

Fenno, a school teacher from Boston, viewed himself as an "editor," not a printer or publisher.[7] He acknowledged that he had writing help from "literary characters"; paramount among these were Secretary of the Treasury Alexander Hamilton and Vice-President John Adams. Despite the overt Federalist financial support which helped Fenno establish his newspaper, he proclaimed it to be "a National, Impartial, and Independent Conveyancer to all parts of the Union, of News, Politics, and Miscellanies." At three dollars a year, the paper was expensive, and would have absorbed about a week's pay for common laborers.[8]

Fenno's circulation differed little from successful pre-Revolution circulations. Operating first in New York, with a 1790 population of 33,000, and then in the nation's largest city, Philadelphia, with a population of 42,000, Fenno's circulation was 1,400 in December 1791.[9] One-hundred-twenty copies were sent free to editors and postmasters throughout the nation.[10]

Despite subsidies, Fenno faced financial difficulties and appealed regularly to Secretary of the Treasury Hamilton to keep his newspaper functioning during its first five years. By early 1797, the subscription price — in part because of inflationary pressures — had risen to eight dollars a year. Its front page was given over completely — as was often the style for the day — to brief advertisements. Peter Blight offered "A Quantity of Brandy, FIRST & 2d proofs" plus gin, rum, "Window-glass, in boxes, of different sizes Hazelnuts in sacks."

Fenno's newspaper carried continuing reports from the debates in the House of Representatives on tariffs, taxation, and smuggling as well as foreign news.

Meanwhile, on the heels of charges of scandalous speculation by Federalists and fiscal misconduct involving Secretary of the Treasury Alexander Hamilton, Thomas Jefferson resigned as secretary of state effective on the last day of 1793. The *Gazette of the United States*, for which Hamilton often wrote, accused Jefferson of disloyalty. The *National Gazette*, writing in support of Jefferson, complained bitterly that under Hamilton, the bankers, speculators, the privileged, and wealthy merchant interests gained far more than was their due.

William Cobbett and *Porcupine's Gazette*

William Cobbett, a British journalist, arrived in America in 1793. Fearing that Jeffersonian Republicans would lead the United States to terrors like those produced by the French Revolution, Cobbett became a pamphleteer. He produced *A Bone to Gnaw for the Democrats*, and in 1797 issued a prospectus for a Federalist newspaper, *Porcupine's Gazette*. Cobbett claimed that the newspapers of the country had done it more injury than its enemies could do by exciting the people to acts of violence against Britain and by promoting falsehoods. He promised to meet the editors of such newspapers "on their own ground; to set foot to foot; dispute every inch and every hair's breadth; fight them with their own weapons, and return two blows for one."[11]

Cobbett did not restrict the festering quills of the *Porcupine's* political attacks to the Jeffersonians, however, and by 1799 President John Adams considered deporting Cobbett under the Enemy Alien Act of 1798. Adams' action wasn't necessary, because Cobbett, whose Philadelphia assets were seized in a $5,000 libel judgment, returned to England in 1800.

Benjamin Russell's *Columbian Centinel*

The disreputable *Porcupine's Gazette* grew to be a political embarrassment to all but the most extreme Federalists. On the other hand, Benjamin Russell's *Columbian Centinel*, founded in 1784, was more moderate than John Fenno's

William Cobbett.

Good Master Young,
    I cannot send the whole amount
        With Christian pat'ence watch and wait;
    Take fifty dollars on account,
        And give the bearer a receipt.
                    Wm Cobbett.

P.S. Though I know it is very difficult to rhyme a presbyterian out of his money, yet when, in the measure of Watts's psalms, rhyme ought to have some weight. —— I will discharge the rest of your bill as soon as possible which, I hope, will be before Saturday night.
Monday, 5 Feb. 1798

William Cobbett, the "Porcupine." (Library of Congress Collection) stridently partisan newspaper or the wild invective of William Cobbett. Russell's *Centinel* tolerated little criticism, however, of the Federalist government. In 1798, after passage of the Alien and Sedition Acts, Russell loudly proclaimed, "It is Patriotism to write in favor of our Government; it is Sedition to write against it."[12]

JEFFERSONIAN (REPUBLICAN) NEWSPAPERS

Philip Freneau and the *National Gazette*

The *National Gazette*, edited by a man labeled the "Poet of the American Revolution," provided an effective newspaper voice for the Anti-Federalists and, later, for the Jeffersonian Republicans. A 1771 graduate of Princeton, Freneau had roomed there with James Madison. In 1791 Madison and Jefferson persuaded Freneau to move to the nation's capital city, Philadelphia, for the salary of $250 a year.

Madison and Jefferson expected that Freneau would establish a newspaper to fire answering journalistic volleys at John Fenno's *Gazette of the United States*. Indeed, Freneau did attack Federalist men and measures. He lambasted Hamiltonian-Federalist financial measures, including the Bank of the United States, and made fun of the aristocratic airs of the Federalists, airs which seemed to Freneau to reflect a fondness for monarchy.

Freneau's satirical thrusts stuck home, and his support of the French won him enemies. Hamilton, writing anonymous letters for publication in the *Gazette of the United States*, accused Secretary of State Jefferson of using public monies to pay an editor who turned on the government. Hamilton claimed Jefferson had departed "from the rules of official propriety and obligation, and from the duty of a discreet and patriotic citizen."[13]

President Washington indicated to Jefferson that he wanted Freneau fired from his job as a translator clerk in the State Department.[14] Later in 1793, Washington referred to charges that Jefferson was responsible for the *National Gazette's* attacks on the president and the government. Jefferson wrote to Washington, pleading that he had no direct influence on Freneau's paper. Jefferson swore that he never wrote for the *National Gazette* unless his name, or that of his office as Secretary of State, was used with a written statement.[15] Jefferson's letter to Washington added that

> he [Freneau] & Fenno are rivals for the public favor. The one courts them by flattery, the other by censure, & I believe it will be admitted that one has been as servile, as the other severe. . . .

> No government ought to be without censors: & where the press is free, no one ever will.

The *National Gazette* lasted only two years, suspending publication October 26, 1793. The paper was halted after Jefferson made known his intent to resign as secretary of state. Its demise was doubtless insured not only by the reluctance of subscribers and advertisers to pay their debts, but also by the yellow fever epidemic scourging Philadelphia that fall. The *National Gazette*, quite clearly a money-loser, nevertheless had a circulation of more than 1,500 that reached throughout the union.

Six months before the paper suspended publication, Jefferson gave it high marks: "His paper has saved our constitution which was galloping fast into monarchy. . . ."[16] Freneau, by no means the most vitriolic of the editors in a vituperative age, nevertheless taunted President Washington into an uncharacteristic outburst during a Cabinet meeting. Washington denounced "that rascal Freneau."

Benjamin Franklin Bache and the *Aurora*

Benjamin Franklin was circumspect, cautious, and diplomatic as a journalist, businessman, and statesman. However, his grandson, Benjamin Franklin Bache, was one of the most ferocious journalists in American history. Bache grew up near his grandfather, and accompanied him to France during Franklin's service as ambassador. Angered at the Federalist's treatment of his grandfather, who had grown suspicious of the aristocratic group of officers under Washington, Bache seethed at what he perceived to be slights upon the old statesman.[17] When Franklin died in 1790 and Bache inherited the publishing house, he began a newspaper to oppose Federalist thought and action. The newspaper, grandiloquently called the *General Advertiser, and Political, Commercial and Literary Journal*, was soon mercifully shortened to *General Advertiser* and later also was known as the *Aurora*.

Bache's residence in France clearly helped shape his sympathies, and his paper favored France and his friend, the soon-to-be discredited French envoy, Citizen Genet. By the end of 1793, Freneau's *National Gazette* had disappeared and Bache's newspaper emerged nationally as the prime Jeffersonian Republican paper. In late 1796, the *Aurora* cast a savage light on President Washington's farewell address:

> If ever a nation was debauched by a man, the American nation has been debauched by Washington. If ever a nation has suffered from the improper influence of a man, the American nation has suffered from

the influence of Washington. If ever a nation was deceived by a man, the American nation has been deceived by Washington. Let his conduct then be an example to future ages. Let it serve to be a warning that no man may be an idol.[18]

The combative Bache—dubbed "Lightning Rod Junior" in reference to his grandfather's experiments with electricity—declared Washington's retirement should be cause for celebration: ". . . there ought to be a JUBILEE in the United States." After all, Bache asserted, Washington, "the source of all the misfortune of our country is this day reduced to a level with his fellow citizens, and is no longer possessed of power to multiply evils upon the United States."[19]

Publication of such verbiage about the beloved Washington proved dangerous. A shipbuilder thrashed Bache, and later John Ward Fenno, son of the editor of the Federalist's chief paper, attacked Bache in the streets. Undaunted, Bache published a secret letter from French Foreign Minister Talleyrand; he accused the administration of hiding the letter in order to avoid negotiating with France. Federalists accused Bache of treason; the poison-penned Federalist editor William Cobbett claimed the "infamous Lightning-rod, jun. was a hireling of, and in correspondence with the despots of France."[20]

Margaret Bache and William Duane

Benjamin Bache did not publish the *Aurora* unaided. His wife, Margaret Markoe Bache, proved to be an able manager. And in 1796, William Duane, a thirty-six-year-old wanderer who had published a newspaper in Calcutta, India, joined Bache as assistant editor of the *Aurora*.

In September 1798, while being prosecuted on charges of sedition, Benjamin Franklin Bache remained in Philadelphia to continue publishing his newspaper. Yellow fever struck the city and Bache died within a week of contracting the disease. After a brief suspension of the *Aurora*, Margaret Bache, as publisher, and William Duane, as editor, resumed publication. The two married in 1800 and continued the newspaper until 1822 as a Republican voice.

ALIEN AND SEDITION ACTS OF 1798

When John Adams was inaugurated as the second president of the United States March 4, 1797, the First Amendment had been in effect for more than five years. During those years relationships with France had deteriorated dramatically. French raids on American shipping outstripped the British raids of earlier years. France treated American diplomatic emissaries with open contempt, while at the same time trying to exact funds from the new country to help France with its many-sided war erupting from the French Revolution.

Nationalism and anti-French enthusiasm grew, and the Federalist leadership increasingly equated political opposition with disloyalty to country. The Federalists disliked the French sympathies of the Republican party, and of Republican journalists in particular. In fact, some Republicans were immigrants, and had not yet applied for citizenship, and the Federalists increasingly looked for methods to silence the opposition. In that setting, Congress passed and President Adams signed provisions affecting aliens and freedom of expression.[21]

THE NATURALIZATION ACT

This legislation, passed June 18, 1798, extended the period of residence necessary to become a citizen from five to fourteen years, with the proviso that five of those fourteen years had to be spent in the state or territory where the individual was being naturalized. The one softening feature applied to persons who were living in the United States before 1795; they had a year in which to take advantage of the preexisting five-year naturalization law.

THE ENEMY ALIEN ACT

This legislation placed despotic powers in the hands of the president, allowing him to deport all males over fourteen who were subjects of any government at war with or who had threatened United States territory. The legislation, in effect, would have allowed Adams to deport all French-speaking unnaturalized citizens in the United States if he had chosen to declare France's actions acts of war.

THE SEDITION ACT

The Sedition Act made it illegal to conspire to oppose measures of the government. This specifically included any persons who, with criminal intent, ". . . shall counsel, advise or attempt to procure any insurrection, riot, unlawful assembly, or combination," whether or not the activity had the proposed effect. Punishment for violating the law was a fine of up to $5,000 and imprisonment for up to five years.

The second section of the act hit at the heart of newspapers and the publication of opposition voices:

> That if any person shall write, print, utter or publish, or shall cause or procure to be written, printed, uttered or published, or shall knowingly and willingly assist or aid in writing, printing, uttering or publishing any false, scandalous and malicious writing or writings against the Government of the United States, or the President of the United States, or either house of the Congress of the United States, with intent to defame the said government, or either house of the said Congress, or the said President, or to bring them, or either of them into contempt or disrepute; or to excite against them, or either of them, the hatred of the good people of the United States, or to stir up sedition within the United States . . . shall (upon conviction) be punished by a fine not exceeding two thousand dollars, and by imprisonment not to exceed two years.

The law provided for truth as a defense and the right of the jury to determine the law and the fact of the case. An expiration date for the Sedition Act, approved July 14, 1798, was included in the legislation. The law was in force until March 3, 1801.

Supporters defended the Sedition Act by arguing that such restrictions were necessary because of possible war with France, and that press freedom as guaranteed by the First Amendment meant absence of prior restraint, not the ability to "make false, scandalous, and malicious publications against the government."[22] Some historians have argued that it represented an improvement over the common law of sedition, because it allowed a jury to decide both the law and the fact of a case, and it made truth a defense. Further, the intent of speakers or writers, plus criminal tendencies of their words, would be taken into account.

Such safeguards, however, saved few Anti-Federalists. Federalists appointed the federal court judges (and marshals and bailiffs), and controlled jury selection processes. The matters of "intent" of the speaker or writer and the "tendency" of words, far from being items of mitigation for the defendant, were indeed easily interpreted as evil in troubled times.[23]

James Morton Smith, leading scholar of the Alien and Sedition acts, put them in chilling perspective, noting that they raised the basic question of whether residents of the United States were to be free to criticize their government:

> The meaning of the First Amendment did not crystallize in 1791, when the Bill of Rights was added to the Constitution. Not until the years from 1798 to 1801, when the Sedition Act was debated and enforced, did the limits of liberty of speech and press become an issue

which focused attention squarely on its definition as a part of the American experiment in self-government.[24]

THE VIRGINIA AND THE KENTUCKY RESOLUTIONS, 1798 AND 1799

The Republicans protested the Alien and Sedition Acts in 1798 and 1799 by passing the Virginia and Kentucky resolutions. James Madison secretly wrote the Virginia Resolution, and Jefferson clandestinely supplied the Kentucky Resolution. Both resolutions claimed the Sedition Act violated the Constitution. The Virginia Resolution of December 14, 1798, declared that the national government's defiance of the Constitution would "transform the present Republican system of the United States into an absolute, or at best, a mixed monarchy." Not only did the Alien and Sedition Acts subvert government by uniting legislative and judicial powers with the powers of the president, those Acts exercised a power "not delegated by the Constitution, but on the contrary, expressly and positively forbidden" by the First Amendment. The resolutions maintained that the power of the Alien and Sedition Acts "is levelled against the right of freely examining public characters and measures, and of free communication among the people, thereon, which has ever been justly deemed the only effectual guardian of every other right."[25]

PROSECUTIONS

Perhaps the most remarkable aspect of the Sedition Act prosecutions was their scope. In 1790, about 100 newspapers existed, and by 1800 that number had grown to 235.[26] Between 1798 and 1800 about twenty-five persons, primarily Republican journalists and printers, were charged under federal or state sedition laws.[27]

Benjamin Franklin Bache

A prime target for prosecutorial eagerness was "Lightning rod, jun.," Benjamin Franklin Bache. On June 26, 1798—the same day that the Sedition Bill was introduced in the U.S. Senate—Bache was indicted under a claim of violating a federal common law crime.[28] Bache was personally obnoxious to the Federalists for his name-calling; Abigail Adams had been urging passage of a sedition law to deal with the editor who described her husband as "old, querulous, bald, blind, crippled, toothless Adams."[29] The incident triggering the common-law prosecution of Bache was the *Aurora's* publication of diplomatic correspondence and charges that the Adams Administration had forged or tampered with that correspondence before showing it to Congress. Arrested on June 26, 1798, Bache was allowed to remain free until June 29, when his bail was set at $4,000.[30]

Bache's trial was set for October 1798, but a greater power than the Federalist prosecutors interceded: Bache died of yellow fever September 10, 1798. The *Aurora* continued its fight against the Federalists and editor William Duane later was made a sedition target but never was brought to trial.[31]

Luther Baldwin

By all odds the most ludicrous prosecution was of Luther Baldwin, a resident of Newark, New Jersey. With Congress adjourned in July 1798, President and Mrs. Adams left the vaporous heat of Philadelphia, riding in an open carriage. Preparations had been made to celebrate the President's passage. With cheers of "Huzzah!" and, as the Adams carriage pulled off into the distance the distant booming of cannon firing a salute could be heard.

One customer of a Newark tavern observed that the cannon were firing at the President's arse. Luther Baldwin, perhaps too long in the tavern, said he did not care if they fired *through* his arse. Federalists overhead the remark and the unfortunate Baldwin was prosecuted and fined $150 for sedition.[32]

The Special Case of the "Spitting Lyon"

Vermont Congressman Matthew Lyon probably garnered the most colorful nickname in the sordid history of the Sedition Act. This restless immigrant from Ireland was elected to Congress, and objected vigorously to the passage of the Sedition Act, predicting he would be the act's first victim. His Irish birth and his Republican views set him apart from the congressmen representing New England: one member of Congress even suggested that the Irish-born Lyon came from an inferior bloodline. Lyon, a feisty wordsmith, suggested, unlike the New England Federalists, he did not claim to be

> descended from the bastards of Oliver Cromwell, or his courtiers, or from the Puritans who punished their horses for breaking the Sabbath, or from those who persecuted the Quakers, or hanged the witches.[33]

Lyon, one of Vermont's legendary Green Mountain Boys in the Revolutionary War, was briefly removed from the military, evidently on ill-considered charges of leaving his post, before being reinstated and serving heroically in battle. Nevertheless, Federalists made slighting references in newspapers about his military record. And when Federalist Congressman Roger Griswold of Connecticut denigrated that record, Matthew Lyon spat in Griswold's face,

Chapter 5 **A New Nation**

right in the House of Representatives. Federalist efforts to get the two-thirds vote needed to remove Lyon from Congress failed.[34]

Lyon responded to the attack with a letter to a Federalist newspaper, criticizing the president's "unbounded thirst for ridiculous pomp, foolish adulation, and selfish avarice. . . ."[35]

That, and similar attacks on the presidency, brought Lyon within range of the Sedition Act. Lyon, meanwhile, tiring of not being able to get his responses to Federalist-newspaper attacks accepted for publication, established his own paper in 1798 with the marvelous title: *The Scourge of Aristocracy and the Repository of Important Political Truths.* Lyon's protests that the Sedition Act was unconstitutional did him no good, nor did his assertion that his articles were harmless and published without bad intent. Lyon was convicted by a Federalist judge, jailed for four months, and fined $1,000.[36]

After Lyon's conviction, Federalist newspapers crowed that by punishing Lyon for licentiousness, true freedom of the press was being saved.[37] Republican papers such as William Duane's *Aurora* declared that Lyon was a martyr, a hero of press freedom. His jailing in a vile, cramped cell won sympathy for Lyon, as did his letters from his cell, widely published by Republican newspapers. While still in jail, Lyon was reelected to Congress by a comfortable margin, and he emerged from jail a hero.

The Sedition Act Expires

Prosecutions did not end with the expiration of the Sedition Act in 1801. In 1803, Harry Croswell, editor of the Federalist *Wasp*, was charged under a state charge of seditious libel. Croswell claimed that Jefferson paid James Callender (who had been convicted under the Sedition Act) to call Washington a traitor, robber, and perjurer. Alexander Hamilton, a supporter of the Sedition Act, defended Croswell before the New York Supreme Court. Although maintaining that governments could be defamed, Hamilton argued that seditious libel law should not be used to stifle truthful criticism of public men and public measures. Although Croswell was convicted despite Hamilton's efforts, the New York legislature responded by passing a libel act that same year that made truth a defense and gave the jury the power to decide both law and fact.

JEFFERSONIAN DEMOCRACY

Puzzled by Thomas Jefferson's seemingly contradictory statements, historians have long debated the third president's position on freedom of the press. Although Jefferson fully supported freedom of the press to criticize government, he was less inclined to support criticism of individuals in the public arena. Jefferson's reputation for upholding freedom of the press is based on statements such as the one to his friend Edward Carrington in 1787:

> The basis of our governments being the opinion of the people, the very first object should be to keep that right; and were it left to me to decide whether we should have a government without newspapers or newspapers without a government, I should not hesitate a moment to prefer the latter.[38]

In 1794, Jefferson expressed a more fully developed theory of freedom of the press in his "Notes for a Constitution:" "Printing presses shall be free except as to false facts published maliciously either to injure the reputation of another, whether followed by pecuniary damages or not, or to expose him to the punishment of the law."[39]

In 1803, after he had been subjected to the vicious partisan wars during his first term as president, Jefferson's works had a different ring as he wrote to Chief Justice Thomas McKean of Pennsylvania, suggesting that "nothing in a newspaper is to be believed," and that "a few prosecutions of the most prominent offenders would have a wholesome effect in restoring the integrity of the press."[40] In context, however, Jefferson's stance remains consistent if one assumes he was referring to the prosecution of personal libel cases.[41] Jefferson said existing state laws were sufficient to prosecute and continued to denounce the "gag law" of the Federalists. Jefferson's suggestions appeared to have been taken seriously, and several state prosecutions resulted.

Both Jeffersonians and Federalists urged the use of civil libel suits as a press control. William Coleman's *New York Evening Post* recommended that Federalists file suits against the Republican papers. William Duane, editor of the Republican *Aurora*, was said to have so many libel suits against him that no "reputable lawyer could offer only one defense to any new suit: Duane's own reputation was so bad that his slanders could no longer injure his targets."[42]

NEWSPAPERS OF THE JEFFERSONIAN PERIOD

The *National Intelligencer*, 1800–1812

Partisan journalism continued as the norm after Jefferson's election, but a newspaper of record, the *National Intelligencer*, begun by Samuel Harrison Smith in 1800, developed methods for extensive coverage of Congress. The *Intelligencer*'s extended verbatim excerpts of debates in the House and the Senate were exchanged with newspapers around the nation. It provided an invaluable fund of in-depth information until it was sold by one of Smith's successors, W.W. Seaton, in 1864.

Smith began the newspaper when President Jefferson persuaded him to leave his Philadelphia publishing venture to set up shop in the new national capital, the "malarial swamp" as John Adams once called it, Washington, D.C. During his Philadelphia days, Smith learned shorthand from Joseph Gales, Sr., one of the first reporters to cover sessions of Congress, and who acquired the *Independent Gazetteer* after Eleazer Oswald died in 1794.[43] Gales, fearful of Philadelphia's repeated yellow fever outbreaks, sold the paper to Smith in 1797 and moved to North Carolina, where he founded another Jeffersonian paper, *The Raleigh Register*.

The House of Representatives had been open to the press and the public since the beginning, but the Senate continued to meet secretly. In 1800, when the nation's capital was moved to Washington, the new galleries in the House were so far from the floor that it was difficult to hear the delegates. Smith tried to secure a desk inside the rail, but was refused. Until the next congressional election, when Smith finally was granted his request, he reported information given to him by the clerk of the House. His troubles were not over, however, and he was expelled from the House for a session for reporting that James Lane had been arrested for disorderly conduct after applauding from the gallery.[44] In addition, the Federalist judiciary attempted to indict him for libel, but a grand jury refused. Smith responded, "Inasmuch as governments may err, every citizen has a right to expose an error in HIS OPINION comitted [sic] by them."[45] By 1802, however, Smith's position was secure as he was readmitted to the House and admitted to the Senate.

Smith's triweekly newspaper was a remarkable accomplishment, supporting "liberal policies in a conservative manner." The shorthand reporting from Congress provided a service not otherwise available to editors throughout the young nation.[46] Smith produced the paper single-handedly, except for printing. He wrote the news, reported the debates, clipped from other newspapers, solicited advertising, and kept accounts. In 1809, however, Smith left the business for banking and sold his newspaper to a trusted associate. In 1808, Joseph Gales, Jr., son of the man who taught Smith shorthand, joined the staff as "stenographer." By January 1809, the younger Gales became a partner, and in August 1810 he assumed full responsibility for the newspaper.

The New York Evening Post

In an intensely political United States, of course, the *National Intelligencer* was not universally admired. The Federalists of the early nineteenth century loathed anything Jeffersonian. To counteract the influence of the *Intelligencer*, arch-Federalist Alexander Hamilton started a new paper in New York City, which by 1800, with 60,000 residents had become the nation's largest city.[47] Although New York already had three Federalist-leaning newspapers and a strong Republican sheet, Hamilton and some Federalist friends secured the editorial services of William Coleman, a Princeton graduate, an attorney, and a man acclaimed as one of the day's most accomplished public speakers. The Federalist stalwarts each signed a founders' list and each was expected to contribute at least $1,000, with about $10,000 regarded as necessary for initial capitalization. The first list of subscribers added up to 600, and included names as prominent as that of John Jacob Astor.

On November 16, 1801, the first issue of the *New York Evening Post* appeared:

> The design of this paper is to diffuse among the people correct information on all interesting subjects, to inculcate just principles in religion, morals and politics; and to cultivate a taste for sound literature.[48]

In addition to its weekday efforts—which soon netted it a respectable circulation of 1,100, the *Evening Post* reused its already set type to produce a weekly edition, called the *Herald*. This weekly *Herald* was sent to out-of-town subscribers from Boston to Savannah. It featured fewer advertisements but more news and comment than its cousin, the *Evening Post*.

Coleman, perhaps the best-educated journalist of his day, relied heavily on Hamilton's knowledge and also took dictation from Hamilton to write articles. Although the *Evening Post* remained a lively paper, the relationship between Coleman and Hamilton was ended by a duelist's bullet. Aaron Burr, incensed over Hamilton's opposition, which may have cost Burr both the presidency and the governorship of New York, fatally wounded Hamilton on July 11, 1804.

THE *NATIONAL INTELLIGENCER* OF GALES AND SEATON

The *National Intelligencer*, under Joseph Gales, Jr., continued to be the nation's most important—and politically potent—newspaper for at least a decade. Gales was only twenty-four years old when he took over the *Intelligencer*. He had worked for his father's *Raleigh Register* after being expelled from the University of North Carolina, then moved to Philadelphia and ultimately to Washington to respond to Samuel Harrison Smith's advertisement offering the *Intelligencer* for sale. When the rigors of putting out the triweekly put an exhausted Joseph Gales, Jr., in his bed for a lengthy recuperation in 1812, his brother-in-law William Winston Seaton moved from the *Raleigh Register* to

National Intelligencer *Office in Washington, at 9th & E. Streets, N.W. (Library of Congress Collection)*

become a partner in the *Intelligencer*. The Gales and Seaton partnership lasted forty-eight years, through truly cataclysmic changes in the nation.

Although the *Intelligencer* offered a gold mine of information on government, with Seaton taking shorthand notes on the debates in the Senate, and Gales covering the House, the paper went through difficult financial times. Smith, as owner of the *Intelligencer*, had received congressional printing (worth perhaps $5,000 a year in 1801) and some printing work for executive departments. When Congress began to award printing and stationery contracts to lowest bidders, non-newspaper printers gained much of the business until 1819, when a patronage system was reestablished by Congress. Subscribers and advertisers apparently were longer in promises than hard cash, and such government printing as the newspaper received was not enough to allow the partners to turn a solid profit. Even so, the paper was regarded as both a valuable service and as an organ of the presidential administration, from Jefferson through the administrations of Madison (1809–1817) and Monroe (1817–1825).

Madison's tenure found a nation in the throes of awkward adolescence and spoiling for a fight. Although President Madison retained the lingering distrust of standing armies and large navies left over from his memories of British colonial rule, the nation took up arms against Indians and defended itself against other nations' interference with American shipping. In response to local congressmen referred to as the War Hawks, Madison, urged annexation of Canada and Florida.

At the onset of the War of 1812, Gales and Seaton volunteered for service in a District of Columbia infantry company, alternating with one serving under arms while the other edited. The size and quality of the paper suffered and friends maintained that the editors would be of more service to their country by remaining full-time editors.[49]

The *National Intelligencer* worked hard to prepare its readers for war, editorializing to remind the nation of grievances against the British: impressment of seamen, interferences with U.S. trade, and efforts by the United States to keep the peace, including embargoes and other trade restrictions. But other newspapers posed considerable opposition. The *Columbian Centinel* of Boston and the *Boston Repertory* both claimed the declaration of war on June 18, 1812, to be dreadful news.

When the British fleet and British soldiers reached Washington, most of the *Intelligencer*'s printers were called away from their work to defend the capital. Troops were badly trained, poorly deployed and too few in number to be effective. Humiliation mounted upon humiliation, as American gunboats were destroyed so the British would not capture them, and British troops swept into the capital. The government of the United States fled to Virginia, while on August 25, 1814, the British put most of Washington to the torch.

The chief incendiary, Admiral George Cockburn, ordered the *National Intelligencer*'s offices destroyed. Clearly Admiral Cockburn felt that the newspaper was not merely private property, which generally was spared throughout the city.[50] It was even said that Admiral Cockburn orders the *C*s in the type cases smashed so the editors would not be able to print — or denounce — his name.

The *Intelligencer* recovered after the war, although finances remained a troubling issue. By 1818, Joseph Gales, Jr., owed a bank $6,500, a large sum in that day. As he put up the *National Intelligencer* for collateral, Gales told the Bank of the United States that he and Seaton also owed money to private parties because of the difficulty of collecting the $80,000 to $100,000 owed to the *Intelligencer*.[51]

The political ambition of Senator Henry Clay of Kentucky, maneuvering for a presidential bid, helped rescue Gales and Seaton. In 1819, Clay promoted a patronage system allowing both houses of Congress to select a printer

> **CRITICISM OF THE GOVERNMENT SPRINGS ETERNAL**
>
> The expenditures for the fiscal year ending June 30, 1857, independent of the public debt, as appears from the report of the Secretary of the Treasury, are $65,032,597.
>
> The first question is, whether those expenditures are greater than what they should be under an economical administration of the Government. We think they are.
>
> SOURCE. National Intelligencer, editorial, August 23, 1858.

of choice, without regard to low bids. From 1819 until 1846, Clay's patronage legislation directly affected political newspapers in the capital.

Not only could each house select its own printer, but other printing projects appeared as the activities of Congress and the Executive Branch expanded. At times, particularly during the Jackson presidency in the 1830s, the patronage system helped support newspapers opposing a dominant party. Political horsetrading allowed a number of opposing splinter factions to subsidize newspapers through contracts to print the *Annals of Congress, American Archives* and the *American State Papers*. Such publishing projects were handled by Whig editors who fought against the Jackson administration at every turn.[52]

Gales and Seaton held House printing contracts from 1819 to 1829 and Senate contracts from 1819 to 1826. In the first five years, they received nearly $160,000, a remarkable amount when a printer's wages added up to about $500 a year.[53]

THE ELECTION OF 1824

With the jockeying for position during the election of 1824, each candidate representing a different constituency selected a newspaper to espouse his views. John Quincy Adams of Massachusetts, secretary of state under President Monroe, was the son of the second president of the United States. Educated in Europe and graduated from Harvard, he read law and had represented the United States in the Netherlands, Prussia, England, and Russia. He led the American delegation negotiating the 1814 Treaty of Ghent, which ended the War of 1812. Adams was supported by the *National Journal*, a sober, proper newspaper founded in 1823 by Peter Force to support Adams' candidacy for President.

A second candidate, John C. Calhoun of South Carolina, an aristocratic southerner, also claimed extensive government experience. A Yale graduate and attorney, he was elected to the House of Representatives in 1810 and was a leading War Hawk. In 1817, he became President Monroe's secretary of war. When he failed to gain the support of the *National Intelligencer*, Calhoun and his friends founded *The Republican*, edited by Thomas McKenney, to support his candidacy.

Henry Clay of Kentucky, known as the great orator, represented western interests. He advocated a high tariff to protect American manufacturers and supported using proceeds from the tariff to build roads, helping farmers and other producers of raw materials to get their goods to market. Clay had helped reach the Missouri Compromise of 1820, setting a pattern by admitting a "slave state" into the Union for every new "free state." Clay was hoping for the support of the *Intelligencer*, since his patronage system of 1819 had been a great financial boon to that newspaper.

William Harris Crawford, also a candidate for president, withdrew his candidacy, but not until he founded the *Gazette*, edited by an able scholar Jonathan Elliott, and partially funded by the Treasury Department.

Andrew Jackson of Tennessee, the symbol of the Common Man, was the hero of the Battle of New Orleans. He stood for the West, but not for the more genteel West of Henry Clay. General Jackson also garnered substantial support among workers in the burgeoning cities of the East. Jackson was fifty-seven in 1824, and had been elected to both the House and Senate from Tennessee. He also served as a judge before retiring. After eight years at The Hermitage in Tennessee, he volunteered to fight in the War of 1812. Nicknamed "Old Hickory," he led troops to a masterful performance at New Orleans—his troops suffered only sixteen casualties while inflicting some 2,000 on the British. Washington, D.C., had a Jacksonian paper, edited by the mercurial Duff Green—who later turned against Jackson after he became president.

The fortunes of the newspapers of the day to some degree depended on the fortunes of their candidates. The *National Intelligencer*'s co-editor, William Winston Seaton, was a friend of candidate John C. Calhoun, and the *Intelligencer* certainly owed Calhoun a great deal for his 1819 patronage bill. Meanwhile, many suspected the *Intelligencer* of hanging back in hopes of seeing Crawford elected president. After much waffling, the *Intelligencer* announced its support for Crawford, even though he was much weakened from a stroke suffered some ten months earlier.

Soon afterward, John C. Calhoun abandoned the race and his newspaper, the *Republican*, ceased to exist. In the presidential election, electoral votes counted December 1, 1824, showed Jackson leading with ninety-nine, over John Quincy Adams with eighty-four, William H. Crawford with forty-one, and Henry Clay with thirty-seven.

Because there was no majority, the election was thrown into the House of Representatives. John Quincy Adams, the prim and high-minded man who said in 1821 that he would never stoop to "cabal and intrigue, or purchasing newspapers, bribing by appointments, or bargaining for foreign missions," was elected when Henry Clay threw support to him. Adams named Clay secretary of state, leading to irate "corrupt bargain" charges by supporters of Jackson.

The political bargaining and tying of newspapers to candidates was illustrated clearly in the election of 1824. Thereafter, a more independent press began to emerge, although newspapers retained their loyalties to particular candidates and to parties well into the twentieth century. The rise of mass advertising in the 1830s, however, substantially freed leading northern urban newspapers from government and party financial support.

Magazines and Some Questions about Audience

Benjamin Franklin and Andrew Bradford attempted to publish magazines in 1741, but both failed to create economically viable subscription lists. In 1743, Jeremiah Gridley made a more successful attempt, and published the *American Magazine and Historical Chronicle* for three years. Five other magazines were started before the Revolution, but none survived long. In 1800, only twelve magazines existed, but by 1825 their numbers increased to one hundred.

The successful establishment of magazines depended on obtaining content significantly different from that of the general press, on a paying audience, and on a distribution system. The assumption usually has been made that magazines in colonial and revolutionary America did not survive because the magazines consisted primarily of English reprints, and that a professional group of writers did not exist in America to produce magazine content. Furthermore, magazine content often seemed elitist, and because prices were high, audiences generally have been considered to be elite as well.

In a recent study of *The New-York Magazine; or, Literary Repository*, historian David Nord suggested that at least one magazine included content that appealed to working-class groups in the city, and that half of the magazine's subscribers were artisans and shopkeepers. Only half was made up of the upper-class merchants and professionals. The editors claimed to design their magazine to appeal to different groups, stating that "The universality of the subjects which it [a well-conducted magazine] treats of will give to every profession, and every occupation, some information, while its variety holds out to every taste some gratification." The editors further claimed every "class of society" would be able to afford the magazine.[54] Nord concluded that the content did appeal to all but the lowest economic classes because of its republican themes: virtue portrayed as public virtue, suspicion of luxury, and a belief in the power and democratizing influence of knowledge.

Magazines such as *The New York Magazine* tended to circulate locally because magazines did not enjoy the favored postal rate status of newspapers. The 1792 postal act required that magazines pay letter rates if sent through the mails. Two Philadelphia magazines—the *Columbian* and the *Museum*—suspended publication. Others survived by creating alternative distribution systems.

In 1794, the postal act set more favorable mailing rates for magazines, but gave postmasters the right to determine whether the mails could handle the added bulk. If subscribers could receive the publications, they paid 20 to 40 percent of the subscription price for postage.

In 1815, the postmaster general decided that magazines and pamphlets interfered with regular mail, and excluded all except the publications of "Bible societies." Exempt from the postmaster's ban, religious publications gained the largest national circulations.[55]

CONCLUSION

Newspapers of the early national period reflected the party discussions and antagonisms of the Federalists and the Anti-Federalists, but also promoted party cohesion and the expression of diverse political and social views. Editors of partisan newspapers sometimes were chosen for political reasons and were not always entrepreneurs or members of the printing network established in colonial days. By 1815, postal laws and a patronage system protected newspapers from high distribution costs and subsidized them through contracts for government printing. Advertising continued as a source of revenue, consisting primarily of announcements for goods and services by those who subscribed to the newspapers.

Developing alongside the political press and sometimes integrated with it were commercial dailies in the burgeoning cities. Expanded trade, particularly after 1812, created a need for commercial information. In addition, changing social relationships altered traditional relationships between workers, and artisans may have provided an enlarged audience for new publications.

In 1798, as Federalists faced growing political opposition and feared war with France, Congress enacted alien and sedition laws. Supporters of the acts argued they were necessary because of the threat of war and that they did not violate freedom of press, which they interpreted to mean absence of prior restraint. Jefferson and Madison, however, through the Kentucky and Virginia resolutions, argued that the acts were a clear violation of the First Amendment. Federalists used the acts to vigorously prosecute Republican editors. The debate over the use of the Alien and Sedition Acts brought into sharp focus differing viewpoints that had existed long before the creation of the Bill of Rights.

When Jefferson became president in 1800, he pardoned those convicted under the Alien and Sedition Acts. Although historians have been puzzled by Jefferson's seemingly contradictory statements, he continuously adhered to a theory of freedom of the press, although he became weary of personal criticism during his tenure as president. Both Federalists and Republicans advocated the use of civil libel suits to control vicious criticism of individuals, and Jefferson was no exception.

Although the Continental Congress had acted in secrecy, the House of Representatives opened its doors to the press from the beginning, and the Senate soon followed suit. The *National Intelligencer*, although sympathetic to the Republican cause, became known as a newspaper of record and provided news from the nation's capitol through printers' exchanges for much of the nation.

NOTES

1. Alexander Hamilton died after a duel with Aaron Burr in 1804. Jeffersonian Republicans have no relationship to the Republican party of the twentieth century. The current Republican party was begun in the middle of the nineteenth century.
2. Richard E. Ellis, "The Meaning of Jeffersonian Ascendancy," in Stanley N. Katz and Stanley Kutler, *New Perspectives on the American Past, 1607–1877* (New York: Little, Brown, 1972), pp. 171–172.
3. David Paul Nord, "A Republican Literature: A Study of Magazine Reading and Readers in Late-Eighteenth-Century New York," paper presented to the History Division, Association for Education in Journalism and Mass Communication, Norman, Okla., August, 1986.
4. Richard B. Kielbowicz, "The Press, Post Office, and Flow of News in the Early Republic," *Journal of the Early Republic* (Fall 1983), p. 269. One must be aware, however, that the postmaster was an Anti-Federalist, and perhaps assumed that rural papers would tend to support his party rather than the opposition.
5. The frontier press is discussed at length in chapter 7.
6. Cited in Kielbowicz, "The Press, Post Office, and Flow of News in the Early Republic," *Journal of the Early Republic* (Fall 1983), p. 280.
7. Willard G. Bleyer, *Main Currents in the History of American Journalism* (New York: Houghton-Mifflin, 1927), p. 106.
8. *Gazette of the United States,* April 15, 1789. For wage/subscription comparison, see Alfred McClung Lee, *The Daily Newspaper in America* (New York: The Macmillan Co., 1937).

PART 2 EXPANSION AND CONFLICT

9. *Gazette*, December 7, 1791.
10. Bleyer, *Main Currents*, p. 107.
11. Cobbett's prospectus appeared in the *Gazette of the United States* February 13, 1797. For full discussion of Cobbett, see Karen K. List, "The Role of William Cobbett in Philadelphia's Party Press, 1794–1799," *Journalism Monographs* 82 (May 1983).
12. *Columbian Centinel*, Boston, October 5, 1798. James Morton Smith, *Freedom's Fetters: The Alien and Sedition Laws and American Civil Liberties* (Ithaca, N.Y.: Cornell University Press, 1956), p. 179n, also found that statement quoted in the *Albany Centinel* for October 12, 1798.
13. *Gazette of the United States*, September 15, 1792.
14. Bleyer, *Main Currents*, p. 110.
15. Jefferson to Washington, 1793, in Paul Leicester Ford, ed., *Writings of Thomas Jefferson*, vol. 6, p. 108, cited in Bleyer, *Main Currents*, p. 111.
16. Cited in Bleyer, *Main Currents*, p. 111.
17. Margaret A. Blanchard, "Benjamin Franklin Bache," Perry J. Ashley, ed., *Dictionary of Literary Biography*, (Detroit, Mich.: Gale Research Press, 1986), vol. 43: pp. 14–15.
18. The *Aurora*, December 23, 1796.
19. The *Aurora*, March 6, 1797.
20. *Porcupine's Gazette*, June 1798, cited in Smith, *Freedom's Fetters*, pp. 194, 195.
21. For account of tensions of the period, see Smith, *Freedom's Fetters*.
22. Jeffery Alan Smith, *Printers and Press Freedom: The Ideology of Early American Journalism* (New York: Oxford University Press, 1987), p. 59.
23. Smith, *Freedom's Fetters*, pp. 421–422; Leonard W. Levy *Emergence of A Free Press*, (New York: Oxford University Press, 1985), p. 297.
24. Smith, *Freedom's Fetters*, p. 426.
25. Henry Steele Commager, ed., *Documents of American History*, (New York: Appleton-Century Crofts, 1949), p. 182. Jefferson's motives may have been two-fold, one, to protest the sedition act, and two, to insure the supremacy of states rights.
26. Alfred McClung Lee, *The Daily Newspaper in America* (New York: The Macmillan Co., 1937), p. 711.
27. Smith, *Printers and Press Freedom*, p. 58.
28. Smith, *Freedom's Fetters*, pp. 188–192.
29. Cited in Page Smith, *John Adams*, (Westport, Conn.: Greenwood Press, 1969), vol. II, p. 361.
30. Smith, *Freedom's Fetters*, p. 202.
31. Smith, *Freedom's Fetters*, p. 204.
32. Smith, *Freedom's Fetters*, p. 271.
33. Annals of Congress, 5th C, 1S (June 2 and 3, 1797,) pp. 232–235, cited in Smith, *Freedom's Fetters*, pp. 222.
34. Smith, *Freedom's Fetters*, pp. 223–224.
35. *U.S. v. Lyon*, Wharton's State Trials, 333. Case No. 8646, *The Federal Cases* (St. Paul, 1895), vol. 15, pp. 1183–1191.

Chapter 5 **A New Nation**

36. *U.S. v. Lyon*, Wharton's State Trials, p. 335.
37. See *Connecticut Courant*, November 26, 1798; Spooner's *Vermont Journal*, October 15, 1798, cited in Smith, *Freedom's Fetters*, p. 236.
38. Jefferson to Edward Carrington, January 16, 1787, in Julian P. Boyd, ed., *The Papers of Thomas Jefferson* (Princeton, N.J.: Princeton University Press, 1955) vol. 11, p. 49.
39. Cited in Smith, *Printers and Press Freedom*, p. 89.
40. Jefferson to Thomas McKean, February 19, 1803, in Paul Leicester Ford, ed., *The Writings of Thomas Jefferson* (N.Y.: G.P. Putnam's Sons) vol. 9, p. 451.
41. Smith, *Printers and Press Freedom*, p. 89.
42. Norman L. Rosenberg, *Protecting the Best Men*, (Chapel Hill: University of North Carolina Press, 1986) p. 107, citing the Portsmouth, N.H., *Oracle*, December 10, 1808.
43. Harry Stonecipher, "Samuel Harrison Smith," Perry J. Ashley, ed., *DLB* vol. 43, p. 420.
44. William E. Ames, *A History of the National Intelligencer* (Chapel Hill: University of North Carolina Press, 1972), p. 26.
45. *National Intelligencer*, October 26, 1801, cited in Ames, p. 29.
46. Ames, *National Intelligencer*, pp. 19, 66, 67.
47. Allan Nevins, *The Evening Post: A Century of Journalism* (New York: Boni and Liveright, 1922), p. 12.
48. Cited in Nevins, *Evening Post*, p. 19.
49. Sallie A. Whelan, "William Winston Seaton," *DLB* vol. 43, pp. 20; 415–416.
50. Ames, *National Intelligencer*, pp. 98–99; Whelan, "William Winston Seaton," p. 416.
51. Ames, *National Intelligencer*, pp. 109–111.
52. William E. Ames and Dwight L. Teeter, "Politics, Economics and the Mass Media," in Ronald T. Farrar and John D. Stevens, eds., *Mass Media and the National Experience: Essays in Communications History* (New York: Harper & Row, 1971).
53. United States House Report 298, Twenty-Sixth Congress, First Session, and United States Senate Report 18, Fifty-Second Congress, First Session, cited in Ames, *National Intelligencer*, p. 111.
54. *New York Magazine*, 1 (April 1790), p. 197, cited in Nord, "A Republican Literature," p. 7.
55. Kielbowicz, "Press, Post Office and Flow of News," pp. 267–269.

CHAPTER 6

PENNY PAPERS IN THE METROPOLIS

The introduction of newspapers that sold for a penny into the nation's largest commercial city, New York, represented a commercial venture in the midst of an industrializing and modernizing nation that was undergoing immense social, cultural, and economic change. The newspapers challenged elite authority within the city by developing a new attitude toward advertising, by aiming at new audiences, and by paying reporters to cover local news. By circulating to diverse audiences within the city and to country audiences through weekly editions, the newspapers sought to break down geographical and local cultural barriers by disseminating news of national interest.

Prior to 1830, the metropolitan press, especially that of New York and other major cities, directed itself toward a commercial and political elite. These newspapers, dominated by commerce and vehement political rhetoric, were, as one historian described them, "little more than bulletin boards for the business community."[1] Newspapers cost six cents per issue and readers paid in advance for a year's subscription. Names such as *Commercial Advertiser* emphasized their particular appeal, and their circulations averaged about 1,500.[2]

With the beginning of Benjamin Day's *New York Sun* in 1833, followed by the *Evening Transcript* in 1834 and by James Gordon Bennett's *New York Herald* in 1835, the "new" New York press represented a truly dramatic departure from its elite predecessors and commercial rivals. The penny press, so labeled because each issue sold for a penny, championed the growing city population — immigrants and the middle class — rather than the commercial elite. Its content included day-to-day events such as police court news within its more traditional format of social and political news. By 1836 and 1837, the penny idea spread to Boston, Philadelphia, and Baltimore. William Swain's *Philadelphia Public Ledger* first appeared March 25, 1836, and in eight months circulated to 10,000 readers, at a time when the city's previous largest newspaper sold about 2,000 copies.[3]

In order to produce the "new" content for the penny papers, newspaper editors created "new" staffing patterns. Prior to the 1830s, newspaper editors simply took what walked in the door. Ship captains' letters, legal documents, campaign material, and legal documents constituted a good deal of the news. Publishers primarily were printers and collectors of news — not producers or creators. In the 1830s, the pattern began to change, and publishers hired managing editors and reporters, creating a staffing pattern that with modifications and expansion is still in place today. Technology boosted the collection of news, the printing of the newspaper, and its distribution. Faster presses and the use of steamships, railroad, and telegraph fostered faster, more timely news, printed for greater circulations, and delivered news more quickly to the readers.
The development of advertising on a larger scale promoted the inexpensive newspaper, and although newspaper editors, relying on advertising instead of political party support, claimed political independence, they often retained strong partisan loyalties. Their assertions of independence related more to the lack of political financing than to the lack of neutrality of political opinion.

Although the independent press claimed to reach the "masses," many groups still perceived themselves to be outside mainstream society as defined and reported by the newspapers. Therefore, a specialized press for labor, for various immigrant groups, and for blacks developed alongside the penny press.

Traditionally, journalism historians have depicted the 1830s as a period of revolution in United States journalism. Although such might be the case in describing the beginning of staffing patterns and the speed of delivery, it is not an accurate model for explaining the United States press as a whole. Rather, the period from 1820 to 1860 represented change and continuity, with reporter-originated stories gaining prominence over clipped second-hand news, particularly in urban dailies, and with increased speed in the delivery of news, but with content and style remaining rather stable.[4] Major changes did occur in New York, and other cities began to imitate the New York products; reporters and editors trained in the city also carried the idea to smaller cities. Nevertheless, the penny press model rarely was duplicated in the smaller towns of middle America.

Perhaps the most interesting question is why the change occurred. Researchers differ in their interpretations of what caused the penny press, with some attributing the change to a new focus on an immigrant class, and others to more attention to the middle class. Still others relate the change to broader changes in American society.

CHARACTERISTICS OF THE PENNY PRESS

The penny press was distinguished by a variety of characteristics. The most obvious of these involved financing, price, and salesmanship. Newspapers sold for a penny a copy, were hawked by street vendors, and were financed primarily through advertising. If debts were incurred, they were based on collateral provided by the value of the newspaper and the accompanying property such as presses and buildings. This differed from former newspaper owners who received money either directly from particular political or business interests or through banks supported by particular interests. Newsboys hawked the newspapers on the street rather than promising discreet delivery.

INFIRMARY.

DR. SHERRILL

HAS TAKEN A HOUSE, WITH GOOD AND AIRY ROOMS,

PLEASANTLY SITUATED AT

540 HUDSON ST., N. Y.

And fitted up an Institution often desired by those who have not a regular home,—to receive respectable patients and invalids to board, and furnish them Medical attendance. This will be made a comfortable home and quiet asylum for invalids. Careful attention will be paid to those who place themselves in this institution.

Dr. Sherill will continue to visit and attend patients at their residences, as usual.

For assurance of judicious Medical treatment and counsel, and for kind attention, reference may be had to—

Dr. V. Mott,	Dr. Alex. H. Stevens,
" W. Parker,	" Jno. F. Gray,
" F. W. Johnston,	" A. D. Wilson,
" J. W. Francis,	Willam Bard Esq.,
Rev. J. Pound,	Smith Dunning, Esq.
Ephraim Stephens, Esq.	

Early advertisement. (Library of Congress Collection)

The orientation toward advertising helped earn the penny press its label of sensationalism. Although unethical advertising existed prior to the penny press, editors of the elite newspapers that preceded the penny press claimed they screened their advertising. Editors of the new papers adopted a "let the buyer beware" attitude, attracting nearly all comers with a product to sell. The *Philadelphia Public Ledger* announced, for example:

> Our advertising columns are open to the "public, the whole public, and nothing but the public." We admit any advertisements of any thing or any opinion, from any persons who will pay the price, excepting what is forbidden by the laws of the land, or what, in the opinion of all, is offensive to decency and morals. . . . Our advertising is our revenue, and in a paper involving so many expenses as a penny paper, and especially our own, the *only* source of revenue.[5]

Editors who saw the penny press as a rival attacked its advertising policies, particularly those regarding patent medicines. In truth, however, many commercial dailies as well as colonial newspapers had carried patent medicine ads before the advent of the penny press. Benjamin Towne's Pennsylvania paper in 1784 advertised such genuine patent medicines as Hooper's Female Pills, Turlington's Balsam of Life, and Dr. Anderson's Scots Pills.[6] Fiercely antagonistic toward the New York penny papers, the city's *Journal of Commerce* rejected theater ads as being indecent, but accepted ads for patent medicines, and at the same time printed unfavorable comments on the medicines issued by medical societies.[7] Sociologist Alfred McClung Lee suggested that the objections directed at the new advertising represented a shift in the nature of the advertising process itself. In colonial and pre-penny newspapers, those who advertised were also those who subscribed to and financed the journal. An advertisement was seen as a mechanism for spreading information by means of a paid insertion. The penny press separated the advertising function from its subscribers and catered to the needs of all businesses to advertise and to the supposed desire of readers to recognize available new products.

Newspaper ownership is another important factor in change. Although there are significant exceptions, colonial editors were entrepreneurs—merchants, book dealers and shopkeepers trained in printing either in England or in the colonies. Early republic editors often were printers hired by political factions to represent a particular point of view. Ownership of the penny press rarely was apolitical, but the first aspiration of the editor was to succeed as a businessman.

The issue of content has been debated extensively. Some argue that penny papers changed content, focusing on crime news, the day-to-day events of the household and the streets, and on local happenings. They have been characterized as "news" papers rather than "views" papers. "One might say," wrote sociologist Michael Schudson, that, for the first time, the newspaper reflected not just commerce or politics but social life. To be more precise, in the 1830s the newspapers began to reflect, not the affairs of an elite in a small trading society, but the activities of an increasingly varied, urban, and middle-class society of trade, transportation, and manufacturing.[8]

Some historians maintain that a change in content was not readily apparent between 1820 and 1860 for the American press as a whole. In analyzing 3,000 sample newspapers, Donald Shaw found that newspapers did not become less political and more social, and that they focused on politics, social and intellectual aspects of communities, and economic concerns. He argued that social news did not develop in the context of the penny press, but that it existed prior to the 1830s. "In terms of press content the story of the 1820–1860 period is one of continuity, not change," Shaw wrote. However, Shaw also noted that the number of stories written by reporters began to replace news gathered from other newspapers. News also began to focus more concretely on local events. The most apparent change was in the employment of reporters to cover news, and the developing technology which greatly accelerated the speed with which news was gathered.[9]

THE NEW YORK LEADERS

BENJAMIN DAY AND THE *NEW YORK SUN*

Benjamin Day, an entrepreneur with newspaper and publishing experience, began learning the printer's trade on the Springfield (Mass.) Republican in 1824, when he was fifteen years old. At twenty, he went to New York and worked as a compositor at the *Evening Post* and the *Commercial Advertiser*. With the small savings he accumulated, he began a job-printing business. He subsequently started the *New York Sun*, not out of political or moral principle, but because he thought it would promote his printing business.[10] Other businessmen had tried the same concept—that of a penny paper—and failed, so it was not the first attempt to break away from the more staid metropolitan dailies.

Day issued the first edition of the *Sun* September 3, 1833, with an old press printing 200 sheets an hour. It was a day of free advertising for those who appeared in the *Sun*. The contents of the paper consisted of rewritten items and ads that Day reprinted from other newspapers. The four-page newspaper was printed on an 11¼ inch by 8 inch page, roughly similar to a piece of today's standard typing paper. In the first issue, Day announced his ambitions:

> The object of this paper is to lay before the public, at a price, within the means of every one, ALL THE NEWS OF THE DAY, and at the same time afford an advantageous medium for advertising. The sheet will be enlarged as soon as the increase of advertisements requires it—the price remaining the same.[11]

The subscription price was three dollars per year. Advertisers who signed for a year got ten lines a day for an annual rate of thirty dollars.

Two months later Day claimed success, with 2,000 subscribers and a "steadily increasing advertising patronage."[12] On December 17 he acquired a machine press that would print 1,000 impressions an hour, and his circulation surpassed 4,000. With the initial promise of success, Day hired a young reporter, George W. Wisner, and promised him four dollars a week to rise at 4 A.M. to cover daily police court sessions. Wisner, an ardent abolitionist, who sometimes sneaked an editorial or two into the *Sun*'s pages on that subject, became half-owner of the *Sun* in 1834. A year later, when Wisner decided to leave New York for the fresh air of Michigan, Day purchased Wisner's share for $5,000. Day's pattern for success became the historians' formula for describing the penny press. It contained the essential elements: expanded advertising, low cost, additional technology, street sales, and paid reporters to cover local news. As far as Colonel James Watson Webb of the old style *Courier and Enquirer* was concerned, those reporters could have been hired guns. He found the practice of hiring reporters scandalous, the results shoddy, and the success frightening.

When Wisner left Day's *Sun*, the editor hired another reporter, Richard Adams Locke, for twelve dollars a week. Locke was no mere hack, but an educated man interested in recent scientific discoveries and in astronomy.[13] Edgar Allen Poe said Locke's prose style "is noticeable for its concision, luminosity, completeness."[14] His prose style also was adaptable—he wrote poetry, political stories, and stories involving the nature of the universe. It was his interest in philosophy that led him to propose to Ben Day the possibility of a series of stories that would boost circulation—a series that resulted in the now infamous Moon Hoax. The series exploited the discoveries of Sir John Frederick William Herschel, the greatest astronomer of his time, who had established an observatory near Cape Town, South Africa. On August 21, 1835, an announcement appeared on page 2 of the *Sun*:

> CELESTIAL DISCOVERIES—The *Edinburgh Courant* says—"We have just learnt from an eminent publisher in this city that Sir John

> **POLICE COURT**
>
> Harriet Shultz, charged with committing a violent assault on the person of Henry Shultz, one of her husbands, who appeared against her as complainant; he stated that his wife was generally pretty clever to him, but, by some means or other, she was more ill-natured than usual last night, and took occasion to give him something of a flogging—he stood on the defensive when his wife made the attack, but finding himself unable to cope with her in the matrimonial combat, he bawled "murder," which brought a watchman to his assistance. The injured husband, with the assistance of the watchman, succeeded in capturing his tyrannical rib, and brought her, a prisoner, to the watch-house. On their promising to live together peaceably for the future, they were discharged.
>
> SOURCE. The Sun, September 3, 1833.

Herschel, at the Cape of Good Hope, has made some astronomical discoveries of the most wonderful description, by means of an immense telescope of an entirely new principle.[15]

Four days later Locke's first story appeared in the *Sun*. The source cited was a supplement to the Edinburgh *Journal of Science*, which ceased publication before 1835. The first story, which left readers in great suspense, detailed the new telescope Herschel was using and claimed he had "made the most extraordinary discoveries in every planet of our solar system; has discovered planets in other solar systems; has obtained a distinct view of objects in the moon." The following day the *Sun* printed four columns of Herschel's great discoveries, which described lunar vegetation, the moon's atmosphere, fine forests, and "continuous herds of brown quadrupeds" similar to the American bison, although smaller. Subsequent installments revealed the existence of winged creatures, much like men and women, on the moon, as well as magnificent structures, such as the great Temple of the Moon, built of polished sapphire.

The *Sun* fooled not only the general public, but the scientific community as well, including a delegation of scientists from Yale. But it was Locke himself who exposed the hoax. Gerard Hallock, who was David Hale's partner on the *Journal of Commerce*, sent a young reporter to retrieve extra copies of the *Sun* containing the moon story so the *Journal* could reprint it. Locke warned the young reporter not to reprint the story. "I wrote it myself," Locke said. When the *Journal* revealed the hoax, the *Sun* made light of the whole thing, praising the story's "useful effect in diverting the public mind, for a while, from that bitter apple of discord, the abolition of slavery, which still unhappily threatens to turn the milk of human kindness into rancorous gall." The *Sun* stated that while some called the moon story "an adroit fiction of our own," other readers "construe the whole as an elaborate satire upon the monstrous fabrications of the political press of the country and the various genera and species of its party editors." Locke was known to be annoyed with many of the period's popular books on astronomy, which often mixed fiction with fact. He later claimed he had intended the whole thing to be taken as a satire, rather than as truth. "I am the best self-hoaxed man in the whole community," he said.[16]

Dan Schiller suggested in *Objectivity and the News* that the hoax really was a "clever attempt to outwit the papers of New York City."[17] The penny papers were annoyed because the six-penny papers were reprinting their stories without credit. Deceived by the detailed scientific description in the stories about the moon, six-penny editors could not ignore the soaring circulation of moon-hoax issues of the *Sun*. When the hoax was revealed, James Gordon Bennett, editor of another famous penny paper, the *New York Herald*, claimed the *Sun* had gone too far in ignoring the truth in the order to make money. But the six-penny dailies, some of whom wrote of the moon discoveries as though they too had read them in the *Journal of Science* and not in the *New York Sun*, were indeed reduced in stature.

The moon hoax boosted circulation; during publication of the pseudo-scientific stories in August 1835, the *Sun* editors claimed a circulation of 19,360. (The largest competitor in New York City was the *Courier and Enquirer*, with a circulation of 4,500.) Advertising absorbed so much space that often news appeared in only five of the twenty columns. The publisher sometimes apologized for leaving out advertisements, or for having so little space for news. To help the situation, Day expanded the paper in January 1836. It remained a four-page sheet, but the size of the newsheet increased to 14 by 20 inches. By 1837 the *Sun*'s advertising revenues exceeded $200 a day. These reviews came not from the display advertising we are familiar with today, but with "liners," the common form of advertising in the 1830s. Liners looked like this:

> A CARD—TO BUTCHERS—Mr. Stamler, having retired to private life, would be glad to see his friends, the Butchers, at his house, No. 5 Rivington Street, this afternoon, between the hours of 2 and 5 P.M., to partake of a collation.

> SIX CENTS REWARD!—Run away from the subscriber, on the 30th of May, Charles Eldridge, an indented apprentice to the Segar-Making business, about 16 years of age, 4 feet high, broken back. Had on, when he left, a round jacket and blue pantaloons. The above reward and no charges will be paid for his delivery to
>
> John Dibben, No. 354 Bowery

In June 1837, Benjamin Day sold the *Sun* to Moses Beach, his brother-in-law, for $40,000. For a couple of years during Day's ownership, profits at the *Sun* had been as high as $120,000. The six months net return ending October 1, 1836, as claimed by the *Sun*, was $12,981.88; however, in June 1836, when Day sold the *Sun*, it was barely breaking even. The editor was only twenty-eight years old and had amassed a sizable fortune. There was speculation the drop in advertising was related not to a decreasing popularity of the *Sun*, but instead to the 1835 New York fire, which destroyed more than twenty blocks around Wall Street, and to banking failures of the year.

After the purchase of the *Sun* by Moses Beach, the newspaper continued to be innovative, both in terms of content and new methods of acquiring news. Before becoming involved with the *Sun*, Beach invented a rag-cutting machine for paper mills, but lack of speed in securing a patent prevented him from earning the income he otherwise might have gained from the process. Beach began the use of an express service operated by William F. Harnden to bring news from the harbors, using boats from New York to Providence and rail from Providence to Boston. With the express, New York newspapers could obtain English newspapers from the Boston Harbor within a day after the ships landed. In June of 1839, as the *Sun*'s own sailing vessels met the incoming steamships down the bay, the *Sun* boasted of its speed in collecting the news:

> In consequence of our news-boat arrangements we receive our papers more than an hour earlier than any other paper in this city. On the arrival of the Liverpool [July 1, 1839], we proceeded to issue an extra, which will reach Albany with the news twelve hours before it will be published in the regular editions of their evening papers, and twenty-four hours ahead of the morning papers.

While waiting for the telegraph to reach New York, which did not occur until 1846, the *Sun* used horse express, special trains, and carrier pigeons to speed up collection of news:

> Carrier-pigeons have long been remarked for their sagacity and admired for their usefulness. They are, of all birds, the most invaluable, and as auxiliary to a newspaper cannot be too highly prized. Part of the flock in our possession were employed by the London *Morning Chronicle* in bringing intelligence from Dublin to London, and from Paris to London, crossing both channels; therefore they are not novices in the newspaper express.

New technology was necessary to keep up with expanded news gathering and

Chapter 6 **Penny Papers in the Metropolis**

circulation. During the three years that he owned the *Sun*, Day bought two new Napier presses from Robert Hoe for $7,000 so that he could run 3,200 papers an hour on each press. In 1846, Beach bought two new presses at a cost of $12,000, each capable of printing 6,000 copies of the *Sun* an hour.

Within a dozen years, the first penny paper was no longer a small operation. On September 3, 1843, the *Sun* employed eight editors and reporters, twenty compositors, one hundred carriers, sixteen pressmen, and twelve folders and counters. Daily circulation was 38,000. The *Weekly Sun* had a circulation of 12,000. The *Sun* still filled four pages, with seven columns per page. Of the twenty-eight columns per issue, about twenty-one were filled with advertising, three with news and editorial, two with court reports, and one with reprint.

The coming of the Mexican War raised the cost of having news delivered quickly. Battle news from Mexico to New York took about eighteen days, traveling by steamer to New Orleans or Mobile, then by railroad to the nearest telegraph. The *Sun* had no correspondent, but relied on George Kendall's accounts written for the New Orleans *Picayune*. The expense of each newspaper collecting such news on its own led to a meeting in the *Sun* offices presided over by Gerard Hallock, editor of the *Journal of Commerce*. Representatives for the *Sun*, the *Herald*, the *Tribune*, the *Courier and Enquirer*, and the *Express* attended and formed the Harbour News Association. A fleet of news boats would be operated in cooperation to retrieve the news from afar, and the New York Associated Press, connected with the Harbour News Association, would pool resources for gathering news in centers like Washington, Albany, Boston, Philadelphia, and New Orleans.

Beach retired in 1848 at the age of forty-eight and turned the paper over to his sons. The newspaper retained its respectable position through the Civil War and was sold by the Beach family to Charles A. Dana in 1868. Dana spent almost thirty years with the *Sun*. Those thirty years kept the *Sun* in the forefront of developing news-gathering and news-organization techniques.

Benjamin Day's influence carried further than New York. Penny papers did not pop up accidentally in other cities; men trained by Day and familiar with his approach moved to other cities to start those newspapers. William M. Swain, who was Day's foreman on the *Sun*; Azariah H. Simmons, another New York printer; and Arunah Shepherdson Abel, who worked for the New York *Mercantile Advertiser* and who was a close acquaintance of Day's, started the Philadelphia *Public Ledger* in March 1836. The newspaper sold for a penny and claimed to be "neutral in politics." The *Ledger* struggled for nearly a year before its returns were in the black. Once the *Ledger* was on a solid financial footing (where it remained for more than thirty years), Abell, financed in part by his two Philadelphia partners, went to Baltimore in May 1837, to start the *Baltimore Sun*. Writing one hundred years later about the *Sun*, the authors of *The Sunpapers of Baltimore* noted that judged by modern standards, the *Sun* "was almost fabulously bad. But in the realm of the blind, a one-eyed man is king and American journalism, in the early part of the nineteenth century, was a realm of the blind. What lay at its own doors it could not by any chance perceive." The authors described the early issues of the Baltimore *Sun*:

> For instance, its early police court stories were frequently characterized by such remarkable statements as 'the defendant, a middle-aged man whose name we did not ascertain,' and again and again cases were reported in every detail *except* the decision of the court. The stories were full of editorial opinion, frequently written in what was intended to be a humorous vein, but which seems pretty heavy-footed to the modern reader, while occasionally the reporter indulged in what any modern newspaper man would identify at a glance as an outrageous fake. Names, dates and addresses, the things in which absolute accuracy is most rigidly exacted by the modern city editor, were treated by the early SUN with a casualness which makes a present-day reporter gasp. But on one point THE SUN from the very beginning maintained the same policy to which it adheres after a hundred years — it was extremely reluctant to run puffs as a reading matter.[18]

JAMES GORDON BENNETT AND THE *NEW YORK HERALD*

James Gordon Bennett began the *New York Herald* with $500 of capital and a desk of wooden planks placed across two barrels. He was about forty years old, and some might have termed him, at that point in his life, a failure. A Scotsman, Bennett immigrated to New York in 1822. After a few months of struggling to get work, he moved to Charleston, South Carolina, to work for the *Charleston Courier*, translating Spanish documents as they arrived in port.

In 1823, he returned to New York and wrote for the *Mercantile Advertiser*. He assumed ownership of the *New York Courier*, but within a few months turned it back to its original owner, unable to turn it into a paying proposition. Bennett then wrote for the *National Advocate*, and in 1827 went to Washington as a correspondent for the *New York Enquirer*. In 1829, after the *Enquirer* merged with the *Courier* into a single newspaper, Bennett fell out of favor with the new *Courier and Enquirer* publisher, Colonel James Watson Webb, over the issue of the national bank. In 1832, Bennett tried his hand at publishing once more, but the *New York Globe* failed in a month. From an editorial position in Philadelphia, Bennett then attacked the Wall Street bankers as enemies of the people. Returning to New York, he tried to enlist Horace Greeley's backing to start a newspaper, but Greeley turned down the offer. In the 1840s, Greeley became a competitor of Bennett's as the editor of the *New York Tribune*.

After many attempts at reporting and publishing, Bennett turned to his basement office and began a new newspaper, claiming it would support no party. From the beginning, Bennett was not popular among the old-line New York editors. He had clashed bitterly with James Watson Webb of the *Courier and Enquirer* over the issue of the national bank. Bennett supported Andrew Jackson's 1832 veto of a congressional resolution to recharter the bank (its charter was due to expire in 1836) and accused Webb of accepting political bribes in the form of loans from Nicholas Biddle, the bank's president.

The daily covered Wall Street and attacked its competitors, both old-line newspapers and Benjamin Day's new penny sheet. In August 1835, after an eighteen-day suspension of the paper caused by a fire in the printing shop, Bennett invited friends and patrons to stop by with bits of news or advertising, "barring always discoveries in astronomy, which our friends of the *Sun* monopolize."[19] By October, Bennett began to hire help and the twenty columns of the paper included fourteen columns of advertising.

Bennett's florid writing style was put to good use in April 1836, and it gained him notoriety and expanded circulation. A young woman by the name of Ellen Jewett was found murdered in a fancy brothel. When Richard P. Robinson, a merchant's clerk, was accused of the hatchet murder, Bennett defended him. The various newspapers in New York disagreed about who was responsible, but the attraction of Bennett's coverage was that he visited the scene of the crime and described the corpse of the beautiful courtesan in detail. Circulation during the stories of murder varied from 5,000 to 15,000 per day, and Bennett gleefully announced, "We are rapidly taking the wind out of the big-bellied sails of the *Courier and Enquirer* and *Journal of Commerce*."[20]

Bennett was a truly irreverent man, mocking the social set and attacking other editors. After writing a malicious editorial about James Watson Webb, Bennett was beaten in the street by Webb, an event chronicled by Philip Hone, who was a wealthy merchant and former mayor:

> There is an ill-looking, squinting man called Bennett, formerly connected with Webb in the publication of his paper, who is now the editor of the *Herald*, one of the penny papers which are hawked about the streets by a gang of troublesome, ragged boys, and in which scandal is retailed to all who delight in it, at that moderate price. This man and Webb are now bitter enemies and it was nuts for Bennett to be the organ of Mr. Lynch's late vituperative attack upon Webb, which Bennett introduced in his paper with evident marks of savage exultation. This did not suit Mr. Webb's fiery disposition, so he

> **BENNETT'S MARRIAGE ANNOUNCEMENT**
>
> To the Readers of the Herald—Declaration of Love—Caught At Last—Going to be Married—New Movement in Civilization.—I am going to be married in a few days. The weather is so beautiful; times are getting so good; the prospects of political and moral reform so auspicious, that I cannot resist the divine instinct of honest nature any longer; so I am going to be married to one of the most splendid women in intellect, in heart, in soul, in property, in person, in manner, that I have yet seen in the course of my interesting pilgrimage through human life.
>
> SOURCE. James Gordon Bennett, New York Herald, June 1, 1840.

attacked Bennett in Wall Street yesterday, beat him, and knocked him down.[21]

There were others, in addition to Philip Hone, who considered Bennett a scandalmonger. His practice of printing news of bankruptcies (one mistake cost him $500 in a libel suit) and his intrusive accounts of exclusive society dinners made him less than popular with the New York social set.

In addition to introducing thorough news coverage of Wall Street and writing florid accounts of murders and social dinners, Bennett made substantial contributions to the field of news gathering. After returning from a European trip in 1837, Bennett hired six correspondents to cover Europe and put correspondents in the field in Mexico, Texas, and Canada. He, like the *Sun* editors, organized a ship news service and contracted with light sailing craft to collect news from foreign ship captains before they landed in U.S. harbors. He also covered court news and experimented with the use of illustrations, primarily in the form of maps and drawings. In 1839, he began printing religious news. His coverage of church conferences was regarded as near sacrilege. Bennett emphasized a personal Christianity and attacked the "new Protestantism that seemed to equate true Christianity with money and empire."[22] Bennett wrote that real Christianity did not consist "in believing the dogmas of any church."[23]

New York society took out its anger on Bennett by organizing a moral war against him in 1840, the same year he was married. The war ostensibly was organized against his attack on prudish language. Words such as pants, legs, shirts, and trousers were considered forbidden and Bennett campaigned against what he thought represented insanity of speech. The editor rubbed it in thoroughly: "Petticoats—petticoats—petticoats—petticoats—there—you fastidious fools, vent your mawkishness on that."[24] Philip Hone wrote in his diary, "The evil has reached a pitch of enormity which renders further forbearance criminal, and a simultaneous attack is made upon the libellous paper, its editor, and those who, from fear or a fellow-feeling, support it."[25] A boycott was organized to force hotels and clubs to dispose of Bennett's paper, but circulation continued to hold and in 1840 combined circulation of the daily, a weekly edition, and extras reached 51,000.[26]

In 1841, with the inauguration of President John Tyler, Bennett decided to open a Washington bureau. In Washington, however, he encountered resistance from the Senate leaders and from the Washington press. The *Herald*'s correspondents were excluded from the Senate floor on the basis of an old rule that allowed only reporters of local papers to cover the Senate. Bennett responded with a bitter attack:

> It is caused by the selfish and malignant influence of the Washington newspapers, in order to maintain a monopoly of Washington news, and to rob the public treasury, under the color of public printing, in order to gratify their extravagant habits of life.[27]

Bennett noted that the Washington *Globe* was receiving $90,000 and the *Madisonian*, $330,000, from the public treasury for printing contracts. A third Washington paper, the *National Intelligencer*, also received government printing contracts. Bennett did not win his challenge immediately, however, and his correspondents were forced to develop inside sources.

In his continuous effort to speed up the collection and delivery of news, Bennett was delighted with the introduction of the telegraph. "What has become of space?" he asked in 1844, after "What God Hath Wrought" was telegraphed from Washington to Baltimore. "The magnetic telegraph at Washington has totally annihilated what there was left of (space) by steam and locomotives and steamships."[28] In January 1845, in the midst of the Mexican War, Bennett established a courier system between New Orleans and New York to convey exchanges between the *Herald* and the *Crescent City* of New Orleans. His courier system was faster than the U.S. mails, and he was forced to stop it under a law prohibiting the moving of mail by private means. Bennett was the only New York editor to send correspondents to Mexico. Two New Orleans newspapers, the *Picayune* and the *Delta*, also had correspondents in Mexico.

The personal war on Bennett continued. In 1850, two men who opposed his choice of mayor beat him with whips. A package containing a bomb was delivered to his office. Libel suits also continued. Promoters sued him for his criticism of an opera company; despite appeals and a reversal, he was found liable and paid $6,000 in damages.

By the 1850s, however, the *Herald* was an established New York Institution. Politicians and businessmen alike feared Bennett's power coupled with his apparent southern sympathies and his influence in England. The paper continued to be a fierce competitor to other New York sheets through the years prior to and during the Civil War.

REASONS FOR DEVELOPMENT

Historians have argued a variety of causes for the development of the penny press. The standard explanations have focused on (1) an expanding literate and urban population, (2) the development of technology to support mass circulations, and (3) the brilliance of individual editors. Another explanation, advanced by Walter Lippmann, a prominent twentieth-century journalist and early media theorist, assumed that the penny press emerged in the context of the natural and inevitable growth and progress of the newspaper industry. Sociologist Michael Schudson viewed the press as a development within the political and social context of Jacksonian democracy and an expansion of individual rights. Others viewed it as a commercial development, a product for which the times were right as U.S. manufacturing and commercial development made possible an advertising-based newspaper product. Dan Schiller argued that rather than appealing to an upwardly mobile middle class, the penny press appealed to a downwardly mobile artisan class. Communications historians Arthur Kaul and Joseph McKerns linked the development of the penny press to economic and ideological cycles in American life.

Sociologist Michael Schudson effectively eliminated expanded technology and literacy as sole causes for the development of a mass press. Although penny newspapers took advantage of new technology and, indeed, often supported inventors, they existed before the technological developments were in place. The first edition of the *New York Sun* was printed on a flatbed hand-run press making 200 impressions an hour. Until 1800, the wooden, hand-powered press had been the standard press in use. It was replaced by an iron press, which was easier to operate and which produced better quality. The use of steam power and the development of the cylinder press were introduced in varying degrees after the turn of the century.

Federick Koenig invented a steam press first used in England, and by the 1840s a similar press dominated the American market. The first two-cylinder press was the "Hoe-Type Revolving Machine," initially used by a newspaper, the *Philadelphia Public Ledger*, in 1847. Further improvements in the 1850s and 1860s occurred with the adaptation of "stereotyping," or the use of a paper mat created from an impression and used to create cylindrical molds.[29] Another major development came with an improvement by N. L. Robert in the process used to make paper from rags. Robert's Fourdrinier paper-making

The hand press and hand-set type was in common usage in many parts of the country as late as 1850, despite the introduction of more sophisticated technology. (State Historical Society of Wisconsin)

machine was first imported to the United States in 1827. Wood pulp as the raw product for paper was not used in the United States until 1866.[30]

Other technological advances occurred in the transportation system, facilitating the collection and distribution of news. In 1830, the United States had twenty-three miles of railroad; by 1840, it had 3,000 miles and by the Civil War, 30,000 miles of track were in place. The telegraph was another important factor in news development. From 16,735 miles of telegraph line in 1852, the wires extended to 110,727 miles in 1880 and to 237,990 in 1902.[31]

Although technology was a critical factor during the nineteenth century in the expansion of the newspaper press, its impact came too late to explain the development of the penny idea.

Schudson's argument negating expanded literacy as a primary cause in the development of the penny press centers on the fact that equally advanced literate societies such as Sweden and Scotland did not produce a similar press. As a singular cause, expanded literacy does not explain the development of the penny press. Certainly the population was increasing. About three million more people lived in the United States than had been there in 1820, representing an increase of about one-third across the decade. The increase, however, represented steady growth, not a departure from the norm. In 1830, 91.2 percent of the population was still rural. By 1840, that figure dropped only 2 percent. However, growth in New York surpassed national averages. From 1830 to 1840 New York's population doubled, a rate of growth not equaled by any other city. Daniel Schiller suggested it was the composition of this growing population, rather than the quantity itself, that had the major impact on development of the penny press.

A third argument posed is that of inevitability. In 1931, Walter Lippmann suggested that "any nation's press will naturally pass through stages of development."[32] Lippmann described four stages: (1) a monopoly controlled by government; (2) political party control; (3) a commercially supported press; and (4) a professional stage in which newspapers would institutionalize "trained intelligence." Lippmann claimed that in the professional stage newspapers would divorce themselves from the changing tastes and prejudices of the public itself. What Lippman did was to view developments of American newspapers, and from these developments, as he viewed them, construct a "natural" or "inevitable" development of all newspapers. Comparative studies show such development is not inevitable in all societies.

After "debunking" the arguments of literacy, technology and natural tendency, Schudson offered his own explanation of the development of the penny press. He suggested that it developed in a context of Jacksonian Democracy, or the Age of Egalitarianism, which he defined as a period in which the skilled craftsmen, the small and large merchants, and tradesmen were able to wield influence in politics and business. This rise of an urban middle class,

Schudson wrote, accounted for the qualities of the penny press—relative independence from party, low price, high circulation, emphasis on news, timeliness, and sensation.[33]

The commercial aspect of egalitarianism should not be forgotten. James Murphy, commenting on the expansion of the press in the early nineteenth century, said the "accessible masses of buyers and advertisers and their never-ending sources of story ideas, formed a natural newspaper market." The market, Murphy emphasized, was a greater social equalizer than were politics.[34] But it was not until several decades after the start of the penny press that expanded advertising made its major impact.

Schiller, in his quest for determining the origins of objectivity in the U.S. press, claimed that the major public for the penny papers were the artisans and mechanics of New York City.[35] Rather than a responding upwardly mobile urban middle class that bought the penny newspaper, Schiller claimed it was a downwardly mobile artisan class shouting its last battle cry. An expanding and changing economy, beginning to move toward national distribution, and a developing transportation system were forcing local artisans to compete with production of out-of-town goods. The same steamship that allowed James Gordon Bennett to deliver news more quickly upset the familiar trading patterns within cities and regions. Even the law was changing in regard to the workmen, with more attention focused on the promotion of business and less on protection of the workman. The primary function of law became one of protecting commerce and maintaining law and order. The maintenance of order had its biggest impact on the artisans and mechanics, whose daily lives became suspect. Vagrancy, drunkenness, and other vices were not to be tolerated.

In the late 1820s and 1830s, a burgeoning labor press developed in New York, with newspapers such as *The Mechanics' Press* and the *Workingman's Advocate* asking questions about "equality for all," about the politically affiliated press, and about the status of workingmen in relation to the law. However vigorous it was, the labor press was not able to sustain itself through the depression of 1837, which put nearly 50,000 New Yorkers out of work, leaving one-third of the labor force unemployed. During that period the penny press "claimed to speak alike to the politicized and the less-politicized, the journeyman and the merchant," and "appropriated and softened the anger of the labor press into a blustery rhetoric of equal rights, enlightenment, and political independence . . . ."[36]

The penny papers flaunted their independence, openly admitted their conversion from politics to business as a source of income, and often supported tradesmen and the right of workers to organize. Schiller argued that the focus on crime news, rather than serving up the sensationalism a mass public desired, was instead designed to protect the rights of workingmen and to assure that justice would be meted equally. The penny press focused not only on the integrity of the state but also on the unequal effect of social class on the political nation and, specifically, in the law. The cheap papers had only to station reporters at the police courts to pick through a constant flow of cases that might be used to reveal and dramatize the status of the citizenry's rights.[37]

During the Robinson-Jewett murder case, for example, the penny papers railed against the privileged of the city and asked whether, for the right amount of money, an acquittal could be purchased. In addition, the Robinson case was being heard by the same judge at the same time as a case in which twenty journeyman tailors were convicted for their part in a "conspiracy" to resist wage deductions. The explanation, Schiller argued, for the boisterous crowd at the Robinson hearing was not "in some abstract 'sensationalism,' but in the journeymen's rage against unequal justice, which barred their union as a conspiracy but allowed their masters to combine to lower wages."[38]

The penny papers, however, did not carve out their major role in taking up the cause of labor. After the depression of 1837 and the decline of the labor press, the penny papers freely moved into the circles of respectability. While maintaining a position that championed equality of opportunity and the public good, the penny papers also adhered to the principles of laissez-faire economics and the rights of property. This contradictory philosophy enabled penny papers to rationalize their support of the laborer's equality under the law while denying the laborer the right to unionize and to strike against employers. Such a position led the newspapers to more conservative stances emerging from a developing framework of objectivity (reporting, rather than making the news), and provided them a solid financial base from which to operate.

Kaul and McKerns viewed penny-press development within a larger context of developing journalistic ethics and ideology within a structure of American capitalism, claiming that "American capitalism has generated cyclical 'long waves' of qualitative structural change in the economy of journalism, prompting economic reconstruction and ideological revitalization in response to life-threatening crisis."[39] The authors described a "long wave" as a forty-to-sixty-year cycle comprised of alternating periods of vigorous growth and expansion followed by a period of sustained stagnation and contraction. For example, a period of expansion occurred from the 1780s to the mid-1820s, with a period of contraction from the mid-1820s to the mid-1840s, the period in which the penny press developed. The penny papers, they contended, represented a new medium that radically shifted the "economic infrastructure of newspapers from political patronage to marketplace competition."

As the century progressed, however, size and complexity of newspapers increased during a phase of economic expansion, and competition intensified, culminating in the great newspaper wars like those William Randolph Hearst and Joseph Pulitzer waged in the 1890s. Dependence on the marketplace "produced a formidable turn-of-the-century public backlash that further threated newspapers' marketplace existence." In an attempt to deal with the economic crisis of the 1830s, newspaper editors resorted to new commercial strategies (dependence on advertising) and to new ideologies (claims to political independence). This American tendency to "translate economic crisis into moral terms, commercial strategies into professional ideologies," wrote Kaul and McKerns, "mystifies the linkage of culture to economics." In other words, the American desire to intertwine commercial interest and moral obligation obscures the facts for those of us who look to history to help to explain the present.

Conclusion

The penny press represented a transition from limited circulation newspapers designed primarily for a commercial and political elite to newspapers with large circulations aimed at expanding audiences, including the middle class and possibly the downwardly mobile artisan class. Publishers of penny newspapers were entrepreneurial businessmen, much like colonial printers, and were not tied by finances to partisan politics as were some editors of the early national period.

During the 1830s as products became available for distribution, editors relied more heavily on institutional advertising to support their newspapers. Advertisements moved away from simple announcements by subscribers to become a mechanism for promoting the wares of developing manufacturers.

Although the content of the press represented significant continuity with the past, changes did occur, particularly in reporter-originated stories. Editors paid reporters to cover police courts and to develop stories that would boost circulations. Editors focused on expanded news gathering, development of paid staffs, and organization of cooperative news gathering. The coverage of Washington by New York newspapers challenged the *National Intelligencer*'s monopoly on congressional news.

The penny press emerged during a period of political rhetoric that endorsed egalitarianism. Shifting work and labor patterns created new audiences among the working classes, while technology enabled circulations to expand and the development of manufacturing created a new type of advertising to support newspapers independently of party coffers.

PART 2   EXPANSION AND CONFLICT

NOTES

1. Michael Schudson, *Discovering the News* (New York: Basic Books, Inc., 1978), p. 16.
2. Alfred McClung Lee, in the *The Daily Newspaper in America* (New York: The Macmillan Co., 1937), p. 730, estimates that in 1830 the eleven newspapers in New York circulated to 16,000 people, For description of commercial qualities of newspapers prior to the penny press, as well as for description of early penny newspapers and expansion after 1837, see Alexander Saxton, "Problems of Class and Race in the Origins of the Mass Circulation Press," *American Quarterly* 36:2 (Summer 1984) pp. 211–34.
3. Schudson, *Discovering the News*, p. 18.
4. Standard histories such as those already cited in this book tend to describe the 1830s as a major breaking point. Recent research, including Donald Shaw, "AT THE CROSSROADS: Change and Continuity in American Press News 1820–1860," *Journalism History* 8:2 (Summer 1981), pp. 38–50, notes that the New York journalistic world did not represent an accurate picture of the United States press as a whole.
5. Cited in Lee, *The Daily Newspaper in America*, p. 181.
6. Lee, *Daily Newspaper in America*, p. 58.
7. Lee, *Daily Newspaper in America*, pp. 316, 317.
8. Schudson, *Discovering the News*, pp. 22, 23.
9. Shaw, "AT THE CROSSROADS," pp. 38–50.
10. Much of the information about the *New York Sun* is taken from Frank M. O'Brien, *The Story of The Sun* (New York: George H. Doran Co., 1918). The story of the beginning of the *Sun* appears on p. 22.
11. The *New York Sun*, September 3, 1833, p. 1.
12. O'Brien, *Story of The Sun*, p. 50.
13. Phil Cohan, "Heavenly Hoax," *Air and Space*, May 1986, pp. 87–95.
14. O'Brien, *Story of the Sun*, p. 66.
15. The story of the moon hoax is detailed in O'Brien, *Story of The Sun*, pp. 68–72.
16. Cohan, "Heavenly Hoax," p. 94.
17. Dan Schiller, *Objectivity and the News: The Public and the Rise of Commercial Journalism* (Philadelphia: University of Pennsylvania Press, 1981).
18. Gerald W. Johnson, Frank R. Kent, H.L. Mencken, and Hamilton Owens, *The Sunpapers of Baltimore* (New York: Knopf, 1937), pp. 34–37.
19. Don Carlos Seitz, *The James Gordon Bennetts—Father & Son, Proprietors of the New York Herald* (New York: Beekman Publishers, Inc.: 1974), p. 44. (Reprinted from Bobbs-Merrill, 1928.)
20. Cited in Seitz, *The James Gordon Bennetts*, p. 47.
21. From *The Diary of Philip Hone, 1828–1851*, (N.Y.: Arno Press, 1970), cited in Seitz, *The James Gordon Bennetts*, p. 49.
22. Judith Buddenbaum, "The Religion Journalism of James Gordon Bennett," Unpublished paper presented to the History Division of the Association for Education in Journalism and Mass Communication, Norman, Oklahoma, 1986.

23. James Gordon Bennett, "Religion and Salvation," *New York Herald*, December 14, 1838, p. 2, cited in Buddenbaum, "Religion Journalism."
24. Cited in Seitz, *The James Gordon Bennetts*, p. 74.
25. Hone, cited in Seitz, *The James Gordon Bennetts*, p. 76.
26. Seitz, *The James Gordon Bennetts*, p. 77.
27. Cited in Seitz, *The James Gordon Bennetts*, p. 90.
28. Cited in Seitz, *The James Gordon Bennetts*, p. 120.
29. Stereotyping was brought to the United States as early as 1811 or 1812 by type founders who learned the process in England. The first book printed from stereotype in the United States was in 1813; the process was used by the New York Bible Society long before newspapers adapted the technique. See David Paul Nord, "The Evangelical Origins of Mass Media in America, 1915–1835," *Journalism Monographs* (Columbia, S.C.: Association for Education in Journalism and Mass Communication, 1984), 88: pp. 8–9.
30. Schudson, *Discovering the News*, p. 32.
31. Lee, *Daily Newspaper in America*, p. 67.
32. Lippmann, "Two Revolutions in the American Press," *Yale Review* 20 (March 1931), p. 440, cited in Schudson, *Discovering the News*, pp. 39–40.
33. Schudson, *Discovering the News*, pp. 49–50.
34. James Murphy, "Tabloids as an Urban Response," in Catherine L. Covert and John D. Stevens, eds., *Mass Media Between the Wars* (Syracuse University Press, 1984), p. 57.
35. Schiller, *Objectivity and the News*, p. 17.
36. Schiller, *Objectivity and the News*, p. 46.
37. Schiller, *Objectivity and the News*, p. 57. See also Saxton, "Problems of Class and Race," pp. 211–34.
38. Schiller, *Objectivity and the News*, p. 63.
39. Arthur J. Kaul and Joseph P. McKerns, "Long Waves and Journalism Ideology in America, 1835–1985," unpublished paper presented to Association for Education in Journalism and Mass Communication, Memphis, Tenn., August 1985, pp. 5–6. See also David L. Eason, "Review Essay: The New Social History of the Newspaper," *Communication Research* 11 (January 1984), pp. 141–51; Arthur J. Kaul, and Joseph P. McKerns, "The Dialectic Ecology of the Newspaper," *Critical Studies in Mass Communication* 2 (1985), pp. 217–233; and John C. Nerone, "The Mythology of the Penny Press," *Critical Studies in Mass Communication* 4 (1987), pp. 376–404.

CHAPTER 7

WESTWARD HO!

In America there is scarcely a hamlet that has not its newspaper. . . . The facility with which a newspaper can be established produces a multitude of them . . . Alexis de Tocqueville Democracy in America

The common conception of the frontier journalist has been that of the inexperienced printer moving westward, carrying a shirttail full of type and a portable press. Once he arrived at the site of a possible new community, he set up his press and began promoting his community to the world. Dates? It didn't matter much—1820 or 1880—he was moving West. First to Pennsylvania in the 1780s, beyond the Alleghenies; then to Kentucky, beyond the Appalachians; then to Michigan, Minnesota, Texas, Oregon, or California; then to Kansas; and finally to the territories of New Mexico, Utah, and Wyoming. The frontier journalist was conceived of as a man of his own will and daring, one of the first to arrive in a western town. As he produced his newspaper, the town grew and the journalist became a leader of the community. He was partisan in his politics, vociferous when attacking his enemies, and no mincer of words.

Despite this picture, it did matter when and where the newspaperman went. And where he went and how he operated depended on specific historical conditions. The financial conditions under which he operated, the territory to which he moved, the political issues of

The National Telegraphic Union published its own newspaper, The Telegrapher. *This masthead appeared on the* Telegrapher *in 1865. (Library of Congress Collection)*

the time, and the availability of transportation contributed to a diversity of frontier newspapers. Although frontier editors often relied on older technology, they utilized the telegraph for quick transmittal of important news items.

Although white men certainly dominated as editors, as they did in most aspects of nineteenth-century public life, minorities such as Native Americans and women were not without representation on the frontier. Nearly 250 women have been identified as frontier editors, and as many as 250 Native American newspapers were printed in Indian Territory before 1900.[1]

The movement westward

Settlement of Kentucky began in 1769, culminating in statehood in 1792. The first newspaper, the Kentucky *Gazette*, was founded in 1787. Presses were active in Michigan, Minnesota, Indiana, Wisconsin, and other midwestern states by the 1830s. Settlers began moving to Texas and Oregon in the 1820s, a process which culminated in statehood for Texas in 1845 and settlement of a dispute with the British over Oregon in 1846. California, Utah, and Washington Territory also boasted settlers by this time. By the mid-1850s, settlers poured into Kansas and Nebraska.

Chapter 7 **Westward Ho!**

The extensive movement westward in the 1840s reflected a period of a nationwide interest in expanding settlement and acquiring additional lands. When settlement began in Texas, California, and New Mexico, these territories belonged to Mexico. Britain held major claims to parts of Oregon and Washington. Americans, however, were enamored with the concept of Manifest Destiny, a belief that the United States was destined to expand and conquer and control. The belief was supported in part by the romantic myth of adventure on the frontier, the desire to develop trade with the Far East (thus the interest in Oregon and California ports), and fears of foreign intervention at isolated borders.

The first wave of migration occurred in the 1820s, when settlers crossed the Appalachians. In 1810, only one-seventh of the American people lived beyond those mountains; by 1840, more than one-third of all Americans lived in the "West." During a similar time period, the Mexican government invited settlers into Texas, as long as they agreed to abide by Mexican law. By 1830, East Texas was occupied by about 20,000 U.S. white citizens and by about 1,000 black slaves. But settlement did not proceed without conflict. In 1830, Mexico halted U.S. immigration and the importation of slaves and imposed duties on American goods. Mexican General Santa Anna, who had seized power, then reneged on a promise to Mexican and U.S. settlers to make the province of Texas a state of Mexico. Angered by Santa Anna's change of heart, Texans revolted and declared their independence March 2, 1836.

At the same time they declared independence, many Texas settlers expressed a positive attitude toward being incorporated as a state into the Union. However, northern Whigs feared war with Mexico and accused the South of trying to increase its political power by admitting another slave state. The North feared the South would gain additional votes to be used against industrial legislation favorable to their interests. Texas was one of the big questions during the presidential campaign of 1844, and Democrat James Polk won against the Whig Henry Clay, on an annexation platform. In December 1845, Texas gained its statehood.

The early settlements in Oregon occurred in the 1830s, when missionaries went west to convert Indian tribes to Christianity. Once there, the missionaries wrote letters to eastern friends about the beneficent climate and fertile soil of Oregon. Taking the Oregon Trail, which began at Independence, Missouri, the first major caravans of settlers arrived in Oregon in 1843. By 1845, 5,000 settlers from the states lived there. Although Great Britain and the United States had never settled their dispute over how much of Oregon each owned, in 1818 the two countries agreed the territory would be open to citizens from either country. As U.S. settlers began to dominate the territory, they petitioned the government to settle the border question. After political sparring by both sides and threatening disputes on the Mexican border, Congress approved dividing Oregon at the 49th Parallel with Britain retaining Columbia River navigation rights and Vancouver Island.

Friction with Mexico increased dramatically during the Texas dispute, and after the United States annexed Texas in 1845, Mexico broke off diplomatic relations with the United States. Increased settlement in California and New Mexico irritated the Mexican government, and although the Nueces River had formed the traditional southern boundary of Texas, Texans disputed the southern boundary line, claiming the Rio Grande as the southern border. President Polk sent troops to defend the Texas claim at the Rio Grande, further angering the Mexicans. After a failed attempt by President Polk to purchase California and New Mexico, Congress declared war May 13, 1846, on Mexico. Better equipped in terms of men, supplies, and arms, the United States rather easily won the war, occupying New Mexico and California and then moving to the capital, Mexico City. On March 10, 1848, the Treaty of Guadalupe Hildalgo gave California, New Mexico, and the Rio Grande Boundary to the United States.

The desire to expand the borders of the United States did not end with the Mexican War, however, and attention shifted to the Kansas and Nebraska territories. In Kansas from 1855 to 1857 an ideological press developed, based on sectionalist conflict and the slavery issue. Such newspapers preceded the booster town or promotional press that aligned itself with business and attached itself to the power structure of the community. Kansas editors well knew the value of promotion, and did not ignore it, but they viewed resolution of the slavery issue as their first task. In the bloody battle for statehood, editors were as extremist as other groups, and their battles of wit and word contributed to the conflict itself rather than to its resolution. Further, the editors did not represent purely Kansas interests, but rather represented factions outside the state which saw Kansas as a battleground for the perpetuation of sectional disputes.

When Missouri was admitted as a slave state in 1820, the South agreed that any other states to be carved out of the territory above the line 36°–30′ north latitude, which bounds Missouri on the South, would be free. Then in 1850, a compromise was effected to admit California as a free state. One of the concessions to the South was that New Mexico and Utah would be organized as territories with no reservations about slavery. The compromise was hailed as an end to the slavery issue, and at the 1852 conventions both parties claimed the sectional controversy would never again be renewed.

But that was not the case. In 1854, the Kansas-Nebraska law killed the Missouri Compromise. Stephen A. Douglas, who wrote the bill that subsequently was enacted, claimed settlers of all new territories must be allowed to decide whether their land should be slave or free. Into the law was written the right of squatter sovereignty, and thus, with Missouri on the east and abolitionist fervor in the North rising, the bloody battle for Kansas began.

Chapter 7 **Westward Ho!**

TRANSPORTATION AND COMMUNICATION

Transportation was a critical factor in the development of the frontier press. Hazel Dicken Garcia, in a study of the development of the Kentucky press between 1769 and 1792, the years between settlement and statehood, noted that newspapers carried "distant" information, rather than local news, because word-of-mouth distributed local news faster than did newspapers. Because newspapers appeared irregularly and depended on available postriders and horses and on expensive equipment, which had to be transported across the mountains, letters were the primary conveyors of news in the early years in Kentucky.[2]

Editors continuously faced transportation problems in collecting news. In the 1830s and 1840s, James Gordon Bennett and other editors experimented with the use of pigeons, sailing craft, and other forms of transportation in order to gather news quickly from Washington and from abroad. Transportation was a critical factor in determining the source of news, even in states that composed the original thirteen colonies. In a study of South Carolina newspapers, Gerald Baldasty wrote that during the first third of the nineteenth century, South Carolina editors depended heavily on the Washington newspapers for news from the capitol. Much of their news came from the *National Intelligencer*, whether the South Carolina editors agreed with the views expressed or not. However, by the late 1840s, with the development of the telegraph, "the Washington political press provided only a small fraction of national political news to South Carolina papers."[3] Editors had clamored for better transportation even before the penny press developed.

POSTAL EXPRESS

The first postal express, a mail service that traveled faster than ordinary post, was developed in 1825. Several such expresses operated between 1825 and 1861. From the beginning, the U.S. Postal Service, as well as private express services, granted newspapers special privileges. Newspaper postage rates were less expensive than postage rates for other customers, and editors exchanged newspapers at no charge through the mails. This magnanimous gesture was prompted not solely by a philosophical attitude about the importance of newspapers, but rather by a commercial need. Market information, if acquired by one New England merchant, put that merchant at a definite advantage in timing his purchase of southern cotton to be sold to England. That advantage could be eliminated only if all merchants had equal access to market information. The 1825 Express, which operated between Boston and Augusta, Georgia, was designed to equalize that kind of information.[4]

The overland mail—the start from the Eastern side. Wood engraving in Frank Leslie's Illustrated Newspaper, *October 23, 1858. (Library of Congress Collection)*

The development of improved mail transportation was accomplished through a blend of public and private enterprise. Between January 14, and February 1, 1833, David Hale and Gerard Hallock, owners of the New York *Journal of Commerce*, established an express from Philadelphia to New York. Riders would pick up news from Washington and the southern states from the mail in Philadelphia, and then forward it to New York by private postrider, beating the *Journal*'s competitors by a day. The Post Office, embarrassed at being beaten at its own game and wanting to create commercial balance, established its own express January 31, 1833. In response, the *Journal* moved its express to carry news from Washington to Philadelphia and gave its material to the official Post Office express in Philadelphia, thereby still beating its competitors by a day. Other New York papers complained and the postmaster general ordered the Philadelphia mail riders not to accept any material from the *Journal*'s Washington express. The *Journal* then attempted an express from Washington to New York, carrying mail between February 12 and March 5, 1833. When called before a Senate committee, editor Hale testified that although his express was an expensive proposition at $7,500 a month, it was still less expensive to operate than was the government's.

The Post Office Act of July 2, 1836, authorized the first nationwide

Chapter 7 **Westward Ho!**

express service. Complaining New York editors spurred passage of the act, as did Postmaster General Amos Kendall, a Kentuckian, who wanted to free readers from their dependence on eastern dailies. As privileged customers, newspaper editors sent digests and proofs free, while one thin sheet of express mail shipped up to thirty miles cost eighteen cents. During the next few years, various routes were operated, including ones from New York to New Orleans, New York to Washington, with stops in Philadelphia and Baltimore, and from Washington to New Orleans, with stops in Richmond, Columbia, Charleston, Mobile, and Montgomery. Most express routes cut regular mail times in half. For example, in 1835, regular mail traveled from New York to Washington in thirty-two hours; in 1837, by express, the same mail reached its destination in twenty-four hours. In 1839, however, regular mail had speeded up enough that expresses lost their advantage and were discontinued.[5]

Private express companies competed at times with the Postal Service and at other times operated routes where the Post Office did not operate. They usually carried newspapers free in return for free advertising.

The Mexican War brought new demands for fast mail service, and from January to March 1845, James Gordon Bennett operated an express to transport war news from New Orleans to New York. Postmaster General Charles Wickliffe threatened to arrest the New Orleans newspaper cooperating with Bennett for carrying private mail on public postal roads.

Probably the most famous private express was the western Pony Express, which operated during 1860 and 1861. For eighteen months the company carried mail between St. Joseph, Missouri, and San Francisco, California. Before the arrival of the Pony Express, news traveled largely by ship down the Atlantic, to the Isthmus of Panama, then by horse or rail to the Pacific Coast, and by steamers to California towns.

Nearly fifty years after Kentucky became a state, the news of President William Henry Harrison's death took three months and twenty days to reach Los Angeles.[6] The first California newspaper, the *Californian*, appeared in 1846 and twelve years later eighty-nine newspapers and periodicals, including nineteen dailies, published regularly. News still moved slowly, taking twenty-three to twenty-six days to arrive by ship and twenty-two days to arrive overland from St. Louis. In 1860, Pony Express riders cut this time in half by carrying mail 1,900 miles from St. Joseph, Missouri, to Sacramento, California, in about ten days.[7]

Newspapers used the expensive Pony Express for bulletin-style information, following it up a few days later with more complete information acquired through the less expensive regular mail routes. For example, Colorado's *Rocky Mountain News* carried a short report on Lincoln's inaugural address, acquired through the express, then the full text, which was received in later mail. Newspapers in Salt Lake City formed a cooperative to jointly use news arriving by Pony Express, thereby cutting their costs.

159

Samuel Morse, "What God hath wrought." (State Historical Society of Wisconsin)

TELEGRAPH

When Samuel Morse opened the nation's first telegraph line May 24, 1844, with the searing question, "What hath God wrought?" he also opened the modern era of communications, for the first time separating communication from the limits of geography and transportation.[8] The introduction of the technology created fear of the technology itself as well as anticipation at the possibilities the technology introduced. "What might the telegraph," wondered the nation's populace, "augur for thought, politics, commerce, the press, and the moral life" of the nation?[9] Fear was directed at the electrical lines themselves, and in 1844, when Ezra Cornell was putting in place experimental lines, he was forced to hire an eminent professor to assure the public there was no danger to their safety.

But fear was outweighed by the level at which entrepreneurs marveled at the possibility of instantaneous communication between the West and the cities of the East. The Reverend Ezra Gannett told his Boston congregation that electricity was both "the swift-winged messenger of destruction" as well as the "vital energy of material creation." Others predicted the telegraph would link men by a single mind in universal peace and harmony.[10]

From the beginning, the telegraph was inextricably linked to the newspaper press and cooperative news-gathering functions. The seven New York newspapers that had formed the Harbor News Association in 1849 quickly shifted their attention from gathering marine news to gathering telegraphic news. In 1851, they organized as the Telegraph and General News Association. From the beginning, the organization, soon to be known as the Associated Press, enjoyed favored rates from the various telegraph companies.

Morse tried to interest the government in taking over telegraph lines and preserving them as common carriers of information, but the government refused. During the early years, many telegraph companies and lines proliferated, but by 1866 Western Union had a virtual monopoly.

After October 1861, with the completion of the transcontinental telegraph, news delivery across the nation was quick and usually reliable. Commemorating the great event on October 24, 1861, the *Sacramento Union* wrote:

> The opening of this line for over 2,000 miles will produce a more marked revolution in the means of transmitting news than has yet occurred in California. The change produced by the establishment of the Pony Express was great; but that produced by the telegraph will prove much greater.[11]

The telegraph did have a major impact. Newspapers off the main telegraph lines, however, and with limited resources, still did not have unlimited access

The telegraph constructed. (Library of Congress Collection)

to news. When the southern stage route was abandoned at the beginning of the Civil War, the *Los Angeles Star*, for example, found it difficult to obtain news, although a telegraph line linked Los Angeles and San Francisco. The line was often out of order and rates were high.

However, between 1860 and 1862, the Pony Express and the telegraph reduced the time lag between events occurring in the East and news of those events being transmitted to western readers; newspapers used more hard news, made typographical innovations, and became increasingly competitive. Because of high rates the telegraph resulted in fast, but brief, accounts of newsworthy events of the Civil War and the politics involved.

COVERING THE MEXICAN WAR

During the Mexican war, enterprising printers followed the Army, setting up at least twenty-five publications in fourteen occupied cities. These papers provided news for soldiers at the front and those at home. Supplementing this war news information were Mexican newspapers and metropolitan newspapers in the states, which devised elaborate news collections and delivery schemes.[12]

Although the press was relatively free to comment during the Mexican War, at least ten newspapers in the war zone were restricted or closed down. These closings were accomplished under General Winfield Scott's martial law regulations, designed to allow military commanders to enforce behavior within military zones. Scott and other commanders were not partial to the American or the Mexican Press — Professor Tom Riley cited five of each type that were closed. One example: *El Liberal*, a Spanish-language anti-American newspaper in Matamoros in northern Mexico, denounced the "barbarians from the north." U.S. newspapers commented that the outrageous tone of *El Liberal* was certain proof of freedom of the press in the United States. The *New Orleans Courier* claimed the continued existence of *El Liberal* was "proof of the respect of our people for the liberty of the press." It did not remain proof for long, because the military shut down the press.

NEWSPAPERS ON THE FRONTIER

Frontier newspapers were started for a variety of reasons, including: (1) governmental need for the publication of laws, (2) desire of a literate population for information and general reading matter, (3) excess production capacity of job printers, (4) promotion of political points of view, and (5) boosterism.[13] Although information is not available for every state, in Wisconsin newspapers often came into existence six or seven years after the establishment of post offices and tended to develop in towns with more stable populations. Their editors used caustic language, mixed styles of type from whatever was available in the type case, and generally used outdated equipment brought from the East.

Because newspapers were expensive to start, a variety of financing plans were used. In Wisconsin during the 1850s and 1860s, the capital investment for a weekly averaged $1,500. Techniques used for financing included subscription drives, chattel mortgages, joint stock companies, and individual investments. Editors financing newspapers with a subscription drive attempted to get subscribers to promise money in response to a prospectus specifying the newspaper's political position. Editors sometimes solicited financing by mortgaging their equipment to companies who sold presses and types. Often terms were unrealistic and mortgages were sold or foreclosed on. A third method of financing, the joint stock company, was created by stockholders owning shares and hiring an editor. Usually the stockholders held a common interest in ideas and politics, as well as in their investment. The fourth method included individual politicians or developers financing an editor's venture.[14]

In Iowa and Utah, handwritten newspapers preceded printed ones. Iowa newspapers included news, features, and editorials written for local residents, and editors may have used them to recreate cultural worlds the editors had known before they migrated westward. Roy Atwood, who studied Iowa papers, suggested:

> It is also possible, based on the identity of the editors as lawyers, politicians and educators, that these men represented a distinct group or class within their agricultural frontier social order and consequently shared a common interest in the newspaper as a mode of public expression especially well-suited to their professional perspectives and goals. These editors may have tried to create a communications environment that could embody their cultural and professional values and facilitate a mode of discourse to which they had grown accustomed. Until further research is completed, however, each of these explanations remains speculative.[15]

NATIVE AMERICAN MEDIA

The movement of the frontier created an Anglo-frontier press and a Native American press. When Columbus arrived in America, about 14 million Native Americans lived within what is now the United States. Three hundred years later, the Native American population was less than 1 million. The first newspaper, *The Cherokee Phoenix*, was one method of protesting the continual crowding of the Native Americans onto reservations and further westward. The weekly newspaper was begun in 1828 when the Cherokees, who inhabited millions of acres in North Carolina, Georgia, and Tennessee, were displaced by the federal government.

A second newspaper was begun February 24, 1835, by a Baptist missionary and printer in Kansas Territory. The *Shawanoe Sun* was printed entirely in Sioux. Richard LaCourse, Native American media historian, labeled the Indian use of media, "acculturation without assimilation," meaning that Native Americans used technologies and techniques they learned from whites, but they used them to preserve their own cultures, not to adapt to a white culture. For example, the *Cherokee Phoenix*, which lasted six years, did not only utilize the Roman alphabet (a . . . b . . . c . . .) but also an eighty-six character alphabet designed by a Cherokee, Sequoyah.

Like Anglo-frontier newspapers, nineteenth-century Native American newspapers published infrequently, were primitive in format and content, had short lives, and operated with minimal staff and resources. Because few issues were saved, it is difficult to know how many Native American newspapers existed, but one historian estimated 250 newspapers were published in Indian Territory before 1900.[16] The papers served an informational and educational function. They carried advertisements, steamboat schedules, and legal notices. Papers were produced from presses in tents, wagons, schoolhouses, and open fields. They averaged fifteen by twenty-four inches in size and were between four and sixteen pages. Circulation ranged from 100 to 1,000 and subscriptions varied from one to three dollars per year. Newspapers were financed not only by tribal governments, but like other frontier newspapers, were financed by outside interests, including real estate and stock companies. Native American editors formed the Oklahoma Press Association in 1888 in Indian Territory, and other press associations followed throughout the years. Sharon Murphy, historian of Native American newspapers, noted:

> Editorial policies were explicitly stated in most papers. Press directories announced the papers' political affiliations and stances; but depending on the directories consulted, a paper could be listed as Democrat, Republican and independent simultaneously. The politically outspoken papers openly invited dispute and bitter controversies. Often, this led to name-calling, libel suits and even murder.[17]

Native American journalists also produced about twenty magazines before 1900, and women editors were not uncommon. Despite the efforts of Native American publications to protest emigration forced on them by the United States government, displacement occurred for all the five civilized tribes:

Ignoring treaties, property deeds, and the sacredness to Indians of their ancestral homes and burial grounds, the United States government, in the late 1830s, herded more than 17,000 peacefully-living, educated Indians on westward forced marches, to satisfy the greed of land-hungry whites. These forced emigrants were refined, well-established people. Many of their leaders were college educated. Many of them owned large plantations; others were skilled teachers, outstanding craftsmen, successful tradesmen. Over one-fourth of the Indians died enroute and many of those who did survive died shortly after resettling. Once wealthy tribes now had nothing. They had been driven at gunpoint by federal troops, from their farms and plantations, to be deposited, with little or no possessions, in new 'homelands.'[18]

The Cherokee Phoenix

The *Phoenix* was edited for its first four-and-one-half years in New Echota, Georgia, by Elias Boudinot, a Native American who was educated at a seminary in the North. He was paid $300 a year for his services by the Cherokee National Council, but apparently printers were considered more valuable than editors because a pressman was hired at $350 a year. Europeans, as well as Cherokees, subscribed to the newspaper. It portrayed standards of life within the Cherokee Nation, reflected problems of intemperance, and covered government attempts to relocate the Cherokee tribe. When Boudinot resigned in 1832, the paper ceased publication for two years. The August 11, 1832, issue of the *Phoenix* carried his resignation letter:

> Were I to continue as Editor, I should feel myself in a most peculiar and delicate situation. I do not know whether I could satisfy my own views and the views of the authorities of the nation at the same time. . . . I do conscientiously believe to be the duty of every citizen to reflect upon the dangers with which we are surrounded, . . . to talk over all these matters. . . . I could not consent to be the conductor of the paper without having the right and privilege of discussing these important matters. . . . I love my country and I love my people. . . . and for that very reason I should think it my duty to tell them the whole truth, or what I believe to be the truth.[19]

Boudinot later was murdered for his support of the 1835 treaty that "surrendered Cherokee lands to the U.S. government and set the scene for removal and the Trail of Tears."[20] Although the Cherokees attempted to move their

Elias Boudinot, editor, Cherokee Phoenix. *(Library of Congress Collection)*

press to Tennessee, Georgia authorities seized it and refused to relinquish the press and type.

Cherokee Advocate

Removal did not destroy the Native American press, however, and by 1843, the Cherokee National Council authorized a new national press, the *Cherokee Advocate*. John Ross, president of the national council, purchased a press in Boston, along with type in the Cherokee and English languages. By this time editors had gained stature over printers. William P. Ross, a Princeton University graduate, was named editor at $500 a year. A translator and four printers were paid $300 each. The first issue appeared September 26, 1844, and carried the slogan, "Our Right, Our Country, Our Race."

The Civil War multiplied the problems the Native Americans already faced. Although native leaders assumed a neutral stance during the war, many Northerners believed Native Americans to be pro-southern, because some leaders had owned slaves. Many publications were suspended during the war years. After the war, increased pressure by white settlers to occupy Oklahoma Territory continued to place hardships on the Native American nation and its presses. The *Cherokee Advocate* closed shop March 4, 1906, and the press and type were sold several years later. The *Daily Oklahoman* wrote:

> Useless, out of date, and covered with mould and rust, the plant, type and fixtures of the old Cherokee Advocate . . . was this week sold as junk.[21]

POLITICAL AND IDEOLOGICAL NEWSPAPERS

Newspapers that operated in the 1850s and 1860s in Bleeding Kansas and on the Kansas-Nebraska border serve as good examples of newspapers that were begun as political or ideological tools. The primary issue was slavery and editors excelled in flagrant thought and word.

Legh Richmond Freeman and his brother, Frederick Kemper Freeman, were highly political, pro-Democratic Southerners, who edited the *Frontier Index* in various Union Pacific Railroad construction towns in Nebraska and Wyoming. Representative of frontier language was a notice to advertisers, in which the *Index* was billed as the emblem of American Liberty,

> perched upon the summit of the Rocky Mountains; [it] flaps its wings over the Great West, and screams forth in thunder and lightning

tones, the principles of the unterrified anti-Nigger, anti-Chinese, anti-Indian party—Masonic Democracy!!!!!!![22]

The newspapers in Kansas sharply divided over the slavery issue from the point the territory was created in 1854. Two types of settlers soon arrived: "free soilers" from the industrialized North and pro-slavery Southerners, primarily Missourians. Two of the most extreme in their positions were the *Atchison Squatter-Sovereign*, organized and edited by J. H. Stringfellow of Missouri, and the *Lawrence Herald of Freedom*, an organ of the New England Emigrant Aid Society, edited by George Washington Brown.

Although Brown bitterly denied that his newspaper was a society organ, and the slogan below the flag read "A Family Newspaper—Independent on All Subjects," the newspaper was financed by the New England Emigrant Aid Society. The newspaper sold for two dollars per year—in advance. The motto: "Be just: Let all the ends thou aimest at be thy country's, God's and Truth's."

The emigrant aid company's goal was to establish a newspaper at "the first point selected for settlement, which was to be the organ of the company —not a newspaper representing the sentiments and interests of the community."[23] First issued October 21, 1854, the first copy was published in Pennsylvania and labeled the *Herald of Freedom*, Wakarusa, Kansas Territory. The second issue was published in Lawrence, labeled "Yankee Town" by Missourians.

The adamantly pro-slavery John H. Stringfellow competed for readers with Brown. Publisher of the *Atchison Squatter-Sovereign*, begun February 3, 1855, Stringfellow devoted his newspaper to "Politics, Literature, Agriculture, Mercantile Affairs and Useful Reading." The motto: "The Squatter Claims the Same Sovereignty that He Possessed in the States." The first issue included a series titled "Negro Slavery, No Evil."

The *Squatter-Sovereign* and the *Herald* were similar in format, with small headlines and long columns of type. However, the *Squatter-Sovereign* was a bit more splashy, was divided into seven columns, and ran four pages. The *Herald* was eight columns wide, with a bit smaller type, and ran an average of eight pages. The *Squatter-Sovereign* usually carried nearly two pages of advertising, while the *Herald* often carried only about half a column. The lack of advertising in the *Herald* indicated the newspaper received outside support, since both newspapers claimed circulations of about 2,000 and the *Squatter-Sovereign* continually made appeals for more support in order to survive financially.

Brown's newspaper was the more solemn of the two, carrying stories about religion in Japan; making promotional appeals for immigrants who would help settle Kansas as a free state; and describing the virtues of Kansas Territory. The first issue carried "The Freeman's Song" on page one, which fully described the newspaper's position on slavery:

> **THE NEED FOR REVENUE**
>
> It is all important that we should have papers of the "right stripe" in the [Kansas] Territory; and it is evident that, for a year or two, they must be supported by the South. We then appeal to our friends for that material aid, which is so necessary to the success of a newspaper. We shall strive to make the Squatter Sovereign what the true Southern man would wish it — an uncompromising pro-slavery print — and with this end in view, we appeal to our friends to sustain us.
>
> SOURCE: J.W. Stringfellow, Atchison Squatter-Sovereign, April 3, 1855.

> Men, who bear the Pilgrim's name,
> Men, who love your country's fame,
> Can ye brook your country's shame,
> Chains and slavery?

The first issue also carried a story warning settlers to avoid staking claims on treatied land, an anonymous letter noting that in Kansas an acre would produce sixty-five bushels of corn or twenty bushels of wheat, and correspondence concerning the history of the slavery question.

The *Squatter-Sovereign's* first issue was somewhat different in tone, although fully as rabid on the question of slavery. It lacked the missionary zeal of the *Herald*, had a column titled "The Funny Corner," and carried poetry titled not "The Freeman's Song," but "Tempt Me Not To Drink Again" and "Every Man Has His Faults."

Slavery was the primary issue, and Stringfellow and Brown engaged in mutual denunciation before Brown ever arrived in Kansas. Brown claimed the repeal of the Missouri Compromise would create a slave state unless sufficient northern immigration prevented it. Stringfellow's first issue warned Missourians of Brown's arrival. He noted that leading abolitionists under the name of "Emigration Aid Societies" were arriving, "the avowed purpose of which is to throw into Kansas a horde who shall not only exclude slaveholders from that territory, but in the end abolish slavery in Missouri." Stringfellow commented about the "Negro thieves" among them and the "free negroes, most of them, as usual of bad character. He was convinced the abolitionists were determined to convert Missouri, then move South. "Missouri vanquished, Arkansas and Texas are looked upon as easy victims."

Regarded almost as a foreign news event, Kansas attracted correspondents from the East to cover the border wars. William A. Phillips came to Kansas for the *New York Tribune*, sent by Horace Greeley. His letters were collected in an 1856 volume, *The Conquest of Kansas by Missouri and Her Allies*.

From a sketch of the Free State Convention in Topeka in December 1855, with rifles ready in case of attack. Printed in Frank Leslie's Illustrated Newspaper. *(Library of Congress Collection)*

Other correspondents such as Thomas Wentworth Higginson of the *New York Tribune*, Samuel F. Tappen of the *New York Times*, and Richard Hinton of the *Boston Traveller* covered "bleeding Kansas."

THE BOOSTER PRESS

Historian Daniel Boorstin claimed that frontier newspapers began as advertising sheets, then turned into news sheets, and that their primary purpose was to advertise nonexistent towns.[24] Although there was some truth in his statement, the booster press performed a wider function — recruiting additional settlers to already established towns in the West.

Many booster editors became leading men of the community. The first press across the Alleghenies was the *Pittsburgh Gazette*, which first appeared July 29, 1786, in the town of 300 population. It was edited by John Scull and Joseph Hall from Philadelphia. Hall died shortly after his arrival, but Scull

171

> **FIGHT OVER A COUNTY SEAT**
>
> Although in the interest of humanity, common decency and honest government we desire that this enterprising, God fearing and progressive city of Ravanna shall be and remain the permanent county seat of this magnificent county, dowered by nature with a climate that makes the most favored part of Italy seem by comparison like a fever-breeding, miasmatic swamp, yet we refuse, in speaking of the denizens of that nondescript collection of bug-invested huts which its few and scabby inhabitants have the supreme gall to call a town, a few miles distant, to descend to the depths of filth and indecency indulged in by the loathsome creature who sets the type for an alleged newspaper in that God-forsaken collection of places unworthy to be called human habitations.
>
> SOURCE. Garfield (Ks.) County Call, October 21, 1887.

became a community leader—a postmaster, bank president, and one of the incorporators of Western University of Pennsylvania. When he died in 1828 the population was 12,000.[25]

A year later—in 1787—the Kentucke *Gazette* first appeared. John Bradford, not related to the colonial printers, and who indeed knew nothing of journalism, was recruited by Kentucky settlers to set up a press. He sent his brother to Pittsburgh to learn printing from Scull. He also became a community leader and gained a good deal of his income from being printer to the territory.[26] Daniel Richards, who came to Milwaukee at the call of a real estate promoter, issued Milwaukee's first newspaper, the *Advertiser* in 1836. James M. Goodhue issued the *Minnesota Pioneer* April 28, 1849. It also played a booster role.

Many western printers did a thriving business publishing legal notices. Such business was aided by the Homestead Act, which required homesteaders to indicate they had fulfilled all obligations on their claims by printing notices six times in the paper nearest their claim. After the notices were printed the claims were final.

THE PENNY PRESS MOVES WEST

The booster press was not confined to the frontier, nor was it the sole province of rural newspapers. As the penny press moved westward, boosterism was one of its primary functions.

Chicago Tribune

The *Chicago Tribune*, often credited with major influence in helping to elect Abraham Lincoln president of the United States in 1860, and which gained an arch conservative reputation as an anti-New Deal newspaper under Robert P. McCormick, began June 10, 1847. For the first eight years it struggled under the hands of various owners, at times successful and at times floundering. Before Joseph Medill and Charles Ray assumed part ownership and control in 1854, the paper was in dire straits, partially due to its support of the Know-Nothing Party. The natavistic party's attacks on Germans and Catholics won little popularity in ethnic Chicago.

Joseph Medill, a Presbyterian Whig, lawyer, and newspaper man, assimilated many ideas of the penny press as editor of the *Cleveland Morning Leader*. Instrumental in establishing the Republican Party in the 1850s, Medill and Ray, an Illinois publisher, changed the paper's politics to Republican as soon as they gained financial control over the *Tribune*, which they began editing in September 1855. Medill supervised the news-gathering operation, advertising, circulation, and printing, and Ray wrote editorials. They departmentalized the news, ended the natavistic bias and argued vehemently to exclude slavery from the territories. Medill viewed Chicago, with its rapidly growing population of 86,000 and expanding railroad industry, as a booming town that would support a lively newspaper.

Medill's and Ray's abolitionist fervor and support of Republicanism led them to cover the Kansas-Nebraska conflict extensively, even holding a free-soil benefit in Chicago and contributing $2,000 to the *Herald of Freedom*.[27]

By rejecting compromise as a solution and promoting continued pressure on the South, the *Tribune* earned a radical reputation in the early days of the Civil War. Before War broke out, Medill traveled to Washington as the newspaper's capital correspondent and during the war the *Tribune* placed correspondents in the field, with the editors remaining at home to coordinate publication of war news and other information.

But abolitionism and war news were not the only issues for the *Tribune*. The newspaper also exposed local corruption, and in 1865, condemned corrupt "street railway swindlers."[28]

The *Tribune* was not without competitors in the early years. The *Chicago Democrat*, begun in 1833, and the Whig *Daily Journal* represented other political viewpoints. In 1854, shortly before Medill arrived in Chicago, and as other newspapers moved to a more neutral stance on the slavery and sectional issues, Senator Stephen Douglas of Illinois began another newspaper, the *Chicago Times*, to represent the Democratic viewpoint. By 1855, the city had seven daily newspapers. Throughout the Kansas-Nebraska disputes, the *Times*, which considered politics the mainstay of its editorial content, accused the *Tribune* of supporting a fraudulent government. The *Times* remained loyal to

> **THE LANGUAGE OF BOOSTERISM**
>
> The growing importance of this metropolis of the West, and the daily extension of its commerce, almost ensure the success of any undertaking which would tend to facilitate our merchants in those dealings which are the foundation of the greatness of our city. With the increase of its commerce, New Orleans itself increases; and in the ratio of this commerce we will see new improvements and ameliorations rise up in every quarter.
>
> SOURCE. On Establishing a Reading Room, New Orleans (La.) Picayune, January 25, 1837.

Douglas through the presidential campaign of 1860 and fervently opposed the *Tribune*.

The Texas Business Press

The *Galveston News*, established in 1842, represented the growing alliance between booster editors and the business communities of western towns. The newspaper grew rapidly and by 1878 intensified its coverage of the state, adding to its offices in Austin and Houston ones in San Antonio, Dallas, Fort Worth, and Waco. The partnership that had governed the *Galveston News* since 1876 was converted into a joint stock company under a state charter.

By the 1880s, the *Galveston News* moved toward the impersonal journalism to become popular in the 1880s, declaring that the newspaper, not its editor, must not be a distinct personality. "A great newspaper," the *Galveston News* said, "must be serenely indifferent to personal likes and dislikes . . . which would interfere with its functions as a faithful collector and disseminator of news."[29] The *News* also claimed that a great newspaper was "the work of a vast ramification of costly agencies and services, held in coordination and maintained in cooperation by a system as highly organized and as vigorously administered as that of a regular army equipped and thoroughly disciplined."

The publishers of the *Galveston News* recognized that Dallas was a growing city, and they decided to extend their influence by establishing a newspaper in Dallas. From this background *The Dallas Morning News* emerged October 1, 1885. Dallas, then a city of about 10,000 people, welcomed the new newspaper. A Dallas spokesman offered to raise $25,000 in subscriptions to stock in the *News* corporation, and a prominent Dallas banker, attorney, and cattle king built a $10,000 brick structure and leased it to the *News*. Because the existing *Dallas Herald* controlled the local franchise of the Western Associated Press, the *News* contracted with United Press for national wire coverage. The

News represented one of the first examples of chain journalism in the United States and still claims to be "the oldest business institution in Texas."[30] The *News* was clearly a businessman's newspaper, and noted that at times the best approach to "persistent evils" in "politics, in public affairs, in society, in industrial and business arrangements" was "philosophic resignation."[31]

CONCLUSION

Press movement westward was linked to settlement and transportation. Editors in western communities often used old technologies to create newspapers on the frontier. Transportation, improved through the introduction of the express and improved mail systems, shortened the time lag between events occurring in the East and information arriving in the West. The introduction of the telegraph, which separated communication from transportation, provided news quickly, but at considerable expense, to western newspapers.

The move westward represented hardship for settlers, who struggled against the elements and fought to carve a living from land that proved productive at times, barren at others. As white men moved westward, Native Americans coped with hostile action and displacement, and their newspapers reflected the resistance and the compromise. For urban planners, real estate promoters, and others who shaped the urban west, the move represented new opportunity and failed dreams. By 1880, all except a few of the eventual urban centers were firmly in place. Each of these urban places, and many that failed, needed promoters. "With gusto these persons—sometimes owners of real estate, but frequently journalists with little personal wealth and at best a tenuous financial interest in the community they championed—portrayed even the smallest of way stations as the next Babylon and Tyre, or depending on the chief forms of business and recreation, Sodom and Gomorrah."[32]

Many journalists in successful towns, or even in those not so successful, stayed and became leading members of their communities. Others, like Joseph Medill, carried their profession with them as they moved, in his case, from Cleveland to Chicago. From the early beginnings of the frontier press, came a stable small town press and associations of editors active in the political and economic lives of their communities. They were boosters, politicians, reformers, and journalists.

NOTES

1. Sherilyn Cox Bennion, "A Working List of Women Editors of the 19th Century West," *Journalism History* 7:2 (Summer 1980), pp. 60–65.

2. Hazel Dicken Garcia. "Letters Tell the News (Not 'Fit to Print'?) About the Kentucky Frontier," *Journalism History* 7:2 (Summer 1980), pp. 49–53, 67.
3. Gerald Baldasty, "The Charleston, South Carolina Press and National News, 1808–47," *Journalism Quarterly* 55:3 (Autumn 1978), pp. 519–26.
4. This discussion of the development of postal expresses relies primarily on Richard B. Kielbowicz, "Speeding the News by Postal Express, 1825–1861: The Public Policy of Privileges for the Press," *Social Science Journal* 22:1 (January 1985), pp. 49–63.
5. For discussions of tensions evident in federal postal policy of the mid-1800s, see Richard B. Kielbowicz, "Modernization, Communication Policy, and the Geopolitics of News, 1820–1860," *Critical Studies in Mass Communication* 3 (1986), pp. 21–35.
6. Helen L. Moore, "California in Communication with the Rest of the Continent with Reference Chiefly to the Period before the Railroads," vol. 13 of *Historical Society of Southern California Annual Publications 1924–27* (Los Angeles: McBride Printing Co., 1924), p. 72, cited in Arthur C. Carey, "Effects of the Pony Express and the Transcontinental Telegraph Upon Selected California Newspapers," *Journalism Quarterly* 51:2 (Summer 1974), p. 320. Carey's article provides the information included in this chapter on carrying mail to California.
7. See Glenn D. Bradley, *The Story of the Pony Express* (Chicago: A.C. McClurg Co., 1913).
8. For a discussion of contemporary reaction to the introduction of the telegraph see Daniel Czitrom, *Media and the American Mind: From Morse to McLuhan* (Chapel Hill: University of North Carolina Press, 1982), pp. 3–29. For analysis of cultural implications of the telegraph, see James W. Carey, "Technology and Ideology: The Case of the Telegraph," *Prospects*, ed. Jack Salzman, vol. 8, pp. 303–323. Carey argues that the telegraph created the wire services and introduced standardization of news, which gave the news function of newspapers preeminence over the editorial function. See also Donald L. Shaw, "News Bias and the Telegraph: a Study of Historical Change," *Journalism Quarterly*, 44 (Spring 1967), pp. 3–12; 31; and Robert L. Thompson, *Wiring a Continent: The History of the Telegraph Industry in the United States, 1832–1866* (New York: Arno Press, 1972).
9. As expressed by Czitrom, *Media and the American Mind*, p. 3.
10. Czitrom, *Media and the American Mind*, pp. 7–9.
11. Cited in Carey, "Effects of the Pony Express," p. 323.
12. Tom Reilly, "Newspaper Suppression During the Mexican War," *Journalism Quarterly* 54:2 (Summer 1977), p. 262.
13. See William H. Lyon, *The Pioneer Editor in Missouri, 1808–1860* (Columbia, Mo.: University of Missouri Press, 1965), and Oliver Knight's review of Lyon's book, *Journalism Quarterly* 42 (Summer 1965), pp. 478–79.
14. Carolyn Stewart Dyer, "Economic Dependence and Concentration of Ownership Among Antebellum Wisconsin Newspapers," *Journalism History* 7:2 (Summer 1980), pp. 42–46.
15. Roy Atwood, "Handwritten Newspapers on the Iowa Frontier, 1844–1854," *Journalism History* 7:2 (Summer 1980), pp. 56–59, 66–67.

16. Carolyn Foreman, *Oklahoma Imprints, 1835–1907: Printing Before Statehood* (Norman: University of Oklahoma Press, 1936), cited in Sharon Murphy, "Neglected Pioneers: 19th Century Native American Newspapers," *Journalism History* 4:3 (Autumn 1977), p. 79.
17. Murphy, "Neglected Pioneers," p.80.
18. Murphy, "Neglected Pioneers," p. 82.
19. Cited in Barbara Luebke, "Elias Boudinott, Indian Editor: Editorial Columns from the Cherokee *Phoenix*," *Journalism History*, 6:4 (Summer 1979), p. 51.
20. Murphy, "Neglected Pioneers," p. 82.
21. Murphy, "Neglected Pioneers," p. 100.
22. *Frontier Index*, May 19, 1868, p. 3, cited in Thomas H. Heuterman, "Assessing the 'Press on Wheels': Individualism in Frontier Journalism," *Journalism Quarterly* 53:3 (Autumn 1976), p. 424.
23. William E. Connelley, *Kansas and Kansas* (Chicago: Lewis Publishing Company, 1918).
24. Boorstin, Daniel, *The Americans: National Experience* (New York: Vintage Books, 1965), p. 127.
25. Boorstin, *The National Experience* p. 126.
26. Boorstin, *The National Experience*, p. 127.
27. Lloyd Wendt, *Chicago Tribune: The Rise of a Great American Newspaper* (New York: Rand-McNally, 1979), p. 67.
28. Wendt, *Chicago Tribune*, p. 200.
29. Sam Acheson, *35,000 Days in Texas: A History of the Dallas News and its Forbears* (New York: The Macmillan Co., 1938), pp. 95–101.
30. See Acheson and the *Texas Almanac* (Dallas, Tex: A. H. Belo Corp., 1982).
31. *The Dallas Morning News*, October 1, 1885, cited in Acheson, p. 106.
32. Lawrence H. Larsen, *The Urban West at the End of the Frontier* (Lawrence: The Regents Press of Kansas, 1978), p. 5.

CHAPTER 8

SECTIONAL CONFLICT AND ABOLITIONIST AGITATION

"Hell is about to enlarge her borders and tyranny her domain." A Quaker editor reacts to the Missouri Compromise.

The Civil War, beginning with South Carolina's secession and the firing on Fort Sumter in 1861, evolved from sectional conflicts as old as the nation itself. Slavery, while legal in all thirteen colonies, became an issue during the War for Independence as colonists began to consider their own enslavement by England. Those who regarded the formation of the new nation as a way of escaping from the corrupt medieval institutions of the past feared that slavery would endanger the new nation's ability to survive. The issue of states' rights versus national power also produced sectional conflict and often revolved around slavery and the issue of the protective tariff, a tax on imported goods.

In 1832, South Carolina threatened to secede from the Union if the federal government insisted on increasing the tariff. This "nullification" crisis (declaring federal law null and void) was averted through a compromise bill, but the issue of the federal government's power over the states was not resolved. The tension over the tariff evolved from a question of whether the government was exacting a tariff on imported goods in order to raise revenue, or whether the tariff was really a protection of northern industry—a means by which southerners, whose economy was based on exporting raw agricultural materials, were being penalized by buying manufacturing products from abroad rather than buying them from struggling northern manufacturing concerns.[1]

Throughout the first half of the century, the admission of new territories to the Union focused attention on slavery as a political issue. In the writing of the Constitution, the three-fifths compromise allowed states to count slaves as three-fifths of a person for the purpose of population counts that determined representation in Congress. States with large slave populations could therefore count on greater political representation. A series of compromises in 1820, 1850, and 1853 made it clear that slavery and its implications in terms of political power were far from resolved.[2]

Editors were deeply involved in many of the sectional issues, varying in their attitudes toward slavery, as well as in their attitudes toward the development of manufacturing. Although many northern editors regarded blacks as inferior, they wanted an end to slavery because they feared it eventually would destroy the Union. Others were willing to compromise, hoping that sectional disputes could be resolved.[3]

Political issues, however, were not all encompassing. Penny papers continued to develop throughout the 1830s and 1840s, with Horace Greeley establishing the *New York Tribune* in 1841 and Henry J. Raymond the *New York Times* in 1851. As the century progressed, women increased their participation in journalism.

Existing alongside the mainstream press was the abolitionist press, largely owned and funded by whites, and varying in its degree of intensity and purpose. The abolitionist press served an important networking function for the antislavery movement, connecting geographically distant, but ideologically similar, groups. The antislavery movement grew out of a conservative evangelical organization of private, voluntary societies designed to revive religion in the face of the Enlightenment and to preserve American society from "infidelity and ruin."[4] Using new technologies, the Anti-Slavery Society in 1835 flooded the mails with literature, thereby exaggerating the power and influence of the abolitionist group.[5] The public reacted to mass distribution of abolitionist materials by orchestrating mobs to destroy abolitionist and black newspapers, passing legislation restricting the flow of information in the South, tampering with the U.S. mail, and instituting a gag rule in Congress.

The black press, underfunded and poorly circulated, was significant in educating free blacks and in documenting the intellectual capabilities of blacks.

NEW DEVELOPMENTS IN THE PENNY PRESS

The newspapers of Horace Greeley and Henry Raymond for the most part rejected the sensationalistic format of the *Sun* and the *Herald*, but used the same technological innovations and gained large circulations with popular editorial formats. The *Tribune* provided a forum for the exchange of ideas aimed at a wide audience and circulated its weekly edition into the Midwest, gaining a following outside of New York. The *Times* gained a reputation for thorough coverage of political and economic issues and avoided sensationalism. The formation of the Republican party in 1854 gave these two newspapers an opportunity to affiliate with a new party that allowed them to adhere to what they considered the best of Whig politics, but to oppose slavery, to support the growing western and northern alliance, and to address themselves to wider audiences.

Women were active from colonial times in the press, but until the 1840s their involvement usually was related to the position of a husband or son. However, with the advent of the penny press, and then later in the 1870s with an increased attention to female readership, women became more active in the daily press. Cornelia Walter, who edited the *Boston Transcript* from 1842 to 1847, took over a newspaper specializing in theater and literature. It was founded in 1830 by her brother Lynde, and she assumed the editorship on his death. Her contemporaries called her "the brilliant lady editor of the Transcript," and after she attacked Edgar Allan Poe in her account of his Boston

Horace Greely at his Desk. (Library of Congress Collection)

recital, he called her a "pretty little witch"—which she resented. Following a traditional pattern, she remained editor until her marriage in 1847 and then retired from journalism.

HORACE GREELEY AND THE
NEW YORK TRIBUNE

Horace Greeley was known in a variety of capacities between 1841, the year he began the *New York Tribune*, and 1872, the year he ran for president of the United States, lost the campaign, and died a month later. He was known as a contentious individual who advocated a variety of not-always-consistent ideas, who believed the United States was destined to greatness and that agriculture and industry combined would produce a great nation in which all people, black and white, could enjoy a share of prosperity. He could be a great moralist, yet would print articles about sex and crime if they made a point; he accepted all forms of patent medicine advertising, but used his profits to

MARGARET FULLER WRITES FROM ROME

The bombardment became constantly more serious. The house where I live was filled as early as the 20th with persons obliged to fly from the Piazza di Gesu, where the fiery rain fell thickest. The night of the 21st-22nd, we were all alarmed about two o'clock, A.M. by a tremendous cannonade. It was the moment when the breach was finally made by which the French entered. They rushed in, and I grieve to say, that, by the only instance of defection known in the course of the siege, those companies of the regiment Union which had in charge a position on that point yielded to panic and abandoned it. The French immediately entered and entrenched themselves. That was the fatal hour for the city. Every day afterward, though obstinately resisted, the enemy gained, till at last, their cannon being well placed, the city was entirely commanded from the Janiculum, and all thought of further resistance was idle.

SOURCE. Margaret Fuller, Letter XXXIII, July 6, 1849, to the New York Tribune, as reproduced in Maurine Beasley and Sheila Gibbons, Women in Media.

---

expand the editorial department and to hire and train good reporters and writers.

Greeley was involved in journalistic endeavors for many years before he began his highly successful *New York Tribune* in April 1841. He began his career as a printer, worked on the *New York Evening Post*, printed several Whig publications as part of his own printing business, and edited the *New Yorker*, a literary publication with 9,000 subscribers, for seven and one-half years. In 1841, with $1,000 of borrowed money, $1,000 of his own money, and a mortgage of about $1,000, he began the *Tribune*.

Greeley's newspaper was the first cheap Whig publication. It consisted of four pages with five columns each on a sheet about the size of a modern tabloid. Within two months he claimed a circulation of 11,000. In September 1841, Greeley began his weekly edition, which quickly circulated to 200,000 subscribers at a cost of two dollars per year, and which gained for him a reputation in the West. He offered one-dollar subscriptions to club members —groups of twenty who subscribed together.

The *Tribune* distinguished itself as an intellectual newspaper for a nonelite audience. Greeley was self-taught, and took great delight in playing with new ideas; the *Tribune* often explored topics in depth for a period of weeks or months, and then dropped those ideas to go on to something new. His fascination with ideas confused his contemporaries and some historians, and his inconsistencies earned him a reputation for being erratic and undependable. He remained active in Whig politics until he joined the Republican party, and while he continued to write for the newspaper, he also traveled the lecture

> **GREELEY'S PRAYER OF TWENTY MILLIONS**
>
> We complain that the Union cause has suffered, and is now suffering immensely, from mistaken deference to Rebel slavery. Had you, sir, in your inaugural address, unmistakably given notice that, in case the Rebellion already commenced were persisted in, and your efforts to preserve the Union and enforce the laws were resisted by armed force, *you would recognize no loyal person as rightfully held in slavery by a Traitor*, we believe the Rebellion would therein have received a staggering if not fatal blow. . . . Had you then proclaimed that Rebellion would strike the shackles from the slaves of every traitor, the wealthy and the cautious would have been supplied with a powerful inducement to remain loyal. . . .
>
> SOURCE. Horace Greeley, New York Tribune, August 20, 1862.

circuit to increase his income. He advocated abstinence from alcohol, popular education, land for the landless, and abolition of slavery. He adhered to Whig principles of the high tariff, a stable monetary supply, internal improvements, and national pride. Greeley, who supported the Homestead Act as a solution to social ills, encouraged people to abandon New York City, promoting the phrase, "Go West Young Man, Go West." In the 1850s he used the pages of the *Tribune* to investigate socialism, and hired Karl Marx as a London correspondent.

Greeley's paper became known as a school for journalists, much as Dana's *Sun* became known in the later years. Henry J. Raymond, who became editor of the *New York Times*, worked for Greeley, as did Margaret Fuller, a transcendentalist writer, Charles Dana, who later edited the *Sun*, and Whitelaw Reid, who eventually took over editorship of the *Tribune* itself. Greeley willingly committed money to improving the editorial side of the paper and in the 1850s hired a dozen editors for special departments. As the years progressed, circulation leveled off and remained steady at about 35,000 to 40,000 for the daily, and 100,000 for the weekly. In 1848, Greeley was appointed to Congress to serve out an unexpired term. He ran several times for a House seat, twice for the Senate, and once for New York comptroller, but always lost his political bids. His last campaign was for the presidency, and while he earned the support of some Liberal Republicans and Democrats, many editors viewed his candidacy with alarm.

Greeley ardently opposed slavery because he felt the institution was not in the national interest, and that it would retard development and destroy the Union. He often received credit for persuading Lincoln to free the slaves through his famous "Prayer of Twenty Millions," but evidence indicates

New York Tribune *Press Room, 1861, as depicted in* Frank Leslie's Illustrated Weekly. *(Library of Congress Collection)*

Lincoln's plans were set long before Greeley published the famous editorial on August 20, 1862. Lincoln and Greeley were well acquainted, however, and not only met, but corresponded about the future of the Union. At the end of the war, Greeley led a campaign to free former Confederate President Jefferson Davis, arguing that a trial would reopen rather than heal the wounds of war. He also supported the move to impeach Andrew Johnson, calling him "America's most degraded son." In 1872, Greeley ran for president on the Liberal Republican and Democratic tickets.

The daily and weekly editions of the *Tribune* continued for thirty-one years until Greeley's death in 1872. He was widely known, primarily because of the weekly, and because of his attitude toward westward expansion. Greeley's success could not be measured in business terms, and many claim that if he had not gone into partnership with Thomas McElrath in 1841 the paper would have floundered financially. In 1849, the Tribune Association was organized, with *Tribune* property divided into shares. Some were sold to supervisory personnel, and when Greeley died he owned very little of the Tribune company.[6] Whitelaw Reid became the new editor of the *Tribune*.

HENRY JARVIS RAYMOND

Henry Raymond, born in western New York state in 1820, began his newspaper career while a student at the University of Vermont as a free-lancer for Horace Greeley's *New Yorker*. By 1840, when he received his degree, Raymond had considerable experience in Whig politics and was hired as Greeley's assistant at the *New Yorker*. He added election returns, read foreign newspapers, wrote book reviews, and read proof. Although unhappy with his salary of $600 a year, Raymond was able to earn another $400 from outside work and he stayed with Greeley as chief assistant at the *New York Tribune*. Raymond objected to Greeley's interest in Fourierism (a form of socialism), and wrote, "Some delectable asses here (among whom I am sorry to say is Greeley) have started a plan for reorganizing society—elevating the social condition of universal dogdom and allowing puppies to hold their proper rank in the scale of being."[7]

Greeley praised Raymond for his hard work and often left him in charge of the newspaper, but Raymond was becoming embittered over his low wages. In 1843, James Watson Webb offered him $25 a week and editorship of the New York *Courier and Enquirer*. Raymond left his post at the Tribune, accepted Webb's offer, and remained at the *Courier* until 1851, when he left to begin the *New York Times*. To potential backers Raymond proposed a newspaper of wide coverage, including city news, with emphasis on public meetings, sermons, religious gatherings, ship news, market information, and stock news. He wanted to avoid what he considered the "crudeness" of Bennett and the radicalism of Greeley. He was aware the *Tribune* made $60,000 a year and "expressed his decided conviction that a new paper could be started in New York, which would make as much money as the Tribune."[8] Raymond secured the Associated Press franchise, remained a moderate voice, and gained the reputation for good news reporting. After the first year the newspaper made about $100,000, and on its first anniversary Raymond doubled the paper's size and raised the price to two cents. He returned to political life and in 1854, broke from the Whigs, joined the Republican party, and addressed a conference of party leaders in Pittsburgh, earning himself the title "Godfather of the Republican Party." He was credited with outlining principles of the new party, for appealing to the party to resist slavery, and for warning of the approaching Civil War.[9] In 1854, he took leave from the *Times* when he was elected lieutenant governor of New York. In 1857, when his term was over, he declined offers to run for governor.

By 1857, Raymond had moved the *Times* into an improved printing facility. In 1861, he covered the first Battle of Bull Run, and spent his time during the war between the battlefields, Washington, and New York. After the war, he supported Andrew Johnson's presidency and was elected to Congress in 1865. Disappointed with Johnson, Raymond ended his political career

Chapter 8 **Sectional Conflict and Abolitionist Agitation**

in 1867 at the age of forty-seven. When he died in 1860, Thurlow Weed, New York politician; Greeley; and Colonel Watson Webb temporarily laid aside their differences to be pallbearers at Raymond's funeral.

The *Times* continued under the editorship of John Bigelow, who was named by the newspaper's three directors: George Jones, Leonard Jerome, and James B. Taylor. Jones, who had been Raymond's partner, saved the paper in 1871 from the hands of William Marcy (Boss) Tweed, who was trying to shut down the voice that opposed his corrupt New York administration. The *Times* declined and suffered bankruptcy before Adolph Ochs bought it in 1896.

ABOLITIONIST PRESS

Abolitionist activity existed in the United States as early as the 1700s, with Quaker groups opposing slavery because it violated their religious principles of brotherly love. While some hoped slavery would be abolished under the newly written Constitution, the three-fifths compromise indicated that compromise rather than principle would rule the day. However, by 1804, Pennsylvania and states north of its boundaries had passed acts of emancipation. The number of freed blacks also multiplied in Maryland and Virginia, as slaveowners voluntarily freed many slaves. In addition, Congress ended the foreign slave trade in 1807, the same year that the English Parliament passed a similar law. Abolitionists continued their work, assuming that moral persuasion and information would cause enlightened Southerners to change their minds about the "peculiar institution."

Abolitionists were a minority, and the movement to free the slaves was not approved by a majority of society until the South actually declared war on the Union. In addition, abolitionists disagreed among themselves. Working-class whites often feared the competition a freed black labor force would supply, and upper-class whites had difficulty freeing themselves from racial prejudice. From 1816 onward, abolitionists divided into two factions: one advocating colonization, or the return of blacks to Africa, and the other emancipation, or the freeing of blacks within the United States. Emancipationists further divided themselves into two groups: those who fought for gradual emancipation and those who decreed that legal, if no social, change could occur immediately.

During the 1820s, abolitionists generally supported the colonizationists and agreed that slavery was a state issue, not a federal one. They hoped that with education, southern whites would learn the error of their ways and voluntarily free their slaves.

Throughout the 1830s, many abolitionists turned to immediate emancipation as an answer and rejected colonization, but the movement still retained a moral and religious focus. In 1835, utilizing new publishing technology such as the steam press and stereotyping, the American Anti-Slavery Society was able to produce materials for nearly half the going rate of the year before. Thus they were able, the Executive Committee reported, to distribute nine times the material at only five times the cost of 1834. The society took advantage of cheap postal rates reserved for pamphlets and newspapers, and flooded the country with a variety of publications. Thus, wrote historian Leonard Richards, "the transformation in printing indirectly contributed to the anti-abolitionist notion of a monstrous Anti-Slavery Society stimulated both by foreign influence and by foreign funds."[10]

By 1840, many abolitionists turned to political action as an alternative, resulting in the formation of the Liberty party and the running of abolitionist James Birney for president. The 1850s saw a revival of religious fervor and the publication of Harriet Beecher Stowe's *Uncle Tom's Cabin*, which propelled the issue of slavery into the popular culture of the day.

In response to an 1850 amendment to the Fugitive Slave Act of 1793, abolitionists more frequently rejected their former pacifistic approach, and in some cases promoted slave insurrections and violent overthrow of the "peculiar institution." The law required citizens to help apprehend fugitive slaves and imposed severe penalties on those who helped slaves escape. The law jeopardized the position of free blacks as well, because a suspected fugitive was not guaranteed the rights of calling witnesses, trial by jury, or writs of habeas corpus.

One of the earliest formal organizations opposing slavery was the American Colonization Society, organized in 1816. Society members feared God's wrath over slavery would destroy the union. They compared slavery to the bondage of Israelites in Egypt, and argued that as God led the Israelites across the Red Sea, so should blacks be led out of bondage in the United States. Because the colonizationists did not fully accept the concept of equality between the races, they argued that blacks in the United States would sink to the bottom of society, and therefore strived to create their own promised land for blacks—the land of Liberia along the Atlantic coast of Africa. Exporting blacks to Liberia, colonizationists argued, would preserve the union by eliminating the racial issue, and would provide blacks with an opportunity to create their own society.[11]

One of the most widely known early abolition editors was Benjamin Lundy, who edited the *Genius of Universal Emancipation* from 1821 to 1839. Lundy, although a believer in equality, supported the colonizationists and made some attempts early in his career to investigate the possibility of creating a black colony in Mexico.

Lundy's work attracted many who became principal figures in the abolitionist movement, including William Lloyd Garrison, who quickly moved away from the position of gradual emancipation and colonization to what was considered radicalism: a demand for immediate emancipation and a position that the Constitution was a pro-slavery document which should be abolished. Garrison and twelve friends formed the New England Anti-Slavery Society in 1831; eventually about a quarter of the members were free blacks. In 1833, the Garrisonians, New York reformers, and Pennsylvania Quakers organized the American Anti-Slavery Society, a national organization of blacks and whites. The group agreed the first target should be the churches, and the movement therefore became religious in tone.

WILLIAM LLOYD GARRISON

Born in Massachusetts in 1805, William Lloyd Garrison was apprenticed at thirteen as a printer in the *Newburyport Herald* office. He quickly became a rapid compositor and wrote his first article anonymously—then set it in type himself. In 1826, at the close of his apprenticeship, he edited several small papers, becoming involved in the temperance movement. Converted to the work of Benjamin Lundy, he became manager of *The Genius of Universal Emancipation* in 1829. While enroute to joining Lundy, he made his first public speech on slavery:

> I stand up here . . . but to obtain the liberation of two millions of wretched, degraded beings, who are pining in hopeless bondage—over whose sufferings scarcely an eye weeps, or a heart melts, or a tongue pleads either to God or man . . .[12]

Lundy's position on gradual emancipation was jeopardized in 1828 when Garrison demanded immediate emancipation in an issue of the *Genius*. The newspaper was closed down and Garrison was jailed.[13] In January 1831, when he was twenty-five years old, Garrison began his own weekly journal in Washington, *The Public Liberator and Journal of the Time*. The motto of the *Liberator* was "Our country is the world—our countrymen are mankind." For thirty-four years the paper continuously demanded immediate and unconditional emancipation, but remained loyal to the tactics of nonviolence.

Garrison's position was not a popular one, and Nat Turner's bloody rebellion of 1831 sparked new attacks on Garrison's extremist position. Despite Garrison's continued pleas for nonviolence, many believed Garrison's rhetoric contributed to insurrection. Nevertheless, Garrison's publications endured. The *National Anti-Slavery Standard* was published weekly in New York for thirty years and the *Liberator* continued for thirty-five years. Neither probably ever exceeded a circulation of 3,000, but they were read, noted, and responded to by supporters and antagonists.

> ### THE LIBERATOR'S PREAMBLE
>
> Whereas, we believe that Slavery is contrary to the precepts of Christianity, dangerous to the liberties of the country, and ought immediately to be abolished; and whereas, we believe that the citizens of New England not only have the right to protest against it, but are under the highest obligation to seek its removal by moral influence; and whereas, we believe that the free people of color are unrighteously oppressed, and stand in need of our sympathy and benevolent co-operation; therefore, recognizing the inspired declaration that God 'hath made of one blood all nations of men for to dwell on all the face of the earth' and in obedience to our Saviour's golden rule, 'all things whatsoever ye would that men should do to you, do ye even on to them,' we agree to form ourselves into a Society and to be governed by the following CONSTITUTION.
>
> SOURCE. The Liberator, February 9, 1833.

JAMES BIRNEY

James Birney, a southern aristocrat, slaveholder and successful attorney, seemed an unlikely candidate to run for president of the United States on an abolitionist ticket. Born in 1792 into a socially prominent family in Danville, Kentucky, he moved to Alabama in 1818 and established himself as a large slaveholding planter. Birney's father and grandfather had opposed slavery in the Kentucky legislature, but believed that until the laws were changed the best approach was to be kind to one's slaves, a position which led Birney to support the American Colonization Society. Birney served as an Alabama legislator for one term, as mayor of Huntsville for a term, and on the Alabama Board of Regents.

About 1832, Birney moved back to Danville, where he freed his slaves and decided to publish an abolitionist newspaper. No one in Kentucky would sell him a press because his views were well known, and he moved across the river to Cincinnati. The *Louisville Journal* wrote, "Not having been permitted to open his battery in this state, he is determined to cannonade us from across the river."[14] After being warned by Cincinnatians that they might respond to violent talk with violent action, Birney published the first issue of the *Philanthropist*, January 1, 1836. Birney charged that southern states were restraining freedom of the press and stirring up violence in the North. While Birney was out of town in June 1836, a mob, organized by the mayor, attacked Birney's office in Cincinnati and threw his press into the Ohio River. But Birney resumed publication, hiring an assistant editor so he could spend more time lecturing. In 1837, Birney turned the paper over to his assistant to become the secretary of the American Anti-Slavery Society. In 1840 and 1844 he ran for president on the Liberty Party ticket. Birney died before slavery was abolished.

ELIJAH LOVEJOY

Elijah Lovejoy began publishing the *Observer* in Alton, Illinois, after being driven from St. Louis for expressing anti-Catholic and antislavery views. In January 1837, the Illinois legislature, fearing southern economic reprisals, urged resistance to antislavery activity. After publishing a call to establish an antislavery society in the state, Lovejoy was asked to stop printing. When he refused, a mob destroyed his press and the Illinois attorney general ruled the action was justified. Lovejoy's printing presses were destroyed twice and his house invaded by proslavery groups. When a third press arrived, determined to protect it, he armed himself, but was gunned down by a mob as his press went up in flames.

Lovejoy's death was the first event to clearly link abolition with civil rights. The American Anti-Slavery Society responded by carrying the motto: "LOVEJOY the first MARTYR to American LIBERTY. MURDERED for asserting the FREEDOM of the PRESS. Alton, November 7, 1837."

CASSIUS MARCELLUS CLAY

Cassius Marcellus Clay was living proof that abolitionists made strange bedfellows. Born in 1810 to Kentucky wealth and the owner of slaves, he fought to abolish slavery. He was a man of intellect, but also a man of violence and passion. Clay attended Yale University, and moved in the circles of the wealthy and powerful, meeting and dining with cousin Henry Clay, General Andrew Jackson, Martin Van Buren, and Daniel Webster. He also came in contact with William Lloyd Garrison.

In 1832, Cassius Clay made an antislavery address to his Yale graduating class. By 1843, Clay freed his own slaves, and in 1845, he denounced slavery's economic, moral, and cultural disadvantages in an "Address to the People of Kentucky." The *Lexington Observer and Reporter* denounced Clay's opinions as militant and provocative, and closed its columns to him. Clay responded by issuing his own newspaper, the *True American*, on June 3, 1845, and proposing that constitutional measures be used to overthrow slavery. But reaction was so intense that he charged his opponents, the editors of the *Lexington Observer and Reporter* and of the *Kentucky Gazette*, of taking the position that "the subject of slavery shall not be discussed, and . . . violence shall suppress our press."

Within two months, about 3,400 people were subscribing to the *True American*. Only 700 of the subscribers were Kentuckians. Horace Greeley of the *New York Tribune* praised the paper as the first "which ever bearded the monster in its den, and dared him to a most unequal encounter." Clay's arguments were economic, as well as moral. The *True American* tried to convince the 600,000 citizens of Kentucky that their interests were not the same as those of the 31,000 slaveowners in the state. Clay argued that the continued existence of slavery in Kentucky destroyed the possibility for industrialization and progress.

In August 1845 while Clay was suffering with typhoid fever, a group of townspeople packed his printing press and printing apparatus and took it to the railroad station to be shipped out of Lexington, hoping to end publication of the antislavery organ. Clay survived his bout with typhoid and by October began publishing the *True American* once more, this time from Cincinnati, although Clay continued to live in Lexington. He later sued the "Committee of Sixty" which had stolen his press and was awarded $2,500. He continued to edit the paper until he volunteered for service in the Mexican War, leaving it in the hands of John Vaughnn. In December 1847, the *True American* was succeeded by the *Louisville Examiner*.

Clay continued his abolitionist work when he returned from the Mexican War, and in 1846 he was stabbed and beaten by a pro-slavery man, Cyrus Turner. Clay managed to bury his knife in Turner's abdomen, even though he had blood gushing from a lung wound. As Clay lost consciousness, he cried, "I died in the defense of the liberties of the people."

But Cyrus Turner lived, and Cassius Clay recovered. Clay's bloody self-defense was denounced by the Garrisonian abolitionists, who advocated nonresistance. Throughout the 1850s, Clay was active in the new Republican party and in 1860 Lincoln appointed him minister to Russia. Clay returned to American permanently in 1869, worked to obtain the vote for black people, and supported Horace Greeley's nomination for president in 1872. He divorced his wife in 1878, and in 1894 when he was eighty-four, he married a fifteen-year-old girl. He endured Ku Klux Klan attacks, a posse that demanded he give up his young wife, and finally died of a kidney ailment in 1903, when he was ninety-three years old.

JANE GREY SWISSHELM

Jane Grey Swisshelm, born in 1815, began her newspaper career when she was twenty-five years old by (writing) anonymous newspaper articles opposing capital punishment. In 1842, she expanded her work, publishing stories and poems for the Pittsburgh, Pa., *Spirit of Liberty*, and articles on slavery and women's rights for a Pittsburgh abolitionist journal.[15] In 1848, she began publishing her own antislavery newspaper, the *Pittsburgh Saturday Visitor*. Swisshelm also included material about women's rights and once described the

> **THE WORK OF COUNTRY GIRLS**
>
> The plow, harrow, reap, dig, make hay, rake, bind grain, thrash, chop wood, milk, churn, do anything that is hard work, physical labor, and who says anything against it? But let one presume to use her mental powers—let her aspire to turn editor, public speaker, doctor, lawyer—take up any profession or avocation which is deemed honorable and requires talent, and O! bring cologne, get cambric kerchief and feather fan, unloose his corsets and take off his cravat! What a fainting fit Mr. Propriety has taken!"
>
> SOURCE. Jane Grey Swisshelm, Letters To Country Girls.

position of women as "something better than that of a baboon, but lower than that of a Negro slave."[16] Jane Swisshelm was not willing to support what she considered to be radical women feminists, however, but emphasized improving the legal rights of married women. In 1853, she collected a book of columns called *Letters To Country Girls*, which claimed that women were expected to work hard physically, receive little pay and scorn their own mental abilities.

Swisshelm moved to Minnesota in the 1850s, where she began the *St. Cloud Visitor*, attacked the Democratic power structure, and was put out of business by a libel suit. She started a new newspaper, the *St. Cloud Democrat*, attacked slavery, and urged federal action against the Sioux Indians, whom she viewed as a threat to Minnesotans. While in Washington pleading for action against the Sioux she appealed to Vice-President Millard Fillmore for a seat in the press gallery, which she occupied for only one day. During the Civil War she worked as a nurse and in 1866 returned to Pennsylvania to write her autobiography.[17]

RESTRICTIONS ON PUBLISHING

In 1832, Virginia legislators reacted to the Nat Turner rebellion and to abolitionist publications by enacting a law that punished those who wrote books or pamphlets "advising persons of colour within this state to make insurrection." The law provided for punishment of thirty-nine lashes for the first offense and death without benefit of clergy for the second offense.[18]

Virginia was not the only state to invoke such a law. In 1829, a former slave, David Walker, published "Walker's Appeal in Four Articles Together with a Preamble to the Colored Citizens of the World." He advised slaves to use violence to free themselves and, according to one source, "set off legislation to curb expression in several states beginning with Georgia."[19]

By 1835, in response to increased abolitionist printing activity, laws prohibiting distribution of antislavery literature were so severe that all antislavery societies below the Mason and Dixon Line had disappeared.

Restrictions, while sometimes legal in nature, also came in the form of aggressive public opinion. When the Anti-Slavery Society mailed more than a million pieces of literature in 1835, including monthly journals, a children's newspaper, woodcuts, and chocolate wrappers, the reaction neared hysteria.[20] In addition to the hostility they encountered in southern society, abolitionists were not always welcome in the North. In 1835, William Lloyd Garrison was assaulted and dragged through the streets of Boston, and another abolitionist barely escaped death after being beaten by a mob in Concord, Massachusetts.

The attacks on abolitionists and on publication of materials attracted more supporters than antislavery societies could garner, although some newspapers defended freedom of speech. During the 1830s, the columns of *Niles' Weekly Register* vigorously protested the proslavery party's attempts to silence its opposition. The *Boston Courier* expressed its support through rhyme:

> Rail on, then "brethren of the south"—
>   Ye shall not hear the truth the less -
> No seal is on the Yankee's mouth,
>   No fetter on the Yankee's press!
> From our Green Mountains to the sea
>   Our voice shall thunder—WE ARE FREE![21]

Even the *New York Herald*, with its pro-South stance, told the South if it demanded the North "to pass laws infringing the liberty of the press we must tell them frankly that they are running into a similar degree of fanaticism to that which they object to in the abolitionists."[22] But the mainstream press did not always support the abolitionists' appeals to freedom of speech and press. The abolitionist minister William E. Channing wrote to James G. Birney that the press had "countenanced, by its gentle censures, the reign of force,"[23]

The federal government also tried to restrict the spread of "incendiary" literature. In December 1835, President Jackson proposed that Congress be given the right to determine which newspapers were incendiary. Even the proslavery forces recognized his proposal as being unconstitutional, but later that year, Postmaster General Amos Kendall, President Jackson, and John C. Calhoun joined forces seeking a federal law to prohibit abolitionist mail from traveling South. The group was not successful, but a combination of southern postmasters and public groups succeeded where legislation did not. When the citizens of Charleston discovered abolitionist materials that were being sent to South Carolina from the American Anti-Slavery Society in 1835, they forcibly seized and burned them on the Charleston Parade Ground. Acting on the postmaster general's advice, the New York and Charleston postmasters announced they would forward no more antislavery matter to the southern address. Kendall wrote to the Charleston postmaster that while he had no legal authority to exclude newspapers from the mail, he was not prepared to order the South Carolina official to deliver abolitionist materials:

> The post office department was created to serve the people of *each* and *all* of the *United States* and not be used as an instrument of their destruction. . . . We owe an obligation to the laws, but a higher one to the communities in which we live, and if the *former* be perverted to destroy the *latter*, it is patriotism to disregard them.[24]

Congress also instituted a "gag rule," under which all petitions from citizens regarding slavery were received without being presented, printed, or considered by Congress. Abolitionists continued to protest the rule, however, and thereby appeared as champions of the Constitution rather than as radicals.

THE BLACK PRESS

During the first sixty-five years of the nineteenth century, 90 percent of America's blacks lived in the South. In the North two-thirds of blacks were illiterate. The very fact that a black press began and survived in this environment is a remarkable feat. The newspaper press was not the first evidence of expression by blacks in America, but was preceded by oratory, primarily in the form of sermons, poetry, spirituals, and narratives of escaped or freed slaves.

Samuel Cornish and John Russwurm usually are credited with producing the first black newspaper, *Freedom's Journal*, in 1827, in response to a black-hating editor, Mordecai M. Noah. The paper was termed "a thoroughgoing abolitionist sheet" and carried the motto, "Righteousness Exalteth a Nation."[25] The newspaper contained original and reprinted articles, poetry, and news of slavery in the United States as well as in other countries. Russwurm and Cornish were divided over the issue of colonization, and during the first six months the *Journal* opposed colonization. Once Cornish resigned to return to the ministry, Russwurm reversed the position.

Russwurm graduated from Bowdoin College in 1826, the first black to graduate from a college in the United States. Before the more restrictive measures taken in the 1830s, *Freedom's Journal* circulated through Virginia, Maryland, North Carolina, Louisiana, and Washington, D.C. Russwurm lost favor because of his position on colonization, and eventually became editor of the *Liberia Herald*. In 1829, when Russwurm left, Samuel Cornish resumed the editorship, changed the name to *Rights of All*, and promised to fight for black citizenship. But lack of finances and support crippled the publication, and it died in October 1829.

Some accounts indicate several issues of black newspapers may have been published in the 1830s, but it was nearly six years after the death of the *Journal* that a continuous publication, *The Spirit of the Times*, was founded in New York City, and it was published there for six years. In January 1837, Phillip A. Bell founded *The Weekly Advocate*, which became *The Colored American*. This four-page newspaper, edited by Samuel Cornish of *Freedom's Journal*, lasted until 1842. *The Colored American* focused on a family audience, strived for humanity and justice, attacked colonization, and charged northern newspapers, clergymen, and businessmen with holding slaveholding sympathies. Its circulation reached 2,000 and reached subscribers from Maine to Michigan.

More papers originated during the 1840s, with some lasting for as long as two to twelve years. Among the best were Frederick Douglass' *Ram's Horn*, *The North Star*, and *Frederick Douglass' Paper*. Black editors continued to initiate publications through the Civil War.

FREDERICK DOUGLASS

His best guess was that he was born in February 1817 in Talbot County on the eastern shore of Maryland. Born a slave, Frederick Douglass knew neither his name at birth, his date or place of birth, or his white father. Douglass's mother died when he was young, and after his master also died he was sent away with other slaves. In his new home he met a kind mistress, who attempted to teach him to read, but his master scolded her, saying "A nigger should know nothing but to obey his master—to do as he is told to do."[26]

Douglass endured slavery under the hands of several masters before he escaped in May 1838, and went to New York City, where he found a benefactor. He supported himself first as a carpenter, then, because of his moving speeches at the Massachusetts Anti-Slavery Society, he became a full-time, paid abolitionist lecturer. In the 1840s, Douglas was the prize speaker of the Massachusetts society, traveling the lecture circuit with William Lloyd Garrison and Wendell Phillips. Part of Douglass's convincing appeal was the experience he had as a slave. In his first public address he captivated his listeners, arguing that emancipation would "blot out the insults we have borne, will heal the wounds we have endured and are even groaning under, will pacify the resentment which would kindle to a blaze were it not for your exertions. . . ."[27] Douglass told his audience the worst feature of slavery was not the lash, but the separation of friends and families.

In 1845, Douglass traveled to Britain to speak for the society. The British were so impressed by his performance they raised enough money to buy his freedom. He also continued his own self-education, learning to write well and speak eloquently.

In 1842, Douglass had begun writing for William Lloyd Garrison's *Liberator*. Commenting on a series of letters Douglass wrote to Garrison from abroad, Horace Greeley of the *New York Tribune* said some passages in the letter, "which, for genuine eloquence, would do honor to any writer of the English language, however eloquent." Thurlow Weed, of the *Albany Evening Journal*, said of the same letter that it gave Douglass "rank among the most gifted and eloquent men of the age."[28]

In 1845, when he was twenty-seven years old, he published his first autobiography, the *Narrative of the Life of Frederick Douglass*. In August 1847, he became associate editor of *The Ram's Horn* and wrote regularly for the *New York City Standard*. Later that year, he began publishing his own newspaper, *North Star*, which continued publication for sixteen years, an unusual lifespan for an abolitionist newspaper. Douglass named the newspaper from a tune sung by runaway slaves, "I kept my eye on the bright north star, and thought of liberty. . . ." Douglass printed a prospectus for the paper in the columns of the *Anti-Slavery Bugle*, promising a weekly that would "Attack Slavery in all its forms and aspects: Advocate Universal Emancipation; exalt the standard of Public Morality; promote the Moral and Intellectual improvement of the Colored People; and hasten the day of FREEDOM to the Three Millions of our Enslaved Fellow Countrymen." In 1851 the name was changed to *Frederick Douglass' Paper*.

Douglass's paper was received with mixed reviews. While his Massachusetts friends were demonstrably happy over the newspaper's appearance, James Gordon Bennett of the *New York Herald* suggested the editor be exiled to Canada and his equipment thrown into a lake. Local hostility, however, was feeble and of short duration. The printers association welcomed Douglass's paper to Rochester and the printers and publishers of the city invited Douglass to a celebration of Benjamin Franklin's birthday. Douglass was proud of his printing establishment, which was the first ever owned by a black in the United States. His press, types, and other printing materials cost between $900 and $1,000 and were, he said, the best that could be obtained in the country. In the modest, single-room office, Douglass's children and a white apprentice set type.

Continuing to lecture on slavery and on women's rights, Douglass published an autobiography in 1855, *My Bondage and My Freedom*. In 1859, he took his message abroad, lecturing in Canada, England, and Scotland. A tireless supporter of the Union Cause, Douglass helped recruit blacks for a Massachusetts regiment, thereby earning an invitation to the White House from President Lincoln. After the war, he moved to Washington, D.C., and in 1869 began publishing *The New National Era*. In 1872, he served as a presidential elector.

While Garrison and Douglass began their acquaintance as friends and political allies, they parted company because Garrison sought dissolution of the Union, rejected the right to vote, and labeled the Constitution a pro-slavery document. Douglass felt that to abstain from voting was a refusal to exercise a legitimate and powerful means for abolishing slavery. He said the Constitution not only carried no guarantee in favor of slavery, but on the contrary, was in "its letter and spirit an anti-slavery instrument, demanding the abolition of slavery as a condition of its own existence as the supreme law of the land."[29] When Douglas resisted a proposition not to support any newspaper that did not assume the Constitution to be a pro-slavery document, Garrison immediately exclaimed, "there is a roguery somewhere," and moved to have the *North Star* stricken from the list. The Garrisonian papers, *The Liberator, The Standard*, and *The Freeman* assailed Douglass, charging him with treachery, inconsistency, and ingratitude.

Douglass turned sixty in 1877, but he didn't hesitate to continue actively working at home and abroad. He was appointed U.S. marshall for the District of Columbia in 1876 and held the office for five years before becoming recorder of deeds in the district. He also served as secretary of the Santa Domingo Commission and as U.S. minister to Haiti.

By January 1882, he had written the last of his three autobiographies. In August of that year, his wife died. In 1884, he remarried and sailed to Europe, Greece, and Egypt to continue his lecture circuit. Highly criticized for his second marriage—to a white woman—Douglass replied that he was quite impartial. His first wife "was the color of my mother, and the second, the color of my father."[30] Douglass died in 1895, after attending a woman suffrage convention the day of his death.

In 1963, *Ebony* magazine, on the centennial of the Emancipation Proclamation, used his photograph on the cover of the magazine, editorializing:

> Frederick Douglass, father of the protest movement, is a worthy subject to grace the cover of any publication commemorating the centennial of the Emancipation Proclamation. . . .
>
> After Emancipation was achieved, Douglass went on fighting for a wide variety of reforms in the areas of black voting rights, urban development, pacifism, social justice, and especially women's rights.[31]

Slavery's Defenders

EDMUND RUFFIN

Edmund Ruffin, born January 5, 1794, an agricultural expert deeply involved in revitalizing agriculture in the South, was also a rabid secessionist and defender of slavery. Originally from Virginia, he declared that if South Carolina seceded, he would renounce his state of birth if it did not secede as well. Ruffin believed in government by the elite and considered the black race as generally inferior, admitting only the possibility that "one Negro in a hundred thousand" might be capable of obtaining a college education. He contributed to Robert Barnwhell Rhett's *Charleston Mercury* and was a pamphleteer, writing "The Political Economy of Slavery," and "Anticipation of the Future," in which he argued for secession and the "glories of an independent South." Ruffin was a member of the Palmetto Guard of South Carolina and on April 12, 1861, is created with firing the first shot on Fort Sumter. After the fall of New Orleans, Ruffin said,

> Rather than submit to Yankee domination . . . it would be better for all to be killed in battle. If we are to be held as subject provinces, I would prefer that our despotic ruler and master should be any power of Europe, even Russia or Spain, rather than the Northern States.[32]

When the South crumbled, so did Ruffin. He lost all his property and carried on disputes with two of three children. At seventy-one years old, he was a beaten man, and less than a week after Lee's surrender he shot himself in the head rather than take an oath of allegiance to the North. He wrote, "I cannot survive the liberty of my country."

CONCLUSION

During the late 1830s, the penny press appealed to a diverse audience of varying socioeconomic characteristics. In the early 1840s, Horace Greeley and Henry Raymond established penny newspapers that, while claiming to avoid the sensationalism of Benjamin Day's *New York Sun*, still appealed to a broad audience. Greeley, with the *New York Tribune*, valued the exchange of ideas and endeavored to create an intellectual newspaper for a nonelite audience. Raymond, producing the *New York Times*, disliked what he saw as Greeley's erratic behavior, and focused on thorough coverage of events.

Despite the attempts of these newspapers to create mass audiences and to define the functions of newspapers, penny editors were not the sole providers of information. The American Anti-Slavery Society and various abolitionist editors, as well as black editors, appealed to specialized groups within antebellum America.

Mainstream editors, as well as abolitionist editors, used new technologies such as the steam press to reduce costs and to achieve wider circulation. While the use of such technologies increased profits and provided for expanded editorial staffing for editors like Greeley and Raymond, abolitionists were rewarded with the wrath of state legislators and public opposition. State legislatures enacted restrictive legislation, Congress instituted a gag rule, and southern postmasters, encouraged by the postmaster general of the United States, refused to distribute abolitionist materials. Mainstream editors, who responded little to abolitionist appeals to destroy slavery, reacted more intensely when they saw government impose limitations on publishing and distributing materials.

The black press, on the other hand, relied on old technology to distribute its message. Ranging from conservative to radical, the black press presented its editors as role models for black society and documented the intellectual achievements of black Americans.

NOTES

1. For general discussions of the Jacksonian period, see Arthur M. Schlesinger, Jr., *The Age of Jackson* (Boston: Little, Brown, 1945); Robert P. McCormick, *The Second American Party System: Party Formation in the Jacksonian Era* (Chapel Hill: University of North Carolina Press, 1966), p. 115; Robert B. Remi, *Andrew Jackson and the Course of American Democracy, 1833–1845* (New York: Harper & Row, 1984), p. 271.
2. For details about the series of compromises, see chapter 7, Westward Ho!
3. For the role of the public lecture system in defining national issues, see Donald M. Scott, "The Popular Lecture and the Creation of a Public in Mid-Nineteenth Century America," *The Journal of American History* (March 1980) 66, pp. 791–809.
4. John L. Thomas, "Romantic Reform in America, 1815–1865," *American Quarterly* (Winter 1965), pp. 656–81.
5. David Paul Nord, "The Evangelical Origins of Mass Media in America, 1815–1835," *Journalism Monographs* (Columbia, S.C.: Association for Education in Journalism and Mass Communication, 1984), 88, pp.23–24. See also Leonard L. Richards, *"Gentlemen of Property and Standing"* (New York: Oxford University Press, 1970), pp. 72–73.
6. For full-length biographies of Greeley, see Don C. Seitz, *Horace Greeley: Founder of the New York Tribune* (Indianapolis: Bobbs-Merrill, 1926); Henry Luther Stoddard, *Horace Greeley: Printer, Editor, Crusader* (New York: Putnam, 1946); or Glyndon G. Van Deusen *Horace Greeley: Nineteenth Century Crusader* (Philadelphia: University of Pennsylvania Press, 1953). For an excellent summary see "Horace Greeley" by Daniel W. Pfaff, in *Dictionary of Literary Biography: American Newspaper Journalists, 1690–1872* (Detroit: Gale Research Co., 1986), vol. 43.
7. Francis Brown, *Raymond of the Times* (New York: W.W. Norton, 1951), p. 39.
8. Augustus Maverick, *Henry J. Raymond and the New York Press for Thirty Years. Progress of American Journalism from 1840 to 1870.* (Hartford, Conn.: A.S. Hale and Company, 1870), p. 90.

9. Meyer Berger, *The Story of the New York Times 1851–1951*. (New York: Simon and Schuster, 1951), p. 21.
10. Richard, *"Gentlemen of Property and Standing,"* p. 73.
11. For information on the abolitionist movement, see Louis Filler, *The Crusade Against Slavery, 1830–1860* (New York: Harper and Brothers, 1960); Russel Nye, *Civil Liberties and the Slavery Controversy, 1830–1860* (Urbana: University of Illinois Press, 1972); H.L. Perkin, "The Defense of Slavery in the Northern Press on the Eve on the Civil War," *Journal of Southern History* (February-November 1943) 9, pp. 501–32; and Eugene Genovese, *The Political Economy of Slavery* (New York: Vintage, 1965) and *The World the Slaveholders Made: Two Essays in Interpretation* (New York: Pantheon Books, 1969).
12. V. Tehertkoff and F. Holah, *A Short Biography of William Lloyd Garrison* (London 1904; rpt. Westport, Conn.: Negro Universities Press, 1970), p. 24.
13. Charles S. Miller and Natalie Joy Ward, *History of America: Challenge and Crisis* (New York: John Wiley & Sons, Inc., 1971), p. 297.
14. Betty Fladeland, *James Gillespie Birney: Slaveholder to Abolitionist* (Ithaca, New York: Cornell University Press, 1955), p. 42. See also William Birney, *James G. Birney and His Times* (New York: D. Appleton & Co., 1890).
15. For a fuller account of the suffrage press, see chapter 12, Reform Is My Religion.
16. Robert E. Riegel, *American Feminists* (Lawrence: University of Kansas Press, 1963), p. 104.
17. Marion Marzolf, *Up From the Footnote: A History of Women Journalists* (New York: Hastings House Publishers, 1977), p. 16.
18. *Supplement to the Revised Code of the Laws of Virginia* (Richmond: Samuel Shepherd & Co., 1833), pp. 246–247.
19. Harold L. Nelson, ed., *Freedom of the Press from Hamilton to the Warren Court* (Indianapolis: Bobbs-Merrill, 1967), p. 167.
20. Nord, "Evangelical Origins of Mass Media," p. 23.
21. Lucy M. Salmon, "Five Crises in American Press Freedom" in *The Press and Society: A Book of Readings* (New York: Prentice-Hall, 1951), p. 69.
22. Salmon, *Press and Society*, p. 70.
23. William Ellery Channing, from "The Abolitionists: a Letter to James G. Birney," *Works of William E. Channing* (Boston: American Unitarian Assn., 1887), p. 746.
24. Letter of Amos Kendall to postmaster at Charleston, S.C., August 4, 1835, *Niles Register*, XLVII (1835), p. 448, cited in Nelson, *Freedom of the Press*, p. 213.
25. Cited in Carter R. Bryan, "Negro Journalism in America Before Emancipation," *Journalism Monographs* 12 (September 1969).
26. Frederick Douglass, *Narrative of the Life of Frederick Douglas, an American Slave* (Boston: 1945), p. 58.
27. John W. Blassingame, *The Frederick Douglass Papers* (New Haven and London: Yale University Press, 1979), p. 3.
28. Philip S. Foner, *Frederick Douglass* (New York: The Citadel Press, 1950), p. 77.

29. Rebecca Chalmers Barton, "Witness for Freedom," *Harpers*, June 1948, pp. 172–174.
30. *Dictionary of American Biography*, p. 407.
31. See also Dickson J. Preston, *Young Frederick Douglass, the Maryland Years* (Baltimore and London: The John Hopkins University Press, 1980) p. xiv.
32. See William Kauffman Scarborough's *The Diary of Edmund Ruffin*, (Baton Rouge: Louisiana State University Press, 1972).

CHAPTER 9

COVERING
THE CIVIL WAR:
CORRESPONDENTS
AND CENSORSHIP

Secession came in South Carolina in December 1860. The election of Abraham Lincoln as president of the United States represented a shift of power to the North and West, to the anti-slavery factions, and to the Republican party. The results of the electoral college made it clear that the South, with only a third of the nation's population, would no longer have the power to control decisions regarding slavery, the tariff, or other economic measures. The Democratic party lay temporarily in shreds, as its inability to agree on a strong candidate to confront Lincoln had proven. Although a variety of sectional issues had caused the split, the issue of expansion of slavery into the territories had severed the party as well as the nation.

By February, the entire lower South had left the Union, but the eight remaining slaveholding upper south and border states remained in. They were in a difficult position. If they remained in the Union, they had little power to retain their slaveholding status, yet they were reluctant to put their faith in fire-eating secessionists and regarded secession as impractical. They hoped for compromise, and prayed for peace. Attempts at compromise failed, however, and on April 12, 1861, the Palmetto Guard of South Carolina fired on

Fort Sumter. The Civil War had begun. The Confederate States of America was made up of eleven states: South Carolina, Georgia, Alabama, Mississippi, Louisiana, Texas, Florida, Arkansas, Tennessee, North Carolina, and Virginia. Delaware, Maryland, Missouri and Kentucky, slaveholding states before secession, adhered to the Union. The war was longer and bloodier than any had imagined. Of 2.1 million Union men, 360,000 died. About 225,000 of those died from disease. Of 1.6 million Confederate soldiers, 400,000 died.[1]

Covering the Civil War was a challenge for North and South alike. With a few exceptions, correspondents for the expanding U.S. press had not covered a war, and the country itself had little experience in dealing with press in wartime. Richard McCormick of the *New York Evening Post* had covered the Crimean War, an Associated Press correspondent covered struggles in Turkey, Palestine, and Egypt, and George Williams had covered an 1858 action against the Mormons. Newspapers responded quickly to the public's desire for war news and devoted a third of the editorial columns to the conflict.

The war increased editors' desire for speed and competition in gathering the news and probably spurred the northern urban papers to greater growth, while southern papers faced financial hardship and often were destroyed as Union armies advanced through the South. News gathering benefited from expanded use of the telegraph, and correspondents began to move toward the inverted pyramid style of writing, leaving behind their nineteenth-century rhetoric. In the North, newspapers directed war coverage from the home office, and the number of correspondents increased dramatically.[2] Nevertheless, the period represented only four short years in the development of the nineteenth-century press, and expanded technology and developing reportorial techniques already in place contributed to coverage of the war.

Chapter 9 **Covering the Civil War: Correspondents and Censorship**

PRESS IN THE NORTH

Newspaper editors developed news coverage through expanded use of the telegraph, home-office organization to assign reporters and handle incoming reports, and by the use of "specials" or correspondents.

The war dramatically increased the use of and need for telegraph facilities, and the unreliability of the wires caused major problems for correspondents. Telegraph lines were limited to start with, and they frequently broke or were commandeered by the military or commercial business. The uncertainty of telegraph wires also contributed to reporters' changing from a chronological style to a style which recorded certain facts first, although the degree to which reporters used a "news lead" varied. Telegraphing was expensive, and reporters began to curtail their flowery nineteenth-century style to fit the needs of telegraphic news. The *New York Herald*'s account of the battle of Fort Sumter was presented chronologically, and the reader had to struggle through thirty paragraphs to discover that Major Anderson surrendered the fort to the Confederates.[3] Dr. Charles Ray's account of the July 1861 Battle of Bull Run, the first major battle of the war, reported the news first: "The battle is lost. The enemy have a substantial victory." The story did not follow in inverted pyramid style, but mixed editorial comment with news and reverted to a more chronological order. The account continued:

> The result, so unexpected, dangerous and mortifying, is due to causes that the country will bye and bye discuss. Men who have been inattentive observers of the field of operations and of the tendency of the popular mind, will say that popular clamor has outrun military preparation; but this is not true. The well-appointed and magnificent army that is now coming back broken and disorganized into the entrenchments on the opposite side of the river, ought never to have been beaten.[4]

The battle represented some of the difficulties reporters would have in covering the war, as well as some of the misconceptions newsmen and the public held about the certainty of a "short war." When the battle began on Sunday afternoon, Washingtonians fully expected a rout of Confederate troops. Henry Raymond, editor of the *New York Times*, wired his newspaper at two that afternoon that a Union victory was in progress. But Raymond filed his report too soon—the Union troops began to straggle back to Washington, defeated and in disarray. Raymond's newspaper was not the only one in error—the New York press on Sunday night of the battle and Monday morning printed accounts of Union victory. Press accounts had been prepared

Cloth campaign banner supporting Abraham Lincoln for President and Hannibal Hamlin for Vice President in 1860. Lincoln won the nomination, but Hamlin did not succeed. (Library of Congress Collection)

in Washington early enough to meet the Monday morning edition deadlines, but censorship of the telegraph wires held up the news. Henry Villard's accounts in the *New York Herald* ran for three days. On July 21 Villard wrote, "I am en route to Washington with details of a great battle. *We have carried the day.* The rebels accepted battle in their strength, but are totally routed. Losses on both sides considerable." On July 22, the *Herald* account read "Our troops, after taking three batteries and gaining a great victory at Bull's Run, were eventually repulsed and commenced a retreat on Washington."[5]

Emphasis on telegraphic news and the high cost of news gathering during the war spurred editors to further develop cooperative news gathering. The Associated Press, known under various names since its organization in 1848, made agreements with Western Union that gave AP preferred treatment and rates and a virtual monopolistic position. In 1858, with the opening of the Atlantic cable, AP made arrangements with European news agencies to acquire news. Reuters in Britain, Havas in France, Wolff in Germany, and Stefani in Italy contributed news to the AP.

> **THE PRESS ASSERTS THE RIGHT TO CRITICIZE**
>
> In response to the *Chicago Times* suppression, the leaders of the New York press community met on June 8, producing a list of four resolutions. The third resolution contained the thrust of the argument:
>
> *While we emphatically disclaim and deny any right as inhering in journalists or others to invite, advocate, abet, uphold or justify treason or rebellion; we respectfully but firmly assert and maintain the right of the press to criticize freely and fearlessly the acts of those charged with the administration of the Government, also those of all their civil and military subordinates, whether with intent directly to ensure greater energy, efficiency and fidelity in the public service, or in order to achieve the same ends remotely through the substitution of other persons for those now in power.*
>
> SOURCE. New York Times, June 9, 1863

As the AP expanded, an AP franchise became a valuable asset for a newspaper and western papers had difficulty securing international news without the franchise. In 1862, angered by the dominance of AP by the New York newspapers, a group of western editors formed the Western AP, charging that New York papers overcharged local papers, that they dictated what news would be in the daily report, and that local newspapers had little power in decision making. Both APs existed until 1892, when the New York AP folded and the Associated Press of Illinois emerged.[6]

Although focusing heavily on news gathering, northern editors did not relinquish their right to editorialize, and Lincoln's friends, as well as his enemies, criticized the president for the mistakes of his military commanders, for his reluctance to free the slaves, and for the repeated drafting of additional men to the army.

The *Chicago Tribune* first demanded military action in the West, then criticized Major General John C. Fremont, who commanded the Western Army headquartered in St. Louis. When, prior to Lincoln's Emancipation Proclamation, Fremont declared martial law and freed the slaves within his military jurisdiction, the *Tribune* supported the emancipation position but took him to task for what the *Tribune* considered military misjudgment and for his precipitous action without Lincoln's consultation. Such a position angered abolitionist newspapers such as Greeley's *Tribune*, the *New York Post*, and the Chicago rivals, the *Times*, the *Journal*, and the *Post*. In response to the attacks, the *Tribune* published an editorial stating that a newspaper during wartime was "regarded as watchmen on the walls. . . ." and that military men, as well as civil servants, should not be exempted from editorial criticism.[7]

PART 2 EXPANSION AND CONFLICT

THE CONFEDERATE PRESS

Pre-war journalism in the South was dominated by the partisan press. With the exception of a few newspapers, primarily the *Picayune* in New Orleans and the *Dispatch* in Richmond, the "penny idea" had not moved South. Although the numbers of newspapers had greatly increased from 1830 to 1860, as they had in the North, southern newspapers were rarely profitable and needed government and party printing contracts to survive. At the beginning of the war, 800 papers were operating in the eleven states of the Confederacy. Ten percent, or 80 of those, were dailies.

The typical newspaper was four pages and varied from four to eight columns wide. The first page carried news and advertisements. Other content included editorials, a limited amount of telegraphic news, marketing and commercial reports, and serialized fiction. International news was viewed as important or more important than local news. Technology had not moved south to any great extent, either, and most southern newspapers at the start of the Civil War were printed on hand presses.[8]

Probably the most successful and influential of the newspapers was the Richmond press. After the war, Whitelaw Reid, famous correspondent for the New York *Tribune*, wrote:

> The newspapers of Richmond, throughout the war, were in many respects the ablest on the continent. Their writing was often turgid, but it was always effective; and it shaped the public sentiment of the whole Confederacy. . . . In the midst of their destitution they managed to keep up double the number of average dailies that we had in Washington, and the editorials of each were generally the productions of educated thinkers, as well as red-hot partisans.[9]

The Richmond papers during the war, as papers elsewhere in the South, contained a variety of points of view within a limited framework. Although the newspapers criticized the Confederate Congress and President Jefferson Davis, they did not criticize the institution of slavery. Like northern papers, once the war began, newspapers quickly rallied to the cause. The war caused a great deal of hardship for many southern newspapers, but some managed to survive and actually flourish. The Richmond *Examiner*, for example, made a net profit of $50,000 during the last two years of the war, and maintained a subscription list that far surpassed the boundaries of Virginia. Other Richmond newspapers included the *Enquirer*, which early in the war had a reputation for being an organ of the Davis administration. The *Whig*, as its name implies, was a Whig paper that opposed secession; its editor, however, was

"Newspapers in Camp," a pencil and Chinese white drawing by Edwin Forbes. (Library of Congress Collection)

forced out in April 1861 and the *Whig* changed its editorial policies overnight. The Richmond *Dispatch*, patterned after the *Baltimore Sun*, represented the penny paper of Richmond. In March 1861 its circulation exceeded that of all Richmond newspapers combined; by the end of the war it was circulating to 30,000 readers. The *Sentinel*, which first appeared in March 1863, replaced the *Enquirer* as the organ of the administration. Another publication developed during the war was the *Southern Illustrated News*, highly sought after because *Harper's Weekly* was no longer available.[10]

In addition to the Richmond newspapers, strong press centers were located in New Orleans, Charleston, Augusta, Savannah, Atlanta, and Mobile. In Charleston, the *Courier* represented the moderate southern position, while the *Mercury* was the mouthpiece for the irascible Robert Barnwell Rhett, Jr., a fire-eating secessionist who was highly critical of Confederate President Davis.

One of the most interesting of the Southern newspapers was the *Memphis Appeal*, sometimes dubbed the "Moving Appeal," which kept ahead of advancing Union armies and published from various cities in Georgia, Mississippi, and Alabama as well as from a railroad flat car. Valued at $75,000 at the start of the war, the *Appeal* was considered one of the "finest examples of Confederate journalism."[11]

Many changes that occurred in newspapers in the North during the war also characterized changes in southern journalism, but southern newspapers were harder hit with rising news costs and difficulties of obtaining news. In the South, as in the North, newspapers ran more prominent headlines, not often crossing the column rule, but extending for many decks vertically. Southern newspapers were characterized by a marked increase in telegraphic news, "extras," the development of newsboy sales over subscriptions, employment of "specials" or correspondents, and the development of cooperative news gathering. News and editorials gradually replaced the advertisements on page one.

However, the high cost of and sheer lack of newsprint forced editors to print on standard writing paper and, at times, even the reverse side of wallpaper. At the start of the war, only 5 percent of the nation's paper mills were located in the South, and once the war was underway, no paper could be imported from the North. Imports from England were unlikely and, as the war progressed, nonexistent. Newspapers that cost five dollars a year before the War sold for fifty to sixty dollars, and on occasion reached $125 at the end of the war. Editors reduced the size of their newspapers; by 1865, the Charleston *Courier* was publishing only a single ten-by-fifteen inch sheet. Editors also used homemade ink substitutes, such as shoeblack.

Manpower was another problem. Of the 800 printers in the South in 1863, by June 1864, 75 percent had been in the army. During the first year of the war forty newspapers in Virginia collapsed; fifty out of sixty in Texas did not survive. Many ceased from lack of economic support, manpower, and supplies, and others were destroyed in the wake of advancing Union armies. By the time that Lee surrendered at Appomattox in April 1865, only twenty dailies were still publishing.

CORRESPONDENTS

After the Battle of Bull Run, newspapers geared up for a longer war, and began to send correspondents or "specials" to the field. Estimates of cost and numbers vary. Some historians claim the *New York Herald* spent half a million dollars covering the Civil War and had as many as sixty-three correspondents in the field. Other estimate that together, the *Times*, the *Tribune*, the *Post* and the *Herald* in New York spent $100,000 a year covering the war. The *New York Times* and the *New York Tribune* may have had as many as twenty reporters covering a major battle. The *Chicago Tribune* claimed to have had twenty-

"News from the front—the Army Correspondent," a pencil and Chinese white drawing by Edwin Forbes, circa 1876. (Library of Congress Collection)

seven reporters in the field, although it is not likely that many wrote simultaneously.[12] On South Mountain, Maryland, a stone arch memorializes 147 artists and reporters who covered the war. The arch reads:

> To the Army correspondents and artists 1861–1865 whose toils cheered the camps, thrilled the fireside, educated provinces of rustics into a bright nation of readers and gave incentive to narrate distant wars and explore dark lands.[13]

Northern correspondents generally were fairly well educated, with several graduates of Harvard, Yale, and other universities among the corps. Many later distinguished themselves as correspondents in other wars, in other areas of newspapers or as professionals in other fields.

Correspondents on both sides were regarded as combatants and often were as endangered as were the soldiers. Standard equipment for reporters included a revolver, field glasses, notebook, blanket(s), a sack for provisions,

> **PERSONNE REPORTS FROM GEORGIA**
>
> Augusta, Ga., March 1, 1862
>
> Notwithstanding all the predictions which the public ear has heard for the last month concerning the fall of Charleston and Savannah, that event appears to be just as far in the distance as the first. In fact, time has so narrowed down the probabilities of a Federal success, that the people of Savannah, at least, are now satisfied of their ability to hold the city against any odds. Yet the preparations for defence still continue. Fortifications against approaches by land are nearly, if not quite complete, and those protecting the water front are deemed equally efficient to resist an attack from that division.
>
> The city is eminently free from excitement — there is marrying and giving in marriages, parties and sociables are mighty woven into the web of social life, while business continues active and undisturbed. Along the river many of the planters have removed their negros, rice and valuables, in accordance with a military order to that effect; but from the town itself there have been comparatively few withdrawals of refugees to the interior. One can hardly say the same for Charleston.
>
> SOURCE. Felix de Fontaine (Personne), reprinted in the Collections of the Georgia Historical Society, June 1959.

and a horse; outfitting a correspondent was an expensive venture. They were, in some cases, a picturesque lot; the *New York Tribune* took special pride in having its correspondents look more dashing than the next. Probably the most colorful, however, was William Howard Russell of *The Times* of London, who arrived in a khaki "himalayan" suit. He was entertained at the White House and covered the First Battle of Bull Run. After his account of the "disgraceful conduct of the troops . . . a miserable causeless panic . . . scandalous behavior," however, he lost favor, and the *New York Illustrated News* pictured him as a "swinish boozer who viewed the battle from a safe remove through bleary eyes and a spyglass."[14] Northern newspapers were not ready to accept a negative English account of their beloved Northern Army.

Competition to get the news first governed the actions of correspondents and, in some cases, wrote Louis Starr, "drove them to bribery, subterfuge, plagiarism, and outright fakery. It fueled the whole news revolution. It left a residue of anecdote and legend which enriched the lore of American journalism."[15] Among the most well-known of the northern correspondents were Murat Halstead of the *Cincinnati Commercial*, Henry Stanley of the *New York Herald*, Whitelaw Reid of the *Cincinnati Gazette*, and Albert D. Richardson and George W. Smalley of the *New York Tribune*.[16]

More than 100 army correspondents represented the Confederate press during the war. Reporters commonly used pseudonyms, and if they wrote for more than one newspaper, might use several pseudonyms. Felix de Fontaine thus wrote under the pseudonym "Personne," a still-anonymous correspondent under the name of "Shadow," and another preeminent southern correspondent, Peter Alexander, under the initials of PWA. Salaries varied from six dollars per day to twenty-five dollars a week. One reporter, during a two-and-one-half year period, earned about $12,000.[17]

CENSORSHIP IN THE NORTH

Censorship in the North began shortly after the outbreak of the war. It was carried out not only by official decree by the departments of State and War, but also individually by commanders of troops. For the most part it was ineffectual. Although the government could successfully prohibit the transmission of news from Washington via the telegraph or the railroad, it could rarely stop dissemination of news from the fields of battle. Defying the censors, however, was not an idle move. Many reporters were arrested, and some court-martialed, for their refusal to cooperate with often rigid restrictions.

In 1861, after two attempts by Secretary of State Seward and General Scott to quash the telegraphic transmission of news about troop movements, the press and Scott agreed on censorship procedures about two weeks before the first major Union defeat, the Battle of Bull Run. Scott agreed that no prior censorship would be required if newsmen would not report by telegraph troop movements, mutinies or riots among soldiers, or predictions of troop movements. As the Sunday afternoon of the battle approached, Washingtonians drove to Manassas in their carriages, carrying picnics and expecting to watch a rout of rebel troops and an end to the Civil War. What they found was a Confederate victory.

As correspondents rushed to correct earlier accounts predicting a Union victory, General Scott imposed strict censorship on the telegraph. Not until reporters found that Monday morning editions of the New York papers carried news of a Union victory did they realize their stories had been stopped. Although Washington newspapers could carry the news of the dramatic defeat, out-of-town newspapers were stuck with old and grossly inaccurate information.

Attempts at cooperative agreements broke down on both sides—military and press. In the summer of 1861, General McClellan attempted another cooperative agreement, but it was ineffective, and on August 10 the War Department issued orders that no information regarding troop movements would be telegraphed from Washington except directly after battles. Newspaper correspondents also were prohibited from writing any information about troop movements or information "respecting the troops, camps, arsenals, entrenchments, or military affairs within the several military districts."[18] Correspondents printed such information with the threat of court-martial and the death penalty under the 57th Article of War.

In February 1862, telegraphic censorship was transferred from the State Department to the War Department and all telegraph lines were transferred to military control. The War Department ordered that any newspaper transmitting information not approved specifically by the War Department or a commanding general would no longer receive or distribute information or publications by telegraph or rail. Editorial opposition was so strong the order was modified the next day to allow publication of some "past facts". A vague Post Office order issued in March further restricted the press and confused the situation. The War Department also harassed several reporters after threatening to seriously enforce its regulations. On April 12, Secretary of War Stanton, in an attempt to standardize censorship, abolished local control and replaced it with a parole system. Correspondents were again prohibited from printing information about locations of generals, divisions, numbers of troops, kinds of arms, rations, transports used for movements, references to camp locations, or pictorial representations of lines of defense. The restrictions were rigid, but were not rigidly enforced.

Although criticism or praise of generals often influenced access to information for correspondents, reporters probably faced more difficulties with General William T. Sherman than with any other general. Criticism of Sherman in the 1861 Kentucky campaign started the feud. The *Cincinnati Commercial* called the general "stark mad," and erroneously claimed he had been relieved of his command. Sherman tried to expel all reporters from his army thereafter, but they were determined to follow him and report military activities. He is reputed to have said about newsmen:

> They come into camp, poke about among the lazy shirks and pick up their camp rumors and publish them as facts, and the avidity with which these rumors are swallowed by the public makes even some of our officers bow to them. I will not. They are a pest and shall not approach me and I will treat them as spies, which in truth they are.[19]

In December 1862, Sherman's battle with the press culminated in the court-martial of Thomas Knox, a *New York Herald* reporter who violated Sherman's order against reporting an abortive Union attempt to seize Vicksburg, Mississippi. Knox enclosed a map with his story and sent it to a collaborator in Cairo, Illinois, but one of Sherman's aides opened the letter. Knox then went to

Cairo by boat and telegraphed a story claiming that Sherman was incompetent. Sherman ordered Knox's arrest and charged him with disobeying orders and giving intelligence to the enemy. Knox was convicted of disobeying orders but escaped the heavier charge, which carried the death penalty, because Sherman could not prove he was giving the enemy information. Knox was told not to return to the war front. Lincoln, however, revoked the sentence and told Knox he had to stay away from the army unless he received permission from General Grant to accompany the troops, permission which Grant would not give without Sherman's approval. Sherman's battle with the press continued, and he once remarked that the only two successful campaigns in the war succeeded because of the absence of the newspaper reporters. When Sherman completed his successful march to the sea, he cut the telegraph wires to delay the transmission of information. And, after the war, it is said that he refused to shake hands with Horace Greeley because the *Tribune* revealed certain details of his Carolina campaign in 1863, which resulted in heavy losses.[20]

Lincoln was generally tolerant of the press, even though it often criticized his administration and the actions of his commanding generals. In June 1863, when General A. E. Burnside ordered the *Chicago Times* closed and prohibited the *New York World* from circulating in the Midwest, Lincoln remanded the order. He directed the secretary of war to say that the irritation produced by such acts would be more harmful than publication of critical information. Lincoln then ordered that arrest of civilians and suppression of newspapers could not be initiated except under presidential order.

Even Lincoln, however, could be pushed too far. In May 1864, he ordered the New York *Journal of Commerce* and the *New York World* closed and their proprietors arrested for publishing a forged presidential proclamation announcing a draft of 400,000 men. Major General John A. Dix investigated the incident and reported to Secretary of War Stanton that the editors were honestly duped. The men were freed after two days when Dix discovered the forgerer, a *New York Times* reporter, Joseph Howard. Howard confessed that the editors had nothing to do with the fraud.

CENSORSHIP IN THE SOUTH

The Confederate government kept tight control of information issued from the early Confederate capital of Montgomery, Alabama, from the first declaration of independence from the Union. The meeting of the Confederate Congress in secret session made it even more difficult for correspondents to obtain hard news in the Confederate capital. When the capital was moved to Richmond, Virginia, in late May 1861, reporters followed, but the same tight rein on news dissemination continued. During the same month the Provisional Congress of the Confederate States passed a bill empowering the president to censor telegraphic dispatches, an act that encountered little public opposition. The act authorized agents to censor telegraph messages, required telegraph employees to take an oath of allegiance to the Confederacy, and prohibited coded messages. The act also imposed penalties of fine and imprisonment for persons convicted of "sending news detrimental to the Southern cause by telegraph."[21]

Brigadier General Braxton Bragg, commanding forces in Pensacola, Florida, with the intent of reducing the federally occupied Fort Pickens, also was reluctant to give correspondents free rein. The same day that Fort Sumter surrendered Bragg ordered L. H. Mathews of the *Pensacola Observer* arrested and charged him with alerting the enemy to a possible attack on Fort Pickens. Mathews was acquitted and released within a few days, but the incident demonstrated the heavy hand of Bragg in dealing with the press. Throughout the fall campaign secrecy was heavily imposed on southern correspondents and they risked being treated as spies in almost every instance. In October, the *Mobile Advertiser and Register* said, "The Richmond papers announce that all civilians are now rigidly excluded from our lines at Manassas."[22]

By June, the censorship that postmasters had practiced before the war in prohibiting abolitionist and other mails from the North was enacted into law. Sometime between the summer of 1861 and 1862 the press and government agreed to voluntary censorship. Newspapers agreed to avoid news of troop movements, locations of forts, munitions, or gunboats. They were permitted to publish any military information regarding the enemy taken from northern newspapers.

Although southern newspaper editors strived to remain cautious and loyal, even they objected when in January 1862, a bill was proposed to subject any newspaper to severe penalties for publishing information vital to Confederate security. The bill did not pass. Military censorship, however, continued to severely restrict reporting.

The Confederate Press Association (PA), was formed in 1863 partly as a response to the severe censorship. Its general manager, J. S. Thrasher, exacted promises from the major military commanders to provide news when it was compatible with the public interest. He secured half-rates for telegraphing dispatches across military and civilian telegraph lines, and employed about twenty news agents to report the news. He instructed reporters to be objective, to discriminate carefully between fact and rumor, and "never to be beaten by a special correspondent."[23]

The association provided weekly reports of 3,500 words for a flat rate of twelve dollars. Newspapers were required to pay ten cents a word for additional material. During the first three months the PA spent from $17,000 to $18,000 for collecting and transmitting copyrighted news to the dailies and a

Photographer's Wagon by T.H. O'Sullivan, Carson desert, Nevada, 1870. (Library of Congress Collection)

few triweeklies of the Confederacy. The service also acted as a cooperative, with individual newspapers providing information from their own locales. The association encountered many difficulties with the military, and with maintaining the cooperation of the newspapers themselves, but on the whole succeeded in a way that individual newspapers would not have been able to.

The effectiveness of Confederate censorship declined after 1863, partly due to the formation of the PA, but also due to the declining morale and level of control of the government itself.

PHOTOGRAPHY AND PICTORIAL ILLUSTRATION

Entrepreneurs, artists, and scientists experimented with various forms of cameras as early as the days of the Renaissance, but not until the 1830s did photographic development proceed enough to allow the recording of permanent images. Louis Daguerre in 1837 designed a process to develop positive photographic plates, which used burnished copper as a base and a thin silvered negative emulsion with unexposed particles that could be washed away in a solvent. Although the daguerreotype was received with acclaim, the process was limited because copies could not be made and subjects had to stand frozen for twenty to thirty minutes, the time required to expose a plate.

From 1837 to 1840, the development of an improved camera lens provided a more brilliant image, the light sensitivity of photographic plates was increased by recoating the plates with different chemicals, and the harsh tones of the daguerreotype were softened by gilding the plate with gold chloride. These developments made it possible to create a portrait that closely resembled the subject, but they did not shorten exposure time.

Daguerre's work coincided with the development of a positive-negative process by British scientists William Henry Fox Talbot and Sir John Herschel. Such a process allowed for multiple prints. In 1851, however, the emergence of the collodion process, which provided durable glass negatives and a shorter exposure time, revolutionized the portrait business, for which photography was commercially used. Glass plates were coated with collodion, a mixture of guncotton in alcohol and ether, developed in silver nitrate, exposed while wet and then developed. In 1871 the use of dry plates replaced the initial collodion process, cutting exposure time to seconds.

Photographers in the United States usually came from the ranks of graphic artists, and sought to record information rather than to produce art. However, the large format technology that was available precluded the capturing of action shots. During the 1850s, the perfection of shorter focal-length stereographic cameras enabled photographers to freeze some types of action, and ultimately led to the photographing of war. Although Roger Fenton, a British photographer, photographed British army personnel during the Crimean War, the American Civil War was the first conflict to be photographed thoroughly. Mathew Brady, the photographer with the eye of an historian, directed most of the pictorial coverage.[24]

Brady was a popular portrait photographer in 1844 in New York. Although some of his photographs were published before the war, technology had not yet arrived to make photographic publication inexpensive. Even during the Civil War, the *New York Herald*'s maps had to be engraved by hand in pieces by several engravers to meet edition time. Similarly, Brady's photographs could only provide models for artists and line engravers. The lack of adequately reproduced photographs is attested to by the fact that in 1864, after Grant's victories, the Washington press corps did not know the general by sight.

By July 1861, Brady had acquired permission from the federal government to accompany troops at his own expense. He photographed the Union

"*Showman in Camp,*" *at the Culpeper Virginia Court House, about September 1863. This pencil drawing by Edwin Forbes appeared in* Frank Leslie's Illustrated Newspaper *January 9, 1864. (Library of Congress Collection)*

flight at the Battle of Bull Run, following the army with a traveling dark room, supplied with photographic plates, plate holders, negative boxes, tripods, and cameras. Exactly how many of the famous photographs that carried the byline, "by Brady," were actually taken by him is debatable; Brady hired twenty photographers, but always retained the credit for himself. One historian suggests that Brady, whose eyesight was failing by the time of the war, may not personally have photographed any of the Civil War.[25] Historians agree, however that Brady's organization and leadership secured the pictorial history of the Civil War we now have. Because he traveled with Union armies, his photographs of Union soldiers, camps and battle action are more varied than his coverage of the Confederate Army, which consists primarily of dead and wounded soldiers and destroyed southern towns. Brady's photographs, as reproduced by artists, gave the public something to digest other than the glory of war, and one *New York Times* writer described it well:

> Mr. Brady has done something to bring home to us the terrible reality and earnestness of war. If he has not brought bodies and laid them on our dooryard and along our streets, he has done something very like it.[26]

The tragedy of Mathew Brady is that at the end of the war, the public no longer wanted to be treated to blood at the doorsteps, and demand for his photos was not what he had expected. The government ignored him also, and he died in poverty.

Conclusion

Newspaper editors entered the Civil War with small staffs in place and with a history of constantly attempting to expand news coverage and the speed with which it was delivered. They had limited experience in covering wars, however, and the nation had limited experience in dealing with the problems of press coverage of war.

Northern newspapers continued in the pattern set before the war and increased the size of their staffs, directed war coverage from the home office, and took greater advantage of the telegraph to speed news. Reliance on the expensive and erratic telegraph wires encouraged reporters to put the most critical information at the beginning of the story and to write short, eliminating the flowery phrases of the past. Nevertheless, despite such encouragement, reporters did not quickly give up their familiar styles. Editors criticized Lincoln, his military commanders, and his strategies for winning the war.

Southern newspapers retained a more partisan flavor, and the high cost of supplies, the unavailability of materials toward the end of the war, and the Union occupation of southern cities took a heavy toll on the Confederate press. Organized under the Confederate Press Association, newspapers did, however, criticize southern military strategy within a narrow framework.

Censorship in the North remained in the official channels of the State and War departments, as well as in the hands of commanders in the field. Telegraph lines remained under military control, and reporters were restricted from writing about troop movements and other specific military information. The Confederate government also imposed censorship of the telegraph and of the reporting of military details. Abolitionist and other antislavery materials were excluded from the mails as well.

Pictorial illustration, as well as words, characterized coverage of the war. Mathew Brady and his crew of twenty photographers followed the army with a traveling darkroom and produced a pictorial record of the war.

Chapter 9 **Covering the Civil War: Correspondents and Censorship**

NOTES

1. For general information on the Civil War, consult Emerson David Fite, *Social and Industrial Conditions in the North During the Civil War* (New York: Ungar 1963); Allan Nevins, *The Emergence of Modern America, 1865–1878* (New York: The Macmillan Co., 1927); James M. Woods, *Rebellion and Realignment* (Fayetteville: University of Arkansas Press, 1987); and C. Vann Woodward, *Origins of the New South* (Baton Rouge: Louisiana State University Press, 1951).
2. This chapter synthesizes material from the definitive accounts of Civil War reporting by J. Cutler Andrews, *The North Reports the Civil War* (Pittsburgh, Pa.: University of Pittsburgh Press, 1955) and *The South Reports the Civil War* (Princeton, N.J.: Princeton University Press, 1970.) See also Phillip Knightley, *The First Casualty* (New York: Harcourt Brace Jovanovich, 1975). Knightley portrays Civil War reporters as "ignorant, dishonest and unethical," and their dispatches as "inaccurate, often invented, partisan and inflammatory." (p. 21).
3. Bernard Weisberger, *Reporters for the Union* (Boston: Little, Brown, 1953).
4. Lloyd Wendt, *Chicago Tribune: The Rise of a Great American Newspaper* (Chicago: Rand McNally & Company), 1979, p. 155.
5. Calder Pickett, ed., *Voices of the Past* (Columbus, Ohio: Grid, 1977), p. 128.
6. For a dramatic, but undocumented account of the early years of the Associated Press, see Oliver Gramling, *AP: The Story of News* (New York: Farrar, Straus & Giroux, 1940). For relationship of AP to European agencies, see Jonathan Fenby, *The International News Services* (New York: Schocken Books, 1986).
7. *Chicago Tribune*, October 3, 1861, cited in Wendt, *Chicago Tribune*, p. 163–4.
8. Andrews, *The South Reports the Civil War*, pp. 24–26.
9. Whitelaw Reid, *After the War* (Cincinnati and New York, 1866), p. 319, cited in Andrews, *The South Reports the Civil War*, p. 26.
10. Andrews, *The South Reports the Civil War*, p. 26.
11. Andrews, *The South Reports the Civil War*, p. 40.
12. See Meyer L. Stein, *Under Fire: The Story of American War Correspondents* (New York: Julian Messner, 1968) Wendt, *Chicago Tribune*; and Andrews, *The North Reports the Civil War*.
13. Stein, *Under Fire*, p. 14.
14. Stein, *Under Fire*, p. 15–16.
15. Louis Starr, *The Bohemian Brigade: Civil War Newsmen in Action* (Madison: University of Wisconsin Press, 1987), p. 232. Copyright first granted to Alfred A. Knopf, who published the book in 1954.
16. For Smalley's reminiscences, see *Anglo-American Memories* (New York and London: G.P. Putnam's Sons, 1911). See also Joseph J. Mathews, *George W. Smalley* (Chapel Hill: University of North Carolina Press, 1973). For other correspondents see F. Lauriston Bullard, *Famous War Correspondents* (Boston: Little, Brown, 1914).
17. See Jean Folkerts, "Felix Gregory de Fontaine (1834–1896)," *Dictionary of Literary Biography*, Perry Ashley, ed. (Detroit: Gale Research Co., 1985), vol 43: pp. 147–151.

PART 2 **EXPANSION AND CONFLICT**

18. Cited in Andrews, *The North Reports the Civil War*, p. 151 (f. 42).
19. Stein, *Under Fire*, p. 18.
20. See Andrews, *The North Reports the Civil War*, pp. 575–584.
21. Andrews, *The South Reports the Civil War*, p. 529.
22. *Mobile Advertiser and Register*, October 27, 1861, cited in Andrews, *The South Reports the Civil War*, p. 103.
23. Andrews, *The South Reports the Civil War*, p. 57.
24. Naomi Rosenblum, *A World History of Photography* (New York: Abbeville Press, 1984), pp. 162–184.
25. *Civil War Times*. August 1978, p. 20.
26. *New York Times* October 20, 1862, p. 5.

The "Lightning Steam Press," along with the electric telegraph, the locomotive, and the steamboat, was considered the "Progress of the Century" in this photograph taken from an 1876 Currier & Ives print. (Library of Congress Collection)

PART 3

MODERNIZATION
AND
REFORM

During the last half of the nineteenth century and the early years of the twentieth century, newspapers and the periodical press became intertwined with a dramatically changing society experiencing the effects of rapid modernization. The role of business grew dramatically as corporations formed to raise capital for large-scale enterprises, creating national markets, traversing the land with railroad tracks, and converting a largely agrarian society into an urban, national market economy.

Although the political debate of the early half of the nineteenth century — the relationship between local and national government — was not resolved, the debate now centered on the relationship of government to business. Only the national government could effectively respond to full development of the telegraph and railroad, which eliminated geographical boundaries and spanned many local governmental entities. However, the rapid urbanization that accompanied change during the period spawned the growth of huge cities, which posed new questions for local governments regarding city utilities, sanitation, and transportation.

As mass production quickly replaced artisan craftsmanship, a third major issue confronting the society was the increasing perception of capital and labor as separate classes. Critics of rapid modernization wondered whether the traditional values of democracy and social mobility could be retained in a society in which commercial values dominated, wealth became more concentrated, and social stratification became increasingly rigid. Critics also feared that massive immigration from Europe would bring to the United States a class oriented view of labor. Cultural chaos and corruption characterized one result of modernization, just as progress and wealth characterized another side of the Gilded Age.

Within the modernizing society, the newspaper and periodical press developed as large business institutions, although corporate or chain ownership did not expand as rapidly as in other industries. Rapid urbanization lent increasing credibility to metropolitan editors, who were viewed as cosmopolitan rather than local in outlook, and who advocated progress and used the new technologies to advance their own interests. Newspapers became bigger, more costly to start and to produce, and reliant on commercial advertising. Although political parties had influenced newspapers during the early half of the century, commercial interests transformed the press of the Gilded Age. Favorable postal legislation, new technology, national advertising, and a growing class of writers contributed to a rapidly growing magazine industry. Magazines appealed to elite interests, to women consumers, and, toward the end of the century, to the middle classes interested in reform.

As businessmen, newspaper editors declared their independence from party, and sought to influence government through the American Newspaper Publishers Association. Publishers cooperated with the U.S. Post Office to achieve favorable postal legislation in Congress. They also sought to control the activities of the organization of labor within the printing shops of newspapers. The Associated Press, through monopolistic agreements with Western Union, dominated the national and international news market. Reporters had little bargaining power over wages and time schedules, and sought to rationalize their own positions. Although they identified themselves as professionals, their status was more similar to that of laborers.

Newspaper publishers, who identified strongly with local business, often formed coalitions with political groups or other coalitions to attack the problems of the metropolis. Although they often were seen as antagonistic to monopolies, they also benefited from the public relations efforts of the railroad companies, which issued free travel passes to publishers, or from the efforts of others who sought favor with local publishers.

The content of newspapers reflected the celebration of city life and the diversity of its populations as well as the problems of the city and the issues of corruption and business exploitation. Some publishers created dramatically innovative layouts, complete with photographs and blaring headlines, striving for an expression of the teeming metropolis. Such sensational treatment offended the more traditional newspaper readers, who sought refuge in newspapers with an orientation toward information. The sensational trend in content represented the exuberance of growth and progress, while the informational trend sought to confront the new order with a mass of rational explanation.

The celebration of progress was not without trauma, and reform groups flourished during the period, fighting partially for what they viewed as traditional values of early nineteenth-century democracy, and partly for improved status of groups whose interests had been ignored or denied. Women, blacks, and agrarian radicals developed their own presses to share information not regarded as "news" by the mass press, to build a sense of community, and to legitimize their organizations.

In 1917, with the beginning of United States involvement in World War I, the nation, not quite at ease with the ramifications of the massive changes that had occurred during the past fifty years, reacted fearfully to independent expression. Socialist newspapers, foreign-language sheets, and pacifist publications lost the right to publish. Once again, the Post Office assumed the role of censorship, and the majority of metropolitan editors uttered scarcely a word of protest.

CHAPTER 10

GROWTH
AND
REUNIFICATION

There was a South of slavery and secession—that South is dead. There is a South of union and freedom—that South, thank God, is living, breathing, growing every hour.[1]

In December 1886, Henry Grady, prominent southern editor of the *Atlanta Constitution*, incorporated these words into his speech, "The New South," presented to the New England Society in the City of New York. Grady spoke eloquently of the New South, which he claimed had "sowed towns and cities in the place of theories and put business above politics." The South Grady described had "fallen in love with work," and had created "close and cordial" relations with the black. "The New South," Grady said, "is enamored of her new work. Her soul is stirred with the breath of a new life. . . . She is thrilling with the consciousness of growing power and prosperity."

Although Grady's description of the South was romanticized and exaggerated, he bespoke an attitude of prominent southern editors, who, in arguing that it was time to put the past behind and to industrialize, represented the modernizing forces of the South. These editors were "public figures of supreme importance," according to C. Vann Woodward, renowned southern historian. They were regarded in the 1880s as metropolitan and progressive, while local editors were considered merely to reflect local interests.[2] The metropolitan editors of the New South argued that the North should allow the South to rebuild without undue interference, and that rebuilding equaled industrialization.

A fascination with industrialization crossed geographical and sectional boundaries. Northern urban newspapers increasingly became a part of the industrial world they championed. First, they relied primarily on advertising, which in itself represented a developing industry, for financial support. Second, editors not only commented on dilemmas of modern industry—labor, technology, consolidation—but they also had to resolve the issues for their own increasingly large businesses. For the most part, newspaper editors responded as reactionary businessmen, using the First Amendment to champion private property rights as much as freedom of speech. Their traditional attitudes toward individualism, private property, and free enterprise limited their ability to deal with the problems of urbanization, which required an orientation toward a collective public community.[3] Although many editors advocated civil service reform to combat corruption and deplored the impersonalization of the business conglomerate, they were at a loss to provide remedies to the problems of industrialized, modern life in the metropolis. The consolidation of the Associated Press and its relationship to Western Union, which by 1866 held a virtual monopoly of telegraph services, further indicated the broad institutionalization of the press, dominated by commercial news values.

Reconstruction

Reconstruction did not occur within a vacuum. The North, faced with economic hard times during the panic of 1873, was dealing with other problems of immigration and unionization. The country expanded its territory, as Secretary of State Seward purchased Alaska from Russia in 1872 for $7.2 million.

He was laughed at for "Seward's folly," but the purchase was completed. The United States also took control of the Midway Islands during 1872, islands that would remain unknown to most citizens until World War II.

What brought the South to industrialization and the North to abandonment of equal rights? In April 1865, the surrender of Lee's army at Appomattox signaled the end of the Civil War. If one is to believe Henry Grady, in twenty years the South rejected the slavery and agriculture of its past, welcomed freed blacks with, if not open arms, at least equal and protective legislation, and forged new coalitions to industrialize and prepare for the future. The transition had not been easy, and it was not so complete as Henry Grady presented it to be.

The years of 1865 to 1880 represented not only years of industrial growth for the South, but also the loss of the dream of equality for southern and northern blacks. Political reunification was achieved, but cheap labor in the South that promoted local industry also contributed to and benefited from industrial strife in the North.

After Lincoln's assassination, the southern president, Andrew Johnson, created a reconstruction plan that pardoned most Southerners, permitted antebellum aristocrats to regain power, and witnessed the development of black codes that carried many provisions of the former slave codes. But northern Republicans rejected Johnson's reconstruction plan when Congress convened in January 1866, and initiated a plan of their own. They ran into quick conflict with the president as they refused to seat Southerners elected under Johnson's reconstructed civilian governments.

In 1866, a Republican Congress enacted two bills: one that expanded the duties of the Bureau of Refugees, Freedmen and Abandoned Lands, and a Civil Rights Act, which granted freedmen protection of federal citizenship and authorized troops to enforce the act. Although Johnson vetoed both bills, Congress overrode the vetoes. Congress was afraid that the conservative Supreme Court would declare the laws void, and thus turned to the work of creating the Fourteenth Amendment. Although the amendment was not adopted until 1868, its basic content was determined in 1866. The first section conferred citizenship on freedmen and prohibited states from abridging constitutional "privileges and immunities." The amendment also prevented states from taking a person's life, liberty, or property "without due process of law" and from denying "equal protection of the law." This section later was interpreted to mean that corporations were to be regarded legally as individuals. This interpretation gave corporations in the 1880s and 1890s broad protection from prosecution by states. In the 1960s, the amendment gained yet another meaning in enforcing civil rights legislation during that decade. The amendment represented major compromises, however, especially in allowing states to deny blacks the right to vote, as long as their representation was reduced proportionately.

In the congressional elections of 1866, Republicans gained strength, and sentiment against Johnson grew. In 1867, with the passage of the Military Reconstruction Act, Johnson's civilian governments were replaced by military authority until new elections could be held. Freedmen were guaranteed the right to vote in elections for state constitutional conventions and state governments. Each southern state was required to ratify the Fourteenth Amendment, ratify its new constitution and submit the constitution to Congress for approval. President Johnson's objections to Congress's actions and further conflict resulted in the impeachment of the president. However, he was not removed from office, for the Senate failed by one vote to convict. But Johnson's days were numbered and Ulysses S. Grant, former Union general, became president in 1868.

The few years after the war represented some gains for blacks, although the time was short and the gains limited. Black people immediately gave education a high priority, and black students flocked to schools and books, both of which had been prohibited under slave codes. Between 1866 and 1869, the American Missionary Association founded seven black colleges. The Freedmen's Bureau helped establish Howard University in Washington, D.C. And by 1877, 600,000 black children were attending elementary school. Blacks focused on educational, political, and economic gains during those years and for the most part did not protest the segregation that was rapidly developing. Black leaders, particularly those who won public office, tended to be prewar elite, rather than former slaves. Land reform, which initially was given some attention by radical Republicans, never was achieved. Sharecropping originated as a desirable compromise, giving blacks freedom from daily supervision or working under a white overseer, and maintaining control by whites. The system soon became one of abuse as blacks and whites suffered from the decline in cotton markets and blacks suffered from the unscrupulousness of white landowners and furnishing merchants.

Republicans won majorities everywhere except in Georgia in the 1868 elections, and sixteen blacks were elected to Congress. Although these numbers raised cries of "Negro Rule" and spearheaded the formation of the Ku Klux Klan in the South, blacks continued to participate in government in far lower proportions than they were represented in the population. The claims of the South were grossly distorted. The reconstruction governments that followed the election produced more democratic constitutions, broadened voting and property rights, and stimulated industry. Manufacturing in the South doubled between 1860 and 1880, and the railway system was rebuilt. But such growth had consequences. Taxes had to be increased to support growth, and charges of graft and corruption reverberated throughout the South. Unfortunately, the charges were true, but corruption was not just a southern problem; it was a national problem.

During and after the Civil War, blacks left the South to seek a better life. This photograph shows fugitive blacks crossing the Rappahannock River in Virginia in 1862. (Library of Congress Collection)

The new governments failed to alter the social structure or distribution of wealth in the South. To reform the social order Congress would have had to redistribute land, a reform that was never seriously considered. At the end of Reconstruction, despite some political and educational gains, blacks remained dependent on whites for food, work, and land.

During the 1870s, many Democrats regained control of state governments. The North tired of the situation and wanted reconciliation with southern states. In addition, the Supreme Court aided the northern retreat from equality for blacks through interpretations of the Fourteenth and Fifteenth amendments that narrowed the meanings and gave the states power once again to disenfranchise blacks. In 1870 and 1871, federal laws were passed against the Ku Klux Klan, and the Klan went underground, replaced in part by local vigilante groups. In 1872, Congress adopted a sweeping amnesty act for most Confederates.

By 1876, Reconstruction was over. Samuel J. Tilden, New York Democratic governor, ran for the presidency against Rutherford B. Hayes. The election deadlocked in Congress, and the South exacted concessions, while letting the Republican Hayes gain the presidency. Kentucky editor Henry Watterson, now in Congress, strictly opposed the compromise but relented in the end. Watterson's Louisville *Courier-Journal* and Dana's *New York Sun* were on the same side in this election, supporting Tilden. In 1877, dismayed at the state of affairs in the South, blacks banded together to move to Kansas in what became known as the "Exoduster" movement. Between 1880 and 1918, more than 2,400 blacks were lynched in the South. Even northern newspapers abandoned the black. Woodward wrote that the *Nation*, edited by Edwin Godkin,

> thought the government should "have nothing more to do with him," and Godkin could not see how the Negro could ever "be worked into a system of government for which you and I would have much respect." The New York *Tribune*, with a logic all its own, stated that the Negroes, after having been given "ample opportunity to develop their own latent capacities," had only succeeded in proving that "as a race they are idle, ignorant, and vicious."[4]

Although the number of farms doubled in the South between 1860 and 1880 and the size of the average farm decreased by half, the statistics are misleading; in 1880, one-third of southern farmers were tenants and sharecroppers; that number had grown to two-thirds by 1920. But industrial development progressed. The 1870s witnessed wide development of textile mills employing cheap, unorganized labor; from 1890 to 1900, the iron, steel, and lumber industries expanded as northern capital and companies moved southward.

Manufacturing and advertising

Before the Civil War, manufacturing industries included flour and grain milling, lumber, and sawmills—the type of industry primarily devoted to processing raw materials and agricultural products into materials consumers used to make bread, build houses, or create other products. "It would be hard to conceive of developing a consumer allegiance to the flour of a local grist mill or the lumber of a particular saw mill," wrote advertising historian Daniel Pope. At that time advertising as an industry was nonexistent. Between 1860 and 1880, the sheer numbers of manufacturing industries grew dramatically, and the type of manufacturing changed as well. While the largest pre–Civil

This advertisement for Payn's Sure-Raising Flour indicated the move toward brand-name products which spurred the development of advertising. (Library of Congress Collection)

War factory was the Merrimack Textile Mill, which employed 2,000 individuals in 1854, by 1900, at least seventy plants each employed as many people.[5] As industries became more capital intensive and increased their output, manufacturers needed to sell more products to stay in business.

Other changes accompanied the rapid growth of manufacturing. Transportation networks developed that broadened the market, allowing a volume of goods to be shipped to a single place. Specialized distribution systems created marketing and service areas, and specialized media such as streetcar placards developed to advertise products in particular locales. Urban Americans bought more goods and services, producing fewer at home. Large scale capitalism appeared in response to excess capacity and destabilizing price competition.[6]

SPACE BUYERS

In 1842, when a few entrepreneurs began to see income-earning potential in advertising, the emphasis was on buying space in volume from a publisher at a discount and, after levying a heavy markup, selling it to advertisers. Volney Palmer, considered to be the first advertising agent, earned as much as 25 percent commission on his sales, but his business was limited because he refused to guarantee payment to publications carrying advertisements he solicited, and he demanded exclusive agreements. In 1865, George P. Rowell, operating in New England, began buying and selling space. He offered businessmen an inch in 100 newspapers per month for an annual fee of $100 and calculated that if he sold half the space he bought he would net $5,500 on an investment of $7,500.

In 1867, Carlton and Smith, a New York agency, bought space in religious magazines, then resold it to advertisers and soon dominated this specialized market. In 1870, it was estimated the religious market had a potential of 400 weeklies with a total circulation of 5 million.[7] A popular employee, J. Walter Thompson, took over the agency in 1878, expanded into the general magazine field, and headed an agency that today is still one of the largest in the field.

In the late nineteenth century, the advertising business had its share of charlatans, as well as its share of respectable businessmen. This fact, coupled with questions about whether the agent's loyalty was to the publisher or to the advertiser, placed the ad man in a dubious position. Publishers grumbled about the discounted rates the agent demanded, and advertisers complained that they had no guarantee of circulation rates or their ads being placed in the most suitable publications. While both publisher and advertiser needed the agent to negotiate the buying and selling of space, both also viewed him as the exploiter.

During the late 1800s, N.W. Ayer, a major advertising agency founded in 1869, experimented with the "open contract," charging advertisers directly for their work, rather than basing their fee on the commission paid by the publisher. However, few agencies followed suit and the commission controversy remained strong through the 1920s.

By 1900, space agents were experiencing many difficulties. Newspaper directories, such as the one designed by George P. Rowell, provided advertisers with a variety of information about newspapers and other publications, which made it possible for them to place their own advertising. Advertisers no longer were quite so blind in regard to their market. A multiplicity of agents and heavy competition further took its toll, and many of the early agencies collapsed. Newspapers also experimented with employing their own people to sell space, a method that worked only for large, metropolitan papers because small rural newspapers could not afford to send an agent to New York to negotiate for national advertising. Newspaper publishers continued to balk at the heavy commission, and in the 1890s, they often were successful in reducing the commission to 10 or 15 percent.

NEWSPAPERS AFTER THE CIVIL WAR

Between 1860 and 1878, the growth and modernization of newspapers intensified. Newspapers developed platforms attacking massive corruption in national and local politics, and responded to widespread industrial and economic change. Editors in the 1870s often responded to local issues similar to the way magazines would respond to national problems in the late 1890s and early 1900s. By 1870, nearly 10 million people lived in the nation's cities, and by 1890, those cities had installed mass transit, a process that spawned urban spread and real estate development. As cities grew and changed, metropolitan newspapers gained increasing credibility as purveyors of news, as mediators in city life, and as social arbiters of the community. The newspaper, from the penny-press days until the 1890s, was "intimately connected with the complexity of life in the modern city," Gunther Barth noted in his study of nineteenth century cities. A shift in values saw the minister replaced by the editor as the conscience of the community, and migrants from the countryside and immigrants from abroad regarded the newspaper as providing information that would help them adapt to city life and to a new language and culture.[8]

Barth wrote that the metropolitan newspaper was the bridge between over-the-fence gossip and telephone chatting. But the newspaper also was concerned with political aspects of the city: crime and corruption. In the years following the war, the focus was on exposing, rather than on reforming, but the exposure helped pave the way for serious reform efforts.

CRIME AND CORRUPTION

Thomas Leonard, in his study of political reporting, *The Power of the Press*, suggested that crime reporting of penny papers was connected to exposures of local and national corruption later in the century. When James Gordon Bennett's *Herald* reported the Robinson-Jewett affair in 1836, it connected personal crime to societal stability: "The death of Ellen Jewett is the natural result of a state of society and morals which ought to be reformed. . . . It as naturally springs from our general guilt and corruption as the pestilence does from the waters of death stagnating under an August sun." Leonard noted that "Bennett was just as sure that powerful men were corrupt as he was that fallen women were violent. . . . In turning vice into big news the press of Jacksonian America insisted that an investigation of the sordid facts revealed a general pattern of corruption in society."[9] Leonard further wrote that "the muckrakers of the first years of the new century were the legitimate heirs of the crime story and the first to make the whole nation take notice."[10] Such a contention describes development of editorial attitudes and news conventions as evolutionary, rather than as representing isolated characteristics of newspapers in a particular period.

POLITICAL INDEPENDENCE AND CORRUPTION

In the 1870s, newspapers intensified their claim of independence from political parties, recognizing that commercial interests now made strong partisan affiliations a liability. Joseph Pulitzer, writing in St. Louis, was one of the first editors to claim that partisan politics in covering local issues no longer paid. As advertisers became more essential to newspapers than did powerful political groups, newspapers covered city life from the bottom up as well as covering municipal corruption. In St. Louis, Pulitzer criticized the high profits and poor service of gas and streetcar monopolies, published questionable real estate deals, described fraud at the polls, and attacked the traditional institutions of vice—the brothels and the gambling halls.

But although Pulitzer may have been responsible for putting a few men in jail and improving a few public services, corruption continued in St. Louis.[11] Similarly, the *New York Times* and *Harper's Weekly*, despite their vivid pictorial and factual criticism of Boss Tweed and Tammany Hall corruption in New York City, were unable to punish most of those who had stolen from the city's treasury or to destroy the city's political machine, although Boss Tweed eventually went to jail in disgrace. As the taste for exposure of one situation faded, journalists were seldom able to present remedies or persuade citizens to think about alternative forms of city government.[12] In some cities in the 1890s, this situation changed as newspapers limited competition among themselves, decreased their partisanship, and joined forces with broad based municipal reform groups.[13]

LABOR

Newspapers were concerned with labor disputes and unionization from the 1830s on, not only in terms of editorial content but also in terms of negotiat-

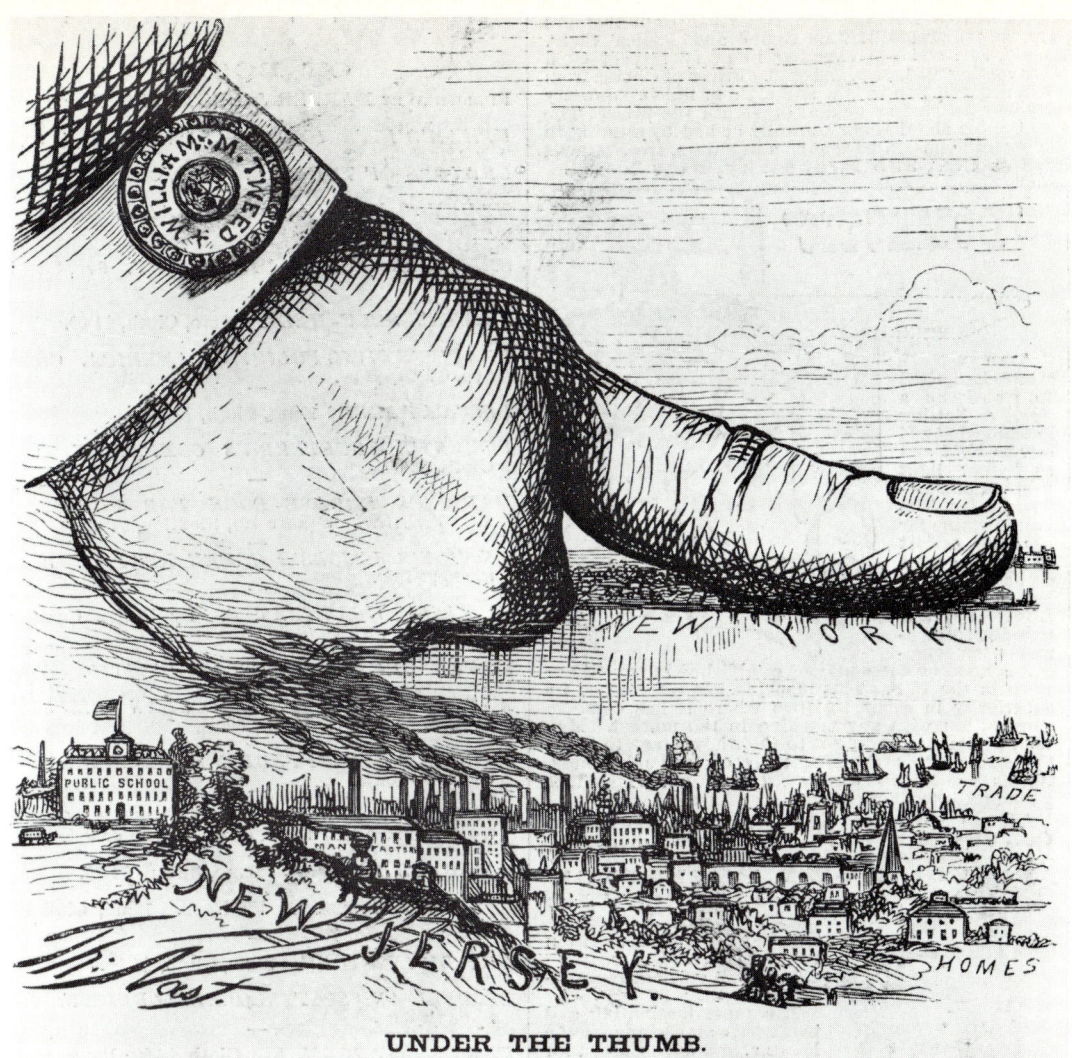

UNDER THE THUMB.

THE BOSS. "Well, what are you going to do about it?"

This political cartoon, titled "Under the Thumb," was created by Thomas Nast and appeared in Harper's Weekly *during the summer of 1871. (Library of Congress Collection)*

ing with labor unions in the production and distribution of the newspaper as a manufactured product. The Typographical Association of New York in 1831 began to object to increased mechanization and to child labor, an issue that followed editors into the second decade of the twentieth century. The union also fought against editors' efforts to increase immigrant labor, a practice designed to decrease wages. Although various printers' unions operated with some success until 1837, the financial recession hit labor hard, and by 1840 the New York association folded.

Printers began to reorganize in the 1840s, and found support from some editors. Horace Greeley, editor of the *New York Tribune*, was president of the New York Printers' Union, organized in 1850. James Gordon Bennett editorialized in the *Herald* April 8, 1850, noting that "strikes which commenced among the mechanics and workingmen of this city a short time since are still going on, and we must again express our satisfaction at the manner in which these strikes and meetings continue to be conducted."[14] Such support by newspaper editors soon faded, however.

In 1852, the National Typographical Union, predecessor to the International Typographical Union, was officially organized. Membership grew dramatically after the Civil War, and the union worked to assure that as new machinery was developed, union men were trained and ready to operate that equipment. The union focused on specialization and effectively adapted in most cases to the introduction of new technology.

As early as 1860, the union promoted the idea of an eight-hour working day for printers, and twenty years later it joined the nationwide, industry-wide movement for the eight-hour day. Although some gains were achieved in setting hours for different types of workers, it was not until 1908, a series of strikes, and strong opposition from the American Newspaper Publishers' Association, that the eight-hour day was incorporated into general practice. During the years after World War I, the union movement was labeled un-American and denounced even more thoroughly by America's publishers.

NEWSPAPER TECHNOLOGY

Rapid developments in newspaper technology after the Civil War paralleled growth in manufacturing as a whole. The interplay of technology, continued urbanization, and the concept of covering the city from the bottom up produced newspapers that were graphically different, incorporated display advertising, and continued to expand in new areas such as evening and Sunday editions.

Newsprint

Rapid advances in processes for converting wood to paper reduced the price of newsprint. Although a variety of attempts to substitute cotton for linen rags, and wood or straw pulp for rags had been experimented with since 1800, only in the 1860s did successful processes for converting wood pulp take hold.

This perfecting press was built by A.B. Taylor & Company for Frank Leslie's Illustrated Newspaper *(Library of Congress Collection)*

In 1870, eight woodpulp plants in the United States produced newsprint; by 1880, 50 plants were in operation, and by 1890, 82 plants were in production. The price of paper had surged during the Civil War, due not only to the war itself, but also to collaboration by paper makers and the development of trade associations. The price surged again briefly about 1868, but then dropped steadily until the beginning of World War II. From the 1880s on, there was a sharp increase in newsprint consumption, which reflected increased circulation, additional pages and the decline in the price of newsprint.

Other Technology

Stereotyping had been experimented with as early as 1727, and the *New York Herald* began using stereotyped plates, along with *La Presse* of Paris and *The Times* of London. The process used a papier-mâché mat made from type forms instead of putting the type forms on the press. The method much reduced the wear and tear on the type, which was a considerable problem for publishers.

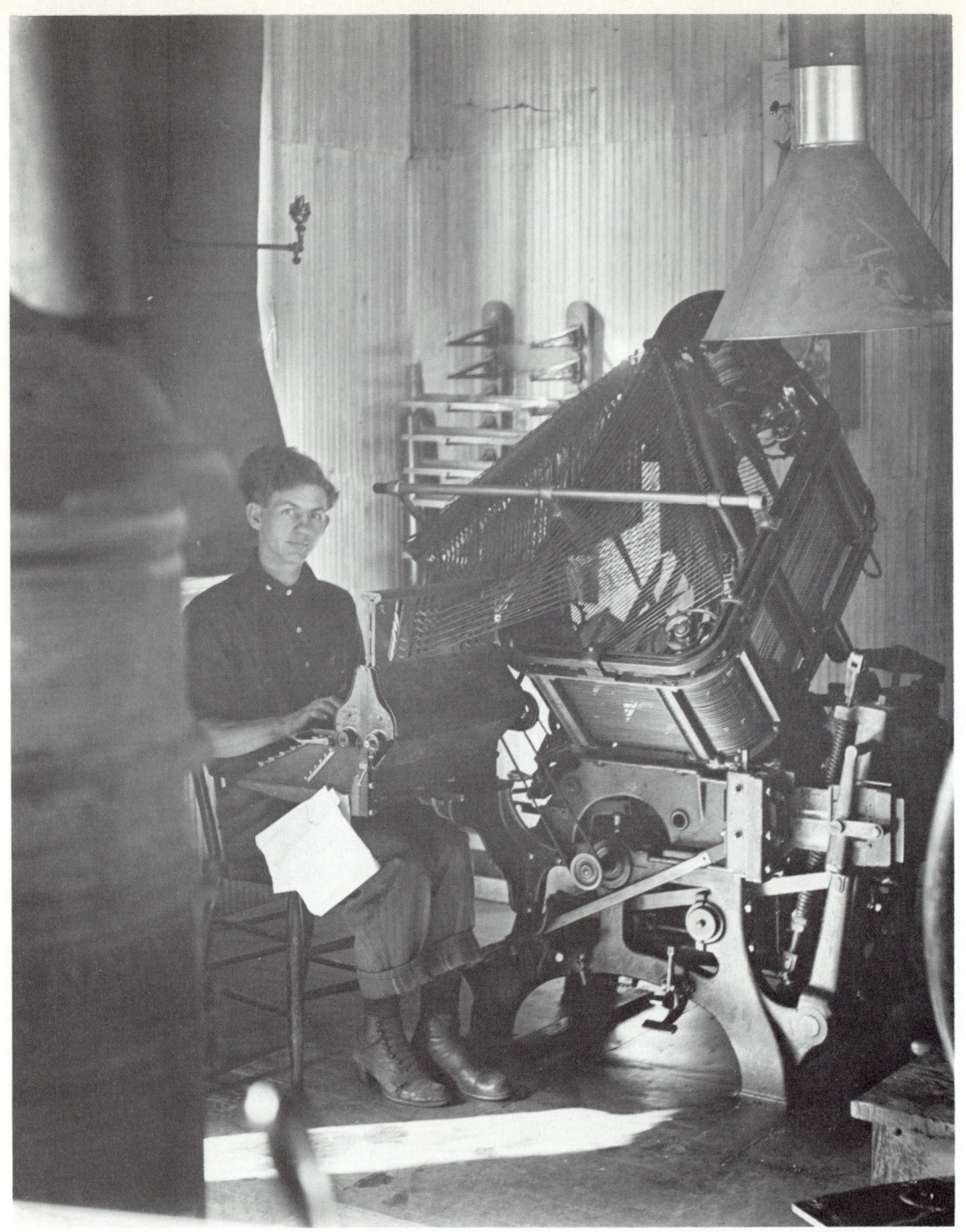

This early linotype was still in use in Waupaca County, Wisconsin, in 1900. (State Historical Society of Wisconsin)

For example, in 1846, the *New York Sun* needed a complete new set of type every three months in order to make a clean impression.[15] Although other newspapers used the process in the 1850s, the invention of a press developed specifically for the process by R. Hoe & Company further promoted stereotyping. Its advantages were great, because not only did it cause less wear on type, but it also allowed for removing of column rules and created the possibility of full-page, rather than column-bound advertisements.

By 1870, the web-perfecting press, a press that printed on both sides of a sheet of paper on a continuous roll (a web) of newsprint, came into popular use. Cutting and folding also were developed during the 1860s and 1870s, further speeding the process and reducing the labor involved.

The most significant development of the 1880s was the perfection of Ottmar Mergenthaler's Linotype machine in 1886. Operated by a keyboard similar to that of a typewriter, the machine released type matrices, assembled them into a line of type, automatically justified them and cast them in a "slug" of lead, returning the matrices to the magazine for reuse. Prior to this development, compositors were required to set each piece of type by hand. Each letter had to be handled individually, arranged in a line of type, justified with metal spacers, and returned to the typecase. Not only did Mergenthaler's machine increase the speed of setting type, it also solved the problem of type wear and tear.[16]

Photographs

Although pictures had been included in publications during the Civil War years, the production of photographs required hand engraving. In the early 1870s photoengraving made it possible for the *New York Daily Graphic* to carry a full-page picture seventeen by twenty-six inches in size.[17] But the revolution in the use of photography was not strictly technological. Thomas Leonard suggested that the impact of *Harper's Weekly's* exposé of Boss Tweed was stronger because it was one of the first attempts to encourage an audience to think visually about the political life of a city. Pictures were unfamiliar to American audiences and many public figures were not visually recognizable, even by the press. Furthermore, pictures were regarded as an inappropriate waste of space, and many newspapers through the 1880s fought against including photographs on their pages.[18] Photographs, when used, were carefully posed and conventionally presented, and it took the pen of Thomas Nast to "puncture the pretty pictures" while presenting the Tweed Ring as bullies and thugs. Nast played on New York's prejudices and stereotypes, incorporating thug-like Irishmen into his cartoons to signify non-Irish political criminals. As conventions broke down, and Hearst and Pulitzer entered the New York field in the late 1880s, photographs became a valued addition to metropolitan papers.

The Associated Press

By 1860, the seven New York dailies that had formed the Harbor News Association in 1848 controlled most U.S. foreign and domestic news gathering through their telegraphic news-gathering service, The Associated Press. The New York dailies spent more than $200,000 annually collecting and distributing news, and their customers outside the city paid them back for more than half the expense.[19]

Rebelling at New York's control, in 1865 a group of midwestern publishers organized the Western AP. They complained that the New York group focused too much on commercial interests of the city and not enough on events concerning the West. They also protested the high cost of cable news from Europe. In 1867, however, the two groups reached an agreement that respected each service's territorial rights and, in conjunction, reached a monopolistic agreement with Western Union.

Western Union, which in 1866 squeezed out its two remaining competitors, forged agreements with the two AP groups that assured that the AP would use the wires of Western Union alone and would oppose additional telegraph companies, while Western Union agreed not to enter news gathering and to grant discount rates to the associations.[20]

During the latter part of the century the public, through congressional action, through pamphlets, and through the press, attacked the monopoly. In 1872, the House Committee on Appropriations pointed out the dangers of the monopoly, and in 1874, a Senate investigation documented instances in which Western Union cut off transmissions of information critical of Western Union or the AP. The report read:

> The power of the telegraph, continually and rapidly increasing, can scarcely be estimated. It is the means of influencing public opinion through the press, of acting upon the markets of the country, and of seriously affecting the interests of the people.[21]

The Associated Press defended its domination of news access to the wires and the granting of franchises to papers of its choice by declaring that the organization was an association of businessmen dealing in a commercial commodity —news.[22] Not until the turn of the century would AP face significant competition from a rival news agency.

Chapter 10 **Growth and Reunification**

EDITORS OF THE TIMES

HENRY WATTERSON

Essentially a southern aristocrat, Henry Watterson remembered himself as a person who used his fifty years on the *Louisville Courier-Journal* to heal the South's wounds by minimizing the race issue through legal equality for blacks and by promoting southern industrialism. Nevertheless, Watterson was a conservative Southerner, who conceded that some advancements for blacks were necessary to preserve states' rights and to keep the federal government from interfering in Kentucky politics.[23]

Watterson was about twenty years old at the start of the Civil War. He was familiar with the nation's capital, having lived there with his politically oriented father. He was a Southerner, a Democrat, and a Unionist. He believed secession was wrong. However, when the South seceded, the Southerner in Watterson triumphed, and he returned to Tennessee and joined the Confederate Army. In 1858, he took over the *Louisville Courier-Journal* and edited it for fifty years, gaining fame as a Democratic party leader, a Kentucky gentleman (earning the nickname "Marse Henry"), and a writer of florid but persuasive and powerful editorials. During Reconstruction he argued for industrialization and political independence of the South. In 1918, at the start of World War I, he was awarded a Pulitzer Prize for his editorials calling America to action.

In 1858, Watterson moved to New York, wrote at "space rates" for Charles Dana, who then was an assistant to Horace Greeley on the *New York Tribune*, and became a music critic for the *New York Times*. Within two years he had returned to Washington, writing political news for *The Daily States*. In 1861, the newspaper closed its doors and Watterson returned to Tennessee reluctantly to join the Confederate Army. In 1862, he began editing *The Rebel*, which became a Confederate Army organ. Wanting to be near the news, Watterson loaded his press on a wagon and printed an issue whenever he had enough copy.

Near the end of the war, Watterson began working for, and ultimately became editor of the *Cincinnati Evening Times*. Missing the South, he moved to Nashville to help revive the *Republican Banner*. After traveling abroad for a short time he began working in 1867 at the *Louisville Journal*. Watterson persuaded the owners of the *Journal* and *Courier* to merge the two papers, and at the age of twenty-eight became the editor and owner of one-third of the stock. The paper was a personal one, never matching the news coverage of a *New York Times*, but it was powerful editorially.

Watterson reflected contemporary southern viewpoints on the issue of race, and only belatedly argued for legal equality of blacks and opposed black codes, which eventually were removed from Kentucky statute books. In 1868,

245

he blasted the night raids of the Ku Klux Klan and said the black must be given "a white man's chance."[24]

In 1872, Watterson joined the "New Departure" Democrats and Liberal Republicans to support Horace Greeley, whom he had admired while working in New York. Watterson believed such a coalition would give the South a voice in national affairs, bring an end to Reconstruction and break through sectional politics.[25] A staunch Democrat, in 1876 Watterson completed an unfilled term in Congress and strongly supported Tilden in the disputed presidential election.[26]

Watterson was highly critical of all presidents, including the Democrat Grover Cleveland, whom he felt had no experience in national affairs. A sound-money advocate, Watterson argued that William Jennings Bryan was a threat to the nation. However, during his fight against Bryan, the Democratic nominee for the presidency in 1896, Watterson lost half his circulation in less than a year. By 1900, he had regained his position, and changed his political attitude toward Bryan. He opposed Theodore Roosevelt and William Howard Taft, calling one too progressive and one too conservative. In 1912, he suggested that Roosevelt was "as mad as a march hare." Although Watterson supported the Democratic candidate Woodrow Wilson in 1912 and 1916, he argued that Wilson was a "schoolmaster and not a statesman." He counseled reason at the beginning of World War I, but had no use for Germany, calling it the nation "of the black hand and bloody heart." Marse Henry, the beloved Kentuckian, died in 1921, a few years after having relinquished the *Courier-Journal* to Judge Robert Worth Bingham.

Watterson's local fame was as a Kentuckian, loyal to his state and committed to the rebuilding of the South. Nationally he was recognized as a superb editorialist, and his editorials often were reprinted as news stories throughout the nation. Although he lived through the 1890s and the period of Pulitzer and Hearst, he resisted their innovations of banner headlines, comic strips and the exploitation of crime.

Although Watterson was highly regarded by many editors and politicians, he was not without his critics. Harry Thurston Peck, writing for *The Bookman* in February 1904, labeled his style "rabid rhetoric." He claimed Watterson aimed his appeals to emotion and prejudice and lacked logic and reason. Henry Pringle, writing in *Scribner's*, said logic was not Watterson's forte, and commented that the editorials denouncing Theodore Roosevelt "are certainly among the most astonishing in the history of journalism."[27]

HENRY WOODFINE GRADY

Labeled the "spokesman for the New South," Henry Grady believed the only way the South could escape depression and become prosperous was to become industrialized, and therefore independent of the North and West for the

> ## THE NEW SOUTH
>
> The new South is enamored of her new work. Her soul is stirred with the breath of a new life. The light of a grander day is falling fair on her face. She is thrilling with the consciousness of growing power and prosperity. As she stands upright, full-statured and equal among the people of the earth, breathing the keen air and looking out upon the expanding horizon, she understands that her emancipation came because in the inscrutable wisdom of God her honest purpose was crossed and her brave armies were beaten.
>
> SOURCE. Henry Woodfine Grady, speech as reported by the New York Tribune, December 23, 1886.

processing of its raw materials. He often spoke in the North on the South's behalf and asked that the South be left alone to solve its own problems. In an attempt to minimize the race issue, he tried to persuade Northerners that on the whole blacks were treated with kindness and respect. His eulogies of the Old South, his companionship with Joel Chandler Harris, and his promotion of industrial growth represented a balance between modernism and tradition that made him a popular individual indeed.

Henry Grady was born in Athens, Georgia, May 24, 1850. His father was a successful merchant who became a colonel in the Civil War and was killed in battle. Grady was graduated from the University of Georgia in 1868 and attended the University of Virginia for a year, enrolling in a law course. After several unsuccessful newspaper ventures in rural Georgia, he became a reporter for the *Atlanta Constitution* and a correspondent for the *New York Herald*.

After buying part of the *Constitution* in 1880 with a $20,000 loan from Cyrus Field of Chicago, Grady spent huge sums of money to gather news and continued to report on politics and other major news events. By 1887, the weekly edition of the *Constitution* claimed the largest subscription list in the South and the following year it claimed the largest circulation for any paper of its type in the United States. Unlike Watterson, Grady avoided personal editorializing and detested denunciation and personal controversy. His emphasis was on news gathering and promotion. He also was one of the first reporters and editors to use the interview technique extensively in reporting and interpreting the news.

Grady also gave immense publicity to Southern resources for industrial development, disregarding any subsequent consequences. C. Vann Woodward wrote:

> His oratorical poems picturing "mountains stored with exhaustless

treasures, forests, vast and primeval, and rivers that, tumbling or loitering, run wanton to the sea" were one long hymn of invocation to preemption and exploitation. "He did not tamely promote enterprise and encourage industry," wrote an admirer; "he vehemently fomented enterprise and provoked industry until they stalked through the land like armed conquerors."[28]

CHARLES A. DANA

Charles Dana bought the *New York Sun* from Moses Beach in 1868 for $175,000. His co-owners and backers represented a distinguished group of prominent men, and he earned the reputation of fair play to aspiring journalists. The *Sun* office was known as "the best school of journalism" and the newspaper as "the newspaper man's newspaper."[29]

As a young man, Dana attended Harvard, then became involved in the collective Brook Farm experiment, where he met literary figures such Nathaniel Hawthorne, Margaret Fuller, Henry Thoreau, and Horace Greeley. At the end of the Brook Farm experiment, he went to work as a typesetter for the *Boston Daily Chronotype* for five dollars a week, and in 1847, moved up to city editor of the *New York Tribune* for ten dollars a week. In 1848, he traveled abroad, writing for Horace Greeley and several other editors, earning a combined salary of about forty dollars a week. After about eight months, he returned to become managing editor of the *Tribune*.

During the prewar years, Dana campaigned for the end of slavery and argued vehemently for the integrity of the Union. During the Civil War he became assistant secretary of war under Edwin Stanton. He resigned his position in July 1865, and moved to Chicago to edit the *Daily Republican*. After a year he left the paper, which suffered due to lack of adequate financial backing. When he bought the *Sun* in 1868, he was forty-nine years old.

Dana's *Sun* was the first aggressively independent Democratic newspaper in the city and expressed the ideology of artisan republicanism, a philosophy which advocated that all, including working men, should share equal rights and full participation in the political system. Dana's willingness to accept the diversity of the city and to champion the working class made him immensely popular in New York City in the 1870s.[30] Dana's paternalistic ideology could not compete, however, when confronted with Joseph Pulitzer's *New York World*, which developed an editorial and news policy that promoted common interests and a "pragmatic, collectivist urban vision."[31]

Dana responded to Pulitzer's challenge with a conservative retreat into the middle class and reestablished the *Sun* as a newspaper that ultimately defended the rights of capital over those of labor.[32]

> **NOTE TO WORKINGMEN**
>
> We believe that sincere respect can only be won by manly honesty, and while we take the workingman's side, we claim also the privilege of being their critics and advisers. This course . . . will render our services doubly useful. It will point out to the workingmen the mistakes they are in danger of committing, and compel the rest of the world, seeing our impartiality, to respect the principles we advocate.
>
> SOURCE. New York Sun, March 17, 1869.

E. L. GODKIN

Edwin Godkin, born and educated in England, began his journalistic career as a Crimean War correspondent for *The London Daily News*. In 1856, at the end of the war, he traveled to New York and through the southern states, writing letters about slavery and the poor whites of the South to the London newspaper. He regarded southern planters as "ignorant provincials clinging with desperation to an institution which was doomed and which was economically unsound," but often thought northern abolitionists were unfair in their "frenzies."[33]

When the Civil War broke out, England sold arms to the Confederates, worried about repayment, and lamented the lack of cotton being shipped from southern ports — cotton that fueled their textile industries. But Godkin had no sympathy for such concerns, and countered southern sympathy in England with his letters to the *Daily News*.

In 1865, Godkin, together with James Miller McKim of Philadelphia, raised $100,000 to begin *The Nation*, a magazine that proclaimed it would be a journal "of politics, literature, science and art" and that would report topics "with greater accuracy and moderation than are now to be found in the daily press." *The Nation* called for legislation that would be "likely to promote a more equal distribution of the fruits of progress and civilization," and that would erase artificial distinctions between blacks and whites. Contributors included such literary greats as Henry Wadsworth Longfellow, James Russell Lowell, and John Greenleaf Whittier.

Godkin soon encountered difficulty with his backers, each of whom had a singular idea of what *The Nation* should represent.

> The editor learned, as editors nearly always do, that each stockholder had a different conception of the best editorial program. The free traders quarrelled with the protectionists. The abolitionists were chagrined when anything except appeals for the Negro was discussed.

This 1857 lithograph depicts reconstruction of the South. *(Library of Congress Collection)*

Finally, Godkin himself was subjected to absurd provincial criticism. He was an Englishman and therefore incompetent. *The Nation*, said the Anglophobes, had been financed with British gold and was seeking to undermine the sacred institutions of America.

Godkin reorganized the company, relying only on close friends for backers, and continued publishing *The Nation*. The journal, never a great money-maker, provided him with a $5,000 annual salary, a generous salary but not enough to allow Godkin to live in the style that he preferred. In 1881, *The Nation* became a weekly edition of the *New York Evening Post*, owned by Henry Villard. Godkin became one of three editors of the *Post*, including Carl Schurz and Horace White. Godkin was fifty years old.

The three agreed, as Godkin wrote, that the *Post* should specialize in "being the paper to which sober-minded people would look . . . instead of hollering and bellering and shouting platitudes like *The Herald* and *Times*." But the three agreed on little else, and when Godkin denounced an 1883 strike of railway telegraphers, Schurz informed Godkin he could no longer continue working with him. Schurz abandoned his post.

Godkin objected to crime news, was offended by public accounts of private matters and abhorred Dana's *New York Sun*, claiming that it was sensational and scandalous. Dana returned the compliments, shouting that the *Post* was as "heavy as it was dull." Godkin joined the campaign against Tammany Hall, writing articles between 1884 and 1890 without much success. He hated jingoism, admired Grover Cleveland, and condemned the Spanish-American War. By 1899, Godkin was in ill health, and he died in 1902 while visiting England.

Godkin, unlike Dana, was not a friend to his reporters, but was known for an aloof austerity. He did not understand the labor movement or problems of the general public. He wholly divorced his journalism from commercialism. "When his freedom was questioned," wrote Edward Mitchell, "he lost his temper completely and refused to give way an inch. It was very seldom questioned, for Godkin's wrath, once aroused, was as noisy as it was sincere. His curses rang through the offices of *The Evening Post*. Even the reporters, who disliked him, smiled as they bent over their tasks. For if Godkin was a free man they were free men, too.

"And *The Evening Post*, under Godkin, was a free newspaper."

CONCLUSION

During the period of Reconstruction, southern editors such as Henry Grady and Henry Watterson championed industrialism as the wave of the future and a solution to the ills of the South. Such editors gained credibility as metropolitan voices for progressive action, while local editors were labeled provincial and backward looking. Watterson and Grady used their political connections to further their economic platforms.

Northern urban newspapers experienced rapid growth, attacked corruption much as they had attacked crime during the antebellum years, and, with significant exceptions, opposed organization of labor, especially when it affected newspaper operation. Traditional values of individualism, free enterprise, and private property characterized most editors' reactions to the new challenges.

Technology rendered newsprint cheaper, which enabled publishers to extend circulation and number of pages, while advertising in a manufacturing economy grew in proportion with the products produced. More efficient presses allowed for display advertising and multiple column headlines and photographs, while the Linotype decreased production time. The introduction of photographs, based on improved technology, required cultural adaptation of the audience as well as technological implementation.

Throughout the period, the Associated Press increased its dominance of the transmission of news, creating a monopoly in 1866 through agreements with Western Union.

By the 1880s, editors such as Charles Dana, who championed the working classes of New York City, but who remained loyal to the ideology of artisan republicanism, lost circulations in the face of newspapers like those of Joseph Pulitzer, which promoted a collective vision of the urban community.

NOTES

1. The words were quoted from Benjamin Hill, who spoke them at Tammany Hall in 1866.
2. C. Vann Woodward, *Origins of the New South* (Baton Rouge: Louisiana State University Press: 1951), p. 145.
3. For a discussion of the *Chicago Daily News* in comparison to the *Chicago Times* and *Chicago Tribune* in regard to attitudes toward urban life, see David Paul Nord, "The Public Community: The Urbanization of Journalism in Chicago," *Journal of Urban History* (August 1985) 11:4, pp. 411–441.
4. *Nation*, vol. 24 (1877), p. 202; and *New York Tribune*, April 7, 1877, cited in Woodward, *Origins of the New South*, p. 216.
5. Daniel Pope, *The Making of Modern Advertising* (New York: Basic Books. 1983), p. 32.
6. For analysis of the evolution of a consumer culture, see Michael Schudson, *Advertising, the Uneasy Persuasion: Its Dubious Impact on American Society* (New York: Basic Books, 1986).
7. Pope, *Making of Modern Advertising*, pp. 117, 118.
8. S. N. D. North, "History and Present Condition of the Newspaper and Periodical Press of the United States, with a Catalogue of the Publications of the Census Year," in U.S. Department of the Interior, Bureau of the Census, *Tenth Census* (Washington, 1884), VIII, p. 51, cited in Gunther Barth, *City People: The Rise of Modern City Culture in Nineteenth-Century America* (New York: Oxford University Press, 1980), p. 62.
9. New York *Herald*, 13 April 1836, p. 1 cited in Thomas C. Leonard, *The Power of the Press: The Birth of American Political Reporting* (New York: Oxford University Press, 1986). Other quotes from Leonard, p. 149.
10. Leonard, *Power of the Press*, p. 153.
11. Leonard, *Power of the Press*, pp. 177, 178.
12. Leonard, *Power of the Press*, p. 130.
13. David Paul Nord, *Newspapers and New Politics: Midwestern Municipal Reform, 1890–1900* (Ann Arbor: University Microfilms, Intl., 1981).
14. Alfred McClung Lee, *The Daily Newspaper in America* (New York: The Macmillan Co., 1937) p. 138.

15. Lee, *Daily Newspaper in America*, p. 117.
16. See Corban Goble, "Rogers' Typograph Versus Mergenthaler's Linotype: The Push and Shove of Patents and Priority in the 1890s," unpublished paper presented to the History Division of the Association for Education in Journalism and Mass Communication (August 1986) Norman, Okla., for controversies involving the developing of this technology. For press technology, see James Moran, *Printing Presses* (Berkeley: University of California Press, 1973).
17. Lee, *Daily Newspaper in America*, p. 128.
18. Leonard, *Power of the Press*, p. 102.
19. Daniel Czitrom, *Media and the American Mind* (Chapel Hill: University of North Carolina Press, 1982), p. 24–25.
20. Czitrom, *Media and the American Mind*, p. 25.
21. From government reports cited in Czitrom, *Media and the American Mind*, p. 26.
22. Czitrom, *Media and the American Mind*, p. 27.
23. Robert K. Thorp, "'Marse Henry' and the Negro: A New Perspective," *Journalism Quarterly* (Autumn 1969), pp. 467–474.
24. Isaac F. Marcosson. *"Marse Henry" A Biography of Henry Watterson* (New York: Dodd, Mead and Company, 1951), p. 85. Marcosson, unlike Thorp, credits Watterson with a more progressive attitude.
25. "One Clause of the Message," *The Weekly Courier-Journal*, December 16, 1874, p. 2.
26. Henry F. Pringle, "Kentucky Bourbon: Marse Henry Watterson," *Scribner's* (January 1935), p. 15.
27. Pringle, "Kentucky Bourbon," p. 17.
28. Cited in C. Vann Woodward, *Tom Watson: Agrarian Rebel* (New York: Oxford University Press, 1983), p. 90.
29. For biographical information about Dana see Candace Stone, *Dana and the Sun* (New York: Dodd, Mead and Co., 1938); Edward P. Mitchell, *Memoirs of an Editor* (New York: Scribners, 1924); Frank M. O'Brien, *The Story of the Sun* (New York: D. Appleton and Co., 1928); and Charles J. Rosebault, *When Dana Was the Sun* (New York: R. M. McBride and Co., 1931). For a more recent, interpretive account see Janet E. Steele, "From Paradise to Park Row: The Life, Opinions and Newspapers of Charles A. Dana, 1819–1897," unpublished Ph.D. disser., Johns Hopkins University, 1985.
30. Steele, *Paradise to Park Row*, pp. 7–8, chapter 6.
31. Nord, "Public Community," p. 436. See also George Juergens, *Joseph Pulitzer and the New York World* (Princeton, N.J.: Princeton University Press, 1966).
32. Steele, *Paradise to Park Row*, p. 234.
33. Citations in this section on Edwin Godkin are taken from Edward Mitchell, "Godkin of 'The Post'," *Scribner's* (December 1934), p. 329.

CHAPTER 11

THE PRESS AND MODERNIZATION

The press emerged from the intensely political years of sectionalism, partisan politics, the Civil War, and Reconstruction to confront a new order.[1] Adaptation to an increasingly urbanized society, rapid technological and scientific growth, corporate consolidation, and questions about the rights of men, women and children as laborers troubled the burgeoning society of the 1890s.

Emerging from the fray were captains of industry, leaders of consolidated corporate giants. Through vertical and horizontal integration of industry, the captains amassed great wealth. They introduced mechanization, which created new jobs and products but destroyed craftsmen and subjected laborers to rigid schedules and routine tasks. The captains sympathized little with labor, and in the years of financial panic — 1873, 1884, and 1893 — they lowered wages while they lengthened hours, and they rarely installed safety equipment or followed safety procedures. Between 1900 and 1917 in the railroad industry alone, 72,000 workers were killed and 2 million injured.[2]

Editors, consumers, and municipal reformers railed against monopolies even as they supported business in general, promoted growth without always considering the costs, and struggled with how to curtail corruption in city services and government. As the press expanded in numbers and in size, critics questioned the reform positions of editors, asking whether indeed, some editors were not captains of industry themselves. Joseph Pulitzer's and William Randolph Hearst's circulation and sensationalism wars of the late 1890s sparked even greater criticism.

The foundations of the modern press were firmly in place, incorporating technologies of rapid printing, mechanized typesetting, and cheap papermaking. Editors and reporters established news-gathering processes such as interviews, beats, and telegraph news. The business function and the editorial process became clearly separate entities, although each influenced the other.[3] Furthermore, the cost of doing business escalated. Newspapers in urban areas frequently sold for $100,000 or more, and some for as much as $250,000.[4] The census of 1880 explained the spectacular growth of the urban press by noting the "conditions of daily life" required "some general medium of communication between man and man." Also recorded in the census was the fact that the "rate of growth of the news industry seemed unparalleled in any other country of the world and hardly equaled by any other phase of industrial development in the United States."[5]

Newspapers now depended on large circulations and expanded advertising bases, and relied little on political-party support. However, government job-printing contracts continued to be important sources of income for many editors of small-to-mid-sized papers. Although partisan politics still played important roles in how newspapers addressed issues, editors were reluctant to emphasize party loyalties if it meant excluding too many strata of the urban societies they served. In some cities, newspapers joined forces with each other and with reform groups to achieve nonpartisan municipal control of city services, including utilities and transportation. It was a new kind of politics, in which local issues gained supremacy over party loyalties. In other cities, fragmented political and business groups and party-loyal newspapers failed to bridge their differences, and city services remained in the hands of the politicians.[6]

Newspapers and magazines chose a variety of paths along a continuum from sensationalism or entertainment to information and fact finding. Some newspapers jumped on the successful Hearst-Pulitzer

A *Harper's Weekly* engraving March 21, 1868, of the "*A Race for the Wires—Energy of the Reporters.*" (Library of Congress Collection)

bandwagon. Others shunned the large, bold headlines and colorful comics that Pulitzer and Hearst used to garner mass circulations; and some adopted the successful graphic techniques, but rejected the sensational quality of the articles, the self-promotion, the intrusions of privacy and the fictionalizing of news associated with the *Journal* and the *World*. Still others, like the highly profitable *New York Times*, shunned it all and remained graphically, editorially, and politically conservative, printing "all the news that's fit to print." Almost all newspapers, however, became distinct parts of the business communities they served.

Although many of the new techniques grew out of the need to compete with other newspapers in the spectacular cities of the late nineteenth century, and much of the growth took place within the cities, the press was not entirely urban, at least in a "city" sense, but the issues of the city—municipal reform, the status of labor, and the effects of sensational presses—did not escape the smaller towns. Editors such as William Allen White of Emporia, Kansas, rejected the editorial techniques of the Hearsts, professed political independence but remained party-oriented, and championed municipal reform.

Newspapers differed tremendously in treatment of subject matter and in graphic presentation while they catered to audiences as different as New York immigrant laborers to Chicago businessmen to the rural readers of White's *Gazette*. Their purposes varied from entertainment to information to interpretation as they cajoled readers to vote for their candidates, to support non-partisan reform and to admire the dramatic growth of the cities, the western states, and the country at large.

Within the newspaper industry, reporters assumed new importance, but received low pay and experienced minimal social status as they began to confront the conflicts inherent within their roles.

Chapter 11 **The Press and Modernization**

NEW STYLES AND GREATER NUMBERS

NEWSPAPER GROWTH

The newspaper industry, one might say, was on a roll. The number of morning, evening, and Sunday dailies grew steadily between 1880 and 1900, a growth that would continue until the close of World War I. In 1870, only 574 daily newspapers were published, but by 1890 that number grew to 1,536. Weeklies grew as well, with 4,295 weeklies publishing in 1870 and 12,600 in 1890. Simultaneously, circulations grew until in 1900 more than 26 percent of the population subscribed to a newspaper. In 1870, dailies circulated to slightly more than 2.5 million people; in 1890 about 8.5 million daily copies entered homes of American people. Foreign-language newspapers, in line with the rising immigration levels, grew from 315 in 1870 to 1,159 in 1900. In 1880, 80 percent of the foreign-language journals were German; by 1900, as immigrants arrived from different countries, only 64.5 percent were German.[7]

Evening newspapers increased rapidly, as editors and advertisers targeted women as primary purchasers within the home. One trade journal argued:

> The morning paper is the business man's paper, and will never be the home paper so long as women are confronted with household duties. When it is fresh, they are too busy to read it and when they are at leisure, it is old, for the evening paper has been born.[8]

Department stores preferred the evening papers because they were more likely to go to the home and be read by women.

THE PRESS AND MUNICIPAL REFORM

Beginning as early as the 1850s, with the *Harpers' Weekly* and *New York Times'* exposure of Boss Tweed, newspapers critically examined local governments. Although the nature of the exposés varied across time, the content often remained similar. Editors generally favored electing better men to office. The "better men" usually came from whichever political party the editor preferred.

As cities multiplied and populations doubled, then doubled again, new problems of sanitation, lighting, and transportation emerged, and editors focused more exclusively on municipal issues as separate from national and state political issues. Historian David Paul Nord, in a study of Chicago and St.

Louis newspapers in the 1890s, suggested that reform groups and newspaper editors in Chicago positively affected the development of city services through a broad-based coalition free from party exclusivity. "Reformers learned to use mass communication, largely through newspapers," Nord wrote, "in part because they lacked the elaborate interpersonal communication networks of the political machine." Newspapers, therefore, played "information" and "agenda-setting" roles, rather than persuasive roles. The new politics, Nord wrote, were issue oriented rather than party oriented; newspapers transcended class and social boundaries to join with consumers, citizens, and taxpayers to achieve specific purposes:

> In this new politics, the newspaper's job was to provide the public with a vision of what the unified, organic city could be. Reform issues, schemes, plans, and proposals were kept always bubbling on the back burners of the public agenda through constant repetition in the newspapers.[9]

Although Chicago's newspapers varied in style and political loyalty, they successfully allied themselves with a broad-based citizens' group, the Chicago Civic Federation, to champion municipal ownership. In St. Louis, also a city of varied newspapers, politics continued to get in the way. Only the *Post-Dispatch*, Pulitzer's paper in St. Louis, supported the fight against privately owned utilities, and even it was not consistent. The other newspapers in St. Louis were mere "house organs" for the street railway companies. But it was not a communication question alone. The failure in St. Louis also was related to the lack of a broad-based coalition that transcended politics and failed to work with the newspapers to keep municipal issues on the public agenda. Nord's *Newspapers and New Politics* directs historians to look beyond the persuasive influence of prominent newspapers and their editors and to analyze the informational aspect of newspapers and the cultural-political milieu in which they operated.

Varying degrees of reform were achieved in the different cities, and in some areas it was not until the muckraking magazines of the early twentieth century sent reporters to town that newspapers and officials paid attention. Even then, reform often was slow to arrive and even slower to succeed. Richard Kielbowicz suggested that in Minneapolis after the turn of the century, that although the newspapers' and magazines' exposure of a corrupt, but popular, mayor succeeded eventually in removing certain officials from office, it did little to effect changes in laws governing prostitution, gambling, and police operations.[10]

Municipal reform was not an issue for cities alone, but for smaller incorporated towns as well. William Allen White, editor of the *Emporia Gazette*, advocated governmental control of public utilities as early as 1897 and cau-

William Allen White edited the Emporia (Ks.) Gazette *from 1895 until he died in the mid-1940s. (State Historical Society of Wisconsin)*

> **WHITE PRAISES REPUBLICAN BUSINESSMEN**
>
> It was a Republican administration that conceived and executed the idea of brightening the home of the farmer, educating his children, increasing the value of his land, compelling the improvement of the roads, and bringing him news of the markets and of the weather, so as to secure him a better price for his crops by delivering his daily mail to him on his farm.
>
> SOURCE. William Allen White, Emporia Gazette, October 24, 1900.

tioned Emporia citizens to seek a maximum-rate clause in the ordinance to protect the people. But he also was interested in protecting local business, and he wanted to ensure that the Kansas and Missouri Telephone Company (an out-of-town company) would not be granted any favors a home company would not enjoy. He also considered Emporia's municipal ownership of the waterworks to be a successful experiment, which he attributed to the high average intelligence of a community that kept party politics out of this branch of municipal affairs. Nevertheless, White thought that most often Republicans were more enlightened than Democrats, and to him "businessmen" were usually synonymous with Abe Lincoln's party.

As far as White was concerned, Republicans simply were better businessmen and better social leaders than were Democrats, who represented the party that had attempted to destroy the Union and that "bossed" the eastern cities. Yet many themes that appeared in White's newspaper were similar to those that appeared in the city sheets.[11]

INFORMATION vs. SENSATION

If one describes the 1890s as a period of "New Journalism" evidenced by Joseph Pulitzer's *New York World* and William Randolph Hearst's *New York Journal,* one has to ignore the more generalized claims that in the late 1800s journalists concerned themselves more than before with "facts" and "reality." One also has to ignore the *New York Times,* the *Chicago Tribune* and the *Kansas City Star,* which denounced the tactics of Hearst and Pulitzer, but which nevertheless gained prominence in their communities, succeeded financially, and continued for many years to provide information and to editorialize about a variety of local and national issues. Any student of the period has to ask how these two threads are connected.

Michael Schudson suggested in *Discovering the News* that the emphasis on facts coincided with a developing American belief that the cure for the ills of the cities and of the society could be found through empirical precision, the advice of the expert and the application of factual information. Although

Americans always had been fascinated by science, as indicated by the *New York Sun*'s successful moon hoax, citizens now turned to science in new fashion, expecting it to solve the ills government and politics failed to answer. Reporters, in a search for credibility and respectability, partially justified their role in society as providers of information designed to solve problems.

But the *World* and the *Journal* operated not in the problem-solving mentality of the emerging progressive mind, but in the city of New York, a city teeming with immigrants who spoke a variety of languages and little or no English. It was an exciting city that provided literary giants with picturesque paragraphs and social commentators like Jacob Riis with endless material about the abhorrent condition of the slums. It was a city of hope, of color, and of opportunity as well as a city of graft, corruption, and squalid living conditions. The newspapers of this New York, unlike the respectable *New York Times*, which appealed to the business classes, provided entertainment. This is not to say the business classes did not read the *New York World*, or that the working classes did not read the *Times*, but the newspapers had definite appeals. Upperclass businessmen and social matrons read the *World* (with perhaps a shade of guilt as they commented on its disgracefulness) and working-class people also sought the information the *Times* provided.[12] Why was one considered respectable and the other not? Schudson wrote:

> Perhaps, then, the *Times* established itself as the "higher journalism" because it adapted to the life experience of persons whose position in the social structure gave them the most control over their own lives. Its readers were relatively independent and participant. The readers of the *World* were relatively dependent and nonparticipant. The experience engendered by affluence and education makes one comfortable with a certain journalistic orientation, one which may indeed be, in some respects, more mature, more encompassing, more differentiated, more integrated. It may also be, in its own way, more limited; refinement in newspapers, people, and sugar, is bleaching. If the *World*'s readers might have longed for more control of their lives, the readers of the *Times* may have wished for more nutrients in theirs.[13]

Communications theorist John Pauly has suggested that public talk about "the news" and the concept of independence allowed Americans to adjust their democratic ideals to the conditions of industrial society and "expressed Americans' belief in the possibility of a morally purified style of commercial journalism that kept faith with earlier political ideals." The ideology of an independent press minimized the severity of political conflicts, proclaimed that metropolitan dailies acted in the public interest, and symbolized a renunciation of the Civil War and a quest for national unity.[14]

Although urban printing plants began to look like modern corporations by the turn of the century, the country newspaper remained a significant force in dissesminating news. (State Historical Society of Wisconsin)

LOCAL PRESS

The movement toward the ideology of independence affected urban newspapers more than it did the local press, which had evolved from its frontier origins into a healthy network of weeklies and dailies. As late as 1931, 34 percent of the 1,500 weeklies in the South and 42 percent of the 8,300 weeklies in the North declared loyalty to either the Republicans or the Democrats. Although many small papers relied on the patronage of county printing contracts, some editors also viewed partisanship as a responsibility, not as a liability, and accused their city cousins of "cold commercialism." "It is only the country newspapers," wrote John Kautz, editor of the Republican *Tribune* of Kokomo, Indiana, "that are willing always to make their party's cause their own, to fight under its standard, to stand or fall with it in the fiercest contests."[15]

Even partisan newspapers were influenced by the independents, and became more willing to print news even-handedly, without regard to party considerations. Party slogans on mastheads disappeared, and newspapers stopped "parading partisan loyalty."[16]

CRITIQUE OF THE PRESS

Criticism of the large city dailies sprang from a variety of sources. Social scientists feared the impact of crime news on juvenile delinquency, while ministers and priests criticized the daily for having an immoral impact on conduct, and condemned the increasingly popular Sunday newspapers for affronting the traditional day of worship. Educators denounced newspapers as cheap reading and called for better forms of leisure and recreation. Elites condemned the focus on mass readership as moral erosion of cultural authority.[17]

SENSATION AT ITS HEIGHT

JOSEPH PULITZER AND THE *NEW YORK WORLD*

Joseph Pulitzer, born in 1847, earned his way in the world of newspapers by refining sensational techniques, hiring a qualified staff, and achieving one of the all-time largest circulations in New York City. His establishment of the Pulitzer Prizes and his endowment of the School of Journalism at Columbia University further secured his reputation. He clamored for fair distribution of wealth and appealed to popular tastes. His key to success lay in his use of technology as well as in his ability to promote the cause of the working class, which needed city services that could be provided only through a sense of collective public community.[18]

Pulitzer was born in Hungary, the son of a Magyar Jew and a German Catholic. He left home when he was seventeen and after being rejected by the Austrian, French, and British armies he arrived in the United States in 1864, where he served for seven months in the Union Army. Because he could not find work in New York, and spoke very little English, he moved west to St. Louis to seek employment.

From 1865 to 1868, Pulitzer worked at a variety of jobs, finally securing a position on the *Westliche Post*, a German-language St. Louis paper published by Carl Schurz. He started reading law, learned English, and eventually became a U.S. citizen. He was elected to the Missouri legislature, but after shooting and wounding a lobbyist who opposed Pulitzer's attempts at reform, His Missouri

> **PULITZER'S PLATFORM**
>
> 1. Tax Luxuries.
> 2. Tax Inheritances.
> 3. Tax Large Incomes.
> 4. Tax Monopolies.
> 5. Tax the Privileged Corporations.
> 6. A Tariff for Revenue.
> 7. Reform the Civil Service.
> 8. Punish Corrupt Officers.
> 9. Punish Vote Buying.
> 10. Punish Employers who Coerce their Employees in Elections.

political career ended. Following Schurz's lead into the reform Republican movement, Pulitzer campaigned vigorously for Horace Greeley in 1872, the same year he bought controlling interest in the *Westliche Post* from Schurz and his partner. He soon relinquished his interest in the *Post* and bought the *Staats-Zeitung*, a bankrupt paper that had an AP franchise. By selling the AP franchise to the St. Louis *Globe* and the machinery from the *Zeitung* to another group, Pulitzer made enough money to retire.

In 1878, Pulitzer purchased the bankrupt evening *Dispatch* and merged it with the *Post*, published by John Dillon. The newspaper was an immediate financial success, netting $45,000 in 1881. The publisher moved away from the reform Republican camp, dismayed by its inability to create a strong platform, and joined the Democratic party. His aim was to publish the leading Democratic paper in the state, with an emphasis on reform and the middle class. Although Pulitzer left St. Louis in 1883 for New York, he retained ownership of the *Post-Dispatch*.

In New York, Pulitzer purchased the foundering *New York World* from Jay Gould for $346,000, a figure considered too high for the 15,000-circulation paper. In 1861, the *World* absorbed the old New York *Courier* and *Enquirer*, but despite its longevity never made money. In 1883, however, New York's only Democratic voice was that of Charles Dana, and Pulitzer planned to broaden the newspaper's base and "to talk to a nation, not a select committee."

On May 17, 1883, Pulitzer announced to New York his plan to tax the rich. He printed an editorial platform, which he recommended to politicians "in place of long-winded resolutions."[19] The ten-point platform, very similar, in fact, to the Democratic political platform, attacked corruption and the accumulation of wealth.

MR. PULITZER AS A LEADER OF LIBERAL REPUBLICANISM.
(Cartoon by Joseph Keppler in the St. Louis *Puck*, March 30, 1872.)

This cartoon, depicting Pulitzer as a leader of liberal republicanism, appeared in the St. Louis Puck *March 30, 1872. (Library of Congress Collection)*

> **IN LA BELLE FRANCE**
>
> We landed at Bologne. Here, I think, my baggage was examined, but I did not see it done as one of the men in the boat with me took charge of it and also found us places in the train bound for Amiens. In the meantime we went into the restaurant on the edge of the pier and had something to eat. I found the waiters able to speak English and willing enough to take American money. The trip to Amiens was slow and tiresome, but I was fully repaid for the journey by meeting M. Jules Verne and his wife, who were waiting for me at the station in company with THE WORLD's Paris correspondent.
>
> SOURCE. Nellie Bly, *New York World*, January 26, 1890, *reporting her trip around the world.*

Part of Pulitzer's success could be credited to his commitment to hiring good reporters and building a strong staff, although his record for paying reporters well is somewhat in doubt. In 1884, the *World* paid reporters $7.50 a column for space and 50 cents an hour for time, less than the *Herald*.[20] Pulitzer also apparently would pit two staffers against each other and encourage them to compete for the same position, a practice that fostered distrust and animosity.

Nevertheless, Pulitzer was able to entice an able staff. One popular reporter was Elizabeth Cochrane (Nellie Bly), who as a writer for the *Pittsburgh Dispatch*, wrote so convincingly of Mexican government corruption that Mexican leaders evicted her from the country. After her return, she published *Six Months in Mexico*, then began working for Pulitzer's *World*. Her undercover approach made her famous, first as a disguised insane woman admitted to Blackwell's Island, which resulted in an investigation into the system for caring for New York's mentally ill. She also posed as a woman prisoner to reveal injustices to women in prison; she posed as a patent medicine manufacturer's wife to expose a bribing lobbyist, and she even danced in a corps de ballet.

She achieved her highest level of notoriety with a trip around the world, designed to see if she could beat the fictitious Phileas Fogg in Jules Verne's classic *Around the World in 80 Days*, while using new forms of commercial transportation. She made the trip in seventy-two days, six hours and eleven minutes. Pulitzer gave her front-page space where she entertained readers with exotic and exciting tales. Her career was cut short by her marriage to a seventy-two-year-old businessman in 1895. After his death, she worked for a time on the *New York Journal* but never regained her popularity. She died of pneumonia at age fifty-six.

Other respected reporters who worked for the *World* included Arthur Brisbane, Frank Irving Cobb, Herbert Bayard Swope, Walter Lippman, Heywood Broun, and David Graham Phillips. William Randolph Hearst, by promising higher salaries, hired many of these *World* reporters to staff his competing *New York Journal*.

Pulitzer used many of the techniques instituted by Bennett and Day, but he added his own flair. He created "ears" on both sides of the flag, promoting the newspaper and printing tiny news clips; he introduced column-spanning headlines; and he developed a world-wide news service. Pulitzer also introduced the widespread use of photographs, beginning with a four-column cut of the Brooklyn Bridge in May 1883. He used diagrams, drawings, and cartoons. He emphasized the coverage of sports for the working man and emphasized women's news, walking a fine line between ignoring and endorsing feminism. The *World*, recognizing the importance of women as buyers, included articles on correct etiquette, decoration, and child care.

Pulitzer also focused more on the working classes than he had in St. Louis and championed crusades for reform aimed at the immigrants, the poor, and other have-nots. By the end of the first year the *World* had a circulation of 60,000; in 1887 circulation reached 200,000 to become the largest in the United States. Pulitzer was printing twelve to fourteen pages daily and thirty-six to forty-four pages on Sunday. The Sunday edition was a laboratory, used to test new ideas and techniques. In 1887, he added an evening edition and in 1889 built the World Building to house his newspaper enterprise.

Pulitzer developed sensationalistic techniques before William Randolph Hearst arrived in New York in 1895. In May 1883, when eleven people were trampled to death as panic broke out on a pedestrian causeway while a Memorial Day crowd picnicked near the newly constructed Brooklyn Bridge, the *World*'s headline read BAPTIZED IN BLOOD.[21] In March 1884, while the *Times*' most sensational front-page lead headline was A PAYMASTER'S OFFICE ROBBED, the *World*'s headlines included dramatic promises of tales such as AN ENTIRE FAMILY ANNIHILATED BY ITS MURDEROUS HEAD; DIED A DESPERADO'S DEATH and A BRUTAL NEGRO WHIPS HIS NEPHEW TO DEATH IN SOUTH CAROLINA.[22]

Although Pulitzer was in the business of selling news, he was not without principle. To his secretary he said,

> It is not enough to refrain from publishing fake news, it is not enough to take ordinary care . . . you have got to make everyone connected with the paper . . . believe that accuracy is to a newspaper what virtue is to a woman.[23]

When accused of pandering to public taste to sell newspapers, Pulitzer replied in the *World*, "Of course newspapers are made to sell, and in that respect they resemble the highest work of art and intellect as well as the sermons preached in pulpits."[24]

Pulitzer attacked the intellectual elite as well as those who violated the law in order to achieve wealth; he demanded justice and attacked ostentatious displays of wealth, noting that it was "false Americanism" to create an aristocracy.[25] Pulitzer revealed his prejudices about women's education as well as his disdain for intellectual snobbery when he commented on Vassar College's commencement in 1884: "There is something appalling in the amount of transcendental erudition which Vassar College poured out at its Commencement."[26] Pulitzer said the country needed sensible wives and mothers, not philosophers. Pulitzer crusaded against religious bigotry, opposed prohibition as destructive to personal liberty, urged the poor to educate their children rather than sending them to work, and supported labor in its struggles against the corporations. But when unions tried to organize businesses such as his own he had difficulty understanding the purpose of unionism.

Pulitzer's wealth increased, he served four months in Congress, and sought social acceptance continuously denied to him because of his Jewish heritage, his poverty-stricken background, his lack of social graces, and his attacks on the wealthy in the pages of the *World*. In 1890, with his vision failing, he retired from active leadership of the *World*, but he continued absolute control of the paper through constant communication with editors.

Pulitzer's major challenge came in 1895 with the arrival of William Randolph Hearst, who purchased the *New York Journal*. Hearst raided Pulitzer's office for staff members and imitated many of Pulitzer's inventions. Although Pulitzer often opposed imperialism, during the Spanish-American War the *Journal* and the *World* distorted news from Cuba, competing to top each other's circulation figures. In 1898, Pulitzer, disgusted with the sensationalistic treatment of the war, gave orders to his staff to clean up its act—the time of immoderacy was over. Pulitzer died in October 1911, aboard his yacht, but the *World* continued to publish until 1931, when it was sold to the Scripps-Howard chain. Pulitzer's long-time rival, William Randolph Hearst, wrote an obituary honoring the prominent editor. It began:

> A towering figure in National and international journalism has passed away; a mighty democratic force in the life of the Nation and in the activity of the world has ceased; a great power uniformly exerted in behalf of popular rights and human progress is ended. Joseph Pulitzer is dead.[27]

WILLIAM RANDOLPH HEARST AND THE *NEW YORK JOURNAL*

William Randolph Hearst, an admirer of Joseph Pulitzer and Pulitzer's main competition during the 1890s and early 1900s, was born into a world vastly different from that of Joseph Pulitzer. He was the son of a wealthy investor and United States senator, and had he not flaunted arrogance in the face of his mentors, would have been a privileged graduate of Harvard University. Hearst was a man of contradiction. Accused for being emotionally childlike and demanding, at times seemingly given to principle while at other times to mere profit or to power, he amassed one of the greatest fortunes in the first half of the twentieth century. Although many despised his sensationalism, his promotion of war before and during the Cuban conflict, and his turn to conservative anti-Communism in the post-Depression years, he was a man to be reckoned with. When Hearst died he left a publishing empire with assets of $160 million. His organization published eighteen newspapers in twelve cities, the Sunday newspaper magazine *The American Weekly*, and nine magazines. In addition the organization owned King Features Service, International News Service, and International News Photos. Hearst owned seven castles and one of the largest private art collections in the United States.

Hearst was born April 29, 1863. He was the son of an ambitious father and a protective mother, and his painful shyness contrasted with his flamboyance and flair for the dramatic. He entered Harvard in 1882, but was suspended after a variety of pranks on professors, including one in which he sent chamber pots with their pictures displayed on the bottom to Harvard faculty. While at Harvard, Hearst became business manager of the financially failing *Lampoon* and soon turned it into a profit-making enterprise. Fascinated by newspapers, he secured a letter of introduction to *Boston Globe* publisher Charles H. Taylor and spent many hours in the *Globe* offices. After leaving Harvard he worked for Pulitzer at the *World*, and then returned to the West to edit the *Examiner*, a financially failing newspaper his father used to support his Senate campaign.

Hearst's father, who regarded journalism as less than a wholesome occupation, reluctantly agreed to let his son take over the San Francisco paper. Hearst launched several crusades, hired good and high-priced talent, and began a campaign against the Southern Pacific, whose officials had dominated California politics for many years. Although the *Examiner*'s circulation increased dramatically under Hearst's aggressive news strategy, it lost money — $300,000 during the first few years. However, by 1895, the *Examiner* was making money indeed, and Hearst looked for greater challenges.

In 1895, Hearst continued his experiment in New York, after purchasing the *Journal*, a newspaper founded in 1882 by Joseph Pulitzer's brother Albert. The paper had struggled through the years as an unprofitable and somewhat scandalous sheet. Within a year, Hearst had only the *World* left as a top competitor, since his circulation had by-passed that of the other New York papers. Hearst raided Pulitzer's staff, introduced color printing, and hired Pulitzer's comic-strip producer, Richard Outcalt, creator of the "Yellow Kid" comic strip. Hearst aimed for sensationalism of the highest order and ultimately demanded the United States engage in a war with Cuba.

Richard Outcault created this "Hogan's Alley" cartoon for Pulitzer's World *in 1896, before moving to Hearst's newspaper. The cartoon is titled, "Two very obstinate gentlemen: or, impoliteness rebuked." (Library of Congress Collection)*

In 1900, Hearst began to expand his newspaper chain and to pursue his political ambitions. Although his primary ambition was to be president of the United States, he never achieved significant political success in the role of an officeholder. He ran twice for Congress, twice for New York City mayor, and once for the New York governorship. In 1900, he became president of the National Association of Democratic Clubs and was elected to Congress in 1902 and 1904; in 1904 he placed second in balloting for the Democratic nomination for president.

Hearst's unrelenting criticism of President McKinley contributed to his lack of success in politics. The assassination of the president in 1901 followed a series of Hearst attacks and an article by Hearst writer Ambrose Bierce after the assassination of a Kentucky governor: "The bullet that pierced Goebel's breast/Can not be found in all the West;/Good reason, it is speeding here/To stretch McKinley on his bier." After claims that McKinley's assassin Leon F.

William Randolph Hearst's residence, "Beacon Towers," at Sands Point, Long Island. (Library of Congress Collection)

Czolgosz carried a copy of the *Journal* at the time of the assassination, many subscribers boycotted the Hearst newspapers and Hearst was hanged in effigy.

Hearst still was able to achieve some political success with his election to Congress, but his political career ended in defeat in 1909. Not content to stay out of the fray, however, Hearst plunged into criticism of U.S. support of Britain in 1914 as European powers declared war. Hearst's fear of Japanese domination of the Pacific and of Mexican collaboration with the "yellow peril" resulted in a film made by his International Film Service in 1915 that earned him a pro-German label. The film's bitter attack on the British and the Japanese sparked a Senate Judiciary Committee investigation of Hearst's activities and a Canadian boycott of Hearst's International News Service.

Hearst's empire continued to expand, with more than 38,000 people on the payroll and a $90 million annual operation. Hearst paid top writers well—Arthur Brisbane earned $250,000 a year. But Hearst publications often were supported by his other enterprises in mining and real estate. The depression strangled the operation, and for several years Hearst feared having to declare bankruptcy. He turned increasingly conservative, strongly opposed the American Newspaper Guild in the 1930s, became loudly anti-Communist and fought against war with Germany until the bombing of Pearl Harbor in December 1941.

Hearst developed serious heart problems in the postwar years and died August 14, 1951, in Beverly Hills.

COVERING THE SPANISH-AMERICAN WAR

The Spanish-American War of 1898 represented the culmination of at least three decades of Cuban struggles for independence and a desire on the part of the United States to acquire additional land and power. From 1868 to 1878 the Cubans fought the Spanish, and although they gained some concessions — the abolition of slavery, for example — they did not achieve their ultimate goal — independence from Spain. The United States meanwhile maintained a heavy investment in the Cuban economy through the imports of sugar. Until 1894, Cuban sugar entered the United States free of duty, but the Wilson-Gorman Tariff of 1894, which placed duties on Cuban sugar, disrupted the economy and perhaps contributed toward Cuban agitation for independence.

As a second insurgent uprising began in the 1890s, the Spanish put Commander Valeriano Weyler in charge of the island. Weyler instituted a policy of reconcentration, separating Cubans in camps from the insurgents in the hills. Disease took its toll in the camps, and more than one-fourth of the population died. During the mid-1890s American investments of $50 million were jeopardized by the conflict, and the $76 million worth of Cuban imports in 1894 declined to $15 million in 1898. While Spain attempted reform in Cuba, Spanish loyalists on the island rioted against the proposed reforms, and the United States sent its battleship *Maine* to the Havana Harbor. On February 16, 1898, the battleship exploded. Although recent evidence indicates the explosion may have resulted from an internal mechanical problem, Americans, including William Randolph Hearst, were quick to blame the Spaniards for the explosion of the ship.

The U.S. government demanded that Spain end its reconcentration policy and declare an armistice. Although Spain agreed to these concessions, Congress declared Cuba independent on April 19, 1898, and authorized the president to use military force to evict the Spanish from the island. Unwilling to relinquish its hold on Cuba, Spain declared war April 24 on the United States, three days after McKinley blockaded the island. During the short conflict 5,400 Americans died in Cuba. Only 379 of those deaths resulted from combat; more than 5,000 died of malaria and yellow fever.

At least a sizable minority in the United States believed that going to war over Cuba was determined more by extensive sugar investments on the island than by a desire to free Cuban citizens. Indeed, despite extensive agitation by yellow journalists such as Hearst and Pulitzer, the war resolution passed the Senate by a vote of only forty-two to thirty-five. The sentiment of the Senate was echoed in much of the local press, which eschewed the warmongering of Hearst and Pulitzer.[28] When the Spanish signed the Treaty of Paris in 1898, they granted Cuba its independence, ceded the Philippines, Guam, and Puerto Rico to the United States, and received $20 million for relinquishing the territory. In 1898 and 1899, the United States continued to acquire new land, annexing Wake Island, Hawaii, and Samoa.

Editors were mixed in their approaches to imperialistic motives and in the early days of the conflict the *Herald*, the *Post*, the *Tribune*, the *Times* and even the *World* attempted to discuss the complexities of the Cuban situation. Pulitzer's first correspondent, William Shaw Bowen, traveled throughout Cuba into insurgent camps and across Spanish lines without restriction because the Spanish respected his fair treatment. Such an approach, however, could not compete with Hearst's jazzy treatment of murderer/victim. One of Pulitzer's biographers, Swanberg, wrote:

> The majority of the public found it more exciting to read about the murder of Cuban babies and the rape of Cuban women by the Spaniards than to read conscientious accounts of complicated political problems and injustices on both sides.[29]

Some correspondents, such as George Rea of the *New York Herald*, doubted the stories of Cuban oppression. Rea, who had lived in Cuba for five years by the time of the second insurgency, was reluctant to fault the Spanish entirely. Rea accused the insurgent general, Maximo Gomez, of using reporters to perpetrate insurgent lies.[30] United States coverage in favor of insurgency escalated, however, and by 1896 the Spaniards were so incensed by American coverage of the insurgents that they restricted reporters' movements and kept them away from the front.

In 1896, both Pulitzer and Hearst escalated their calls for war, a tactic followed by immediate increases in circulation. By 1897, Pulitzer's New York circulation was 800,000, and Hearst was close behind with 700,000. Pulitzer's correspondent James Creelman, who later was employed by Hearst, urged President McKinley to act:

> No man's life, no man's property is safe. American citizens are imprisoned or slain without cause. American property is destroyed on all sides. . . . Blood on the roadsides, blood in the fields, blood on the doorsteps, blood, blood, blood! . . . A new Armenia lies within

80 miles of the American coast. Not a word from Washington! Not a sign from the president![31]

The Spanish, irate at Creelman's lack of restraint, evicted him from the island.

In December of that year, Hearst sent a highly celebrated writer, Richard Harding Davis, and the artist Frederick Remington to Cuba. Each was paid about $3,000 a month, a salary that far exceeded the normal $40 a week Cuban correspondents received.[32] Remington, legend has it, wired Hearst soon after his arrival:

Everything is quiet. There is no trouble here. There will be no war. I wish to return — Remington.

Hearst replied:

Please remain. You furnish the pictures and I'll furnish the war. — W. R. Hearst[33]

Hearst's desire to promote Davis and Remington backfired. He published an article in the *Journal* that Davis had already penetrated insurgent lines. The heavy Spanish surveillance that prevailed after such an article kept Davis from ever reaching Maximo Gomez.

In February 1897, Hearst further angered the Spanish and tried to enlist the American public in his campaign for war with an account of three Cuban women who were searched aboard an American ship off the coast of Cuba. Davis's story that Spanish officers rushed aboard an American vessel, searching for illegal documents, was accompanied by a Remington drawing of Spanish male officers and a naked Cuban woman. Once the ship reached the United States, Pulitzer's *World* reporters interviewed the women, who said they had been searched privately in a cabin by matrons — not by male Spanish officers on deck of the ship. Davis protested Hearst's treatment of his story, claiming that Remington had not been present and was responsible for the distortion. An irate Congress withdrew resolutions it had introduced to investigate the situation and the *Journal* was publicly exposed as "fictionalizing" the facts.

Hearst's greatest endeavor to create news as well as report it came with the tale of Evangelina Cisneros, the beautiful Cuban "Joan of Arc," a woman who voluntarily accompanied her imprisoned father in his exile by the Spanish to the Isle of Pines. While she claimed the island governor, Colonel Jose Berrez, had attempted to rape her, and that she had been jailed for defending her virtue, some evidence indicates she had been involved in an insurrection of the island and had framed the Spanish colonel.

The *Journal* wrote a heart-rending account of the young woman's brutal treatment by the Spaniards, and appealed to American women to sign petitions urging the Queen Regent of Spain and the pope to free her from the barbarous hands of the soldiers. When some newspapers, such as the *Commercial Advertiser*, tried to print a more factual account of the case, the public paid little attention. Meanwhile, Hearst sent reporter Karl Decker to free the maiden; he succeeded, dressed the maiden in a sailor's uniform and escorted her from the island.[34] Once she arrived in New York, Hearst dressed her in the latest fashions and presented her to society and to the president of the United States.

After the explosion of the *Maine*, Hearst pressed even harder for war, personally funding a junket to Cuba for senators and congressmen, including members of the House Foreign Affairs and Naval Affairs committees.[35]

From February to August 1898, the months of U.S. involvement in the war, Hearst spent seventeen days in Cuba as a foreign correspondent directing the activities of a staff of twenty. The war had boosted circulation, but by the end the *Journal* was still losing money.

LIFE OF A CORRESPONDENT

The life of a correspondent, with the exception of a few stars like Richard Harding Davis, was difficult. Few reporters were paid well enough to acquire the needed supplies of a horse, saddlebags, blankets, and adequate food and shelter. The guerilla-style warfare made it difficult for reporters to talk to insurgents, and left them dependent on guerillas for food and protection. It was difficult to get information outside official Spanish channels, and many reporters knew they failed to get accurate information from either side.

After the United States entered the war, reporters relied primarily on cable operators and military officers for information. Cable offices in New York and Key West were manned by censors, and reporters spent some time trying to evade the censors' cuts. Reporters also disliked General William J. Shafter, who led the Fifth Army Corps, the U.S. invading army. Not only did he weigh more than 300 pounds and smell strongly of tropical body odor, he also disclosed information reluctantly. Reporters generally more positively reported the activities of General Wood's Rough Riders, although photographer Jimmy Hare and Davis both said the Rough Riders' egos occasionally got out of line.[36]

From inland the only way to obtain information was on horseback or on foot, and in order to get information back to civilization a reporter either had to endure the arduous journey from jungle to shore, or hire a courier — whose dependability was suspect at best. Because cable lines between Cuba and the U.S. mainland had been cut at the beginning of U.S. involvement, newspapers chartered boats to transport correspondents to Key West to dispatch information. The dispatch boats were essential for speedy news delivery, but cost $5,000 to $9,000 a month. Cable costs also taxed the budgets of newspapers, varying from fifty to eighty cents a word. Melville Stone once claimed cable costs for one story exceeded $8,000.[37] Newspapers editors urged brevity.

In retrospect, news coverage of the Cuban conflict represented dramatic new attempts to obtain information in the midst of war. Editors faced a continuation of Civil War dilemmas regarding issues of national security versus the need for information in times of war. Correspondents struggled with the physical aspects of war reporting—heat, traveling through enemy lines, and living on inadequate rations. In addition, the relationships to editors on the mainland and the desire of editors to color the news often placed reporters in difficult situations with the Spanish, as well as with other reporters.

INFORMATION AS A GOAL

NEW YORK TIMES

Adolph Ochs rescued the *New York Times* from bankruptcy and circulation decline in 1896 when he bought it for $75,000. Ochs, who had worked as a typesetter and had successfully edited the *Chattanooga Times*, quickly installed new typographic equipment, bought new typewriters, and added telephones to the office. He reduced the price of the paper, but never attempted to gain the huge circulation figures of Hearst and Pulitzer. His credo: "To Give the News Impartially, Without Fear or Favor." Objectivity and accuracy were his bywords, and he sought to make the newspaper one of record. Although Ochs deplored photographs on page one, and allowed them only on the occasion of great news events, such as Charles Lindbergh's flight to Paris in 1927 or Franklin Delano Roosevelt's presidential victory in 1932, he introduced an illustrated Sunday supplement featuring the good life in New York. He rejected sensationalism in content and style, and refused even to allow comic strips within the *Times*.[38]

Ochs hired Carr Van Anda, who was managing editor of the *New York Times* from 1904 until 1925. Van Anda complemented Ochs's style with his interest in scientific achievement and pursuance of verifiable facts. Van Anda gained experience on the *Cleveland Herald* and the *Baltimore Sun*, and moved in 1888 to the *New York Sun* as desk man and reporter. After five years as a reporter, Van Anda became Dana's night editor, and then in 1904 moved to the *Times*. He worked twelve hours a day, seven days a week. He stayed at the

Chapter 11 **The Press and Modernization**

THE
Remington

Standard Typewriter

Has demonstrated its superiority for all kinds of Library Work

For **CARD INDEXING** it greatly excels the pen. It is more convenient and easy to operate, and its work is far neater, more rapid and more legible.

The **REMINGTON** is strong, simple, and durable. It never fails at critical moments. It can always be depended upon to do the highest grade of work.

Among the libraries in which the Remington Typewriter is now in successful use for card indexing are the following:

Library of Congress and Public Library at Washington; Pratt Institute, Brooklyn Library, Cooper Union Library, Library of Columbia University and Lenox Library in New York; Free Library and Library of the Philosophical Society in Philadelphia; Public Library, Newberry Library and Field Columbian Museum in Chicago; Wisconsin State Historical Library and the Library of the University of Wisconsin at Madison; Library of the Rhode Island Historical Society in Providence; McGill University Library at Montreal; Howard Library at New Orleans; State Libraries at Harrisburg, Pa., and Columbia, Mo.; and the Free Public Libraries at Minneapolis, Minn., St. Louis, Mo., Jefferson City, Mo., Milwaukee, Wis., Denver, Col., New Orleans, La., Allegheny, Pa., London, Ont., Newark, N. Y., New Haven, Conn., Jackson, Mich., Grand Rapids, Mich., Muskegon, Mich., Erie, Pa., Bradford, Pa., Warren, Pa., Westfield, N. Y., Gloversville, N. Y., Cedar Rapids, Ia., Grinnell, Ia., Iowa City, Ia., Beverley, Mass., Nahant, Mass., Springfield, Mass., and a number of other cities.

Send for special pamphlet giving specimens of card work

Wyckoff, Seamans & Benedict
327 Broadway, New York.

The typewriter revolutionized newsrooms. This advertisement appealed especially to librarians, who could use the typewriter to create card indices. (Library of Congress Collection)

Times until he was sixty, when he took a leave of absence because of severe pneumonia. He officially retired in 1932 at sixty-seven and died of a heart attack in 1945 at eighty years old.

Van Anda set high standards for news reporting and emphasized proper usage, placing a high value on the role of the copy editor. He strived for completeness, accuracy, and objectivity. His motto was that all news is fit to print if handled properly. Van Anda also introduced the rotogravure section of the Sunday supplement to America, an innovation necessary for the illustrated magazines that later would take advantage of the rotogravure technology. He founded the *New York Times Index*, insuring that the *Times* would be a newspaper of record.

WILLIAM ROCKHILL NELSON

Rather than look for a newspaper to edit, William Rockhill Nelson searched for a city in which to start a newspaper. He was a man willing to take a risk, as he had earned $200,000 as a road contractor in Indiana by the time he was twenty-five, and lost it all in a business venture with a friend. Nelson and Samuel E. Morss first bought a Fort Wayne, Indiana, newspaper, *The Sentinel*, in 1879 and edited it as an independent Democratic newspaper. Deciding that Fort Wayne lacked the wide scope they needed, they chose Kansas City, a sprawling and ugly town in 1880. Muddy streets, wooden sidewalks, mule-drawn streetcars, and political corruption characterized the city.

The *Kansas City Star*, an afternoon paper, appeared in September 1880. The four-page paper had narrow columns and sold for two cents, three cents less than its local competitors. Eugene Fields, editor of the competitor *Times*, called the new paper the "Twilight Twinkler."[39] Nelson's subscription list was no problem, but it was difficult to acquire enough advertising to support increased costs of an expanding subscriber base, and he had to borrow money to keep the paper afloat and to install a new perfecting press. During the first year, Morss retired and Nelson became sole owner of the newspaper.

Nelson, like Dana, wrote little for the newspaper, relying on and trusting his reportorial staff. In 1882, he was able to acquire a small evening paper with an Associated Press franchise, which strengthened the *Star's* news sections. In 1901, he bought the *Times*, and published it as a separate morning edition. Nelson's *Star* campaigned against monopoly in the street-railway system, crusaded against city corruption and election fraud, and campaigned for beautification of Kansas City's parks and boulevards. He educated residents about the importance of parks and fought for increased taxes to support such improvements. He fought saloons, offered a reward for the capture of Jesse James, and built model rental homes to demonstrate the possibilities for quality moderate-priced construction.[40]

"Anybody can print the news," he declared, "but the *Star* tried to build things up. That is what a newspaper is for."[41] Nelson avoided the sensationalistic devices of the 1890s and during his lifetime the *Star* never carried colored comics, halftone illustrations, or large headlines.

Nelson, originally a Democrat, ran an independent newspaper and supported Theodore Roosevelt in 1900, turning to the Progressive Party in 1912. In 1914, Nelson began to cope with severe health problems. He died in 1915 from uremic poisoning and stipulated that his fortune be used to establish what is now known as the Nelson Art Gallery.

REPORTERS AND EDITORS

Although being an editor or publisher in the latter half of the nineteenth century signified involvement in a definite profession, being a reporter was more of "a way station on the highway to politics, business, literature or editorial work than a profession itself."[42] Despite the increased amount of news resulting from reporter-generated stories, reporters received low wages, often on space rates, were subject to erratic dismissals, and gained little prestige from their work. Correspondents such as Richard Harding Davis and Jack London, who gained significant reputations as war correspondents, were exceptions rather than the rule. Such treatment propelled journalists to move into editorial capacities or to change professions altogether. In addition, the increased commercialization of the daily press presented a conflict for those reporters who considered themselves to be social critics.

Although some reporters received salaries, more were confined to the space-rate system, which meant that reporters were paid only for the number of column inches printed. In 1884, the trade magazine *The Journalist* claimed New York reporters received from fifteen to twenty dollars per week. Outside New York, reporters received less. By 1900, experienced New York reporters received as much as sixty dollars a week, although hundreds of writers earned only twenty dollars a week. In smaller cities, seventeen to twenty-seven dollars was the norm. Reporters' salaries compared more favorably to that of craftsmen such as compositors and plumbers than they did to professionals such as physicians or teachers. Edwin Shuman, writing in 1903, explained: "Newspaper writing, in the essential qualifications required, is a learned profession; but in its exact comparative insecurity it more nearly resembles a trade."[43]

Reporters engaged in various forms of moonlighting by writing advertisements, working as court stenographers, or producing news and features for independent Sunday papers. It also was possible to supplement one's income by dropping names into stories, including product names in stories and by

This 1885 lithograph by T. Sinclair & Son depicts representative journals of the United States. (Library of Congress Collection)

assisting politicians. Because editors checked the opposition newspapers to decide whether their own reporters were being accurate, reporters often cooperated in agreeing on such facts as addresses and the spelling of names, even if the facts were incorrect. Reporters on space rates also tended to "overwrite," hoping that by producing more inches they would be paid more.[44]

The career patterns of metropolitan editors also changed toward the latter part of the century; in the earlier years editors normally started work as young apprentices, worked their way up to own a small paper, then expanded the publication or bought a larger one. Social and economic mobility decreased by the 1890s. From 1875 to 1890 the apprenticeship system faded, and college educations and successful fathers more directly affected editorial success. By the latter part of the century editors usually acquired college degrees, began newspaper work as reporters, and did not always own a controlling interest in the paper for which they worked.[45] In this sense, top editors belonged to a group comparable to that of industrial leaders.

PRESS CLUBS

Declining social mobility of the reporter coupled with low job security posed a conflict for a reporter who viewed himself as a professional. Katherine Lanpher described the metropolitan reporter as "a hard-drinking bohemian who was socially dexterous, traversing the lines of social class with ease, moving in the circles of both the raw and the refined," but who "eked out" his existence amid a "clash of image and reality."[46]

Lanpher suggested that in the late nineteenth century, reporters formed press clubs to fulfill their need to legitimize their roles within society. Reporters leaned toward identifying themselves as professionals and sought with other groups to identify themselves by their skills.

Press clubs performed several services. For example, the Press Club of Chicago, organized in 1880, aimed to elevate the professional and integrate journalists into the professional and social elite of the community. The Whitechapel Club, formed in Chicago in 1889, on the other hand, was a setting for radical political discussions and a theater for satirical pranks.

Prominent editors and publishers such as Melville Stone, Victor Lawson, and Samuel and Joseph Medill belonged to the Press Club, but the bohemian reporters of the city also belonged. This rather formal club included a variety of kinds of individuals in its membership, but tailored its membership and its activities to be receptive to society as a whole. The Whitechapel Club, on the other hand, preserved its bohemian status, claimed to be "intolerant of pretense," and served as a radical political forum for ideas that did not appear in Chicago newspapers. Reporters were the mainstay—publishers and editors were not allowed.

Lanpher suggested the two Chicago clubs served two functions. Although the Press Club of Chicago sought to convey the image of the reporter as a dignified and valued member of society who could easily assimilate into the complex of men's clubs, the Whitechapel Club pressed for recognition of the reporter as social critic. The clubs presented an image of the reporter that was both tangible to those outside the field and acceptable to the reporters themselves. Press clubs did not dissolve the constraints of working on a newspaper turned commercial institution, but they offered journalists a chance to bring about a kind of reconciliation between the constraints they struggled with and the expectations they nurtured.[47]

PUBLISHERS' ASSOCIATIONS

Regional publishers' associations existed from time to time, but national organization began in 1887 with the development of the American Newspaper Publishers' Association (ANPA). From its first meeting, the organization began to develop policies on labor, but closed-door meetings and lack of adequate records present difficulty in reconstructing early policy. During the 1890s, the association intensified its severe stance against striking labor unions, and during the first two decades of the twentieth century, the association developed a strong antiunion policy.

The record of newspapers on labor organization is mixed. Although Chicago newspapers in reaction to the railroad strikes of 1877, the eight-hour-day movement of the 1880s and the Pullman Strike of 1894, urged conflict resolution in the interest of commercial order and social harmony, they were not so quick to participate in conflict resolution themselves. In 1898, Chicago dailies suspended for four days to fight the demands of the stereotypers and formally agreed not to deal separately with a striking union.[48]

In the early years of ANPA work, the national office dealt primarily with newspaper-agency relations, postal arrangements, newsprint and labor, and interchanged advertising information among members.

CONCLUSION

The newspaper industry grew substantially from the end of Reconstruction through the close of the nineteenth century. Although the total number of dailies and weeklies grew, particular growth was noticeable among Sunday and evening newspapers. Advertisers selected evening editions because of their particular appeal to women, who were regarded as the primary purchasers in the home.

By the 1890s, the newspaper industry was firmly established as a commercial institution, with a division of editorial duties among particular employees and a distinct business department that courted advertisers. For the most part, newspapers relied on advertising rather than on party patronage as a primary means of support, although local government printing contracts continued to be important to some smaller newspapers.

As the press responded to increased urbanization, it developed a variety of models. Some newspaper publishers helped build coalitions with other parts of the community and pursued a consumer-oriented program aimed at solving urban problems and building broad-based city services. Others assumed an aloof, informational role, attempting to present scientific information to solve problems and to promote national unity. Others took the sensational route and described the city in sweeping, celebratory terms, championing the underdog and presenting the diversity of urban life. Although not all newspapers were urban in orientation, even small-town publishers were concerned with developments in business and town services.

Newspapers expanded their editorial staffs and adopted new technologies as they covered the Spanish-American War. Hearst and Pulitzer adopted a sensational approach, which engendered increased criticism of the press. Correspondents covering the war had difficulty getting information from insurgents and relied primarily on official channels of information.

Although reporters became increasingly important in covering the news of the late nineteenth century, they were poorly paid and had little security. Metropolitan reporters organized themselves in press clubs, striving to achieve an identity they and the world around them could recognize, and trying to resolve the conflicts presented within their jobs. Editors also organized, particularly as the American Newspaper Publishers Association, to share advertising and circulation information, to fight labor organization, and to lobby for favorable postal regulation.

NOTES

1. For analysis of the cultural transformation of the United States and its relationship to modernization, see Richard D. Brown, *Modernization: The Transformation of American Life, 1600–1865* (New York: Hill and Wang, 1976). Brown argues that modernization is a process that began in the United States at the moment of colonial settlement and continues today. See also Alan Trachtenberg, *The Incorporation of America: Culture and Society in the Gilded Age* (New York: Hill and Wang, 1982).

2. See Naomi Lamoreaux, *The Great Merger Movement in American Business, 1895–1904* (New York: Cambridge University Press, 1985), for description of merger movement as a means of business survival. For other interpretations see Allen F. Davis and Harold D. Woodman, *Conflict or Consensus In Modern American History* (Washington, D.C.: D.C. Heath and Co., 1968) and Samuel P. Hays, *The Response to Industrialism* (Chicago: University of Chicago Press, 1957).

3. For a description of the cultural development of the nineteenth-century newspaper, see John Pauly, "The Search for the Ideal Newspaper," unpublished paper presented to the American Journalism Historians Association, October 1986, St. Louis, Mo.; "The Professionalization of Newspaper Reading," unpublished paper presented to American Journalism Historians Association, October 1984, Tallahassee, Fla; "News and the Culture of Democracy," unpublished paper presented to the Popular Culture Association/American Culture Association Convention,

April 1980, Detroit, Mich.; and "The Ideological Origins of an Independent Press," unpublished paper presented to American Journalism Historians Association, October 1985, Las Vegas, Nev. Pauly argues that news, as defined by late nineteenth-century and early twentieth-century editors, does not give the public the type of knowledge they need to create a democratic order.

4. Gerald J. Baldasty and Jeffrey B. Rutenbeck, "The Economic Environment of Press Partisanship in the Late Nineteenth Century," unpublished paper presented to the Association for Education in Journalism and Mass Communication Convention, San Antonio, Tex., August 1987, p. 14.
5. S. N. D. North, "History and Present Condition of the Newspaper and Periodical Press of the United States, with a Catalogue of the publications of the Census Year," in U.S. Department of the Interior, Bureau of the Census, *Tenth Census* (Washington, 1884), VIII, p. 51, cited in Gunther Barth, *City People: The Rise of Modern City Culture in Nineteenth-Century America* (New York: Oxford University Press, 1986), p. 59.
6. David Paul Nord, *Newspapers and New Politics: Midwestern Municipal Reform, 1890–1900* (Ann Arbor: University Microfilms, Intl., 1981).
7. All daily figures were compiled from data from the census and Rowell's as cited in Alfred McClung Lee, *The Daily Newspaper in America* (New York: The Macmillan Co., 1937).
8. *Advertising World* (Columbus, Ohio) June 14, 1897, p. 1, cited in Baldasty and Rutenbeck, "The Economic Environment of Press Partisanship in the Late Nineteenth Century," p. 18.
9. Nord, *Newspapers and New Politics*, p. 19.
10. Richard B. Kielbowicz, "The Limits of the Press as an Agent of Reform: Minneapolis, 1900-1905," *Journalism Quarterly* 59:1 (Spring 1982), p. 27.
11. Jean Folkerts, "William Allen White as Businessman and Editor During the Reform Years (1890–1900)," *Kansas History* 7:2 (Summer 1984), pp. 129–138.
12. For elaboration of this theme, see Michael Schudson, *Discovering the News: A Social History of American Newspapers* (New York: Basic Books, 1978) pp. 88–120.
13. Schudson, *Discovering the News*, pp. 119–120.
14. Pauly, "Ideological Origins of an Independent Press," pp. 4, 8.
15. Michael McGerr, *The Decline of Popular Politics: The American North, 1865–1928* (New York: Oxford University Press, 1986), pp. 130–131.
16. McGerr, *Decline of Politics*, pp. 131–132.
17. See Pauly, "The Search for the Ideal Newspaper." Pauly cites contemporary critiques in *The Arena, The Delineator, The Literary Digest, The Homiletic Review*, and *The Atlantic Monthly*.
18. For a contrast of editors who espoused traditional business values and those who sought a more visionary image of the city as a collective enterprise, see David Paul Nord, "The Public Community: The Urbanization of Journalism in Chicago," *Journal of Urban History* 11:4 (August 1985), pp. 411–441.
19. *World*, May 17, 1883, cited in W. A. Swanberg, *Pulitzer* (New York: Charles Scribner's Sons, 1967), p. 76.

20. Ted Curtis Smythe, "The Reporter, 1880–1900: Working Conditions and Their Influence on the News," *Journalism History* 7:1 (Spring 1980), p. 3.
21. *World*, May 31, 1883, cited in George Juergens, *Pulitzer and the New York World* (Princeton, N.J.: Princeton University Press, 1966), p. 63.
22. Juergens, *Pulitzer*, pp. 67–68.
23. Ireland Alleyne, *Joseph Pulitzer, Reminiscences of a Secretary* (New York: Mitchell Kennerley, 1914), p. 110, cited in Juergens, *Pulitzer*, pp. 30–31.
24. *World*, May 6, 1884, p. 4, cited in Juergens, *Pulitzer*, p. 69.
25. *World*, December 16, 1883, p. 4, cited in Juergens, *Pulitzer*, p. 187.
26. *World*, June 13, 1884, p. 4, cited in Juergens, *Pulitzer*, p. 227.
27. Swanberg, *Pulitzer*, p. 412.
28. See Robert C. Hilderbrand, *Power and the People* (Chapel Hill: University of North Carolina Press, 1981).
29. Swanberg, *Pulitzer*, p. 117.
30. Mary Mander, "Pen and Sword" Ph.D. Disser., University of Illinois at Urbana, 1979, pp. 31–32.
31. *World*, May 17, 1896, cited in W.A. Swanberg, *Citizen Hearst* (New York: Charles Scribner's Sons, 1961), p. 108.
32. Mander, "Pen and Sword," p. 22.
33. James Creelman, *On the Great Highway*, pp. 177–78, cited in Swanberg, *Citizen Hearst*, pp. 107–108.
34. *Journal*, October 10, 1897.
35. Swanberg, *Citizen Hearst*, p. 139.
36. Mander, "Pen and Sword," pp. 38–39.
37. Mander, "Pen and Sword," p. 46.
38. Gay Talese, *The Kingdom and the Power* (New York and Cleveland: The World Publishing Co., 1969), pp. 53, 74.
39. Icie F. Johnson, *William Rockhill Nelson and the Kansas City Star* (Kansas City, Mo.: Burton Publishing Company, 1935), p. 49.
40. Frank Luther Mott, *American Journalism* (New York: The Macmillan Co., 1962), p. 472.
41. Willard Grosvenor Bleyer, *Main Currents in the History of American Journalism* (Hougton Mifflin Company, 1927), p. 313.
42. Ted Curtis Smythe, "The Reporter, 1880–1900," p. 8.
43. Edwin Shuman, *Practical Journalism: A Complete Manual of the Best Newspaper Methods* (New York: D. Appleton and Co., 1903), p. 25, cited in Smythe, "The Reporter, 1880–1900," p. 2.
44. Smythe, "The Reporter, 1880–1900," pp. 6–7.
45. Jack Hart, "Horatio Alger in the Newsroom: Social Origins of American Editors," *Journalism Quarterly* 53:1 (Spring 1976), pp. 14–20.
46. Katherine Lanpher, "The Boys at the Club: An Examination of Press Clubs as an Aspect of the Occupational Culture of the Late 19th Century Journalist," Paper

presented to the History Division at the Association for Education in Journalism Annual Convention in Athens, Ohio, July 1982.

47. Lanpher, "Boys at the Club," p. 14.
48. For discussion of Chicago newspapers see David Paul Nord, "The Business Values of American Newspapers: The 19th Century Watershed in Chicago," *Journalism Quarterly* 61:2 (Summer 1984), p. 265. For discussion of nineteenth-century newspaper labor disputes, see Lee, *Daily Newspaper*, p. 153.

CHAPTER 12

REFORM
IS MY
RELIGION

Despite the modernization of the metropolitan press, reform newspapers of all kinds continued to flourish in the late 1800s. The suffragists, agrarian radicals, labor, blacks, and immigrants established their own newspapers, often using older technology, in an attempt to disseminate information the mainstream press ignored. Indicative of the intensity of reform movements during the latter part of the nineteenth century was Iowa Greenback-Labor Congressman Leman Weller's cry, "Reform is my religion." The congressman knew the value of a sympathetic press, and supported a variety of reform newspapers in Iowa.

Although the concept of a mass press was firmly in place by the last half of the century, the presence of these specialized publications clearly marked the limits of advertising-supported newspapers aimed at a large and diversified audience. A press supported by the marketing of commercial products did not address the needs of the variety of people and groups who lived within the United States.

Acquiring the vote for women (suffrage) did not receive major attention from mainstream newspapers until persons outside the movement began to perceive it as a legitimate demand. In Oregon, for example, women gained little coverage of their ideas in the mainstream press from 1870 to 1905. In 1905, when Portland was chosen as the site of the National American Woman Suffrage Association's national convention, the amount and nature of coverage changed.[1] The suffragist press, although divided at times on the scope and tone of women's issues, treated such issues in a serious way and promoted a sense of community among women.[2]

The black press discussed the issue of whether blacks eventually would be incorporated into mainstream society. Because the white press ignored the accomplishments of black leaders and the day-to-day events of their lives—weddings, births, deaths—the black press provided an important social, as well as political function.

Members of the Farmers' Alliance published newspapers to provide information about droughts and crop failures the mainstream press avoided because they feared declining investments in the West by eastern capitalists. Like the suffrage press, farmers' newspapers also provided a sense of community and presented the alliance movement as a legitimate effort to oppose the dominant political and economic structures. Although the agrarian movement was largely ignored by the eastern metropolitan press, the farmers' activities were noted by midsize dailies in the Midwest. These newspapers tried first to laugh the farmers out of business, but as the agrarian radicals achieved more political success, the press began to take them seriously. Agrarian newspapers, however, were ignored by their contemporary editors and by historians, despite their circulations, which in some cases reached 100,000.[3]

The ethnic press, founded largely by immigrants, peaked in 1917 with a total of 1,325 different foreign-language newspapers in the United States. Throughout the nineteenth century these newspapers helped immigrants adapt to life in the United States, helped maintain sociocultural heritages, provided unique information not available in mainstream newspapers, enriched American thought, and played an influential political role in their own communities.

Chapter 12 **Reform Is My Religion**

THE SUFFRAGIST PRESS

In 1900, many Americans still could not vote. Many immigrants, all blacks, Native Americans, and women were excluded from the political process. There were some exceptions. A Wyoming woman, Esther Morris, who migrated with her husband to the western territory in 1869, helped convince the territorial legislature to allow women to vote. Twenty years later, when Wyoming applied for statehood, its constitution contained the right of women to vote in state elections. It was the first state to extend the right to women. So controversial was women's suffrage that Congress petitioned Wyoming to drop the clause from its constitution. Southerners, who usually argued for states' rights, vehemently opposed allowing women to vote, but the Wyoming legislature threatened to remain out of the Union rather than come in without women. In a close vote, the House and the Senate finally admitted Wyoming, with women's suffrage intact.

Although some local school boards permitted women to vote on school issues and in municipal elections, women basically were disenfranchised. It was not until 1920, with the passage of the Nineteenth Amendment, that all women obtained the right to vote in all elections. Throughout the struggle the suffragist press was a vital, although limited part of American communication.[4] It existed because the mass press did not, on the whole, cover women's issues from a sympathetic point of view, nor did it adequately chronicle the organization of the women's movement.

The first wave of feminism in the United States began in the 1840s, and coincided with the most intense period of the abolitionist movement. Legally, women were the property of men, isolated in their domestic sphere. Women active in the abolitionist movement appeared more frequently in public life, and black publications like the *North Star* and William Lloyd Garrison's *Liberator* called for enfranchisement of women as well as that of blacks.

The women's movement formally began July 20, 1848, with a meeting in Seneca Falls, New York. After that meeting a handful of women's publications began to appear. Amelia Bloomer started the *Lily* in 1849, first as a temperance (anti-alcohol) publication, but continued it as a suffrage organ. By 1852, the eight-page monthly was devoted totally to suffrage. Paulina Wright Davis presented women's issues in *Una* from 1853 to 1856, appealing to intellectual women. Two other pre-Civil War suffrage journals were *The Sibyl* in New York and *The Pioneer and Woman's Advocate* in Rhode Island.[5] Although the circulation of the suffrage press was small in comparison to that of its mainstream counterparts, its importance to readers was expressed by an Ohio reader of *The Mayflower*, the only suffrage paper published during the Civil War:

This 1871 illustration in Frank Leslie's Illustrated Newspaper *depicted a delegation of female suffragists presenting the case for women's voting rights to the Judiciary Committee of the House of Representatives. (Library of Congress Collection)*

> How dear your little paper has become to me — how it cheers and strengthens me, even as the voice of a friend . . . it seems endowed with almost human sympathy; perhaps because the writers do not write coldly from the head alone, but warm their glowing thoughts by the pure light of a true and earnest purpose that emanates from the heart.[6]

After the Fourteenth Amendment to the U.S. Constitution was passed in 1868 enfranchising all male voters, a second wave of feminism began. The movement was divided, however, among women who believed they should concentrate on getting the vote, and women who longed for more substantial political and social reform. Lucy Stone's moderate *Journal*, which emphasized the importance of the right to vote, attracted only 6,000 subscribers at its peak. By 1893, the official suffrage organization had only 13,000 members. But suffrage journals, small and medium-sized, mushroomed across the nation. The suffrage editors lacked support even from the suffrage organizations themselves, which refused to grant funds. Prominent women journalists like Jane

> **GOALS OF *THE REVOLUTION***
>
> The enfranchisement of women is one of the leading ideas that calls this journal into existence. Seeing its realization, the many necessary changes in our modes of life, we think The Revolution a fitting name for a paper that will advocate so radical a reform as this involves in our political, religious and social worlds.
>
> SOURCE. Elizabeth Cady Stanton, The Revolution, January 8, 1868.

Gray Swisshelm, one of the first women journalists to actually work in an office—some called it putting herself on public display—reacted to the suffrage issue with mixed feelings.[7] At least one newspaper emerged from the belief that women's interests would not be served by ordinary papers or typical ladies' magazines, because their concerns either would be crowded out or mixed up with others of an undesirable nature.

Despite their lack of political and social homogeneity, publications warned women against apathy and encouraged converts to feminism by celebrating women's accomplishments. Women's publications provided women with a sense of community by acknowledging common goals "and shared interests, participation in cooperative activity, self-conscious emphasis on loyalty and commitment." They made available information for those women unable to attend national suffrage conventions.

The newspapers also provided opportunities for women to develop management skills. Women owned, published, and edited the publications. The papers "taught suffragists how to argue, why to sacrifice, when to renounce; they explained and exhorted; they glorified both the togetherness of this community and its apartness from the larger society."[8]

THE REVOLUTION

Susan B. Anthony, an ardent suffragist, argued that women should not only have the vote, but should have expanded rights in social and political arenas. In 1868, she began publishing *The Revolution*, a sixteen-page weekly, which continued for two and one-half years. The editor, Elizabeth Cady Stanton, argued for voting rights, liberalized divorce laws, equal pay and equal employment opportunities for women, unionization, and elevation of the place of women in organized religion. The motto, "Men, Their Rights and Nothing More; Women, Their Rights and Nothing Less," was considered too radical and unfeminine by many women, who turned to more moderate publications.

WOMAN'S JOURNAL

Lucy Stone's *Woman's Journal*, coedited with her husband, Henry Blackwell, was considered moderate because it focused on voting rights and not on expanded roles for women. This journal's moderation may have prolonged its life. Begun in 1870, it lasted until 1917, shortly before passage of the suffrage amendment. Lucy Stone assured women that a suffragist "could be courageous, dedicated and active, yet still be "a genuine woman, gentle, tender, refined and quiet." The *Journal* emphasized feminism and believed men were necessary as bridge builders to the rest of society and to the political system. Still the *Journal* roused women to an indignant "sense of itself and its value."

WOODHULL AND CLAFLIN'S WEEKLY

At the other end of the spectrum was a radical publication, *Woodhull and Claflin's Weekly*, considered not only too radical but downright scandalous by many women. The newspaper was a joint venture of Victoria Woodhull and her sister Tennessee Claflin. Woodhull campaigned for president of the United States through the pages of the weekly, and she and her sister discussed free love, prostitution, abortion, and venereal disease.

THE WOMAN REBEL

Women became more vociferous after the turn of the century, and Margaret Sanger, famous for her campaign to legalize birth control, began publishing *The Woman Rebel* in 1914. Authorities declared an article about contraception "indecent, lewd, lascivious and obscene" under the Comstock (anti-obscenity) Law. Sanger was indicted for sending birth-control information through the U.S. mails, forcing her to flee the country. She did not give up, however, and in 1921 she formed the American Birth Control League.

The variety of publications showed that although suffrage organizations were developed in eastern states, their publications knew no geographical boundaries. They existed in Oregon, Utah, Illinois, Colorado, Ohio, Arkansas, and Florida. In addition to these individually organized newspapers, about 3,000 publications originally begun as women's professional journals to support various clubs were in existence by the turn of the century. Publications advocating a full range of women's rights issues existed, but suffrage retained the primary focus.[9]

Chapter 12 **Reform Is My Religion**

BLACK PRESS AFTER THE CIVIL WAR

With the end of the Civil War and the passage of the Fourteenth Amendment black Americans looked forward to an era of freedom. In the South blacks moved off the plantations, flocked to the new schools set up for black adults and children and began to practice trades and share cropping. But many of the hopes for political and economic equality were shattered abruptly. As Republican politicians attempted to organize the black vote in the South, white Democratic Southerners became more antagonistic toward blacks. During the late 1860s, the Ku Klux Klan systematically organized violence against blacks and lynching became an increasingly southern and racist phenomenon. Although the paths to black opportunity were wider and more diverse in the North, prejudice and immigrant competition for jobs exacted their toll.

By the 1880s, reconstruction and the promise of black equality gave way to segregation and institutionalized racism. In civil rights cases in the 1880s the Supreme Court declared the 1875 Civil Rights Act, which forbade segregation in public places, unconstitutional. Public consensus in both North and South was that the black was on the bottom of society because he deserved to be.

It was in such a climate that Booker T. Washington, president of Tuskegee Institute, rose to prominence as the new leader of his race with a speech at the opening of the Atlanta Cotton States and International Exposition. Washington advocated a new position of accommodation between northern whites, southern whites and blacks. To the white South, Washington expressed his love and devotion. "I was born in the South," he said, "and I understand thoroughly the prejudices, the customs, the traditions of the South." Washington said "these prejudices are something that it does not pay to disturb," and "that the agitation of questions of social equality is the extremist folly." He renounced northern intervention and advocated that blacks improve themselves through industrial education and economic opportunity. He reminded the South of the black's devotion during the Civil War and encouraged the South to rely on black labor rather than on those who had produced labor strife in the North. He won the admiration and respect of Northern capitalists by denouncing labor unions, revolutionary tactics, and socialism and by professing devotion to the laissez-faire theory of government.[10] His speech, which became known as the "Atlanta Compromise," won the admiration of nearly all whites and espoused a philosophy of equal opportunity, rather than equality, for blacks.

Booker T. Washington became a powerful man. He was the chief distributor of patronage in the South for federal appointments during the administrations of Presidents Theodore Roosevelt and William Howard Taft, and a

Booker T. Washington, speaking to a Louisiana audience. (Library of Congress Collection)

broker for the distribution of northern white patronage. He was invited into southern homes that had barred black people since the war's end, and until his death in 1915 he exerted much influence over the black press. Washington developed what became known as the Tuskegee Machine, a national network of editors and other influential black leaders loyal to Washington. Although he never achieved unanimous support from black leaders, he in time exerted a good deal of influence through the distribution of subsidies to a black press, hard pressed to find better financial support.[11]

His accommodationist tactics, however, were opposed by many, including his chief rival, W. E. B. DuBois. DuBois, who in 1910 founded the *Crisis*, the magazine supported by the National Association for the Advancement of Colored People (NAACP), described those editors who accepted Washington's subsidies as "bribe-takers" and the "worst type" of blacks.[12] Among other newspapers opposing Booker T. Washington's philosophy was William

Monroe Trotter's Boston *Guardian*, founded in 1901. He fought with Washington over control of the Afro-American Council, was jailed after a rally, and found himself at the unpleasant end of a libel suit.[13]

Despite division within the ranks of black leaders and editors, the black press thrived. Although about forty black newspapers were started before 1865, more than 1,000 were added from the end of the war to the turn of the century.[14] Many, although vigorous during their lifetimes, did not last long due to economic hardship and social pressure.

AGRARIAN PRESS

The agrarian press of the 1890s primarily served the Populist party, which grew out of the Farmers' Alliances, first organized in Texas in 1877. These alliances were groups of farmers who banded together after the agricultural depression of the 1870s to protest national policies they believed hampered their growth. The alliances were not without precedent. Indeed, rural America had a rich history of resistance to economic domination by corporations, railroads, and the "robber barons" of the 1880s. Farmers supported the Union Labor Party, in some cases the Socialist Party, and joined the Grange, a nonpolitical organization of farmers designed to promote agrarian social life and cooperative business arrangements. The Farmers' Alliances spread throughout Texas, then through other southern states. Similar organizations developed throughout the Midwest, with Kansas as a key state. Farmers formed cooperatives to combat the crop-lien system, which bound southern farmers to the furnishing merchant. (Southern merchants often would lend farmers money for seed in return for their crop. Farmers were never able to pay off the debt and save enough money for the next year's crop, so they were continually in debt.) In the Midwest the emphasis was on eliminating differential railway rates that hampered the shipment of crops.

For example, rates from one major point to another major point were much less expensive per mile than were rates from rural areas to a major city. It might cost a farmer the same amount to ship his crop from Topeka, Kansas, sixty miles west of Kansas City, Missouri, as it would cost him to ship it the 496 miles from Kansas City to Chicago. To offset these problems, the farmers wanted government ownership of railroads and other land and monetary reforms. Another major concern was the short money supply. As the movement developed, farmers who joined the Populist Party supported the free coinage of silver, a measure they believed would increase the supply of money and help halt the agricultural depression.[15]

PURPOSE

One of the greatest problems facing the Farmers' Alliances, and later the Populist Party, was educating the farmer about economic issues that directly affected him. By this time some mainstream newspapers were served by "telegraphic" reports, but most of these newspapers did not carry detailed news about the farmers' plight. In fact, as the farmers' movement gained momentum, the mainstream newspapers actively campaigned against the alliances.

For example, in 1886 the Texas Alliance Journal, the *Dallas Southern Mercury*, lamented the drought conditions in West Texas. The *Mercury* requested that each local alliance donate seed and food because "already the depopulation of many sections of the West has begun, and trains of farm wagons with their freight of miserable, half-starved humanity is winding their way over the barren plains eastward in search of food." The Texas State Alliance donated $7,000, its total treasury, to the drive. At the same time, the mainstream daily papers, most conspicuously *The Dallas Morning News*, challenged the reports, claiming only the cattlemen, not the farmers, would be hurt. The *News*, which represented urban financial interests, was more concerned about declining property values for land speculators and dropping cattle prices than they were about starving farmers.[16]

The reform press struck back at the city dailies with ferocity. The editor of the *Kansas Workman* said the Republican press was "thoroughly unreliable."

> It lacks both honor and intelligence. It is an unsafe teacher. Its ideas of morals are exceedingly low. One day it abuses and the next it praises. One day it exposes fraud and corruption and the next it lionizes the guilty parties. Under its guidance this nation is rapidly approaching the end of nations.[17]

CONTENT AND STYLE

To provide information the daily newspapers ignored, the Farmer's Alliance first formed a lecture circuit, sending leaders to small towns and farms to present lectures about the developing movement. This strategy consumed too much time and money for a movement that was starving for both. The development of periodicals and newspapers was the answer. During the peak years of the movement the *National Economist*, the farmers' national newspaper, attained a circulation of more than 100,000. Populists had more than 1,000 newspapers in circulation and in Kansas and Texas, both Populist strongholds, 300 newspapers were published. Some like the *Kansas Advocate*

> **HOW TO START A REFORM NEWSPAPER**
>
> You will have two sources of income—from subscriptions and advertisements.
>
> A dollar a year is the popular price for a weekly paper. You ought to be able to obtain from 200 to 1,000 subscribers at that price.
>
> Fifty dollars for a column advertisement for one year will be a low rate for you to charge, making it proportionately more for a smaller advertisement or for a shorter time than one year. For local reading notices 5 cents a line is low enough. For business cards of one inch charge $5 per year. You ought to be able to secure four to six columns of advertising all the time in any live town. You can also count on securing from $50 to $100 in railroad advertising which they will pay in transportation—or mileage books. It would be safe to count on at least $300 for advertising. You ought to be able to get $500 out of subscriptions—I am counting about an average county. This will be an income of $800 a year. Now as to expenses.
>
> The paper, say 600 copies, or 25 quires, will cost you laid down at your office about $3 per week. Any boy or young man who has worked in an office a year or so could set the type. Plenty of such can be had at from $1 to $5 per week—say $5. Count incidental expenses at $2 more, making total expenses $10 per week or $520 per year. This leaves a margin of about $300 to pay you for your trouble. At the end of the year you will know enough about the business to dispense with the services of the boy and save that much.
>
> SOURCE. W. S. Hardy, National Reformer, March 1, 1895.

reached a circulation of 80,000 and others, such as Leonidas Polk's *National Farmer*, saw jumps of 1,200 to 12,000 in circulation.[18]

Just as the mainstream press was composed of the big-circulation leaders and the smaller, unassuming small-town newspapers, so were the Populist party newspapers. They often were eight pages, with little advertising. The sizes of the newspapers were varied, and often unusual. Because the papers were published on limited budgets, editors would purchase off-size paper at a discount. The newspapers, like other small-town and country newspapers, rarely separated editorial content from news content. Stories were not, however, consistently biased toward the editor's viewpoint. Often, opposing views were run. The newspapers also contained drawings, songs, and poetry, as well as letters to the editor. It was through the songs and letters that farmers communicated across the miles with each other.

The newspapers existed in small towns where they usually competed with at least one other weekly, either of mainstream Democratic or Republican persuasion. The editors and the newspapers differed little from their mainstream counterparts, however. Most editors were middle-aged, owned some property, usually a house, and were stable community members. Reform editors tended to migrate west a generation later than did their mainstream counterparts. The main difference between the reform editors and mainstream editors was their different political persuasions.

The Populist newspapers were criticized heavily by mainstream editors, who claimed reform editors simply took up journalism for political purposes. They accused reform editors of being party hacks, of ignoring the technical quality of their newspapers and of taking money from the Populist party instead of remaining independent or relying on advertising. Reform editors were, indeed, in trouble when it came to advertising. Merchants who supported the dominant Republican and Democratic parties wouldn't buy advertising in the reform newspapers. But Morgan's instructions indicated that Populist editors expected to support their newspapers primarily from advertising and subscriptions, rather than from party coffers.

Another technique used to improve the quality of the reform newspapers, as well as to spread party-oriented political information, was the National Reform Press Association, founded in 1891. This internal communications network provided boilerplate, or preprinted material which could be inserted into any local newspaper. The association lasted until 1897, a year after the popular orator William Jennings Bryan was defeated in his presidential campaign.[19] The press association enabled reform editors to meet with one another and escape the isolation from other editors they could sometimes experience in their home communities. The publications were many and varied; some gained national circulation, and other tiny weekly sheets circulated to only a few hundred subscribers. One of the most successful was Leonidas Polk's *Progressive Farmer*. Another newspaper, which will be discussed later, represented the other type of newspaper. The *Jacksboro Rural Citizen* was a small rural sheet with a limited circulation.

THE PROGRESSIVE FARMER

Leonidas Polk began editing *The Progressive Farmer* in Winston, North Carolina, in 1886. Polk previously edited North Carolina newspapers, all locally oriented, but with an interest in state and national affairs. His experience as North Carolina's first commissioner of agriculture also prepared him for the task of educating farmers. *The Progressive Farmer* claimed to be a newspaper for the North Carolina farmer and his family. Like other farm and reform editors, Polk was interested in educating his readers. The first issues contained news about ensilage and silos, potato culture, beekeeping, egg production, fruit canning, and tobacco managing.

Correspondents who were experts on particular items wrote to the newspaper, and Polk guided them as an experienced editor. He wrote to one correspondent: "Article too long. Besides you are too fond of theorizing. This is a practical age. Our readers want *facts*. If you have produced an extra yield of Potatoes, Corn, Wheat, Hay, Cotton, Tobacco, &c., tell us how you did it and stop. One such *fact* is worth ten columns of *theory* as to how it might be done." Polk also was concerned about clean advertising, and promised his readers that advertisements of questionable character would have no place in *The Progressive Farmer*.[20]

Polk also supported farmers' organizations, emphasizing their importance in allowing farmers to express their political views, to discuss neighborhood agricultural problems and to enjoy the advantages of social interchange. By January 1887, just less than a year after Polk began *The Progressive Farmer*, farmers in North Carolina were organized for state-wide action.

Polk continued to support agricultural organization through the 1890s, becoming involved in campaigns in Kansas and other midwest and northwest states. The Republican editors of Kansas were not happy to see a radical out-of-state editor working with local farmers. The Topeka *Capital* attacked him, accusing him of cowardice in the Civil War, of embezzling funds while he was North Carolina's commissioner of agriculture, of letting his partners suffer from his failures in business, and of cheating farmers out of their money. But the efforts of Polk and his Kansas Alliance friends were successful, and they succeeded in replacing John J. Ingalls, a Kansas Republican senator who specialized in patronage and who paid little attention to farmers, with another senator, William Peffer, a member of the alliance and editor of the *Kansas Farmer*. Polk also supported public education and teacher training for young women.

Polk eventually came to the complicated decision that faced many Farmers' Alliance editors. As the alliances began to turn political—that is partisan—the connections became frayed with the other party members. In North Carolina, it meant a split between Democratic and Populist members of the alliance. As Polk became more involved in national Populist politics, he left the editing of *The Progressive Farmer* to others.

JACKSBORO RURAL CITIZEN

The Texas *Jacksboro Rural Citizen* represented a far different kind of reform newspaper. J. N. Rogers, the editor, championed the alliance cause in his first issue September 24, 1880. This rural newspaper, printed during its first few months at the owners' farm, continued as an alliance organ through June 1886, when it changed its name to the *Jacksboro Gazette*.

In the first issue the editor's statement of journalistic principles indicated he was more than a mere reformer with no knowledge of journalism. He said he would not accept free advertising disguised as editorial matter. "Omit anything like the 'puff' of one's business, whether it be politics, merchandising or anything that advances the pecuniary or political interests of anyone," Rogers wrote.

This Texas newspaper, in addition to alliance news, gave what the editor termed "full and impartial" news and opinions of different parties. Reports discussed crop diversification, planting, and harvesting. "We need articles giving the experience of our farmers and stockmen in this and adjoining counties on stock raising and the cultivation of various crops," the editor wrote.[21]

The newspaper also carried "exchanges" from other newspapers and a good deal of correspondence from its readers. These writers were not men of stature, but men and women of the farm community. Thus the newspaper contributed to the community of farmers.

This small paper was more fortunate than some alliance papers its size. Although Rogers became involved in the same political dilemma as Leonidas Polk, he did not approve of the alliance going into politics. As he became more vocal in his disapproval, and as the Farmers' Alliance moved more deeply into politics, he lost alliance support, changed the name of the newspaper, and refused to leave the Democratic Party. Thus, the newspaper did not share the fate of many alliance papers, but survived in one form or another until the present day.

THE DEMISE OF THE AGRARIAN REFORM PRESS

In 1896, in fear of not being able to accomplish its goals as a separate party, the Populist party joined with the Democratic party to support a joint candidate for president, William Jennings Bryan. In the wake of the Republican triumph, the Populist press, as an institution, died. At a meeting of the National Reform Press Association a year after the defeat, only eight editors responded to the summons. In 1891, about six years before, the association had welded more than 1,000 Populist newspapers, providing boilerplate material, financial and psychological support, and printed praise of each other. Shortly after the turn of the twentieth century, and after bitter division within the Populist Party over the issue of silver, the party lay in shreds and its press was buried with it.

This 1900 lithograph in Puck *portrayed William Jennings Bryan, the Populist candidate for President, as swallowing the Democratic Party. (Library of Congress Collection)*

ETHNIC PRESS

By the late 1920s, at the end of the great migrations to the United States, 35 million individuals had made the country their home. Although inaccurate records and changing terminology used on those records restrict the ability to measure exactly where immigrants came from, ethnic populations were highly visible in a variety of communities. During the second half of the nineteenth century, for example, about half of Chicago's population was foreign-born, and by 1900 more than half of the industrial labor force in the North was foreign-born. Members of ethnic groups often hoped to return to their home countries, and some spoke little or no English, so the mainstream, English-language press offered them little information or entertainment.

Prior to the massive waves of immigration in the 1890s, the predominant foreign-language press was German. In 1885, 653 of 822 foreign-language newspapers and magazines were German. Although the German press continued to account for more than half the total foreign-language publications in the United States until 1913, newspapers and magazines in a variety of other

The De Pere, Wisconsin, Volkstem *was produced in this busy shop. (State Historical Society of Wisconsin)*

languages also flourished. Next to the church and the school, the ethnic newspapers served as the single most important social and educational institution in the immigrant communities.

Different newspapers served different purposes. For those who could not read English, the newspapers provided important information that helped immigrants adjust to life in a new country, publishing information about registering to vote, becoming citizens, and conforming to American modes of behavior. Readers could learn from various contributors about the Texas prairies or the wilds of North Dakota, about homesteading, laws, and regulations. The information function of ethnic newspapers reached a peak during World War I, a time marked by a nearly pathological fear of foreigners.

Ethnic newspapers also helped preserve the sociocultural heritage of various groups, fostering the sharing of traditional values and contributing to cultural renewal in different time periods. In addition, ethnic newspapers reported information about immigrants, helping to locate family members and supplying news about countries of origin. Further, these newspapers often served as watchdogs of foreign governments, often aware of and reporting foreign government policy more quickly than the mainstream newspapers.

Ethnic newspapers also played an influential political role in communities, helping to select and support candidates for local office.

Similar to the black, agrarian, and suffrage presses, the ethnic press suffered from financial difficulty. Between World War I and World War II, many newspapers survived not from subscription financing, but from advertising revenues generated by American companies advertising for skilled labor and by department stores hoping to sell to people in certain communities. By the end of World War II, as the old generation died out, subscribers often left ethnic neighborhoods and were assimilated into mainstream suburbia, resulting in a dramatic decline of the ethnic press.[22]

CONCLUSION

The agrarian, suffrage, black, and immigrant presses are examples of publications produced by minority voices. In the 1800s to be a majority voice, a citizen had first to be white and male, and second, to own property. Only within this framework were ideas considered seriously and authoritatively by the mainstream press. The publications of minority groups gave more than half the population—white women, blacks, farmers, and immigrants—a vehicle for expressing their ideas, hopes, aspirations, and solutions. Some of these ideas later were incorporated into majority opinion. For example, some legislation Populists promoted in the 1890s was adopted by the Progressive Party in the 1920s, and was enacted into law. Margaret Sanger's struggle for readily available contraceptives finally resulted in changes in laws which enabled women to make their own decisions about the practice of birth control. Other ideas never gained prominence.

NOTES

1. Lauren Kessler, "The Ideas of Woman Suffragists and the Portland *Oregonian*," *Journalism Quarterly* 57 (Winter 1980), p. 4.
2. For a full discussion of the role of the suffragist press in developing a sense of community among women, see Linda Steiner, "The Importance of Early Suffrage Papers in Creating a Community," unpublished report prepared for presentation to Association for Education in Journalism and Mass Communication, Michigan State University, August 1981. See also Steiner's article, "Finding Community in Nineteenth-Century Suffrage Periodicals," *American Journalism* 1:1 (Summer 1983), p. 15.
3. For development of the thesis that the Farmers' Alliance newspapers served an important function in building community, providing information the mainstream

press ignored, and legitimizing the movement, see Jean Folkerts, "Functions of the Reform Press," *Journalism History* 12:1 (Spring 1985), pp. 22–25. For other information about the agrarian radical press, see Lauren Kessler, *The Dissident Press* (Beverly Hills: Sage, 1984), pp. 115–120.

4. For classic studies on women's suffrage, see Eleanor Flexner, *Century of Struggle: The Woman's Rights Movement in the United States* (Cambridge: The Belknap Press, 1975); Aileen S. Kraditor, *The Ideas of the Woman Suffrage Movement, 1890–1920* (New York: Columbia University Press, 1965); William O'Neill, *Everyone Was Brave: The Rise and Fall of Feminism in America* (Chicago: Quadrangle, 1970); William Chafe, *The American Woman: Her Changing Social, Economic, and Political Roles, 1920–1979* (New York: Oxford University Press, 1972); and Carl Degler, *At Odds: Women and the Family in America from the Revolution to the Present* (New York: Oxford University Press, 1980). These studies focus on the suffrage movement as a white, middle class, conservative political struggle that abandoned the goals of civil rights at the end of the nineteenth century and focused on obtaining the right to vote. For a more complex view of the women's movement, see Elinor Lerner, *Immigrant and Working Class Involvement in the New York City Woman Suffrage Movement, 1905–1917* (Ann Arbor, Michigan: University Microfilms, 1982); Carole Nichols, *Votes and More for Women: Suffrage and After in Connecticut* (New York: The Haworth Press, 1983); Barbara Leslie Epstein, *The Politics of Domesticity: Women, Evangelism, and Temperance in Nineteenth Century America* (Middletown, Connecticut: Wesleyan University Press, 1981) and William Leach, *True Love and Perfect Union: The Feminist Reform of Sex and Society* (New York: Basic Books, 1980).

5. Kessler, *Dissident Press*, pp. 74–87.

6. Steiner, "The Importance of Early Suffrage Papers in Creating a Community," pp. 12–13.

7. Maureen Beasley and Sheila Gibbons, *Women in Media: A Documentary Source Book* (Washington, D.C.: Women's Institute for Freedom of the Press, 1977), p. 10.

8. Steiner, "The Importance of Early Suffrage Papers in Creating a Community," pp. 2, 6.

9. For biographical information on other women editors, see Madelon Golden Schlipp, and Sharon M. Murphy, *Great Women of the Press* (Carbondale: Southern Illinois University Press, 1983).

10. This introductory discussion relies heavily on C. Vann Woodward's *Origins of the New South, 1877–1913* (Louisiana State University Press and the Littlefield Fund for Southern History, The University of Texas, 1951). Quotations are from the 1967 paperback edition. Washington's quotes, cited in Woodward, are taken from his autobiography *Up from Slavery* (New York, 1901) and from his *My Larger Education; Being Chapters from My Experience* (Garden City, 1911). See pp. 357–358 in Woodward.

11. For more information on Washington's dealings with black editors, see August Meier, *Negro Thought in America, 1880–1915* (Ann Arbor: University of Michigan Press, 1964), pp. 226, 230; Emma I. Thornbrough, "American Negro Newspapers," *Business History Review*, 11 (Winter 1966), pp. 483–484; and Louis R.

Harlan, *Booker T. Washington: The Making of a Black Leader, 1856–1911* (New York: Oxford University Press, 1972), pp. 254–271.

12. *Correspondence of W. E. B. DuBois*, ed. by Herbert Apetheker (Amherst: University of Massachusetts Press, 1973), vol. 1, p. 101, cited in Willard B. Gatewood, Jr., "Edward E. Cooper, Black Journalist," *Journalism Quarterly*, pp. 269–275, 324.

13. August Meier and Elliott Rudwick, *From Plantation to Ghetto* (New York: Hill and Wang, 1970), p. 206.

14. For information on other black editors, see Stephen R. Fox, *The Guardian of Boston: William Monroe Trotter* (New York: Atheneum, 1971), pp. 31–58, and Armistead Pride, *The Black Press: A Bibliography*, (Jefferson City, Mo.: Lincoln University Department of Journalism, 1968). Other prominent editors of the period include DuBois, of the *Crisis*, Robert S. Abbott of the *Chicago Defender*, W. Calvin Chase of the *Washington Bee*, Edward Cooper, of the *Freeman* and the *Colored American*, T. Thomas Fortune of the *New York Age*, John H. Murphy, Sr., of the *Afro-American* papers, William Monroe Trotter of the *Boston Guardian*, and Robert L. Vann of the *Pittsburgh Courier*.

15. Lawrence Goodwyn, *The Populist Moment* (New York: Oxford University Press, 1978), p. 33. For background on the Populist movement see Norman Pollack, who in *The Populist Response to Industrial America: Midwestern Populist Thought* (Cambridge, Mass.: Harvard University Press, 1962) argues effectively for populism as a class movement, with a broad base including intellectuals and urban labor. For a thorough description of Populist disaffection with the political system, see Pollack's *The Populist Mind* (Indianapolis, Ind.: Bobbs-Merrill Co., Inc., 1967). For comments on the return of prosperity and the decline of Populism, see John Hicks, *The Populist Revolt* (Minneapolis: The University of Minnesota Press, 1931) and Richard Hofstadter, *The Age of Reform: From Bryan to F. D. R.* (New York: Vintage Books, 1955). For efforts on the part of the corporate power structure to thwart Populist efforts, see Goodwyn, *The Populist Moment*. Other sources on populism include Bruce Palmer's *"Man Over Money:" The Southern Populist Critique of American Capitalism* (Chapel Hill: University of North Carolina Press, 1980); and Stanley Parson's *The Populist Context: Rural Versus Urban Power on a Great Plains Frontier* (Westport, Conn.: Greenwood Press, Inc., 1973).

16. *Dallas Southern Mercury*, 23 July; 6, 20, 27 August 1886; and *The Dallas Morning News*, July, August 1886.

17. *Kansas Workman*, October 22, 1886, cited in Seymour Lutzky, "The Reform Editors and Their Press" (State University of Iowa, June 1951), p. 153.

18. Kessler, *Dissident Press*, pp. 117–118.

19. Bryan was a fusion, or joint, candidate of the Populist and Democratic parties. His nomination reflected a renewed emphasis on the issue of free silver, and the relinquishing by the Populists of many other reform measures. The fight over whether to join with the Democrats split the Populists decisively.

20. Stuart Noblin, *Leonidas Lafayette Polk: Agrarian Crusader* (Chapel Hill: University of North Carolina Press, 1949), p. 152.

21. *Jacksboro Rural Citizen*, February 18 and October 13, 1881.

22. This discussion is based on research notes generously provided by Owen V. Johnson, Czechoslovakian press historian at the University of Indiana, Bloomington. See also Robert Park, *The Immigrant Press and Its Control* (New York: Harper and Bros., 1922, reprinted 1970 by Scholarly Press, St. Clair Shores, Mich.); Edward Hunter, *In Many Voices: Our Fabulous Foreign Language Press* (Norman Park, Ga.: Norman College, 1960); Yaroslav J. Chyz, *225 Years of the U.S. Foreign Language Press* (New York: American Council of Nationalities Service, 1959); and Marion Marzolf, *The Danish-Language Press in America* (New York: Arno Press, 1980).

CHAPTER 13

THE MUCK AT OUR FEET

Although some attempts were made to develop magazines in the colonial and revolutionary periods in the United States, it was not until the mid-1850s that magazines could claim success. Before the *Saturday Evening Post* began publication in 1821, only one magazine, the *North American Review*, had survived for more than five years. Developing technology certainly contributed to the expansion of magazines, but more significantly, Congress enacted postal regulations in 1879 to allow for less expensive distribution of non-newspaper periodicals. Furthermore, a class of professional writers was emerging to contribute to literary and news publications. The arrival of national advertising agencies and national product advertising significantly broadened the appeal to national audiences. The number of magazines grew from a total of 700 in 1865 to 3,300 in 1885.

Beginning in the mid-1800s, quality monthlies such as *Scribner's, The Century, Atlantic Monthly* and *Harper's,* created outlets for writers, while serving up biography, travel and fiction. The qualities sold for twenty-five to thirty-five cents a copy and sported elegant covers. The cost, a quarter, which seems today to be minimal, was in fact expensive for the times. These genteel magazines catered to the wealthy and educated in medium-sized towns and in cities. They resisted the forces of modernization and tended to be politically conservative, emphasizing a rational, slow approach to changing times and issues.

General interest magazines and specialized magazines for women developed during the mid- to late-1800s. Weekly magazines such as *Frank Leslie's Illustrated Weekly* and *Harper's Weekly* stressed news and pictures, and were for the most part more like newspapers than magazines. Women's magazines, such as the *Ladies' Home Journal*, begun in 1883, expanded and gained subscribers. In the late 1890s the *Journal* began to address women's issues and even ventured into highly taboo social issues such as venereal disease and birth control. The *Saturday Evening Post*, a general interest magazine, became a literary and informative weekly after Cyrus Curtis bought it in 1897.

By the end of the nineteenth century, rapid corporate growth and social change created an ideal market for inexpensive periodicals aimed at a mass audience. The development of the dime magazines coincided with a period of reform in the United States characterized by the emergence of a third party—the Progressive party. This political party promoted legislation to curb excesses of business, to assure that food and drugs were pure and uncontaminated, and to regulate other aspects of American life the progressives believed had gotten out of control. The muckraking, or the dime magazines, publicized these social and industrial issues and promoted scientific solutions to modern problems.

Quality monthlies

The quality monthly magazines represented a major development in American periodical literature. Initially associated with publishing houses, such as Harper & Brothers and Scribners', the magazines were viewed as vehicles for serializing books the publishing companies later published, and therefore became advertising outlets for the publishing houses. They were supported by subscriptions, newsstand sales, publishing house subsidies, and minimal advertising.

The monthlies played an important role in developing outlets for American writers, creating a forum for American art and art criticism, and for establishing markets for national advertising. The offices of quality monthlies "echoed the temper of a gentleman's voluntary association," wrote Christopher Wilson, and editing reflected a cooperative literary venture among editors, authors, and subscribers. Articles generally were not solicited, but rather editors perused voluntarily submitted manuscripts for their literary qualities and good taste.[1] Because subscription lists for Gilded Age publications were closely guarded as private documents, little can be said about the audiences, although presumably the magazines were aimed at a northeastern elite.

From 1865 to 1870, the number of American periodicals grew from 700 to 1200 (not including newspapers). By 1870, *Harper's*, which relied heavily on British authors, had a circulation of 150,000. The *Atlantic Monthly*, founded in 1857 with James Russell Lowell as editor, focused on New England contributors and readers. Into this milieu came *Scribner's Monthly Magazine*, which later changed its name to the *Century Illustrated Monthly Magazine*. The *Century*, originally *Scribner's*, is not to be confused with another quality monthly also named *Scribner's*.

HARPER'S NEW MONTHLY MAGAZINE

A student once described the *Harper's* of today as a magazine that you wouldn't find at the Kwik-Shop between *True Detective* and *Modern Bride*, but one that you might find at a "quality" newsstand.[2] It is an apt description because, although *Harper's* has undergone many changes, its reputation for quality has remained throughout its life.

Harper's began in 1850 as a stepchild to the Harper brothers publishing enterprise in New York. One of its purposes was to be an advertising vehicle for the publishers' selections both through advertisements and through serializations of forthcoming books by popular British authors.[3] From its beginning, *Harper's* attracted the attention of wealthy, upper-middle-class, educated Americans. It offered fiction from the most prominent British authors of the day, including Thomas Hardy, Charles Dickens, and William Makepeace Thackeray. In addition, the magazine published elegant etchings, travelogues, historical biographies, scientific essays, and articles concerned with life's pleasures: yachting, hunting, and vacationing. Navy heroes, newly betrothed maidens, well-mannered children, and pedigreed dogs abounded. The magazine's editors avoided news articles, and left politics and social reform to the weekly magazines and newspapers.

By 1890, *Harper's* circulation peaked at 200,000. Competition from muckraking magazines slowly forced *Harper's* to change, and editors reluctantly began to include more topical articles among the literary works. From 1885 to 1930, *Harper's* gradually responded to such contemporary issues as American imperialism, national reform, and the "Jazz" era of the 1920s. In doing so, however, it never abandoned its class bias.

For example, *Harper's* treatment of subjects such as the "country club" as a welcome get-away from the bustle of the metropolis ignored issues of membership restriction and focused instead on blue sky and green grass. The country club, wrote the author, "is one of the results of a final ebullition of animal spirits too long ignored in a work-a-day world; it is nature's appeal for recognition of the body in cooperation with the mind."

On the other side of the poverty line, other kinds of clubs existed, but an attempt by one *Harper's* contributor to analyze some of these groups fell flat when its moral tone turned menacing. The author of "Club Life Among the Outcasts" depicted as "vagabonds, rowdies and outcasts" those who were either born out of, or turned out of respectable society. The author insisted, "Vice must be punished and the vicious sequestered. . . . The best method of handling them is to destroy their clubs and punish them."[4]

Harper's covered the Spanish-American War thoroughly, running a six-part series on the war written by Henry Cabot Lodge. Lodge viewed the Spanish as barbarian and brutal, romanticized the war, and condemned Spain's attempt at imperialism, without questioning the motives of the United States in seizing Puerto Rico, Guam, and the Philippines.[5]

By the turn of the century, *Harper's* became more involved in social issues and printed stories about the education of immigrants, women's feminist activities, and the development of American medicine and evolution. In the midst of the race riots of 1919 the magazine's writers chastised Americans for hiding their heads in the sand and blamed white-controlled newspapers for misrepresenting blacks as inferior.[6]

Despite varied attempts to be socially relevant, the magazine was in financial trouble. In 1953, John Fischer assumed responsibility for *Harper's* as the seventh editor in the magazine's history. He estimated 85 percent of his readers were college graduates, and kept the tone of the magazine scholarly; circulation and revenues continued to decline. The magazine relied heavily on the publishing company for financial support. A decade later, Willie Morris, controversial ex-editor of the University of Texas' *Daily Texan* and well known as a modern-day muckraker, took over the magazine. Morris promised a public affairs approach, and the magazine ran long articles, oriented toward social and political change. The magazine's circulation continued to drop and in 1965, the magazine was sold to the Minneapolis Star and Tribune Co. Lewis Lapham took over in 1971, and most of the *Harper's* staff resigned as a stormy controversy raged over publication of a Norman Mailer essay on women's liberation. During Lapham's tenure *Harper's* hammered away at the decline and fall of America, but the magazine's readers did not respond and in June

1980, *Harper's* announced it would fold.[7] High postal rates and production costs put *Harper's* $1.5 million in debt, and advertising revenues dwindled because the ad men found it difficult to define *Harper's* audience, no matter how prosperous it was.[8]

Before the ink dried on *Harper's* obituary, however, a nonprofit organization saved it. The John D. and Catherine T. MacArthur Foundation of Chicago bought *Harper's* for $250 thousand and convinced Atlantic Richfield to kick in $3 million for operating expenses. Michael Kinsley, former editor of *The New Republic*, took over and promised to make *Harper's* "scintillating and profitable."[9]

CENTURY MAGAZINE

Probably the most elegantly printed of the quality monthlies, the *Century* was an outgrowth of *Scribner's Monthly Illustrated Magazine*, developed in 1870 as an independent arm of Scribner's publishing house. It incorporated *House and Home*, which was published directly by the publishing company. The three individuals responsible for the magazine were Dr. Josiah Gilbert Holland, a religious man and educator, Roswell C. Smith, an astute businessman, and Charles Scribner, member of the publishing firm. Smith and Holland insisted on separate editorial control, and the firm was organized with Scribner owning 40 percent interest, and Holland and Smith each owning 30 percent. This organizational policy was significant because the question of independence later became the issue over which *Scribner's Monthly* was dissolved and reestablished as the *Century*. Scribner died only two years after his monthly began, and his two sons, who took over the publishing business, quarreled with Smith and Holland, who wanted to publish books through the magazine company. The sons sold their interest in 1881 and five years later began *Scribner's Magazine*.

The men who probably deserve most of the credit for the success of the *Century* were Smith, who provided good business management, and Richard Watson Gilder, who edited the magazine from 1881 until his death in 1909. Gilder was a popular poet who had worked for *House and Home* and who organized the Society of American Artists and Authors as well as the Authors Club of New York. The *Century*'s content was similar to that of *Harper's*, with an emphasis on education, religion, history, and biography.

The *Century*'s entry into the quality monthly market was difficult because *Harper's* had cornered the British market, and American writers were scarce, except for those New Englander's already loyal to the *Atlantic*. The *Century*'s unique qualities were its appeal to women readers, its appeal to southern readers, its focus on visual impact, with quality paper, elegant covers, and faultless print, and its emphasis on illustration.

> **THE *CENTURY* CELEBRATES NEW YORK**
>
> The rich and well-to-do people, of all parts of the country, should be able to find in New York that which will make it a delightful home to them. The opera, the theater, the picture gallery, the museum, the library, the literary and scientific lecture, the choicest eloquence of pulpit and platform, bright and stimulating society in multiplied and multiform organization — all these should combine to make a winter residence in New York so desirable that all who have money and leisure, wherever they may live, will indulge in the luxury.
>
> SOURCE. Josiah Gilbert Holland, Scribner's Monthly, June 1877.

Evidence exists after 1914 to indicate the *Century* also attempted to spread its circulation beyond the East. In 1914, the first year figures are available to determine the geographical spread of the magazine's circulation, the total circulation was 92,000, with 34,000 sales in the Middle Atlantic states, 14,000 in New England, 11,000 in the Far West and 26,000 in the Midwest from Ohio to Kansas. These figures indicate that magazines circulated in rural areas and small towns, as well as in the metropolis.

The magazine was a quality showcase for writers, with emphasis on accuracy. Gilder, generally a pleasant man to work for, rushed into the office one day with a copy of a new issue in hand, exclaiming, "We ought all to resign!" He had discovered a typographical error. In 1890, the *Century* was at no loss for writers with 10,000 manuscripts reaching the offices every year. Gilder, as editor, could accept fewer than 400.

Gilder was known to be as sympathetic to writers as he was to employees. His staff read every manuscript the magazine received and notified writers immediately of the receipt of their manuscripts. It paid on acceptance — an uncommon practice in the nineteenth century. It sent acceptances on *Century* stationery, but mailed rejections in plain envelopes, so as to not damage an author's ego. It also returned all manuscripts — even if an author forgot to enclose postage.[10] Authors were paid as well as at any magazine. Some reports indicate payment was from $10 to $100 per printed page, but rarely did it reach the top of that scale. Mark Twain at his peak was paid only $75 per page by the *Century*.

The magazine, always well managed financially, encouraged employees to buy stock and thus develop a self-interest in the company. The magazine also made great strides in developing national advertising. By the late 1880s, circulation was at 250,000, and it peaked from 1884 to 1887 with a major Civil War series. By 1890, the circulation leveled off at 200,000 and the *Century* outstripped all other monthlies in circulation. Advertisements sold in 1870 for $100 for a regular page and $200 for a page placed next to reading material. By 1880, the standard page rate was $270.

Mark Twain was a contributing writer for Century *magazine. (State Historical Society of Wisconsin)*

The *Century*'s prestige in arts and letters, as well as its financial success, was mirrored in its offices:

> The *Century* office was the visible symbol of its power and opulence. No other publication in the world was so magnificently housed. The visitor to its fifth-floor home on Union Square entered a world of polished floors, rich Turkish carpets, broad windows, stained-glass doors, and walls hung with the originals of the monthly's most famous drawings. Only Twain dared keep his hat on and smoke cigars in this atmosphere of elegance and dignity. "You never saw anything like those lovely rooms. And aesthetic furniture," wrote Mrs. S. S. McClure to her sister. "Oh, you Americans are all so rich" was Matthew Arnold's outburst as he gazed about him . . . [11]

The *Century*'s language was as elegant and dignified as its offices, avoiding the harsher situations and worlds of American life. It did not discuss sexual activity, profanity was barred, and other situations that might be "questionable" stayed out of the *Century*. Its political and social stance was a conservative one, with concern about corruption and other immoral aspects of American life, but with a focus on individual responsibility and noblesse oblige.

During the 1890s circulation dropped to 150,000 and it further declined after 1900 to about 125,000 where it leveled off for some years. The competition with mass magazines such as *McClure's* contributed to the demise of the *Century*, with subscribers and advertisers shifting to the less expensive, mass circulation magazines. In 1899, the same year *Harper's* faced bankruptcy and was bailed out by the banking interests of J. P. Morgan, the *Century* faced financial crisis. Another major factor in the decline of the *Century* was the development of photomechanical engraving and the halftone screen, which allowed mass circulation magazines to produce pictures at a tenth the cost of the former procedure. For a time the *Century* refused to lower its standards, although eventually it used the new process.

The *Century* managed to last until 1930, when it merged with the *Forum* and ceased its independent existence.

SCRIBNER'S MAGAZINE

Scribner's Magazine published for 52 years — 1887 to 1939. Priced at twenty-five cents, the magazine sold for a dime less than its competitors, *Harper's, Atlantic Monthly,* and *Century*. Within two years of its beginnings, its subscriptions totaled 100,000. The magazine covered the arts, travel in the Western United States and foreign countries, and natural disasters. Serial stories and other fiction, biographies, and poetry were an integral part of each issue.[12]

> ### ROOSEVELT AND THE ROUGH RIDERS
>
> One of our men and most of the Spanish dead had been found by the vultures before we got to them; and their bodies were mangled, the eyes and wounds being torn.
>
> The Rough Rider who had been thus treated was in Bucky O'Neill's troop; and as we looked at the body, O'Neill turned to me and asked, "Colonel, isn't it Whitman who says of the vultures that 'they pluck the eyes of princes and tear the flesh of kings?'" I answered that I could not place the quotation. Just a week afterward we were shielding his own body from the birds of prey.
>
> SOURCE. *Theodore Roosevelt, Scribner's, July 1898.*

The magazine adhered to the concept of "social evolution" rather than radical social change or revolution. Although it suggested that labor had legitimate grievances, it cautioned against "expecting too much too soon." When dealing with the issue of the woman's vote, one article noted that eventually while the laws of all civilized nations would give women a voice in politics, "there seems to be no pressing haste for action . . . there is a good deal of the old Eve left in the woman of to-day. And bless her sweet heart, Adam is in no haste to have it otherwise."[13]

During the Spanish-American War, *Scribner's* carried stories written by Richard Harding Davis, Hearst's first-hand observer who covered the war with artist Frederick Remington. Many of the stories focused on Teddy Roosevelt and his "Rough Riders." As soon as Roosevelt returned from the war and was elected governor of New York, *Scribner's* commissioned him to write his recollections of the war, which appeared in serial form during the first six months of 1899. This series reversed the magazine's readership decline and signaled the beginning of the "heyday" of the magazine (1900–1915.).

As the new century opened, *Scribner's* remained fairly oblivious to the muckraking going on around it. The magazine touched briefly on social topics—the problem of the saloon and the immigrant, but made few changes in its format in the early 1900s. Stories focused on the exotic—China and Russia. The magazine also covered the nostalgic—picturesque farming in Iowa and hospitality and pride in the Kentucky hills.

Scribner's described itself in 1908 in an article titled, "The Business of a Great Publishing House," claiming it had a "distinct and individual place among periodicals." "No aspect of modern life" was without consideration and "many of the great names representing the transition period from the 19th and 20th centuries have appeared in its pages." Its topics, according to the writer, were history, sociology, the study of the varying conditions of modern life, travel, essays, sports and athletics, music and art, and natural history.[14]

By the 1920s, *Scribner*'s circulation declined from the 200,000 of the early 1900s to 100,000 by 1911 and 70,000 by 1924. Its use of full-color illustrations and quality of paper also declined. Advertising, previously placed at the back of the book, became highly visible from 1920 to 1923, but by 1924 much of it had disappeared. Public issues were given greater emphasis in the 1920s, with arguments that unions were a threat to property rights. Another article lamented the popular "myth" that doctors were overpaid. Shortly before *Scribner*'s demise in 1929, Ernest Hemingway's *A Farewell to Arms* appeared, the event many credited for the momentary upturn in circulation during that year. New authors, including Langston Hughes, William Faulkner, and F. Scott Fitzgerald, appeared in the 1930s, but the magazine continued to lose readers. Circulation dropped below 40,000 by 1936. Although circulation climbed the following year, the magazine continued to lose money, and it stopped circulation after May 1939.

A few months later *Esquire* bought the subscription list. The name was sold to *Commentator*, and the magazine became *Scribner's Commentator*. In 1942, Joseph Hilton Smyth, the publisher, pleaded guilty to an indictment for accepting money from the Japanese to publish their propaganda in the magazine. Historian Frank Luther Mott described this unfortunate demise:

> When a respectable magazine dies it should emulate Stevenson's hunter and lay itself down with a will, and not pass its name on for some other periodical to disgrace.
>
> Throughout its long life, however, *Scribner's* was a credit to the name it bore—a magazine notable for its service to American literature and art, and for its urbane criticism of our national life and culture.[15]

GENERAL INTEREST AND WOMEN'S MAGAZINES

General interest and women's magazines, which gained popularity in the late 1800s, varied widely. They attracted a broader-based audience than did the quality monthlies, aiming not only at the northeastern elite, but also at families of slightly lower incomes. Editors also sought new regional elite audiences in cities of more than 10,000. Unlike the literary editors of the qualities, editors of the mass-circulation magazines often apprenticed in daily journalism and treated their magazines as news commodities, focusing on timely information. They planned their magazines, sought specific contributions from specific writers, and promoted the content as well as the publication. Such editors, wrote Christopher Wilson, "rehabilitated gentle culture by infusing it with managerial skills and work values."[16] These editors covered the realm of business and politics, deliberately aiming at increasing their male readership, and encouraged articles that conveyed tones of authority, authenticity, and expertise.

One man responsible for the development of women's magazines and general interest publications was Cyrus H. K. Curtis, who started the *Ladies' Home Journal* and later the *Saturday Evening Post*. While still a boy, Curtis at age 13 published his own newspaper. He woke at 4 A.M., delivered papers until 7 A.M., attended school, and then spent his evening setting, typing, printing and selling his four-page paper, *Young America*. When a fire destroyed the Curtis home, and young Curtis's office with it, he quit school to help support his family by working as an advertisement solicitor for the Boston *Times*. He started another newspaper, *The Independent*, in Boston, but that newspaper failed. He then went into partnership with his brother-in-law, Hamilton Mayo, and began publishing *The Tribune and Farmer*. This four-page weekly catered to farmers and sold for fifty cents a year. Curtis attempted to expand the paper by developing a woman's section, entitled "Woman and the Home," with reprints of articles from other publications. When Curtis took the new section home to show his wife, she laughed at his choice of content. She became the new editor of the women's section.

LADIES' HOME JOURNAL

The *Ladies' Home Journal* set a standard for women's magazines for many decades. In addition, it paved the way for magazines to crusade in the public interest. Curtis's wife, who edited the women's section of the *Tribune and Farmer* under her maiden name, Louisa May Knapp, assumed the editorship of Curtis's new magazine, first named *Ladies' Journal and Practical Housekeeper*, in 1883.

A businessman rather than an editor, Curtis firmly believed that advertising was the key to the production of high-quality magazines offered at a low price. He also used group subscriptions to lure readers. With a group subscription, four readers could subscribe for one dollar. The regular rate was fifty cents a year. This plan doubled his circulation in six months. With this steady subscription base, Curtis was able to turn his attention to selling advertising.[17] Although expanding advertising continuously, Curtis adhered to a policy of not accepting questionable advertising, and proved that a magazine could be ethical and successful at the same time.

Within six years, monthly circulation stabilized at 440,000 and Curtis

Engravings were essential features in magazines in the mid-nineteenth century. Pictured here is the engraving room of Leslie's Illustrated Newspaper. (Library of Congress Collection)

hired a new editor, Edward Bok. Although Bok would be called sexist today for his belief that women arrived at conclusions by instinct rather than by reasoning, he successfully made content decisions that appealed to women.[18] In his magazine he included homemaking, sewing, fashion, cooking, needlework, theater and fiction, celebrities, and accounts of a society active in the "Gilded Age." In 1895, he published house plans, and architect Stanford White said Bok influenced American architecture through his appeals to women more than any other individual of his time. From 1898 to 1906, he emphasized social concerns and the possibility of the breakdown of the American family. One article by Theodore Roosevelt, "The American Woman as a Mother," reflected concern about the growing lack of discipline of children, of the man who is not a good husband and father, and the woman who had "lost her sense of duty and is sunk in vapid self-indulgence." He claimed good morals and discipline at home would create a moral, disciplined nation.

In 1893, Bok and Curtis took a bold step and cut patent medicine advertising from the *Journal*'s pages. Earlier issues advertised such products as

Ayer's Cathartic Pills, which claimed to cure "heartburn, sickness, headaches, and all disorders of the stomach, liver, and bowels."[19] In another issue a music teacher from North Carolina asserted that a nine-year-old student had become "thin and weak and nervous" due to an awful cough, only to be cured in less than a month's time by Scott's Emulsion.[20]

The *Ladies Home Journal* ended patent-medicine advertising in 1893, but it was not until 1904 that Bok's editorial campaign against the makers of nostrums gained momentum. In the May 1904 issue Bok wrote an editorial titled "The Patent Medicine Curse," which featured an analysis of the alcohol in various brands of cures. For example, Parker's Tonic contained 41.6 percent alcohol. Bok noted that although most magazines were rejecting patent medicine advertising, until they outlawed it, it was woman's duty to refuse to buy any medicine without being fully aware of its ingredients. He also told women who were members of the Women's Christian Temperance Union that they had a special obligation not to allow advertisements to be posted on their barns or fences and to end all subscriptions to religious newspapers that continued to run patent-medicine advertising. After all, these nostrums were attacking the very soul of a child and "planting the seed of a future drunkard."[21] Alcohol was not the only dangerous ingredient. Among others were morphine, opium, and digitalis—all extremely addictive.

In 1908, Bok began to publish statistics and convincing photographs about venereal disease, a topic hardly mentioned in good homes of the time. He criticized parents for not teaching their children the "evils of some of their actions." He demanded children be educated about positive and negative points of sex instead of treating it like a closed issue. The *Journal* lost 70,000 readers, but after eighteen months Bok began to receive letters of inquiry instead of protests. He published a series of *Edward Bok Books* that answered the most common questions about sex and paved the way for parents to tell their children the entire story.[22]

Under the leadership of Curtis and Bok the *Ladies' Home Journal* developed many "firsts." It was the first popular magazine to sell for one dollar a year and ten cents a month, which was to become the prevailing popular price. It also was the first magazine to originate the idea of changing its cover every month. It was the first to refuse questionable advertising and to contain personal correspondence between the editor and readers. The *Ladies' Home Journal* also introduced, as an award, free education to young men and women who gathered subscriptions. It used color printing and originated two- three- and four-color printing. It was the first magazine to contain a garden department and have a kitchen in which recipes were tested before they were published.

Although Bok resigned in 1919, the magazine continued to flourish and by 1928 had a circulation of 3 million.

SATURDAY EVENING POST

Advertising also played a major role in the development of another Cyrus Curtis magazine, the *Saturday Evening Post*. Under Curtis's watchful eye, with George Lorimer as editor, the magazine appealed squarely to middle America. The magazine lauded businessmen whom Curtis revered, and published well-known American writers.[23]

The magazine claimed to have originated as the *Pennsylvania Gazette*, with Benjamin Franklin as original publisher. However, Samuel Keimer was the original editor of the *Gazette*, and it was a newspaper, not a magazine. Franklin bought the *Gazette* in 1729 and as a newspaper it was defunct by 1815. The *Saturday Evening Post* actually was founded in 1821 by two printers.[24] By 1897, when it caught Curtis's eye, it consisted primarily of reprints from other magazines. Intrigued with the history of the magazine, Curtis bought the *Post* for $1,000, hired George Horace Lorimer as editor, and invested at least $1,250,000 in the *Post* before it showed a profit. In 1899, the first full-page advertisement appeared. Less than a year later one issue carried 32 columns of paid advertising. Circulation of the five-cent magazine grew quickly from 2,000 at the time Curtis purchased the magazine in 1897 to 315,000 in 1902. Circulation reached 3 million in 1928.

George Lorimer edited the *Post* until 1936, when he retired. His long editorship was rivaled by another — that of Ben Hibbs who edited the magazine from 1942 to 1961.

The *Saturday Evening Post* paid on acceptance, and manuscripts were reviewed and decided upon within 72 hours of arrival. This practice was favored by writers, and many of the fiction and non-fiction writers of the early 1900s sent manuscripts to the *Post* for review.

MUCKRAKING

Magazine historians generally have explained the development of the muckraking magazines as a form of journalistic exposé aimed at middle-class readers and interrelated with national reform politics from about 1900 to 1916. Many individuals, including writers, were concerned about the direction the nation's economic growth was taking in 1900. They viewed wealth as being more concentrated than before in the nation's history, and in fact, it was. It is estimated that in 1860, just before the start of the Civil War, there were only three millionaires in the United States, but by 1900, only forty years later, the number of millionaires increased to about 3,800. About one-tenth of the population owned nine-tenths of the wealth of the nation.[25] In this social context muckrakers began writing about the social and economic ills of the nation.

The name was bestowed on the magazines by Theodore Roosevelt, who likened the social commentators to the Man with the Muckrake in Bunyan's *Pilgrim's Progress*:

> A man who could look no way but downward with the muck-rake in his hands; who was offered the celestial crown for his muckrake, but would neither look up nor regard the crown he was offered, but continued to rake the filth of the floor.

The term muckraking encompassed a variety of magazines. Some, like *McClure's*, were investigative magazines containing well-researched articles based on fact. Others jumped on the bandwagon with sensational stories lacking in research and detail.

The muckrakers who took their charge seriously were primarily magazine journalists sympathetic to Theodore Roosevelt's Progressive party. They flourished in response to an already aroused middle class and viewed their exposures of the evils of American life as a genuine tool for social reform. Using extensive research, appeals to middle-class guilt and sensationalism, they emphasized individual responsibility in American life, attacked the evils of the privileges of class and money, and sought change through the middle class, hoping to avoid mass conflict between labor and capitalists, and therefore to secure a stable society.[26]

The muckrakers' media were cheap, mass-circulation magazines, although newspapers also were a forum for muckraking in the late nineteenth century. At the peak of the movement, muckrakers were reaching about 3 million people, primarily urban middle-class readers. These journalists developed the magazines as responsible tools for public education, informing the people of the close alliance of business and government, giving evidence of corruption and pointing out the advantages of the privileged. These writers were not trained as historians or as sociologists but as observers, researchers, and writers. They believed exposure would create change and thereby offset revolutionary tactics by underprivileged groups. By 1912, the magazine emphasis on reform had declined, and lack of public interest, deliberate attempts by business to curtail muckraking, and the coming of World War I combined to silence these reform voices. During the 1920s and the New Deal many muckrakers assumed more conservative positions and turned away from their earlier reform work.[27]

Some historians argue that the muckrakers created or caused much of the public protest that defined the first decade of the twentieth century. However, the muckrakers and the protest movement more likely were intertwined. Some reform groups like the Anti-Saloon League, the National Municipal

Reform League, and attempts to reform civil service practices began before muckraking magazines came into existence. Samuel McClure, one of the most famous muckraking publishers, said he began muckraking with no formulated plan, but in response to problems that were beginning to interest people.

The muckrakers were not interested in creating a new society, but in perfecting democracy. Ray Stannard Baker, who wrote many articles about labor organizations for *McClure's* and other magazines, said the muckrakers wrote "not because we hated our world but because we loved it." He emphasized the informational value rather than the reform aspects of his work. Ida Tarbell, who wrote an expose of the Standard Oil Company, claimed, "the things we were advocating were not advocated with a view to overturning the capitalist system." The muckrakers, although occasionally contemplating theories of socialism, usually did not advocate revolution. They were full of hope and optimism about American democracy, and hoped to encourage its development by preventing big business and monopoly from controlling the economics or politics of the country.

The muckrakers saw democracy as a moral force as well as an economic system and believed political institutions should be more responsive to popular will. They tended to believe that corruption of individual politicians and businessmen was the major problem in American society. In addition to viewing individuals as a source for evil, the muckrakers also held individuals responsible for positive change. The muckrakers therefore expected change would come from the middle class and act as a buffer between owners of the major resources and the workers. The muckrakers advocated class harmony and were as upset by violence on the part of miners as they were by violence of owners.

Muckraking was a short-lived phenomenon and by 1913 it was on the decline. Some writers were becoming disillusioned with reform. But the decline was not merely a result of writers' changing perspectives. The American News Company, the major magazine distributor, discriminated against some of the more radical publications. Big-business interests absorbed other publications. When J. P. Morgan and Thomas Lamont interests (banking) in the form of Crowell Publishing Co. purchased the *American Magazine* in 1916, the owners claimed there would be no change in policy. Even Ray Stannard Baker, a writer for *McClure's*, and then for the *American Magazine*, saw no reason for the new business connection to disrupt established policies or restrict freedom of expression. The staff of the *American* either was kidding itself, or it did not understand the power of big business.[28] The *American Magazine* did not survive its new ownership.

Other factors also contributed to decline. The public grew tired of exposure, and *McClure's* circulation actually increased immediately after its muckraking period, as the muckrakers became heavily involved in promoting World War I. During the 1920s, the newer generation, rather than continuing in the muckraking tradition, became expatriates who directed their scorn against the American middle class. The older muckrakers turned their attention to their own careers and families. Many became biographers and, disillusioned, turned to America's past as well as to travel and religion, losing faith in the masses who failed to respond to middle-class altruism.

McCLURE'S MAGAZINE

By the time the muckraking period began in about 1902, *McClure's Magazine* had a history. In other words, it didn't begin as a muckraking magazine, but instead began as a general interest magazine, similar to the quality monthlies.

Samuel McClure, a graduate of Knox College in Galesburg, Ill., began *McClure's* in 1893. His earlier involvement in journalism had been in college publishing, editing a bicycling magazine, and in creating a news-syndicate business. During the summer of 1881, McClure and his friends captured control of the *Knox Student*, and McClure had the magazine chartered by the state. He expanded the magazine, printed book reviews, and organized an intercollegiate news service. Many of his fellow students later joined him in more extensive after-college publishing adventures.

After graduation, McClure worked in Boston and New York, editing the *Wheelman* and writing for *Century*. In 1893, relying on capital from friends, McClure began his magazine with $7,300 worth of capital. Colonel Pope, a bicycle manufacturer, who owned the *Wheelman*, contributed $6,000; Arthur Conan Doyle, the mystery writer, gave McClure $5,000. Of the 20,000 copies that McClure published of the first issue, 12,000 were returned by the distributor, but by 1894 he had 60,000 subscribers and 60 pages of advertising per issue. By 1900, *McClure's* circulation of 370,000 outstripped all his competitors except *Munsey's Magazine*, and by 1907, *McClure's* circulation reached a half million.

From 1895 to 1900, *McClure's* emphasized individual success in American life.[29] Character sketches often revealed the traits of famous political figures, and sometimes focused on businessmen responsible for certain monopolistic practices *McClure's* later denounced during the muckraking period. For example, one article referred to meat-packing magnate Philip Armour as representative of "American life, ideas, ability—representative in success, and . . . personal character."[30] The magazine also referred to Andrew Carnegie, the steel king, as skillful rather than greedy, a man who gave away as much as he earned. The magazine differentiated between good and bad entrepreneurs, good and bad millionaires.[31]

Despite the fact that *McClure's* didn't move into the muckraking stage as early as 1894, that year it identified some problems with industrialization. In July 1894, one writer said that he could not understand how any human being could tolerate working in the Carnegie steel plant. "They all die young," the writer said. "Very few men well along in years are found anywhere about the mills. Yet these men go on for a number of years, and anyone of them could do twice the work in the heat that any man could who had worked as the men work in the East."

Why did *McClure's* change? One historian suggests that Samuel McClure, founder and publisher of the magazine, realized in early 1897 that his success-oriented articles didn't correspond to the reality of American life. He watched the bitter 1896 presidential campaign and wondered what was missing from his magazine. At first he retreated into the past, emphasizing individual successes of historical figures. Then he began to assign stories that dealt with complex issues to experienced writers such as Ida Tarbell. In 1897, he wrote an editorial, saying "We, like other men, wish to gain material success, but we want to gain it by those means which appeal to our intellectual as well as to our moral self-respect."[32]

McClure's might have become a muckraking magazine at that point except for the intervention of the Spanish-American War, which absorbed much of the editor's energies. Coverage of the Spanish-American War focused not only on the horrors of war, but also on the commercial implications for the United States. Major General Fitzhugh Lee, a former consul general of the United States to Havana, wrote in *McClure's* in June 1898, that human life was being "taken by both contestants under the most aggravating circumstances; and that commerce was being extinguished, entailing great loss to the United States and to the American citizens resident on the island."[33]

In the same issue McClure explained that many of its June pages had been set aside to add war material. He promised that representatives, contributors, photographers, and artists would observe and write "with every branch of the army and navy and at every scene of probable action."[34] *McClure's* would offer personal observation, interpretation, comment, and illustrations, hoping to attain a record "of permanent historical value."

The magazine often speculated about the commercial advantages of controlling Cuba. Speaking about the tobacco industry, one writer said, "Under the fostering care of American enterprise and capital, this industry should develop into many fold its present value, and the time easily come when the laboring man, as well as the millionaire, enjoys his after-dinner 'Havana' or 'Philippine.'" Imperialism, or expansion, was seen by some as a way of providing the luxury to the common man of America.

It was not until 1901 that the magazine began to evolve as a muckraking magazine.[35] By this time *McClure's* reflected in many ways the changing of the times. Cities were growing, the West and the South were expanding, immigration was of growing concern, transportation was rapidly developing, emancipation of women was at issue, religion, literature and art were changing, labor organizations and vast corporations were developing.

Chapter 13 The Muck at Our Feet

The exaltation of American accomplishment and an emphasis on Manifest Destiny was pitted against a concern over the increasing chasm between wealth and poverty. It was not until after the Spanish-American War, however, that magazines began attacking expansion as a problem, rather than as an achievement.

In 1902, McClure hired Lincoln Steffens, city editor of the New York *Commercial Advertiser*. Steffens joined a capable staff, including Tarbell and Ray Stannard Baker, whom McClure hired in 1899. Baker was a reporter and editor for the Chicago *Record* and had written free-lance articles for McClure. The three writers — Tarbell, Steffens, and Baker — together with McClure as editor deserve the credit for initiating magazine muckraking, and it was perhaps their influence that made the years of 1902–1907 a significant period for the magazine. Some historians credit the writers, rather than McClure, for developing the muckraking tradition.

Ida Tarbell was born in 1858, the daughter of Pennsylvania Republicans. One brother, an acquaintance of Lincoln, lost an arm at Gettysburg and another served as a major of "colored troops," appointed by Lincoln.[36] Raised on stories told by abolitionists, Tarbell vividly remembered the tragedy of Lincoln's assassination, as well as those of her own family. Rockefeller's Southern Improvement Company forced her father, an oil producer in Titusville, Pa., where oil production began, out of business, leaving him to labor in the oil fields. It was this background that spurred Ida Tarbell to spend four years researching the life of Lincoln and later to delve into the history of the Standard Oil Company.

Ray Stannard Baker was the oldest son of a Wisconsin family. His father was president of a land company and sent his son to Michigan State College. Baker's first contact with *McClure's* stemmed from his fascination with Tarbell's Lincoln study. Baker wrote the editor that an uncle of his had been in command of the party that captured John Wilkes Booth. Baker was commissioned to write an article. During the Spanish-American War, Baker traveled with Stephen Crane and others to the front to write for *McClure's* about scandals in the military administration, about the Rough Riders, and about Theodore Roosevelt. Later Baker went to Germany to write scientific articles.

The third writer in this muckraking trio was Lincoln Steffens. Born in San Francisco, Calif., in 1866, the son of naturalized citizens, Steffens grew to adulthood conscious of the political turmoil about him. After graduating from the University of California and studying in Germany, he returned to the United States broke, jobless, and married. After a stint on the *Evening Post*, he was hired by McClure as managing editor, and although his job was not carefully defined, his salary was the same as Baker's — $5,000 per year.[37]

In October 1902, Steffens printed an article, "Tweed Days in St. Louis," and in November, Tarbell began her series on "The History of the Standard Oil Company." In January 1903, the three writers each contributed an article.

> **CONCERNING THREE ARTICLES...**
>
> How many of those who have read through this number of the magazine noticed that it contains three articles on one subject? We did not plan it so; it is a coincidence that the January McCLURE'S is such an arraignment of American character as should make every one of us stop and think. How many noticed that?
>
> The leading article, "The Shame of Minneapolis," might have been called "The American Contempt of Law." That title could well have served for the current chapter of Miss Tarbell's History of Standard Oil. And it would have fitted perfectly Mr. Baker's "The Right to Work." All together, these articles come pretty near showing how universal is this dangerous trait of ours. . . .
>
> SOURCE. Editorial in McClure's, January 1903.

Steffens wrote "The Shame of Minneapolis," Tarbell continued her history of Standard Oil, and Baker wrote "The Right to Work." These three highly documented articles reflected the writers' talents, as well as McClure's commitment to spend time and money on quality editorial copy. In the same issue an editorial noted that it was "a coincidence that the January *McClure's* is such an arraignment of American character,"[38] and that the three articles combined to demonstrate a glaring American contempt for law. Steffens commented on the disgrace of city governments dominated by boss rule; Tarbell discussed capitalists conspiring to break the law; and Baker wrote about how unions deliberately kept nonunion men from working.

By 1906, however, *McClure's* underwent a variety of organizational changes. Sam McClure devised a grandiose plan for a great industrial combination to include a printing plant, expanded magazine, publishing company, life insurance company, bank, and even ideal housing projects. The result of his plan was that many of the writers and John Phillips, the managing editor, parted company with McClure. At that time McClure bought Phillips's interest and proceeded with his plan. In 1907, the magazine suffered a major loss of circulation and advertising, and McClure abandoned his scheme and worked to secure the magazine's financial health.

By 1911, McClure's health had declined, as well as the magazine's business. The magazine changed hands several times and McClure resigned the editorship. In 1915 *McClure*'s adopted the quarto size (about eleven by fourteen inches) and combined text and advertising. By 1918, *McClure's* increased circulation, reaching its highest point of 563,000. In 1919, with a decline of 20,000 in circulation, the magazine was again sold. Circulation continued to drop and McClure Publications petitioned for bankruptcy. However, the magazine was not to die so easily. It was purchased once more and Sam McClure was reinstated as editor. It returned to the old standard (small quarto, about 8 1/2 by 11 inches) but it rapidly lost money. In 1926, Hearst money once again revived the magazine, but in 1929 it was combined with another publication. The last two years of its life bore no resemblance to the original *McClure's*.

MUNSEY'S MAGAZINE

Although *Munsey's Magazine* was a muckraking magazine, Frank Munsey's claim to fame was that of a consolidator of newspapers rather than as a muckraking publisher. During his lifetime, American newsmen hated him because of his reputation for combining newspapers to make a profit. When Munsey died, William Allen White, a famous Kansas publisher, wrote,

> Frank Munsey, the great publisher, is dead.
>
> Frank Munsey contributed to the journalism of his day the talent of a meatpacker, the morals of a money changer and the manners of an undertaker. He and his kind have about succeeded in transforming a once-noble profession into an eight per cent security.
>
> May he rest in trust.[39]

Although treated unkindly by the newsmen of his day, in some ways Munsey was more visionary than they. His goal was to consolidate, combine, and decrease the competition, a trend that represents business practices even today.

Born in Mercer, Maine, in 1854, Munsey had little schooling and was ill during much of his childhood. At fifteen, he hired himself out to a postmaster for $100 a year. He worked in a country store, where he learned telegraphy. He soon began working for Western Union Telegraph Company in Portland, Maine, as a night and Sunday operator. Before long he became manager of the Augusta, Maine, office. In 1882, he launched his first magazine, the *Golden Argosy*, a children's magazine that showed little if any profit. He changed the magazine to the *Argosy*, an adult pulp magazine. In 1897, he established the *Puritan*, and in 1900, the *Junior Munsey*. These magazines were merged with *Argosy* in later years.

Munsey founded *Munsey's Weekly* in 1889 and changed it to *Munsey's Magazine* in 1891. The magazine limped along, gathering a debt of $100,000, until, in 1893, Munsey cut the price from twenty-five cents to ten cents an issue in a desperate attempt to boost circulation. The price cut propelled the

Lincoln Steffens wrote muckraking articles for McClure's, *then joined Ida Tarbell and John Phillips to create the* American Magazine. *(State Historical Society of Wisconsin)*

magazine into a position that enabled it to lead the world in circulation by 1907.[40]

Munsey was better known as a newspaperman than as a magazine editor. He claimed that the same law of economics applied to newspapers as to other businesses and that small units were no longer competitive. His history of buying and selling was extensive. In 1892, he purchased the *Boston Journal* that published until 1913. In 1901, he bought the *Washington Times* and the *New York Daily News* as a foundation for a proposed chain of daily newspapers to cover several large cities. In 1908, he founded the *Philadelphia Times*, only to abandon it in 1914. He bought the *Baltimore News* in 1908, sold it in 1915, and bought it again in 1917. He acquired the *New York Sun* in 1915. In 1920, he bought the *New York Herald*, the *Evening Telegraph*, and the *Baltimore Star* and *Baltimore American*. In that same year, 1920, the *Sun* was absorbed by the *Herald*. Three years later he bought the *New York Globe* and merged it with the *Sun*. He also sold his Baltimore papers to William Randolph Hearst.

Although Munsey was known as the "dealer in dailies" and for "killing" newspapers, he also was known as a millionaire.[41] His dealings paid him more than $20 million. And, although other editors criticized him for combining newspapers, he also strengthened them. Munsey, for example, poured enough funds into the dying *New York Herald* to give it once again the success it enjoyed under James Gordon Bennett. Then, in 1924, he sold it to Ogden Reid of the *New York Tribune* for an unprecedented $5 million.

Munsey's newspapers were conservative, and journalists claimed they lacked distinction because of that position. But his dailies were clean, respectable, free from bitterness, and fair to advertisers. He supported the Republican party without deviation except for one foray into the Progressive party. When Theodore Roosevelt, Munsey's friend, led the Bull Moose Progressives out of the Republican party in 1916, Munsey followed. Frank Munsey died in 1925. After taxes and payments of debts, his estate was valued at almost $20 million. He had no heirs nor family and most of his money was donated to the New York Metropolitan Museum of Art. During his life he owned eighteen newspapers and twelve magazines.

AMERICAN MAGAZINE

American Magazine, although a concern independent of *McClure's*, certainly had ties to the earlier magazine. Tiring of McClure's schemes for expansion, John Phillips, McClure's able editor, and Ida Tarbell, Lincoln Steffens, and Ray Stannard Baker, the trio of muckraking writers, broke away from Samuel McClure and began their own magazine. In 1906 they bought *American Magazine*, formerly *Frank Leslie's Illustrated Monthly*, for $360,000. Although their hopes were high, their finances were unstable. Lincoln Steffens wrote to his father, "We are buying an old magazine, which we propose to make the greatest thing of the kind that was ever made in this world."[42] The writers vigorously departed from the old standard of muckraking and approached American life with what Phillips described as "a song of optimism based on facts."[43] Such an approach failed to acquire the needed circulation and the constant shortage of working capital persuaded the investors to sell the magazine to the Crowell Company in 1911. Crowell Company was backed by the banking interests of J. P. Morgan and Thomas Lamont. For a year the new arrangement seemed to work fairly well, but in 1915 after numerous disputes over content and with advertisers, most of the staff resigned. From 1915 to 1923, the magazine made a sentimental appeal to the family audience and circulation passed 1,700,000.

SCHOLARLY MAGAZINES

Among the other media involved in reform during the early 1900s were scholarly publications such as *The Annals of the American Academy of Political and Social Science*. The magazine thoroughly documented the problems of the tenement houses, focusing its attention on the "evil," "poor," and "deplorable" conditions of the tenement houses in several northeastern cities. The magazine investigated the possibility of inspection of tenement houses and the licensing of tenement landlords. The magazine dealt with the issue of tuberculosis, lack of adequate fire escapes, and lack of sanitation. The articles pointed out that as many as four families shared one toilet and people washed at sinks in public halls. Water pressure at times was insufficient to allow water to reach the upper floors and the main drain pipes of the plumbing system were buried beneath cellar floors where they could not be examined.[44]

CONCLUSION

Scholars have long debated the chicken vs. the egg question in terms of muckraking magazines and social reform. Did the muckrakers create a reform climate or did a reform climate create muckraking? The answer to the question surely is much more complicated than yes or no. Undoubtedly the climate for reform existed or muckraking magazines would likely have been unsuccessful, but how far they went in terms of promoting legislation and getting results is difficult to measure. We do know, however, that the hue and cry raised by the magazines and by reform groups resulted in some change. The Food and Drug Act passed in 1906, and by 1900 twenty-eight states had passed some regulations establishing a minimum age of employment, thus eliminating some child labor. However, the laws often were revised by the industries affected before legislation was passed and they rarely contained substantial enforcement provisions.

Magazines as a whole continued to be important in American life. During the Gilded Age their content reflected many of the conflicts in society, and their audiences were readers with varied tastes. Some of the quality monthlies and general-interest magazines have never ceased publication and can be found on newsstands today. General-interest magazines suffered in the 1950s with the advent of television as a national advertising market. However, despite hardship, many of the old magazines persist, and in response to new demands, special-interest magazines developed in the place of magazines that died.

NOTES

1. Christopher Wilson, "The Rhetoric of Consumption: Mass-Market Magazines and the Demise of the Gentle Reader, 1880–1920," in *The Culture of Consumption*, Richard Wightman Fox and T. J. Jackson Lears, eds. (New York: Pantheon, 1983), pp. 39–64.
2. Dara Trum, "*Harper's*: Food for Thought 1850–1982," unpublished paper written for *The Magazine in American Society*, seminar at Washburn University, Topeka, Kan., taught by Jean Folkerts.
3. Theodore Peterson, *Magazines in the 20th Century* (Urbana: University of Illinois Press, 1956), p. 409.
4. Caspar W. Whiting, "Evolution of a Country Club," *Harper's*, December 1894; Josiah Flynt, "Club Life Among the Outcasts," *Harper's*, April 1895.
5. Henry Cabot Lodge, "The Spanish-American War," *Harper's*, February–August 1899.
6. See *Harper's*, Elizabeth Breuer, "What Four-Million Women Are Doing," December 1923; Howard Edsall, "Whisky Below Decks," July 1929; Ellwood Hendrick, "The Changing View of Evolution," December 1920, and "Sell the Papers: The Malady of American Journalism," June 1925.
7. *Newsweek*, June 30, 1980.
8. *Time*, September 28, 1980.
9. *Time*, September 28, 1980.
10. Arthur John, *The Best Years of the Century* (Urbana: University of Illinois Press, 1981), p. 147.
11. John, *Best Years of Century*, p. 140.
12. The author is indebted to Cynthia Steele for her unpublished paper, "Chronicle of *Scribner's Magazine*."
13. Robert Grant, "The Art of Living: The Case of Woman," *Scribner's Magazine*, October 1895, p. 476.

14. "The Business of a Great Publishing House," *Scribner's Magazine*, January 1908, p. 134.
15. Frank Luther Mott, "Scribner's Magazine," *A History of American Magazines* (Cambridge, Mass., 1957), vol. 4, p. 732.
16. Wilson, "Rhetoric of Consumption," p. 45.
17. Walter Deane Fuller, *The Life and Times of Cyrus H. K. Curtis* (New York: The Newcomen Society of America, 1948), pp. 11–13. See also John Tebbel, *The American Magazine* (New York: Hawthorne Books, 1969), p. 181.
18. Tebbel, *American Magazine*, pp. 183–84.
19. *Ladies Home Journal*, December 1892, p. 32.
20. *Ladies Home Journal*, December 1892, p. 32.
21. *Ladies Home Journal*, May 1904, p. 18.
22. James Playsted Wood, *Magazines in the United States* (New York: Ronald Press Co., 1971), pp. 112–113.
23. Wood, *Magazines in the United States*, pp. 147–165.
24. Roland Wolseley, *Understanding Magazines* (Ames, Iowa: The Iowa State University Press, 1969), p. 28.
25. Arthur and Lila Weinberg, eds. *The Muckrakers* (New York: Simon and Schuster, 1961), p. xiii.
26. For elaboration of this thesis, see David M. Chalmers, "The Muckrakers and the Growth of Corporate Power: A Study in Constructive Journalism," *American Journal of Economics and Sociology* 18 (April 1959), pp. 295–311.
27. For discussion of the demise of muckraking magazines, see Robert D. Reynolds, Jr., "The 1906 Campaign to Sway Muckraking Periodicals," *Journalism Quarterly* 56:3 (Autumn 1979) pp. 513–520, 589.
28. John E. Semonche, "The *American Magazine* of 1906–15: Principle vs. Profit, *Journalism Quarterly* 40:1 (Spring 1963), pp. 37–44, 86.
29. Fred F. Endres, "The Pre-Muckraking Days of *McClure's* Magazine, 1893–1901," *Journalism Quarterly* 55:1 (Spring 1978), pp. 154–157. See also Jeanne G. Goldfarb, "McClure's in Fact and Legend: Muckraking the Muckraker Historians," Master's thesis, The University of Kansas, December 1970.
30. Arthur Warren, "Philip D. Armour," *McClure's*, February 1894, p. 260, cited in Endres, "Pre-Muckraking Days of McClure's Magazine, p. 154.
31. Endres, "Pre-Muckraking Days of McClure's," p. 156.
32. *McClure's*, October 1897, p. 1101, cited in Endres, "Pre-Muckraking Days of *McClure's*."
33. *McClure's*, June 1898, p. 100.
34. *McClure's*, June 1898, p. 206.
35. Endres, "Pre-Muckraking Days of *McClure's*," pp. 156–157.
36. Harold S. Wilson, *McClure's Magazine and the Muckrakers* (Princeton, N.J.: Princeton University Press, 1970), p. 74.
37. Wilson, *McClure's Magazine*, p. 89.

38. Wilson, *McClure's Magazine*, p. 146.
39. George Britt, *Forty Years—Forty Millions, the Career of Frank A. Munsey* (New York: Farrar & Rinehart, Inc., 1935), p. 17.
40. Britt, *Forty Years—Forty Millions*, p. 81.
41. Oswald Garrison Villard, *Some Newspapers and Newspaper-Men* (New York: Alfred A. Knopf, Inc., 1923), p. 81.
42. Lincoln Steffens to father, June 3, 1906, in *The Letters of Lincoln Steffens*, vol. 1, pp. 176, 173–4, cited in Semonche, "The 'American Magazine' of 1906–15," pp. 36–44, 86.
43. From John S. Phillips to William Kent, Kent papers collection, cited in Semonche, "The 'American Magazine' of 1906–15," p. 38.
44. See *The Annals of the American Academy of Political and Social Science,* vol. 20.

CHAPTER 14

THE GREAT WAR

During the early years of the twentieth century, newspapers experienced increased costs and raised their prices accordingly. Consolidation affected most cities and as competing newspapers died, circulation and price wars came to an end. By the end of World War I, the percentage of advertising carried had increased, and advertising supported greater percentages of the cost of newspapers than before. After 1909, the number of newspapers declined, as circulation and number of pages increased. The newspaper industry experienced a period of stability, with a solid profit base supporting the product.

The reform movement, which provided such viable content for magazines during the early years of the century, also forced newspaper editors to confront growing resistance to child labor, which provided the "newsies" who delivered the growing number of evening newspapers.

The beginning of World War I prompted editorial enthusiasm for a sense of American nationalism and diverted reform energies to winning the war for democracy. Citizens during World War I feared the results of the period of massive change they had just undergone, and responded to massive immigration, unionization, and a lack of homogeneity with repression of rights, rather than extension of civil liberty. The Espionage and Sedition acts created a

This Charles Dana Gibson drawing appeared in an April 1917 issue of Life. In this drawing the mother gives her son to Uncle Sam. (Library of Congress Collection)

legal basis for shutting down newspapers or for restricting their second-class mailing privileges, and therefore dramatically increasing the cost of circulation.

Not reserved for Germans alone, the attack on printed matter was aimed at all Americans who seemed different. Socialist newspapers were hard hit. The most famous, *The Masses*, survived from 1911 to 1917, when its editors were indicted under the Espionage Act. Black newspapers also had serious decisions to make, often protesting discrimination within the Armed Services. W. E. B. DuBois advocated segregated training camps for officers, arguing that blacks would never be incorporated into white society. Robert Abbott of the famous *Chicago Defender* was appalled at this suggestion, arguing that blacks should be incorporated into the mainstream of military life.

Most metropolitan dailies, however, supported the war, often cooperating with George Creel's Committee on Public Information, and uttering barely a cry of protest as other newspapers came under the heavy hand of the post office and the courts.

On foreign fronts, the war also had an impact on United States media. War correspondents, confronted with heavy censorship, moved from the front to centralized headquarters. Reports were based more heavily on military reports than on first-hand accounts, and censorship was a major problem.

GENERAL CHARACTERISTICS

During and after World War I, the price of daily newspapers rose slightly. Gone were most of the penny papers from the Hearst and Pulitzer days and in their place were two- and three-cent papers. The rise in cost was due to a higher cost of newsprint, higher labor costs, increased volume of news and features, and higher postage rates. In addition, consolidation reduced competition, ending circulation and price wars.

Newspapers were about the same size as standard metropolitan newspapers of today (an eight-column, 18-by-22-inch sheet). At the start of the war, news occupied about 50 percent of the space, and advertising the other 50 percent. During the war the percentage of news dropped. Advertising paid for a greater percentage of newspaper costs, increasing from 64 percent in 1909 to 75 percent in 1929.

A desire for war news prompted increased membership in the Associated Press from 1914 to 1920, but membership slumped slightly after the war. In 1914, nearly 900 news organizations belonged to AP. The number peaked in 1920 at 1,250, then dropped in 1924.

GROWTH AND RECESSION

The rapid growth of newspapers ended before the war. The combined total of morning and evening newspapers peaked in 1909, with 2,600 newspapers. By 1919 there were only 2,441. The major transportation and communication developments that prompted increased numbers of newspapers slowed down. Growth of railroad mileage stabilized, the telegraph was firmly in place and rural free delivery routes grew only slightly in the war and postwar years.

Circulation was a different story, however, with the number of readers growing at a rate similar to the rate of growth of the urban population. In 1870, only 11.5 percent of the literate population subscribed to a daily newspaper. By 1930, 45 percent of the literate population subscribed. Newsprint consumption also continued to increase, indicating the growth in the number of pages of dailies. Average circulation of a daily newspaper in 1919 was 13,531. Sunday circulations hovered around 30,000.

The geographical location of daily newspapers also was changing. In 1880, dailies printed in six cities (New York, Chicago, Philadelphia, Cleveland, Boston, and San Francisco) constituted 51.1 percent of the country's dailies. By 1919, that figure had dropped to 34.7 percent and by 1929 it dropped further to 33.7 percent.

The weekly newspaper picture also showed a decline in numbers during the war years. In 1909, about 16,135 newspapers were in existence. The numbers fluctuated only slightly until 1917, when the total number dropped to 15,587. The weeklies experienced a steady decline through 1935, when 10,505 weeklies were printed.

Chain ownership was growing, although its greatest period of growth came in the early 1920s. In 1900, ten chains owned thirty-two dailies; by 1923, thirty-one chains owned 153 dailies, or 32.4 percent of all daily circulation. Newspapers begun in the previous decades continued to be major forces in the South and Midwest. The *Chicago Tribune*, the *Kansas City Star*, the *St.*

Louis Post-Dispatch, and the *Denver Post* continued as financially strong and independent voices. The *Louisville Courier-Journal* and the *Atlanta Constitution* provided similar strength in the South.[1]

THE INDUSTRY CONFRONTS REFORM

The reform years of the early twentieth century provided content for magazines, but it also resulted in pressure on newspapers to treat their employees differently. Child-labor reform groups were concerned about low pay and poor working conditions for newsboys, a concern which culminated in the 1920s in educational programs for news carriers. David Nasaw suggested that newsies were the product of the boom of afternoon dailies that began in the 1880s and continued through the war. Newsboys bought newspapers from the circulation manager at a discounted rate, then sold them to their customers for a specified price. Newspapers depended on the little distributors and fought for their loyalty with Thanksgiving dinners, theater tickets, and baseball leagues. Occasionally newspapers employed thugs to harass newsboys of other newspapers, hoping to defeat the competition. Although such violence generally was short-lived and rarely prevalent, Chicago newsboys endured battles fought by adult hoodlums hired specifically to challenge the competition.[2]

Newsboys came from every ethnic group, and almost exclusively from the working class. Selling newspapers on the street was a common childhood occupation in all major cities, and newsboys, for the most part, enjoyed the autonomy of being an independent dealer away from the watchful and disciplining eyes of teachers and parents. But it was a demanding occupation as well, which required boys to exercise judgment about how many papers to buy, where to sell them and how to get the best tips. If a boy bought too many papers, he made no profit and was stuck with the extras, but if he bought too few, he would alienate his regular customers. Boys chose particular street car stops, theater exits, and other heavily populated districts in order to sell the most papers. They wept, pled poverty, or begged for a customer to buy a "last paper" so they could go home to bed—all to gain the tips that gave them real profit. Reformers urged customers not to tip, not to encourage the practice of children "begging," but others looked at it differently:

> The more prosperous Americans, on their way home from business or pleasure, saw what they wanted to see in the city left behind. The children of the street were not, to their eyes, the exploited, deprived children the reformers had described, but a band of little merchants selling their wares. Some were dirty, some ragged; some scowled,

Newsboys formed the distribution network for newspapers during the early twentieth century. (Library of Congress Collection)

"POST-BELLUM"

In this poem Dean Collins, a Portland (Ore.) newsie, described the dry news days after World War I which made it difficult for newsboys to sell papers. The poem was printed in a newspaper published by newsboys to raise money for their club and activities:

A newsboy with his papers sat sighing on the street
For the cruel war was over and the foe had met defeat.
And the scare-heads in the dailies, they had vanished like a spell,
And the liveliest thing the newsie had was market heads to yell.
"O, maybe Sherman had it right," said he, "but wars must cease—
And Sherman never tried to peddle papers when 'twas peace."

"They used to saw an extra off each half hour by the clock.
And we used to wake the echoes when we whooped 'em down the block.
War may be just what Sherman said it was, but just the same,
If Sherman were a newsie, O, I wonder what he'd think
Of peddling papers after peace had put things on the blink?"

"How can I jar the people loose to buy the sheet and read,
If I start yelling 'bout the rise in price of clover seed?
When they are used to war and smoke and sulphur burning blue,
Will they warm up to read about the W.C.T.U.?
O, Maybe Sherman had it right on war—but wars must cease—
And Sherman never tried to peddle papers after peace."[3]

---

some whimpered; but they were all on the streets for a noble cause: to make money for their families—and themselves. Here were scores of children who had adopted the American credo, who believed in hard work, hustle, and long hours, who were on their way up the ladder to success. With the help of kindly benefactors who bought their goods and left tips, these children would raise themselves from poverty to prosperity.[4]

It was not only newsies, or reformers, who were concerned about the working people on newspapers. Journalists' organizations, comprised of reporters who were concerned about wages and working conditions, began to take shape. These early struggles culminated in the 1930s with the formation of a newspaper guild. Newspapers were not immune from labor strikes as production personnel struck for higher wages and shorter hours.

Postal acts in the early part of the century required newspapers and magazines to make honest statements about circulation and provide specific ownership information. The American Newspaper Publishers Association, organized in 1887 to lobby for legislation favorable to newspapers and against restrictive legislation, gained momentum during the war years and became a significant force in later decades.

WORLD WAR I

In 1914, when the nations of Europe became embroiled in World War I, the United States shunned involvement. War had been brewing for more than a decade, with Germany, Austria-Hungary, and Turkey organized as the Central Powers fighting against what eventually became America's allies: France, England, Russia, and Italy. Members of Theodore Roosevelt's Progressive party, which included the group of journalists who had been involved in muckraking, believed the European nations were fighting merely over commercial rivalries. They also believed the role of the United States should be that of a model of peace and democracy, uninvolved in imperialistic wars.

However, in 1917, when the German government threatened American ships and suggested that Germany would involve Mexico in the war, and the Bolshevik Revolution in Russia freed the United States from the embarrassment of being allied with a tyrannical power, President Woodrow Wilson went before Congress to argue that the world must be made safe for democracy.

Despite Wilson's plea for democracy, citizens during World War I feared the results of the period of massive change they had just undergone, and sought to create a restrictive, homogeneous society. In early 1917, in a small rural community in north central Kansas, a group of farmers arrived at the parochial school of a German Lutheran Church and painted the schoolhouse yellow. Only months before, the members of the church had seemingly been friends with their neighbors. The Germans were admired for their hard work and thrift. But the intense reaction against German peoples during World War I defied reason. It was, as social historian John Higham wrote, "the most spectacular reversal of judgment in the history of American nativism."[5]

This was not an isolated incident. In his book on the First Amendment, legal historian John Stevens recalled many similar examples from Wisconsin, home for many individuals of German descent.

> Libraries burned German-language books, symphonies removed all German compositions from their repertoires, schools stopped teaching German, and universities fired professors of German. The federal

> ## WILSON CALLS FOR WAR
>
> The world must be made safe for democracy. Its peace must be planted upon the tested foundations of political liberty. . . .
>
> It is a fearful thing to lead this great peaceful people into war . . . But the right is more precious than peace, and we shall fight for the things which we have always carried nearest our hearts,—for democracy, for the right of those who submit to authority to have a voice in their own governments, for the rights and liberties of small nations, for a universal dominion of right by such a concert of free peoples as shall bring peace and safety to all nations and make the world itself at last free.
>
> SOURCE. War Message to Congress, 1917.

government clamped down on German-language newspapers. By the thousands, citizens, banks, businesses, and even towns lined up to anglicize their names.[6]

Why the sudden reversal of attitude against the Germans? Stevens suggested that Americans, partially because they had been able to avoid foreign entanglements, believed the country was unique, and that its homogeneity contributed to that uniqueness. The possibility a sizeable minority of American citizens would disagree on foreign policy, as war threatened, shocked the rest of the populace.[7]

Antagonism toward immigrants also had been on the increase since the economic hard times of the 1880s. Laborers viewed immigrants as threatening their jobs, and capitalists were afraid immigrant labor would stimulate strikes and other forms of what they termed "anarchism," or disrespect for government and authority. In addition, the German government threatened to sink American ships.

During the early stages of the European phase of the war, German-language newspapers in the United States often supported Germany's victories. Once the United States entered the war, however, most German-language newspapers avoided discussing the war, became pacifist or supported United States policies.[8]

LEGAL RESTRICTIONS DURING THE WAR

At the beginning of World War I, the only acts regarding freedom of expression still on the books were the Treason Act and the Conspiracies Act from the Civil War. Neither of these acts punished individuals for uttering disloyal remarks, and both of them required proof of conspiracy to convict. In fact, during the Civil War, President Abraham Lincoln was disturbed because it sometimes seemed that civilians—particularly those associated with the press—had more rights than those who defended the Union. He wrote to a friend, "Must I shoot a simple-minded soldier boy who deserts, while I must not touch a hair of a wily agitator who induces him to desert?"

Such was not the case during World War I. In 1917, Congress introduced a draft, increased restrictions on aliens, and enacted the Espionage, the Sedition, and the Trading-with-the-Enemy Acts. At least 2,000 persons during the war were indicted under the Espionage Act alone.

The Espionage Act, initially designed to prevent interference with military operation, was aimed at those who attempted to cause "insubordination" or "disloyalty," or to obstruct enlistment or recruiting.[9] The act also allowed the postmaster to refuse to mail materials he thought violated the act. In 1918, the Sedition Amendment expanded the original intent, making it a crime to write or publish any "disloyal, profane, scurrilous or abusive language about the form of government of the United States" or the Constitution, military or naval forces, the flag or the uniform, or to use language to bring those ideas or institutions into contempt or disrepute. This amendment made punishable speech that in World War II would have been deemed mere political comment. The Trading-With-the-Enemy Act, passed in 1917, authorized censorship of communications moving into and outside of the United States, and required that foreign-language newspapers file translations with the government.

One Wisconsin editor criticized the army's requirement that all recruits be vaccinated for smallpox, and because he did not file a translation, he was indicted under the Trading-with-the-Enemy Act and the Espionage Act. His son testified that he was senile and did not understand the requirement. The son, who claimed the newspaper was unimportant and read by only a few of the editor's friends, begged the judge to be lenient, but the judge sentenced the old editor to a year at Leavenworth, where he died while imprisoned.[10]

Through this legislation and court interpretations of it came the most important decisions made by the Supreme Court in the area of freedom of the press. Not since the Alien and Sedition Acts of 1798 had the United States suppressed, to such a great extent, unpopular ideas. These decisions were continued and expanded through the 1930s. The first major legal case to arise out of the legislation was *Schenck vs. United States*.[11] Schenck, who was general secretary of the Socialist party, mailed about 15,000 leaflets to men who had been called to military service, urging them to oppose the Conscription Act, or draft. He was indicted for trying to mail unlawful documents and for conspiracy to cause insubordination in the military service of the United States. In reviewing the case on appeal to the Supreme Court, Justice Oliver Wendell Holmes articulated the famous clear and present danger rule. He noted that what must be ascertained was whether the words were used in such circumstances as to "create a clear and present danger which would have brought about substantive evils which Congress had a right to prevent. It is a question of proximity and degree." Holmes argued that statements made in times of war differed substantially from those made in peacetime.

POSTAL CONTROL AND THE *MILWAUKEE LEADER*

Shortly before the beginning of World War I, broad powers for press control fell into the hands of Postmaster Albert S. Burleson. Burleson had the power of determining what could and what could not be sent through the second-class mails, and he used that power not wisely, but well. This power used by the Post Office Department was sanctioned by the Espionage Act of 1917. The extent of the Post Office's activities to control "disloyal" publications was substantial. An estimated seventy-five newspapers had been interfered with by the Post Office by mid-1918, a professor wrote in the magazine *Contemporary Review*, and forty-five of those were Socialist papers. Four were suspended and many others continued only because they agreed not to comment on the war.[12]

The postmaster general's wartime activities ultimately were upheld as legal by a 1921 decision of the Supreme Court of the United States.[13] Even though publications that had their second-class privileges withdrawn had the right to judicial review, the court battles were often so drawn out as to be ruinous to the publishers. The Socialist *New York Call* lost its privileges in November 1917, and its court fight did not end until March 1921, when the Supreme Court upheld the withdrawal of mailing privileges from the *Milwaukee Leader*.

The denial of second-class rates did not mean that publications were barred completely from the mails. For a publication that depended on circulation by mail, however, higher cost of third-class or first-class rates were prohibitive. Second-class rates were eight to fifteen times lower than third-class for printed matter.[14]

As John Lofton noted in his book, *The Press as Guardian of the First Amendment*, "Not only did the *Leader* lose its second class rate, but the paper was deprived of the right to receive or send first class mail. The withholding of first class mail caused the *Leader* to lose $70,000 in subscription money and $50,000 in local and national advertising. The paper lost approximately fifteen thousand subscribers."[15]

Victor Berger was an important man for a variety of reasons. Born in Austria in 1860, he came to the United States at age eighteen. Over the years, he helped found the Socialist party in the United States; was editor of the

MAIL PRIVILEGES REVOKED

List of publications whose second-class mail privileges were revoked after a hearing on account of violation of the Espionage Law, together with the date of revocation.

Publication	Location	Date
Arbeiter Zeitung	Buffalo, N.Y.	Oct. 9, 1917
Bull	New York, N.Y.	Aug. 16, 1917
Cultura Obrera	"	Aug. 28, 1917
Elore	"	Sept. 24, 1917
Hlas Svobody	"	Sept. 12, 1917
L'Avvenire	"	Aug. 15, 1917
Mother Earth	"	Sept. 25, 1917
The Masses	"	Aug. 15, 1917
New York Call	"	Nov. 10, 1917
New Yorker Volkszeitung	"	Oct. 6, 1917
Novy Mir	"	Oct. 3, 1917
Obrana	"	Aug. 28, 1917
Solidarity	Chicago, Ill.	Oct. 26, 1917
American Socialist	"	Aug. 8, 1917
Das Wochenblatt	"	March 18, 1918
La Parola Proletaria	"	Sept. 25, 1917
The Decatur Labor World	Decatur, Ill.	March 21, 1918
Il Proletario	Boston, Mass.	Aug. 28, 1917
Cronaca Sovversiva	Lynn, Mass.	Aug. 9, 1917
Kova	Philadelphia, Pa.	Jan. 12, 1918
The Peoples Press	"	Aug. 28, 1917
Philadelphia Tageblatt	"	Sept. 21, 1917
Die Freie Presse	Glencoe, Minn.	Jan. 4, 1918
Allarm	Minneapolis, Minn.	Sept. 26, 1917
Referendum — Four Page Home Print	Fairbault, Minn.	Aug. 11, 1917
Missouri Staats-Zeitung	Kansas City, Mo.	Feb. 16, 1918
Saint Louis Labor	Saint Louis, Mo.	Aug. 17, 1917
Social Revolution	"	Oct. 3, 1917
El Rebelde	Los Angeles, Calif.	Aug. 31, 1917
Vorwarts der Pacific Kuste	San Francisco, Calif.	Oct. 12, 1917
The New Critic	Grand Junction, Colo.	Oct. 11, 1917
Jeffersonian	Thomson, Ga.	Aug. 8, 1917

continued

The Thomson Guard	"	Oct. 1, 1917
Watson's Magazine	"	Oct. 12, 1917
Die Washtenaw Post	Ann Arbor, Mich.	Oct. 10, 1917
New Jersey Freie Zeitung	Newark, N.J.	Oct. 6, 1917
Volksfreund und Arbeiter Zeitung	Cleveland, Ohio	Feb. 23, 1918
The Josephinum Weekly	Columbus, Ohio	April 6, 1918
Scimitar	Abbeville, S.C.	Sept. 26, 1917
Charleston American	Charleston, S.C.	Dec. 20, 1917
The Rebel	Hallettsville, Tex.	Aug. 7, 1917
The Battle Axe	Danville, Va.	Aug. 8, 1917
Spokane Socialist	Spokane, Wash.	Sept. 12, 1917
The Milwaukee Leader	Milwaukee, Wis.	Oct. 1, 1917

SOURCE. National Archives

German-language newspaper, the *Milwaukee Leader*; and was a member of Congress from 1911 to 1913, the first Socialist to serve in Congress. Berger opposed U.S. involvement in World War I, as did many other Americans. But as Zechariah Chafee, Jr., noted, "Unlike the great majority of Americans, Berger and other Socialists did not consider the German submarine campaign of February 1917 a sufficient reason for changing their minds, but maintained that war was justified only in case of invasion."[16]

In October 1917, the third assistant postmaster general withdrew second-class mail privileges from Berger's *Milwaukee Leader*. The *Leader* fought the withdrawal in court, but the U.S. government countered with articles and editorials published in the *Leader* which the Post Office Department claimed clearly violated the Espionage Act. One government exhibit against the *Leader* included a Berger editorial captioned "War and Insanity," which began with this claim: "For the first time, an army has been forced to provide a field insane asylum." Quoting a neurologist, Berger's editorial continued:

> In the present war the number [of cases of battle-induced insanity] frequently reaches 40 to 1,000 men. Think of it! An army of 1,000,000 men might have 40,000 insane—more than are housed today in all the state hospitals of Illinois, Ohio and Indiana.
> It is said that in France there are certain closed cars which are used for the purpose of transporting the insane away from the front, and that there are sometimes long trains made up exclusively of these.[17]

Other newspapers rarely came to the defense of Victor Berger and his *Milwaukee Leader*, and often they seemed to be cheering efforts to keep his

Victor Berger, editor of the Milwaukee Leader, *opposed U.S. involvement in World War I. (State Historical Society of Wisconsin)*

newspaper out of the mails. In January 1918, during some of the early actions against publications suspected of being opposed to the war or otherwise "disloyal," the *New York Times* editorially criticized Berger and seemed to ask for harsh enforcement of the Espionage Act. The *Times* approved of a Court of Appeals decision that upheld the power of the postmaster general to withhold second-class mailing privileges from newspapers he saw as "seditious." The editorial said:

> Now . . . Victor Berger will probably be more convinced than ever that our government is not a democracy. The Socialist ex-Representative reached that conclusion when the United States Supreme Court declared the draft law constitutional, and in his paper, The *Milwaukee Leader*, expressed his opinion with what some editors would regard as rather dangerous frankness.[18]

After having wreaked havoc on the *Leader* by manipulating its powers over the mails, the federal government then moved against the *Leader*'s editor. In February 1918, Berger and four other Socialists were indicted for conspiracy to violate the Espionage Act of 1917. In that time of war hysteria, Berger was convicted. Berger's conviction was reversed early in 1921—more than two years after the end of the war—because Judge Kennesaw Mountain Landis (later the Commissioner of Baseball) was obviously prejudiced against Berger and his codefendants. Landis had made derogatory remarks about German-Americans during the trial. After the trial, Landis is said to have expressed regrets the law did not permit him "to have Berger lined up against a wall and shot."[19]

Furthermore, even though Berger was reelected to Congress in 1918 while under indictment for a supposed violation of the Espionage Act, Congress refused to seat him. As Lofton has shown, major newspapers had no compunctions about denouncing Berger; evidently, Berger's freedom of the press extended only far enough to agree with those worthy publications about the rightness of World War I. The *New York Times* said that Berger's contentions that he should be seated in Congress had no merit. The *Boston Transcript*, Lofton reported, even endorsed an American Legion resolution asking that Berger be deported.[20]

THE COMMITTEE ON PUBLIC INFORMATION

World War I brought with it not only legislation silencing the press, but an active propaganda effort promoting American war policy. In April 1917, President Wilson established the Committee on Public Information. Serving

This 1918 Joseph Pennell poster exhorted citizens to buy bonds to support the war. (Library of Congress Collection)

on the committee were the civilian director, former newspaperman, George Creel, who was paid $8,000 annually for his efforts, and the secretaries of the departments of War, Navy, and State. The total cost of the committee's effort came to about $4.5 million, financed from a fund granted to the president for the general defense of the country and by admission fees for committee exhibits and films shown to the public.

The task was to change antiwar opinion to enthusiasm for an organized military operation and to intensify a feeling of national solidity. The Creel Committee, in the two years of its existence, mailed 6,000 news releases that generated about 20,000 columns of newsprint each week. It also published an official daily bulletin with a circulation of about 118,000, and sponsored 75,000 speakers who in small towns of America "roused the righteous wrath" of U.S. citizens toward the Germans.[21]

The Creel Committee also established a foreign-language division, which monitored foreign-language newspapers and translated pamphlets into other languages, published a newsletter for schools, *The National School Service*, supported the creation of propaganda films, developed cartoons, created posters supporting the war effort, solicited more than $1.5 million in free advertising in magazines, trade journals, and newspapers, and developed an extensive propaganda effort abroad. John Mock and Cedrick Larson, who wrote a comprehensive history of the committee's efforts, described the totality of the effort:

> And every item of war news they [a rural family] saw — in the county weekly, in magazines, or in the city daily picked up occasionally in the general store — was not merely officially approved information but precisely the same kind that millions of their fellow citizens were getting at the same moment. Every war story had been censored somewhere along the line — at the source, in transit, or in the newspaper office with "voluntary" rules issued by the CPI. . . . Patriotic advertising in all of these papers had been prepared by the CPI. . . . Cartoons were those inspired by the Committee staff. At the state fair the family viewed war exhibits under Committee sponsorship, and the movies at the county seat began with one of the Committee's patriotic films and paused briefly for oratory by one of the Committee's Four Minute Men, who had gained his ideas for the talk from the Committee's "suggestions."
>
> At the township school the children saw war photographs issued by the Committee. . . . The postoffice bulletin board was adorned with copies of the Committee's *Official Bulletin*, and posters in the general store and on telephone poles up and down the countryside were those designed by the Committee's artists. . . . On Sunday the pastor

George Creel headed the Committee on Public Information. (Library of Congress Collection)

thanked Providence for blessings that had been listed by one of the Committee's copywriters.[22]

Creel's appointment was viewed with skepticism by editors, both those on the right and those on the left. Before the war, as a writer for the *Denver Post* and editor of the *Rocky Mountain News*, Creel vehemently criticized mining companies and working conditions of miners. Staunch Republican editors accused him of being a socialist and others accused him of being a censor. The *New York Times* described Creel's career prior to the war as "turbulent," and expressed doubt that "he is qualified for any position of authority over the press."[23]

Despite such criticisms, Creel successfully orchestrated press coverage of the war and the attempt to garner public opinion. In addition to publishing news releases, school bulletins, and other printed pieces, he organized exhibits of war and trophies captured from the Germans, and charged the public admission to view them. Creel was assisted in his efforts by a variety of liberal, reform-minded journalists and intellectuals, who feared that German militarists posed a new threat to democracy.[24] Charles Dana Gibson designed posters based on his popular Gibson Girls in support of the war. Professors from prestigious universities such as the University of Chicago, the University of Illinois, and Columbia University wrote pamphlets and made speeches for the committee. Film stars such as Mary Pickford and Douglas Fairbanks sold liberty bonds.

Within two months after he was appointed, Creel issued regulations to the press requesting voluntary cooperation. He organized news into three categories: "dangerous" or not to be published news, which included information about military maneuvers and threats against the president; "questionable" news, which involved technical inventions and rumors, to be published with caution and preferably with the approval of the committee; and "routine" news, which required no authorization. Press reaction varied. The Pittsburgh Press Club organized an intelligence bureau to disseminate war news and to monitor the patriotism of newspapers in twenty-seven Pennsylvania counties, and the Hearst papers and the *Washington Post* violated the regulations quite consistently. Cooperation was the rule, however, rather than the exception.

MEDIA REACTION TO THE WAR

The United States remained neutral from 1914 until 1917, although it aided the allies, particularly Britain, during the first three years. In 1917, when the German government threatened to sink American ships and to engage Mexico on its side, President Woodrow Wilson asked Congress to declare war.

Journalists reacted in various ways. Used here to illustrate several reactions are a biographical sketch of the liberal journalist Walter Lippmann, a discussion of the reaction of major metropolitan newspapers, and a sketch of the socialist publication, *The Masses*.

WALTER LIPPMANN

The reaction of the liberal journalist was typical of that of Walter Lippmann, a brilliant Harvard graduate who as a college student claimed to be a socialist and who, at the time war was declared, was an editor of the *New Republic*, a liberal journal of opinion financed by benefactors, rather than by advertising. In 1914, Lippmann claimed that wars stemmed from colonialism and imperialism and that the United States should not become involved in Europe's quarrels. He claimed ignorant rulers led people to war. However, in 1917, on the eve of Wilson's declaration, Lippmann persuaded himself that the war was a noble cause.

> "We are living and shall live all our lives now in a revolutionary world," he wrote the week after America went to war. There would be a "transvaluation of values as radical as anything in the history of intellect." Concepts like liberty, equality and democracy would have to be reexamined "as fearlessly as religious dogmas were in the nineteenth century."[25]

Lippmann's newly found zeal was reflected in his desire to help in the war. He applied for an exemption from selective service and went to work for Secretary of War Newton D. Baker, temporarily severing his ties to the *New Republic*. Although Lippmann promoted the war under Baker's supervision, he was disturbed by the government's censorship of socialist publications. He advocated benign neglect of socialist journalists, fearing censorship would create bitter enemies and leave ugly scars. He suggested censorship should not be left to those who might be intolerant, a comment aimed at George Creel, whom Lippmann did not trust. But Lippmann also noted that "in the interest of the war it is necessary to sacrifice some" free speech.[26]

Although he had little impact on preventive censorship or persecution of socialist journals, Lippmann was highly regarded by Wilson and his cabinet and helped draft the president's Fourteen Points, an initial peace proposal. He then joined a group of intellectuals on a special inquiry board and finally traveled to Europe with the Military Intelligence Branch, where he wrote propaganda leaflets to be dropped behind enemy lines. At the peace talks in Paris he became discouraged at what he regarded as impossible demands by the Allies in carving up European nations, as well as by Wilson's capitulation, and he returned to the United States to argue against Wilson's proposal for the League of Nations. He returned to the *New Republic* and in 1922 joined Pulitzer's *New York World*, which he later edited. At the *World* Lippmann became widely known as an editorialist and columnist. Lippmann's ardor in supporting the war and his idealism about extending democracy to all nations of the world ended in disillusionment. His antipathy toward war later was apparent in an extensive attack on President Lyndon Johnson's military commitments in Vietnam.

If Lippmann, whose mentor was the old muckraker and socialist radical Lincoln Steffens, could move from a position of antiwar to serving the cause with vigor and enthusiasm, one might wonder about the position of editors who had not objected so greatly in 1914.

METROPOLITAN NEWSPAPERS

Initial reaction to war in Europe generally was one of dismay coupled with a hands-off policy. The *Detroit Free Press* treated the war as a European phenomenon until German submarines began to attack American shipping. When Wilson declared war, the *Free Press* editorialized that this was a war not against the German peoples, but a war against the "barbarous governmental regime of Berlin."[27] Others were not so generous. The *New York Times* and the *Literary Digest* urged readers to report "any utterances or writings that appeared seditious."[28]

The attitude of newspapers toward censorship varied. When the Espionage Act was first introduced into Congress, many newspapers fought the inclusion of a specific censorship amendment. Once that amendment was eliminated, however, few seemed to recognize the significance of the act and the impact of the Sedition Amendment. Although cooperation with George Creel's Committee on Public Information was, on the surface, voluntary, Creel certainly had the legislation he needed to back up any requests he made to newspapers that violated his regulations.

E. W. Scripps' chain of newspapers, before the beginning of the war, advocated no U.S. involvement, but supported the allies. Hearst papers heartily opposed the war. Although most newspapers were not overjoyed at the prospect of Creel's regulations, they generally submitted to them.

Technical aspects of coverage were greatly enlarged, and although newspapers probably could not be commended for impartiality and calm reason on the home front (they tended to whip up fear against "hordes of invading Huns"), they could be commended for the zeal with which they pursued coverage of foreign fronts against great censorship odds.

This anti-war drawing entitled "Ammunition" appeared in The Masses *in 1914. (Library of Congress Collection)*

THE MASSES

Some regarded it as a socialist rag, others as the intellectual guardian of its time, and still others as simply a vehicle for radical thought and writing. Many writers for *The Masses*, including John Reed and Louise Bryant, subjects of the film, *Reds*; the poet Carl Sandburg; Upton Sinclair, author of *The Jungle*; and even Walter Lippmann for a time, spent the early teens discussing radical politics in Mabel Dodge's fashionable Greenwich Village flat. Mabel Dodge, not an artist or writer herself, collected radicals as some others might collect statues or paintings. Those in her coterie included anarchist Emma Goldman, muckraker Lincoln Steffens, people like Lippmann, and other intellectuals like Reed, who never abandoned his faith in the Communist party, and Max Eastman, who edited *The Masses* and whose disillusionment came with Stalin's purges in Russia in the 1930s.

> **JOHN REED WRITES ABOUT REVOLUTION**
>
> No matter what one thinks of Bolshevism, it is undeniable that the Russian Revolution is one of the great events of human history, and the rise of the Bolsheviki a phenomenon of world-wide importance. Just as historians search the records for the minutest details of the story of the Paris Commune, so they will want to know what happened in Petrograd in November, 1917, the spirit which animated the people, and how the leaders looked, talked and acted. It is with this in view that I have written this book.
>
> In the struggle my sympathies were not neutral. But in telling the story of those great days I have tried to see events with the eye of a conscientious reporter, interested in setting down the truth.
>
> SOURCE. John Reed, in the Introduction to Ten Days That Shook The World, January 1, 1919.

Eastman, a graduate of Williams College in Massachusetts and a logics professor at Columbia, began editing *The Masses* in 1912. A man of great personal force, he first faced the task of clearing up the magazine's debt. His charm paid off, both in terms of recruiting money from little old ladies who knew little about socialism and who regarded Eastman as a romantic poet, and in terms of recruiting writers.

Under Eastman's leadership, *The Masses* was a successful publication from 1913 to 1916. The magazine published poetry, art, and literature as well as socialist-oriented political articles. The most serious question debated in the open staff meetings was the question of art versus propaganda. Eastman made the final decision if agreement could not be reached. He attempted to publish anything he considered interesting that did not compromise *The Masses* revolutionary character. He wrote in his first editorial notice:

> We plan a radical change of policy for *The Masses*, and we appeal to our subscribers and contributors to help us put it through. . . .
>
> We are going to make *The Masses* a *popular* Socialist magazine—a magazine of pictures and lively writing.
>
> Humorous, serious, illustrative and decorative pictures of a stimulating kind. There are no magazines in America which measure up in radical art and freedom of expression to the foreign satirical journals. We think we can produce one, and we have on our staff eight of the best known artists and illustrators in the country ready to contribute to it their most individual work.[29]

The Masses dealt with the separation of capital and labor by covering labor

This John Sloan drawing appeared in the January 1914 issue of **The Masses** *to illustrate "Class war in Colorado." (Library of Congress Collection)*

strikes in a different vein than did metropolitan dailies. In June 1914, Eastman described the Colorado state militia attack on a tent colony of striking miner families:

> I put the ravages of that black orgy of April 20th, when a frail, fluttering tent city in the meadow, the dwelling place of 120 women and 273 children, was riddled to shreds without a second's warning, and then fired by coal-oil torches with the bullets still raining and the victims screaming in their shallow holes of refuge, or crawling away on their bellies through the fields—I put that crime, not upon its perpetrators, who are savage, but upon the gentlemen of noble leisure who hired them to this service.[30]

The Masses could not continue in this vein without legal difficulty. The first lawsuit against the magazine occurred when *The Masses* accused the Associated Press of having suppressed a West Virginia strike at the request of employers. Eastman and a second editor were charged with criminal libel, pleaded not guilty, and were released on $1,000 bail. Eventually that charge was dropped.

But *The Masses*' difficulties with the legal system continued. Its support of contraception, free love, and feminism drew unkind attention from the Post Office and it had difficulty retaining its postal permit. The difficulty increased as Eastman argued against intervention in World War I. *The Masses* argued that revolution was necessary to rout the capitalists, but that World War I was merely a struggle between imperial powers, not a revolution aimed at freeing the proletariat, or the worker. After subsequent attacks on the conscription act (the draft) Eastman and four other editors were indicted under the Espionage Act. Twice *The Masses* editors went to trial. Both trials ended in hung juries, but in August 1917, *The Masses* lost its mailing privileges, which forced the editors to suspend publication.

Although *The Masses* could no longer publish, Eastman was not silenced and joined with his sister to publish the *Liberator*. In 1922, Eastman traveled to the Soviet Union, where he was disillusioned by what he termed "the misuse of the sacred scriptures of Marxism. . . . Instead of liberating the mind of man, the Bolshevik Revolution locked it into a state's prison tighter than ever before."[31] When Eastman returned to the United States, he was boycotted not only by those who opposed socialism but also by his friends who could not accept his disillusionment. They branded him a traitor to the cause. In the 1930s Eastman accused the *New York Times*' correspondent, Walter Duranty, of obscuring the truth about famines, liquidations, and purges within Stalinist Russia. In the late 1930s, when Stalin formed a pact with Adolph Hitler of Germany, others joined in Eastman's disillusionment and he regained some prestige within the community of writers. Ironically, he worked as a roving editor for the conservative *Reader's Digest*. He continued writing until his death in 1969 and despite his extensive political involvement, he considered his best writing to be two books: *The Enjoyment of Poetry* and *The Enjoyment of Laughter*.[32]

ON THE FRONT

During the Spanish-American War, correspondents faced great physical hardships—lack of food, lack of proper quarters, difficulty in obtaining physical access to the places the war was being fought. By World War I some of these problems were alleviated. Correspondents were well fed and were housed in some of Europe's best hotels.[33]

Although transportation was available, the extensive rerouting of trains and long-distance journeys, sometimes by steamer, proved exhausting to war correspondents. But their biggest problem was the distance of press headquarters from the front and the problems of censorship by the various governments involved. At the very beginning of the war, correspondents moved freely in covering the advance of German armies, but by the fall of 1914 correspondents were kept entirely away from military zones. This ban lasted until April 1915, when the British began to allow a few American reporters behind the lines. Eventually French, Austrian, and German governments also provided glimpses at the front, but the movements of correspondents were strictly regulated. In addition to restricting the correspondents' movements, governments also strictly regulated their copy. In Britain the willingness of publishers to accept severe controls brought them social prestige and political power, but also undermined the faith of the public in the press.[34] In 1915, Theodore Roosevelt wrote a letter to the British foreign secretary, claiming British and French controls of the press were so tight that the only source of information for American reporters was from Germany. Roosevelt told the foreign minister censorship was hurting Britain's cause in the United States.[35]

One of the most well-known American correspondents was Richard Harding Davis, who sailed on the *Lusitania* to Europe in 1914, at the outset of the war. Davis, a famous reporter during the Spanish-American War, went straight to Brussels to report the entrance of the German Army into the city.

Davis encountered severe German restrictions in reporting the war and was subjected to arrest and overnight imprisonment after being accused of being a British officer. After the British and French also refused to let him near the front, Davis returned home. "I'm not about to write sidelights," he

> ### THE MARCH INTO BRUSSELS
>
> BRUSSELS, FRIDAY, AUGUST 21, 2 P.M.—The entrance of the German army into Brussels has lost the human quality. It was lost as soon as the three soldiers who led the army bicycled into the Boulevard du Regent and asked the way to the Gare du Nord. When they passed the human note passed with them. . . .
>
> For seven hours the army passed in such solid columns that not once might a taxicab or trolley car pass through the city. Like a river of steel it flowed, gray and ghostlike. Then, as dusk came and thousands of horses' hoofs and thousands of iron boots continued to tramp forward, they struck tiny sparks from the stones, but the horses and the men who beat out the sparks were invisible.
>
> SOURCE. Richard Harding Davis, London News Chronicle.

said.[36] Other correspondents, acting in violation of censorship, had no choice. They were returned home. But some, including reporters for the *New York Times*, managed to elude the censors by writing in code. American ingenuity allowed a few uncensored stories to slip through the lines.

After America's entrance into the war, U.S. regulation of correspondents abroad represented a bureaucratic nightmare. Stringent regulations were imposed and reporters who did not cooperate made no progress. Some, like Heywood Broun, returned to New York in 1918, disgusted with the lack of access to information.

THE BLACK PRESS DURING AND AFTER THE WAR

The black press found it difficult to support a war to "make the world safe for democracy," while black people in the United States felt democracy hardly extended to them. Although on the whole the black press did support U.S. involvement in the war, black editors vociferously attacked discrimination in the armed forces and in domestic life. Editors such as Robert Abbott of the *Chicago Defender* crusaded for integration and equality of opportunity, while others, such as W. E. B. DuBois, argued for segregated training camps. DuBois believed segregation was a necessity, and blacks would never be given an equal chance within an integrated training situation. Separate but equal was his battle cry.

George Creel viewed the situation as alarming and tried to persuade black editors that foreign propagandists were stirring up the equal-rights crusade, and in 1919 the Justice Department claimed racial propaganda was caused by Russian sympathizers. Black editors, pressured to support the war effort while maintaining their own integrity, met in June 1918 to voice their support of the struggle against Germany.[37]

Some historians regard the period beginning with World War I and continuing through the 1930s as the period of prime influence of the black press. The dramatic story of World War I and its contradictions—blacks carrying arms in defense of their country—carrying arms with white approval for the first time since the Civil War, coupled with discrimination at home and in the armed forces, gave the black press news content and crusade material. Another major story—that of urbanization of blacks—provided another area of leadership for the black press. Coinciding with these news events was a reawakening and rediscovery of black culture that preceded the renaissance of the 1920s and its promotion of jazz and other cultural developments. War-industry employment also improved the overall economy, and the black economy. Black newspapers, always on the brink of financial disaster, benefited greatly from good economic conditions. The postwar years were difficult years for blacks. Returning white veterans looking for jobs resented inroads blacks had made during the war. The tension resulted in massive race riots in the late teens.

Black newspapers avoided competition with white newspapers, emphasizing black issues and black accomplishments. In 1900, about 200 black publications existed; in 1920 the figure grew to 500. By the 1970s it dropped once more to 200. The rising black middle class and accompanying economic power of blacks in the 1980s forced media to direct not only programming content, but advertising as well, toward blacks in greater degree. This development had a "mainstreaming" effect, an effect that did not benefit a strictly black press.

During the war and postwar years the most significant publications included Marcus Garvey's *Negro World*, sponsored by the Universal Negro Improvement Association. In the 1920s, this newspaper was the first black paper to top a circulation of 200,000. Three rivals bypassed that circulation in the 1920s. They were Robert L. Vann's Pittsburgh *Courier*, Carl Murphy's Baltimore *Afro-American*, and Robert Abbott's *Chicago Defender*. The vast majority of black papers were small-town southern papers, and editors faced not only discrimination but restriction of freedom of expression. These papers dared not endorse the National Association for the Advancement of Colored People, trade unions, socialism, or black nationalism. Thus it was left to the big-city papers to champion the cause for equality and to promote the northward migration.[38]

THE CHICAGO DEFENDER

The Chicago Defender probably was one of the best known of the black papers, particularly in the 1920s. Robert Abbott, who founded the paper in 1905, was born in 1868 to former slaves on St. Simons Island off the coast of Georgia. When he began publishing the *Defender*, it was a one-man operation, although many of his friends donated time and energy to writing, printing, and distributing the paper. The *Defender* covered not only Chicago, but served as a national chronicler of events in the black community. In his autobiography Malcom X wrote, "And every time Joe Louis won a fight against a white opponent, big front-page pictures in the Negro newspapers such as the *Chicago Defender*, the *Pittsburgh Courier*, and the *Afro-American* showed a sea of Harlem Negroes cheering and waving and the Brown Bomber waving back at them from the balcony of Harlem's Theresa Hotel."

Abbott utilized sensational techniques of the day, foreshadowing modern American journalism by compartmentalizing news. Departments included sports, editorials, women's news, and state news. He advocated abolishing race prejudice and opening trade unions to black membership. He championed representation in the president's Cabinet, representation in departments of police forces and on railways and buses, admission of all Americans, white and black, to public schools, federally mandated abolishment of lynching, and full enfranchisement of all Americans.

The *Defender* was at its peak during the teens, when race riots broke out in Chicago and other major cities of the nation. At first it joined the sensational coverage of other Chicago newspapers. The *Chicago Daily News* falsely claimed that black men had attacked and killed white women and the *Defender*, just as falsely, informed its readers:

> The homes of blacks isolated in white neighborhoods were burned to the ground and the owners and occupants beaten and thrown unconscious into the smoldering embers.

As the riots continued, the editor sought to calm his readers:

> Do your part to restore quiet and order. . . . Every day of rioting and disorder means loss of life, destruction of property, loss of money for you and your families, and for some of us these losses will be large and irredeemable.

When the rioting stopped, Governor Frank O. Lowden appointed a commission of race relations, and Robert Abbott was one of six blacks appointed to the twelve-member commission. The causes of the riots were many, but one major factor was the heavy migration of southern blacks to the North. Stifled by prejudice and lack of employment opportunity in the South, blacks responded to the calls of northern newspapers like the *Defender*. Historian William Tuttle reported that Chicago's black population nearly doubled from 1916 to 1920 and that perhaps "the most effective institution in stimulating the migration was the *Defender*, which prompted thousands to venture North."[39] In October 1916, the *Defender* said, "to the North we have said, as the song goes, 'I hear you calling me,' and have boarded the train singing, 'Good-bye Dixie Land.'"

Abbott finally achieved financial security during the 1920s, and although he changed his mind on a variety of issues, he never wavered on integration. Abbott was proud of his financial success and contributed to the Chicago Urban League, became a life member of the Art Institute of Chicago and joined a variety of social clubs. During the Depression years the *Defender* and its finances declined, but it survived. When Abbott died, the *Defender* devoted most of its space to his death. But the racial line was still drawn in Chicago, and although prominent individuals, black and white, attended Abbott's funeral, the *Chicago Tribune* carried his obituary of several paragraphs in the standard obituary columns at the back of the newspaper.

Conclusion

The era of massive growth and expansion in numbers of newspapers was over. Circulation growth, expansion in newspaper size, and developments in distribution and collection of news were still to come. The industry stabilized, and with stabilization and a time of national crisis came a resistance to rapid change and decreased tolerance of competing voices. Reform voices urged newspapers to change their practice of hiring children to sell newspapers, and journalists began to organize to protest wage scales and working conditions. In response, the American Association of Newspaper Publishers strengthened its organization to confront the complex problems of the modern world.

Expression of opinion was guaranteed during the war years only for those in the mainstream of American thought. Newspaper publishers usually supported the war once it was declared, and many cooperated with George Creel's propaganda machine, the Committee on Public Information. Reform voices joined in the plea for nationalism, fearing that German militarism posed a threat to democracy even greater than did monopolistic capitalism. Those expressing unpopular opinions were indicted under the Espionage and Sedition acts, or faced restriction of their second-class mailing privileges.

Foreign correspondents encountered restrictions abroad as well as from the U.S. government. Black editors, while generally supporting the war, protested the discrimination in the armed forces and in domestic life.

NOTES

1. Ernest C. Hynds, *American Newspapers in the 1980s* (New York: Hastings House, 1980), p. 75.
2. David Nasaw, "The Newsies," chapter 5 of *Children of the City: At Work and at Play* (Garden City, N.Y.: Anchor Press/Doubleday, 1985), p. 65.
3. *The Hustler*, February 1918, p. 4, cited in David Nasaw, *Children of the City*, p. 80.
4. Nasaw, *Children of the City*, p. 86.
5. John Higham, *Strangers in the Land* (New York: Atheneum, 1972), p. 196.
6. John D. Stevens, *Shaping the First Amendment: Development of Free Expression* (Beverly Hills: Sage, 1982), p. 46.
7. Stevens, *Shaping the First Amendment*, p. 45.
8. Lauren Kessler, *The Dissident Press* (Beverly Hills: Sage, 1984), pp. 139, 140.
9. Harold L. Nelson and Dwight L. Teeter, Jr., *Law of Mass Communications*, 5th ed. (New York: The Foundation Press, 1982), p. 38.
10. Stevens, *Shaping the First Amendment*, p. 49.
11. 249 U.S. 47, 39 S.Ct. 247 (1919).
12. Lindsay Rogers, *Contemporary Review*, vol. 114 (August 1918). The list of newspapers in the National Archives names only 45 newspapers that lost second-class privileges.
13. *U.S. ex rel Milwaukee Social Democrat Publishing Co. v. Burleson*, 255 U.S. 407 (1921).
14. Zechariah Chafee Jr., *Free Speech in the United States* (Cambridge, Mass.: Harvard University Press, 1946), p. 300.
15. John Lofton, *The Press as Guardian of the First Amendment* (Columbia, S.C.: University of South Carolina Press, 1980), p. 176, citing U.S. Congress, Special (House) Committee on Right of Victor Berger to be Sworn In, Hearings, 1: 535, 681, and 719, and Chafee, *Free Speech*, p. 248.
16. Chafee, *Free Speech*, p. 247.
17. Quoted in Seymour, Stedman, et al., *The Case of the Chicago Socialists* (brief in the United States Court of Appeals for the Seventh Circuit, Oct. term, 1918), p. 32.
18. *New York Times*, Jan. 17, 1918, p. 12. This editorial apparently referred to the decision in *Masses Publishing Co. v. Patten*, 216 F. 24 (1918), overruling Judge Learned Hand's decision in the same case, at 244 Fed. Supp. 535 (1917).
19. Quoted in Lofton, *Press as Guardian*, p. 203.
20. Lofton, *Press as Guardian*, p. 199, citing the *New York Times*, November 12, 1919, p. 12, and *Boston Evening Transcript*, November 12, 1919, p. 2 of editorial section. See also Chafee, *Free Speech*, pp. 250–269.

21. Phillip Knightley, *The First Casualty* (New York: Harcourt, Brace, Jovanovich, 1975), p. 123.
22. James R. Mock and Cedric Larson, *Words That Won the War: The Story of the Committee on Public Information, 1917–1919.* (Princeton, N.J.: Princeton University Press, 1939), pp. 6, 7.
23. Cited in Mock and Larson, *Words That Won the War*, p. 59.
24. Stephen Vaughn, *Holding Fast the Inner Lines* (Chapel Hill, N.C.: University of North Carolina Press, 1980), p. 37.
25. Ronald Steel, *Walter Lippmann and the American Century* (New York: Vintage Books, 1981), pp. 114–15.
26. Steel, *Lippmann*, p. 125.
27. Frank Angelo, *On Guard: A History of the Detroit Free Press* (Detroit: Detroit Free Press, 1981), pp. 141–143.
28. Kessler, *Dissident Press*, p. 141.
29. William L. O'Neill, *Echos of Revolt: The Masses 1911–1917* (Chicago: Quadrangle Books, 1966), p. 28.
30. O'Neill, *Echoes of Revolt*, p. 150.
31. Daniel Aaron, *Writers on the Left*, (New York: Avon Books, 1965), p. 124.
32. The authors would like to thank Bill Frisbie, a student at the University of Texas, for contributing to the research on *The Masses*.
33. Mary Sue Mander, *Pen and Sword: A Cultural History of the American War Correspondent: 1895–1945.* Ph.D. Disser., University of Illinois at Urbana-Champaign, 1979, p. 62.
34. Knightley, *The First Casualty*, pp. 80, 81.
35. Knightley, *The First Casualty*, pp. 94, 95.
36. Knightley, *The First Casualty*, p. 116.
37. Kessler, *Dissident Press*, pp. 41–42.
38. Theodore G. Vincent, ed., *Voices of a Black Nation: Political Journalism in the Harlem Renaissance* (San Francisco: Ramparts Press, 1973), pp. 19–38.
39. This discussion relies heavily on the entry by Jean Folkerts on Robert Abbott in the *Dictionary of Literary Biography* (Detroit, Mich.: Gale Research Press, 1984), vol. 29, pp. 12–18. See also the primary research materials used for the article: Roi Ottley, *The Lonely Warrior* (Chicago: Regnery, 1955); Henry G. La Brie III, *Perspectives of the Black Press* (Kennebunkport, Maine, 1974); Metz Lochard, "Robert S. Abbott—Race Leader," *Phylon*, 8 (Second Quarter, 1947), pp. 124–132; and William M. Tuttle, Jr., *Race Riot: Chicago in the Red Summer of 1919* (New York: Atheneum, 1970).

FDR addresses a nation. (Trans Lux Theatre, Library of Congress)

PART 4

MEDIA IN A MODERN WORLD

The nation emerged from World War I wary of foreign wars, prosperous, and modernized. The relationship of government to business that had been debated during the nineteenth century became solidified as the progressive fascination with regulation and the expert held sway. Mass media, now expanded far beyond the periodical press, became integrally interconnected with the business-government relationship. Consolidation accelerated within all forms of media, and as the broadcast media of television and radio developed, the federal government and the broadcast industry devised mutually powerful and satisfactory roles. Regulation, nevertheless, represented a critical departure from First Amendment protection of print media. Although industry recommendations historically dominated government regulation, by the 1980s both industry and some individuals in government were advocating abandoning regulation of broadcasting. The news media continually maintained their right to be free of government censorship, but simultaneously lobbied the government for preferential treatment in regard to labor law and antitrust actions.

The nature of the community also changed as rapid forms of transportation and communication reduced the size of the nation and the world. Although tabloids in the 1920s still expressed the diversity of urban life and the social agenda characteristic of the progressive years, documentaries of the 1930s were more concerned with the effects of a depression economy. Content and style became interrelated issues and trends toward increased interpretation in various forms alternated with objectivity as an ideal goal. Journalists explored forms of the documentary through photography and newsreels, and introduced political columns and bylines, but feared the partisanship of the past and the haunting spectre of nonobjective journalism. The adherence of wire services to the objective form during the antiCommunist hysteria of the 1950s, however, convinced many that the old forms promulgated lack of understanding and intolerance. In the 1960s new styles of investigation as well as new forms of writing resulted in a subsequent assertion of control and concern with ethics on the part of publishers.

Introduction of new technology profoundly affected the twentieth century, with portable cameras creating a new journalistic tool; radio allowed the nation's leaders to bypass editors and exert new types of news management; television brought live pictures of war, poverty, success, and celebration into the nation's living rooms. Audiences rushed to their television sets, sometimes leaving their newspapers behind. Technology altered the face of newspapers as well, but the personal and financial costs of adaptation were severe.

Alternatives to mainstream media existed throughout the century. Socialist publications and other forms of radical thought flowered in the 1930s, and the black press fought before and during World War II for a double victory at home and abroad. Although consensus politics and culture dominated the late 1940s and early 1950s, individuals such as Dwight Macdonald and I. F. Stone kept alive the voice of dissent. In the 1960s the underground, advocacy, and alternative media gained prominent national attention. The magazine industry presented another alternative, first in the form of thoughtful, opinion magazines, then in the mass circulation magazines, and finally in specialized information for targeted audiences.

At the close of the 1980s, the broadcast industry showed signs of major reorganization. The high costs of news gathering had prompted the networks, which were losing audience shares to cable television, to reduce news budgets and rethink their news agendas. Media companies, now not only big business, but public companies, dealt with the direct effects of stock-market trading and hostile takeover possibilities. Chain ownership controlled more than 60 percent of the nation's newspapers, and although critics searched for answers through scholarly research of mass media, voices of dissent in the 1980s were faint.

CHAPTER 15

THE ROARING TWENTIES: THE MYTHICAL DECADE

The 1920s has been characterized as the flapper age, with prosperity running high, sexual mores changing dramatically, and the world adopting a "devil may care" attitude. Depicting that kind of world were the motion pictures produced in Hollywood, and the New York tabloids, half the size of regular metropolitan newspapers, carrying large photographs and screaming headlines. But the world of the 1920s was more complex than it appeared in such dazzling modern images. Amidst rapid social change and conflict, Americans faced often contradictory images of themselves and their society as they attempted to adapt to a modern urban, technological, consumer society.

The relationship between communication and transportation shifted, as individual travel superseded mass transit, and radio broke through the technological barriers that had restricted news dissemination. The number of automobiles increased as people traveled more miles and the federal government funded road development. Rapid-transit track mileage dropped and intercity railway systems declined. Railroads faced tight regulation as the country poured its resources into airline development, both for carrying passengers and for delivering mail.[1] Although the telegraph broke the link between transportation and gathering news, until the advent of radio, the distribution or dissemination of communication to a mass audience was tied to the transportation system. The introduction of radio into the American household during the 1920s evoked the hopes, fears, and anxieties of a nation already in the midst of cultural disruption. Some hoped radio would provide the technological means to realize utopian dreams of unifying the nation, democratizing society, and ending persistent social problems. Fears surfaced about the lack of face-to-face communication and traditional authority, the growing specter of technology, and increasing alienation. These fears were expressed in the ongoing debates in the 1920s about how radio would take shape, how it would affect politics, religion, music and the arts, and whether it would be educational or commercially entertainment oriented.[2]

Corporate consolidation, increasing productivity, and the change from a debtor to creditor nation came with the close of the war. The growth of the advertising industry promoted adoption of consumer products and differentiation of brand names. Coupled with increasingly available credit opportunities through automobile-sales finance companies and by banks and other financial institutions, advertising promoted the purchasing of more consumer, particularly major durable, goods, than ever before in American society.[3] The darker side of the 1920s reflected an uneven distribution of wealth, high unemployment, plummeting farm prices and increased fears of immigration. Lack of tolerance was exhibited in the developing Ku Klux Klan and fears of socialist activity that followed the Bolshevik Revolution and increased organization of labor.

In the face of such turmoil, the sensational tabloids portrayed the glamour of the twenties as well as the seamier side of prosperity. Newspaper chains or groups became more common, representing increased concentration in ownership. Government and business hired public relations professionals to interpret events and policy for the press and the public. National advertising, the professionalization of advertising, and the creation of the agency promoted the advertising dollar. Radio struggled through an initial decade of adjustment and began to capitalize on consumer advertising. After an initial period of technical chaos, the broadcast industry and the government worked together to form the beginnings of broadcast regulation. The movies attracted large audiences as they moved from silent entertainment to rudimentary sound-tracked productions, and as the large movie houses concentrated the production of American film in Hollywood.

TABLOIDS

The standard view of the tabloids is that they reflected what some termed the declining moral values of the decade, publishing screaming headlines about divorce, murder, and crime. Improvements in photographic technology provided the newspapers with the opportunity to display large pictures. The *New York Graphic* led the way, splashing on page one the execution of Ruth Snyder, first woman to die in the electric chair. The photograph was sensational in content, but even more sensational in context, for the photographer talked his way into the execution chamber and took the photo with a camera strapped in a trouser leg.

A newer view of the tabloids suggests they helped city dwellers to create order in their chaotic lives, and to "understand and to cope with their own experience in relationship to a new and increasingly complex society."[4] The tabloid pictures of city life helped citizens to view the city with amazement, while their day-to-day lives consisted of factory or assembly-line jobs.

The tabloid was not a creation of the 1920s, nor was it a creation of metropolitan U.S. editors. A British publisher's experiment with the tabloid form on the *New York World* in 1901 probably was preceded by similar British publications. The *New York Illustrated Daily News,* the first regularly published tabloid in the United States, began June 23, 1919. Published by Chicagoans Joseph Patterson and Robert McCormick, the *Daily News* circulated to 400,000 within two years. Although the circulation of other New York dailies remained fairly constant from 1919 to 1926, the *Illustrated Daily News* soared to a new height of one million by 1926. By 1924, two competing tabloids entered the market: Hearst's *Daily Mirror* and Bernarr Macfadden's *Evening Graphic.* The *Graphic,* never a close contender in circulation, failed after six years. The major innovation of the tabloids was the extensive use of photographs and composographs, or faked photos.

The tabloids raised the ire of newspaper publishers and of elite society.

The literary world referred to the half-size sheets as "Tabloid Poison," "that new black plague," and "jungle weeds in the journalistic garden." Some claimed, however, that the tabloids were no worse than their full-size metropolitan competitors. "The *News* is cheap and frothy but not, as a rule, antisocial," wrote one critic. "It is, from the social point of view, on a par with a considerable portion of the American press which, like this first of the tabloids, is given its character by triviality and slight constructive contest."[5]

THE 1920S NEWSPAPER

CONTENT

The information-versus-sensation dilemma of the late nineteenth century continued to appear in the newspapers of the 1920s. Newspapers either maintained an elite attitude, with serious but dull coverage of important national and international news, or they increased their coverage of events associated with the jazz age of the 1920s, and provided little serious news. Such newspapers included more human-interest stories, murders, crime, natural disasters, train accidents, and sports. Silas Bent, a harsh critic of the metropolitan press in the 1920s, wrote in 1927 that it was not uncommon "to see in New York newspapers as much as twenty columns devoted to a single day's proceedings in two second-rate murder trials."[6]

CHAINS AND CONGLOMERATES

Commercial agreements among newspapers existed as early as the 1700s, but generally these agreements were designed to handle short-term problems or create short-term gains. In the 1700s, collective agreements were made to hold down the price of labor or to stabilize the price of subscriptions. In the 1830s, a variety of attempts were made to facilitate cooperative news gathering, and after the Civil War several companies secured profits by providing boilerplate, or ready-made sheets to be included in the weeklies of the country.

Nine groups existed from the 1890s through 1900; each chain owned from two to five newspapers. By 1900, ten chains controlled thirty-two dailies, just over one percent of the nation's total dailies, and about 12 to 15 percent of the nation's total circulation. The development of chains spread rapidly

> **INS REPORTS A FAMOUS MURDER**
>
> A chilly-looking blonde with frosty eyes and one of those marble, you-bet-you-will chins, and an inert, scare-drunk fellow that you couldn't miss among any hundred men as a dead setup for a blonde, or the shell game, or maybe a gold brick.
>
> Mrs. Ruth Snyder and Henry Judd Gray are on trial in the huge weatherbeaten old courthouse of Queens County in Long Island City, just across the river from the roar of New York, for what might be called for want of a better name, The Dumbbell Murder. It was so dumb.
>
> They are charged with the slaughter four weeks ago of Albert Snyder, art editor of the magazine, *Motor Boating*, the blonde's husband and father of her nine-year-old daughter, under circumstances that for sheer stupidity and brutality have seldom been equaled in the history of crime.
>
> SOURCE. Damon Runyon, April 19–May 9, 1927.

after 1900 and boomed during the 1920s, with the number of chain newspapers doubling between 1923 and 1933, and chain control of daily circulation rising from 32.4 to 37.4 percent. In 1923, thirty-one chains owned 153 papers; in 1928, fifty-four chains owned 280 papers; and in 1930, fifty-five chains owned 311 papers.

The six largest chains in 1933 were Hearst, Patterson-McCormick, Scripps-Howard, Paul Block, Ridder, and Gannett. These six chains controlled 69.7 percent of the total daily chain circulation and 26.1 percent of the nation's total.[7]

One of the earliest modern chains was formed by J. E., G. H. and E. W. Scripps and J. S. Sweeney. By 1880, the Scripps Publishing Company controlled five dailies. E. W. Scripps then expanded and formed a partnership with M. A. McRae and subsequently launched other groups. In 1920, E. W. Scripps owned twenty-two newspapers. Scripps' method was to lend money to an enterprising young publisher and let the publisher run the paper; if he succeeded Scripps took 51 percent of the profits; if he failed, Scripps took the loss. In 1922, the Scripps-Howard chain was organized, formed by E. W. Scripps and the twenty-five-year-old Roy Howard. This chain grew to twenty-five dailies by 1930, most of which were evening papers. Howard, who headed the United Press (UP) wire service, had come to Scripps newspapers in Indianapolis and Cincinnati after an earlier stint with the St. Louis *Post-Dispatch*.

Although some newspaper publishers and press critics argued that chain ownership would decrease the diversity of the news media, there was even more concern expressed about conglomerates, or companies with extensive business interests that also owned media properties. The fear was that a company with an interest in one aspect of business outside the media would try to influence or dictate how media treated that business.

One major example of the 1920s is the case of the International Paper Company (IPC), which almost monopolized the American newsprint industry and owned interests in fourteen American newspapers, including the Boston *Herald and Traveler,* the *Chicago Daily News,* and the Chicago *Journal,* as well as four Gannett papers. Furthermore, the International Paper Company (IPC) was owned by International Paper and Power Company (IP&PC), a holding company that also owned large electricity-producing subsidiaries and was a member of the so-called "Power Trust."

In 1928, the Federal Trade Commission, on directions from the U.S. Senate, began an investigation of the IP&PC and seventeen other holding companies. The IPC's newspaper investments were a secret until the FTC hearings, and although no direct evidence was presented, the fear was that the parent company had invested in newspapers in order to assure a lack of criticism of the power and utility industry. As soon as the hearings made the newspaper investments known, Gannett repaid its loans to IPC and withdrew completely from any dealings with the company. By the end of 1929, the IPC sold all its holdings.

The IPC president argued that there had been no intention to influence public opinion in regard to the utilities industry, but that the company had purchased the newspaper companies to assure long-term contracts with the paper company. Gannett testified that his newspapers had opposed the power trust and that IPC had put no editorial pressure on him. His dealings with IPC had only to do with tonnage of paper, he testified.

Whether the power trust intended eventually to use the newspapers editorially or not is a matter of conjecture, but the investigations and the fear of the possibility of control by business interests set the stage for increased complaints about the corruption of the press in the 1930s.[8]

CHARACTERISTICS OF DAILIES

From 1914 to 1934 the average price of a newspaper doubled; in the late 1920s most dailies cost three cents and were approximately the same size as newspapers of today (eighteen- by twenty-two-inch sheet carrying eight columns). In 1920, the average size of a daily was twenty pages, a number that grew to thirty from 1927 to 1929, then shrank to twenty-two during 1933, in the midst of the depression. Newspapers carried about 60 percent advertising, and newspapers expanded by creating branch plants and neighborhood edi-

> **WHAT READERS WANT**
>
> On the editorial page we have only two columns of editorials. But they are crisp and to the point. We have several Harvard professors writing editorials for us. But I do not believe in too much quantity of that sort; for it is the *average* man and woman to whom I want to appeal.
>
> SOURCE. Edwin A. Grozier, Editor, Boston Post, *speaking to a reporter in 1923 for an American Magazine* article.

tions. Associated Press membership expanded rapidly during World War I, then stabilized during the 1920s.

Before the war, the cost of a newspaper varied from one to three cents, but several factors forced newspapers to raise their prices slightly after the war. Higher newsprint costs, expansion of news and features, and higher postage rates contributed to the standard of the three-cent paper. Further, the cost of labor increased as newspaper editors began to upgrade notoriously low wages.

DEVELOPMENT OF PUBLIC RELATIONS

Although public relations activities had been visible in ancient and modern societies in a variety of forms, the term, public relations, used to describe promotion, press agentry, and publicity, was coined by Edward Bernays in the 1920s. Bernays believed an understanding of social and behavioral science would lead public relations practitioners to better communicate the public's ideas to management, and the ideas of management, or business, to the public.

Although press agents have been credited with the creation of characters as diverse as western hero Buffalo Bill Cody and Jenny Lind, the "Swedish nightingale," and although various volunteer associations, such as the American Bible Society, the abolitionists, and the suffrage organizations used public relations techniques, the development of the modern public relations agency is a twentieth-century phenomenon.

Common, however, to the nineteenth century was the practice of press agentry. Foremost among the press agents was Richard F. Hamilton, press agent to Phineas T. Barnum, famous director of the Barnum & Bailey Circus. Even before the formation of the circus in the 1870s, Barnum successfully promoted a variety of scams, such as the story of Joice Heth, who Barnum claimed had taken care of George Washington nearly 100 years earlier. People flocked to see the ancient black woman, but when she died an autopsy showed her to be only eighty years old, not 160 as Barnum said she was.

Meanwhile, Barnum had been collecting as much as $1,500 a week from those who wanted a look at the pipe-smoking old woman.[9]

Nineteenth-century leaders in governmental-relations strategy and public-relations technique were large railroad corporations. In 1850, capitalizing on fears of a coming Civil War, the Illinois Central Railroad organized a public relations campaign to construct a north-south railway that the company claimed would bind North and South together "so effectually that even the idea of separation" would vanish from the nation's vocabulary. The company's successful campaign to obtain federal funds for railway construction altered a historic pattern of local business funding for railroad building.[10]

In the late 1870s, in an attempt to alter the public's negative image of pools and other cooperative arrangements, railroad executives paid for "puffery" pieces, and issued free railroad passes, which, according to Norfolk and Western vice-president Frederick J. Kimball, was the "cheapest form of advertising we can get." As railroad executives confronted the instability of private rate-fixing agreements in the 1880s, they used their previously established relationship with the press to gain discussion of government regulation of the industry, and to create a positive public image of the necessity of governmental regulation. Meanwhile, railroad executives were instrumental in helping to guide the writing of the legislation that resulted in the Interstate Commerce Act of 1886, an act that created a commission sympathetic rather than antagonistic to the industry.[11]

By the turn of the century, public relations personnel were regarded as invaluable by the utility industry and other business enterprises, and practitioners became skilled at providing "news" that journalists readily used. Ivy Ledbetter Lee, a newspaperman turned publicist, earned a reputation for "objective" public relations in his work for the Pennsylvania Railroad, the Rockefeller family, and the anthracite coal operators. Lee argued that informing the press and the public, rather than operating in secret, would earn greater public favor, even if the news was not positive. In 1906 Lee issued a "Declaration of Principles," claiming that all work was done in the open. He claimed his material was accurate and that he would assist any editor in clarifying detail. "In brief," Lee wrote, "our plan is, frankly and openly, on behalf of the business concerns and public institutions, to supply to the press and public of the United States prompt and accurate information concerning subjects which it is of value and interest to the public to know about."[12]

Despite his claim to accuracy and objectivity, Lee was despised by many journalists and castigated as "Poison Ivy" by Upton Sinclair in *The Brass Check*. "Journalists were bewildered," wrote Genevieve Caspari in an analysis of public relations ethics, "by Lee's ability to deny that persuasion was his purpose but still get publicity, and even accurately predict its news placement."[13]

Ivy Lee's work and the creation of pioneering public relations agencies preceded the massive propaganda efforts of George Creel's Committee on Public Information during World War I. The Publicity Bureau, formed in Boston in 1900, a second agency formed by journalist William Wolff Smith in Washington in 1902, and Parker & Lee, Lee's agency formed in partnership with George Parker, began to set standards for public relations work. The Creel Committee, which employed former journalists and intellectuals, provided a training ground for many who practiced public relations after the war.

Public relations expanded after World War I in a variety of areas, including associational activities as well as in corporate business. The war stimulated causes for public relations, as well as the activities themselves. The Red Cross, the Salvation Army and the YMCA Community Chests developed publicity campaigns based on wartime models. Will Irwin claimed that by 1920 there were nearly a thousand "bureaus of propaganda" in Washington based on such models. Samuel Insull, Chicago Edison's electric-power baron, adapted propaganda techniques learned during his tenure in the American branch of the British Propaganda Office to the Illinois Public Utility Information Committee. By 1923, other utilities followed suit and "were turning out a stream of utility publicity that almost matched the volume of patriotic publicity during the war."[14]

One of those trained on the Creel committee was Edward Bernays, who opened his own office in 1919, and who envisioned the role of the public-relations practitioner as an agent of change — not as an agent of the press. Bernays advocated principle over profit and "personal accountability for professional conduct."[15] Bernays' three books, *Crystallizing Public Opinion* (1923), *Propaganda* (1928), and *Public Relations* (1952), written across a thirty-year period, emphasized the importance of understanding the public and communicating that understanding to business management. Bernays argued that publicity was not the point when the practitioner started his activity, but rather the stage at which it ended.[16]

ADVERTISING

By the 1920s, advertising was an established industry, developed in response to changes in business and marketing strategies. Advertisers were becoming aware of their markets and newspapers were experimenting with hiring employees to sell advertisements. The difficulties that space agents were experiencing in placing advertisements in competition with in-house attempts to control advertising made it clear that if agencies were to survive, changes were imperative. These changes came in the area of added services.[17]

This 1922 advertisement depicted a popular movie star, Betty Compson, eating Eskimo Pie. (Library of Congress Collection)

FROM SPACE TO SERVICE

By the late 1880s, large department stores began to make a commitment to employing advertising copywriters. When Wanamaker's opened in Philadelphia, the store management hired John E. Powers to write advertisements. By 1899, Wanamaker's of New York spent $300,000 in ads. By hiring their own copywriters and because they dealt in large volume, such stores could bypass the agency and deal directly with the media. Manufacturers dealing with brand name goods also began to recognize the value of good advertising copywriting. Developing technology in stereotyping and photography enabled more creative layout and design to take place as well.

Agencies that succeeded in this new market adapted quickly to the change in demand. By 1900, N. W. Ayer regarded preparation of copy as a standard service of the agency. Albert D. Lasker, who in 1898 began to work for the major Chicago agency, Lord & Thomas, rapidly expanded the copywriting staff. Lasker bought out the agency in 1912 and gained a reputation for training younger men in the business. Lasker claimed he made his men so good he couldn't keep them. Men in the business joked that getting fired from Lord & Thomas was a credential for getting hired elsewhere.[18]

Rudimentary marketing surveys were experimented with at Ayer's as early as 1879 and became a standard service about 1900. By 1910, other companies had followed suit. In the early 1900s, Stanley B. Resor, trained in history and economics at Yale and employed by J. W. Thompson, published *Population and Its Distribution,* a collection of demographic and economic data compiled from the federal census. In 1916, Resor bought the Thompson agency for half a million dollars and developed departments of planning and statistical investigation. Resor managed "by consensus, distrusting what he called Individual Opinion, and thought that brilliance was dangerous."[19] He abandoned hierarchical authority, preferring instead "cross fertilization" from assorted minds.[20]

The industry was trying to professionalize and made claims to being as valuable to American society as were engineers and physicians. In 1917, the American Association of Advertising Agencies was formed; by that year, agencies had become powerful institutions, handling 95 percent of all national advertising.

Why the agencies were so successful is difficult to analyze. Clearly there were some alternatives. Some of the bigger companies were capable of efficiently creating in-house agencies; boilerplate advertising from the American Press Association provided smaller newspapers with preset advertising copy from a variety of advertisers, and free-lancers were available for work on specific projects. The agencies, however, argued they had a preferred position in buying space in media, they offered specialized services, and they provided the advertiser with an independent, unbiased view. As the agencies made these arguments and strived to maintain their position in the advertising exchange, the commission system of charging publishers a commission continued to provoke controversy. The Periodical Publishers Association and the American Newspaper Press Association helped preserve the agency/commission system, arguing that the commission kept the agencies loyal to the press, not to the advertiser, and that agencies made it possible for the press to get and keep national advertising. Meanwhile, the American Association of Advertising Agencies developed standard procedures requiring media to pay commissions only to established service organizations, stabilizing the commission at 15 percent, and discouraging the paying of rebates to clients. By 1918, they had preserved and stabilized the system, and by the end of World War I further guidelines were in place. Agencies, as a rule, did not handle competing accounts, they reduced their high-pressure soliciting tactics (taking clients away from other agencies) and they continued to encourage avoiding price competition.[21]

Another problem, in addition to the dispute over the commission, resulted from unaudited circulations. Advertisers continually complained that publishers inflated circulation statistics and that they had no means of verifying the accuracy of how many individuals their ads actually were reaching. After several attempts by various agencies and a push from Congress, which in 1912 required publications using the mails to print sworn annual circulation statements, the Association of National Advertising Managers and the American Advertising Association joined forces in 1914 to create the Audit Bureau of Circulation. Although the bureau had financial difficulties in the early years, it was successful in establishing standards for circulation claims and for auditing those claims.

Other changes in the early years of the century were apparent as New York advertising agencies changed their places of business. They moved from an area dominated by publishers to one dominated by business—Madison Avenue. They opened branch offices in various cities and expanded their work force. In 1900, Ayers employed 163 people; by 1910, 298 individuals were employed in the agency; in 1920 that number expanded to 426. Billings for Ayer were $1.5 million in 1900; by 1921 they surpassed $11 million. The ad agencies, in tune with the progressive period, moved toward systematic, scientific management.

The agency workforce was 95 percent male. In 1916, half the men associated with agencies had attended college and one-fourth held bachelor's degrees. Only one in ten was older than fifty and about half were from the Middle West. They were predominantly Protestant, middle-class, middle-American males. One of the few women in the advertising business, Helen Rosen Woodward, lamented the change to the formal business stature. She wrote:

> Advertising has the solid mentality usual in a large established business with heavy investment. It no longer attracts the lovers of chance, but rather those who look for safety. It has a pontifical dignity which robs it of much of its earlier fire. If [sic] never occurred to any of the pioneers to think about the dignity of advertising. It was much too interesting for that.[22]

By the 1920s, Daniel Pope wrote, agencies were selling "access to American consumers. To use a chilling but revealing phrase of modern marketing, advertising agencies dared to offer their corporate clients a share of the American mind."[23]

ETHICS AND REGULATION

Another hotly debated issue of the early 1900s was that of ethics. Although some publishers and a few agencies had rejected fraudulent advertising, agents took responsibility only for the ads, not for the product. More publishers became involved at the turn of the century; for example, in 1892 Cyrus Curtis rejected all medical ads for the *Ladies' Home Journal.* Some agencies turned away lucrative accounts on ethical grounds. As the truth-in-advertising movement gained credence, agents began to argue that false advertising injured the product's credibility and created financial losses; that the truth paid. Agencies were concerned about their own status as professionals and could little afford claims of false advertising. Although agencies opposed government interference in the 1890s, by the time the Pure Food and Drug Act was passed in 1906 there was little opposition. The act was aimed at penalizing fraud and misstatement, primarily in labeling, and was not aimed at the harmfulness of a product; furthermore, the bill carried few enforcement procedures. However, by 1910 most patent medicine advertisements were placed directly by manufacturers or distributors rather than by agencies.

The first real enthusiasm for a truth-in-advertising movement came with the 1911 convention of the Associated Advertising Clubs of America (AACA). Although postal regulations and some state laws contained provisions against fraudulent advertising, all required proof of intent to deceive and required that a transaction must be complete before the law applied. In 1911, *Printer's Ink* ran a series on unfair competition, and within that series of articles proposed a model statute banning dishonest advertising—a statute to be enforced by the states and that would not require proof of intent to deceive. The article that proposed this statute also suggested local advertising-club surveillance would be essential to the success of any statute. By 1921, twenty-three states enacted the statute recommended by *Printer's Ink,* although some exempted publishers from liability and some required proof of deception. In 1914, Congress passed the Federal Trade Commission (FTC) Act, which made the FTC the most powerful regulator of advertising, but until 1938, with the passage of the Wheeler-Lea Amendment, the FTC had to prove that a false ad harmed a competing business.

In 1912, an eighteen-member National Vigilance Committee (NVC) was created from the Associated Advertising Clubs, and many cities established local clubs. Energy was primarily devoted toward local cases, the movement was clearly in advertising's self-interest and there was a heavy dependence on enlightenment rather than on prosecution. Vigilance groups were careful when dealing with large corporations, although the NVC and other groups denied such charges. Under the guise of truthfulness in advertising, the movement also managed to eliminate much comparative price competition.

The movement remained directed at the truthfulness of words used within an ad, and never evaluated the social impact of advertising or the ethics of using a variety of persuasive techniques. In fact, Daniel Pope suggests that the decline of the lie led to the introduction of new and more powerful persuasive techniques.

PERSUASIVE STRATEGIES

Advertising copy and persuasive strategies were intertwined with the continuing success of old products and with the introduction of new consumer products in the 1920s. Roland Marchand wrote in *Advertising the American Dream* that in a single year, "major advertising campaigns rescued two fading products so successfully that the entire advertising industry had to ponder the lessons they offered in modern advertising technique."[24] Fleischmann's Yeast, which had been used primarily to bake bread, was fast becoming a victim of urbanization and the fact that people were buying bread, not making it. The J. Walter Thompson company within a year transformed Fleischmann's into a "potent source of vitamins, a food to be eaten directly from the package."[25] Two years later, the agency assisted in once again transforming the product, this time into a natural laxative. Human-interest advertising copy arranged much like an editorial feature was a major component in the campaign. In three years, sales increased 130 percent, and the agency called in physicians who recommended eating yeast to counteract "intestinal fatigue." Although the American Medical Association prohibited its doctors from participating in the advertising campaign, European doctors readily testified, and their prestigious names only aided the campaign.

The transformation of Listerine from a general antiseptic to a breath freshener represented another advertising success story of the 1920s. After advertising copywriters hit upon the term "halitosis," and explained how a man with wealth, good looks, and charm, who labored under the dread "bad breath," could lose everything, Listerine's parent company increased its profits from $100,000 per year in 1920 to $4 million in 1927. In 1926, *Printer's Ink,* a major trade journal, credited the copywriter of the Listerine campaign with having "amplified the morning habits of our nicer citizenry — by making the morning mouthwash as important as the morning shower or the morning shave."[26] Listerine later was promoted as a cure for dandruff, a cure for colds, and a deodorant.

Advertising copywriters did not exist in a vacuum; one of the great dilemmas of the decade was deciding on the true nature of the audience. Did an advertiser aim at the great general mass of people, or at the more cultured elite? Many agencies took the position of aiming at those who read the tabloids, and patterned their copy on techniques used by tabloid and confession-magazine writers. Others maintained the more elite position. Advertisers often aimed at women, because although women constituted only about 50 percent of the audience, they were regarded as the family purchasing agents. Men were depicted almost universally as businessmen dressed in business suits. Working-class men never appeared as consumers; in the advertising industry policemen, factory workers, government officials, and architects never existed.[27]

Other techniques attracted women consumers. The emphasis on color increased, with kitchen appliances, Hoosier cabinets, and bathroom fixtures produced and advertised in color; the importance of the first impression also was emphasized. Many women in 1920s advertisements lamented the fact they had made a poor first impression in a social or business circle, and therefore had doomed their husband's career forever. Urbanization, mobility, and feared cultural disintegration of the 1920s was incorporated into advertising strategy. According to advertising copy,

> first impressions brought instantaneous success or failure. In a relatively mobile society, where business organizations loomed ever larger and people dealt far more often with strangers, the reasons one man gained a promotion or one woman suffered a social snub had become less explicable on grounds of long-standing favoritism or old family feuds. One might suspect that almost anything—especially a first impression—had made the crucial difference.[28]

By the end of the decade, the full-service agency was firmly in place. The advertising industry had moved from a position in the late nineteenth century, when its primary function was to sell space in media to advertisers to sophisticated businessmen and creative individuals writing copy, designing marketing research, and appealing to a variety of consumers by incorporating the social tensions of the day into advertising copy and strategy. The industry had developed its own professional standards, abolished the more blatant competitive strategies, and had gained legitimacy through a "Truth in Advertising Movement."

RADIO

Radio was a technological innovation that was to change the pattern of communication in the nation. Within less than a decade, radio moved from a technological "miracle" to a household necessity provided by and controlled

By 1929 the radio had become a necessary furnishing in middle-class households. (Library of Congress Collection)

by corporate interests. Its history is a story of technical development, corporate leadership versus entrepreneurship, industry battles, congressional regulation, and social impact.[29] The debates of the 1920s centered on who would pay for radio development, who would control it and how it would be used. Legislators and industrial giants viewed it as a new tool of influence; educators debated its usefulness as a teaching tool; cultural elites worried about the effect it would have on concerts and other cultural events. In many ways, radio became the sounding box for the contradictions of the twenties and as a new communications medium played a major role in disseminating debates about those contradictions to Americans who were trying to retain traditional values and behavior and at the same time adapt to modern conveniences and freedoms.[30]

By the end of the 1920s, the fundamental contours of an American system of broadcasting were in place. With little public debate about the significance of the new technology in relationship to freedom of expression, commercial broadcasters quickly took control of the medium and strongly influenced congressional regulation that enhanced the commercial enterprise.[31] The development of radio as a commercial, primarily entertainment enterprise loosely regulated by the federal government was neither inevitable, nor the result of "happenstance." It resulted from a complex interplay of technology, military and government needs, corporate enterprise and congressional action within a volatile social and cultural milieu.[32]

TECHNOLOGY

Technological inroads toward developing radio telephony, as it was called, began as early as 1870, and by the close of World War I the instruments were ready. In the 1870s, a British scientist named James Clerk-Maxwell discovered the transmission of radio waves was theoretically possible, and shortly after that a German scientist, Heinrich Hertz, showed that energy actually could be transmitted, without connecting wires, between two points. Thrilled with the possibility of implementing Hertz's discovery was an Italian youth, Guglielmo Marconi, who saw radio as a means of supplementing or replacing telegraphy. Because the Italians were not interested in his experiments, he went to London, where the British government, because of its colonial empire, was very much interested in the development of improved means of communication.[33]

In 1897, he secured the necessary patents and, backed by English investors, formed the Marconi Wireless and Signal Company. His efforts in areas of the world where it was impossible to lay telegraph wires attracted international attention, and resulted in an international radio conference in Germany in 1903. By the early twentieth century some pioneering individuals envisioned using wireless telephony to transmit the human voice and music. On Christmas Eve 1906, Reginald A. Fessenden sent music and voice over the air

> ### WHAT HAPPENED TO RADIO?
>
> What have you done with my child? You have made him the laughing stock to intelligence, surely a stench in the nostrils of the gods of the iconosphere. Murder mysteries rule the waves by night and children are rendered psychopathic by your bedtime stories. This child of mine is moronic, as though you and your sponsors believe the majority of listeners have only moron minds.
>
> SOURCE. Lee De Forest, inventor of the audion tube.

to previously alerted amateurs and shipboard operators. At about the same time Lee De Forest invented the audion tube, which allowed modulation and amplification of electrical currents and which made small, reliable receivers possible. Prior to World War I and the subsequent corporate venture into commercial broadcasting, a variety of amateurs broadcast music and other programming across the air waves, and at least four universities made use of the airwaves for educational broadcasting.[34]

GOVERNMENT AND INDUSTRY JOIN HANDS

In 1912, Americans attended an international conference in London, where nations agreed that each country would regulate the use of radio within its own territory. That same year the U.S. Congress passed the Radio Act of 1912, requiring radio operators to obtain a license from the U.S. secretary of commerce and labor. The secretary issued licenses and frequencies nonselectively and to all comers.

World War I provided a boom in radio research. Wartime military needs provided more systematic, heavily financed research, as well as the pooling of patents. Cooperative research between American Telephone and Telegraph, General Electric, and Westinghouse ultimately resulted in the technological sophistication of wireless telephony and the creation of the powerful Radio Corporation of America (RCA). Between 1914 and 1918, radio was strictly regulated by the U.S. Navy for use in ship-to-shore communications. During those same years, the navy became increasingly uncomfortable about the fact that a foreign company, British-owned American Marconi, was the sole supplier of most U.S. radio equipment. At the close of the war, the U.S. government applied pressure to General Electric chairman Owen D. Young to propose a new corporation to hold all American patents. General Electric created a $2.5 million fund to buy out American Marconi and, with American Telephone & Telegraph, United Fruit, and Westinghouse Electric, formed RCA.

David Sarnoff, who had risen from the position of radio operator to commercial manager of American Marconi, became president of RCA. The companies operated under joint ownership until 1926, when AT&T withdrew from broadcasting.[35]

The creation of RCA and its pooling arrangement strongly affected the development of radio. In essence, the new alliance allowed its members to continue their wartime control over major radio patents. Radio historian Elaine Berland wrote that the arrangement also "provided member corporations with strong financial bases, a public image of promoting national interest, and friendly relations with the federal government and the military." These factors put alliance members in an advantageous position to influence the field of domestic broadcasting in the 1920s.

Amid the postwar experimentation with receivers and transmitters and the negotiations over patents, Dr. Frank Conrad, like many other amateur operators, received permission to put his amateur station on the air, and began playing victrola music from a small transmitter above his garage in Pittsburgh, Pennsylvania. People responded in droves to his suggestion that they request specific tunes. His success spurred Westinghouse to ask Conrad to build a station, KDKA, which went on the air with advertised programs to help listeners form the "listening habit." Programming was not the primary interest. Westinghouse established the station to sell receivers and goodwill for the company name. On November 2, 1920, KDKA went on the air with a broadcast of results of the race between presidential candidates Warren G. Harding and James M. Cox, setting into motion what conventionally has been regarded as the birth of broadcasting in the United States. What created radio as a communications medium was not the perfection of technology, but rather the realization that a popular market existed and could be reached for a relatively small investment. In the fall of 1921, Westinghouse opened three more stations; General Electric and RCA established stations in 1922 and 1923.

Radio was so popular that RCA sold $11 million worth of receivers in 1922. By 1925, sales jumped to $50 million. The five stations that existed in 1921 grew to 576 stations by 1923 and 700 by 1927. By the end of the decade, 618 stations and two networks were firmly in place. Set sales paralleled the growth of stations. In 1924, $45 million worth of sets was sold, a figure that jumped to $135 million in 1929. In 1923, only 1.5 percent of the households in the United States owned a radio set; by 1930, almost 50 percent owned sets.[37]

It soon became apparent that establishing a broadcast station was an expensive venture, one that could not be supported indefinitely by the sale of radio receivers. Who should pay for the programming became a critical question for the infant industry. As early as 1922, AT&T announced it would sell time to individuals who wanted to send a message over the air. Initially, the public and press reacted negatively. Many observers such as Herbert Hoover envisioned radio as a public service and feared that "if a speech by the President is to be used as the meat in a sandwich of two patent medicine advertisements there will be no radio left."[38] Despite such reservations, AT&T's station WEAF ventured into what it termed "toll broadcasting," making a pitch for a cooperative apartment complex in New York City. The commercial lasted less than fifteen minutes, was repeated for five days and cost $100. By the end of 1924, other stations attempted to imitate AT&T's approach, but the company claimed it was a new phase of the telephone business and, as such, was their sole domain.[39]

Disputes over who would control patents, who would manufacture sets, and who had the right to sell advertising and thereby turn radio into a profitable medium created controversy and competition within the industry. The industry also faced technological problems of interference that had not been solved by the allocation of frequencies under the 1912 legislation. Foreseeing problems, Secretary Hoover urged Congress to pass new legislation. Between 1921 and 1927, twelve bills that would have repealed the 1912 Act, and forty others that would have amended it were introduced into Congress. But Congress failed to act because its members could not agree. Meanwhile, Hoover organized conferences attended by industry representatives, educators, engineers, and others to discuss the problems of jammed air waves and proliferating stations that threatened set sales and the industry itself. Industry representatives specifically recommended to Congress that broadcasting be left under private control with limited federal supervision of the technical aspects of the medium. They recommended the federal government assign licenses, limit the number of stations, abolish low-powered stations (many of these were educational), support trade-name advertising, and issue licenses on the basis of "public interest."

As Congress and those attending Hoover's conferences debated the various issues, RCA members sought to renegotiate their earlier cross-licensing agreements. The giants were divided into two groups — AT&T and its subsidiary, Western Electric, or the Telephone Group; and Westinghouse, RCA, and GE, the Radio Group. AT&T claimed it had exclusive rights to manufacture and sell radio transmitters for broadcasting, to sell time for advertising, and to connect stations by wire for network or chain broadcasting. The Radio Group claimed the right to manufacture and sell radio sets to the public, to recoup program expenses from sponsors, and to interconnect stations by any available means. The industry resolved its disputed claims in 1926, with AT&T withdrawing from the broadcast industry. RCA bought AT&T's station, WEAF, for $1 million and guaranteed AT&T $1 million a year by agreeing to use its telephone lines to interconnect stations. RCA, GE, and Westinghouse formed the National Broadcasting Company (NBC), the nation's first network. By adopting commercial sponsorship as well, NBC represented a solid organizational and financial base for the development of radio broadcasting—a red network fed by WEAF and a blue network fed by WJZ, formerly a Westinghouse station.

At last having settled their own differences, the industry magnates were ready to urge Congress to pass legislation. In January, Congress, following most of the industry's recommendations, passed the Federal Radio Act of 1927, creating a five-member commission to regulate radio. Believing that radio was too valuable a resource to be operated as a monopoly, the regulation stated that the airwaves belong to the American people, and that stations must operate in "the public interest, convenience, or necessity." Nevertheless, most of the responsibility for programming and the ability to profit was left in private, corporate hands.[40]

Regulation of broadcasting represented a strict departure from the relationship between print communication and government. Licensing was justified on the "scarcity principle": there simply were not enough broadcast frequencies for all comers, so the Federal Radio Commission would choose among applicants "in the public interest." So it was that a kind of "shotgun wedding" took place between government ownership of the airwaves—a resource in theory belonging to all people (and crossing state and national boundaries, too)—and a media system based on private enterprise.

GOING TO THE MOVIES

The modern film industry came of age during World War I, and the economics of war enabled the United States to move rapidly ahead of other countries in the development of film for a commercial audience. In France, Germany, Great Britain, and Italy, where film production had flourished, photographic supplies such as cotton and nitric and sulphuric acids, were diverted into the manufacture of explosives. Because U.S. involvement in the war was shorter and marginal compared to that of the European powers, American film producers were at a distinct advantage. The U.S. economy, stimulated by the war, provided a large domestic audience, and the industry was based on business expertise not available to other countries.[41]

The development of photography was essential to modern film, but people were fascinated with the concept of moving images long before the technology to support any kind of photography was developed. The Greeks passed on the concept of the projected illuminated image to the Arabs, and later Italian Leonardo da Vinci experimented with the camera obscura, or a room with a pin hole that permitted viewing an outside image on the opposite wall. A seventeenth-century Jesuit priest built a portable camera obscura, added a candle, a lens, and glass slides with images, thereby creating an entertainment

This 1896 lithograph depicted Edison's Vitascope. The New York Herald *noted that the vitascope produced life size pictures full of color that made "a thrilling show." (Library of Congress Collection)*

popular throughout Europe. Through the nineteenth century various individuals developed increasingly sophisticated narrative slide shows.

The next step involved putting pictures on both sides of a wheel and spinning it, creating an optical toy called a Thaumatrope. Various advanced forms of the toy combined a shutter principle, light, and angled mirrors. In the late 1880s, in Paris, the Theatre Optique at the Musée Grevin presented stories projected on screen by shining a bright light through long strips of translucent material.

In 1878, Eadweard Muybridge achieved a semblance of motion by setting up a battery of cameras alongside a race track and pulling the shutter several intervals apart. It was only slightly later that the French physician and scientist Etienne Jules Marey devised a camera that produced twelve pictures a second on a single plate. In 1888, gelatin emulsions allowed photographing of real movement. Combined with the production of celluloid, available in 1888, the moving-picture industry celebrated its infancy.

From 1891 to 1894 Thomas Edison's labs developed and publicized a new entertainment machine, the Kinetoscope, which moved fifty-foot loops of film in less than a half minute over a series of spools. The machine was about the size and weight of an upright piano. In 1895, Luis and Auguste Lumière made portable equipment and carried their Cinematographe into Eastern Europe, the Far East, and the United States. The Cinematographe and competing machines soon earned a place in the vaudeville programs across the United States.

At first the novelty of captured motion rather than content dominated productions, which were about a half minute long. Two American films, produced in 1903 by Edwin S. Porter, "Life of an American Fireman" and "The Great Train Robbery," were about twelve minutes long and introduced editing techniques, which allowed film to emerge as its own artistic form.

Films were instantly popular, and by 1907 three thousand nickelodeons in America were attracting audiences. "There was no better place for this classically democratic phenomenon," wrote film historians Louis Giannetti and Scott Eyman:

> Here, immigrants who couldn't speak English and illiterate laborers attended a new invention, learning about their new land and its customs, transported by the magic of storytelling drama for the first time in their lives, many of them learning English bit by bit, word by word in the bargain. For millions, the movies were art, science, and schooling all in one.[42]

Edison retained significant control over the industry, using lawsuits to preserve and extend his control of patents. By 1908, he had persuaded the major competing companies to join with him in organizing the Motion Picture Patents Company. The members pooled sixteen patents for film, cameras, and projectors. The company secured an agreement with Eastman Kodak to monopolize raw film stock, and they firmly controlled distributors and exhibitors, blackballing those who broke the rules. At first the pooling arrangement eliminated competition, but by 1912 independent firms, many begun by European immigrants, produced almost half the feature films, and were experimenting with longer features and new techniques. During the politically charged late summer of 1912 the government charged the Motion Picture Patents Company with violating the 1890 Sherman Anti-Trust Act, and in 1915 declared the group to be illegally restraining trade. By 1915, however, the independents had already gained considerable ground, attracting middle-class audiences by building larger theatres and producing longer and more expensive films.[43]

The transition of ten-minute entertainments to "films" was accomplished by 1915, with David Wark Griffith's three-hour production, *The Birth of a Nation*. The film yielded $5 million on an investment of less than $100,000.

> ### NEWSBOY'S POEM
>
> All what I see wit' me own eyes I knows an' unnerstan's
> When I see movin pitchers of de far off, furrin' lan's
> Where de Hunks an' Ginnes come from—yer betcher life I knows
> Dat of all de lan's an' countries, 'taint no matter where yer goes
> Dis here country's got 'em beaten—take my oat dat ain't no kid—
> "Cause we learned it from de movin' pitchers, me an' Maggie did.—
>
> This anonymous poem by a newsboy in 1910 evoked an image of immigrant boys being uplifted by the movies, an impression popular among some civic leaders.[44]

The editing techniques, the full-story length, the sensitive construction of visual images made the film an artistic milestone. But the film also created great controversy because of its "outrageously racist" message. Nevertheless, "Looking beyond the ever-widening social gulf between modern attitudes and those that were the norm in 1915, *The Birth of a Nation* remains a remarkable achievement," wrote Giannetti and Eyman. Griffith made later films, although none achieved the recognition of *Birth of a Nation*. Never a businessman, he suffered financial difficulty and did not adapt to changes within the industry.

From 1914 to 1916, a few independent distributors, such as the Paramount Group, gained power by contracting with producers such as Adolph Zukor for exclusive distribution of Zukor's films. In the Paramount case, Zukor, unhappy about working for a distributor, bought out several Paramount partners, took control, and consolidated his power through block-booking. The next step was to buy theatres and begin to establish vertical integration within the industry. Such was the beginning of the powerful studio system.[45]

By the 1920s, the film industry was centered in Hollywood, where twenty studios produced features and shorts for a weekly audience of 40 million people. Throughout the decade the formation of large studios such as Metro-Goldwyn-Mayer and Warner Brothers produced large fortunes. One 1923 film, for example, cost $120,963 and grossed $1,588,545. The silent comedies of Charles Chaplin and Buster Keaton, leading actresses such as Gloria Swanson and Mary Pickford, teamed with Rudolph Valentino and Douglas Fairbanks, reigned supreme. In the mid-1920s, the American film industry produced 82 percent of the world's movies. The twenty thousand theatres in the states grossed about $360 million. But the film industry was soon going to have to make large capital investments—investments to produce and play in theaters the talking movies that rapidly were gaining ground.

By 1928, mediocre films with sound sequences were rapidly outdistancing highly artistic silent films. In 1929, Warners' profits topped $17 million, in comparison to $2 million the year before. Paramount cleared $15 million and Fox $9 million.

The decade also witnessed the solidification of the industry into large movie houses, rather than centering its film making in the hands of independent producers. By 1929, five companies monopolized the industry. Paramount, Warner Brothers, Fox, Metro-Goldwyn-Mayer (MGM) and Radio-Keith-Orpheum (RKO) controlled production houses and theatre outlets, and heads of studios dominated decision making about film topics and production. The studio system, combined with the focus on top stars, reached its peak in the 1930s and 1940s, when movie-going audiences were at their peak as well.

Conclusion

By the end of the 1920s, most of the modern forms of communication were in place, but a lively debate ensued about how those forms—newspapers, motion pictures, and radio—would affect American life. Critics wondered whether new forms, which separated the dissemination of information from transportation, would help preserve traditional values or whether they would modernize the world so that it would be unrecognizable to an older generation.

The debate over whether newspapers would provide information or sensation continued throughout the decade. The tabloids, with screaming headlines, reflected the diversity of city life and used advances in photographic technology to attract their readers. The number of newspaper chains doubled between 1923 and 1933 and fear of conglomerates evoked much criticism. Sixty percent of the newspaper content was advertising, and costs and prices increased.

The development of public relations techniques continued from the latter half of the nineteenth century to promulgate business into the foreground as makers of news and disseminators of news. Skilled practitioners urged business leaders to abandon secrecy and to convince the public of their honorable intentions by explaining situations and policies.

Advertising practitioners responded to the development of differentiated products, and by the 1920s moved from selling space to newspapers to creating agencies that provided services from market research to copywriting. Agencies soon dominated the business, championed professionalism, moved slowly toward truth-in-advertising policies, targeted women as primary consumers, and incorporated the social tensions of the day in their persuasive strategies.

PART 4   MEDIA IN A MODERN WORLD

Radio, a social as well as a technological innovation, caused cultural and political leaders to explore the possibilities of the new medium. Within less than a decade, an American system of broadcasting was in place. Initial profits from the sale of sets gave way to a commercialized industry, which relied on advertising for its profits. Proliferation of individual local stations, linked by the National Broadcasting Corporation, dominated the radio industry. The Federal Radio Act of 1927 incorporated most of the demands of the industry and created the Federal Radio Commission to administer technical aspects, which stabilized the industry for commercial growth. Although licensing of the broadcast industry introduced stabilization, it also represented a critical departure from First Amendment protection granted to the print media.

By the end of the 1920s, motion pictures had become full-length entertainment films, moving from twelve-minute novelties to a full-fledged industry dominated by five major Hollywood studios.

NOTES

1. Richard Schwarzlose, "Technology and the Individual: The Impact of Innovation on Communication," in Catherine L. Covert and John D. Stevens, *Mass Media Between the Wars* (Syracuse, N.Y.: Syracuse University Press, 1984), p. 97.
2. Elaine Prostak (Berland), "Up in the Air: The Public Debates Over Radio Use During the 1920's," Ph.D. disser., University of Kansas, 1983.
3. For analysis of the roles of consumer credit and advertising in the consumer-durables revolution of the 1920s, see Martha Olney, "Advertising, Consumer Credit, and the Consumer Durables Revolution of the 1920s," Ph.D. disser., Berkeley, 1982.
4. James E. Murphy, "Tabloids as an Urban Response," in Covert and Stevens, *Mass Media Between the Wars*, p. 55.
5. Douglass W. Miller, "The New York Tabloids," *Journalism Quarterly* 5: (1928), pp. 39–40, cited in Covert and Stevens, *Mass Media Between the Wars*, p. 60.
6. Silas Bent, "The Art of Ballyhoo," *Harper's* (September 1927), p. 493, cited in James L. Baughman, *Henry R. Luce and the Rise of the American News Media* (Boston: G.K. Hall/Twayne), p. 54.
7. For statistics, see Alfred McClung Lee, *The Daily Newspaper in America* (New York: The Macmillan Co., 1937), pp. 214–215.
8. For a complete description of the International Paper Company investigation, see Cathy Packer, "Conglomerate Newspaper Ownership: International Paper Company, 1928–29," *Journalism Quarterly* 60:3 (Autumn 1983), pp. 480–483, 567.
9. For this story and a short history of public relations organized around four models (press agentry, public-information, two-way asymmetric model and two-way symmetric model), see James E. Grunig and Todd Hunt, *Managing Public Relations* (New York: CBS College Publishing, 1984). For a captivating account of Barnum's

promotional efforts, see Neil Harris, *Humbug! The Art of P. T. Barnum* (Chicago: University of Chicago Press, 1981).

10. See Marvin Olasky, "The Development of Corporate Public Relations, 1850–1930," *Journalism Monographs* 102 (April 1987), pp. 2–3. For quote, see Carter Goodrich, *Government Promotion of American Canals and Railroads, 1800–1890* (New York: Columbia University Press, 1960), p. 171, cited in Olasky, p. 3.
11. Olasky, "Corporate Public Relations," pp. 2–15.
12. Ray Eldon Hiebert, *Courtier to the Crowd: The Story of Ivy Lee and the Development of Public Relations* (Ames: Iowa State University Press, 1966), p. 48.
13. Genevieve G. Caspari, "Ethical Thought in Public Relations History: Seeking a Relevant Perspective," presented to Public Relations Division, Association for Education in Journalism and Mass Communication, Memphis, Tenn., August 1985.
14. Michael Schudson, *Discovering the News: A Social History of American Newspapers* (New York: Basic Books, 1978), p. 143.
15. Caspari, "Ethical Thought," pp. 5, 8.
16. Caspari, "Ethical Thought," p. 7.
17. For a critical view of advertising and consumer culture, see Stuart Ewen, *Captains of Consciousness: Advertising and the Roots of Consumer Culture* (New York: McGraw Hill, 1976) and T.J. Jackson Lears and Richard Wightman Fox, eds., *The Culture of Consumption.* (New York: Pantheon, 1983).
18. David Ogilvy, *Ogilvy on Advertising* (New York: Crown Publishers, Inc., 1983), p. 191.
19. Ogilvy, *Ogilvy on Advertising*, p. 192.
20. Stephen Fox, *The Mirror Makers* (New York: William Morrow and Company, Inc., 1984), p. 83.
21. See Daniel Pope, *The Making of Modern Advertising,* (New York: Basic Books, 1983) for full discussion of why advertising agencies dominated the advertising industry.
22. Helen Woodward, *Through Many Windows* (New York: Harper & Brothers, 1926), pp. 348–349, cited in Pope, *Making of Modern Advertising,* p. 180.
23. Pope, *Making of Modern Advertising,* p. 183.
24. Roland Marchand, "Two Legendary Campaigns," *American Heritage* 36:3 (April/May 1985), p. 76. See also Marchand, *Advertising The American Dream: Making Way for Modernity, 1920–1940* (Berkeley: University of California Press, 1985).
25. Marchand, "Legendary Campaigns," p. 76.
26. Marchand, "Legendary Campaigns," pp. 76–77.
27. Marchand, "Legendary Campaigns," p. 80.
28. Marchand, "Legendary Campaigns," p. 85.
29. For analysis of industry battles and congressional legislation, see Erik Barnouw's classic three volume-work, *A History of Broadcasting in the United States*, vol. 1, *A Tower in Babel* (New York: Oxford University Press, 1966); Philip T. Rosen, *The Modern Stentors: Radio Broadcasters and the Federal Government, 1920–1934* (Westport, Conn.: Greenwood Press, 1980); Daniel E. Garvey, "Secretary Hoover and

the Quest for Broadcast Regulation," *Journalism History* 3 (Autumn 1976): pp. 66–70, 85; and Donald G. Godfrey, "The 1927 Radio Act: People and Politics," *Journalism History* 4 (Autumn 1977), p. 78.

30. For discussion of contemporary public debates over educational, political, cultural, and religious use of the airwaves, see Prostak, "Up in the Air."

31. For extensive account of the debate over the meaning of free speech on the radio, with emphasis on the debate in the legal community, see Louise M. Benjamin, "Radio Regulation in the 1920s: Free Speech Issues in the Development of Radio and the Radio Act of 1927," Ph.D. disser., University of Iowa, 1985. See also Robert W. McChesney, "Free Speech and Democracy: The Debate in the American Legal Community over the Meaning of Free Expression on Radio, 1926–1939," unpublished paper presented to Law and History Divisions, Association for Education in Journalism and Mass Communication, San Antonio, Texas, August 1987.

32. Prostak, "Up in the Air," p. 22. For important discussion of the complex interplay between opposing forces and implications of technology, see Daniel Czitrom, *Media and the American Mind* (Chapel Hill: University of North Carolina Press, 1982).

33. For development of radio technology see Hugh G. J. Aitken, *Syntony and Spark: The Origins of Radio* (Princeton, N.J.: Princeton University Press, 1985) and *The Continuous Wave: Technology and American Radio, 1900–1932* (Princeton, N.J.: Princeton University Press, 1985).

34. Werner J. Severin, "Commercial and Non-Commercial Radio During Broadcasting's Early Years," *Journal of Broadcasting* 22 (Fall 1978), p. 491.

35. Barnouw, *Tower in Babel,* pp. 185–186.

36. Prostak, "Up in the Air," p. 31. See Aitken, *Syntony and Spark,* pp. 472–474.

37. Prostak, "Up in the Air," pp. 23–24. For figures on station ownership see Christopher Sterling and John M. Kittross, *Stay Tuned: A Concise History of American Broadcasting* (Belmont, Calif.: Wadsworth, 1978), pp. 510–533.

38. Herbert Hoover at the Third National Radio Conference, October 1924, cited in Sterling and Kittross, *Stay Tuned,* p. 49.

39. Prostak, "Up in the Air," p. 38. See also Catherine L. Covert, "We May Hear Too Much: American Sensibility and the Response to Radio, 1919–1924," in Covert and Stevens, *Mass Media Between the Wars,* and Mary S. Mander, "The Public Debate About Broadcasting in the Twenties: An Interpretive History," *Journal of Broadcasting* 28:2 (Spring 1984), pp. 167–185.

40. For information on the congressional debates, see Daniel E. Garvey, "Secretary Hoover and the Quest for Broadcast Regulation," *Journalism History* 3:3, (Autumn 1976) pp. 66–70, 85; Joseph P. McKerns, "Industry Skeptics and the Radio Act of 1927," *Journalism History* 3:4 (Winter 1976), pp. 128–131, 136; and Donald G. Godfrey, "The 1927 Radio Act: People and Politics," *Journalism History* 4:3 (Autumn 1977), pp. 74–78.

41. Jack C. Ellis, *A History of Film,* 2nd ed. (Englewood Cliffs, N.J., Prentice-Hall, 1985).

42. Louis Giannetti and Scott Eyman, *Flashback: A Brief History of Film* (Englewood Cliffs: Prentice Hall) 1986, p. 15.
43. Robert Sklar, *Movie-Made America: A Cultural History of American Movies* (New York: Vintage Books, 1975), pp. 35, 36, 40, 87.
44. This stanza of the newsboy's poem is cited in Czitrom, *Media and the American Mind,* p. 51.
45. Sklar, *Movie-Made America,* pp. 144–45.

CHAPTER 16

DEPRESSION
AND
DISILLUSION

First of all, let me assert my firm belief that the only thing we have to fear is fear itself—nameless unreasoning, unjustified terror.—Franklin Delano Roosevelt

I am serving notice that I am firing 25 percent of the staff now, and when I return from my vacation in Hot Springs I am going to fire 25 percent more.—Publisher Lucius Tarquinius Russell, Newark Ledger.

In his inaugural address in March 1933, President Franklin Delano Roosevelt attacked the widespread fear that gripped the people of the United States, caught in the despair of a depression. The fear, however, was based on reality, as the *Newark Ledger* publisher's remarks indicated. The prosperity of the twenties faded as a dream, as 13 million unemployed workers and farmers struggled to feed their families in the face of plummeting prices and loss of savings. Among those workers were compositors, reporters, and editors.

The press, as well as stock-market analysts, ignored the economic warnings of the late twenties. From 1925 on, the number of commercial failures increased relatively unnoticed, while the automobile and construction industries steadily declined. On Black Thursday, October 24, 1929, Wall Street crashed. A record number of shares sold, but those that sold were priced low, and others remained on the market for lack of buyers. Wild speculation preceded Black Thursday, with buying on margin, and investors borrowing 50 to 90 percent of the purchase prices from brokers, who increasingly borrowed from the banks at rising interest prices.

By 1933, corporate profits fell from a 1929 high of $10 billion to $1 billion, and the gross national product dropped by half. Stockholders and depositors lost $2.5 billion during those four years in savings-account failures, and farm income was cut in half. In 1930, four million Americans were jobless, and by 1933, one-fourth of the labor force — 13 million — was unemployed. From 1928–1932 labor income dropped 40 percent.[1]

Despite its now vast resources, the press failed to adequately inform the public prior to the stock-market crash of 1929. And although the periodical industry would suffer some of the same business losses as other industry, the press proved surprisingly resilient. Newspapers suffered little, radio's profits accelerated, and the technology for television developed throughout the decade. Nevertheless, reporters made few economic gains, and some news staffs responded to the low pay and poor working conditions by organizing the American Newspaper Guild.

The industry remained not only strong, but innovative. The muckrakers and other progressive journalists had relied on presentation of facts to convince American readers. Artists, filmmakers and photographers of the 1930s, influenced by international experimentation with the documentary film and newsreel, led a developing documentary movement to chronicle the emotional, as well as the factual reality of the decade. The camera earned middle-class respectability, and at the beginning of the '30s, nearly fifty million people viewed newsreels and full-length features every week.[2]

The journalism of synthesis, the photojournalistic essay, and the development of the newsreel opened new dimensions of interpreta-

> **THE SPANISH CIVIL WAR**
>
> BARCELONA, MARCH 17—Barcelona has lived through twelve air raids in less than twenty-four hours, and the city is shaken and terror-struck. Human beings have seldom had to suffer as these people are suffering under General Francisco Franco's determined effort to break their spirit and induce their government to yield.
>
> SOURCE. Herbert Matthews, writing in the New York Times, March 18, 1938.

tion.[3] Some newspapers, codes of ethics, and textbooks suggested that in order to inform the American public adequately, newspapers would have to go beyond presenting facts. Interpretation spawned a new generation of newsmen—the columnists and editorial writers. Newspapers also took advantage of gains in social science, using polls to predict the outcome of elections.

Innovation, traditional patterns of reporting, and alternative news media competed for the bewildered audience of the 1930s. The wire services maintained an objective tradition that continued to flourish throughout the 1950s. Henry Luce, with college friend Briton Hadden, in 1923 successfully introduced *Time*, the news magazine that synthesized and organized information appearing in U.S. newspapers. Luce also developed a highly successful photojournalism magazine, a business magazine, and a radio program and newsreel, "March of Time." Other journalists, such as Dorothy Day and Ralph Ingersoll, abandoned the mainstream press and established alternative publications.

President Franklin Delano Roosevelt, the personality leading government intervention during the depression, reinstituted and expanded government supply of news to the media. His open style and continuous flow of information to members of the press endeared reporters to him, while his challenges to publishers alienated the industry and the editorial page.[4]

THE NEWSPAPER INDUSTRY

The number of dailies continued a decline that began about 1910, dropping from 2,580 in 1914 to 2,441 in 1919, to 2,080 in 1933. Weeklies also declined from about 1916 on, dropping from 13,964 in 1919 to 11,931 in 1935. Circulations showed a slight decline from a 1929 peak. Concentrated in the nation's big cities, 47.4 percent of the nation's dailies in 1929 and 41.8 percent of the nation's Sunday papers originated in six cities.[5]

Loss of advertising resulted in a newspaper and periodical revenue decline from $1,580,565 in 1929 to $937,114 in 1933. But the total income of the news and periodical industry compared to the income of all other American industries was proportionately higher during the depression years than it had been previously. By cutting wages and paying less for raw materials, newspapers remained relatively stable despite adverse financial conditions. One newspaper reported that operating expenses in 1929 comprised 67 percent of its gross income and in 1932 only accounted for 73 percent of the gross. Evaluating the large, relatively stable and monopolistic newspaper enterprises, Albert McClung Lee noted in 1937:

> Their publishers believe in such old-fashioned catchwords of democracy as "freedom of the press" largely because the price of the chips defines the character and the number of those who can now play the journalistic game.[6]

REPORTERS AND EDITORS

WOMEN IN THE INDUSTRY

Although women made professional strides in the 1920s, during the 1930s when jobs were scarce, employers hired men before women. Women were viewed as second-income earners in a nation without enough jobs to go around. Although in 1920, 11.9 percent of all professionals were women, and by 1930 14.2 percent, by 1940 the percentage dropped to 13.[7] Women doubled their numbers in reporting and editing jobs during the 1920s, representing 24 per cent of the profession or 12,000 women at the end of the decade. During the 1930s, the number of women in journalism grew by only one per cent. Women journalists of the 1920s and 1930s often represented

Women became country editors, as well as city reporters. In 1939 the editor of the Valley News in Brown's Valley, Minnesota collected news items by telephone. (Library of Congress Collection, Farm Security Administration photo)

"firsts:" the first woman to achieve a certain position, or to gain an interview or a privilege. Women still most frequently covered women's issues or worked for society pages. In a study of autobiographies of working women, Donna Born concluded that professional women were compared to men, usually remained single, and rarely mentioned their husbands or children if they were married. Many women journalists were well educated, some at journalism schools, and all that Born studied had wanted to be writers since their childhood days. Although these women confronted special problems in what was then a "man's profession," Born revealed that "none were dissuaded from their professional commitment by such attitudes."[8]

THE AMERICAN NEWSPAPER GUILD

In 1933, the average reporter earned $29.47 each week, according to government figures. Responding to that figure and to deplorable conditions for writers and editors in the newspaper industry, on August 7, 1933, popular syndicated columnist Heywood Broun wrote in the *New York World-Telegram*:

> After some four or five years of holding down the easiest job in the world I hate to see other newspapermen working too hard. It embarrasses me even more to think of newspapermen who are not working at all.

Four months later Heywood Broun became the first president of the American Newspaper Guild as it organized reporters in response to publishers' opposition to the U.S. Wage and Hour Code. Thirty-seven delegates from seventeen cities attended the first convention. Initially the guild represented only the editorial staffs of newspapers, but it soon expanded to include commercial staff as well. In 1936, the guild joined the American Federation of Labor, which later merged with the Congress of Industrial Organizations to become the AFL-CIO. Initially the guild fought for a forty-hour, five-day week, a graded scale of dismissal notices, a minimum wage scale of thirty to thirty-five dollars for men with one year's experience, a minimum number of beginners who could be employed, collective bargaining through outside parties, and an annual vacation of two weeks.

Publishers opposed the movement, and after eight students at Washington and Lee University attempted to form a junior guild chapter in March 1934, publishers and university administrators halted student action. The guild's Committee on Education reported to the 1935 convention:

> There is a tendency among schools of journalism, to a degree, to be

publisher-dominated, either because of endowments from publishers or boards of trustees consisting entirely of publishers. . . .

As a result, journalism students represent a potential reservoir of strikebreakers, existing as a constant menace to the Guilds in the localities of such schools. . . .

Those of us who have attended the schools of journalism are aware of the Horatio Alger philosophy that sometimes pervades them. . . .

The result is that many an immature reporter spends the first years on a newspaper wrestling with his delusions and trying to orientate himself to a situation for which he has not been . . . prepared.[9]

In the summer of 1934, the guild adopted a code of ethics stressing the need for accurate and unbiased news and nonprejudicial reporting of crime news, and opposing the power of privileged groups to withhold news. The code further opposed the printing of publicity items as news, publishing stories that newsmen knew to be false or misleading, accepting money from publicists, and using publisher privilege to influence officials in nonnews-gathering situations. Most publishers agreed with the claim of the trade journal *Editor and Publisher* that editorial departments had grown cynical because of their unsuccessful competition with the business department, and that labor unionism "smacks of class-conscious propaganda."[10] There were significant exceptions among publishers, however, some of whom agreed that publishers had contributed to conditions that allowed the development of a reportorial union or guild.

DEVELOPMENT OF INTERPRETATION

As the hard times of the 1930s replaced the roaring excesses of the 1920s, those who held faith in American democracy were losing some of their naiveté. George Creel's propaganda efforts of World War I shook the journalist's faith in facts, and the growing public-relations industry further indicated that even facts were a matter of interpretation. Furthermore, the reporting of facts had not prepared society for the depression.[11]

THE DOCUMENTARY TRADITION

One method of interpretation, the documentation of emotion rather than information, in an effort to show "man at grips with conditions neither

> **FACTS DO NOT SPONTANEOUSLY TAKE SHAPE**
>
> The development of the publicity man is a clear sign that the facts of modern life do not spontaneously take a shape in which they can be known. They must be given a shape by somebody, and since in the daily routine reporters cannot give a shape to facts, and since there is little disinterested organization of intelligence, the need for some formulation is being met by the interested parties.
>
> SOURCE. Walter Lippman, Public Opinion

permanent nor necessary," appeared worldwide, beginning almost as soon as moving pictures developed technically to a point of providing entertainment for viewers.[12] In the 1920s, the documentary focused on man's interaction with his environment and on an effort to capture the essence of city life. By 1930, political ideology had become a third aspect of the documentary film.[13]

At the beginning of the 1930s in Germany and the Soviet Union, where documentary philosophy was determined by government, technically brilliant films glorified national fervor. In England and the United States, independents, often on the political left, produced most of the documentaries. The Film and Photo League of New York City, for example, documented the inhumanity of evicting people from their homes in a 1934 film, *Sheriff*.[14] As the New Deal progressed, the administration funded documentaries that promoted concepts of conservation and government intervention with Pare Lorentz's production of *The Plow That Broke the Plains* (1936), a report on attempts to alleviate dust bowl conditions for Oklahoma farmers, and *The River* (1937), a documentary of the effects of soil erosion in the Mississippi Basin and the positive effects of the Tennessee Valley Authority, a New Deal reclamation project.[15]

During the 1930s, the documentary tradition became a preferred mode of expression because it appealed to emotion as well as to facts, and informed a generation skeptical of abstract promises who believed "what they saw, touched, handled, and—the crucial word—felt."[16] Practitioners of the new mode included photographers such as Margaret Bourke-White and Dorothea Lange, who photographed American life and working conditions for the Farm Security Administration, as well as other artists employed by the Federal Writers Project and other New Deal agencies and programs. The documentary, wrote cultural historian William Stott, "treats the actual unimagined experience of individuals belonging to a group generally of low economic and social standing in the society (lower than the audience for whom the report is made) and treats this experience in such a way as to try to render it vivid, 'human,' and—most often—poignant to the audience."[17]

Henry Luce, with the development of *Life* magazine in 1936, combined the documentary tradition, the new available technology of the portable camera, the tradition of German picture magazines, and some aspects of 1920s jazz journalism to produce the leader in the realm of the photojournalistic essay.

INTERPRETATION IN THE DAILY PRESS

Interpretation in the daily press, unlike the documentary tradition, was not antithetical to the development of objectivity as a reporting ideal. Interpretation in the newspaper, unlike the documentary, less overtly expressed emotion. Recognizing that the citizenry had not been properly forewarned about World War I or about the advent of the depression, journalists began to discuss the need to put facts into context. Such discussion permeated the academic and the professional communities.

Curtis MacDougall's textbook, *Reporting for Beginners*, first appeared in 1932. When he revised it in 1938, its title changed to *Interpretative Reporting*. MacDougall explained that he changed the title and content because "changing social conditions . . . are causing news gathering and disseminating agencies to change their methods of reporting and interpreting the news." MacDougall wrote that the trend "is unmistakably in the direction of combining the function of interpreter with that of reporter after about a half century during which journalistic ethics called for a strict differentiation between narrator and commenter."[18]

In 1933, the American Society of Newspaper Editors accepted interpretive reporting in a resolution specifying that because world affairs were increasingly complex and because citizens were becoming increasingly interested in public affairs, editors should devote more attention to "explanatory and interpretative news and to presenting a background of information which will enable the average reader more adequately to understand the movement and significance of events."[19]

Michael Schudson, in *Discovering the News*, suggested that journalists responded to the new developments by admitting their subjectivity through signed articles and by developing specialties that would enable them to better interpret facts. Bylines appeared sparingly in the *New York Times* in the 1920s, but were used liberally by the 1930s. The Associated Press, bylining its first story in 1925, soon followed suit. And, while *Journalism Bulletin* in 1924 reported that "Truly the age of specialization is at hand," specialization did not grow significantly until the 1930s.[20]

The acceptance of subjectivity as inevitable did not, however, encourage journalists to abandon objectivity, but rather to view it as an ideal. Schudson explained:

> Journalists came to believe in objectivity, to the extent that they did, because they wanted to, needed to, were forced by ordinary human aspiration to seek escape from their own deep convictions of doubt and drift. . . . Surely, objectivity as an ideal has been used and is still used, even disingenuously, as a camouflage for power. But its source lies deeper, in a need to cover over neither authority nor privilege, but the disappointment in the modern gaze.[21]

THE SIGNED POLITICAL COLUMN

Developing along with the new interest in interpretation was the signed political column. In the 1920s David Lawrence, Mark Sullivan, and Frank Kent began to evaluate worldwide political and economic affairs. Heywood Hale Broun's *New York World* column began appearing in 1921, and Lippmann's "Today and Tomorrow" first appeared in the *Herald Tribune* in 1931. By 1937, Lippmann's column was syndicated in 155 newspapers. *The New Republic* noted in 1937 that "much of the influence once attached to the editorial page has passed over to the columnists."[22]

JOURNALISM OF SYNTHESIS

Another form of interpretation involved a journalism of synthesis, or the interpretive news summary, evidenced by the development of news magazines and by the inclusion of weekly summaries in the daily press. Foremost among the developers of interpretative journalistic summary was Henry Luce, who cofounded *Time* with Briton Hadden in 1923 to summarize information found in the daily press. Luce struggled through financial gains and losses during the 1920s, but by the 1930s *Time* was an established financial success.

Luce edged out some competitors, such as *Literary Digest*, but encouraged others, such as *Newsweek*, founded in 1933, and *U.S. News and World Report*, which grew out of the *United States Daily* (1926 to 1933) and other David Lawrence publications. *Business Week*, also a depression baby, was founded in 1929 by McGraw-Hill Publishing Co. *Reader's Digest*, founded in 1922 as a synthesis of articles from other magazines, also flourished in the 1930s.

Dailies followed the lead of Luce and of *Time*, introducing weekend news summaries. In 1931, the *New York Sun* began a Saturday review of the news; the *Richmond News Leader* replaced its Saturday editorial page with an interpretive summary, and in 1935, the *New York Times* began an interpretive Sunday news summary. The Associated Press responded to the development with a weekend review of its own.[23]

USE OF MEDIA POLLS

Although by the late nineteenth century major political parties used canvassing widely to determine party allegiances, advances in the 1930s brought refined methods for gathering statistics and refining mathematical techniques. The first efforts to sample opinions of the general population were made by newspapers in the 1840s to predict the outcome of elections, but not until 1896 did polls become serious business. During that year the Chicago press, greatly concerned with the McKinley-Bryan race, sent reporters to sample various segments of the population. The *Chicago Tribune* determined that McKinley was the choice of 82 percent of the factory hands and 86 percent of the railroaders. The *Chicago Record* mailed postcard ballots to all 328,000 registered voters in Chicago and one voter in eight in twelve midwestern States. The *Record* employed mathematicians to analyze the 250,000 return cards, predicting McKinley would win 57.94 percent of the Chicago vote. Although the prediction was close to the actual Chicago results, the team failed to determine vote percentages in other states.

Newspapers continued their flirtation with polling, and by 1912 a syndicate led by the *Chicago Record-Herald* and the *New York Herald* conducted presidential polls in every state. The Hearst chain polled forty-six states in 1928 and predicted Hoover's win with reasonable accuracy. The *Literary Digest* conducted presidential election polls from 1916 to 1936. Their sample, based on mailings to potential subscribers, then to the public at large, provided reasonably accurate predictions until the Landon-Roosevelt contest of 1936. As a cost-saving measure during the depression, the *Digest* relied on its 1932 mailing list, and failed to correct its interpretation of results based on Landon supporters having a much higher rate of response than Roosevelt supporters. The disastrous prediction that Landon would win led many to discount the validity of mail questionnaires.

Despite the *Literary Digest* disaster, however, refinements in the understanding of random sampling techniques and the need for advertisers to determine consumer preferences led researchers to continue to develop polling strategies. A reawakening of interest in shifting party membership during the New Deal furthered the cause of polling. George Gallup, Archibald Crossley, and Elmo Roper instituted the modern attitudinal polls in 1935. Roosevelt, intrigued with the concept and pleased that the polls had accurately predicted his 1936 landslide, employed Hadley Cantril, a pollster, to help him time his foreign and domestic policy announcements to appeal to public opinion. The industry flourished until every major pollster and political commentator predicted Thomas Dewey would defeat Harry Truman in 1948. From then until the 1960s pollsters relied on answering commercial questions to sustain their incomes. In the 1960s, as politicians began to solicit their own secret polls to assist in developing political campaigns, pollsters again moved into the public arena.[24]

CRITICISM AND ALTERNATIVES

With the continuation of the Hearst empire and other newspaper chains and the formation of new dominant companies such as Time, Inc., publishers faced continuing charges by critics in the field and from without. Franklin Delano Roosevelt claimed 85 percent of the press opposed him, and blamed the owners of the papers, not the reporters. Socialist and communist publications flourished, and social-movement newspapers such as the *Catholic Worker* challenged the daily press's interpretation of the depression and Roosevelt policies. Although an increasing percentage of newspapers claimed political independence, publishers such as Robert McCormick of the *Chicago Tribune*, William Randolph Hearst, and Henry Luce of Time, Inc., held definite political beliefs and did not hesitate to imbue their newspapers and magazines with their ideologies.

George Seldes, a well-known, successful reporter during World War I for the *Chicago Tribune*, launched bitter attacks on what he termed the monopolistic press. His books *Freedom of the Press* (1935) and *Lords of the Press* (1938), although ignored by many newspaper publishers, became best-sellers. From 1940 to 1950, he published *In Fact*, a newspaper funded through subscriptions only. Seldes refused advertising on the basis that it threatened press freedom as much as did government. Seldes later was accused of fronting for the Communist party, although he claimed he did not know the money given to him by his acquaintance Bruce Minton, a contributor to *New Republic*, had been provided by the Communist party. Minton severed his relationship with Seldes after a year because he could not control the editorial content of *In Fact*, nor could he persuade Seldes to run communist political commentary. During the McCarthy years Seldes was cleared of charges of conspiring with the Communist party.[25]

Seldes urged development of codes of ethics and pleaded with journalism schools and the Newspaper Guild to pave the way. He denounced the publishers' criticism of the New Deal, chided them for ignoring research that indicated smoking was harmful to health while cultivating tobacco industry advertisers, and labeled the American Newspaper Publishers Association the "house of lords." Seldes also claimed the great press lords such as Hearst, Chandler, and Gannett were "in bed with business in almost all respects and are using their papers mainly to advance the commercial and political interests of themselves and their cronies."[26]

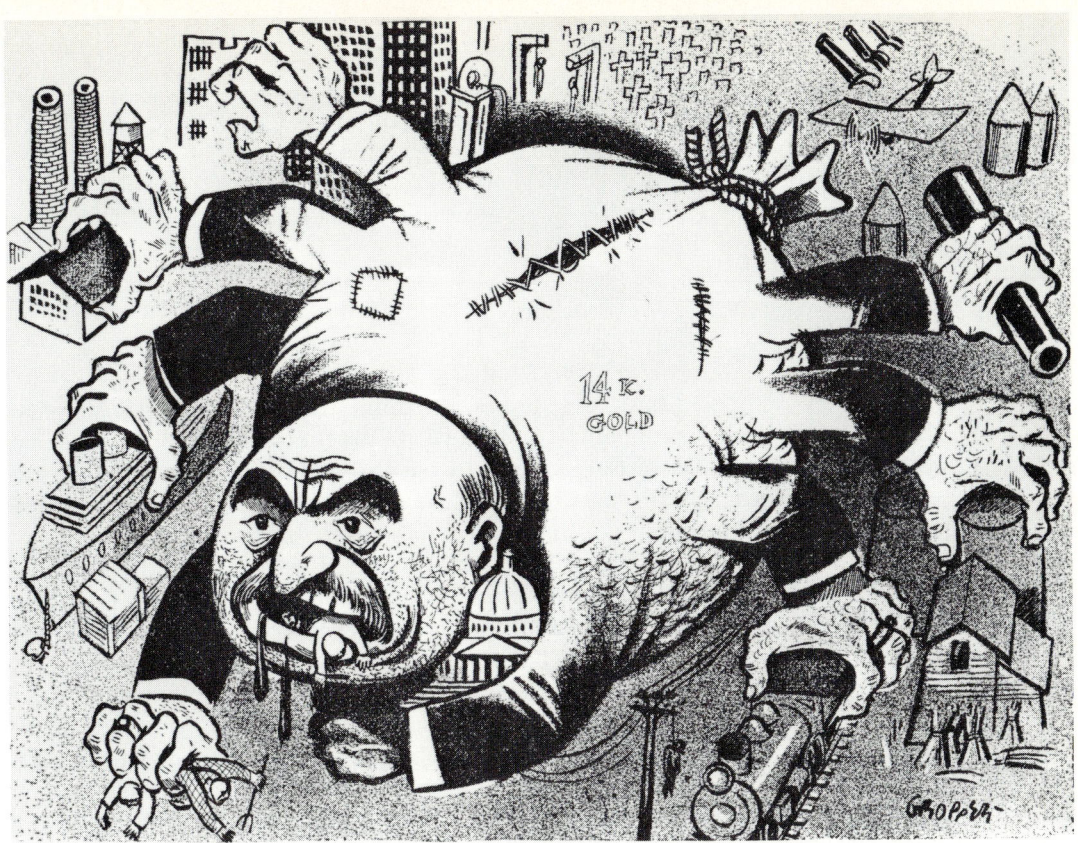

This lithograph by William Gropper in the June 1933 New Masses *caricatured the capitalist as an eight-armed monster grasping everything in sight. The cartoon was titled, "Business Is Picking Up." (Library of Congress Collection)*

ELECTRONIC MEDIA

RADIO

The 1930s was the first of two decades of what some termed the Golden Age of Radio. After a successful battle with newspapers to secure information from the wire services and development of worldwide transmission, radio networks began their own news-gathering organizations and news programming. Sponsored programming in drama, music, and comedy brought elite and popular culture into American homes. Franklin Delano Roosevelt bypassed the comment of hostile newspaper editors, explaining his policies on radio in "Fireside Chats" to a population besieged by the depression. Structurally, the networks consolidated their control of the industry, while turning over much of the programming to agencies that developed programs and negotiated with advertisers to sponsor them. The alliance between industry and government was solidified with the creation of the Federal Communications Commission and the passing of the 1934 Federal Communications Act.

The Federal Communications Act

The Radio Act of 1927 assigned the responsibility for allocating licensing "in the public interest, convenience or necessity," to the seven-member Federal Radio Commission. Despite arguments by educational broadcasters during the ensuing years that radio had become too commercial, in 1934 Congress granted commercial users continued dominance of the medium through the Federal Communications Act. Congress also added telegraph and telephone matters to the agency's responsibilities.[27] The commission did not have the power to censor content, but it did have the power to consider a station's past performance when renewing a license. Although the FCC revoked few licenses over the years, critics argued that the threat of license denial could limit the diversity of program content. Broadcasters clearly did not have the same far-reaching range of freedom of expression that was granted to print media.

Section 315 of the act granted equal time to political candidates, requiring each station that allows any candidate for public office to use its broadcast station to "afford equal opportunities to all other such candidates for that office in the use of such broadcasting station. . . ." Section 315 also denied broadcasters the opportunity to censor material presented by a candidate.

Radio News

By the 1930s, radio was a worldwide force. The capacity for worldwide transmission of radio programs was clear in 1929 when Admiral Richard Byrd transmitted news of his Arctic expedition to Schenectady, New York, and when a symphony concert performed in Queen's Hall in London was heard clearly in the United States. The development of shortwave broadcasting by governments, commercial interests and the networks contributed quickly to establishment of transmitters in world capitals and to the concept of radio news.[28] Radio news, at first mere news bulletins built on a pattern of print news, began to feature talks by politicians or cultural figures. Panel discussions and news commentary successfully won audiences by mid-decade.

The development of news broadcasts put fear in the hearts of newspaper owners and editors, resulting in a press-radio war during the early 1930s. From 1931 to 1934, newspapers successfully prohibited networks from ob-

Modern technology presented stark contrast to the country weeklies of 1939. This Virginia City, Montana newspaper was one of the first in the state. (Library of Congress Collection)

taining wire-service copy. But such reactionary activity on the part of newspapers merely spearheaded development of news departments at both NBC and CBS. Associated Press, an organization dominated and led by newspaper publishers, led the battle against radio news. In 1931, the American Newspaper Publishers Association passed a resolution calling for control of radio news, and at the 1932 national political conventions radio and newspapers confronted each other directly. When United Press decided to provide CBS with election returns, AP agreed as well, not knowing that UP, fearing the consequences of its action, would back out at the last minute. A third wire service, International News Service (INS), also installed teletype, resulting in service to CBS from three wire services. After the election, UP and INS continued to sell to broadcasters, but AP refused to serve the networks. In 1933, AP made its reluctance official and passed a specific resolution not to sell news to radio. The organization also pressured influential clients of UP and INS to refrain from servicing the networks.

CBS reacted by creating its own news bureau with 800 stringers. In 1933, David Sarnoff of NBC's parent company, RCA, NBC president M. H. Aylesworth, and CBS's William S. Paley sought a peace treaty with the newspapers and wire services. A December 1933 agreement required that networks and stations stop gathering news on their own and limit the times and amount of news. The decision of the networks not to gather news was short-lived. In 1934, competition from a new service, Transradio Press, offered news from the wire agency Havas in France and England's Reuters, as well as providing domestic news. By the end of 1934, Transradio had 150 clients. Fear of competition from Transradio and other independent services drove the wire services to service the new medium, despite publishers' opposition.[29] Radio broadcasts now brought news from Japan, speeches of Adolf Hitler, and news about the 1938 Nazi occupation of Austria into American homes.

Radio was viewed as a flexible and innovative medium. Initiated as a device for advertising *Time* magazine, a pseudodocumentary radio program, "March of Time," popularized news events by using actors to recreate events in various formats. The show appeared on both CBS and NBC and varied from a fifteen-to-thirty-minute format. Production required the work of seventy-five staff members and 1,000 hours of labor to get each issue on the air. One of America's most popular radio shows, "March of Time," was on air from 1931 to 1945, immortalizing the expression, "Time—Marches On!" Initially Time, Inc., funded the program, but after 1932 it gained sponsors and network support.

Radio and Popular Culture

News was only a small part of radio's impact on society. One impact was definitely commercial. Radio programs were produced primarily by advertising agencies, and by 1932, more time was spent on commercials than on news, education, lectures, and religion combined.

In the 1930s, the various genres already recognized in literature ascended to the microphone. Comedy, detective stories, westerns, and melodramas crossed the air waves during the evening programming hours. Radio heroes demonstrated the American values of truth, justice, and good. Major Bowes' Original Amateur Hour started the amateur craze in 1934 and contests proliferated throughout the decade. Lux Radio Theatre showcased Broadway stars. On October 30, 1938, Orson Welles's dramatization of "War of the Worlds" concretely demonstrated that American people listened to and believed in radio. Welles had planned the radio script of H.G. Wells's novel about Martians arriving on the shores of the United States as a Halloween trick, but Welles's use of journalistic techniques convinced many listeners that the invasion was real. Although popular accounts depicted listeners who panicked as they waited for the arriving aliens, Hadley Cantril's Princeton University Study indicated that only about one-sixth of the listeners actually were frightened by what they thought was a news program.[30]

NEWSREELS

Newsreels made their debut in 1910 and, like the documentary film, were a worldwide phenomenon. Issued weekly or semiweekly, they momentarily overshadowed the documentary film, but they differed from the documentary in that facts generally were selected for their currency and social significance.[31] During World War I, newsreels were used in the Soviet Union to "unite people by keeping them informed of the ups and downs of agonizing struggle." They also were used in the period following the war to promote Soviet ideology.[32] In the United States, newsreels were first produced by independents commenting on social ills. From 1930 to 1932 the National Film and Photo League organized a "Workers Newsreel," which documented the National Hunger March of December 1932. Later in the decade, the major movie studios dominated newsreel production, discouraged creativity and controversy, but continued to produce the expensive 10-minute capsules of major events because movie audiences liked and expected them.[33]

As a spin-off from the radio program, "March of Time," newsreels began in 1934 and represented the development of motion picture journalism. The newsreels, journalistically suspect because they included "faked" situations and footage, nevertheless dealt with controversial subjects. A. William Bluem, student of the documentary, wrote that the "March of Time" "stretched the limits of journalism by implicitly arguing that the picture as well as the word was, after all, only symbolic of reality. What mattered was not whether pictorial journalism displayed facts, but whether, within the conscience of the reporter, it faithfully reflected the facts."[34]

"March of Time" satirized "Share the Wealth" Louisiana politician Huey Long, commented on development of the Soviet state, and depicted an impersonation of Adolf Hitler. Never a profit-maker, "March of Time" was abandoned in 1951. Shortly before the demise of the program, *New York Times* critic Bosley Crowther wrote on July 15:

> More than a sentimental sadness over the passing of a cinematic friend will be felt by those toilers in the vineyards who have sweat blood over documentary films. For to them, no matter how they may have snickered at the series' recognized conventional form, the March of Time has stood up as a symbol of real accomplishment in the "pictorial journalism" field.[35]

The death of "March of Time" represented a general decline in the newsreel business. As newsreels began to be overshadowed by television, Warner Brothers, Paramount, Fox, and MGM discontinued their newsreel operations.[36]

MOTION PICTURES

The movie industry was not immune from the depression. Company profits plummeted, with Warner Brothers losing $14 million in 1932 and Paramount losing nearly $16 million, resulting in bankruptcy the following year.[37] In addition, special interests pressured the industry to conform to specified standards of morality.

Various cities and states set up censorship boards as early as 1907 to combat what some citizens considered to be immoral influences. By the early 1920s, with Hollywood scandals erupting, such as the drug-induced death of Wallace Reid and the murder of director William Desmond Taylor, the industry organized the Motion Picture Producers and Distributors of America (MPPDA), naming Will H. Hays as its president. In 1934, a group of Catholic Church bishops formed the National Legion of Decency to warn Catholics against objectionable films. Hollywood responded by enforcing its production code, requiring a seal of approval on each film. Violators paid a $25,000 fine. The code forbade sex, excessive violence, and vulgar language. The system remained in effect until 1968, when the industry adopted the present ratings designating intended audiences.

Gangster films, complete with morals that crime doesn't pay, gained popularity in the 1930s and avoided the censor's pencil. Producers emphasized the American success story and environmental causes that explained the rise of gangsters. The "suffering proletariat" appeared often in the gangster films:

> The gangster is the man of the city, with the city's language and knowledge, with its queer and dishonest skills and its terrible daring, carrying his life in his hands like a placard, like a club. . . . It is not the real city, but that dangerous and sad city of the imagination which is so much more important, which is the modern world.[38]

Fred Astaire and Ginger Rogers set a standard for dance musicals, making nine films for RKO during the 1930s. "Screwball" comedies and American success stories were other popular genres.

Shirley Temple, a child star, performed in a variety of box-office hit comedies. In 1932 and 1933, she appeared in *Baby Burlesk,* a series of one-reel

These movie advertisements encouraged the citizens of Harrin, Illinois, to attend the movies in 1939. (Library of Congress Collection, Farm Security Administration photo)

comedies. The song-and-dance number, "Baby Take a Bow," included in her first full-length musical, *Stand Up and Cheer*, of 1934 made her a star. That same year she received a special Oscar, and from 1935 to 1938 she remained the nation's top box office star. In 1938, she made $307,014, reportedly more than the president of General Motors. She earned $5 million before she reached her teens. "I class myself with Rin Tin Tin," she told a *Parade* reporter in 1986. "People in the Depression wanted something to cheer them up, and they fell in love with a dog and a little girl."[39]

Film-maker Frank Capra mastered the American success movie style in "It Happened One Night" (1934) and "Mr. Smith Goes to Washington" (1939). "The movies are energetic, irreverent poems to a civics-lesson America," wrote Louis Gianetti. "Evil is usually represented by one nasty banker or politician; once he is vanquished, the way is clear for the triumph of decency. Capra's world is a middle-class one of marriage, family, the neighborhood—all very much springing from nineteenth century archetypes." Capra's message of depression-era moviegoers was "stand up, stick your chest out, fight for what you know is right."[40]

In 1940, John Steinbeck's *The Grapes of Wrath* portrayed the depression-poor Joad family making the trek to California after losing their Oklahoma land. The characters reflected the despair of much of the farming community: "It's not ownin' it. It's bein' born on it, and livin' on it, and dyin' on it. That's what makes it your'n."[41]

The movie industry battled the Justice Department at the end of the 1930s, when in 1938 the government filed suit against all eight movie companies for restraint of trade. Two years later the department obtained a consent decree against five companies. They agreed to limit block booking, blind booking, and other coercive tactics directed at theatre owners. Disputes among workers and actors over wages led to a revived Screen Writers Guild and Screen Actors Guild by the end of the decade.

THE PRESIDENT AND THE PRESS

Although the art of criticizing government or personalities within government was the province of journalists from colonial days, the news media faced new challenges of dealing with bureaucracy in the mid-twentieth century. Furthermore, broadcasting exacted new governmental regulation that strictly departed from print standards.

William McKinley, during his presidential years of 1897–1901, was the first president to regularly attempt to control the flow of information from the White House to Washington correspondents. Under Theodore Roosevelt, from 1901 to 1909, Gifford Pinchot, chief of the U.S. Forest Service from 1898 to 1910 and Roosevelt's adviser, was particularly adept at encouraging newspapers to cover conservation activities. Pinchot, who like many Progressives, believed informed readers would make informed decisions, established one of the first press bureaus in an executive branch agency. He directed production of hundreds of publicity pamphlets, newspaper and magazine articles, interviews, lecture tours, traveling exhibits, all designed to increase public awareness of conservation policy and to further Roosevelt's conservation policies. Pinchot's policies were considered progressive in that they attempted to spread information about conservation and they valued the importance of public opinion.[42] Although McKinley was interested primarily in gaining favorable recognition of his foreign policy, Theodore Roosevelt used similar methods and his magnetic personality to curry favor for his domestic policies. William Howard Taft, on the other hand, spent four years ignoring, and therefore alienating, the press. However, Woodrow Wilson, elected in 1912, renewed Roosevelt's practices and instituted regularly scheduled press conferences.[43]

George Creel's activities during World War I furthered government's role in news management and at the 1919 Paris Peace Conference, President

Woodrow Wilson's aide, former muckraker Ray Stannard Baker, was dismayed to discover the Paris negotiations would be made in secret. Although Baker did not object to governments keeping some of the details from the public, he saw no reason to keep them secret from the press:

> It had been proved over and over again, that no group of men can be more fully trusted to keep a confidence or use it wisely than a group of experienced newspaper correspondents—if they are honestly informed and trusted in the first place.[44]

Michael Schudson suggested that Baker's protest and the continued concern over publicity during the Paris peace talks signified a new relationship between government and the press. "For the first time in the history of American foreign policy," wrote Schudson, "political debate at home concerned not only the substance of decisions the government made but also the ways in which the government made decisions."[45] The press also considered itself, as is apparent in Baker's comments, as separate from the rest of the public and deserving of additional information.

By the 1920s, regular correspondents often gathered news in Washington from official handouts or briefings. But perfection of government use of the media remained in the hands of Franklin Delano Roosevelt, who believed that information was the key to unlock support of his New Deal policies. Roosevelt wisely hired advisors who were familiar with the press, including Louis Howe, former reporter for the *New York Herald*, Marcus McIntyre, former city editor of the *Washington Times*, and Stephen T. Early, a former Associated Press reporter and Paramount newsreel executive. These former newsmen maintained a high level of credibility with the press, and close relationships with the president, which allowed them during the early years of the depression to circumvent what might have been a more adversarial relationship. Roosevelt's style of keeping open a constant channel of news flow differed so dramatically from Hoover's self-isolation during the last days of his presidency that the press found news-gathering an easy and enjoyable task. Further, both Early, as the press secretary, and Roosevelt provided information on-the-record, rather than forcing reporters to rely on unnamed sources.[46]

For the most part, reporters participated in news management. Their treatment of Roosevelt, for example, showed their continuing willingness to withhold information from the public if only they were allowed to share in the power. The nation's press photographers continuously presented Roosevelt as a strong and vigorous president, despite the fact he was crippled as a result of polio. Through his press secretary and with the help of the Secret Service, Roosevelt managed to control photographers, who agreed not to photograph his wheelchair and other equipment relating to the disease.[47]

However, Roosevelt demanded a high degree of loyalty, tolerating little

This photo indicates the government's effort to encourage Americans to help themselves during the depression. This segment of a Farm Security Administration filmstrip was captioned, "You can do your part by growing and storing your own food and raising a surplus to sell. Ask your farm and home supervisors how you can do the most—in your own home and on your own farm—to help in the war." (Library of Congress Collection, Farm Security Administration photo)

criticism, and reporters soon became suspicious of government news management, recognizing that information not delivered through the president's well-managed office was information suppressed. Further, reporters were ill equipped to understand the economic news of the 1930s, and relied heavily on the president's often condescending explanations. Roosevelt also violated his early policy of not offering exclusive information to specific reporters, and he often tried to acquire favorable publicity by granting favors to individual newsmen.

By 1936, Roosevelt, who claimed that 85 percent of the press opposed him, focused his criticism on publishers, who he claimed were motivated solely by selfish concerns. After his overwhelming victory in 1936, he turned to the radio as a preferred medium for conveying his individual message to the nation.

Broadcasters, constantly aware of their vulnerability to government regulation, cooperated fully with Roosevelt's desired use of radio. The networks extended public-service time to the administration, broadcasting not only Roosevelt's "Fireside Chats," but political education programs as well. By March 1936, at least three government agencies had dramatic radio programs on the air. Broadcasters elected not to comment on administration policy and therefore to avoid incurring the same wrath Roosevelt directed at the newspaper press.

Also adept at relationships with the press, Eleanor Roosevelt instituted press conferences for women only. The press conferences assured coverage of Mrs. Roosevelt and her family on the women's pages of newspapers, and, because men were excluded, motivated editors to hire women. These efforts contributed to the expansion of women reporters in the capital during World War II. In 1933, only nineteen women were allowed in the congressional press galleries. By the end of 1942, sixty-one women were admitted.[48]

INDIVIDUALS, INNOVATION, AND CRITICISM

Five individuals, Henry Luce, Ralph Ingersoll, Margaret Bourke-White, Robert McCormick, and Dorothy Day, represent many of the intricate conflicts involving the press, the government, and the social issues of the 1930s. Although they certainly are not the only important individuals in the press at the time, nor necessarily significant out of context, their professional choices explain various ways individuals reacted to, participated in, and were affected by the decade of the 1930s. Luce, with his rapidly expanding publications, represented innovation and a nationalistic ideology; Ralph Ingersoll, who became dissatisfied with his work under Luce, started a new paper, *PM*, designed to escape the pressure of advertising and to incorporate the new ideals of interpretation. Working for both of them was Margaret Bourke-White, a pioneer in photojournalism, who photographed industry as architecture, who portrayed the people of the depression, who traveled to the Soviet Union, and who was unrelentingly investigated by J. Edgar Hoover's Federal Bureau of Investigation. Robert McCormick espoused nationalism and opposed the growing strength of the labor movement. Dorothy Day flirted with communism and socialism as alternatives to a capitalistic system that seemingly had failed, and then turned to the Catholic Worker movement and developed a long-continuing newspaper, the *Catholic Worker*, to promote individual efforts to relieve the oppressed and to champion pacifism through World War II, the Korean Conflict, and Vietnam.

HENRY LUCE

Henry Luce, who with Briton Hadden had successfully introduced *Time* in March 1923, hardly noticed the depression, introducing in February 1930 his new business magazine *Fortune*, which lauded the business manager-tycoon, and enjoying company profits in 1932 (*Time* and *Fortune*) of $650,000 after taxes. His photojournalism magazine, *Life*, founded in November 1936, initially lost $6 million, but eventually produced enormous profits.

Luce never forgot that he was born in China. He lived there for fourteen years after his birth in 1898, attending a British boarding school at Chefoo on the Shantung north coast, where he was editor-in-chief of the school paper. In 1912, he went to England to attend St. Albans, and then to the Hotchkiss School in Connecticut. He and a classmate at Hotchkiss, Briton Hadden, attended Yale together and competed for positions on the *Yale Daily News*. Luce's experience in China as the son of Presbyterian missionaries and his schooling among the upper classes of England and the United States influenced his attitude toward the necessity of an elite and what he believed to be the proper role of the elite in government. He detested communists even while at Yale, believing in the concept of a "morally superior America."[49]

After a year of study at Oxford and a stint on the *Chicago Daily News*, Luce rejoined his friend Hadden in February 1922 to develop a news magazine that would compete with the *Literary Digest*. By October, primarily through their Yale contacts, the two raised $86,000 to start *Time*, and the first issue appeared March 3, 1923. Giving the news a "jaunty personal point of view," Hadden and Luce sold only 9,000 copies of the first twenty-eight-page issue, which was far below their expectations of 25,000.[50] The magazine remained in the red until 1927.

Luce and Hadden noted in their prospectus that no editorial page would appear in *Time* and that no article would be written to prove a special case, but that the editors recognized

> that complete neutrality on public questions and important news is probably as undesirable as it is impossible, and are therefore ready to acknowledge certain prejudices which may in varying measure predetermine their opinions on the news.

The prejudices they listed indicated a distrust of increasing government authority and expenditures, a respect for old manners and an admiration for the "statesman's 'view of the world.'"[51] Luce and Hadden continued their competitive friendship until Hadden's death at thirty-one in 1928. After his death, Luce and his associates bought enough shares from Hadden's estate firmly to control Time, Inc.

Time introduced a condensed, telegraphic style that challenged the stodgy papers being written for the upper middle class. Luce instructed editors to write stories with a beginning, a middle and an ending, and to avoid the common inverted pyramid style newspapers had adopted.[52]

Time became famous—or infamous—for its language, dubbed Timestyle. Trick words and inverted sentence structure produced a sarcastic, gossipy tone which, although popular with its audience, also produced its share of critics. T. S. Matthews, a rising editor at *Time* who had worked for the *New Republic*, compared the two magazines:

> The contrast felt between the New Republic and Time was a contrast between scholarly, distinguished men and smart, ignorant boys. The New Republic didn't exist primarily to call attention to itself; it had the nobler motive (or so it seemed to me) of trying to recall Americans to their better senses.

Matthews later called *Time* a "strutting little venture" whose style was a "ludicrous, exhibitionistic but arresting dialect of journalese."[53] The magazine was criticized for its sense of omniscience because the magazine relied less on authority figures for quotes and spoke its own mind, despite the fact that it was often wrong. *Time*, for example, predicted that Hitler would not come to power in Germany.[54]

Time was directed toward an upper-middle-class, male audience. A 1931 survey of readers in Appleton, Wisconsin, showed that 60 percent of *Time* readers had an average annual income of $5,000 or more. The average *Time* family income was $21,000. In 1929, nationwide only one percent of all families earned $10,000 or more, and the average income was $2,335. Advertising in *Time* promoted the expensive hotels and private schools available only to upper middle classes. More bankers read *Time* than any other magazine. Although three out of eight college students were women in 1922, the *Time* prospectus, content, and advertising specifically targeted men. Further, Luce hired women only as researchers, who checked facts, not as writers.[55]

In the last issue of *Time* before Black Thursday Luce introduced *Fortune* in a three-page announcement. The monthly would sell at one dollar a copy or ten dollars a year and be produced not by businessmen, but by a staff of amateurs, many drawn from Luce's colleagues at Yale. The first 184-page issue sold in February 1930 to 30,000 subscribers. The magazine was a success, and in 1932, in the midst of the depression, Time, Inc., showed profits of $650,000 after taxes. The magazine lauded the manager of business, but with writers such as Dwight Macdonald, the poet Archibald MacLeish, and the now legendary film critic and novelist, James Agee, *Fortune* expressed skepticism about business, explored the documentary expression popular in the 1930s, and avoided the reactionary tone of other business magazines.⁵⁶ In 1932, Luce bought *Architectural Forum*, which he kept for more than thirty years, although it never made a profit.

While busily at work, Luce fell in love with Clare Boothe Brokaw and divorced his wife Lila in 1935, a fact not mentioned in *Time*, although divorces of the social elite were usually fair game for its columns. Clare Boothe Luce, a playwright, later was elected to Congress and became ambassador to Italy, and her newsworthy plays and speeches often posed a dilemma for Luce editors. Although Luce edited reviews of the plays and some of the coverage of her congressional activities, he played his hand much less heavily than did William Randolph Hearst with his longtime companion Marion Davies.

Life

Luce's next great venture in the magazine world was the introduction of the photojournalistic magazine, *Life*, which incorporated technical and editorial developments of European and American magazines preceding it.

Editors experimented with the use of photographs as early as 1855 with *Frank Leslie's Illustrated Newspaper* and its competitor (1857) *Harper's Weekly*. But technology necessitated the redrawing of photographs, which then were made into woodcuts. In 1880, as technology arrived to permit the reproduction of halftones from a printing press, the *New York Daily Graphic* quickly included such photographs in its makeup. But it was not until the development of the rotogravure press in Germany and the Leica camera after the turn of the century that photographic capturing of images and reproduction reached the kind of quality that allowed a true "picture" magazine. One of the first of these on the American side of the Atlantic to be produced was the *New York Times* weekly rotogravure magazine, the *Mid-Week Pictorial*, which presented photographs of World War I. The magazine lasted until 1937. It adopted a photojournalistic format, integrating pictures and text, hired staff photographers, and imitated German picture magazines.⁵⁷ The German Leica introduced portability, allowing photographers to shoot thirty-six frames before reloading, offering a greater depth of field, and permitting indoor shots without flash. Although dailies resisted the new technology and issued their photographers Speed Graphics or Graphlexes, which required changing film after each shot, Luce capitalized on the new possibilities in creating a magazine based on the candid photograph and the photojournalistic essay.⁵⁸

Building on that tradition and imitating German magazines, particularly the picture magazine *BIZ*, *Life* relied heavily on agency photographers, and its relationship with the Black Star Picture Agency, as well as others, shaped its development as a photojournalistic magazine. Ernest Mayer, who started the Black Star Picture Agency in 1936, had directed a Berlin agency that published books and sold photographs to German magazines such as *BIZ* and *Munchner Illustrierte Presse*. Mayer's special talent was generating photographic essay ideas by clipping stories from regional newspapers. When Hitler came to power in 1933, Mayer and his Jewish associates were "excluded from all professions exerting an influence over German cultural life . . . [including] theater, films, radio, literature, and the arts . . . and—most important of all—the press."[59] Mayer, who already had a number of U.S. contacts, emigrated in November 1935, when he was 42, a few months before he started the Black Star Picture Agency.

The agency became an important component in the development of *Life*, which in its second year of operation had only ten staff photographers while printing about 200 pictures per weekly issue. Eight months before *Life* was published, Black Star signed a contract to supply photographs and photo essays for Time, Inc. Some of these appeared in *Time* magazine before *Life* began in November 1936. Time, Inc., also received first refusal on all pictures imported by Black Star. Many agency photographers ultimately became *Life* staff photographers, and by 1952 more than a quarter of *Life*'s photographers were 1930–1940 emigres from Europe; half of those had been associated with Black Star.[60] *Life* was important to Black Star as well, comprising about a quarter of the agency's sales during the late thirties. Other magazines in the U.S. used photographs, but few showed interest in the photojournalism essay.

Life was instantly successful, selling 435,000 copies of the first issue and achieving a circulation of 760,000 by January 1937. Luce had pegged the advertising rates too low, however, and maintaining the high quality and massive circulation was an expensive endeavor. At first the magazine lost $3 million per year, but by 1939 the magazine broke into the black.[61]

The Cowles family of Des Moines, Iowa, challenged *Life* with the introduction of *Look* in January 1937, but *Life*'s headstart, its higher quality of paper and production and its more serious tone carried it past the competition. But *Life* was not entirely a serious magazine. Although Margaret Bourke-White's photojournalistic essay on Muncie, Indiana, turned the Lynd's classic sociological study, "Middletown," into a "real" town, *Life* also captured the more frivolous sides of life with articles such as "How to Undress for Your Husband."[62]

Luce Politics

Although Luce was widely regarded as the nation's most powerful publisher during the late 1930s, throughout World War II and during the Cold War, his influence probably was overrated. His magazines appealed largely to the upper middle class and never achieved working-class circulation such as did the *Saturday Evening Post*. Although Luce believed in a morally superior America, he publicized American foreign policy more than he created it.[63]

Luce had actively opposed communism from the beginning of the Bolshevik Revolution in 1917. He abhorred the doctrine because it was antireligious, opposed businessmen like himself, destroyed the aristocracy in Russia, and spread throughout his beloved China. In the late 1920s and early 1930s, Luce, like many business leaders and intellectuals, found himself admiring the fascist regime of Italy's Benito Mussolini. In 1928, Luce termed Mussolini the "outstanding national moral leader in the world today."[64]

Laird S. Goldsborough, *Time*'s foreign news editor, drew fire from other *Time* staffers for his support of Franco's ultimately successful attempt to take over Spain. Goldsborough referred to Franco's armies as the "Whites," and to the "Loyalists," or the soldiers of the constitutional government of Spain, as the "Reds." Such a position was contrary to that of many of the expatriate writers such as Ernest Hemingway, who traveled to Spain to defend the Loyalists against inroads of fascism. Although Luce, after much opposition to Goldsborough by the staff, removed him as foreign news editor, in 1944 he appointed Whittaker Chambers to the same position. Chambers was known as a former Communist party member who was so anti-communist that *Time* editors were careful not to let him review books on the subject. Chambers is best known for his testimony in the 1950s against Alger Hiss before the House Un-American Activities Committee.

Luce's foreign news may have been most biased in relationship to China. A strong supporter of Chiang Kai-Shek, Luce introduced Madame Chiang to the American public, arranging a major press tour for her in 1942, and her face graced the cover of *Time*. Luce assisted relief organizations in forming United China Relief, and pressured Roosevelt and other influential leaders to continue military aid to China. His magazines failed to recognize the lack of support for Chiang in his own country. In regard to America's foreign policy in China, Luce was out of step with most prestigious U.S. publishers. Although the Hearst and Scripps chains and Robert McCormick's *Chicago Tribune* agreed with him, most columnists, radio commentators and the *New York Herald Tribune* agreed that Chiang's position was hopeless.[65]

By 1944, Luce's empire included *Time*, with a weekly circulation of 1,160,000; *Life*, with a domestic circulation of 4 million and foreign circulation of 317,000; *Fortune* with a weekly circulation of 170,000; *Architectural Forum* with a circulation of 40,000; radio's "March of Time", broadcast to as many as 18 million U.S. citizens over the NBC Blue Network, of which Luce owned 12.5 percent interest; a daily radio program, "Time Views the News;" and the "March of Time" newsreels which appeared every four weeks in American and Foreign theatres.[66]

During the years that followed World War II, Luce's ideological biases filtered through his publications to a greater extent than they had prior to the war. He viewed the twentieth century as the American Century and attempted to export America's liberties, institutions, and expertise. Although in the early 1940s Luce praised the Soviet Union for carrying the burden of war and for its economic progress, by 1946 *Life* adamantly warned its readers of Soviet aggression, and Luce's prominent cold war stance during the 1950s earned him the reputation of an ideologue.

PM AND RALPH INGERSOLL

Many of the conflicts of the depression years were reflected in the high expectations and the quick demise that characterized *PM*, a New York tabloid newspaper with a magazine format. The newspaper, which began in 1939, was to exclude advertising and rely on subscriptions as a financial base, thus eliminating any possibility of being influenced by advertisers. Such an idea, which today might seem radical to media business magnates, was supported by seventeen of America's major businessmen and women. People such as Chicago department store owner Marshall Field and Sears and Roebuck heirs William and Lessing Rosenwald invested substantial amounts in the experiment. The staffing of the newspaper included professionals from other publications and a variety of nonprofessionals, who argued extensively about the relative merits of capitalism and communism. The first issue benefited from extensive publicity, but *PM* failed partly because of poor business management and ideological conflict among staff members.

PM, begun by veteran magazine man Ralph Ingersoll, experimented not only in form and content, but in the underlying assumptions of how a newspaper or magazine would be financed. *PM* was designed to avoid sensationalism common to tabloids of the thirties, featured compartmentalized news, and was financed through subscription. Ingersoll set up a permanent research staff and covered new beats such as labor, food, radio, and modern living.

Ingersoll began his career as a cub reporter for Hearst's *New York American* in 1923 and soon became managing editor of *The New Yorker*. He moved to *Fortune* as managing editor and then became general manager of Luce's company, Time, Inc. Ingersoll's biographer, Roy Hoopes, argued that Ingersoll was the driving force behind the development of *Life* magazine, and when Luce did not reward him with the editorship of the new magazine, Ingersoll swore he "would never again lose myself in the creation of a magazine that belonged to someone else—even Harry Luce."[67] After working for the conservative Luce, Ingersoll claimed to have been liberalized by his affair with playwright Lillian Hellman. In *PM*'s prospectus, he wrote, "We do not believe all mankind's problems are soluble in any existing social order, certainly not our own, and we propose to applaud those who seek constructively to improve the way men live together. . . ."[68]

By January 1940, Ingersoll acquired $1.5 million and more than 10,000 applicants for positions on *PM*. Joseph Medill Patterson, publisher of the *New York Daily News*, declared a circulation war and threatened newsstand dealers if they distributed the new paper. To further complicate the paper's rocky

PM'S ORIGINAL STOCKHOLDERS

Marian Rosenwald Stern (Sears Roebuck heir)	$200,000
Howard Bonbright (investment banker)	$100,000
John Loeb (partner in investment firm Loeb, Rhoades & Co.)	$100,000
Deering Howe (Deere Tractor Co. heir)	$100,000
Garrard B. Winston (lawyer, former undersecretary of the treasury)	$100,000
Elinor Gimbel (department store heir)	$50,000
Marshall Field (Chicago department store heir)	$200,000
Huntington Hartford III (A&P heir)	$100,000
Harry Scherman (chairman of the board of Book-of-the-Month)	$100,000
Dwight Deere Wiman (Deere Tractor Co. heir)	$50,000
William and Lessing Rosenwald (Sears Roebuck heirs)	$100,000
Philip K. Wrigley (chewing gum manufacturer)	$50,000
Chester Bowles (advertising executive)	$50,000
Lincoln Schuster (book publisher)	$50,000
Ira J. Williams (investor)	$50,000
John Hay Whitney (investor)	$100,000

By Permission of Washington Journalism Review

financial situation, staffers could not find the list of 150,000 charter subscribers, only 50,000 fewer than were needed to break even. Although 450,000 copies sold the first day, within eight weeks circulation dropped to 31,000. Marshall Field bought out the other investors and became sole owner of *PM*, with Ingersoll continuing as editor until he joined the army in 1942. When he returned in 1946, he again assumed the editorship for a few months, but he resigned when Field argued to include advertising in the newspaper. In January 1949, the paper folded. Marshall Field commissioned a study to try to determine why the paper failed. Most of those replying to questionnaires sent to 200 employees said bad business management and biased news were the paper's major faults.[69]

MARGARET BOURKE-WHITE

Margaret Bourke-White (1904–1971), who provided the cover photograph for the first issue of *Life*, became the first accredited woman war photographer, the first woman to fly a combat mission, and the first outsider to thoroughly photograph Soviet industry and life.[70] Her work, which spanned

> **MARGARET BOURKE-WHITE**
>
> No editorialist writing about the human condition in our time had more to say about deprivation or suffering than she did through pictures. And few philosophers or dramatists penetrated more deeply into the wondrous possibilities of human hopefulness and dignity. . . . Margaret Bourke-White was able to make her camera see past the surface into meaning.
>
> SOURCE. Norman Cousins, on Bourke-White's death, September 11, 1971, Saturday Review.

several decades, first earned recognition in the 1920s for architectural and industrial photography. Bourke-White photographed steel mills, shipyards, banks, and skyscrapers, portraying the capitalistic structure of American industry. One critic observed that her work "transformed the American factory into a Gothic cathedral."[71] Henry Luce hired her as the first photographer for *Fortune* and as one of four original staff photographers for *Life*. Her agreement with Luce allowed her six months of the year to pursue her own work for advertising agencies and other clients.

Bourke-White was always a source of controversy, despite her talent and achievements, partly because she espoused liberal causes. In 1944, the House Un-American Activities Committee cited her thirteen times for espousing foreign ideologies and producing un-American propaganda. In the early 1940s, J. Edgar Hoover had recommended that Bourke-White be placed on a list of individuals to be considered for custodial detention in time of emergency. The Post Office monitored her mail, and the Customs Bureau reported to the FBI whenever she left the country and returned. Despite repeated searches of her luggage, the Customs Bureau never found incriminating evidence.

When White was sent to Korea for *Life* to develop and photograph a human-interest story on the impact of the Korean conflict, she voluntarily submitted a statement to the secretary of defense refuting allegations of communist sympathy. She stated:

> I am not a member of the Communist Party, and never have been. I am not affiliated with the Communist Party, and never have been. I have never knowingly been a member of, sponsored, lectured before, or contributed to a Communist-front organization. I have never been sympathetic to the Communist Party or the Communist ideology. I have never voted or campaigned for or provided funds for a candidate of the Communist Party. I have never advocated force or violence to alter the constitutional form of government in the United States.[72]

Bourke-White never learned of the FBI surveillance of her activity, nor of the extensive file they maintained about her friendships and affiliations, and the surveillance did not harm her career.

ROBERT McCORMICK

Robert R. McCormick grew up in Joseph Medill's newspaper family, but not as the chosen son to take over the *Chicago Tribune*. Born in 1880, he was the son of Joseph Medill's daughter, Katherine, and Robert Sanderson, nephew of Cyrus McCormick, who invented the reaper. Robert's brother, Joseph Medill McCormick, was his mother's choice for editor of the *Tribune*. When Joseph Medill died in 1899, control of the *Tribune* went to Robert Patterson, his son-in-law and husband of Medill's daughter Elinor. Under Patterson, both his son Joseph Patterson, who later owned and edited the New York tabloid, the *Daily News*, and Medill McCormick worked on the *Tribune*. Medill died early of alcoholism, and Joe Patterson and Robert McCormick took over the *Tribune*. The two cousins were friends, despite Joe's tendencies toward socialism and Robert McCormick's unswerving conservatism.

McCormick survived major circulation wars in the teens with Hearst's *American* (which was renamed the *Examiner*) and by 1910 the *Tribune* led Chicago morning circulation with a count of 241,000. It slightly trailed the more popular evening *Daily News*. After a trip to the Russian Front and military service in World War I, McCormick became a full colonel, and returned to assume even more control of the *Tribune* when Joe Patterson left in 1919 to begin the *Daily News*. During the 1920s, McCormick established foreign news correspondents for the *Tribune* and continued his successful management of the newspaper.

Although the Depression caused ad lineage at the *Tribune* to decline by half, McCormick was not seriously bothered by hard times. Circulation declined only slightly, and deflation balanced the drop in ad revenues with costs. Net profits for *Tribune* shareholders in 1933 were reported by Luce's *Fortune* magazine to be $2,900,000.[73] Joseph Gies, a McCormick biographer, wrote that *Tribune* copy in the early '30s was hardly controversial: "impassioned demands for reduction in government spending and taxes, and bland appeals for national unity."[74] The *Tribune* dismissed the 1932 veteran's bonus march as communist-inspired, denounced the veterans for demanding early payment of their bonus, considered Roosevelt and Hoover as "firm, middle-of-the-road progressives," and assumed Roosevelt would not undertake any dangerous economic experiments.

Roosevelt and McCormick, old school chums from Groton, remained friendly until they parted irrevocably over the National Recovery Administration's attempt to regulate the business aspects of newspapers. McCormick, who became chairman of the American Newspaper Publishers' Association's

A Chicago landmark since its completion in 1925, the Tribune *tower is "home" to the Chicago* Tribune's *editorial department plus advertising, marketing, and other support wings. The Tribune Company, a publicly-owned company in the 1980s, is also headquartered here. (Chicago Tribune photo)*

Committee on Freedom of the Press when it was established in 1928, urged the ANPA to take a stand that the National Recovery Administration (NRA) was detrimental to freedom of the press.

By 1934, the *Tribune*'s coverage of Roosevelt was avidly accusatory. Gies noted that

> Stories compared him to Kerenski as an ineffective leader paving the way to bolshevism. Agriculture Secretary Henry Wallace, son of a distinguished family of Iowa Republicans, was compared to Lenin, Mussolini, and Hitler. McCormick saw a coincidence in the birthplace of Felix Frankfurter, which was the same as that of Hitler, Hapsburg-ruled Austria-Hungary, a nativity that left him "impregnated with the historic doctrines of Austrian absolutism."[75]

Unlike Luce, McCormick viewed Hitler as a dangerous ruler and informed his readers' about the dangers of the Nazi leader. In 1933, stories from the *Tribune*'s Berlin correspondent, Sigrid Schultz, reported "German Decree Annuls Liberty and Civil Rights," "Nazi Terrorism Grows," and "Jewish Stores Closed."[76]

McCormick earned his reputation as a reactionary with his obviously biased coverage of Roosevelt's reelection campaigns, through his activities with the ANPA designed to limit government regulation of the newspaper business, and by his involvement with the America First Committee, a group of prominent isolationists, on the eve of World War II.

In 1933, the ANPA confronted Congress directly over passage of the National Recovery Act, which provided for establishment of codes of fair competition for all industries. The codes guaranteed the right of collective bargaining and freedom of labor union organization, and empowered the president to license and to revoke those licenses for individual companies in any industry not cooperating under NRA. The ANPA submitted a voluntary code, providing for "open shops" in which union and nonunion members could work side by side, and exempting newsboys from child-labor restrictions. The voluntary code also exempted reporters and other editorial workers from the maximum hour provisions of the law. Publishers also included a phrase in the voluntary agreement which noted that

> Nothing in the adoption and acceptance of this code shall be construed as waiving, abrogating, or modifying any rights secured under the Constitution of the United States or of any state, or limiting the freedom of the press.

In accepting the publishers' voluntary code with modifications to the child-labor provisions and open shop clauses, President Roosevelt replied:

> The freedom guaranteed by the Constitution is freedom of expression and that will be scrupulously respected—but it is not freedom to work children, or to do business in a fire trap or violate the laws against obscenity, libel and lewdness."[77]

Such exchanges further alienated publishers from the New Deal. The final version of the Newspaper Code provided a forty-hour week for employees of newspapers in towns with populations of more than 50,000 and set minimum wages. Children of twelve could work as newsboys as long as they worked during daylight hours and were not required to perform duties that would impair their health or interfere with their schooling. News-editorial employees, as well as others, were granted the right of collective bargaining, paving the way for the formation of the American Newspaper Guild in 1933.

McCormick was not the only publisher who was glad to see the Supreme Court declare the NRA unconstitutional in 1935, but his joy was short-lived, for the next year the Wagner Labor Relations Act contained many of the provisions of NRA, such as collective bargaining. McCormick had little faith in New Deal legislation. When Social Security was instituted in 1935 and many publishers, including his cousin Joseph Patterson, canceled company pension plans, McCormick retained the *Tribune*'s plan, assured that the New Deal would spend the money secured for Social Security and also convinced he could take better care of his employees than could the federal government. As soon as the guild began to organize the Hearst newspapers, McCormick set his employees' salaries at levels higher than those the guild required.[78]

THE *CATHOLIC WORKER* AND DOROTHY DAY

Dorothy Day, daughter of a middle-class family, attended the University of Illinois, ironically on a Hearst scholarship, where she became a member of the Socialist Worker party and expressed rebellion against her background by smoking and swearing. She left school at the end of her sophomore year and began working in New York for the Socialist *Call*. At the beginning of World War I, she joined the staff of *The Masses*. When it shut down, she worked for its successor, *The Liberator*, and entered the social life of Greenwich Village. During the next few years she joined the expatriates in Europe, then worked in Chicago, New Orleans and New York. With profits from the movie rights to her first novel, *The Eleventh Virgin*, she bought a cottage on Staten Island and began to associate with leftist friends.

In 1927, shortly after the birth of her daughter, Dorothy Day's life underwent a major transition when she was converted to Catholicism. In 1933, in the midst of the depression, she started the *Catholic Worker*, which published Catholic social activist Peter Maurin's essays and advocated solutions based on radical Christian personal action. As editor until the late 1970s, Dorothy Day avoided partisan politics and advocated personal action rather than politics as a means of social change.[79] Because the newspaper contained the word "worker" in the title and because of its strong pacifist views during the Spanish Civil War and World War II, the paper was regarded widely as a communist organ. Circulation reflected opposition to the paper's pacifistic views, dropping from 190,000 in 1938 to 50,500 during World War II.[80] The newspaper fought anti-Semitism, including those views expressed in Father Coughlin's *Social Justice*, and the 1938 Nazi attacks on Jews. It also denounced U.S. internment of Japanese during the war.

As early at 1940, the Federal Bureau of Investigation began to investigate Dorothy Day, convinced she was a front for a communist organization; ultimately, however, the FBI became convinced that while radical she was honest and had given up communism. In June 1944, her file apparently was closed. In the fifties the newspaper was again investigated by the FBI, and Dorothy Day was jailed several times from 1955 to 1961 for protesting air raid drills. Her imprisonment in 1957 for refusing to participate in an air raid drill finally gained support for the struggling *Catholic Worker* from mainstream newspapers such as the *New York Times* and the *New York Post*, as well as from the *Daily Worker* and the *Village Voice*. The *Catholic Worker* continued to oppose military conflict and led the opposition to the Vietnam War. Dorothy Day died November 29, 1980, but the newspaper continues today.

Conclusion

During the depression the periodical and electronic media industries remained strong, despite declines for newspapers in advertising and circulation. The motion-picture industry probably faced the most critical economic problems, with profits plummeting dramatically. Newspapers cut costs and wages to maintain a profit margin, and reporters responded by organizing a newspaper guild to fight for better working conditions and better salaries. Jobs went first to the men, and gains women had made within the industry during the 1920s held even but did not increase.

The social events and issues of the decade were described and interpreted in a variety of ways. The documentary movement, which chronicled emotion as well as fact, spurred the development of other interpretive techniques. Newswriters added bylines to their stories, editors experimented with news summaries, columnists expounded on political programs, photographers explained with their cameras, and new research methods contributed to measuring public opinion. The variety of innovation sparked a continuing debate in subsequent decades about the validity of objectivity as a professional norm versus the need for interpretation.

Radio expanded its news operations against dramatic protests by newspaper editors and by the end of the decade became a favorite medium for President Roosevelt, whose voice crossed the airwaves with "Fireside Chats" and news conferences. Eleanor Roosevelt enhanced the position of women journalists by creating press conferences for women only.

Roosevelt cultivated relationships with print journalists during the early years of his presidency, endeavoring to garner favor for New Deal legislation. Angry with publishers who commented, and often fought against, his programs, he then turned to radio as a means of disseminating government information. Broadcasters, always wary of possible government regulation and uneasy about controversy, opened the air waves to Roosevelt as well as to a variety of government agencies.

The social tensions of the decade and reaction to the flapper era of the 1920s created pressure for the motion picture industry, which during the 1930's established procedures for guaranteeing certain codes of morality in American films.

NOTES

1. For a general discussion of the depression and of New Deal legislation, see Mary Beth Norton, et al. *A People and a Nation* vol. 2 (Boston: Houghton Mifflin Co., 1982), pp. 700–750. For a more scholarly evaluation, see William E. Leuchtenburg, *Franklin Roosevelt and the New Deal* (New York: Harper Torchbooks, 1963).
2. Edgar Dale, *The Content of Motion Pictures* (New York: The Macmillan Co., 1935), p. 1.
3. James L. Baughman, in a presentation, "Informing the Mass and the Middle: The Journalism of Synthesis in Twentieth Century America," at the annual Association for Education in Journalism and Mass Communication (AEJMC) in Norman, Okla., August 1986, suggested "synthesis" as a journalistic theme for the twentieth century.
4. See the Introduction to Richard W. Steele, *Propaganda in an Open Society: The Roosevelt Administration and the Media, 1933–1941* (Westport, Conn: Greenwood Press, 1985).
5. The cities were New York, Chicago, Philadelphia, Cleveland, Boston, and San Francisco.
6. Alfred McClung Lee, *The Daily Newspaper in America* (New York: The Macmillan Co., 1937), p. 173. For supplementary data about economics of newspapers in the depression years, see pp. 171–3, 203–204.
7. Lois Banner, *Women in Modern America—A Brief History* (New York: Harcourt Jovanovich, Inc., 1974), p. 143, cited in "The Woman Journalist of the 1920s and 1930s in Fiction and in Autobiography," by Donna Born, AEJMC Qualitative Studies Division, Athens, Ohio, July 1982.

8. Born studied biographies of Fanny Butcher, *Many Lives—One Love* (New York: Harper & Row Publishers, 1972); Bess Furman, *Washington By-Line* (New York: Alfred A. Knopf, 1949); Mary Knight, *On My Own* (New York: The Macmillan Co., 1938); Mary Margaret McBride, *A Long Way from Missouri* (New York: G.P. Putnam's Sons, 1959); Margaret Anderson, *My Thirty Years War* (New York: Covici, Friede, 1930); Edna Lee Booker, *News Is My Job* (New York: The Macmillan Co., 1940); Agness Underwood, *Newspaperwoman* (New York: Harper & Brothers, 1949); and Kathleen Ann Smallzried, *Press Pass* (New York: E.P. Dutton & Company, Inc., 1940).

9. Cited in Lee, *Daily Newspaper in America*, p. 683.

10. Cited in Lee, *Daily Newspaper in America*, p. 686.

11. For elaboration of this theme, see Michael Schudson, *Discovering the News: A Social History of American Newspapers*, (New York: Basic Books, 1978), p. 144.

12. Definition of documentary provided by William Stott, *Documentary Expression and Thirties America* (New York: Oxford University Press, 1973) pp. 8–12, 20.

13. Lewis Jacobs, *The Documentary Tradition* (New York: Hopkinson and Black, 1971), pp. 12–13.

14. Jacobs, *The Documentary Tradition*, p. 72.

15. Jacobs, *The Documentary Tradition*, p. 75.

16. Stott, *Documentary Expression*, p. 73.

17. Stott, *Documentary Expression*, p. 62. See also Karin Becker Ohrn, *Dorothea Lange and the Documentary Tradition* (Baton Rouge: Louisiana State University Press, 1980).

18. Curtis MacDougall, *Interpretative Reporting* (New York: The Macmillan Co., 1938), p. v, cited in Schudson, *Discovering the News*, p. 146.

19. Cited in Schudson, *Discovering the News*, p. 148.

20. Schudson, *Discovering the News*, p. 145.

21. Schudson, *Discovering the News*, p. 159.

22. Schudson, *Discovering the News*, pp. 150–151.

23. Schudson, *Discovering the News*, pp. 145–146.

24. This discussion relies heavily on Richard Jensen, "Democracy by the Numbers," *Public Opinion* (February/March 1980), pp. 53–59.

25. Everette E. Dennis and Claude-Jean Bertrand, "Seldes at 90: They Don't Give Pulitzers for that Kind of Criticism," *Journalism History* 7:3–4 (Autumn-Winter 1980), pp. 85–86.

26. Dennis and Bertrand, "Seldes at 90," pp. 83–84.

27. Erik Barnouw, *The Golden Web* (New York: Oxford University Press, 1968), pp. 28–29.

28. David H. Hosley, *As Good As Any: Foreign Correspondence on American Radio, 1930–1940*. (Westport, Conn.: Greenwood Press, 1984), pp. 8–9.

29. Holsey, *Foreign Correspondence on American Radio*, pp. 18–22.

30. Shearon Lowery and Melvin L. DeFleur, *Milestones in Mass Communication Research: Media Effects* (New York: Longman, 1983), p. 70.

31. Jacobs, *The Documentary Tradition*, p. 29. See also Erik Barnouw, *Documentary: A History of the Non-Fiction Film* (New York: Oxford University Press, 1983), p. 26.
32. Barnouw, *Documentary*, p. 52.
33. Jacobs, *The Documentary Tradition*, pp. 106–107.
34. A. William Bluem, *The Documentary in American Television* (New York: Hastings House, 1965), cited in Jacobs, *The Documentary Tradition*, pp. 104, 105.
35. Raymond Fielding *The March of Time, 1935–51* (New York: Oxford University Press, 1978), p. 302.
36. Barnouw, *Documentary*, p. 206.
37. Louis Giannetti and Scott Eyman, *Flashback: A Brief History of Film* (Englewood Cliffs, N.J.: Prentice-Hall, 1986)
38. Cited in Gianetti and Eyman, *Flashback*, p. 164.
39. *Parade Magazine* December 7, 1986, p. 5.
40. Giannetti and Eyman, *Flashback*, pp. 176, 77. See also Robert Sklar, *Movie-Made America* (New York: Random House, 1975).
41. Giannetti and Eyman, *Flashback*, p. 190.
42. For a full discussion of Pinchot's cultivation of newspaper editors, see Stephen Ponder, "Federal News Management in the Progressive Era: Gifford Pinchot and the Conservation Crusade," *Journalism History* 13:2 (Summer 1986).
43. This discussion relies heavily on the Introduction to Steele, *Propaganda in an Open Society*. See also Robert Hilderbrand, *Power and the People: Executive Management of Public Opinion in Foreign Affairs, 1897–1921* (Chapel Hill: University of North Carolina Press, 1981).
44. Ray Stannard Baker, *Woodrow Wilson and World Settlement*, 2 vols. (London: William Heineman, 1923) vol. 1, p. 137, cited in Michael Schudson, *Discovering the News: A Social History of Newspapers* (New York: Basic Books) 1978, p. 165.
45. Schudson, *Discovering the News*, p. 165.
46. Steele, *Propaganda in an Open Society*, pp. 9–12.
47. Betty Houchin Winfield, "F.D.R.'s Pictorial Image, Rules and Boundaries," *Journalism History* 5:4 (Winter 1978–79), p. 110.
48. Betty Winfield, "Mrs. Roosevelt's Press Conference Association: The First Lady Shines a Light," *Journalism History* 8:2 (Summer 1981), p. 67. See also Ishbel Ross, *Ladies of the Press, The Story of Women in Journalism by an Insider* (New York: Harper & Brothers, 1936) and Maureen Beasley, ed., *One Third of a Nation: Lorena Hickok Reports the Great Depression* (Urbana: University of Illinois Press, 1981.)
49. W. A. Swanberg, *Luce and His Empire* (New York: Charles Scribners' Sons, 1972) p. 42.
50. Swanberg, *Luce and His Empire*, pp. 53–57.
51. Swanberg, *Luce and His Empire*, p. 53.
52. James L. Baughman, *Henry R. Luce and the Rise of the American News Media*, (Boston: G. K. Hall/Twayne, 1987), p. 27.
53. Cited in Swanberg, *Luce and His Empire*, pp. 122–23.
54. Baughman, *Luce and the Rise of the American News Media*, p. 49.

55. Baughman, *Luce and the Rise of the American News Media*, pp. 34, 50–53.
56. Baughman, *Luce and the Rise of the American News Media*, pp. 62–74.
57. Keith Kenney, "*Mid-Week Pictorial*: Pioneer American Photojournalism Magazine," paper presented to Visual Communication Division of the AEJMC, Norman, Okla., August 1986.
58. Baughman, *Luce and the Rise of the American News Media*, pp. 84–85.
59. Herman Ullstein, *The Rise and Fall of the House of Ullstein* (New York: Simon and Schuster, 1943), p. 27, cited in C. Zoe Smith, "The History of Black Star Picture Agency: *Life*'s European Connection," paper presented to Visual Communication Division, AEJMC, Gainesville, Fla, August 7, 1984.
60. Smith, "Black Star Picture Agency," p. 2.
61. Baughman, *Luce and the Rise of the American News Media*, pp. 91–95.
62. Baughman, *Luce and the Rise of the American News Media*, pp. 99–102.
63. See the Introduction to Baughman's *Luce and the Rise of the American News Media*.
64. Swanberg, *Luce and His Empire*, p. 70.
65. Baughman, *Luce and the Rise of the American News Media*, p. 156.
66. Swanberg, *Luce and His Empire*, p. 214.
67. Roy Hoopes, "When Ralph Ingersoll Papered Manhattan," *Washington Journalism Review* (December 1984) p. 26.
68. Hoopes, "Ralph Ingersoll," p. 27.
69. Hoopes, "Ralph Ingersoll," p. 32.
70. Robert E. Snyder, "Margaret Bourke-White and the Communist Witch Hunt," *Journal of American Studies* 19:1 (1985), p. 6.
71. Cited in Snyder, "Communist Witch Hunt," p. 5.
72. Margaret Bourke-White Statement to the Office of Public Information, Office of the Secretary of Defense, 15 January 1951, Bufile 100-3518, cited in Snyder, "Communist Witch Hunt," p. 20.
73. Joseph Gies, *The Colonel of Chicago* (New York: E.P. Dutton & Company, Inc., 1979), p. 117.
74. Gies, *Colonel of Chicago*, p. 123.
75. Gies, *Colonel of Chicago*, p. 129.
76. Gies, *Colonel of Chicago*, p. 130.
77. Edwin Emery, *History of the American Newspaper Publishers Association* (Westport, Conn: Greenwood Press) 1950.
78. Gies, *Colonel of Chicago*, p. 141.
79. Nancy Roberts, *Dorothy Day and the Catholic Worker* (Albany: State University of New York Press, 1984), p. 90.
80. Roberts, *Dorothy Day*, p. 119.

CHAPTER 17

WAR

AND

PROSPERITY

Although the United States did not declare war, and thus become an integral participant in World War II until after Japan bombed Pearl Harbor December 7, 1941, the beginnings of conflict dated to the close of World War I. Germany and its European allies struggled to pay war debts that taxed the economies of the European nations, while Japan and China attempted to resolve internal troubles and resolve border disputes.

Further, the worldwide depression of the 1930s resulted in attempts by various countries to use foreign policy as well as domestic policy to shore up falling economies. Japan, after experiencing an economic expansion from 1925 to 1929, turned to aggressive action on the Soviet border and in Manchuria during the late 1920s. Internal disputes in China between the Nationalists, led by Chiang Kai-Shek, and the Communists, led by Mao-Tse Tung, crippled the country's resistance to the Japanese attempts to control the profitable economic relationships with Manchuria. In 1931, Japan attacked Chinese troops and brought Manchuria under its control. The situation grew even more tense in July 1936 when Japan signed an anti-Comintern pact with Nazi Germany, creating a Germany-Italy-Japan Axis. Japan threatened to invade central China, and war broke out in 1937.

In Spain, the republican government struggled to resist Franco's fascist inroads from 1936 to 1939. England, also facing an economic crisis, fought to keep its empire intact, resisting Indian pleas for independence, appeasing Hitler, and ignoring the Italian invasion of Ethiopia. In 1938–1939, Germany seized Austria and areas of Czechoslovakia. During the same year, Germany and the Soviet Union signed the Soviet-Nazi Pact and a few days later separately invaded Poland. In November 1939, the Soviets attacked Finland.

During the war years wire services, newspapers, and broadcast organizations sent correspondents to Asia and Europe to cover international developments. The costs of such coverage escalated throughout the war and increased the dominance of the prestige newspapers, the wire services, and the networks. Columnists, cartoonists, and photographers depicted the war, presenting a variety of themes and images. But nearly all forms of media complied with government restrictions instituted through the Office of Censorship and the Office of War Information. The Justice Department, the Post Office Department, and the FBI continued their surveillance of "suspicious" journalists and of the black press. Government news management and increased concentration of ownership alarmed publishers such as Henry Luce, who helped fund the Commission on Freedom of the Press, which reaffirmed the importance of a free press in a democratic society and urged publishers to accept the responsibility such a philosophy entailed. Editors, concerned about the lack of information available in other countries, worked to establish a worldwide agreement ensuring freedom of news dissemination. At the end of the war, soldiers returned to a prosperous country, and looked for peace and consensus as they moved to an increasingly suburban America.

Telegraph desk in the news room of the New York Times *in September 1942. (Library of Congress Collection, Office of War Information photo)*

COVERING THE WAR

CORRESPONDENTS AND COSTS

In the mid-1930s, about 300 U.S. press and radio correspondents worked outside the boundaries of the country. During the war the number grew to exceed 2,600, although all correspondents were not in the field at the same time. U.S. correspondents were in Asia as early as 1929 to cover the Japanese/Soviet border dispute and stayed to cover the Manchurian war. Even the

445

movies were there, as Paramount Newsreels depicted the brutality of the Japanese invasion of China soil.

Coverage of the war in Asia assured that correspondents would be in place as the war escalated to become a world war, and further assured that the wire services and the prestige press, who could afford the high costs of coverage, would dominate dissemination of world news. The Associated Press, International News Service, and United Press wired stories home via London at a rate of about thirty-five cents a word.[1] In 1937, United Press coverage of the continuing conflict between China and Japan cost about $2,000 per day. In July of that year, Associated Press spent $12,000 for all its foreign-press coverage, $12,000 more than it had spent in July, 1936. From China and Japan alone, AP was spending $4,000 per day, plus costs for transmitting photographs. The first transmission of a photograph from Tokyo to New York took place in August 1937, took ten hours to transmit, and cost $225 to move.

Costs of coverage continued to escalate throughout the war. By the mid-1940s, CBS and NBC were spending $10,000 a week to bring news roundups from European capitals. Foreign news costs for the *New York Times* in 1941 exceeded $1 million, and in 1942 the Associated Press spent slightly more than $1 million for overseas coverage.[2]

Correspondents faced great personal risks. Because of the bombing, they could rarely escape danger even when not technically at the front. Joe James Custer, a UP correspondent, suggested that correspondents should train on something other than beer and cigarettes to prepare for physical hardships. Nearly every correspondent in the Southwest Pacific, he said, "has had malaria, dysentery and feet and leg sores. . . . It's a hard physical grind, working 24 hours a day, with a nap only now and then. . . . A correspondent is a non-combatant, but if he's surrounded by the enemy . . . he'll be a dead duck." He suggested correspondents train like the Marines did.[3] In March 1943 the *World's Press of London* reported that twenty-three British, British Commonwealth, and U.S. correspondents had been killed, with seven more reported missing and others wounded, captured, and interned. Nine were held as prisoners of war. Of the twenty-three killed, *Editor and Publisher* reported that twelve were U.S. correspondents. After the war thirty-six correspondents received decorations, including the Silver Star, Bronze Star, Air Medal, and special commendations. By 1948, forty-nine U.S. correspondents were reported as having lost their lives between 1939 and 1945.[4]

Marguerite Higgins

Marguerite Higgins, an MA graduate of Columbia University's Graduate School of Journalism in 1942, went directly to her employer, *New York Herald Tribune* publisher Helen Ogden Reid, to plead for a job as a war correspondent. Higgins, who went abroad in 1944, was one of the first American correspondents to cover the U.S. capture of the Dachau Concentration Camp. She also covered the Nuremberg War Trials and became the *Herald Tribune*'s Berlin bureau chief in 1945. She recalled that she had not expected the appointment because she was "wearing a chip on my shoulder about the unlikelihood of my paper's picking a female to run an established newspaper bureau. . . . This attitude offers great and comforting opportunities of fooling yourself because it prevents your facing up to the fact that just possibly the reason you aren't going to receive a certain promotion is that your talents aren't up to it."[5] Higgins continued to work hard and challenge herself, an attitude that paid off as she headed the *Herald Tribune*'s Tokyo Bureau and won a Pulitzer Prize during the Korean War. When an army colonel in Korea warned her there might be trouble and she'd have to leave, Higgins replied, "Trouble is news, and the gathering of news is my job."[6] In 1963, Higgins, taking a hard anti-communist line, covered the early days of the Vietnam conflict for *Newsday*, where she contracted a tropical disease and died in 1966 at age forty-five.

DEVELOPMENT OF BROADCAST NEWS

The need to cover a variety of disturbing world events and the advent of available technology combined with other factors to bring radio news broadcasting to maturity during the 1930s and 1940s. Many of the popular voices of World War II became the familiar television newscast faces in the years that followed. Edward R. Murrow, who joined CBS in 1935 as director of talks and special events, went to London for CBS in 1937 as an administrator and coordinator as well as broadcaster of news. He remained in London throughout the war. One of Murrow's early recruits was William Shirer, who remained in Berlin in 1940 and who later wrote *The Rise and Fall of the Third Reich*.

Mutual Broadcasting Company, which by 1936 had stations coast to coast, reported the Czechoslovak, or Munich crisis during three weeks of September 1938. By 1939, about 800 radio and newspaper correspondents from the United States covered breaking world events.[7]

Hans von Kaltenborn

Hans von Kaltenborn, born in 1878 in Wisconsin, became one of radio's first news commentators. Kaltenborn's extensive experience as a newsman on the *Brooklyn Eagle* and as a Washington and Paris correspondent led to radio broadcast news analyses over Westinghouse's experimental station WJZ in Newark, New Jersey. In 1923, the *Eagle* began sponsoring Kaltenborn on a

Hans Von Kaltenborn, prominent radio commentator during World War II. (State Historical Society of Wisconsin)

regular weekly half-hour commentary over WEAF. His controversial radio broadcasts, which forced him to move from station to station, earned him the nickname, "the wandering voice of radio."[8] In 1930, Kaltenborn left the *Eagle* for CBS. As Kaltenborn broadcast from Spain during the Civil War, listeners heard "machine gun bullets whizzing overhead and the thud of bombs in the distance."[9]

Kaltenborn's name became a household word in 1938 during the twenty days of the Munich Crisis, the discussions between British Prime Minister Neville Chamberlain and Germany's Adolf Hitler. Kaltenborn's task was to coordinate reports from CBS London correspondent Edward R. Murrow and other reporters in Europe. The sixty-year-old commentator described the twenty days, which he spent either behind a microphone or on a cot in the CBS studio, as a "pressure I had never before experienced in seventeen years of broadcasting."[10] Kaltenborn became a celebrity, receiving honorary doctorates and awards and appearing in cartoons. A *New Yorker* magazine cartoon pictured a captain saying to men leaving a sinking ship: "Hold on men. I've got H. V. Kaltenborn on the radio. He's analyzing our predicament."[11]

In 1940, Kaltenborn began broadcasting daily for NBC and in 1952 was named "Radio Father of the Year." He stopped broadcasting, but continued to write. Kaltenborn believed in radio as a force for democracy and as a source for presenting controversy. "If [a news analyst] is worth listening to, he will excite some controversy even if the subject he discusses is not usually considered controversial," he wrote.[12]

Edward R. Murrow

Murrow, a Phi Beta Kappa graduate of Washington State College (now Washington State University) in 1930, was a student leader, and after college became assistant director of the Institute of International Education. Unlike many broadcasters of his time, he had no newspaper experience before becoming CBS director of talks and education.

Murrow led the way in organizing a network of broadcast correspondents for CBS, setting up the coverage of the European theater of World War II. NBC staffed the major European capitals in a similar fashion, but CBS gained recognition with its staff of fourteen skillful newscasters. Best remembered of all were the Edward R. Murrow "This . . . Is London" broadcasts, accounts which, sometimes during air raids, gave Americans a chilling feel for the war.[13]

Murrow, admired for his courage in refusing to go into air raid shelters while the bombs felt dangerously close to him, dismissed accounts of his valor. Eric Sevareid wrote a few years later that he thought it was Murrow who told him he was afraid to go into the bomb shelters, for fear that once he started, he would not be able to stop.[14]

For two years after the war, Murrow was a vice-president of CBS and director of public affairs, but he returned to the air in 1951 with his "See It Now" programs. The most famous probably was his 1954 exposure of Senator Joseph McCarthy during McCarthy's communist-hunting escapades. In 1961, Murrow joined the Kennedy administration as director of the United States Information Agency. Murrow retired for health reasons and died of lung cancer at the age of fifty-seven.

WIRE SERVICES

Until the beginning of World War II, the two major wire services in the United States, UP and AP, had fashioned various agreements with European agencies such as Havas in France, Reuters in Britain, and Wolff in Germany to trade domestic news for foreign news. However, as Hitler gained control in Europe, devastating the resources of the German and French agencies, the American wire services dominated the market. AP put 179 reporters in the field, relied on its strong news-picture service built up in the 1930s and developed a fast-breaking style of news event coverage. Meanwhile, UP carved out its own expertise in developing the human interest story.[15]

AP's strong monopoly, which excluded competitors, was finally broken in 1945 when a Supreme Court decision made UP and AP services available to any newspaper or radio station that paid the fee. AP members could no longer deny competitors service nor prevent its members from subscribing to a second service, such as UP. UP no longer had a captive market from those newspapers denied access to AP, but because news was in such demand in the world war period, UP gained subscribers from the group that previously subscribed exclusively to AP.

After the War, AP continued to expand overseas, competing not only with UP, but with Reuters of Britain and the newly developed French service, Agence France-Presse.

DEPICTIONS OF WAR

COLUMNISTS AND CARTOONISTS

Columnists and cartoonists chronicled not only the events of the war, but the lives of soldiers at the front. Bill Mauldin's Willie and Joe talked about the difference between life at the front and life at the rear — wallowing in mud versus staying warm and well fed — and depicted the unpleasant discrepancies

> **PYLE AND THE INFANTRY**
>
> I love the infantry because they are the underdogs. They are the mud-rain-frost-and-wind boys. They have no comforts, and they even learn to live without the necessities. And in the end they are the guys that wars can't be won without.
>
> SOURCE. Ernie Pyle, New York World-Telegram, May 3, 5, 1943.

between officers and enlisted men. Willie and Joe were critical of bureaucrats at home as well, claiming they sent the boots and jackets to the rear echelon, leaving those at the front in need.[16] Mauldin attacked the pompousness of the military and bureaucracy but his pictures of the infantry were realistic, noting that soldiers at the front "shot the enemy in the back, blew him up with mines, and killed him in the quickest and most effective way." Ernie Pyle, Pulitzer Prize-winning columnist, commented on another discrepancy—the difference between attitudes at home and attitudes at the front. Mary Mander's study of war correspondents summed up the differences:

> When the invasion forces were landed on Omaha beach, GIs in Italy were still under enemy artillery and attack, and over and above that, were enduring some of the most miserable weather ever undergone by a man in uniform. Under wretched conditions such as these, the GIs got letters from home in which a relative said, "I'm so glad you're in Italy while the fighting is in France." People such as Bing Crosby, who entertained the troops, told the folks back home that salutes really snap at the front. Meanwhile, back in the foxholes, the soldiers were saying that the folks at home seemed to think the GIs and Germans were dancing the beer barrel polka together.[17]

When Pyle was killed covering the war in the Pacific, President Harry Truman said "The nation is quickly saddened again by the death of Ernie Pyle. No man in this war has so well told the story of the American fighting man as American fighting men wanted it told. He deserves the gratitude of all his countrymen."[18]

PHOTOGRAPHY AND THE JAPANESE INTERNMENT

In the spring of 1942, 110,000 Japanese-Americans on the West Coast, 70,000 of whom were born in the United States, were "relocated" in ten camps where they spent the duration of the war. The War Relocation Author-

Dorothea Lange, who photographed the Manzanar Relocation Center, took many photographs of the depression years as well. She took this photo in Kern county, California, 1936. (Library of Congress Collection, Farm Security Administration photo)

ity implemented the relocation and hired photographers to document the internment. Among those photographers were Dorothea Lange, famous for her pictures of the depression, and Ansel Adams, known as a landscape photographer.

Both photographed the Manzanar Relocation Center. The record the two produced recorded distinct points of view. Adams's pictures, which focused on the small businesses that grew up in the camp, smiling people and serene

452

landscapes, emphasized the success of the Japanese-Americans in adapting to their environment. Lange, on the other hand, showed oppressive circumstances and attempted to reveal the internment as an injustice.

Few of Lange's photographs were used during the period. Adams's documentation of camp life, *Born Free and Equal*, was published in 1944 and during the same year his photographs were exhibited at the Museum of Modern Art in New York. The exhibit received little attention and Japanese-Americans showed widespread resentment at the work. During the 1960s, Lange's work found more acceptance in a society that recognized a pattern of discrimination against minorities in American life, and in 1972, her work was collected under the title *Executive Order 9066* and widely exhibited.[19]

COVERAGE OF NAZI CONCENTRATION CAMPS

Although the press covered stories of German atrocities toward Jews as early as 1933, many Americans later claimed they had no idea of what was going on in Germany. Most likely it was not lack of information, but a variety of other factors that colored U.S. citizens' perceptions of German behavior. In the early 1930s, American businessmen envied the growth and expansion of the Germany economy. Tourists who visited saw a clean country, devoid of the problems visible in American society. Norman Chandler, attending the 1936 Olympic Games, berated Ralph Barnes of the *New York Herald Tribune* and William Shirer of CBS for their critical stories. Reporters feared expulsion from Germany and revenge on their Jewish sources. Readers, wary of the false atrocity stories generated in World War I, greeted stories with horror, skepticism, and a belief that things just couldn't be as bad as they appeared to be. Also blocking America's perception was a strong strain of anti-Semitism in the United States. These factors combined to color readers' perceptions and to encourage editors to cover the news, but also to moderate the tone of the stories and to avoid treating Nazi restrictions on Jews as a central theme of German coverage. Repeatedly, the press failed to grasp the extent of the institutionalization of anti-Semitism in the German state, although opposition increased considerably after the Nuremberg Laws of 1935 officially disenfranchised Jews and classified them as noncitizens.[20]

In a study of magazine coverage of Nazi exterminations of European Jewry from November 1941 to November 1944, when six million Jews were systematically annihilated, Arlene Rossen Cardozo found that opinion magazines provided much more coverage and analysis of the Jewish situation than did news or feature magazines. *The Nation*, in particular, repeated the theme that Jews must be removed from Europe in order to survive. The magazine also encouraged the British to litt restrictions on admitting Jews to Palestine and advocated a Jewish homeland as a solution to the problem. Another magazine active in analysis was the *New Republic*.[21]

But American citizens, caught in their own worries with the depression, with a strain of anti-Semitism running through the country, and with skepticism produced from untrue atrocity stories in World War I, were dubious at best.[22] In 1945, no doubt remained, as *Life* magazine reported on May 7:

> Last week, Americans could no longer doubt stories of Nazi cruelty. For the first time there was irrefutable evidence as the advancing Allied armies captured camps filled with political prisoners and slave laborers, living and dead.[23]

CENSORSHIP

Correspondents were, of course, subject to the censorship restrictions of the countries they reported from. These were severe at times, especially in Japan and Germany. Once England declared war, the British government also set up fairly strict censorship procedures.

The Federal Communications Act of 1934 gave President Roosevelt the power to take control of radio in a national emergency. Furthermore, in 1941, the FCC ruled in the *Mayflower Broadcast Corp.* case that broadcast license holders could not use the airwaves to air their own views on public issues. This doctrine, declared by the FCC at the same time the industry was cautioning its own commentators to avoid expressing personal judgments, did not change until 1949, when the FCC instituted the Fairness Doctrine and held that broadcasters could air a point of view if they made time available for other persons holding different views. Soon after the war began in Europe, Roosevelt declared a limited national emergency. In its own move to cooperate, the National Association of Broadcasters established a regulatory code, requesting the avoidance of "horror, suspense and undue excitement," and ruled out editorializing. The code called for fairness to all "belligerents" and noted that analysis should explain and evaluate facts, rumors, and propaganda not establish one's own point of view.

Within hours after the attack on Pearl Harbor, the U.S. government moved to secure Japanese, Italian, and German correspondents. They were interned at the luxurious hotel, The Greenbriar, in White Sulphur Springs, West Virginia, until they were exchanged and returned to their countries. The German government reacted by arresting all twenty U.S. correspondents, and the Japanese held about eleven correspondents for almost two years (1941–1943).

A California workman reads a war extra. (Library of Congress Collection, Office of War Information photo by Russell Lee)

CENSORSHIP ON THE HOME FRONT

Agencies for evaluation of press coverage and dissemination of government news proliferated after Franklin Delano Roosevelt became president. In 1933, the President created the Division of Press Intelligence, which evaluated press coverage of New Deal policies and synthesized information into bulletins for the president, Congress, and other members of the administration. After 1942, the Office of War Information, together with the Agriculture Department, assisted Roosevelt in gathering information until conservative congressmen, fearful of government manipulation of public opinion, halted much of the work done by the federal agencies. Other government agencies, including Army Military Intelligence and the Bureau of Investigation (renamed the FBI in the 1930s), active in World War I in monitoring newspaper content, continued to investigate journalists and question their levels of loyalty to the country.

By early 1941, correspondents were required to carry press passes, bearing their photographs, name, institutional affiliation, signature, and fingerprints to attend White House conferences and to gain access to many of the other governmental information sources.

The first move toward wartime censorship occurred in January 1941, when Secretary of the Navy Frank Knox asked correspondents to voluntarily censor news about the navy and shipping in general. The request stemmed in part from the United States Lend-Lease program, which provided material and munitions to favored nations. Although in April Secretary Knox asked that correspondents not report or photograph the comings and goings of British ships, the request had limited effect.

After the attack on Pearl Harbor, the Espionage Act of 1917, which had not been repealed, was invoked. News of casualties was to be cleared through military channels and communications companies were ordered to halt cable, radio, and telephone traffic to or from Japan, Germany, Italy, and Finland. From the Southeast Pacific news passed through General MacArthur's headquarters, correspondents in the Central Pacific had to have naval approval, and those in Hawaii had to pass both fleet officers and Honolulu censors.[24] A Defense Communications Board was authorized to take over or close any radio or other communications facility, and navy censorship was imposed on all news entering or leaving the United States. News of weather and of ship and troop movements could not be reported.

OFFICE OF CENSORSHIP

Censorship procedures gained formality in late December 1941, when the Office of Censorship was organized under the direction of Byron Price, former executive editor of the Associated Press. The staff eventually included 11,500 persons and its budget for 1943 alone was $26,500,000.[25]

The Office of Censorship had three primary tasks. It administered the Code of Wartime Practices, issued in January 1942, which requested news institutions to adhere to a voluntary censorship code; it monitored news entering and leaving the country; and it handled foreign correspondents reporting the war from the United States. Nine newspapermen, on loan to the government, assisted with the domestic censorship operation and it is to their credit that complaints by newspaper editors were so few. The Office of Censorship operated quickly, observing the needs of newspapers and broadcast stations to function on deadline; material cabled to the Washington office experienced a turnaround time of as little as seven minutes. The office backed the press in most instances, although it did issue thousands of letters of complaints of violations of the code to newspapers, from weeklies to major metropolitan dailies. However, the office had little formal censuring power except for materials that left or entered the country.

Fifteen Office of Censorship stations, located in cities where mail was most likely to enter or leave the country, monitored newspapers and magazines being shipped to Alaska, Mexico, and other countries, in addition to material being shipped to the war zone itself. If the office found objectionable material, it either stopped distribution of the publication or clipped the objectional paragraph or page, and then sent the rest of the publication intact to its destination.[26]

Battle of Midway

Probably one of the most serious breaches of military intelligence occurred in the *Chicago Tribune*'s report of the Battle of Midway in June 1942. Stanley Johnston, a *Tribune* correspondent, in an article about the navy repulsing the Japanese at Midway, revealed that it had word of the Japanese plan to strike. A *Tribune* editor submitted the story to domestic censorship in Washington, as the paper was publishing the story under a one-column headline, "NAVY HAD WORD OF JAP PLAN TO STRIKE AT SEA."

What *Tribune* editors did not know was that prior knowledge of the Japanese plan had been obtained by breaking the Japanese naval code. The major question was how Johnston had gotten the information. Johnston claimed that because of his service in the Australian navy and a lifelong study of military and naval subjects, he unraveled for himself the fact that an earlier attack had been a feint. He also claimed the list of ships he listed as involved had come from notes mistakenly picked up in the cabin of the ship. Although authorities were never sure of the source of Johnston's list (they believed he had seen the original message transmitted to Admiral Nimitz because of the unusual misspellings in several ships' names), a grand jury in Chicago found

A meeting on military news in the office of Elmer Davis, director of the U.S. Office of War Information. (Left to right) Gardner Cowles, Jr., Director of Domestic Operations, Nicholas Roosevelt, Milton Eisenhower, Associate Director, Commander Robert W. Berry, representing U.S. Navy Public Relations, Col. F.V. Fitzgerald, U.S. Army Bureau of Public Relations, and Davis. (Library of Congress Collection, Office of War Information photo)

the *Tribune* innocent of publishing information that hurt the war effort. The grand jury refused to indict because it was not presented all available evidence. In order to convict, the government would have had to reveal the classified information it was seeking to protect.[27]

OFFICE OF WAR INFORMATION

The Office of War Information, created in June 1942, handled propaganda and absorbed the Office of Government Reports, the Office of Facts and Figures, and several smaller agencies. Elmer Davis, former *New York Times* staffer, directed the operation.

OWI's domestic and foreign operations in May 1945, at the peak of activity, required the services of 9,600 persons, and the budget was $132,500,000 for the three years of operation.[28] Three experienced editors and publishers directed the domestic operation: Gardner Cowles, Jr., of the *Des Moines Register and Tribune,* the *Minneapolis Star-Journal* and *Tribune,* and *Look* magazine; E. Palmer Hoyt, editor and publisher of the *Portland Oregonian*; and George W. Healy, Jr., publisher of the *New Orleans Times-Picayune.* The government controlled the broadcasting facilities of five companies that had been disseminating shortwave programs from the United States, including CBS and NBC. News and other programs broadcast through these facilities to a variety of enemy and allied countries became known as the Voice of America, an operation still in existence. The Voice of America and related overseas activity comprised 85 percent of the total OWI budget.

THE FILM INDUSTRY

Government opinions of the motion picture industry's activity during the war were mixed. Major producers cooperated to produce war films on what they termed a nonprofit basis. Nevertheless, during 1941 and 1942, the Army Pictorial Division alone spent more than $1 million in Hollywood. Critics claimed the producers filmed for the government during slack times, or when the studios otherwise would have stood idle, and that by cooperating, the industry managed to remain relatively untouched by the war. Therefore, despite Walt Disney's portrayal of Donald Duck as a duck willing to pay taxes with patriotic enthusiasm and Frank Capra's direction of the "Why We Fight" series designed to train new soldiers, the motion picture industry faced a variety of enemies in Congress.

The Motion Picture Bureau, a division of OWI, attempted to influence Hollywood producers to support the war effort. Among its tasks was to try to motivate producers to incorporate more realistic pictures of black life into films. In response to evidence such as a 1942 survey conducted by the Office of Facts and Figures that indicated 49 percent of Harlem blacks thought they would be no worse off if Japan won the war, OWI wanted Hollywood to tone down its racist images of blacks to foster a sense of unity in the country.[29]

Although the industry had catered to the Legion of Decency and various other economic groups, when OWI attempted to promote more positive images of blacks, the industry cried censorship. MGM in 1938 had hand carried its script of Robert Sherwood's antifascist play, *Idiot's Delight,* to Italy for approval after drastically altering it to avoid offending Benito Mussolini. Warner Brothers coal-mining saga, *Black Fury,* was altered to blame labor unrest on union radicals rather than on mine operators—after the National Coal Association protested. OWI efforts had little effect. A 1945 Columbia University study found that of 100 black appearances in wartime films, 75 percent perpetuated stereotypes, 13 were neutral, and only 12 were positive. OWI hesitated to push very far, claiming the war came first.[30]

Throughout the 1940s, different segments of government attacked the motion picture industry. In 1941, Senator Gerald B. Nye, in a series of committee hearings, charged that motion picture moguls lacked American character. In 1943, a special Senate committee again questioned whether movie makers could be counted as loyal citizens. Striking workers and battling unions further provided fodder for the House Un-American Activities Committee to pursue its anti-communism witch-hunt in Hollywood after the war. The industry did not stand solid. Some managers, such as Walt Disney and Louis B. Mayer, cooperated with the government and provided names of those they termed "known communists," and some workers testified against others as well.[31]

The film industry began its decline in the late 1940s when the Supreme Court forced studios to divest themselves of their theater chains, thus limiting the monopoly of production and distribution studios had built over a thirty-year period. In the industry's peak year of 1946, 90 million Americans, or 75 percent of the population, went to the movies each week. For the next two decades, movie audiences declined dramatically and while studios distributed most major films, independents made some gains in production.

MONITORING OF THE BLACK PRESS

The black press more than doubled its circulation between 1933 and 1940, reaching more than 1,276,000 people by 1940. In 1944, five papers represented a total average weekly circulation of 50,000, representing more than 46 percent of the total circulation. Because pass-around readership was extensive, these circulation figures represented only a fraction of the numbers reading such papers as the Chicago *Defender*, the Baltimore *Afro-American*, or the *Pittsburgh Courier*.

Roosevelt's interest in monitoring press attitudes continued from the 1930s through World War II[32] Aided by J. Edgar Hoover's willingness to investigate journalists, Roosevelt's monitoring policies extended to a variety of groups, and the black press was no exception. The black press had been the subject of government interest since World War I, as administration officials during both wars concerned themselves with the possible effects of the attitudes of 13 million black Americans, which comprised 10 percent of the country's population. The black press had grown as an institution during the interwar period, and its increasingly militant stance triggered additional federal concern during World War II. The *Pittsburgh Courier*, the *Baltimore Afro-American*, and the *Chicago Defender* signalled a change in the black press from small sheets of low circulation to mass-circulation, highly influential newspapers in the black community. The revival of the Ku Klux Klan in the

The Pittsburgh Courier *was widely read for its Double V campaign during the war. (Library of Congress Collection, Farm Security Administration photo)*

1920s, segregation of black troops, and general lack of progress toward equal rights for blacks during the interwar years gave blacks reason to doubt whether another world war was, for them, a war to extend democratic participation.[33]

During World War II, the black press was investigated by seven government agencies, including the Department of Justice, the Federal Bureau of Investigation, the Post Office, the Office of Facts and Figures, the Office of War Information, the Office of Censorship, and the Army. An eighth agency, the War Production Board, may have cut newsprint supplies to some newspapers.[34]

> **MARCH ON WASHINGTON, 1942**
>
> We know that our fate is tied up with the fate of the democratic way of life. And so, out of the depths of our hearts, a cry goes up for the triumphs of the United Nations. But we would not be honest with ourselves were we to stop with a call for a victory of arms alone.
>
> SOURCE. A. Philip Randolph, in an address to the Policy Conference of the March on Washington Movement, September 1942.

In mid-June 1942, John Sengstacke, president of the Negro Newspaper Publishers Association, and publisher of the *Chicago Defender*, met with Attorney General Francis Biddle to discuss increased pressure on the black press to tone down its militancy and to support the war effort without reservation. Sengstacke told Biddle that in exchange for interviews with top government officials to obtain information, black newspapers would be glad to cooperate with the war effort. For such cooperation, Sengstacke expected that no black newspapers would be indicted for sedition.[35] Despite continued investigation by the FBI and by the Post Office, no black newspapers were indicted during the war. The lack of indictments probably was due to the influence of Biddle, and his cooperative agreement with Sengstacke, but also may have reflected efforts by other black leaders, who worked for increased liberal policies toward blacks from the federal government.[36] Furthermore, after the bombing of Pearl Harbor in 1941, the black press adopted the Double V platform begun by the *Pittsburgh Courier*, which advocated victory at home and victory abroad.

THE SMITH ACT

On June 28, 1940, the nation's first peacetime sedition act since 1801, the Smith Act, was passed quietly to prohibit advocacy of the violent overthrow of the government. The act ostensibly would prevent military soldiers from being led astray and made it a crime to "interfere with, impair or influence the loyalty, morale or discipline of the members of the armed forces by encouraging insubordination, disloyalty or mutiny."[37] The second part of the act, modeled after the New York Anarchy and Criminal Syndicalism Act of 1902, prohibited "three kinds of conduct: advocacy of the violent overthrow of the government; organization of a group which advocates the violent overthrow of the government; and membership in a group which advocates the violent overthrow of the government."[38]

Although the act was passed in 1940, it was rarely used before 1949, when public opinion turned violently anti-communist and twelve defendants

John Sengstacke was part owner and general manager of the Chicago Defender. *(Library of Congress Collection, Office of War Information photo)*

were indicted for conspiring to organize the Communist party and for advocating the violent overthrow of the government of the United States. The New York case, which became *Dennis v. United States* on appeal, established a pattern for subsequent cases. Judge Harold Medina, who presided at the first communist trial, narrowed the range of punishable speech, stating that the act prohibited only the teaching or advocacy of "action" directed toward overthrowing the government, and that it did not mean the accused could not advocate or teach violent overthrow in the abstract.[39] Medina's interpretation later was upheld by the Supreme Court in *Yates v. United States*, 354 U.S. 298 (1957) when it overturned a lower court's decision to convict. Since the Yates case only one defendant has been convicted. Although it is difficult to predict in what circumstances the Smith Act would be used again, the implications of it remaining on the law books are somewhat frightening. The fact that it exists, wrote Don Pember, provides "a misleading and dangerous balm. Another national panic, another Red Scare, an alleged conspiracy by Negro militants or the New Left—any of these could create the excuse once again to dust off the Smith Act and begin rounding up "subversives."[40]

COMMISSION ON FREEDOM OF THE PRESS

Press critics since the turn of the century had been increasingly concerned about concentration of ownership and what many perceived to be a lack of responsibility on the part of press owners. Concentration, coupled with sponsorship control of the networks, elicited increasing criticism from various sectors of society throughout the 1930s and during the 1940s. Furthermore, some publishers such as Henry Luce were concerned about increasing government control or management of the press. Luce was concerned that the government, by flooding news agencies with information rather than by censoring, was controlling the press's agenda.[41]

In December 1942, Luce suggested to Robert M. Hutchins the formation of an independent inquiry into freedom of the press. In 1943, the commission was formed, financed by $200,000 in grants from Time, Inc., and $15,000 from Encyclopaedia Britannica, Inc. The money was disbursed through the University of Chicago and the commission headed by the university's controversial president, Robert Hutchins.

In its evaluation of the status of freedom of the newspaper press, radio, motion pictures, magazines, and books, the commission elicited testimony from fifty-eight persons connected with the press, recorded interviews with 225 members of industry, government and private agencies connected with the press, and examined 176 documents prepared by the commission staff. Citing the pressing need for information during a time of world crisis, Hutchins said the commission concentrated its efforts on determining the "role of the agencies of mass communication in the education of the people in public affairs."[42] The commission did not address the issue of government publicity.

In 1947, the Commission listed five "ideal demands of society for the communication of news and ideas:"

1. A truthful, comprehensive, and intelligent account of the day's events in a context which gives them meaning;
2. A forum for the exchange of comment and criticism;
3. The projection of a representative picture of the constituent groups in the society;
4. The presentation and clarification of the goals and values of the society;
5. Full access to the day's intelligence.

After evaluating the press in light of its ideal demands, the commission found freedom of the press in the United States to be in danger because of the monopolistic nature of the press. Concentration meant, the commission noted, that fewer people had access to communication channels and that those in charge had not provided a service to society's needs.

Concerned with the potential of new technology to be developed for either good or evil, the commission discussed guidelines for regulation of new technology and international communications systems.[43] The commission, chose, however, to assign the press the responsibility of "accountability," rather than recommending increased government regulation. The commission suggested that retraction or restatement might better serve victims of libel rather than suits for damages and recommended repeal of state syndicalism acts and the Alien Registration Act of 1940, saying they were of "dubious constitutionality." The commission also suggested the government assume responsibility for disseminating its own news, either through private channels or channels of its own.

The commission suggested the press should accept the responsibility of being a "common carrier" of information and should not assume that ownership gave the right to disseminate a personal viewpoint. It encouraged owners to experiment with new activities, especially in areas where profits were not necessarily assured. The commission also encouraged vigorous mutual criticism by members of the press and increased competence of news staffs. In addition, the commission chided the radio industry for giving control away to soap sponsors and recommended it take control of its programs and treat advertisers in the way the "best" newspapers treated them.

Focusing on freedom as "bound up intrinsically in the collective good of life in society," the commission furthermore suggested the public had a social responsibility to ensure continued freedom of the press, requesting that non-profit institutions help supply variety and quality to press service. It requested that educational centers be created for advanced research about communications and emphasized the importance of the liberal arts in journalistic training.[44]

Renewing the discussion of the importance of a free and accessible press to a democratic society, the commission finally recommended that an independent agency be established to appraise and report annually on the performance of the press. The commission worried, however, that too much emphasis was being placed on that recommendation. Nevertheless, it seemed the only solution commissioners could agree on, after acknowledging that neither the concept of laissez-faire, nor government control, would eliminate the effects of monopoly.[45]

Needless to say, the owners of the agencies of mass communication reacted negatively. Many members of the press were critical because no one from its ranks was included on the commission. Responding to the criticism, the American Society of Newspaper Editors in 1950 appointed ten newspapermen and educators to investigate self-improvement possibilities. The editors' findings reaffirmed the concept of laissez-faire and rejected the commission's recommendations, claiming that improvement of American newspapers depended on "the character of American newspapermen," and their "acceptance of the great responsibilities imposed by freedom of the press." The ASNE study suggested that reporters and editors might be more willing to profit by the "intelligent criticism of the newspaper-reading public" than they would by suggestions made by a commission over which they had no control.[46]

THE CAMPAIGN FOR INTERNATIONAL FREEDOM OF THE PRESS

The American news media responded to the dismantling of the press in Axis countries and to severe censorship encountered by correspondents during World War II by waging a campaign to export the First Amendment to the rest of the world.[47] A similar effort was made after World War I, but proposals developed then lay in the archives of the League of Nations, which took no official action on the subject.

The 1940s campaign encountered many difficulties from the start. During the war the press and the government had cooperated at a variety of levels, with the wire services supplying the State Department with news for transmission overseas and with newspapers complying, for the most part, with a voluntary code of censorship. As the war ended, the press became increasingly uncomfortable with its unfamiliar alliance with government. Furthermore, U.S. press motives were suspect in other countries. Other nations often viewed press demands for freedom of expression as a means of establishing American domination of news and analysis of that news.

The movement, spearheaded by the American Society of Newspaper Editors, the Associated Press, and the United Press, was based on a hope by newspaper editors that the government would help them to establish international accords that would grant correspondents freedom to travel, to gain access to information, and to transmit it freely to their own countries. Those supporting the movement did not always agree exactly on the goals of the campaign. Kent Cooper, executive director of the Associated Press, argued for an all-inclusive program to export the American press as an institution to all other countries. Speaking to the ASNE, he called for "freedom of the press of the entire world as we know it here." He said the best press in the world existed in the United States and that "it would be wonderful if the force that is available from that success would be directed altruistically toward the extension of the American accomplishments to the rest of the world."[48] Recognizing that other nations might have different opinions about the goals, behavior, and results of American-style press coverage, Hugh Baillie, United Press director, argued for "equal access to news at its source in all countries, equal transmission rates, no peacetime censorship."[49]

ASNE members began talking with the State Department as early as 1943 about end-of-the-war guarantees, and in May 1947, the Subcommission on Freedom of Information and of the Press, organized under the UN Human Rights Commission, met to establish an agenda for a 1948 Geneva Conference on Freedom of Information. The disputes arising throughout those discussions continued to be ones that would, in the end, negate the development of an international agreement. Critical areas of discussion included accreditation of correspondents, privileges of correspondents versus responsibilities to present the interests of their home countries, permissible levels of censorship, inequitable distribution of communication facilities and supplies, and permissible sanctions for violations.

Resolution of these issues was complicated by considerations of national self-interest. The United States, for example, consumed more than 65 percent of the international supply of newsprint. However, editors saw no reason they should share their wealth. Also, the United States had refused to let some correspondents enter the country on the grounds they were members of subversive organizations. Furthermore, the Polish delegation at Geneva quoted the Hutchins Commission report to claim the press was in the hands of a few and would serve only special interests in the country.

Disagreement on these issues continued to stall debates and limit effective action until 1950, when the State Department and the American press abandoned the crusade. In the end, these two groups believed that the goal of the provisions as written through compromise at the United Nations was to specify information that could be restricted rather than to increase freedom of access to information. Furthermore, reporting conditions abroad had deteriorated rather than improved, and the murder of CBS correspondent George Polk while working in Greece and the three-year imprisonment of William Oatis of the Associated Press in Czechoslovakia on false charges of espionage discouraged hope for viable international accords.

PROSPERITY AT WAR'S END

From 1940 to 1950 suburbia came of age. The population of counties surrounding major cities swelled, while populations of the cities increased only slightly. Personal incomes also skyrocketed, and by 1950, Americans were spending almost twice as much on housing and household operations as was spent in 1945. Tired of war and dissension, most publications stayed within the mainstream of American thought or turned toward a postwar, cold war, mentality.

PART 4   MEDIA IN A MODERN WORLD

Conclusion

During the years just prior to and during World War II, the U.S. press expanded its overseas operations, placing newspaper, wire service, and broadcast correspondents at the many corners of the globe. The costs were astronomical, and continued to escalate throughout the war. The depictions of war were varied, seen through the eyes of columnists and cartoonists who commented on the discrepancies between the front-line operation and the propaganda at home, as well as through the eyes of those who photographed not only the action, but the results of war. Issues such as the internment of the Japanese within the borders of the United States provided material for photographic commentary. Although media reported Nazi repression of the Jews, skepticism stemming from inaccurate World War I atrocity stories and strong anti-Semitic strains within the country moderated editors' coverage of the extermination of 6 million Jews within Germany.

With the advent of war, Congress and the president instituted censorship of correspondents abroad and media at home. Congress renewed the Espionage Act, and the Office of Censorship monitored news entering and leaving the country and imposed a voluntary censorship code. Broadcasters, wary of the powers of the Federal Communications Act and its regulatory implications, ruled out editorializing. Newspaper editors usually complied with the voluntary code. The Office of War Information established the Voice of America in an overseas propaganda operation and attempted to influence the content of motion pictures. The Justice Department, the Post Office Department, and the FBI continued its surveillance of journalists, including those suspected of "leftist" sympathies, and the black press. The Smith Act restricted those who advocated violent overthrow of the government and remains on the books today.

In 1943, the Commission on Freedom of the Press, concerned about increasing government news management, increased concentration of press ownership, and the potential of radio and television technology within a democratic society reaffirmed a doctrine espousing the importance of a free press in a democratic society. The commission encouraged owners to regard freedom of ownership within the context of the common good and to exercise social responsibility with the right to publish. Editors rejected what they regarded as the commission's interference in private enterprise, and established their own study group which reaffirmed the doctrine of laissez-faire.

Toward the end of the war, U.S. editors organized a campaign for international freedom of the press, but questions about whether such a campaign should give license to export U.S. news practices and values or whether it should grant equal access to news at its source in all countries obstructed progress toward international accords.

Increased production of war materiel and full employment brought the prosperity that had eluded the country during the 1930s, despite the structured New Deal programs designed to end the depression. Americans moved to the suburbs, shunned radical thought, and participated in a decade of consensus politics and cold war ideology.

NOTES

1. Robert Desmond, *Tides of War: World News Reporting 1931–1945.* (Iowa City: University of Iowa Press, 1984) pp. 5–9.
2. Desmond, *Tides of War*, pp. 17–18, 95–96.
3. Desmond, *Tides of War*, p. 451.
4. Desmond, *Tides of War*, p. 453.
5. Marion Marzolf, *Up from the Footnote: A History of Women Journalists* (New York: Hastings House, 1977) p. 77.
6. Marzolf, *Up from the Footnote*, p. 77.
7. Desmond, *Tides of War*, pp. 77, 83.
8. Irving Fang, *Those Radio Commentators!* (Ames: The Iowa State University Press, 1977), p. 25.
9. David Holbrook Culbert, *News for Everyman* (Westport, Conn.: Greenwood Press, 1976), p. 72.
10. Hans Kaltenborn, *Fifty Fabulous Years* (New York: G. P. Putnam's Sons, 1950), p. 209.
11. Fang, *Radio Commentators*, p. 34.
12. Kaltenborn, *Fifty Fabulous Years*, p. 301.
13. See Christopher Sterling and John M. Kittross, *Stay Tuned* (Belmont, Calif.: Wadsworth, 1978), pp. 176–177; A. M. Sperber, *Murrow: His Life and Times* (New York: Freundlich Books, 1986), and Eric Sevareid, *Not So Wild a Dream* (New York: Atheneum, 1978 [originally published in 1946]), p. 83.
14. Sevareid, *Not So Wild a Dream*, p. 19.
15. Fenby, Jonathan, *The International News Services* (New York: Schocken Books, 1986), p. 56.
16. Mary Mander, "Pen and Sword: A Cultural History of the American War Correspondent: 1895–1945," Ph.D. disser., University of Illinois at Urbana-Champaign, 1979, pp. 144–45.
17. Bill Mauldin, *Up Front* (New York: Norton, 1944, 1968), p. 78 cited in Mander, "Pen and Sword," p. 147.
18. Lee G. Miller, *The Story of Ernie Pyle* (New York, 1950), p. 427, cited in Ernest C. Hynds, *American Newspapers in the 1980s* (New York: Hastings House, 1980), p. 83.
19. Karin Becker Ohrn, "What You See Is What You Get: Dorothea Lange and Ansel Adams at Manzanar," *Journalism History* 4:1 (Spring 1977) pp. 14–22, 32.

20. Deborah E. Lipstadt, *Beyond Belief: The American Press and the Coming of the Holocaust, 1933–1945* (New York: Free Press, 1986), p. 57.
21. Arlene Rossen Cardozo, "American Magazine Coverage of the Nazi Death Camp Era," *Journalism Quarterly* 60:4 (Winter 1983), pp. 716–718.
22. W. Richard Whitaker, "Outline of Hitler's 'Final Solution' Apparent by 1933," *Journalism Quarterly* 58:2 (Summer 1981), pp. 192–200, 247.
23. Cited in Whitaker, "Outline of Hitler's 'Final Solution'," p. 192.
24. Mander, "Pen and Sword," p. 170.
25. Desmond, *Tides of War*, p. 219.
26. Interview with Patrick S. Washburn, Ohio University, January 1987. Also see Washburn, *A Question of Sedition* (New York: Oxford University Press, 1986), pp. 253–54.
27. A variety of accounts on the Midway incident have been offered, some implying more involvement on the part of the *Tribune* than others. For an explanation of the situation see Dina Goren, "Communication Intelligence and the Freedom of the Press: The *Chicago Tribune*'s Battle of Midway dispatch and the Breaking of the Japanese Naval Code," *Journal of Contemporary History* 16 (1981), pp. 663–90 and Lloyd Wendt, *Chicago Tribune: The Rise of a Great American Newspaper*, pp. 627–637.
28. Elmer Davis, "Report to the President," ed. by Ronald T. Farrar, *Journalism Monographs* 7 (August 1968), p. 39.
29. See Clayton R. Koppes and Gregory D. Black, *Hollywood Goes to War: How Politics, Profits & Propaganda Shaped World War II Movies*. (New York: Free Press, 1987).
30. Clayton R. Koppes and Gregory D. Black, "Blacks, Loyalty, and Motion-Picture Propaganda in World War II," *Journal of American History* 73:2 (September 1986), p. 394.
31. Robert Sklar, *Movie-Made America: A Cultural History of American Movies* (New York: Vintage Books, 1975), pp. 249–251.
32. For analysis of civil rights progress during the interwar period, see Nancy J. Weiss, *The National Urban League, 1910–1940* (New York: Oxford University Press, 1974).
33. See Washburn, *A Question of Sedition*; Lee Finkle, *Forum for Protest* (Cranbury, N.J.: Associated University Presses, 1975); and Harvard Sitkoff, *A New Deal for Blacks* (New York: Oxford University Press, 1978).
34. Washburn, *Question of Sedition*, p. 8.
35. See Washburn, *Question of Sedition*, chapter 4.
36. Richard Gid Powers, *Secrecy and Power: The Life of J. Edgar Hoover* (New York: Free Press, 1987), p. 277, notes that Biddle blocked almost all of Hoover's recommendations for prosecution under sedition laws. See also Powers, *G-MEN: Hoover's FBI in American Popular Culture* (Carbondale: Southern Illinois Press, 1983).
37. Don R. Pember, "The Smith Act as a Restraint on the Press," *Journalism Monographs* 10 (May 1969), p. 5.
38. Section 2385, Title 18, United States Code, cited in Pember, p. 6–7.

39. Pember, "The Smith Act," p. 11.
40. Pember, "The Smith Act," p. 32.
41. Michael Schudson, *Discovering the News*, (New York: Basic Books, 1978) p. 167. See also Jerilyn McIntyre, "Repositioning a Landmark: The Hutchins Commission and Freedom of the Press," *Critical Studies in Mass Communication* 4 (June 1987), pp. 136–160.
42. Commission on Freedom of the Press, *A Free and Responsible Press* (Chicago: University of Chicago Press, 1947) p. vi. See also Margaret Blanchard, "The Hutchins Commission, the Press and the Responsibility Concept," *Journalism Monographs* (May 1977) 49, pp. 1–59, and D. L. Smith, *Zechariah Chafee, Jr.: Defender of Liberty and Law* (Cambridge, Mass.: Harvard University Press, 1986).
43. McIntyre, "Repositioning a Landmark," p. 141.
44. Quotation is from McIntyre, "Repositioning a Landmark," p. 143.
45. McIntyre, "Repositioning a Landmark," p. 150.
46. John H. Colburn, "What Makes a Good Newspaper?" *Saturday Review* (June 9, 1952), pp. 50, 52, cited in Hynds, *American Newspapers,* p. 29.
47. This discussion relies heavily on the comprehensive account of the movement by Margaret A. Blanchard, *Exporting the First Amendment: The Press-Government Crusade of 1945–52* (New York: Longman, 1986).
48. Kent Cooper, "ASNE and Press Freedom—By Kent Cooper," *ASNE Bulletin,* September 1, 1943, p. 7, cited in Blanchard, *Exporting the First Amendment,* p. 19.
49. Hugh Baillie, "Freedom of Information: Open Channels for News," *Free World,* November 1944, p. 433, cited in Blanchard, p. 19.

CHAPTER 18

TECHNOLOGICAL ADVANCEMENT AMIDST A COLD WAR

The United States emerged victorious from World War II, having experienced fewer losses during the war than all the countries in Europe and Asia. The land lay unscathed, the war economy created full employment and advanced the interests of women, and the soldiers returned home to a welcoming populace. Manufacturing turned domestic as consumers moved to the suburbs, bought appliances and automobiles and supported the government in its foreign policy considerations. But beneath the surface churned many of the conflicts that emerged during the depression. Added to the domestic agenda were new issues such as housing shortages and inflation.[1] Richard Lingeman of the *New York Times* wrote: "The fifties under Ike represented a sort of national prefrontal lobotomy: tail-finned, we Sunday-drove down the superhighways of life while tensions that later bubbled up in the sixties seethed beneath the placid surface."[2]

President Harry S Truman, who succeeded Roosevelt in 1945 after the latter's death in Warm Springs, Georgia, practiced less diplomacy than his predecessor and, with the help of the State Department's Soviet expert George Kennan, articulated the policy of containment. The powerful United States, he said, would "contain"

> **FDR IS DEAD**
>
> The heart of this whole, great city welled over with frank, unashamed grief at dusk last night as the news of President Roosevelt's death spread, by rumor, by radio, and by extra editions of the afternoon newspapers. People told the news to each other in hushed, choked voices. In every corner of the metropolis, people clustered about their radios, hurried into the streets, not wanting to believe it.
>
> When it was true — palpably, hopelessly true — men and women wept open, honest tears at the dread news.
>
> SOURCE. The newspaper PM, 1945.

communism, or strike out wherever communism practiced aggression. Truman sought, and was granted, the support of many public opinion leaders, including congressmen of both political parties and journalists, in his effort to carry the policies of the Cold War beyond Kennan's expectations.

In the postwar world the Soviet Union secured its position in countries where it had established considerable military influence. Communist takeovers in China and Korea took advantage of Soviet support. The United States, also a major power, became economically and strategically involved in Europe. Journalistic and public support tenuously granted to the Soviet Union during the world war quickly disintegrated, and public opinion leaders spoke of the responsibilities of America in the postwar world, which some journalists had been demanding since before the war's beginning. Wrote Walter Lippmann in 1939, "What Rome was to the ancient world, what Great Britain has been to the modern world, America is to the world of tomorrow."[3]

In 1947, the United States instituted the Marshall Plan to aid recovery in Europe. In the same year, the National Security Act readied a permanent structure for self-defense and aggressive foreign policy by creating a Department of Defense, which combined the armed services and the Department of War. The Central Intelligence Agency was created for purposes of spying and carrying out covert actions. In 1953, the United States Information Agency became a permanent propaganda unit for dispensing information throughout the world, particularly in Latin America.

Truman's anti-communist rhetoric intensified, and by early 1947 many mass-circulation magazines echoed his pronouncements, supporting the ideology of America as a dominant world power with an altruistic foreign policy. In 1946 *Collier*'s labeled the Soviet Union as a "gangster government," and the *Saturday Evening Post* characterized postwar tensions as a "world-wide contest between the Soviet Union and the West."[4]

The Soviet Union, expanding into what it considered its own spheres of influence, and concerned that the United States call for an open-door trade policy was expansionism under disguise, cut off Western access to Berlin in June 1948. But Truman airlifted supplies to the western sectors of the city until the Soviet Union was forced to lift the blockade in May 1949. Later in the year, the United States entered its first formal European military alliance since 1778 by creating the North Atlantic Treaty Organization. In Korea, which had been divided by the agreements ending World War II, North Korean soldiers marched across the 38th Parallel on June 25, 1950. The United States believed the invasion was Soviet-inspired and took immediate action, although some evidence suggests North Korea started the war for nationalistic purposes. General Douglas MacArthur took command of United Nations forces in Korea, but soon discovered that victory would not be achieved without tangling with Mao Tse Tung's forces in China. MacArthur refused to heed President Truman's caution against such an engagement and called for an attack on China. Truman removed MacArthur from command, and his hesitation about entering another full-scale war cost him considerable popularity in a conservative Congress and public.

The policy of global defense, however, continued unabated as government aid was extended to the French in Indochina, South Korea, and Formosa. Australia and New Zealand joined the United States in a mutual defense agreement and bases were acquired in Morocco, Spain, and other areas. James Reston of the *New York Times* reported from Asia in August 1953 that the "range of American activities in this part of the world is unbelievable."[5]

The consensus in the 1950s was that the United States was the most powerful, most free, wealthiest, and most contented nation on earth. Economists as well as labor leaders predicted that economic growth would produce enough for everyone. Whatever doubts about democracy critics had expressed during the 1930s vaporized. Confidence returned.

A consensus attitude ran through public institutions as well as political decisions. High schools used J. Edgar Hoover's anti-communist polemic *Masters of Deceit* to teach American government; historians attempted to explain conflicts as aberrations in society and stressed what had been continuous throughout the nation's political, social, and economic history; and the press ignored the rumbling underneath in favor of the apparent great gains for the nation's population. Broadcasters focused on technological improvement, and although some newsmen strived for greater issue coverage, the commercial dominance of the sponsor limited such scope. It was a press, wrote University of Massachusetts professor James Boylan in *Columbia Journalism Review*, "mired in a creed of impenetrable smug," of "unquestioning acceptance of authority," and "scorn for matters intellectual." To be a professional, he wrote of his own experience at the Columbia University Graduate School of Journalism, was to get the "technique" right.[6]

The espoused technique, despite the emphasis on interpretation discussed in many circles in the 1930s, was "objectivity." Although the bylined political columnists and editorial writers practiced as energetically as in the past, many news reporters maintained a conventional attitude, reporting the statements of officials and ignoring the undercurrents, the indications of a discontented black population and labor unrest. Publishers and broadcast managers were in collusion, if not consciously, then unconsciously accepting the dominant intellectual frame of the nation's political leaders. Wrote James Boylan, "over the long run even objective journalism disseminates mainly what its managers see as legitimate."[7]

Alternatives existed, although liberal or critical voices declined after the war, and the media became the object of anti-communist investigations in Congress. One of the "lonely voices" on the left was Dwight MacDonald's *Politics*. MacDonald, who spent seven years working for Luce's publications and who flirted briefly with Marxism, began the journal in 1944. *Politics*, which died in 1949, never made a profit, but kept alive the voice of dissent in the late 1940s.[8] Probably the decade's most consistent critic was I. F. Stone, who published his *Weekly* throughout the Korean War, the McCarthy years, and into the 1960s, when his was one of the first voices to speak against the Vietnam War.

Newspapers faced severe competition from television for the advertising dollar in the 1950s, and the number of cities having multiple newspapers continued to decline. The number of women editors and reporters in the periodical industry increased 7 percent during the 1940s, and a slow increase continued into the 1950s, so that by 1960 women claimed 36.6 percent of all those jobs.[9] *Mademoiselle*'s job editor in 1949 wrote that before men returned from the war women "could have had a crack at a beginning job, even on a big-city daily," but that women were being shifted to departments emphasizing the women's angle, and when they dropped out of news jobs, men replaced them.[10]

TELEVISION TECHNOLOGY COMES OF AGE

RADIO IN CRISIS

Radio prospered during World War II, but the popular medium lost listeners in the early 1950s and shifted direction. In heavy competition with television by the mid-fifties, radio turned to music for its content and capitalized on portability.

The 950 stations operating at the beginning of the war years grew to more than 2,000 stations by 1950. Radio-station revenue, at $155 million in 1940, reached $310 million by 1945 and $454 million in 1950. Radio also became the major news medium for most Americans. Polls in 1939 indicated that 25 percent of the public relied on the radio for most of its news, and many listeners said they believed radio was more objective than the newspapers. In

> **RADIO AS MIRROR**
>
> Radio, if it is to serve and survive, must hold a mirror behind the nation and the world. If the reflection shows radical intolerance, economic inequality, bigotry, unemployment or anything else—let the people see it, or rather hear it. The mirror must have no curves and must be held with a steady hand.
>
> SOURCE. Edward R. Murrow, September 16, 1945, as reported in Variety, September 19.

1942, other surveys indicated 73 percent of the public received most of its war news from radio; in 1946, 63 percent of the public said radio was its major source of all news.

The magic of live radio rapidly disappeared, as magnetic tape made palatable prerecorded sound. The wire recording available before the war required hand-tieing and heat fusion for editing, which rarely produced satisfactory sound. Americans discovered and confiscated prerecorded plastic tape when they entered Germany during the war and found automated radio stations.

Radio, which had grown to prominence during the thirties and forties with its controversial commentary about the war, its battle coverage, and its top entertainment, searched for new purpose at the end of the war. Performers, news broadcasters, and children's programmers had encouraged bond sales, savings and other war-directed efforts. Clearly the time for new programming had arrived. Some industry figures wanted to focus on perfecting existing program genres; others argued that radio should become more controversial and explore issues such as racial and religious intolerance, the threat of the atomic bomb, and antidemocratic tendencies within the country.[11] Radio solved the dilemma to some degree by pursuing both directions. Although it perfected existing programming, it also developed in new directions. In 1945, for example, NBC introduced "Meet the Press," and in 1946, it established a documentary unit.

Radio felt the full impact of the conservative swing of the public mind after the war, and by 1949, sponsors began to withdraw support for liberal commentators. When William Shirer lost his sponsor for his prime-time CBS broadcast that year, he resigned, claiming his liberal views were not compatible with the network. Liberal commentators, whose patriotism had been in vogue during the antifascist years, now were draped like weights around the necks of the sponsor-dependent and sponsor-dominated networks. Some commentators changed with the times. Walter Winchell, for example, moved from being an outspoken liberal to being so strongly anti-communist that the Soviet ambassador called him a warmonger. And, in December 1950, when NBC broadcast a public-service affairs program sponsored by the American Civil Liberties Union to mark the 159th anniversary of the adoption of the Bill of Rights, hundreds of letters and telegrams protested the airing of "pro-Communist" material.[12]

But liberal versus conservative politics represented only a small portion of radio's real crisis. Despite expansion in the news area, by 1950 radio was beginning an era of "doldrums." More than one hundred of the network series had been on the air for at least a decade, and the listening audience dwindled, particularly during the evening hours. Furthermore, television, which had been promised as early as 1930, finally arrived. The networks fought for the best talent in the radio business. William Paley hired some of NBC's best, and by December 1949, CBS had sixteen of the top twenty shows in the Nielsen ratings. In contrast, during the first four months of 1949 NBC lost $7 million in advertising revenues.[13] During the early 1950s, despite the fact that radio slashed its advertising rates as much as 25 percent, Kellogg, Pillsbury, and other big advertisers curtailed spending. From 1946 to 1955 the four radio networks' gross revenues declined at the rate of $32 million per year.

Radio continued to fashion new programs, introducing adult fiction and westerns. "Gunsmoke" first appeared on radio in 1952 and "Have Gun, Will Travel" went on the air in 1958. Major dramatic programs such as "Philco Playhouse" and the NBC "Star Playhouse" nevertheless dropped from the top Nielsen ratings by 1955. Although there were 46.6 million radios in homes, only 768,000 people were listening to evening broadcasts.

So radio simply changed its tune. In a tight economic atmosphere the networks encouraged local stations to experiment with multiple, local sponsorship. Turning away from a single national sponsor increased the level of independence in radio programming, as well as the independence of the local station. By the 1960s, the networks provided skeletal radio programming: news on the hour, special events coverage, recorded music, and a few features. Commenting on the new developments, Matthew J. Culligan, NBC's vice-president in charge of radio, told a group of advertising agency officials in 1958 that "Radio didn't die. It wasn't even sick. It just had to be psychoanalyzed." Culligan said the portability of the radio had made it "a companion to the individual" instead of "a focal point of all family entertainment. . . . It has become as personal as a pack of cigarets."[14]

Radio, however, faced one more crisis as the decade closed—payola scandals created by disc jockeys who took money in turn for playing certain records. The scandal ran deeper within the industry than the disc jockey, however, and two federal communication commissioners and an assistant to the president resigned for accepting gifts which influenced decision making.[15]

FREQUENCY MODULATION— A NEW RADIO

Edwin Armstrong, who became a millionaire after inventing circuits for RCA, invented FM in the basement of Philosophy Hall at Columbia University, in response to a comment by RCA president David Sarnoff that he wished someone would invent a black box to take the static out of radio. FM was technically superior to AM, eliminated static, and provided for high-fidelity broadcast of music. When his invention was completed in 1933, Armstrong secured four patents and called Sarnoff to view his invention. After testing the equipment, RCA ignored Armstrong and FM, not wanting to upset the radio structure, and pursued television instead, which Sarnoff saw as competing with FM for the upper ranges of the available frequencies.

After demonstrating the clarity of FM at a November 1935 meeting of the Institute of Radio Engineers, Armstrong went to the FCC in the spring of 1936, seeking spectrum allocation. At the same hearings were David Sarnoff and the RCA attorneys, pleading solely for television frequency allocations. Armstrong managed to obtain an experimental license, and began building a 50,000-watt FM station in Alpine, New Jersey.[16]

In 1940, Armstrong achieved victory when the FCC assigned Channel 1, which had been allocated to the television band, to FM. But just as victory seemed imminent, war began. After World War II, the FCC reversed its position and removed FM to the upper end of the spectrum, rendering prewar sets obsolete. In addition, it approved duplicate programming on AM and FM, further reducing the chance of creative FM development. Nevertheless, once Sarnoff recognized that FM would no longer compete for television frequencies, RCA ended its protest. In the years of television development when radio changed to a nearly all-music format, FM finally gained stature because of its superior capability in broadcasting music.

TELEVISION

Variety in April 1930 advertised that television soon would burst forth on the marketplace. And, while tube technology neared acceptable quality, World War II interrupted the marketing of sets begun in 1938. Still, several stations broadcast throughout the war, and by 1950 in cities such as Los Angeles, Philadelphia, New York, and Baltimore more people watched television than listened to radio. In 1948, a CBS vice-president, Hubbell Robinson Jr., announced, "Television is about to do to radio what the Sioux did to Custer. There is going to be a massacre."[17]

The rudiments of television viewing were in place as early as 1931, but disputes over color and a wartime freeze halted its role as an instrument of mass communication until about 1948. (Library of Congress Collection. Photo by Underwood & Underwood)

TECHNOLOGY AND PROGRAMMING

Television technology can be traced in many ways to the same origins as the technology of the motion picture. Experiments in the 1880s with mechanical scanning, and later electronic scanning, led to development of the iconoscope tube in the 1920s by a Russian emigré, Vladimir Zworykin. From 1935 on, RCA demonstrated television to the trade press, and in 1939 the company presented it publicly at the New York World's Fair. RCA was not alone in the field; CBS and Allen B. Du Mont's experimental stations also were telecasting in New York in 1939.

By 1940, about twenty-three stations were reported to be broadcasting in the United States. The boom halted temporarily, however, as war and the need for military production dominated the electronic industry. The major figures joined the war effort. David Sarnoff, who was a brigadier general by the end of the war, had joined the signal corps; William Paley of CBS worked for the Psychological Warfare Unit; and even Edwin Armstrong, who was experimenting with FM, joined the army.

RCA and CBS, which continued to experiment with television, turned their production forces toward domesticity at the end of the war, and by July 1946, the FCC issued twenty-four new licenses. CBS appealed to the FCC to adopt its new mechanical color system, which would provide a superior color system but render prewar black and white sets obsolete, while RCA promoted its own compatible electronic color system. In March 1947, the FCC approved RCA's system, registering a major defeat for CBS. Only months after FCC action approved the RCA standards, the FCC chairman resigned to become NBC's vice-president and general counsel. In battle before the war, Sarnoff had persuaded the FCC to establish a national television standard. His postwar efforts were also successful, as RCA's black-and-white and compatible-color system dominated the industry and achieved FCC approval. CBS and ABC, created from the Blue Network that RCA sold in 1943, lagged behind in television development, and in the early 1950s they struggled to catch up.

Television growth was phenomenal. Although in 1948, 172,000 homes had television receivers, that number had grown to 42 million by 1958. The three major networks, ABC, CBS, and NBC controlled between 50 and 60 percent of all local programming, and 95 percent of evening programming.

During the late 1940s, CBS and NBC experimented with newsreel-patterned news broadcasts, operating in conjunction with the movie houses, and expecting radio profits to pay the bills for the as yet nonprofitable television operations. But in 1948, the FCC froze television development one more time in an effort to study the problems of interference. The freeze continued until 1952, near the end of the Korean War. New York and Los Angeles, each with seven stations, experienced the most complete television operations, while other cities had no more than one station. The spotty effects of television caused advertisers to hesitate and continue their radio sponsorship, but some advertisers, like Hazel Bishop, catapulted sales through television advertising. In cities where television succeeded, movie houses closed and night clubs experienced large drops in attendance.[18]

Television at first adapted much of its programming from successful radio series. Characterizing what some termed television's "Golden Age" of the early 1950s were live anthologies such as "Philco Television Playhouse," "Kraft Television Theatre," and "U.S. Steel Hour." Each show was individually sponsored by a particular advertiser as the names "Kraft" and "U.S. Steel" indicated. The conservative climate of the early 1950s mitigated against bold or controversial themes, and when Reginald Rose submitted a script for "Thunder on Sycamore Street," which depicted neighborhood prejudice against a black family, Westinghouse's "Studio One" theatre on CBS accepted it only on the basis that Rose change the black family to "something else" so as not to offend southern audiences. Although Rose agreed to change the family to that of an ex-convict, he built the dramatic plot so that viewers did not know the reason for the neighborhood treatment of the family until the show's end, thus creating a controversial image in viewers' minds.[19]

The anthologies, combined with live spectaculars and innovative news programs such as Ed Murrow's "See It Now," provided exceptional fare for the new medium, but between 1956 and 1958 the anthologies and Ed Murrow were canceled, and the industry moved from its New York base to the film capital of Hollywood. Detective shows, westerns, situation comedies such as "I Love Lucy," and highly successful quiz shows replaced the older programming.

Straight news programming in the early 1950s shifted from radio's analysis to an emphasis on "staged events" in fifteen-minute evening broadcasts. NBC's John Cameron Swayze's "Camel News Caravan" and CBS's "Television News with Douglas Edwards" had to cope with new demands for visuals, resulting in too-often staged events. In addition, direct sponsorship exacted other tolls: Camel forbade "No smoking" signs from appearing on any of Swayze's shows.

The quiz shows, which emulated successful radio quiz shows, offered considerably higher stakes, and by 1957, constituted thirty-seven hours of the networks' weekly schedule. The "$64,000 Question," which enabled Revlon to sell out "Living Lipstick," was quickly emulated by "Twenty-One" and other programs. Public disillusionment ran high, however, when Charles Van Doren, a highly successful "Twenty-One" contestant, admitted in 1959 that he had been given the correct answers by the show's producers. Van Doren's admission led to further investigations, revealing that rigged programs prevailed throughout the quiz-show industry.

The early days of television bespoke optimism for the possibilities of mass culture. NBC's president Sylvester L. Weaver, Jr., in 1953, described programs that "serve the grand design of television, which is to create an aristocracy of the people, the proletariat of privilege, the Athenian masses—to make the average man the uncommon man."[20] By 1958, however, Edward R. Murrow in a lecture to the Radio and Television News Directors' Association, attacked television content as consisting of "decadence, escapism, and insulation from the realities of the world." He said networks underestimated their viewers and that mass media content reflected the nation's comfort and complacency.[21] Competition between networks during the early years of the decade, the challenge to defeat the threat of pay television, and the need to

The Television Quiz Hearings of 1959 were lonely indeed, compared to the years of grandiose promotion that preceded them. (Library of Congress Collection, U.S. News and World Report photo)

program for a new medium promoted the development of superior programming. However, by 1958 nearly 90 percent of all homes had television sets, growth rates of advertising were leveling off, and the industry decided to contain costs rather than spend lavishly on expensive programming.[22]

TELEVISION GOES TO THE ELECTIONS

In 1948, Republicans and Democrats convened their national conventions in Philadelphia because it was in that city of the Founding Fathers that television could reach the greatest audience. Truman de-emphasized broadcasting in his campaign, claiming that broadcasters had "sold out to the special interests." He continuously referred to the "kept press" and the "paid radio." On the other side, Thomas Dewey refused the advice of the Republican-hired advertising agency of Batten, Barton, Durstine & Osborne, which urged him to make a number of spot announcements. Instead he relied on lofty speeches. The polls predicted Dewey would win, and on the morning after the election H. V. Kaltenborn remained convinced, noting that although Truman was ahead, he could not win. Truman's victory was ambiguous at best; while he remained in office he fought an antagonistic Congress throughout his second term.[23]

In 1952, the networks offered sponsored television campaign coverage. As historian Erik Barnouw wrote, Betty Furness opened and closed refrigerator doors hundreds of times for Westinghouse before the issues were settled. General Dwight D. Eisenhower of World War II fame and Richard Nixon of the House Un-American Activities Committee fame challenged Illinois Governor Adlai Stevenson and Senator John Sparkman of Alabama. Eisenhower, upon the advice of the same advertising agency that prompted Dewey to use spot announcements, relied on twenty-second "hero-in, hero-out" shots. Saturation coverage during the last two weeks of the campaign cost $1,500,000. Stevenson, refusing to be merchandised "like a breakfast food," relied on speech making, a radio technique not well applied to the visual television era.

Historically, the most studied aspect of the campaign may well have been Richard Nixon's televised "Checkers" speech. The Republican National Committee sponsored a half hour of time for Nixon, accused of irregularity in the use of campaign money, to defend himself. Nixon claimed none of the money ever went for his personal use, and then added:

> One other thing I should probably tell you, because if I don't they'll probably be saying this about me too, we did get something—a gift—after the election. A man down in Texas heard Pat on the radio mention the fact that our two daughters would like to have a dog. And, believe it or not, the day before we left on this campaign trip we got a message from Union Station in Baltimore saying they had a package for us. We went down to get it. You know what it was? It was a little cocker spaniel dog in a crate that he sent all the way from Texas. Black and white and spotted. And our little girl—Tricia, the six-year-old—named it Checkers. And you know the kids love that dog and I just want to say this right now, that regardless of what they say about it, we're going to keep it.[24]

In 1956, recovering from a heart attack, President Eisenhower ran for reelection, relying even more on television than he had in 1952. The networks expanded their coverage of the national conventions, using battery-operated miniature cameras to broadcast live interviews from the convention floor.

Eisenhower used television to his advantage, both in the 1952 election and in this 1959 press conference. (Library of Congress Collection, U.S. News and World Report photo)

Other innovations included split screens, devices for flashing vote totals on home screens and allowing coverage to be coordinated by a TV director instead of the anchor team. However, once the conventions were over, network news about the campaigns consisted only of interview programs and weekly news summaries. The fifteen-minute nightly newscasts provided for little daily coverage of political campaigning.[25]

THE PRESS AND GOVERNMENT

During the late 1940s and the early 1950s, the press found itself in an uneasy alliance with government. Cooperation with the Executive Branch and the State Department during the war years had led editors and broadcasters to question their relationship to federal officials. Although the media promoted the hard-line rhetoric of Truman and other anti-communist political leaders, they also became targets of its abuse. The convention of objectivity, adhered to in part because publishers had rejected the partisanship of nineteenth- and early twentieth-century press lords, as well as because it allowed newspapers to avoid challenging those in power, contributed to the anti-communist hysteria. Often, adherence to objectivity was related to opinions about McCarthy. From 1950 to 1955, the Associated Press Managing Editors Association hotly debated the relative merits of objectivity and interpretation. Those who supported objectivity inevitably supported McCarthy editorially, while those who advocated interpretation opposed the senator and his charges.[26]

THE FEDERAL COMMUNICATIONS COMMISSION

The Federal Communications Commission, created as an independent regulatory agency in 1934, perpetuated unequal media partners in regard to the First Amendment, an arrangement created by the Federal Radio Act of 1927. Although the FCC had the power to grant and revoke licenses to broadcasters, print media were free to publish without license. In 1932, a U.S. Court of Appeals upheld the right of the Federal Radio Commission (which preceded the FCC) to revoke the license of a station that made reprehensible attacks on the Catholic Church, but a year earlier the U.S. Supreme Court, in *Near vs. Minnesota*, held that a "Minnesota rag" scandal sheet could not be shut down even though it was viciously attacking Jews and law enforcement officials. So, although the government could not censor broadcasts, the threat of license removal acted as a constant caution to station managers.

In addition to license allocation, the FCC had been active through the late 1930s in modifying station-network relationships. In May 1941, it issued the "Report on Chain Broadcasting" in an attempt to limit network control over the affiliates and to increase the diversity of programming. The report also forced the partial dissolution of NBC, specifying that a network could affiliate with only one station in a community.

The Supreme Court upheld the FCC's rules in NBC's challenge to the licensing process in *National Broadcasting Co. v. United States*. The court declared that denial of a station license on the grounds of public interest "is not a denial of free speech," and that the FCC, while charged with technical regulation, had considerably more power than that of a traffic cop.[27] In October 1943, NBC sold the less profitable of its two systems, the Blue Network, which then became ABC.

The FCC continued to express its concern over programming by noting the discrepancies between station-license proposals and actual programming. In March 1946 the FCC issued "Public Service Responsibilities of Broadcast Licensees," more commonly referred to as the Blue Book of broadcasting. Although in the Blue Book the FCC stipulated more definite program standards, those standards never were enforced, creating more controversy than change.

Not only did the courts have double standards and logic-tight compartments offensive to broadcasters, the leaders of the print media often were unsympathetic. In the late 1950s, *Wall Street Journal* editor Bernard Kilgore declared that the First Amendment simply did not apply to broadcasters because the First Amendment, passed in 1791, said nothing about broadcasting.

During the 1950s, the regulatory agency was underfunded and like most regulatory agencies of the decade "lost the glamour of the New Deal years, when, so the legend went, the bright young attorneys and academicians rushed to Washington to supervise the American economy."[28] Eisenhower, who disliked patronage, made poor choices in his appointments, and procedural constraints on all regulatory committees limited the possibilities for an activist commission. One chairman dubbed the decade "the whorehouse era," as he noted the 1957 reports of commissioners favoring Republican applicants and accepting gifts and loans from license applications and lobbyists. In 1957, a House investigation committee revealed that commissioners had voted in at least one case in return for money to meet personal expenses.

Nevertheless, the activities of the commission in the 1950s set significant groundwork for subsequent court decisions. In 1959 Congress codified a series of rulings made by the FCC as early as 1949 that became the "Fairness Doctrine." The doctrine required that broadcasters encourage open and robust debate on public issues "by affording reasonable opportunity for the discussion of conflicting views of issues of public importance."

Despite the passing of the Fairness Doctrine, scholars and the public alike questioned the efficacy of the regulatory agency because of its close ties to the industry being regulated. From 1945 to 1971, for example, twenty-one of the thirty-three commissioners (64 percent) who left office went to work for the communications industry.[29]

THE HOUSE COMMITTEE ON UN-AMERICAN ACTIVITIES (HUAC)

Investigation by the House Un-American Activities Committee put fear in the minds and hearts of those who contemplated criticizing the anti-communist stance of the committee. The motion picture industry was the first branch of media to come under the scrutiny of HUAC. Industry leader Jack L. Warner contributed to the hysteria by citing communist propaganda in films which, he said, consisted of "picking on rich men" and "poking fun at our political system." At first Hollywood assumed a courageous stance and seemed to close ranks to protect those who were attacked, but its courage soon failed. On November 24, 1947, a group of top film executives met in New York and decided to clean house to protect the industry's reputation, blacklisting many industry artists.[30]

Late that same year, the broadcast industry was attacked by the American Business Consultants, a group which consisted of three former FBI agents. The complaints by the consultants accelerated a few days before the Korean War broke out, when the group published a 215-page booklet, *Red Channels: The Report of Communist Influence in Radio and Television*, with a cover that depicted a red hand closing on a microphone. The report charged 115 individuals in the industry with having communist sympathies. The list, wrote Erik Barnouw, was a "roll of honor," citing many of the people who had made radio an "honored medium." Although the report was seldom discussed publicly, actors soon began to feel its effects; the industry then institutionalized blacklisting, with CBS requiring a loyalty oath and NBC establishing security channels within its legal department.[31] The impact of the charges continued to be felt throughout the fifties, as networks and sponsors screened actors and writers for any possible leftist ties.

THE PRESS AND JOSEPH McCARTHY

One unscrupulous public official who understood how to manipulate the press through its own endorsement of objectivity as a journalistic convention was Joseph R. McCarthy, the Republican junior senator from Wisconsin. Even though McCarthy joined the hunt for communists in government — in partic-

The television cameras gathered to report the last day of the McCarthy hearings in June 1954. (Library of Congress Collection, U.S. News and World Report photo)

ular, in the U.S. State Department—in March 1950, he was slow to reach the anti-communist bandwagon. Historian Garry Wills suggested that the "McCarthy Era"—as it is sometimes called—did not begin in 1950, when McCarthy made his first accusations of communists in government. That era, Wills wrote, started in 1947, under President Harry S Truman, Attorney General Tom Clark, and FBI director J. Edgar Hoover. These officials provided HUAC—which helped propel Congressman Richard M. Nixon to prominence—with lists of names and with "the loyalty program for which it could demand ever stricter enforcement, the presumption that a citizen is disloyal until proved loyal, the denial of work to any man or woman who would not undergo such a proving process."[32]

Because he realized that a senator's sensational allegations could make news—and increase his power—Senator McCarthy became an expert in making charges—without supporting evidence—claiming there were hundreds (the figures varied from announcement to announcement) of communists in the State Department. He also identified specific government officials as being communists, doing so while the Senate or a Senate subcommittee was in session.

Wire services and "objective" newspaper reporters fell easily into Senator McCarthy's trap. He would unleash a sensational charge shortly before deadline, reducing time for fact checking by the news media. Refuting such charges required extensive reporter initiative and time, and many media offered prompt space or time. Newspapers that relied on the wire services, which operated on tight deadlines and with limited staff, tended to repeat McCarthy's charges without adequate refutation. Nevertheless, a variety of newspapers and magazines, including the *Christian Science Monitor*, the *Washington Post*, the *Milwaukee Journal,* and *Time* challenged McCarthy from the moment on February 9, 1950, that he made his first charges in a speech at Wheeling, West Virginia. The *Post* used in-depth, daily reporting by Murrey Maurder, not only to report McCarthy's charges, but also to examine the charges and to relate McCarthy's comments to earlier charges. Such coverage was supplemented by devastating Herblock cartoons and calm, reasoned editorials by Alan Barth. From the date of the Wheeling speech until McCarthy's death seven years later, the *Milwaukee Journal* published 201 editorials criticizing McCarthy.[33]

Nevertheless, it took four years, charges of communists in the army, and the power of television finally to expose McCarthy in such a way that the American public was no longer willing to believe him. The magic name here—and still a symbol for excellence in television news—was that of Edward R. Murrow of CBS News. The trusted, over-smoked deep baritone voice that had informed Americans of the bombs being dropped over London, on a program called "See It Now," finally exposed Senator McCarthy.

The winter of 1953–1954 was memorable as the depth of the McCarthy Era, months during which an Indiana textbook commissioner called Robin Hood a communist and recommended purging textbooks of references to Quakers, who did not believe in fighting wars. Further, McCarthy had been investigating the army and was beginning to attack individual officers.[34]

On March 9, 1954, Murrow's "See It Now" program devoted all of its thirty minutes to a devastating portrait of Senator McCarthy. As he read the introduction, Murrow offered reply time to the senator. The reply time was offered in that fashion on advice from CBS President William S. Paley. Paley

> ### MURROW CHALLENGES AMERICANS TO THINK
>
> We will not walk in fear, one of another. We will not be driven by fear into an age of unreason if we dig deep in our history and our doctrine, and remember that we are not descended from fearful men, not from men who feared to write, to speak, to associate, and to defend causes that were for the moment unpopular. This is no time for men who oppose Senator McCarthy's methods to keep silent, or for those who approve. We can deny our heritage and our history, but we cannot escape responsibility for the result. There is no way for a citizen of a republic to abdicate his responsibilities. As a nation we have come into full inheritance at a tender age. We proclaim ourselves — as indeed we are — the defenders of freedom, wherever it continues to exist in the world. But we cannot defend freedom abroad by deserting it at home. The actions of the junior senator from Wisconsin have caused alarm and dismay amongst our allies abroad and given considerable comfort to our enemies. And whose fault is that? Not really his. He didn't create this situation of fear, he merely exploited it — and rather successfully. Cassius was right: "The fault, dear Brutus, is not in our stars but in ourselves."
>
> SOURCE. Edward R. Murrow

evidently believed the senator was sure to ask for response time, and offering it before the fact would show the network behaving with a fairness foreign to McCarthy's bullying of witnesses in the hearings of his Senate Subcommittee on Investigations.[35]

The half-hour show broadcast clips of Senator McCarthy making statements, with a counterpoint of contradictions from the senator himself, or, at times, with corrective statements added by Murrow. For example, in A. M. Sperber's words:

> There was McCarthy questioning a witness — "You know the Civil Liberties Union has been listed as a front for . . . the Communist Party?" — with Murrow (intoning an answer) right behind him: "The Attorney General's List (visible in McCarthy's hand) does not and never has listed the A.C.L.U. as subversive. Nor does the F.B.I. or any other federal government agency.[36]

Murrow here stepped far beyond the featureless objectivity that McCarthy had fed upon. He spoke out at a time when few dared to oppose McCarthy publicly. President Dwight D. Eisenhower, despite what evidently was a growing distaste for McCarthy, remained silent or, when out campaigning—gingerly expressed affirmation for McCarthy's anti-communist crusading.

Murrow concluded his broadcast with an intensely personal conclusion. He looked through the camera and seemed to talk one-to-one with the members of the audience as he delivered one of the most famous editorial statements in American journalism. He noted that investigation by legislative committees is necessary to gather information needed to create effective laws, but that the line between investigation and persecution was extremely fine. "We must not confuse dissent with disloyalty," Murrow warned, and "must remember always that accusation is not proof."[37]

Murrow's courageous broadcast—with the support of CBS News when it counted most—was the beginning of the end for Senator McCarthy.[38] McCarthy's famous and disastrous confrontation with canny attorney Joseph Welch just months later—in which Welch castigated McCarthy for smearing one of the young lawyers in Welch's firm—symbolized the senator's growing desperation and political impotence. Welch, a slight, gentle Boston lawyer, rose in fury against the alcohol-fueled cruelty of Senator McCarthy with a much-remembered line: "At long last, Sir, have you no sense of decency?"

EASTLAND HEARINGS

But the press's confrontation with anti-communism did not end with McCarthy's demise. In 1955, the Senate Internal Security Subcommittee, headed by Senator James Eastland, Democrat of Mississippi, held closed hearings to investigate communist influence in American newspapers. The *New York Times* was the focus of the attack; of the thirty-eight witnesses interviewed, twenty-five were *Times* employees and five others had formerly worked for the *Times*. In January 1956, the *Times* wrote that it had been singled out for investigation because it championed desegregation and opposed McCarthyism, issues on which Eastland took the opposite view. The *Times* also said it would not knowingly employ a communist on its staff. Actions of the *Times* are remembered differently, however, by its former reporters. Editor Turner Catledge claimed he persuaded the general manager, Julius Ochs Adler, not to fire people for taking the Fifth Amendment.[39] However, James Aronson recalls that the *Times* fired at least three editorial workers.[40]

AN ACTIVIST NEWS MEDIA

By 1954, then, the basics for an activist news media were in place. The Supreme Court had declared in *Near vs. Minnesota* (1931) that it would protect the press from states' legal meddling, and Murrow had suffered no consequences for his editorial comment on McCarthy. Beyond such legal safeguard, the media had the object lesson of the McCarthy Era to suggest that deadpanned objectivity was insufficient. Objectivity had to be expanded to reporting the facts fully, fairly — and, if facts did not speak for themselves, efforts must be made to put them into meaningful perspective.

CRITICISM AND ALTERNATIVES

"IZZY" STONE

I. F. Stone, born Isidor Feinstein, challenged the establishment throughout his long career as a journalist. A member of the radical left in the 1930s and a *PM* staffer in the 1940s, Stone cajoled, berated, and challenged government officials and the military-industrial complex.

Stone was born in 1908 and began his first newspaper, *The Progress*, when he was fourteen. His father forced him to stop publishing because the newspaper absorbed Stone so much that he nearly flunked out of school. He attended the University of Pennsylvania, but left in 1927 because he claimed school interfered with his reading. He took a job with the *Camden* (N.J.) *Courier*, but quit when he failed to get an assignment to cover the Sacco-Vanzetti anarchist trial. After a short stint with the *Philadelphia Inquirer*, Stone worked from 1938 to 1946 for the *Nation*. He was a staffer on *PM* and then joined the *New York Compass*, which folded in 1952.

In 1946, Stone traveled aboard an illegal ship from Europe to Palestine, writing the account of survivors of the holocaust who ignored Britain's immigration quotas for Palestine to seek a homeland. After spending three months aboard ship and in Palestine, Stone wrote a series for *PM*, which was reprinted in a book *Underground to Palestine*.[41]

In the narrow political atmosphere of the 1950s, Stone was hard pressed to find a job. Even Frieda Kirchwey, editor of the *Nation*, would not hire him back. His critical work, *The Hidden History of the Korean War*, had earned criticism from the right, and his criticism of cold war policies of both the West and the East had earned him the label of apologist from the left.

In 1952, Stone began his own news sheet, *I. F. Stone's Weekly*, a critical, liberal publication aimed at a small audience. With $3,500 in severance pay from the *Compass*, and $3,000 in loans and the old *PM*, *Star*, and *Compass* mailing lists, he gathered 5,300 charter subscribers.

Stone's radical vision of the 1930s faded as the Soviet Union invaded Hungary, and he became fully aware of the lack of regard for human rights within the Soviet system. In May 1956, he traveled through the Soviet Union and returned, noting "This is not a good society, and it is not led by honest men. No society is good in which men fear to think — much less speak — freely." He called Soviet Russia "a hermetically sealed prison, stifling in its atmosphere of completely rigid and low-level thought control."[42]

Stone's criticism of the Soviet Union alienated many of his readers on the left, and coupled with a defense of a homeland for Palestinians, as well as for Jews, lost his *Weekly* about 400 subscribers.[43] Although Stone's fans, ranging from Albert Einstein to Marilyn Monroe, were faithful to his ringing criticism, Vice-President Spiro Agnew referred to the *Weekly* as "another strident voice of illiberalism" and David Eisenhower, Nixon's son-in-law, refused to attend his own graduation because I. F. Stone was the commencement speaker.

Stone's unpopularity in the 1950s and early 1960s began to change, however. One of the first to criticize the Vietnam War, in the 1960s he became a hero of the American left. During the 1960s and early 1970s, he received five honorary degrees, including one from the University of Pennsylvania, and a documentary of his life and work was shown at the Cannes Film Festival in 1974 and later on public television.

Stone's wife, Esther, handled the business end of the weekly, which Stone ended in 1971 because of his own poor health. Though his wife was a Republican at heart, he claimed, she never interfered with his right to be a radical. Although Stone lost his hope for a successful society coming from a socialist framework, he never lost sight of what he considered to be necessities of a good society: freedom of speech and protection of other civil liberties.

THE BLACK PRESS

A trend toward consolidation in the black press was apparent from the 1930s onward, just as it was apparent for the press as a whole. In 1956, John Sengstacke converted the famous *Chicago Defender* from a weekly to a daily and developed a newspaper group with nine papers, including the *Pittsburgh Courier*, which he acquired in 1966. The second largest black newspaper group was the Afro-American Newspapers.

The major development of the 1950s was the expansion of the black-magazine industry. In 1942, John H. Johnson, employed by an insurance agency in Chicago, borrowed $500 to start *Negro Digest*. That publication served as the cornerstone for subsequent magazines and a successful corporation. Johnson started *Ebony*, patterned after *Life*, in 1945. *Ebony* demonstrated the power of the black person as a consumer and was the first publication to garner enough advertising dollars to shift financial reliance from subscription rates to advertising. In 1950, Johnson started *Tan*, and in 1951, *Jet*, a weekly black news magazine.

CONCLUSION

Radio, the dominant news media of the war years, began to give way to television competition and lose its advertisers and listening audience in the 1950s, despite cutbacks in advertising rates. Reflecting the growing conservatism in the country, the industry withdrew its support for liberal commentators and turned toward a new format of noncontroversial news summaries and music formats.

Television technology, which had been available since before World War II, found favorable conditions only after two freezes on licenses and the end of the Korean War. Programming in the early 1950s adapted radio's best shows and promised quality fare with anthologies and live performances. Nevertheless, by the end of the decade industry leaders, assured of large audiences and relieved of the fear of pay television, consolidated costs and turned to less expensive weekly shows. The quiz scandals of the late 1950s propelled the industry toward a greater interest in public affairs programming. Television was used by both presidential candidates in the elections of 1952 and 1956, and although networks covered the political conventions, fifteen-minute evening newscasts provided little in the way of daily political campaign coverage.

The media and government participated in an uneasy alliance during the decade. Although the convention of objectivity was employed to join the country's protest against Communism, the media also became victims of the anti-communist hysteria. Congressional investigations of the motion-picture industry, the broadcast industry and newspapers led to caution on the part of many editors and managers and slowed progress toward the exposure of Senator Joseph McCarthy.

Although liberal voices were nearly silent during the decade, some alternatives existed. Dwight MacDonald's *Politics*, *I. F. Stone's Weekly*, and the black press catered to specific audiences.

NOTES

1. Thomas G. Paterson, *On Every Front: The Making of the Cold War* (New York: W. W. Norton & Co., 1979), p. 119.
2. Cited in Mary Beth Norton, et al., *A People and a Nation*, vol. 2 (Boston: Houghton Mifflin Co., 1982), p. 862.
3. Walter Lippmann, "The American Destiny," *Life* (5 June 1939), pp. 47, 73, cited in James L. Baughman, *Henry R. Luce and the Rise of the American News Media* (New York: G. K. Hall/Twayne, 1987), p. 132.
4. Ronald Samuel Reinig, "America Looking Outward: American Cold War Attitudes During the Crucial Years, 1945–1947, as Reflected in the American Maga-

zine Medium," Ph.D. disser., Syracuse University, 1974, p. 487 and *passim*., cited in Baughman, *Luce and the Rise of the American News Media*, p. 150.

5. Norton, et al., *A People and a Nation*, p. 808.
6. James Boylan, "Declarations of Independence," *Columbia Journalism Review* (November/December 1986), p. 30.
7. Boylan, "Declarations of Independence," p. 31.
8. Lauren Kessler, "Against the American Grain: The Lonely Voice of *Politics* Magazine, 1944–49," *Journalism History* 9:2 (Summer 1982), p. 49.
9. Marion Marzolf, *Up from the Footnote: A History of Women Journalists* (New York: Hastings House, 1977), p. 74.
10. Cited in Marzolf, *Up from the Footnote*, p. 75.
11. Fred J. MacDonald, *Don't Touch That Dial! Radio Programming in American Life, 1920–1960* (Chicago: Nelson-Hall, 1979), p. 77.
12. MacDonald, *Don't Touch That Dial*, pp. 315, 317, 320.
13. MacDonald, *Don't Touch That Dial*, p. 81.
14. *Variety*, February 12, 1958, p. 49, cited in MacDonald, *Don't Touch That Dial*, p. 88. "Cigaret" was the common journalistic spelling through the 1960s.
15. Erik Barnouw, *Tube of Plenty: The Evolution of American Television* (New York: Oxford University Press, 1975), p. 247.
16. Barnouw, *Tube of Plenty*, pp. 77–83.
17. MacDonald, *Don't Touch That Dial*, p. 85.
18. Barnouw, *Tube of Plenty*, p. 114.
19. Barnouw, *Tube of Plenty*, p. 165.
20. Sylvester Weaver, "Television 1953: The Case for the Networks," *Television Magazine* 10 (January 1953), p. 17; address by Weaver, 15 June 1953, Broadcast Pioneers Library, Washington, D.C., File 179, p. 16, cited in James L. Baughman, "Television in the 'Golden Age': An Entrepreneurial Experiment," *The Historian*, vol. 47, no. 2, February 1985.
21. James L. Baughman, *Television's Guardians: The FCC and the Politics of Programming, 1958–1967* (Knoxville: University of Tennessee Press, 1985), pp. 29, 30. Text of the address is in box 7-B-25 of the Murrow Papers and was reprinted in *The Reporter*, November 13, 1958, pp. 32–36.
22. For elaboration of this thesis, see Baughman, "Television in the 'Golden Age.'"
23. Barnouw, *Tube of Plenty*, pp. 111–112.
24. Barnouw, *Tube of Plenty*, pp. 136–138.
25. See Craig Allen, "TV and the 1956 Presidential Campaign: Insights into the Evolution of Political Television," paper presented to History Division, Association for Education in Journalism and Mass Communication, San Antonio, Tex., August 1987.
26. Edwin R. Bayley, *Joe McCarthy and the Press* (Madison: University of Wisconsin Press, 1981), pp. 80–85.
27. Baughman, *Television's Guardians*, p. 9.

28. Baughman, *Television's Guardians*, p. 11.
29. Florence Heffron, "the FCC and Broadcast Deregulation," in John J. Havick, ed., *Communications Policy and the Political Process* (Westport, Conn.: Greenwood Press, 1983), p. 43.
30. Barnouw, *Tube of Plenty*, pp. 108–109.
31. Barnouw, *Tube of Plenty*, p. 129.
32. Garry Wills, Introduction to Lillian Hellman, *Scoundrel Time* (New York: Little, Brown & Co., 1976), pp. 11–12.
33. Bayley, *McCarthy and the Press*, pp. 135, 148–150.
34. A. M. Sperber, *Murrow: His Life and Times* (New York: Freundlich Books, 1986), p. 426.
35. Sperber, *Murrow*, p. 435.
36. Sperber, *Murrow*, p. 437.
37. Edward R. Murrow, "See It Now" for March 9, 1954, in Edward W. Bliss, Jr., *In Search of Light: The Broadcasts of Edward R. Murrow 1938–1961* (New York: Knopf, 1967), pp. 247–248.
38. Although CBS seemed to support Murrow to some degree in the broadcast, Murrow and Fred Friendly were forced to advertise the program with funds from their own pockets.
39. Turner Catledge, *My Life and the Times* (New York: Harper & Row, 1971), pp. 227–30, cited in Bayley, *McCarthy and the Press*, p. 138.
40. James Aronson, *The Press and the Cold War* (New York: Bobbs-Merrill Co., 1970), p. 146.
41. Larry Van Dyne, "The Adventures of I. F. Stone," *The Chronicle Review* (Supplement to the *Chronicle of Higher Education*), February 5, 1979, pp. 4–6.
42. Robert Cottrell, "I. F. Stone: A Maverick Journalist's Battle with the Superpowers," *Journalism History* 12:2 (Summer 1985), p. 64.
43. *Washington Post* July 9, 1979, B 1–2.

CHAPTER 19

AFFLUENCE
AND
ACTIVISM

It was a time when old values were breaking down; new knowledge exploded all around us; people worried about drugs, hippies, and war. We talked of violence, urban disorder, turmoil. New terms like polarization, credibility gap, and counter-culture crept into the language.[1]

The decade of the 1960s represented to Americans a period of cultural upheaval, dramatic change in value systems, and rebellion and experimentation in journalism as well as in other aspects of American life. John F. Kennedy, in his inaugural address in January 1961, aroused high expectations not only in the hearts of many intellectuals, but also in the hearts of young people, and minorities. However, those expectations, inspired by Kennedy's inaugural challenge, became failed expectations by the end of the decade.[2] During the late 1960s, crisis became routine with the Tet Offensive of 1968, balance-of-payment and gold crises, Johnson's decision not to run for reelection, the Martin Luther King and Kennedy assassinations, black protests, student sit-ins, riots at the 1968 Democratic convention, and National Guard interventions and subsequent killings at Kent State.[3]

Emerging during the 1960s was a New Left, a radical student mass movement which championed civil rights, challenged authority, and,

> ### KENNEDY PRESENTS A CHALLENGE
> In the long history of the world, only a few generations have been granted the role of defending freedom in its hour of maximum danger. I do not shrink from this responsibility — I welcome it. I do not believe that any of us would exchange places with any other people or any other generation. The energy, the faith, the devotion which we bring to this endeavor will light our country and all who serve it — and the glow from that fire can truly light the world.
>
> SOURCE: John Fitzgerald Kennedy, Inaugural Address, January 21, 1961.

later in the decade, opposed the Vietnam War. The New Left had few ties to the radical socialist-communist movements of the 1930s, and rather than appealing to the American working class, the movement attracted young, affluent, but often alienated, adolescents and young adults.[4]

The movement had a profound, although perhaps fleeting, impact on American institutions, and the media were no exception. College students of the early 1960s became reporters, and with the move from student to reporter, they carried a concept of professionalism that demanded more autonomy in the newsroom and sparked challenges to the authority of the editor. James Boylan, writing twenty-five years later (1986) in *Columbia Journalism Review*, wrote that the "great surprise, in retrospect, is the speed with which the bedraggled, victimized press of the 1950s came to see itself as an apparently potent, apparently adversary press in the 1960s."

Within the television studio, the correspondent also gained status, primarily as a result of two networks' decision in 1963 to provide half-hour news shows, which incorporated longer reports and more film. Chet Huntley and David Brinkley helped encourage the evening news habit, starting an evening news show on NBC in 1956 and from 1962 to 1967 keeping CBS in second place in the ratings. CBS rejected as anchorman the super-star commentator Eric Sevareid of World War II fame and Edward R. Murrow tradition for a safer, more objective, former wire-service reporter named Walter Cronkite. Cronkite's all-American, trustworthy image balanced the correspondents' reports that unsettled CBS executives and garnered wrath from the White House.[5]

Although the change was apparent in the newsrooms and studios, and extremely visible in the alternative press, the effect on the corporate structure and the hierarchy of the media was minimal. Publishers were concerned with higher costs and competition from television and suburban newspapers, and corporate consolidation accelerated.

The emphasis on the reporter and the story, however, coupled with a generational challenge to authority, promoted the development of an adversarial approach when foreign correspondents tackled the job of covering a new kind of war, a war with no front line, no clear definition of purpose, and a growing opposition at home. Despite claims that television affected the outcome of the war, more reflective accounts written long after the war's end indicate that the media adhered to the concept of objectivity, or "verifiable truth," and followed public opinion more often then led. Although government protested the new approach and continued its news management efforts, dramatic changes in libel law expanded journalists' abilities to continue in a watchdog role.

The resistance of daily newspaper hierarchies to expand reporter power and to allow the use of new journalism techniques momentarily energized the magazine industry, and writers adopted magazines as their favorite medium for challenging institutional structures. But new journalism did not financially enhance the industry—specialization and targeted advertising markets fueled the industry as some of the big circulation leaders died.

The effects on journalism as seen by the public were negative. Journalists had never before been so visible, and at the end of 1968, George Gallup reported that never in his time had media been held in such low esteem. Wrote Ernest Hynds, "As the 1960s closed, it appeared that the press had become the nation's scapegoat for crime, racial troubles, the war in Vietnam, and other problems."[6]

Changes in the Newsroom

CHANGES IN MANAGEMENT

James Boylan, in an analysis of the changes in the press from 1960 to 1986, attributed some of the changes in journalism to a generational change in control of major newspapers. In 1960, Otis Chandler took over what Boylan described as "the disreputable old *Los Angeles Times* and began to overhaul it." Arthur Ochs Sulzberger became publisher at the *New York Times* and appointed A. M. Rosenthal metropolitan editor; Rosenthal subsequently became managing editor. In 1965, Benjamin Bradlee became editor of the *Washington Post*. These individuals shifted more emphasis to reporting and less to editing.

CHANGES IN THE RANK AND FILE

The generational change occurred not only at the top, but at the bottom as well. As other members critical of institutional society in the 1960s questioned authority, reporters also rebelled at taking orders from deskmen, whom they considered to be unexciting enforcers of old technical standards. Furthermore, reporters extended that challenge to authority to those outside the newsroom, to public officials in particular. "Being a pro," wrote Boylan, "came to mean more than being a good soldier; it meant allegiance to standards considered superior to those of the organization and its parochial limitations."[7]

The change came early in the decade. In 1962, William Rivers, in a study of Washington correspondents, found that reporters felt considerably less pressure from their home offices to write stories in certain ways, and that they experienced greater freedom than had been found in a 1937 study.[8] By 1970, John Johnstone and a group of researchers found that autonomy was highly related to job satisfaction, particularly for younger, participant-oriented journalists. Johnstone also found that older, managerial newsmen tended to be more oriented toward neutral, or objective journalism, than did younger reporters.[9]

REACTIONS TO GOVERNMENT ATTITUDES

The combination of changes among management and reporters, as well as a change in government style, encouraged the press to resist government imposed restrictions in the 1960s. As government moved beyond the cooperation mode editors supported throughout World War II and the 1950s and moved into a stage of what editors perceived to be government-imposed, rather than editor-imposed, news management, the press rebelled.[10] Newspaper editors during the 1950s had regarded themselves as members of an American team: they refused an invitation from the Chinese government to send correspondents to China because, as Clifton Daniel wrote, "We did not want to embarrass our government." Editors had withheld information about aerial spying over the Soviet Union before Gary Powers was captured in 1960 in the U-2 incident; in 1961, a *Miami Herald* story about the training of Cuban exile forces in Florida never appeared; and the *New York Times*, the *Miami Herald*, the *New Republic* and the *Washington Post* all either withheld information completely or altered bits and pieces of the story about the 1961 CIA-sponsored Bay of Pigs invasion of Cuba.

Although editors may have regarded cooperating with the government to suppress information as a civic duty, government excluding the press from the knowledge of power was another. Sociologist Michael Schudson traced the press's outrage at news management to a statement by Arthur Sylvester, spokesman for the Pentagon under presidents Kennedy and Johnson, who defended news management during the 1962 Cuban missile crisis. Sylvester claimed the government had an inherent right to lie if it meant saving itself when faced with a nuclear disaster.[11] Schudson maintained that Sylvester's statement threatened the role of the press as the "fourth branch of government" by crossing "a thin moral line the press felt an obligation to patrol." The press objected not only to the government's lying, but to its claim that the government had a right to lie:

> There was at least this virtue to hypocrisy when the government lied while claiming to be truthful: that if the press discovered the lie, it could embarrass the government. The Sylvester statement placed the government beyond embarrassment.[12]

Furthermore, editors and reporters alike may have objected to Kennedy's handling of the press. Historian and journalist Mark Perry suggested that Kennedy's biographers claimed the president "dazzled" the press, knew how to "handle" them, and enjoyed "bantering" with them. But in actuality Kennedy and his advisers regarded journalists as simpletons to be manipulated.[13]

FINANCIAL STATUS AND CORPORATE DEVELOPMENT

CORPORATE BROADCASTING

When the broadcast industry emerged as a commercial enterprise during the 1920s and 1930s, efforts were made to regulate the industry in the public interest. Despite the rulings regarding equal time and fairness made by the

FCC between the 1934 passing of the Federal Communications Act and the 1960s, consumers and legislators have questioned whether the commission operated in the public interest, or whether it operated in the interests of the industry alone. Moreover, since 1934, increased attention has been paid to the large corporate structure of broadcasting, the involvement of parent companies in defense contracts as well as communications issues and to the seeming ineffectiveness of the regulatory agency.

When President Dwight D. Eisenhower left office in January 1961, he warned Americans of a growing military-industrial complex, and urged the nation to avoid letting "the weight of this combination endanger our liberties or democratic processes." He emphasized the importance of knowledge in a democratic society.[14]

Although Eisenhower did not specifically address the role of the media in creating an "alert and knowledgeable citizenry," various media critics have questioned the effects of media companies' involvement in the military-industrial complex on media content and style. Sociologist Herbert Schiller argued that a "monopolized informational apparatus" appeared after World War II that is "inseparably connected to the military establishment." In such an arrangement, Schiller contended, "the objectivity and reliability" of communications content comes "increasingly into doubt."[15]

Schiller argued that top executives of the networks often are connected to the power structure in ways that inhibit full and complete coverage of societal issues. For example, Frank Stanton, 1960s president of CBS, served as chairman of the U.S. Advisory Commission on Information, a four-person panel which assesses the role of the USIA and makes recommendations for its future. Until early 1967, Stanton also was chairman of the board of the Rand Corporation, a nonprofit California research organization funded almost entirely by U.S. Air Force contracts. Stanton also chaired the executive committee of Radio Free Europe, which in 1967 was uncovered as a conduit for the Central Intelligence Agency.[16]

RCA, the parent company of NBC, ranked twenty-fourth among Defense Department contractors in 1965 and during that year obtained $214 million in military contracts. A year later, as the Vietnam War grew more intense, RCA's total rose to $242.4 million. General Electric, with numerous interests in media companies, earned $824.3 million in 1964 and $1.187 billion in 1965.[17]

The question that emerged in the 1960s was whether network ownership by defense-contracting parent companies and the interlocking responsibilities of network executives altered either the approach or the content of coverage of such issues as civil rights and the Vietnam War. Although legends abound to suggest at least occasional interference with specific stories, more concern has been directed at what stories did not get covered.

Stanton had been a friend of President Johnson since 1938, when Johnson acquired CBS affiliate status for his wife's Austin radio station. During the 1960s Johnson regularly was infuriated with CBS coverage of Vietnam, and relayed his dismay through Stanton to top CBS executives. In August 1965, CBS correspondent Morley Safer filed tape and film of the burning of a Vietnamese village, Cam Ne. CBS executives could not fail to use the film, David Halberstam wrote, because it was "awesome, the full force of television, the ability to dramatize, now fastening on one incident, one day in the war, that was going to be shattering to an entire generation of Americans."[18]

The next morning President Johnson got Stanton out of bed with the telephoned attack: "Frank, this is your President, and yesterday your boys shat on the American flag." Halberstam claimed that CBS made extra efforts during the next two weeks to include positive Vietnam information in its reports to balance the Safer story, and that Stanton would have fired Safer if other executives had not protected him.[19]

FEDERAL COMMUNICATIONS COMMISSION

At the beginning of the 1960s, consumer activists challenged the FCC to enforce the Fairness Doctrine and to secure changes in programming. Under the chairmanship of Newton Minow, best known for labeling television programming a "vast wasteland" before the National Association of Broadcasters, shortly after his appointment in 1961, the Federal Communications Commission attempted to address complaints about programming, but its efforts met with little success. Despite wide public acclaim for Minow's speech, he faced challenges from conservative commissioners, from Congress, and from the industry. Minow argued specifically for longer newscasts and for improved children's programming. But whenever Minow commented positively or negatively about programming, congressmen and industry spokesmen accused him of imposing censorship or of decrying public taste. Frank Stanton of CBS responded that broadcasting truly represented a "cultural democracy" and claimed that ratings indicated what viewers preferred. Minow argued for the rights of minorities and for those who did not agree with the ratings, as well as noting that perhaps audiences responded to stimuli offered, not to alternatives which were not presented.

In 1962, Minow attempted to increase competition and the multiplicity of channels through an all-channel bill which would force the industry to sell sets that received both UHF and VHF channels, thereby ending the preferred position of VHF channels. The industry backed the bill as the least of evils—a way to keep regulation off its backs. Minow continued to argue for increased local, live, public affairs programming as well as for elite cultural offerings, in the face of an industry in which the affiliates ran network programming for 95 percent of evening prime time programming.

> **WHAT ABOUT TELEVISION?**
>
> Television is more than just another public resource—like air and water—ruined by private greed and public inattention. It is the greatest communications mechanism ever designed and operated by man. It pumps into the human brain an unending stream of information, opinion, moral values, and aesthetic taste. It cannot be a neutral influence.
>
> SOURCE: Nicholas Johnson, former Federal Communications Commissioner.

Minow, who often stood alone without backing from other commissioners or from the public at large, created more controversy than change during the decade. During his term as chairman, the FCC initiated revocation proceedings against twenty-three stations. Fourteen lost their licenses, but most of those were small radio stations accused of technical violations or of blatantly antisocial programming. When he attempted public hearings, those attending often either represented narrow self-interests or defended local stations against federal bureaucrats like himself.[20]

Furthermore, both Kennedy and Johnson attempted to use the Fairness Doctrine to silence the religious right and spokesmen against the Nuclear Test Ban Treaty.[21] Minow resigned in 1963 and Congress halted further attempts by the FCC to turn the National Association of Broadcasters code into official regulation. From 1964 to 1966, the FCC abandoned all attempts to encourage news and public affairs or local programming.

Throughout the 1960s, the FCC heavily restricted the growth of cable antenna television for fear it would destroy "local" television provided by UHF channels. The industry feared cable would splinter the audience to such a degree that profits would be seriously endangered. The new UHF stations, however, did not provide diversified programming, but instead the stations kept costs to a minimum by using reruns and network syndications. In 1962, Congress passed the Educational Television Facilities Act, which partially subsidized start-up costs for educational stations, and in 1967, the Public Broadcasting System was created, providing for intellectuals the hope that PBS would provide what commercial television had avoided.

Despite broadcasters' continued complaints and efforts to overturn the Fairness Doctrine, its constitutionality was upheld by the Supreme Court in 1969. In this case, known simply as *Red Lion*, radio preacher Billy James Hargis attacked author Fred J. Cook for the views he expressed in the book, *Barry Goldwater: Extremist on the Right*. Cook asked for free time to respond over the Red Lion, Pennsylvania, station owned by Red Lion Broadcasting Co. The broadcaster refused to give Cook the time, and Cook complained to the FCC. The FCC, in turn, told the broadcaster to provide Cook with time. Meanwhile, the Radio-Television News Directors Association, along with CBS and NBC, were challenging the complicated and burdensome rules having to do with broadcasters' responsibilities for notifying people who had been personally attacked or people or organizations who had been the subjects of unfavorable editorial comment.

The Supreme Court held that the FCC's creation of the Fairness Doctrine was a constitutional exercise of the regulatory agency's power. It pointed to Congress' 1959 amendment to Section 315 of the Communications Act of 1934, saying that stations were expected to operate in the public interest and to "afford reasonable opportunity for the discussion of conflicting views on issues of public importance." The court held that because of the scarcity of the airwaves, it was "the right of the viewers and listeners, not the right of the broadcasters, which is paramount.[22]

SATELLITE DEVELOPMENT

At the end of his presidency, Dwight Eisenhower encouraged private enterprise to establish and operate satellite relays. His position that satellite development should be commercial rather than governmental was quickly adopted by President Kennedy. Just as the government had rejected control of the telegraph lines many years before, it now rejected ownership of space communications. Congress passed the Communications Satellite Act in August 1962, and with it adopted the assumptions that private ownership was necessary for speedy development and efficient operation and that satellites were essentially an adjunct of existing facilities. Although Congress recognized that the State Department and the FCC would need to be involved in the international negotiations needed for satellite communication, it maintained that these would best be handled by the "common carriers." Congress further assumed that capital outlay for a satellite system would be extensive and should be borne by private enterprise.[23]

In February 1963, the Communications Satellite Corporation (COMSAT), became a private U.S. corporation, and that summer offered shares to stockholders. The FCC allocated half the shares to individual investors and half to communications carriers. At the end of the trading period, the industry giants, AT&T, IT&T, General Telephone and Electronics Corporation, and RCA Communications held 90 percent of the industry stock and 45.4 percent of the total issue.

The arrangement assured that government would be highly involved, but not in control of, international satellite transmission. McGeorge Bundy, former chief aide to President Kennedy, testified before Congress in August 1966, that "Comsat was established for the purpose of taking and holding a position of leadership for the United States in the field of international global commercial satellite service."[24] In 1967, James McCormack, chairman and chief executive officer of COMSAT, defined his company "as a unique concept in corporate structure and purpose. It is a privately owned corporation, but it also serves as a representative of the United States Government."[25]

The organization needed customers. The consortium, INTELSAT, organized August 20, 1964, was designed to fulfill this function. Nineteen countries signed initially; by 1969 sixty-four countries were affiliated with the consortium. COMSAT held 61 percent of the ownership—ownership distributed on the basis of contributions to capital costs of the system. The United States hold a protected position; no matter how many members eventually join the system, the United States cannot drop below 50.6 percent of ownership.

Western domination of satellite technology has created considerable controversy about the impact of western ideology on developing nations. Marshall McLuhan, popular media guru of the 1960s who coined the terms "global village" and "hot" and "cold" media, suggested that electronic media in the postindustrial society could become new and "benign" agencies of a collective consciousness. Christopher Brookeman, criticizing McLuhan's corporate connections as well as his naiveté, wrote that McLuhan's ideas appealed to corporations and to the U.S. government alike:

> McLuhan's image of a global village joined by a single universal technology of electric circuitry chimed in with America's world role in reconstructing and maintaining the world economic and political system after the chaos of the Second World War. If McLuhan was right, the new systems of information technology could be the basis for a new world order. In the same way that the new criticism assimilated individual quirkiness, McLuhan's theories aimed to integrate the diversity and individuality of the world's cultures into cybernetic unity."[26]

CONTINUED NEWSPAPER CONSOLIDATION

Corporate structure certainly was not unique to broadcasting, for it was a common pattern in newspapers. The trend toward single ownership continued throughout the decade. By the beginning of the 1970s, groups or chains accounted for one-half the nation's dailies and two-thirds of its circulation. In the 1950s, the Samuel I. Newhouse group, based in New York, New Jersey, and Pennsylvania, acquired papers in Oregon, Missouri, Alabama, Louisiana, and Ohio. John S. Knight's group in Ohio, Michigan, and Illinois expanded to include newspapers in North Carolina, Georgia, and Pennsylvania. His acquisitions included the prestigious *Philadelphia Inquirer*. The Tribune group,

These interior views of a hot-type printing plant were taken in 1957. In the 1960s, many newspapers moved to various forms of cold type. (Library of Congress Collection, U.S. News and World Report photo)

which originally consisted of the *Chicago Tribune* and the *New York Daily News*, took over the top circulation position in the 1960s. The older and influential Hearst Group had begun cutbacks in the 1930s and continued to divest through the 1960s, merging the International News Service with United Press in 1958 to form United Press International and giving up the Sunday supplement, *American Weekly*, in 1963.[27] The Scripps-Howard chain remained stable throughout the period. At the beginning of the 1970s, the Tribune Company, Newhouse, Knight, Scripps-Howard, and Hearst led in circulation, while the Thomson and Gannett groups led in the numbers of dailies.

Although newspapers experienced a steady growth in advertising revenues and circulation during the 1960s, they also faced increasing costs. Circulation increased from 52 million in the late 1940s to 62 million in the late 1960s. Despite television's inroads into national advertising revenues, ad dollars still increased from $260 million in the 1940s to more than one billion dollars in the late 1960s. Total newspaper advertising revenues in 1968 were $5.2 billion, compared to $3.1 billion for television. Although some large metropolitan newspapers suffered, in 1966 medium city newspapers averaged a net profit of 23 percent.

Another factor affecting cost was a series of strikes which caused extensive shutdowns. The nation's longest strike in late 1967 and early 1968 closed the *Detroit News* and the *Detroit Free Press* for 267 days.[28]

TECHNOLOGY

Strikes often occurred over disputes about automation and the role of skilled labor as new technology was introduced to the industry. Three major developments in the 1950s and 1960s revolutionized the printing industry. Teletypesetters, available in the early 1950s, produced punched tape that would activate a Linotype or other typesetting machine. Wire services sent tape with their copy, thereby eliminating the need to typeset wire copy. The improved technology also increased the level of standardization because newspapers could print wire copy without having to hire someone to set it. Computers were used to produce text as early as 1963, further eliminating the need for dual typing. No longer did a reporter have to type a story and have a typesetter retype it into the machine. Furthermore, expanded and improved offset printing which used photographic plates rather than stereotypes provided cheaper printing, especially for smaller papers. Computers affected not only the editorial side, but also automated mail rooms and accounting systems. Facsimile transmission allowed wire services to send pictures and newspapers to auxiliary printing plants.

Chapter 19 **Affluence and Activism**

Newspaper Preservation Act

In 1970, the adoption of the Newspaper Preservation Act symbolized the end of meaningful efforts on the part of the Federal government to regulate newspaper consolidation. This law represented a yielding to enormous political clout from a number of powerful newspaper publishers: it provided twenty-two newspapers with "limited exemption from antitrust prosecution."[29] The act legalized preexisting anticompetitive arrangements in eleven cities as worked out by combinations such as the *San Francisco Chronicle* and the *San Francisco Examiner*; the *Wisconsin State Journal* and the *Capital Times*, both of Madison; the *Miami Herald* and the *Miami News*, and the *Honolulu Advertiser* and the *Honolulu Bulletin*.

The act permitted competing newspapers to combine production, circulation, and advertising operations if one newspaper was (or had been at the time the joint operating agreement was entered) in financial distress. Passage of the act was triggered by a 1969 decision in *The Tucson Case* by the Supreme Court. The court held that under U.S. antitrust laws, the only legal justification for two companies' combining operations would be proof that one of the companies was failing financially at the time of the combination. Because the court believed neither one of the Tucson papers was "failing," the papers' Joint Operating Agreement (JOA) violated antitrust laws.

This decision frightened a number of powerful newspaper interests and set off a remarkable scramble in Congress. Within days, legislators from each state with JOA newspapers had submitted bills to create an antitrust exemption for such operations. Despite loud objections from the Antitrust Division of the U.S. Department of Justice, the Failing Newspaper Act—soon to be renamed, more positively, the Newspaper Preservation Act—sailed through Congress with minimal opposition and was signed into law by President Richard M. Nixon. The theory behind the act was that twentieth-century economics often dictate that no more than one newspaper company can survive, even in large cities, and that allowing JOAs will keep more voices in the marketplace of ideas. Under the JOA concept, the news operations of two newspapers remain separate and "competitive," while the business-printing-circulation departments join together to provide efficiency and reduce costs.

In San Francisco, however, publisher Bruce Brugman of the *Bay Guardian* challenged the constitutionality of the Newspaper Preservation Act, charging that it violated the First Amendment by encouraging a journalistic monopoly. The *Bay Guardian*'s legal action complained that the Newspaper Preservation Act of 1970 rubber-stamped approval on the JOA reached in San Francisco in 1965. That agreement spelled the demise of one paper, the already triply merged *News-Call-Bulletin*. The two remaining dailies—the *Chronicle* and the *Examiner*—divided up the market area for dailies, with

511

printing done for both papers by a jointly owned subsidiary. Profits from all operations were shared.

Although the *Bay Guardian* lost its effort to have the Newspaper Preservation Act declared unconstitutional, its contentions that neither the *Chronicle* nor the *Examiner* were "failing companies" and that the *News-Call-Bulletin* should not have been killed had some effect. The *Bay Guardian* was one of the number of parties who shared in a $1,350,000 out-of-court settlement. Even so, the Newspaper Preservation Act—sometimes called the "Newspaper Profit Preservation Act" by its critics—remained in effect.

A 1987 study indicated that newspapers produced under JOAs were more similar to competitive newspapers than they were to monopoly newspapers and that in at least four of twenty-two markets readers had a choice between different op-ed and editorial pages and occasionally between two slightly different news sections.[30]

COVERING VIETNAM

The United States was involved at various levels in Vietnam from the close of World War II. After supporting French reinvolvement in Indochina in 1945, in 1949 the United States committed funds to the French, frightened by the fact that Mao Tse Tung had secured power in China and, together with the Soviet Union, had recognized Ho Chi Minh's communist government in Vietnam. In 1954, with the defeat of the French at Dienbienphu, and the division of Vietnam into two countries, North and South, the United States extended direct economic and military aid to South Vietnam. By the end of 1963, American assistance reached $400 million annually, and 12,000 military advisers operated in the country. The Tonkin Gulf Resolution of 1964 paved the way for direct military involvement, which escalated through the Tet Offensive of January 1968, when a reexamination of commitment sparked the beginning of negotiations. The conflict widened during 1972–1973 before the withdrawal of U.S. troops and the fall of South Vietnam to the communists in 1975.

After the war it became popular for government officials, as well as for some journalists, to blame the news media for losing the war. Because Vietnam was the first war thoroughly covered by television, broadcasters received particularly heavy criticism. In his memoirs, published in 1978, Richard Nixon blamed the news media for reporting "little of the underlying purpose of the fighting." Eventually, he wrote, such "relentless and literal reporting of the war" created a "serious demoralization of the home front, raising the question whether America would ever again be able to fight an enemy abroad with unity and strength of purpose at home."[31]

Views of Vietnamese market life and other village scenes conveyed the reality that human beings were being affected by the war. (Photo by Leroy Towns)

And the *New York Time*'s James Reston wrote in 1975:

> Maybe the historians will agree that the reporters and the cameras were decisive in the end. They brought the issue of the war to the people, before the Congress or the courts, and forced the withdrawal of American power from Vietnam.[32]

The press's role in creating public opinion antagonistic to Vietnam has been exaggerated. Historians Stanley Karnow and David Hallin suggested that public opinion and news media reaction was intertwined, and that media coverage tended to follow, rather than direct, public opinion. Generally speaking, the press and the American public supported U.S. involvement during the early years in Vietnam. In fact, until the U.S. Marines landed in the spring of 1965, only five American news organizations maintained staff correspondents in Vietnam. Little criticism emerged from the first efforts to aid the

French in 1949 until about 1967, shortly before the Tet Offensive in 1968. However, despite that general support, the press at times questioned the involvement, as was illustrated during the Laos crisis of 1961.

The Geneva Convention in 1954 had called on Laos to form a coalition government with Prince Souvanna Phouma at its head, but the United States, fearful that Ho Chi Minh would march through Laos and conquer the rest of Southeast Asia, helped bring to power and militarily supported a government takeover by General Phoumi Nosavan. By 1961, the Pathet Lao, a broad-based pro-communist group, and other factions were engaged in a bitter and destructive civil war in Laos, with the United States supporting General Nosavan and the Soviet Union supporting the Pathet Lao. By the end of February 1961, the Pathet Lao were in an exceptionally good military position, and by March were on the verge of capturing the capital, Vientienne.

On March 23, 1961, Kennedy explained the Laos situation in a press conference and intimated that the United States would take action if the USSR continued to supply the Pathet Lao through Hanoi. At least one reporter doubted the wisdom of the action, asking "Mr. President, perhaps you could tell us just what our $310 million investment in Laos has bought us?"[33] Kennedy responded by emphasizing the immediate danger of communist control of Laos. Walter Lippmann, whom Kennedy often lunched with, criticized the "bully" position on Laos as a "false and imprudent commitment."[34] Ralph McGill, editor of the *Atlanta Constitution*, noted that in eight years in Southeast Asia the French had failed in their program, and that Southeast Asia could well become a Sino/Soviet battleground. "If Laos falls," McGill wrote, "South Vietnam cannot be defended."[35]

Despite criticism of Kennedy's handling of the Laos crisis, the *New York Times* in the early 1960s described the Vietnam War as "a struggle this country cannot shirk."[36] The conflict continued without censorship, which would have required a declaration of war or at least official admission that the conflict was broad enough to require official censorship. However, as the war progressed reporters resisted the military's admonition that they should "get on the team."[37]

The news media were not the only official sources questioning the wisdom of continued Vietnam involvement. In 1962, when Kennedy sent Senate majority leader Mike Mansfield to Vietnam, Mansfield returned with gloomy predictions, claiming that despite the $2 billion the United States had contributed during the past seven years, the same complications remained or had increased.[38]

In October 1963, shortly before South Vietnamese President Ngo Dinh Diem was ousted in a coup supported by the United States, reporters David Halberstam of the *New York Times*, Neil Sheehan of UPI, and Malcolm Brown of AP became increasingly critical of government policy. President Kennedy suggested to *New York Times* publisher Sulzberger that Halberstam was "too close to the story, too involved," hoping to have the reporter removed from Southeast Asia. Sulzberger kept Halberstam in Vietnam for an extended period, just to prove he could not be influenced by such suggestions.[39]

But government was not the press's worst critic during those days. Other reporters and editors jumped on the Vietnam correspondents. Joseph Alsop accused them of carrying on "egregious" crusades against Diem and compared the reporters to Chiang Kai-Shek's press critics, whom he blamed for losing China to the communists. Asserting the still formidable power of the editor over reporter, Otto Fuerbringer, managing editor at *Time*, commissioned an article which charged the Saigon press corps with pooling "convictions, information, misinformation and grievances" to distort the truth. *Time* correspondents Charles Mohr and Mert Perry promptly resigned in protest.[40] Despite the increased criticism, at the time of the Tonkin Gulf Resolution in 1964, opinion polls showed that 85 percent of the public supported the administration; newspaper editorials elected a similar sentiment.[41]

The distance between official reports and verifiable truth emerged more clearly, however, when Harrison Salisbury, assistant managing editor of the *New York Times*, traveled to Hanoi in late 1966 to cover the war from North Vietnam. Although President Johnson had been busy convincing the American people that increased recent bombings were aimed strictly at military targets, Salisbury's reports indicated many cities had been hit and civilians killed. Historian Stanley Karnow reported that while Salisbury's stories essentially were accurate, they did convey the wrong impression that the United States "was indiscriminately trying to destroy North Vietnam."[42] What Salisbury wrote, however, was not the only matter of contention. The fact that he employed objective journalistic conventions as he reported from North Vietnam, and quoted officials there "as though they belonged to the Sphere of Legitimate Controversy," also raised criticism from American officials and journalists.[43]

In 1967, under the direction of Henry Luce's successor Hedley Donovan, *Time* and *Life* altered their perspective with an editorial in *Life* claiming the commitment to Southeast Asia was not "absolutely imperative" to America's interests. Two years later, long after Lyndon Johnson claimed Donovan had betrayed him, *Life* ran pictures of the 250 Americans who had died in Vietnam that week.[44] In January 1968, television coverage of the Tet Offensive involving more than 70,000 North Vietnamese troops, exploded onto America's television screens. According to political scientist Michael Hallin, even in those days television remained "a follower rather than a leader."

> The later years of Vietnam are a remarkable testimony to the restraining power of the routine and ideology of objective journalism. At a time when much of the nation's intelligentsia was in a militant and passionate mood, when members of Congress, employees of the

The faces of Vietnam were portrayed in many United States newspapers. (Photo by Leroy Towns)

U.S. embassy in Saigon, and business executives could be seen demonstrating in the streets against the nation's foreign policy, most television coverage was dispassionate; 'advocacy journalism' made no real inroads into network television.[45]

Nevertheless, when Walter Cronkite returned from Saigon in February 1968, predicting that the Tet Offensive, far from being the military victory reported by U.S. officials, assured "more . . . than ever that the bloody experience of Vietnam is to end in a stalemate," President Johnson and others publicly complained that the news media were losing the war in Vietnam.[46]

Hallin suggested that media became, in part, a scapegoat for a lack of clarity within the U.S. government and for the lack of consensus in society at large. Stressing that cooperative arrangements worked well, and the press did keep important secrets, Hallin doubted whether more external constraints on the press would have altered the outcome of the war.

COVERING THE CIVIL RIGHTS MOVEMENT

At the end of World War II, black and white soldiers returned home, whites to a world of prosperity and jobs, blacks to a nation still characterized by segregation and unequal opportunity. Legally, blacks made some progress in the early 1950s, particularly with the Supreme Court decision in *Brown v. Board of Education of Topeka*, a Kansas case which ruled that separate education was not equal education. Many white communities defied the court order and in 1957, when a black student attempted to enroll in an all-white Little Rock, Arkansas, high school, Governor Orval E. Faubus called out the National Guard to prevent desegregation of the school. In late 1955, a year-long bus boycott in Montgomery, Alabama, signalled the advent of the type of protest advocated by Martin Luther King, Jr., that of nonviolent civil resistance. Volunteers organized by King's Southern Christian Leadership Conference continued to sit-in at white lunch counters, libraries, and bus stations, and members of the Congress of Racial Equality and the Student Non-Violent Coordinating Committee encouraged blacks to resist segregation and to vote. In 1962, President Kennedy ordered U.S. marshals to protect James Meredith, the first black to enroll at the University of Mississippi. In August 1963, King addressed a crowd of 250,000 at the Washington Monument, proclaiming "I have a dream that my four little children will one day live in a nation where they will not be judged by the color of their skin but by the content of their character." In September, white terrorists bombed a Birmingham Baptist church, killing four black girls.

Shortly after the assassination of President John F. Kennedy in Dallas, November 22, 1963, President Johnson declared civil rights a top priority. Johnson signed the Civil Rights Act of 1964, which outlawed discrimination in public accommodations and in jobs. During the summers of 1964 and 1965, racial violence broke out not only in the South, but in northern cities as well. In 1965, Congress passed a voting rights act.

The events of the 1960s, unlike the underlying currents of the 1950s, were, according to any accepted journalistic standards, "newsworthy events." In 1957 and 1962, *Life* carried extensive coverage of school integration in Arkansas and Mississippi, along with feature stories on racism as a social problem. *Life* assured its readers that the North had done more than the South had for black dignity and regarded the Mississippi incident as "a disgrace to themselves, their state and their nation."[47] However, not until the end of the decade did *Life* cover contemporary black life apart from news events. The coverage by *Life* was similar to that of many newspapers and of television: a focus on events. Critics chastised the media for not covering the issues of civil rights and for waiting until civil disobedience commanded their attention.[48]

On April 4, 1968, Martin Luther King died from an assassin's bullet and that June, Robert Kennedy was assassinated by an Arab nationalist.

New York Times vs. Sullivan

In 1964, the Supreme Court, hearing a case on appeal by the *New York Times*, extended a decision Kansas Courts had made in 1908 that public officials carried a heavier burden than did private individuals in libel judgments.[49] The *New York Times vs. Sullivan* case assured the news media that random errors in reporting the activities of public officials would not result in large libel judgments. The case was critically important because it allowed the media to report on controversial subjects on deadline, such as civil rights demonstrations, without fear of heavy recrimination.

The case arose from a *New York Times* advertisement titled "Heed Their Rising Voices," which appeared in March 1960, shortly after whites used violence at Alabama State College in Montgomery against black demonstrators, who were protesting segregation of public facilities. Sixty-four persons, white and black, signed the advertisement, which appealed for financial support for the Alabama State College students. The ad read, in part:

> In Montgomery, Ala., after students sang "My Country, 'tis of Thee" on the State Capitol steps, their leaders were expelled from school, and truckloads of police armed with shotguns and tear gas ringed the Alabama State College campus. When the entire student body

> protested to state authorities by refusing to register, their dining hall was padlocked in an attempt to starve them into submission. . . .
>
> Again and again, the Southern violators have answered Dr. (Martin Luther) King's peaceful protests with intimidation and violence. They have bombed his home almost killing his wife and child. They have assaulted his person. They have arrested him seven times—for "speeding," "loitering," and similar "offenses." And now they have charged him with "perjury"—a felony under which they could imprison him for *10 years.*[50]

Police Commissioner L. B. Sullivan, one of three elected commissioners of Montgomery, Alabama, filed suit in a Montgomery Court, charging he was libeled by the ad's general references to police, and that he was accused of padlocking the hall and of intimidating Dr. King and his family. Witnesses testified much of the material in the ad was in error. For example, students sang "The Star-Spangled Banner," not "My Country, 'tis of Thee." The *Times* advertising acceptability manager testified that he had no reason to believe the ad was false because it was prepared by a reputable agency and signed by persons with good reputations. The Alabama court awarded Sullivan $500,000.

Implications of the lawsuit went beyond the $500,000 it would have cost the *New York Times*. Libel suits were being used by southern states to attempt to control news coverage of civil rights demonstrations. For example, the *Times* was facing eleven other libel suits in Alabama courts that totaled more than $5 million. CBS was defending five libel suits in southern states with a total of almost $2 million at stake. Those were big dollar amounts in 1964, a time when one could buy an up-scale luxury-model automobile for about $5,000.

The *Sullivan* case reached the Supreme Court first, and the court's decision represented a crucial turning point, a reaffirmation of the First Amendment. Even on the surface, the *Sullivan* decision was a great event, for it made it difficult for public officials to use defamation lawsuits as a weapon to punish the press, to try to sue critics until they shut up or folded up. In writing for the court's majority Justice William J. Brennan, Jr., saw that this was not merely a libel suit in which an individual was seeking to protect his reputation. Important as reputation is, there was something far more crucial at stake: the right to be able to discuss and to criticize government and government officials.

The lawsuit strategy against the *New York Times* was the reprehensible repackaging of an old enemy of freedom—the crime of seditious libel—into a new wrapper—civil lawsuits for libel by government officials. Justice Brennan evidently agreed with the late First Amendment scholar Zechariah Chafee: it is not what you *call* the power that matters. Chafee once wrote that it is not the inscription on the sword that matters; it is the existence of the weapon.[51]

The Supreme Court turned aside arguments by lawyers of the plaintiff Sullivan that the *Times* was not entitled to First Amendment protection because the publication complained of was in an advertisement. That was true: up to 1964, commercial advertising, the courts had said, was not entitled to First Amendment protection. But *New York Times v. Sullivan* said that editorial advertising—expressing social or political ideas—did have constitutional protection.

The court's majority in *Sullivan* expressed a willingness to take the risk that freedom of expression entails. Free societies are not always orderly. Justice Brennan's opinion stressed the importance of protecting even erroneous statements in the discussion of public issues:

> Thus we consider this case against the background of a profound national commitment to the principle that debate on public issues should be uninhibited, robust, and wide-open, and that it may well include vehement, caustic, and sometimes unpleasantly sharp attacks on government and public officials. The present advertisement, as an expression of grievance and protest on one of the major public issues of our time, would seem clearly to qualify for the constitutional protection.

The court then ruled that in order for public officials to recover damages for libel, they must prove that the statements were made with "actual malice"—that is, with "knowledge that it was false or with reckless disregard of whether it was false or not." The decision cleared the way for thorough reporting of civil rights issues and for subsequent investigatory articles on government officials but it did not, as some newsmen and lawyers predicted, abolish the law of libel.

THE LANGUAGE OF PARTICIPANT JOURNALISM

As young reporters demanded new levels of autonomy in the newsroom and reacted to events of the 1960s, some abandoned the objective, straightforward approach of "Who? What? When? Where? and Why?" The demands of interpretation and the political and cultural context of the decade demanded new techniques, new language, and incorporation of styles that had distinguished alternative media for many years. Everette Dennis, in the *Magic Writing Ma-*

chine, divided New Journalism into five types: (1) the new nonfiction, also called reportage and parajournalism; (2) alternative journalism, also called "modern muckraking," (3) advocacy journalism, (4) underground journalism, and (5) precision journalism. Although the new nonfiction focused on technique, it also raised questions about objective fact. Alternative, advocacy, and underground journalism became names for the issue-oriented discussions by alternative media. Precision journalism incorporated social science techniques in an attempt to measure empirically objective fact.

NEW NONFICTION

The practitioners of new nonfiction wrote about social trends, celebrities, "little people," and public events. They used fictional techniques to make their articles and books sound like short stories and novels and published their work primarily in magazines. Tom Wolfe's magazine articles, collected in *The Kandy Kolored Tangerine Flake Streamline Baby*, were, according to the publisher's promoters and in true Wolfeian style,

> full of raw talent. . . . Wolfe has caught with his anamorphic prose the grotesque, spastic juggernaut of metropolitan life, or half-life. In a clatter of detail, a char-broil of savory observation, he captures mad memorabilia, from the neon jungle of Las Vegas . . . to the ecstatic carnage of auto-demolition derbies. . . . [52]

The New Journalism went wild in observation, developing its own prose style and, to some extent, its own vocabulary.

Truman Capote, a fiction writer of some note, catapulted himself into the new nonfiction journalistic world with a novel, *In Cold Blood*, an account of a 1959 murder of a western Kansas farm family and the subsequent pursuit, trial, and execution of the murderers five years later. The account stirred considerable controversy and earned Capote $2 million.[53] A good deal of the controversy revolved around the question of accuracy. Capote claimed to have taken no notes during his interviews, but said he was able to recall what people said in minute detail. Many reporters, as well as many of the western Kansas people interviewed, questioned his claim. *Commonweal* magazine deplored the "voyeurism" of the book; *Atlantic Monthly* said that although the publisher of *In Cold Blood* claimed it represented a "serious new literary form" it was, in reality a "high-minded aesthetic excuse for reading about a mean, sordid crime."[54] But others praised the nonfiction work. Tom Greene, writing in *America* (January 22, 1966), praised Capote for capturing on 350 pages "a complete and meaningful human document."

Also experimenting with interpretive reporting, in-depth research, descriptive personal detail, and a dramatic writing style was former *New York Times* copyboy Gay Talese. His experimentation earned him thirty bylined articles in *Esquire* over a period of ten years. Famous for his profiles of celebrities such as Frank Sinatra, Joe DiMaggio, and Peter O'Toole, Talese's articles were collected in three books, *Fame and Obscurity, New York: Serendipiter's Journey*, and *The Bridge*. In 1969, he published an exhaustive history of the personalities and inner workings of the *New York Times (The Kingdom and the Power)*, and in 1971, he published an account of a mafia family, *Honor Thy Father*. The two books displayed the value of Talese's research, his focus on detail, and his fictional style based on fact.

The fictional style, and determining whether the style or the fact is fiction, has been one of the major controversies surrounding the new journalism. Jimmy Breslin, sports columnist for the *New York Herald Tribune* and author of a book about the New York Mets, *Can't Anybody Here Play This Game?*, was an avid follower of Robert Kennedy. Visiting Kansas State University in 1969, a year after Kennedy's death, Breslin wrote a column heavy with inaccuracies, but which he claimed captured the essence of a situation. He inaccurately reported that a black man had been jailed for burning a campus building and referred to the burned building, Nicholls Hall, a gymnasium which also housed the music department and radio station, as an ROTC building.[55]

ADVOCACY AND ALTERNATIVE JOURNALISM

Alternative journalism might be traced as far back as Ben Franklin's older brother, James Franklin, who in 1721 started the *New England Courant* at least partially as a reaction to the government-dominated views of the postmaster papers of Campbell and Brooker, which were published "by authority." Some of the radical publications of the 1930s and 1940s, including Dorothy Day's *Catholic Worker* and Dwight MacDonald's *Politics*, could correctly be labeled alternative publications. Reminiscent of the nineteenth-century reform press, during the 1960s alternative publications provided information not disseminated by mainstream newspapers. Unlike advocacy newspapers, which espoused a cause or distinct opinion, alternative press stories included a ruthless check for accuracy after intensive investigation. Examples of the best included the *San Francisco Bay Guardian*, the *Rocky Mountain Journal*, and the *Village Voice*. Alternative editors did not strongly identify with the counterculture movement, but instead were often middle-aged, old New Dealers, or progressives. These publications were blunt, as this example from the *Rocky Mountain Journal* shows:

> ## HUNTER THOMPSON SPEAKS
>
> So much for Objective Journalism. Don't bother to look for it here—not under any byline of mine; or anyone else I can think of. With the possible exception of things like box scores, race results, and stock market tabulations, there is no such thing as Objective Journalism. The phrase itself is a pompous contradiction in terms.
>
> SOURCE: Hunter Thompson, Fear and Loathing: On the Campaign Trail '72

This newspaper does not trust City Hall on the mass transportation issue. This newspaper does not accept Mayor William H. McNichol's explanation—and here's why. (November 11, 1970)[56]

Another form of alternative news media which developed during the 1960s were the journalism reviews. Two leaders still in the field in 1987 were the *Columbia Journalism Review*, founded in 1961, and the *Washington Journalism Review*, founded in 1977. Although the Columbia review had been somewhat managerial in tone, the *Chicago Journalism Review*, begun shortly after the Democratic convention of August 1968, created a forum of critical discussion of the Chicago and national press. The goal was to create an open forum for critical discussion of journalism, which, as the reaction to the Hutchins Commission had demonstrated, had been absent within the profession, although not from without.

Advocacy journalism was defined as distinctly and admittedly biased, colored with the writer's own point of view. Those who practiced advocacy during the decade argued that such writing came closer to the truth than did the bland surface journalism reported within the constraints of professionalism and objectivity. These writers believed that if journalists present a point of view the public will read a variety of such views and make intelligent decisions. Advocacy journalist Hunter S. Thompson, in *Fear and Loathing on the Campaign Trail '72*, paid scant attention to the journalistic conventions of the regular reporters. Writing in 1972, he said, "As far as I was concerned, there was no such thing as 'off the record.' The most consistent and ultimately damaging failure of political journalism in America has its roots in the clubby cocktail personal relationships that inevitably develop between politicians and journalists."[57]

UNDERGROUND JOURNALISM

Underground journalism flourished in high schools and universities, on military bases, and in urban areas. These newspapers also were advocacy newspa-

Covering the Democratic Convention in 1964 was an easy exercise, compared to the convention of 1968. (Library of Congress Collection, U.S. News and World Report photo)

pers, promoting radical politics and psychedelic art, as well as describing the drug culture and protesting the style and lack of social services. Editors and writers in the movement wrote for newspapers such as the *Berkeley Barb* and *Off Our Backs*. Such newspapers offered forums for discussion of taboo subjects in the mainstream press.

PRECISION JOURNALISM

Precision journalism is at an opposite pole from other types of New Journalism. Precision journalists decried the "Man-on-the Street" interview and the slipshod methods reporters used to gather what they termed public opinion. Precision journalists believed in interpretation based on understanding gained through using social science techniques, such as survey research based on random sampling. Philip Meyer, professor in the School of Journalism at the

University of North Carolina at Chapel Hill, in 1967 became project director for a project sponsored by the Detroit Urban League and financed by Henry Ford II and two foundations. Meyer and his team hired black interviewers to canvass a random sample of black citizens in the main riot areas of Detroit. After analyzing the results on a computer, Meyer and his team combined the statistical data with photographs and quotes into a highly readable series.[58]

Meyer is still practicing precision journalism, and other individuals and publications have used the approach as well, but while newspapers often contract for political-poll information, they have failed to use precision techniques in highly creative ways.

Magazines

Magazines, unlike newspapers, which were aimed at mass audiences, in the 1960s constituted an industry increasingly characterized by selectivity of audience. Although timely, they did not face the same pressure as the daily newspaper and therefore were more able to treat subjects in depth and to pursue editorial platforms over time. As more permanent vehicles of information than newspapers, they were especially well suited for instructing and educating, as well as entertaining. Magazines were national in scope and lacked the local perspective and biases of newspapers, provided low-cost entertainment, and carried considerable advertising.[59]

Although general circulation leaders like *Saturday Evening Post*, *Life* and *Look* enjoyed great popularity and prosperity during earlier decades of the twentieth century, the more common magazines were those which emphasized special interests. As early as 1934, the special interest magazine *Model Railroader* capitalized on increased leisure time and successfully appealed to railroad hobbyists. *Skin Diver*, begun in 1951, experienced similar success.

Magazine readership increased dramatically across the twentieth century, as a growing population with increased purchasing power attracted advertisers who could target specific buyers. Magazines profited as well from increased educational levels and increasing leisure time. By 1950, *Life* magazine reached one in five Americans, and by 1961, the A. C. Nielsen reports indicated it reached one-quarter of the adult population. Other big circulation leaders included *Reader's Digest*, reaching 27 percent of American adults; *Look*, reaching 21 percent; and *Saturday Evening Post*, reaching 18 percent.

But mammoth circulations did not always indicate health. The push for giant circulations began in 1937, when *Saturday Evening Post* garnered 3 million subscribers. From 1942 to 1945, circulations continued to increase, and in the postwar years magazines experienced extensive expansions in circulations. Between 1950 and 1962, *Look* and *McCalls* more than doubled their circulations. Critics argued that magazines were giving up the selectivity of market that had been their strength and some contended that the "race for circulation was a race to the poorhouse."[60]

Lack of advertisers, not subscribers, sounded the death knell for the big magazines. As costs increased 40 to 50 percent in the 1950s, big publishers found it hardest to respond quickly and effectively. Curtis Publications, with its massive, vertically integrated system of subsidiaries, which did everything from grow trees and produce paper to distribute the *Saturday Evening Post*, found it difficult to maintain large overheads in the face of decreasing advertising revenues. In 1961, Curtis Publishing Company lost $4,194,000; the next year losses jumped to $18,917,000. In 1962, the Curtis management attempted to save the *Post*, installing as editor Clay Blair, Jr., who introduced new journalism and "sophisticated muckraking" into the *Post*. The latter shocked some of the magazine's readers, but more importantly, by the end of 1963 it involved the *Post* in $27,060,000 in libel suits.[61] Big publishers were not the only losers. From 1950 to 1960, one out of eight magazines belonging to the Audit Bureau of Circulation died or was merged out of existence.

The old circulation leaders such as *Life* and *Look* declined and died in the late 1960s and early 1970s, but their deaths did not represent a decline in the industry as a whole. The large circulations of *Saturday Evening Post* and other similar magazines resulted in large costs, and advertising revenues could not keep pace with what television could provide. The mass audience became a television market and magazines turned even more to specialized audiences and advertisers. From 1962 to 1971, 160 magazines were sold or merged, while 753 new magazines appeared on the racks.[62]

Conclusion

The 1960s was a decade of cultural upheaval and failed politics of expectation. Reporters, often a part of the generation that comprised the New Left, resisted the authority of the news desk and publisher power, intending to assert autonomy in approaching assignments and writing stories. They often viewed qualities of professionalism as loyalty to an ideal, rather than to an organization. Although editors resisted relinquishing power, they too rebelled when government imposed a new style of news management. Willing to cooperate in the 1950s and early 1960s to withhold information they felt would endanger national security, they mutinied when government tried to withhold information from the editors themselves.

Although reporter and editor power affected changes in the newsroom, it had little impact on the corporate structure of the news media, which grew bigger and more consolidated. Although the FCC probed programming during the decade, congressional and industry pressure saw to it that little real change occurred. Critics worried about the effects of interlocking ownership and directorates, noting that many companies which owned media outlets also held huge defense grants. The government, as it had in the early days of the telegraph, resisted ownership of communications in space and allocated the rights of communication, as well as the cost outlays, to private enterprise. Newspapers continued to consolidate, with chains accounting for ownership of half the newspapers in the country by 1970. Companies faced steady growth and increased costs. New technology created conflict that sometimes resulted in production strikes, and the high cost of competition propelled newspaper publishers to seek relief from Congress in the form of the Newspaper Preservation Act.

As the decade progressed, coverage of the Vietnam War intensified, and reporters sought to verify a truth that seemed elusive. As protest surged in the country over civil rights and the war, the news media reported the conflict. By the end of the decade, the media were convenient scapegoats for the troubles of the nation. Nevertheless, an important decision in *New York Times v. Sullivan* insured that libel suits would not provide convenient mechanisms for limiting coverage of public issues.

Coverage of conflict and the emergence of reporter power also fostered new language and new styles of interpretation, many of which appeared in the few remaining general circulation or opinion magazines. The magazine industry experienced profound change, as targeted advertising suggested the profitability of the specialized journal.

In May 1965, Walter Lippmann, in a speech to the International Press Institute in London, congratulated the press for becoming a profession characterized by intellectual discipline, but he warned against the hazards of the new power and influence gained during the decade of the 1960s, noting that the "crude forms of corruption which belonged to the infancy of journalism tend to give way to the temptations of maturity and power." Lippmann continued, "The most important forms of corruption in the modern journalist's world are the many guises and disguises of social climbing on the pyramids of power. . . ."[63]

NOTES

1. Everette E. Dennis, ed., "The New Journalism: How It Came to Be," *The Magic Writing Machine* (Eugene: School of Journalism, University of Oregon, 1971), p. 1.
2. For expansion of this thesis, see Henry Fairlie, *The Kennedy Promise* (Garden City, N.Y.: Doubleday, 1973).

3. Todd Gitlin, *The Whole World Is Watching* (Berkeley: University of California Press, 1980).
4. For an analysis of the "New Left," see Maurice Isserman, *If I Had a Hammer: The Death of the Old Left and the Birth of the New Left* (New York: Basic Books, 1987) and James Miller, *'Democracy is in the Streets: From Port Huron to the Siege of Chicago'* (New York: Simon and Schuster, 1987).
5. See the Profile of Huntley and Brinkley in the August 3, 1968, *New Yorker*, pp. 34–60. For CBS, see David Halberstam, *The Powers That Be* (New York: Alfred A. Knopf, 1979), p. 242.
6. Ernest C. Hynds, *American Newspapers in the 1980s* (New York: Hastings House, 1980), p. 43.
7. James Boylan, "Declarations of Independence," *Columbia Journalism Review*, November/December 1986, p. 32.
8. See Leo Rosten, *The Washington Correspondents* (New York: Harcourt, Brace and Company, 1937) and William L. Rivers, "The Correspondents After 25 Years," *Columbia Journalism Review* 1:1 (Spring), pp. 4–10.
9. John W. C. Johnstone, Edward J. Slawski, and William W. Bowman, *The News People: A Sociological Portrait of American Journalists and Their Work* (Urbana: University of Illinois Press, 1976), pp. 130–132.
10. Michael Schudson, *Discovering the News* (New York: Basic Books, 1978), p. 172–173.
11. *Editor and Publisher*, November 19, 1962; "The Right to Lie," *Columbia Journalism Review* 5 (Winter 1966–67): pp. 14–16, cited in Schudson, *Discovering the News*, pp. 171–172.
12. Schudson, *Discovering the News*, pp. 172–173.
13. Mark Perry, "Damning with Faint Praise: John Kennedy, The Press and the Laos Crisis of 1961," unpublished manuscript, p. 33.
14. *New York Times*, January 18, 1961, cited in Herbert I. Schiller, *Mass Communications and American Empire* (New York: Augustus M. Kelley, Publishers: 1969), p. 33.
15. Schiller, *American Empire*, p. 53.
16. Schiller, *American Empire*, pp. 54–56.
17. Fred MacDonald, *Television and the Red Menace: The Video Road to Vietnam* (New York: Praeger, 1985), p. 181.
18. David Halberstam, *The Powers That Be* (New York: Alfred A. Knopf, 1979), p.489.
19. Halberstam, *Powers That Be*, pp. 491–92.
20. For a thorough look at FCC activity during the 1960s, see James L. Baughman, *Television's Guardians: The FCC and the Politics of Programming, 1958–1967* (Knoxville: The University of Tennessee Press, 1985), on which this discussion is based.
21. Edward Fouhy, "Killing Freedom with Fairness," *Washington Journalism Review*, October 1987, in a review of Lucas Powe, Jr., *American Broadcasting and the First Amendment* (University of California Press, 1987).
22. *Red Lion Broadcasting Co. v FCC*, 395 U.S. 367 at 385, 80 S. Ct. 1974 (1969).

23. Harvey J. Levine, *University of Pennsylvania Law Review*, 113:3 (January 1965) cited in Schiller, *American Empire*, pp. 129–130.
24. *Progress Report on Space Communications*, Hearings before the Senate Subcommittee on Communications, 89th Congress, 2nd Session, August 10, 17, 18 and 23, 1966, Serial 89–78, Washington, 1966, cited in Schiller, *American Empire*, p. 131.
25. "Comsat's Role in Communications," James McCormack, *Signal*, May 1967, p. 32.
26. Christopher Brookeman, *American Culture and Society Since the 1930s* (New York: Schocken Books), 1984, p. 133.
27. Statistics are from Hynds, *American Newspapers*, p. 88.
28. Hynds, *American Newspapers*, p. 85.
29. Hynds, *American Newspapers* p. 89.
30. Stephen Lacy, "Content of Joint Operation Newspapers," in *Press Concentration and Monopoly: New Perspectives on Newspaper Ownership and Operations* (Norwood, N.J.: Ablex Publishing Co., 1987), p. 159.
31. Richard Nixon, *The Memoirs* (New York: Grosset & Dunlap, 1978), p. 350, cited in David Hallin, *The Uncensored War: The Media and Vietnam* (New York: Oxford University Press, 1986), p. 3.
32. James Reston, "The End of the Tunnel," *New York Times*, April 30, 1975, p. 41, cited in Hallin, *The Uncensored War*, p. 3.
33. Transcript of President Kennedy's Press Conference on Laos, *New York Times*, March 24, 1961, p. 8, cited in Perry, "Damning with Faint Praise."
34. "Laos Crisis Mounting, Britain Interceding," by Walter Lippmann, *Boston Daily Globe*, March 23, 1961, p. 1.
35. Ralph McGill, "Inescapable Wrestling Bout," *Atlanta Constitution*, March 24, 1961, p. 1, cited in Perry, "Damning with Faint Praise," p. 24.
36. Stanley Karnow, *Vietnam, A History: The First Complete Account of Vietnam at War* (New York: The Viking Press, 1983), p. 255.
37. Karnow, *Vietnam*, p. 262.
38. Karnow, *Vietnam*, p. 268.
39. Boylan, "Declarations of Independence," p. 33.
40. Karnow, *Vietnam*, p. 297.
41. Karnow, *Vietnam*, p. 374.
42. Karnow, *Vietnam*, p. 490.
43. Hallin, *The Uncensored War*, p. 147.
44. Karnow, *Vietnam*, p. 489.
45. Hallin, *Uncensored War*, p.163.
46. Karnow, *Vietnam*, p. 548.
47. "Let Glory Wave Alone Over Ole Miss," *Life*, October 12, 1962, p. 6, cited in Mary Alice Sentman, "*Life* in Black and White: Coverage of Black America by *Life* Magazine, 1937–1972," paper presented to Association for Education in Journalism, Michigan State University, August 1981.
48. See Gitlin, *The Whole World Is Watching*, for discussion of how issue groups in the 1960's altered their behavior in response to media coverage.

49. *Coleman vs. MacLennan*, 1908.
50. Harold Nelson and Dwight Teeter, *Law of Mass Communications: Freedom and Control of Print and Broadcast Media*, 5th ed. (Mineola, N.Y.: The Foundation Press, 1986), p. 107.
51. Zechariah Chafee, Jr., *Free Speech in the United States* (Cambridge, Mass.: Harvard University Press, 1941), p. 467.
52. See back jacket cover of paperback edition, Tom Wolfe, *The Kandy Kolored Tangerine Flake Streamline Baby* (New York: Pocket Books 1972), 9th ed. Originally published by Farrar, Straus & Giroux, 1965.
53. Review of *In Cold Blood, Commonweal* (February 11, 1966) p. 561.
54. *Atlantic Monthly*, March 1966, p. 160.
55. Everette E. Dennis and William L. Rivers, *Other Voices* (Canfield Press, 1974), p. 18.
56. Cited in Dennis and Rivers, *Other Voices*, p. 55.
57. Hunter S. Thompson (*Fear and Loathing on the Campaign Trail*) New York: Fawcett Books, 1974) p. 18, cited in Brookeman, *American Culture* p.162.
58. Dennis and Rivers pp. 190–191.
59. Theodore Peterson, in *Magazines in the Twentieth Century*, 2nd ed., (Urbana: University of Illinois Press, 1972), argues that magazines, as major carriers of advertising, and therefore of information about new products, were instrumental in increasing the U.S. standard of living. He also claims they played a significant role in creating a sense of national community.
60. Peterson, *Magazines*, pp. 61—63.
61. Peterson, *Magazines*, p. 178–199.
62. Roland Wolseley, *Understanding Magazines*, (Ames: Iowa State University Press, 1972) p. 27.
63. Cited in Boylan, "Declarations of Independence," p. 35.

CHAPTER 20

TROUBLES IN PARADISE

A style of investigative journalism that was developed during the civil rights activities of the 1960s and during the Vietnam War culminated in the early 1970s with the publication of the Pentagon Papers, a historical record of the war based on secret government documents, and with the coverage of the Watergate affair. Journalists began to take seriously the concept of the profession as a fourth branch of government, and Harrison Salisbury, referring to Justice Potter Stewart's Pentagon Papers opinion, declared that publishing the papers meant that the *Times* had "quite literally become that Fourth Estate, that fourth co-equal branch of government."[1]

The *Times* would have been hard pressed to find verification from the public for its new role. Newspapers again declined as the major source of news for Americans, with television rapidly gaining loyal viewers. In 1961, television bypassed newspapers as the most believable news medium. In 1968, it reached a two-to-one advantage over newspapers, and by 1974 the margin had widened to a two-and-a-half-to-one advantage.[2]

The turmoil of the 1970s engendered considerable criticism for the media in general and for newspapers in particular, and resulted in a renewal of concern about ethics. Newspaper publishers, anxious to heighten their sliding credibility, and reporters, interested in preserving their newly won small share of independence in the newsroom, looked for ways to institutionalize developments of the 1960s. In 1973, The Society of Professional Journalists adopted an ethics code; in 1975, the American Society of Newspaper Editors adopted a revised "statement of principles" and the Associated Press Managing Editors (APME) adopted a similar code.[3] In addition, the National News Council and the use of ombudsmen appeared as attempts to assure fairness of media coverage. But codes and other attempts to assure fairness did not solve the ethics controversy, which came to an embarrassing confrontation in 1981 when Janet Cooke of the *Washington Post* won a Pulitzer Prize for what later was revealed to be a fabricated story about an eight-year-old black heroin addict. The *Post* returned the prize when the discovery was made.

The experience heightened criticism from the political and religious right, as well as from internal organizational structures. Editors began to impose more control over reporters' copy, and by 1982, journalists indicated they felt significantly less autonomy in their jobs and less freedom to determine the emphasis of their stories than they had in 1971. In line with society at large, journalists moved to the political center and became increasingly concerned about job security. Journalists' salaries suffered from inflation; median income in 1982 was $19,000, with $7,000 less in purchasing power than in 1971, and although media companies expanded and profits grew tremendously, particularly in broadcasting, the rewards did not trickle down to more than a few stars in major markets.[4]

Activist movements of the late 1960s and early 1970s also affected newsroom hiring and promotion patterns. In 1968, the Kerner Commission found that minority status in newsrooms had improved only slightly since the 1950s, when an American Newspaper Guild survey indicated only thirty-eight blacks were working in a pool of 75,000 newspaper editorial employees.[5] Women were paid less than men, even when they did comparable work. The bastion of white male dominance in the early 1970s, the APME, maintained that women "had no aptitude for executive roles and that, should they inadvertently be stuck in an executive role, their duty was 'to make a man feel like the boss.'"[6] After the passage of the Equal Employment Opportunity Act of 1972, women and minorities at *Newsweek*, the AP, the *New York Times*, NBC, and the *Reader's Digest* filed suits, which usually resulted in limited settlements. By 1982, women comprised nearly a third of the journalistic work force, although blacks and hispanics had made few gains.[7]

In the 1980s, most reporters came to the field with journalism school degrees, although large media companies in the Northeast tended to hire reporters with liberal arts degrees. Most significantly, by 1982, reporters between thirty and forty-five, those who were the best educated and experienced, expressed a greater desire to leave the field than they had in 1971.

Operating within a political climate that supported deregulation of transportation and communication, the FCC supported deregulation of the broadcast industry, backed away from its "stewardship" role, and, in the 1980s, announced it would no longer enforce the Fairness Doctrine.

The experience of reporters in Vietnam did not translate immediately to coverage of other parts of the world, such as the Middle East and South America, where event coverage still seemed to override issue coverage. When reporters were banned from accompanying troops during the Grenada invasion of 1983, they gained little public support for their protests against managed news. However, the *Washington Post*'s coup of 1986–1987, the uncovering of arms trading with Iran and money diverted to support Nicaraguan Contras, indicated that event politics, if not issue politics, were still prime factors on the news agenda.

Despite a continued interest in political news, newspapers and television increased their reliance on marketing surveys for determining the packaging of the news product. A 1979 study indicated audiences wanted a broadened definition of news, and editors and news directors responded with more soft news, including economic, health, and technology issues. The advent of cable promised a new diversity in programming, but despite some innovations such as twenty-four-hour news programming, cable relied on adolescent movies, violence, and sex, thwarting the hopes of those who anticipated a cultural revolution. *USA Today* entered the national market with a format determined by market research. Meanwhile, quality monthly magazines continued a downward spiral, although new ownership injected needed capital into operations at *Harper's*, *Atlantic Monthly*, and *Saturday Review*. UPI continued its financial struggles as it changed ownership, although in 1987 its problems had not been stabilized.

"WATERGATE" AND THE NEWS MEDIA

In the early 1970s, the *Washington Post* began to investigate a seemingly obscure burglary in the Watergate Hotel in Washington, D.C. That "third-rate" burglary of the national Democratic party headquarters in the Watergate Hotel on June 17, 1972, became the beginning of the unraveling of what William Safire called in 1987, an "abuse of the power of government in order to effect an election." Such abuse, wrote Safire, "was an impeachable offense and rightly resulted in the resignation of the President."[8]

Early in February 1972, President Richard Nixon's former law partner, campaign manager, and Attorney General John Mitchell resigned from the Cabinet to direct the Committee to Re-Elect the President, often called by a prophetic acronym, "CREEP." Former White House aides working with CREEP — G. Gordon Liddy and Howard Hunt — turned out to be macho operatives with a taste for cloak-and-dagger work. Cloak-and-dagger strategy led to the attempted burglary in the Democratic party headquarters, where five men were caught not only looking for political information but trying to plant electronic listening devices.

Two *Washington Post* reporters, young metropolitan desk staffers Carl Bernstein and Bob Woodward, soon tied one of the burglars, James McCord, to the Central Intelligence Agency.[9] Within days, President Nixon in news conferences denounced electronic eavesdropping as alien to the political process of the United States. As subsequent events showed, Nixon and his aides, H. R. Haldeman and John Erlichman, tried to cover up White House connections to the burglars from the outset.

> ## ON WATERGATE
>
> So while Watergate vexes us now as the troubles of the 1860s and 1870s vexed our forefathers, there is little reason to despair. Life is trouble, for both men and nations, but this nation retains deep and abiding strength. The present troubles too will pass away, and the American experiment with freedom will endure.
>
> SOURCE. Robert L. Bartley, Wall Street Journal.

Although other newspapers downplayed the story, Woodward and Bernstein's perseverance paid off. They traced a $25,000 check deposited in a Florida bank to the account of one of the Watergate burglars, Bernard L. Barker. The check was written by the Republicans' Midwest finance head, Kenneth H. Dahlberg, and had been given to former Secretary of Commerce Maurice Stans, Republican campaign treasurer in 1972.

With the 1972 election approaching, necessary details of the Watergate story eluded verification no matter how hard the two young reporters — jointly nicknamed "Woodstein" by editor Ben Bradlee — tried to pin it down. While Nixon claimed the White House was cooperating with the FBI and the Department of Justice investigators, the *Post* pushed on, and on October 10, 1972, broke a major story that the Watergate burglary was not an isolated incident, but was part of a massive Republican campaign of political "dirty tricks" — sabotage — and spying.

At this point, Woodward and Bernstein went to press without sufficient verification. Interviewing a likable White House aide, Hugh Sloan, they took his noncommittal nonanswers to mean that he had told a grand jury that H. R. Haldeman was one of the paymasters who could hand out cash in exchange for spying. Sloan denied that he had told the grand jury such information, and the Republican establishment labeled "Woodstein" and the *Washington Post* irresponsible. Some leading Democrats joined the chorus. Sloan later admitted he had not told the grand jury that Haldeman paid for political spying on the Democrats, but only because the jury did not ask him the direct question that would have elicited that specific testimony.

Meanwhile, the burglars obstinately maintained their silence about what they were doing in the Watergate on that June night. The silence continued for more than six months, well past the November 1972 reelection of President Nixon and Vice-President Spiro Agnew. Meanwhile, President Nixon's popularity soared. Shortly after the Paris agreement to initiate a cease-fire in Vietnam was signed on January 27, 1973, a Gallup Poll found that 68 percent of the public favored the president.

In March 1973, a major break came in the Watergate story. One of the convicted burglars, James W. McCord, admitted to U.S. District Judge John

Sirica that he had been pressured to remain silent. McCord was pointing toward the White House when he suggested that persons higher up the political chain were involved.

Disastrous admission followed upon disastrous admission. FBI director Patrick Gray resigned late in April, conceding that he had destroyed evidence related to Watergate. White House aides G. Gordon Liddy and Howard Hunt admitted they had broken into a psychiatrist's office to try to obtain the records of former Rand Corporation employee Daniel Ellsberg. Ellsberg was accused, along with J. Anthony Russo, of having stolen and leaked a massive, forty-seven-volume set of classified historical materials dealing with years of United States involvement in Vietnam. The materials were classified "Top Secret." Portions of the Pentagon Papers were published by the *New York Times*, the *Washington Post*, and the *St. Louis Post-Dispatch*. Charges against Ellsberg and Russo were dismissed by a U.S. district judge after word reached him that White House aides Liddy and Hunt had invaded the doctor's office.

Meanwhile, President Nixon announced the resignations of chief aides John Erlichman, H. R. Haldeman, and John Dean, as well as that of Attorney General Richard Kleindienst. Nixon told the nation he took responsibility for the actions of his aides, but denied any knowledge of a cover-up on Watergate. Eventually, however, Dean revealed that Nixon was indeed a part of the operation and of the cover-up.

THE NIXON TAPES

When Richard Nixon became president, he denounced President Lyndon B. Johnson's procedure of taping many, if not most, of the conversations involving the office of president. As journalist-historian Theodore White observed, "Ego is the disease of great leaders; some leave pyramids, some leave tapes. . . ."[10] In fact, Nixon had the Army Signal Corps tear out Johnson's tape machines, and none reappeared until 1971. After Haldeman told Nixon about the insistence of archivists and librarians that tape machines be installed, the president changed his mind and allowed the taping to resume. Machines —some with on-off switches, and some voice-activated—were installed, and that included the White House phones most often used by the president. "Thus the tapes ran," wrote Theodore White, "sporadically stopping and starting, spinning and halting as they wove the web that was ultimately to trap Richard Nixon."[11]

In June 1973, a reluctant witness named Alexander Butterfield appeared before investigators of the U.S. Senate committee investigating Watergate. He grudgingly revealed what he said was "probably the one thing the President wouldn't want revealed:" that the President's conversations had been taped.[12]

The Washington Post *gained national prominence after its treatment of the Watergate story. Today the* Post *is the product of a complex, technologically advanced process that combines the talents of more than 3,000 employees. Reporters work on computer terminals in this technologically advanced newsroom. (Washington Post Photograph)*

Shortly thereafter, Bob Woodward got a tip from his shadowy secret source, the now-legendary "Deep Throat." Deep Throat suggested that there were some suspicious gaps on the tapes, and a *Washington Post* story—with an anonymous source—relayed that assertion to the public. Sure enough, there turned out to be an 18½-minute gap in one of the tapes, indicating tampering.

From that point, the Senate Watergate Committee attracted national attention. Particularly chilling was the series of accusations against President Nixon calmly delivered by John W. Dean III, former presidential counsel. He accused the president of complicity in Watergate cover-up efforts. The Nixon Administration absorbed another damaging blow in the fall of 1973 when Vice-President Spiro Agnew resigned from office, charged with tax evasion for accepting illegal payments from contractors while he was Maryland's governor. Nixon replaced Agnew with Representative Gerald R. Ford, the House minority leader.

Other self-inflicted wounds hit the Nixon Administration. President Nixon, squirming under the evidence-gathering of Special Prosecutor Archibald Cox, a Harvard law professor, demanded that Attorney General Elliott Richardson fire Cox. Richardson and his top assistant, William D. Ruckelshaus, resigned instead of obeying Nixon's order. Solicitor General Robert Bork stepped forward, in what became known as the Saturday Night Massacre, and fired Archibald Cox. Bork went on to become a federal appeals judge who in 1987 was nominated for a post on the Supreme Court by President Reagan. Bork's conservative writings—and memories of his role in Watergate—were among the factors leading to the Senate's refusal to confirm him. Three days after Cox was fired, the House Judiciary Committee— with a majority incensed by the firing of Cox—decided to begin considering impeachment charges against President Nixon. The president, meanwhile, reversed his field. Back in July 1973, Nixon refused to obey a subpoena from the Senate Watergate Committee to hand over the secret tape recordings from the Oval Office. But by late October 1973, perhaps in response to growing political pressure, Nixon agreed to release the tapes. He later reneged, instead giving the Congressional committee only edited transcripts, although the transcripts added up to more than 1,200 pages.

On August 8, 1974, President Richard Nixon at long last announced his resignation on nationwide television, and Ford assumed the presidency.

THE SIGNIFICANCE OF WATERGATE

Contrary to popular myth—and to the claims of some journalists—the press, including the *Washington Post*, did not topple President Richard Nixon. As journalist David Schoenbrun wrote, Nixon was doomed neither by his enemies nor by the media. Nixon was doomed by a long record of misdeeds, and of violations of the law, as well as his lies and cover-ups. On one level, then, the Watergate debacle can be understood as a breach of faith, as an effort to subvert the electoral and judicial processes of the nation, rather than as a journalistic coup.

EFFORTS TO RESTORE CREDIBILITY

Despite the press's role in Watergate, or perhaps because of it, the public granted less credibility to the press in the early 1970s than it had in recent years. Outside critics charged that journalists "were out of control and out of line with dominant social values; they had come to constitute a separate and subversive class."[13] News organizations responded to the external critique by creating codes of ethics and devices for monitoring the media.

Some editors viewed the creation of the National News Council and ethics codes, and the positioning of ombudsmen within larger papers as a long overdue effort by the industry to assume responsibility for its vast power and control over public information. Others, however, rejected the council and other devices as an effort to appease government, which would open the door to government control.[14] Whatever the motive, the result was that the press seemed as unwilling to criticize itself as it had when the Hutchins Commission released its 1947 report.

NATIONAL NEWS COUNCIL

News councils in the United States have been modeled after the British Press Council, organized in 1964, which required that individuals asking the council to investigate a complaint must also agree not to bring civil action against the newspaper about which it lodged a complaint. In Britain the council activity corresponded with a drop in libel cases.

The National News Council, begun in the United States by foundation money in 1973, lost its financing in 1984. The National News Council initially had the support of the *Washington Post*, the *Wall Street Journal*, the *Christian Science Monitor*, CBS, the Associated Press, and United Press International. Lined up against the national council was the *New York Times*. Publisher Arthur Ochs Sulzberger declared the *Times*' decision to boycott the council in a memo to his staff: "We will not be a party to Council investigations. We will not furnish information or explanations to the Council. In our coverage, we will treat the Council as we treat any other organization: we will report their activities when they are newsworthy."[15]

Critics have argued that failure of the National Press Council was partly its timidity and early insistence that it limit its cases to "principal national suppliers of news," as well as its reluctance to initiate any investigations on its own.

OMBUDSMEN

In 1967, the *Louisville Courier Journal*, a family-owned newspaper, adopted the concept of employing an ombudsman, a Swedish term denoting a government official appointed to receive or investigate complaints. In the American newsroom, the ombudsman is employed and paid by the employer, not by the government. By 1985, about thirty-five ombudsmen were at work nationwide,

> **ASNE STATEMENT OF PRINCIPLES**
>
> The First Amendment, protecting freedom of expression from abridgment by any law, guarantees to the people through their press a constitutional right, and thereby places on newspaper people a particular responsibility.
>
> Thus journalism demands of its practitioners not only industry and knowledge but also the pursuit of a standard of integrity proportionate to the journalist's singular obligation.
>
> SOURCE. Preamble.

responding to criticism from readers and formalizing internal standards and procedures. Many also were writing columns related to their work. Newspapers have experimented with a variety of organizational patterns, sometimes rotating a staff member into the slot and at other times hiring a person from the outside for a limited term. The latter approach has the advantage of reducing staff pressure on the ombudsman and granting him or her more independence in the role.

CODES OF ETHICS

In addition to adoption by major journalistic organizations of codes of ethics, individual news organizations in the 1970s established codes to limit the involvement of reporters in activities that might embarrass the news organization. CBS, for example, adopted a code of standards for covering demonstrations and other civil disturbances which encouraged the reporter to relay information factually and without participation.[16] Newspaper codes limited the amount of political involvement management considered appropriate and asked reporters to avoid investments that might jeopardize their objectivity.[17]

CORPORATE AND PUBLIC OWNERSHIP

CIRCULATION OF NEWSPAPERS

Although the total circulation of newspapers increased steadily from the mid-twentieth century, despite slight declines in the mid 1970s, in relationship to the population newspaper readership has not grown as expected. Between 1950 and 1984 newspaper circulation grew only 17.6 percent, while the nation's population grew by 55 percent.[18] Newspaper household penetration declined from 124 percent in 1950 to 72 percent in 1985, showing its greatest drop between 1970 and 1980.

CORPORATE OWNERSHIP OF NEWSPAPERS

Group and chain ownership of newspapers continued to increase through the 1970s, and purchases of old-line family newspapers in the 1980s underscored the trend. In 1970, chains controlled 63 percent of the newspaper circulation in the United States and 50 percent of the dailies; by the end of 1985, groups controlled 77 percent of the circulation and 71 percent of all dailies. The $315 million 1986 Gannett purchase of the *Louisville Courier-Journal*, the $200 million purchase of the dominant Iowa paper, the *Des Moines Register*, and the Times-Mirror acquisition of the Baltimore Sun Papers incorporated three major independent newspapers into groups or chains.

The Des Moines paper had been owned by the Cowles family since 1903, when Gardner Cowles, an Algona, Iowa, banker bought the *Register and Leader* for $300,000. Between 1903 and 1986, the combined *Register and Tribune* won twelve Pulitzer prizes. In early June 1986, Times-Mirror purchased the *Baltimore Sun and Evening Sun* for $600 million from the A. S. Abell Co. The Baltimore price escalated because its only competitor, Hearst's *News American*, folded the day before Abell agreed to sell. Times-Mirror owns eleven newspapers, including the *Los Angeles Times*, New York's *Newsday*, the *Hartford Courant*, the *Denver Post*, and the *Dallas Times-Herald*. Its holdings are not restricted to newspapers, but include other media as well.

Critics respond differently to increased chain ownership. Ben Bagdikian, dean of the School of Journalism at the University of California at Berkeley and widely known press critic, wrote that "a very large degree of control of the newspaper industry is in the hands of relatively large companies. Politically and socially, that is something to be concerned with. It gives them enormous power." However, Brian Brooks of the University of Missouri emphasized that the newspaper industry remains diverse. Of the 1,700 daily newspapers in the country, the biggest chain, Gannett, controlled only ninety in 1986. "It is possible," said Brooks, "to envision a scenario, sometime down the road, when the industry becomes so concentrated that there is a problem, but that is a long way off."[19]

MEDIA COMPANIES ON THE STOCK EXCHANGE

Mass media participated in the accelerating spiral of finance capitalism, mergers, and takeovers in the 1970s and 1980s. In terms of historical per-

Media companies are big business. Freedom Center, the Chicago Tribune's "state of the art" production and circulation facility, represents a $186 million investment. (Photograph courtesy of Chicago Tribune)

spective, this development has been remarkably rapid, almost sudden. Although group and chain ownership have been structural components of the industry since the eighteenth century, media corporations issuing publicly held stock is a recent phenomenon.

This trend began in the early 1960s, with Dow Jones, Inc., publisher of the *Wall Street Journal*, issuing publicly traded stock. By the late 1980s, at least fifteen publicly traded corporations owned newspapers. The Times-Mirror Company, headquartered in Los Angeles and formerly a closely held family organization, was listed on the New York Stock Exchange in 1964. Gannett and Media General went public in 1967. In the late 1960s, Ridder Publications and Knight Newspapers (since joined into the mighty Knight-Ridder Corporation), The New York Times Corporation and Lee Enterprises joined the move to go public. In the 1970s, the Washington Post Co. (owner of *Newsweek* magazine and, like the others listed, also an owner of broadcast properties) and Affiliated Publications (*Boston Globe*) went public. Harte-Hanks Communications went public in the 1970s and then, as hostile takeovers threatened autonomy of many corporations, bought up enough of its own stock to go private again in the mid-1980s. The 1980s saw the A. H. Belo Corp. (*Dallas Morning News*) and The Tribune Co. (*Chicago Tribune* and *New York Daily News*) going public. Capital Cities Communications, a major owner of broadcast stations and cable outlets, acquired two major newspapers with the *Ford Worth Star-Telegram* and the *Kansas City Star*.

"Going public" earns companies certain benefits under the tax code, such as maintaining a company after the death of an original owner, while at the same time allowing the distribution of shares to heirs and lessening the tax bite that the Internal Revenue Service takes out of family-owned businesses when a prime owner dies. Mergers are more easily accomplished, and liquidity of shares in publicly held corporations makes possible stock ownership plans for employees. Proceeds from sale of stock shares can be used for technological innovations.

Not all aspects of this corporate "Brave New World" are positive. Some critics of the media fear that earnings-oriented managements of media firms will worry more about how well shares trade on the market and how well regarded they are by financial analysts than about how well the news is covered. Given the finance-school and boardroom backgrounds of many persons heading media conglomerates during the late 1980s, the question of news as entertainment (and the greatly diminished number of troublesome and generally unprofitable news specials) versus news as news was unresolved.

MERGER MANIA OF THE 1980S

The administration of President Ronald W. Reagan supported deregulation begun in the 1970s in a variety of industries, and favored less involvement of the FCC in the media business. On April 1, 1985, the deregulation-minded Federal Communications Commission under Chairman Mark Fowler announced a policy that accelerated mergers of media companies. The change is known by a shorthand number label: "7-7-7" to "12-12-12." Until that April day, no person or corporation could be licensed to operate more than seven AM radio stations, seven FM radio stations, and seven television stations. One other limitation set by the FCC was that no one company could have broadcast stations reaching more than 25 percent of the nation's homes.

Until that change in policy, Capital Cities Communications (owners of the *Kansas City Star* and the *Fort Worth Star-Telegram*, plus a substantial number of broadcast stations) and the ABC Network (also owners of numerous stations within the 7-7-7 rule) eyed each other as suitable merger partners. Such a financial marriage couldn't occur until the 12-12-12 rule was put into effect. That way, the newly merged operation could keep most of its broadcast stations, selling enough to get under the 25 percent viewership limitation.[20]

Also pushing ABC toward the merger with Capital Cities were fears of a "hostile takeover," a ploy by which an entrepreneurial shark tries to buy enough of a corporation's stock to swallow the corporate fish, hook, line, sinker, and assets. Another wrinkle in the hostile takeover maneuver was the use, on occasion, of "junk bonds:" relatively low-security but high-interest bonds providing money for an entrepreneur to buy up enough stock to gain control of a company. Rumors circulated of takeover attempts of ABC by flamboyant operators such as the Bass Brothers of Fort Worth or Ted Turner, who had created a great success out of his Atlanta Super-Station, WTBS, and his much-praised news innovation, Cable News Network (CNN). ABC chairman Leonard Goldenson dismissed those rumors, saying that the friendly merger with Capital Cities had not been effected to avoid someone deemed less desirable.[21]

During the mid-1980s, most journalists looked at the Wall Street interest in buying or merging with media companies with a kind of horrified fascination. This was supposed to be *journalism*, not high finance. Nevertheless, media companies were prized along Wall Street and by hotshot entrepreneurs because they were companies with a high cash return on investment ratio. This encouraged efforts at "leveraged buyouts"—borrowing money to take over control of a company and then allowing the company's earnings to pay off the loan.

BROADCAST TRANSITIONS

The combination of an avid interest in capturing media companies for the fun of profit with technological developments making possible the development of cable television created new questions in the 1980s about the status of the television networks. The advances of cable television throughout the 1970s and 1980s, including the inroads made by Cable News Network, have challenged the traditional superiority of the big three: ABC, CBS, and NBC. The Australian media magnate Rupert Murdoch also was very much a "player" in the United States in the 1980s. His News Corporation in 1985 bought half of Twentieth Century-Fox Corporation, thus gaining access to its enormous film library. Murdoch's evident goal—to establish another television network— was viewed with apprehension by the network old guard. Fox Television Network in 1987 reached more than 80 percent of American homes.

Early in 1986, in what was then the biggest non-oil-company merger in history, General Electric, which was forced out of RCA by the FTC in 1930, acquired RCA Corporation for the incomprehensible sum of $6.28 billion. GE chairman John F. Welch, Jr., was ecstatic: "This is going to be one dynamite company," he told the *Wall Street Journal*.[22]

Tagging along in the RCA corporate mix, of course, was NBC. The GE purchase meant that two of the three major networks had been acquired (ABC purchased in a friendly takeover in 1985 by Capital Cities Communications), and CBS was soon to follow. The financial community's jubilation over the purchase of RCA (including NBC) by GE was not universal. The author of *In Search of Excellence*, Tom Peters, said he was deeply saddened that GE, "with an incredible amount of bucks lying around," could not find a way to invest them internally.

Consumer advocate Ralph Nader was outraged, concerned about problems created for competition and about the close relationship between GE and Pentagon defense industry dollars, and questioning whether NBC could resist the temptation for self-censorship.[23]

CABLE NEWS NETWORK AND METROMEDIA

Begun in 1980, Ted Turner's Cable News Network became the nation's first global television channel, reaching 40 percent of homes in the United States on cable and beaming news to Europe and around the world via satellite.[24]

Rupert Murdoch, owner of Metromedia, sought American citizenship so he could meet FCC rules that forbid foreigners from owning U.S. television stations. Known for his variety of newspaper holdings, including the *Times* of London and the *New York Post*, Murdoch also has been a global force in film and video.[25] His News Corp Ltd. owns television properties in Australia and Europe, the 20th Century-Fox Film studio and six Metromedia television stations in key U.S. cities, including New York, Los Angeles, Chicago, and Washington.

Cable efforts have paid off for these entrepreneurs. While in 1970 cable audiences were too small to be measured, nearly 80 percent of American households had access to cable in 1987. Of those households having cable, nearly 50 percent subscribed to basic service, and other 25 percent subscribed to a pay service. Such growth has had a substantial impact on the networks, bringing forth predictions such as CBS executive Ernest Leiser's column in the *Washington Post*, "That's the Way It Was When Network News Died." From 1980 to 1987 prime-time network share had dropped from 90 to 73 percent.

PUBLIC BROADCASTING SERVICE

By the late 1980s, two of the most respected television reporters headed an hour-long, noncommercial news broadcast. Robert MacNeil and Jim Lehrer's "MacNeil-Lehrer News Hour" performance lacked the star quality of news anchors Dan Rather (CBS), Tom Brokaw (NBC), or Peter Jennings (ABC), but the News Hour garnered a strong following for PBS. The show's format was shaped around fewer stories, with more in-depth treatment than was allowed in the major networks' thirty-minute formats. This depth helped PBS to fulfill some of the high hopes for educational TV that had been expressed throughout broadcast history, especially during the 1950s days of TV channel allocation.

During the 1950s, Frieda Hennock, first woman member of the FCC, fought strenuously during her term from 1948 to 1951 to convince the commission to set aside channels for educational use, despite dire predictions from some commercial broadcasters that government educational channels might lead to totalitarian propagandizing of the public. In 1967, after recommendations from a prestigious study group—the Carnegie Commission on Public Television—President Lyndon B. Johnson advocated, and Congress passed, legislation creating the Corporation for Public Broadcasting. This made available several hundred million dollars to support local educational stations and to link together public television stations. In 1969, Public Broadcasting Service was created to supervise the linkage among stations.

A TALE OF CBS

During 1985 and 1986, CBS was threatened by a hostile takeover by Turner of CNN, a takeover heightened by noisy threats from those on the religious and political far right. As Turner attempted to raise $5.4 billion to buy control of CBS, North Carolina Democratic Senator Jesse Helms and a group of television evangelists organized a group labeled Fairness in Media, declaring that CBS stock should be bought and the network put in what they termed responsible hands. Helms, in particular, wanted Dan Rather, CBS Evening News anchor, fired.[26]

Turner offered to trade stock in the Turner Broadcasting Company plus $5.4 billion in "junk bonds" to gain control of 67 percent of CBS—the amount needed for control under New York law. The prestigious British magazine, *The Economist*, noted that Turner's bid contained not one penny of cash, adding: "Mr. Turner hopes instead to tempt CBS shareholders with an annual dividend" of seven times the 1985 CBS dividend.[27]

The Turner threat to CBS seemed real enough that the network revamped its structure, taking on more debt, but at the same time making itself somewhat less attractive to unwanted takeover efforts. Meanwhile, CBS invited Lawrence Tisch, head of the conglomerate Loew's Corporation and one of the nation's richest men, to join the network's board. Tisch had been quietly buying CBS stock. Once Tisch gained control, he accelerated cuts in the news budget and staff which had already been underway.

Howard Stringer, appointed chief of CBS News under Tisch, continued the cost cutting. In the fourth round of CBS news cuts in two years, March 6, 1987, about 200 employees were fired as part of a $30 million budget reduction ordered by Tisch.[28] Some long-time reporters who were let go included law correspondent Fred Graham and Capitol Hill correspondent Ike Pappas. In the same sweep, CBS cut the sixteen-year-old children's program, "In the

Dan Rather, CBS News Anchorman, confers with Howard Stringer. Stringer, executive producer when this photograph was taken in 1983, has been promoted to chief of CBS News. (Library of Congress Collection, U.S. News and World Report photo)

News," and fired its staff. "CBS Morning News" lost twenty-eight job positions. The news division also closed bureaus in Warsaw, Bangkok, and Seattle.

Tisch's firings resulted in an angry protest from anchorman Dan Rather. Fred W. Friendly, former CBS News president who had been Edward R. Murrow's producer, added his voice to the fray. He charged that Tisch did not understand that the nature of news staffing demands that it must not be cut to a bare minimum; it must have sufficient capacity to cover crises and emergencies, not just routine news. Friendly told the *New York Times*:

> [T]he way you judge a news team is how it acts in a crisis. When President Kennedy was shot, the country was on the edge of chaos. CBS held the country together with hundreds of reporters on five continents reporting on the meaning of it.

Friendly said that CBS News was not losing money; "they're just not making as much as they might make." Claiming that CBS was not in cash registers or pork bellies, he maintained, "They're licensed to operate in the public interest, and that's all been forgotten."[29]

CBS News, long the proud leader in network news, by 1987 was trailing NBC and ABC in the ratings game. Dan Rather's "Evening News" lagged behind NBC's Tom Brokaw and ABC's Peter Jennings. CBS also trailed in the prime-time and morning news ratings in 1986, when it became a three-time loser for the first time in at least sixteen years.[30]

Speaking before a national news conference in New York, Tisch defended the CBS action, citing increased competition by cable and distinguishing between editorial integrity and economic immunity. "Let's be clear," noted Tisch. "The news room—the journalists—must be independent in its preparation of the news.... This is an absolute, sacred principle. It will not be breached." Tisch added, however, that maintaining news quality did not require that "cost management and budget levels be left entirely in the hands of journalists."[31]

DEREGULATION

The controversy over trying to create programming change through the FCC led to disillusionment with the agency's effectiveness by the end of the decade, despite some concessions to reform groups who established citizens' rights to challenge licenses.[32] In 1976, under the leadership of California Congressman Lionel Van Deerlin, Congress began examining possible revisions of the 1934 Communications Act. Before Van Deerlin was defeated in 1979, the subcommittee that he chaired proposed removal of regulations and a return to market-forces regulation. Van Deerlin's committee recommended substitution of three-year licensing with indefinite license terms, abolition of the Fairness Doctrine, and removal of equal-opportunity rules.[33]

Since 1981, with his appointment as chairman of the FCC, Mark Fowler led the move to deregulate the broadcast industry. "Free-market forces and competitive forces are better able to serve the public and police companies" than the government, Fowler told a *Washington Post* reporter in 1987. Fowler's efforts resulted in a significant reduction of paper work, eliminated the need to keep detailed program logs, and reduced licensing renewals to a pro forma operation. In addition, the limits on how many AM, FM, and television stations broadcasters can own were raised from seven of each to twelve.

Despite Fowler's antagonism toward the Fairness Doctrine, under his leadership the FCC adopted sweeping new restrictions on the broadcast of obscene and offensive material.[34] Nevertheless, by the fall of 1987, despite the departure of Fowler in the spring of that year, the FCC announced it would no longer enforce the Fairness Doctrine. Efforts to codify the doctrine by Congress were vetoed by President Reagan.[35]

The possibility of hostile takeovers and deregulation have led some critics to fear that the broadcast industry is losing its sense of stewardship, although others would argue that the industry never took its sense of stewardship seriously. Leonard Goldenson, who owned ABC from 1953 until he sold it to Capital Cities in 1985, told a *Washington Post* reporter that the possibility existed for stations being quickly "flipped from owner to owner for quick profit, with little commitment to their communities."[36]

CHANGING NEWS AGENDA

In 1950, David Reisman, in a classic work, *The Lonely Crowd*, noted that journalists paid more attention to politics than the audience seemed to demand. Michael Schudson, writing in 1982, observed that the same was still true, "journalists accord politics a prestige that it does not have in the public mind."[37] In 1979, a study of *Changing Needs of Changing Readers* by Yankelovich, Skelly and White for the American Society of Newspaper Editors reinforced the concept that readers wanted information more than they wanted political news. The study indicated seven hot areas for newspapers to explore: economic news, business news, financial news, health news, personal safety, technology, and international news. The kind of news readers wanted within these categories, the study emphasized, was news interpreted to explain the impact of events on the local arena. For example, readers wanted to know the effects of decisions made by OPEC on the local oil markets in Texas.[38]

Responding to extensive market research was a highly criticized enterprise conducted by the Gannett Corporation, as it launched a national newspaper that its critics labeled, "McNewspaper."

USA TODAY

USA Today, a five-day-a-week national newspaper begun in 1982 by the Gannett Chain, conducted probably the most extensive market research in the history of newspapering before its first issue was published. Market research indicated readers wanted short stories and would not follow a jump, that they liked sports, charts, and graphs, and wanted information presented in ways that could be absorbed quickly. So extensive was the research that the only

Large circulations demand tons of newsprint. These rolls are lifted by overhead cranes with vacuum lifts. (Courtesy of Chicago Tribune)

addition made after the paper began was a reader-requested crossword puzzle.[39]

USA Today was the first national newspaper in addition to the *Wall Street Journal* to hit the stands since the demise of the *National Observer*, a serious general-interest weekly published by Dow Jones between 1961 and 1976. The *Observer*'s audience was so diverse that its "demographics just didn't grab advertisers," reported Lawrence Armour, director of corporate relations for Dow Jones & Co. *USA Today,* on the other hand, is clearly directed, according to Al Neuharth, chairman of the Gannett Co., at "several million readers across the U.S.A. who are mobile and curious and who have general interest in what's going on around them, not just finance, not just politics, not just sports."[40] Gannett utilized its nationwide editorial, production, circulation, promotion, and delivery networks already in place and by January 1983 reported an audited circulation of 531,438. The newspaper is satellite beamed to a variety of printing locations and makes spectacular use of color and graphics.

In a speech to the Inland Daily Press Association in 1985, Neuharth said readers expect newspapers to "present all the news in the particular arena in which we play. That means the good as well as the bad, the glad as well as the sad. They want reading their newspaper to be as enjoyable an experience as watching television."[41]

William Wright's study of the "good news" qualities of the paper indicated that positioning was the most critical factor, and that 57.4 percent of the good-news stories and only 31.9 percent of the bad-news stories appeared above the fold in *USA Today*.[42] Wright said the newspaper's handling of an income-poverty report in 1984 prompted his study. The first six paragraphs of the article in *USA Today*, headlined "1st Real Income Gain in 4 Years," focused on a U.S. Census Bureau report that median income for various U.S. brackets had increased between 1.4 and 3.3 percent over the previous year. In the seventh paragraph, the newspaper reported that the national poverty rate reached 15.2 percent of the population, its highest level in eighteen years. The *New York Times* and the *Washington Post* coverage of the report led with the increase in poverty.

Critics have called *USA Today* a fast-food newspaper, with "no serious sense of priorities."[43] The question, asked Ben Bagdikian, is "how good is the paper journalistically?" The newspaper represents no gain to the reading public, he claimed, "which gets a flawed picture of the world each day from the new paper, and a serious blow to American journalism, since the paper represents the primacy of packagers and market analysts in a realm where the news judgment of reporters and editors has traditionally prevailed."[44] Others have praised its layout, innovative use of color, and clarity of writing and suggested that similar techniques could be profitably applied to newspapers with more serious agendas.

MAGAZINES

QUALITY MONTHLIES

As the trend toward specialized magazines continued in the 1970s and 1980s, the rescue of three quality monthlies reflected the loyalty of their readership, their importance as cultural artifacts, and their lack of ability to continue to attract advertisers.

Harper's, owned for the last fifteen years by the Minneapolis Star and Tribune Co., appeared dead by mid-summer of 1980. After a six-month search, no buyer had been found, and company chairman Otto Silha admitted to stockholders that *Harper's* "has never been a true financial success" since the company bought it.

In 1971, *Harper's* witnessed a truly sensational walk out by editor Willie Morris and a variety of staff members during a year when it was losing about

$200,000. The Star and Tribune Co., in an attempt to "upscale" *Harper's*, had begun a series of discount circulation offers in the late 1960s and early 1970s, but *Harper's* ended up with a list of subscribers who refused to renew and an artificially high circulation list which boosted mailing costs and did nothing to appeal to advertisers.

Harper's was rescued in 1980 by the MacArthur Foundation of Chicago and the Atlantic Richfield Co. foundation, which assumed the responsibility for the magazine's operating expenses, including the $4 million debt.

The Atlantic Monthly remained a profit-making enterprise, although it too was losing money when Mortimer Zuckerman, the Boston real-estate developer, bought it in 1980. Although Zuckerman said that on economic grounds alone he would not have bought the *Atlantic*, he still predicted the magazine would make money by the mid-1980s.

The third publication to be rescued was *Saturday Review*, which was purchased in 1980 by a successful financial publisher, Robert Weingarten. Weingarten altered the *Review*, from a general interest magazine to a magazine of the arts.[45]

OTHER CHANGES

U.S. News's Mortimer B. Zuckerman, a major real-estate developer, moved into the publishing business in the 1980s with purchases of the *Atlantic* magazine and *U.S. News and World Report*. In the fall of 1984, Zuckerman paid $182.5 million for *U.S. News*, the magazine begun in the 1930s by David Lawrence.

Zuckerman's bid for *U.S. News* guaranteed employees $3,000 for each share of stock they owned. Zuckerman claimed he would not make major changes in *U.S. News*: "It will never be an entertainment-style magazine; it has not been, it is not its tradition. . . . It's not a *People* magazine, and it will never be a *People* magazine. It's a serious magazine—in the best sense of that word."[46]

The *New Yorker*, the envy of the periodical industry from its founding in 1926 until 1967 when the magazine began to lose massive pages of advertising and net profits, shrank from a 1966 level of $3 million to less than $1 million in advertising revenues, although its circulation remained the same. Media critic Ben Bagdikian credited the loss to Jonathan Schell's account of an American assault on the village of Ben Suc in Vietnam. It was that story, Bagdikian claims, that caused nearly 2,500 pages of advertising for products such as Audemars Piguet watches, starting at the price of $10,500, to disappear from *New Yorker* pages.[47]

William Shawn, the editor of the *New Yorker* who chose to publish Schell's account, resigned in January 1987. The Newhouse Media Chain bought the magazine in 1985, and Shawn's exit may result in major changes at the magazine during the next few years. Shawn, the second editor of the *New Yorker*, took over from its founder William Ross in 1952. Replacing Shawn was Robert Gottlieb, former president and editor-in-chief of Alfred A. Knopf, Inc., which is part of Random House, also owned by Newhouse. The magazine quickly made some advertising changes, accepting a Calvin Klein "Obsession" advertisement. The ad's risque content would "have been unacceptable under the magazine's once notoriously stolid criteria."[48] Newhouse also launched a $2 million network television advertising campaign promoting the magazine. Bagdikian described the magazine as "almost the last repository of the style and tone of Henry David Thoreau and Matthew Arnold, its chaste, old-fashioned columns breathing the quietude of Nineteenth Century essays."[49]

UPI'S CONTINUING TROUBLES

Always the financial underdog of the two major wire services, in 1980 UPI faced a threatened strike by employees over a wage dispute during the Republican National Convention. The company at that time was 95 percent owned by the E. W. Scripps Co. in Cincinnati, and 5 percent by the Hearst Corp. Owners claimed it had lost $17 million between 1961, its last profitable year, and 1980. According to the Wire Service Guild, UPI ranked sixty-three in 1980 on a pay scale of 125 U.S. newspapers.[50] Times continued to be tough, however, and in 1984 wire service employees took a 25 percent wage cut to keep the service in business.[51]

In the spring of 1986, Mexican news magnate Mario Vazquez-Rana put $2.5 million into UPI, and pledged $25 million to creditors and $12.5 million in capital to rescue the ailing wire service from bankruptcy. Officials said it was the first major infusion of capital in more than a decade. Vazquez's actions were controversial because he dismissed top editors and shifted the foreign desk overseas. Vazquez acknowledged that the wire service continued to operate in the red, although he declined to say how much, and he admitted that cancellations of service had increased in the first few months after his takeover.[52]

Vazquez's acquiring of UPI caused some dismay among UPI staffers as well as other newsmen, since rumors floated consistently about his being a front man for former Mexican president Luis Echeverria. Vazquez decentralized UPI's administration, cracked down on overtime payments and other newsroom costs. In August 1986, UPI had about 2,800 broadcast and 550

Women broke through the male ranks in the 1970s and 1980s to assume roles as on-air reporters and anchors. Renee Pouissant has become a prominent local anchor at WJLA, Washington, D.C.'s ABC affiliate. (Courtesy of WJLA-TV)

Milwaukee Journal *reporters at work in the newsroom. (Courtesy of* Milwaukee Journal*)*

leaders managed to stay alive, although they made little profit and in some instances lost money continuously. The dominance of Associated Press seemed almost assured as UPI faced continuing financial difficulty.

NOTES

1. Cited in James Boylan, "Declarations of Independence," *Columbia Journalism Review*, November/December 1986, p. 37.
2. "Changing Public Attitudes Toward Television and Other Mass Media," Roper Organization, Inc. 1977, p. 4.
3. Philip Meyer, *Ethical Journalism* (White Plains, N.Y.: Longman, 1987), p. 18.
4. For reporter characteristics in 1982 as compared to 1971, see David Weaver and G. Cleveland Wilhoit, *American Journalists* (Bloomington: Indiana University Press, 1986).
5. Boylan, "Declarations of Independence," p. 39.
6. Boylan, "Declarations of Independence," p. 39.
7. Weaver and Wilhoit, *American Journalists*, 1986), pp. 38–39.
8. William Safire, "Ten Myths About the Reagan Debacle," *New York Times Magazine,* March 22, 1987, p. 22.

newspaper clients in the United States. In November 1986, UPI lost yet another major client — the *New York Times* — changed presidents, and fired its managing editor. Washington staff members protested the firing of Ronald Cohen by pulling their bylines from stories.

The infusion of capital and change of management did not pull UPI out of the red, however, and in late February 1988, Vazquez turned operating control of the wire service over to Paul Steinle, president of cable television's Financial News Network. At that time UPI was reported to be losing $1 million to $2 million every month.

CONCLUSION

The investigative styles of the 1960s culminated in the dogged efforts of the *Washington Post* to uncover the campaign dirty tricks of President Richard Nixon and his subsequent efforts to cover up the details. But the public was not terribly impressed, and newspapers declined in believability and as the prime news source. As the 1970s proceeded, editors began to pull back the control given to reporters in the 1960s and renewed their interest in codes of ethics and other forms of self-criticism. Although some newspapers responded enthusiastically to the creation of a news council and to the role of ombudsmen, others decried it as an open door to government control.

During the 1970s and 1980s, the face of the journalist changed. By 1982, nearly one-third of all journalists were women, reporters moved more toward the political center and sought job security. Low salaries and loss of autonomy led some reporters to look outside the field. The color of the newsroom changed little, however, as blacks and hispanics made few gains.

The development of cable throughout the 1980s challenged the networks, which lost audience share and reacted to ever-increasing news budgets with harsh cutbacks. "Going public" caused new areas of concern for broadcast owners and publishers regarding hostile takeovers and trading shares on the market.

Led by 1980s commissioner Mark Fowler, the FCC began to withdraw from its stewardship role, expanded the numbers of outlets one owner could possess, and announced it would no longer continue to enforce the Fairness Doctrine. In 1987 Congress attempted to codify the Fairness Doctrine, but President Reagan vetoed the bill.

Newspapers and networks alike responded in the 1980s to a changing news agenda, introducing increased soft news and increased information about specific effects of economic and international news.

Magazines turned increasingly to specialization, but some of the big

9. Carl Bernstein and Bob Woodward, *All The President's Men* (New York: Simon and Schuster, 1974).
10. Theodore H. White, *Breach of Faith—The Fall of Richard Nixon* (New York: Atheneum, 1975), p. 244.
11. White, *Breach of Faith*, p. 245.
12. Woodward and Bernstein, *President's Men*, p. 331.
13. Boylan, "Declarations of Independence," p. 41.
14. See Meyer's interpretation in *Ethical Journalism*, pp. 168–171; James Boylan, "Declarations of Independence," p. 42.
15. Philip Meyer, *Ethical Journalism*, p. 170.
16. Clifford G. Christians, Kim B. Rotzoll, and Mark Fackler, *Media Ethics* (New York: Longman, 1987), p. 96.
17. Boylan, "Declarations of Independence," p. 42.
18. Philip Meyer, *Ethical Journalism*, p. 179.
19. James L. Rowe Jr., "Chains Seen Buying More Papers," *Washington Post*, June 1, 1986, F2.
20. David Clark Scott, "ABC Merger Likely to Generate Spinoff Sales," *Christian Science Monitor*, March 20, 1985.
21. "Omaha's Plain Dealer," *Newsweek*, April 1, 1985, p. 54.
22. "GE's Planned $6.28 Billion Acquisition of RCA Is Expected to Take 9 Months," *Wall Street Journal*, February 13, 1986, p. 1.
23. "GE and RCA: A Sampling of Opinions," *Wall Street Journal*, December 13, 1985, sec. 2, p. 27.
24. Michael Schrage and David A. Vise, "Murdoch, Turner Launch Era of Global Television," *Washington Post*, August 31, 1986, H1.
25. Schrage and Vise, "Murdoch, Turner," p. H1. Murdoch was forced to sell the *New York Post* early in 1988.
26. *Newsweek*, April 1, 1985, p. 57; "Network Blockbuster," *Time*, April 1, 1985, p. 60.
27. "When the Junketing Has to Stop," *The Economist*, April 27, 1985, p. 91; see also Alex S. Jones, "And now, the Media Mega-Merger," *New York Times*, Sec. 3, p. 11, March 24, 1985.
28. Meryl Gordon, "If Howard had known . . .," *Channels* (October, 1987), p. 60.
29. Alison Leigh Cowan, "Tisch is Holding a Hot Potato," *New York Times*, March 13, 1987, p. 18.
30. Tom Shales and Trustman Senger, "Bad News at Black Rock," *Washington Post*, July 2, 1986, D1, p. 6.
31. Laurence Tisch, "The Economics of Television News: What Is Happening and What It Means," speech given at "The Changing Economics of News," a national conference sponsored by the Gannett Center for Media Studies, April 28, 1987.
32. For thorough analysis of the effects of consumer reform, see Willard D. Rowland, Jr., "The Illusion of Fulfillment: The Broadcast Reform Movement," *Journalism Monographs* (December 1982), no. 79.

33. Florence Heffron, "The FCC and Broadcast Deregulation," in John J. Havick, ed., *Communications Policy and the Political Process* (Westport, Conn.: Greenwood Press, 1983), p. 43; Manhy Lucoff, "The Rise and Fall of the Third Rewrite," *Journal of Communication* vol. 30 (Winter 1980), p. 47.
34. Caroline E. Mayer and Elizabeth Tucker, "The FCC According to Fowler," *Washington Post,* April 19, 1987, H1, 4.
35. See *Broadcasting*, December 28, 1987, p. 31.
36. David A. Vise, "Concept of a Global Network Wasn't Born Yesterday," *Washington Post*, Business (H) 1.
37. Michael Schudson, "News Conventions in Print and Television," *Daedalus* (Fall 1982), vol. 111, no. 4, p. 107.
38. Robert G. Marbut, "Economics of the Mass Media in the United States," speech presented to Working Journalist Project, College of Communication, University of Texas-Austin, March 1, 1983.
39. Katharine Seelye, "Al Neuharth's Technicolor Baby," *Columbia Journalism Review* March/April 1983, p. 28.
40. Seelye, "Technicolor Baby," p. 28.
41. William F. Wright, "USA Today: Accentuating the Positive: A Study of the Gannett Flagship Newspaper," paper presented to the Association for Education in Journalism and Mass Communication, 1986, Norman, Okla., p. 4.
42. Wright, "USA Today," p. 10.
43. Ben Bagdikian, "Fast-food News: A Week's Diet," *Columbia Journalism Review* March/April 1983, p. 32.
44. Bagdikian, "Fast-food News," p. 33.
45. Lee Lescaze, "In the Nick Of Time: Three General Interest Magazines Rescued . . . For Now," by Lee Lescaze, *Washington Journalism Review* (September 1980), pp. 17–19.
46. Caroline E. Mayer, "Zuckerman: From Boston to Washington, from Property into Publishing," *Washington Post Business,* June 18, 1984, pp. 1, 36.
47. Ben H. Bagdikian, "The Wrong Kind of Readers: The fall and Rise of The New Yorker," *Progressive* (47:5), May 1983, p. 52.
48. Curt Suplee, "New Editor Chosen at New Yorker," *Washington Post,* January 13, 1987, D1, 10.
49. Bagdikian, "Wrong Kind of Readers," p. 52.
50. Louise B. Betts, "UPI Strike Settled at the Wire," *Washington Journalism Review* (September 1980), p. 8.
51. Michael Abramowitz, "Vazquez Wins Court Battle for UPI," *Washington Post*, June 11, 1986, pp. G1, 11.
52. Michael Abramowitz, "Honeymoon Is Over for UPI's New Owner: Rumors Fly as Employes Question Management Style, Personnel Decisions," *Washington Post Business*, October 13, 1986, p. 3.

INDEX

Abbott, Robert, 339, 363–366
Abell, Arunah Shepherdson, 139
Abolitionist press, 180, 187
Actual Malice, 520
Adams, Abigail, 113
Adams, Ansel, 452, 453
Adams, John, 54, 60, 84, 103, 105, 106, 110, 114
Adams, John Quincy, 121, 122
Adams, Sam, 54, 55, 75
Adler, Julius Ochs, 493
Advertising
  after Civil War, 234
  and the penny press, 129, 130, 133
  clubs, 385
  colonial, 18
  Fleischmann's Yeast, 386
  for patent medicines, 94
  history of, 374, 378, 380–387, 392, 397, 398
  in early Republic, 81, 93
Advertising Agencies
  Batten, Barton, Durstine & Osborne, 486
  Carlton and Smith, 236
  Lord and Thomas, 383
Advertising the American Dream, 386
Advocacy Journalism, 517, 521–523
Advocate
  of Kansas, 298
Agee, James, 427
Agence France-Presse, 450
Agnew, Spiro, 495, 535, 537
Agrarian press, 297
  in 1890s, 297–303
Aitken, Robert, 68, 91
Alaska
  Purchase of 1872, 230

Albany Evening Journal, 197
Alexander, James, 40, 42, 43
Alexander, Peter, 213
Alfred A. Knopf Inc., 553
Alien and Sedition Acts of 1798, 105, 113, 124, 110, 111–113, 346
  Enemy Alien Act, 101, 106, 111
  prosecutions under Sedition Act, 113
All-Channel bill, 505
Allen, William, 7
Alsop, Joseph, 515
Alternative Journalism, 501, 520–523
American Advertising Association, 384
American Archives, 121
American Bible Society, 379
American Birth Control League, 294
American Broadcasting Corporation, 482, 488, 543–545, 548, 549
American Civil Liberties Union, 479
American Colonization Society, 188, 190
American Magazine, 324, 331
  of Andrew Bradford, 33
American Magazine and Historical Chronicle, 123
American Marconi, 390, 391
American Missionary Association, 232
American News Company, 324
American Newspaper Guild, 274, 488, 532
American Newspaper Publishers' Association, 284, 344, 414, 417
  and NRA legislation, 436
American Society of Newspaper Editors, 411, 465, 466, 467, 540, 549
  statement of principles in 1975, 532
American Telephone and Telegraph, 390, 391, 392, 507

559

INDEX

American Weekly, 271, 510
American Weekly Mercury
  of William Bradford, 35
American Woman Suffrage Association, 290
Anglicanism
  in America, 13
  in England, 9
  in southern colonies, 15
Annals of Congress, 121
Annals of the American Academy of Political and Social Science, 332
Anthony, Susan B., 293
Anti-Courant, 22
Anti-Federalists, 85, 89, 101, 104, 112, 124
Anti-Slavery Bugle, 197
Anti-Slavery Movement, 180
Anti-Slavery Society, 181, 188–191, 194, 196, 199
Antoinette, Marie, 104
Apprenticeship
  in printing, 31
Architectural Forum, 428, 430
Areopagitica, 10
Armstrong, Edwin, 480, 482
Arnold, Benedict, 66
Arnold, Matthew, 553
Aronson, James, 493
Around the World in 80 Days, 268
Articles of Confederation, 79, 82, 84
Artisan republicanism, 248, 252
Artisans, 29, 31–32, 102
Associated Press, 186, 204, 206, 207, 230, 244, 252, 266, 280, 340, 379, 411, 412, 417, 423, 446, 457, 466, 467, 514, 532, 533, 539, 556
  and Supreme Court decision, 1943, 450
  and telegraph, 161
  of New York, 139
  Western, 244
Associated Press Managing Editors Association, 487
  Ethics Code of 1975, 532
Astaire, Fred, 420
Astor, John Jacob, 118
Atchison (Ks.) *Squatter-Sovereign*, 169, 170
Atlanta Compromise, 295
Atlanta Constitution, 229, 247, 341, 514
Atlantic Monthly, 309, 311, 316, 521, 534, 552
Audience
  of colonial newspapers, 11
  of the penny press, 129
Audit Bureau of Circulation, 384, 526
Aurora, 109–111, 113, 116
Authors Club of New York, 313
Ayer, N. W., 236
Aylesworth, M. H., 418

"Baby Burlesk," 420
Bache, Benjamin Franklin, 109–111
  and Sedition Act, 113
Bache, Margaret, 110–111
Bagdikian, Ben, 541, 551–553
Bailey, Francis, 68
Baillie, Hugh, 466
Bailyn, Bernard
  on revolutionary pamphlets, 64
Baker, Newton D., 356
Baker, Ray Stannard, 324, 327, 328, 331
Baldasty, Gerald, 157
Baldwin, Luther, 114
Ballads
  Broadsheet, 9
Baltimore Afro-American, 364, 365, 468
Baltimore American, 331
Baltimore News, 331
Baltimore Star, 331
Baltimore Sun, 140, 209, 278
Baltimore Sun and Evening Sun, 541
Barker, Bernard L., 535
Barnouw, Erik, 486, 489
Barnum, Phineas T., 379
Barry Goldwater: Extremist on the Right, 506
Barth, Gunther, 237
Bartley, Robert L., 535
Battle of Bull Run
  of July, 1861, 205, 213
Battle of Midway, 457
Battle of Monmouth, 88
Battle of New Orleans, 122
Bay Psalm Book, 12
Beach, Moses, 138, 139
Beasley, Maureen, 183
Bell, Robert, 66, 68
  and *Common Sense*, 67
Bennett, James Gordon, 130, 137, 140–143, 147, 157, 159, 197, 237, 238, 240, 269
  and marriage announcement, 142
  and moral war, 142
  and newsgathering, 142
  and religious news, 142
  and telegraph, 143
  and Washington Bureau, 143
Berger, Victor, 347, 349, 351
Berkeley, William, 13
Berkeley Barb, 524
Bernays, Edward, 379
  and *Crystallizing Public Opinion, Propaganda and Public Relations*, 381
Bernstein, Carl, 534, 535
Biddle, Francis, 462
Bierce, Ambrose, 272
Bigelow, John, 187
Bill of Rights, 81, 85, 94, 112, 125
Bingham, Judge Robert Worth, 246

Index

Birney, James, 188, 190, 191, 194
"Birth of a Nation (The)," 396
BIZ, 428
"Black Fury," 459
Black press, 181, 195, 200, 209, 444,
    460–462, 468
  during reconstruction, 295–297
  during World War II, 460
  in 1950s, 495
  in World War I, 363, 364
Black Star Picture Agency, 428
Blair, Clay Jr., 526
Blind booking, 422
Block booking, 422
Bloomer, Amelia, 291
Blue Book of Broadcasting, 488
Blue Network, 482, 488
Bluem, A. William, 419
Bly, Nellie, 268
Bok, Edward, 320, 321
Bookman, 246
Boorstin, Daniel, 171
Booster Press, 171, 172, 174
Bork, Robert, 538
Born, Donna, 408
"Born Free and Equal," 453
Boston
  as newspaper center, 32
Boston Courier, 194
Boston Daily Chronotype, 248
Boston Gazette, 19, 25
  and circulation, 69
  of Edes and Gill, 52, 54, 75
Boston Gazette and Weekly Journal, 33
Boston Globe, 271, 542
Boston Herald and Traveler, 378
Boston Journal, 331
Boston Massacre, 54
Boston News-Letter, 17, 18, 29, 33, 34
  circulation of, 69
Boston Repertory, 120
Boston Tea Party, 54
Boston Times, 319
Boston Transcript, 181
Boston Traveller, 171
Botein, Stephen, 30
Boudinot, Elias, 166
Bourke-White, Margaret, 410, 425, 429,
    432–434
  and communist charges, 433
  House Un-American Activities Committee,
    433
Bowen, William Shaw, 275
Boylan, James, 476, 500, 502
Bradford
  Andrew, 32, 36, 123
  John, 172

  Thomas, 35, 57, 68, 71
  William, 32, 35, 41, 57, 68, 71
  William, Jr., 57
  William I, 41
  William III, 34
Bradlee, Benjamin, 535
Bragg, Brigadier General Braxton, 216
Brant, Irving, 80
Brass Check (The), 380
Brennan, Justice William J., 519, 520
Breslin, Jimmy, 522
Brinkley, David, 500
Brisbane, Arthur, 268, 273
British Press Council, 539
Broadcast Industry
  corporate, 1950s, 503
  deregulation, 548
  licensing, 416, 480, 482, 487–488
  regulation, 373, 375, 380, 385, 389, 393
  transitions, 544
Brokaw, Tom, 545
Brookeman, Christopher, 508
Brooker, William, 19, 522
Brooklyn Eagle, 447, 449
Brooks, Brian, 541
Broun, Heywood, 268, 363, 408, 412
Brown, George Washington, 169, 170
Brown, Malcolm, 514
Brown v. Board of Education of Topeka, 517
Bryan, William Jennings, 300, 302
Bryant, Louise, 358
Bundy, McGeorge, 507
Bureau of Refugees, Freedmen and
    Abandoned Lands, 231, 232
Burleson, Postmaster Albert S., 347
Burnside, General A. E., 215
Burr, Aaron, 118
Business Week, 412
Busy-Body Papers, 35
Butter, Nathaniel, 10
Butterfield, Alexander, 536
Byrd, Richard, 416

Cable News Network, 544, 545
Calhoun, John C., 105, 122, 194
Californian, 159
Callender, James, 115
Camden (N.J.) *Courier*, 494
Campaign for International Freedom of the
    press during World War II, 466
Campbell, John, 17–19, 33, 522
Can't Anybody Here Play This Game?, 522
Cantril, Hadley, 413
  and "War of the Worlds," 419
Capital Cities Communications, 542–544, 549
Capital Times, 511
Capote, Truman, 521

561

INDEX

Capra, Frank, 421, 459
Carnegie Commission on Public Television, 546
Carrington, Edward, 116
Cartoonists
  during World War II, 450
Catholic Worker, 414, 425, 437, 438, 522
Catledge, Turner, 493
Caucus Club, 54
Caxton, William, 8
Censorship
  in Civil War, North, 213-215
  in Civil War, South, 215-217
  World War II, 444, 454, 456, 457, 459, 461, 466-468
Centinel papers, 85, 89
Central Intelligence Agency, 474, 504
Century, 309-314, 316, 317, 323, 325
Chafee, Zechariah, 349, 519
Chamberlain, Neville, 449
Chambers, Whittaker, 430
Chandler, Norman, 453
Chandler, Otis, 414, 502
Chaplin, Charles, 396
Charles I
  King of England, 9, 14
Charles II
  King of England, 10
Charleston Courier, 140, 209
Charleston Mercury, 199, 209
Chattanooga Times, 278
Checkley, John, 21
Cherokee Advocate, 168
Cherokee Phoenix, 165, 166
Chew, Benjamin, 71
Chiang Kai-Shek, 433
Chicago American, 434
Chicago Civic Federation, 260
Chicago Daily Journal, 158, 173
Chicago Daily News, 365, 378, 426
Chicago Defender, 339, 363-365, 460, 462, 495
Chicago Journal, 207, 378
Chicago Journalism Review, 523
Chicago Post, 207
Chicago Record, 413
Chicago Record-Herald, 413
Chicago Times, 173, 207, 215
Chicago Tribune, 173, 207, 210, 262, 340, 413, 414, 430, 434, 457, 542
  and Battle of Midway, 457
Chicago Urban League
  Abbott as member, 366
Child labor, 341
Christian Science Monitor, 491, 539
Cincinnati Commercial, 212, 214
Cincinnati Evening Times, 245

Cincinnati Gazette, 212
Cinematographe, 395
Circulations
  and modernization, 259
  of colonial newspapers, 69
Cisneros, Evangelina, 276
Cist, Charles, 68
Civil Rights, 499, 504, 527
  coverage of, 517-520
Civil Rights Act
  during Reconstruction, 231
  of 1875, 295
Civil War
  Beginning of, 204
  in England, 4, 10
  in United States, 163, 168, 173, 179, 186, 193, 196, 197, 346
Claflin, Tennessee, 294
Clark, Tom, 490
Class structure
  colonial, 31
  commercial, in England, 9
Clay, Cassius Marcellus, 191, 192
Clay, Henry, 120, 122, 155, 191
Claypoole, David C., 92
Clerk-Maxwell, James, 389
Cleveland Herald, 278
Cleveland Morning Leader, 173
Cobb, Frank Irving, 268
Cobbett, William, 106, 110
Cochrane, Elizabeth
  (Nellie Bly), 268
Cockburn, Admiral George, 120
Cody, Buffalo Bill, 379
Cohen, Ronald, 555
Coleman, William, 118
Collier's, 475
Collins, Isaac, 69
Colonial development, 11-15
Colonization, 187-190, 195, 196
Colored American, 196
Columbia Broadcasting System, 417, 418, 446, 447, 449, 450, 453, 459, 467, 478-483, 489, 491, 493, 500, 501, 504-506, 519, 539, 540, 544-548
  CBS Morning News, 547
  threatened by takeover, 546-548
Columbia Journalism Review, 476, 500, 523
Columbia School of Journalism, 265
Columbian, 124
Columbian Centinel, 106, 120
Columnists, 412, 450
Commentator, 318
Commercial Advertiser, 129, 134, 277, 327
Commission on Freedom of the Press, 444, 464-468, 523, 539

Index

Committee on Public Information, 339, 351, 357, 366, 381
Common Sense, 49, 64, 66–68
Commonweal, 521
Communications Act of 1934, 507
Communications Satellite Act, 507
Communications Satellite Corporation, 507
Communist Party, 358, 414, 430, 433, 492
Compass, 494
COMSAT, 507, 508
Comstock Law, 294
Condy, Jeremy, 32
Confederate Congress, 215
Confederate Press Association (the P.A.), 216
Congress of Racial Equality, 517
Connecticut Gazette, 52
Conquest of Kansas by Missouri and her Allies, 170
Conrad, Dr. Frank, 391
Conspiracies Act, 345
Constitution
　of the United States, 80, 81, 83–87, 94, 102, 113, 180, 187, 189, 190, 195, 198, 229, 232, 247, 229, 232, 247
　of Wyoming, 291
　ratification of, 101
Contemporary Review, 347
Continental Congress, 60, 79, 103, 125
　secrecy in, 57
Continuation of Our Weekly News, (The), 10
Cook, Fred J., 506
Cooper, Kent, 466
Copywriters, 382, 386
Cornell, Ezra, 161
Cornish, Samuel, 195, 196
Corporation for Public Broadcasting, 546
Corrant out of Italy, Germany, &c, 9
Correspondents
　and press passes, 456
　and World War II, 444–447, 449, 451, 454, 456, 457, 466–468
　in World War I, 339, 362, 363, 367
Cosby, Governor William, 40, 42
Coughlin, Father, 438
Cousins, Norman, 433
Cowles, Gardner, 459
Cox, Archibald, 538
Cox, James M., 391
Crawford, William H., 122
Creel, George, 339, 353, 355–357, 364, 366, 381, 409
Crescent City, 143
Crimean War, 204
Crisis
　of NAACP, 296
Cronkite, Walter, 500, 517
Crossley, Archibald, 413

Croswell, Harry, 115
Crouch, Mary, 32
Crowther, Bosley, 419
Cuba, 270, 271, 274–277
Culligan, Matthew J., 479
Culture
　oral, 3
　popular, 7
　scribal, 3, 7
Currency Act
　of 1764, 51
Curtis, Cyrus, 310, 319–322, 385
Curtis Publishing Company, 526
Custer, Joe James, 446
Czolgosz, Leon F., 273

Da Vinci, Leonardo, 393
Daguerre, Louis, 394
Dahlberg, Kenneth H., 535
Daily Republican, 248
Daily States, 245
Daily Worker, 438
Dallas Herald, 174
Dallas Morning News (The), 174, 298, 542
Dallas Times-Herald, 541
Dana, Charles, 184, 234, 245, 248, 251, 252, 266
Daniel, Clifton, 503
Davies, Marion, 428
Davis, Elmer, 458
Davis, Jefferson, 185, 208, 209
Davis, Paulina Wright, 291
Davis, Richard Harding, 276, 277, 317, 362, 363
Day, Benjamin, 129, 130, 133–141
Day, Dorothy, 405, 425, 437, 438, 522
De Fontaine, Felix, 213
De Forest, Lee, 390
De Tocqueville, Alexis, 153
Dean, John, 536
Decker, Karl, 277
Declaration of Independence, 49, 60, 62, 75, 79, 94
Delta, 143
Democracy in America, 153
Democratic Party, 203, 245, 266, 302
Democratization
　of knowledge, 7
Democrats, 233, 246, 262, 264
Dennis, Everette, 520
Dennis v. United States, 463
Denver Post, 341, 355, 541
Depression
　United States, 1930s, 403, 405, 406, 409, 411–415, 420, 421, 423, 425, 426, 427, 431, 434, 437, 438
Des Moines Register, 541

563

INDEX

Des Moines Register and Leader, 541
Des Moines Register and Tribune, 459, 541
Detroit Free Press, 510
Detroit News, 510
Dewey, Thomas, 413, 486
Dickens, Charles, 311
Dickinson, John, 49, 54, 66, 82
Dillon, John, 266
DiMaggio, Joe, 522
Discovering the News, 262, 411
Disney, Walt, 459, 460
Dix, Major General John A., 215
Documentary Tradition, 404, 409–411, 418, 419, 427, 438
   development of in 1930s, 409–411
Donovan, Hedley, 515
Douglas, Senator Stephen, 173
Douglass, Frederick, 196–198
Draper, Margaret, 33
Duane, William, 110, 114, 116
DuBois, W. E. B., 296
Duck, Donald, 459
DuMont, Allen B., 481
Dunlap, John, 68, 91–92
Duranty, Walter, 361

Early, Stephen T., 423
Eastland, James, 493
Eastland Hearings, 493
Eastman, Max, 358, 359, 361
Eastman Kodak, 395
Ebony, 495
Echeverria, Luis, 553
Economist, (The), 546
Edes, Benjamin, 52, 55, 69, 75
Edinburgh Courant, 135
Edison, Thomas, 381, 394, 395
Editor and Publisher, 409, 446
Educational Television Facilities Act, 506
Edward Bok Books, 321
Einstein, Albert, 495
Eisenhower, David, 495
Eisenhower, Dwight D., 486, 488, 492, 504, 507
El Liberal, 163
Eleventh Virgin (The), 438
Elizabeth
   Queen of England, 9, 14
Elliott, Jonathan, 122
Ellsberg, Daniel, 536
Emancipation, 187–189, 196–198
Emigrant Aid Society, 169
Emporia Gazette, 260, 262
Enemy Alien Act of 1798
   see Alien and Sedition Acts
Enlightenment, 7
Erlichman, John, 534, 536

Espionage and Sedition Acts
   of World War I, 337, 339, 346, 347, 349, 351, 357, 361, 456
Esquire, 522
Ethics, 531, 532, 539, 540, 555
   codes of, 540
Ethnic press, 290, 303, 305
Executive Order 9066, 453
Exoduster Movement, 234
Eyman, Scott, 395

Fairbanks, Douglas, 355, 396
Fairness Doctrine, 454, 488, 489, 505–507
Fame and Obscurity, 522
Farmers' Alliance, 290, 298, 301, 302
Faubus, Governor Orval E., 517
Faulkner, William, 318
Fear and Loathing on the Campaign Trail '72, 523
Federal Bureau of Investigation, 444, 456, 461, 462, 468, 489, 490
Federal Communications Act, 416
   of 1934, 454
   Section 315, 416
Federal Communications Commission, 416, 454, 480, 482, 487, 488, 504–507, 527, 533, 543, 545, 546, 548, 549, 555
Federal Radio Commission, 393, 398, 487
Federal Trade Commission, 378, 385
Federalists, 83–85, 89, 101, 104–106, 108–112, 114, 116, 117, 124
Fenno, John, 105–106
Fessenden, Reginald A., 389
Field, Marshall, 431, 432
Film and Photo League of New York City, 410
Film Industry, 375, 393, 395, 396, 459, 460
   and Justice Department in 1930s, 422
   during World War II, 459
   in the 1930s, 420
First Amendment, 85, 87, 110, 112, 125
   and property rights, 230
Fischer, John, 312
Fitzgerald, F. Scott, 318
Fleet, Thomas, 45
Fogg, Phileas, 268
Foner, Eric, 67
Force, Peter, 121
Foreign language Press
   and modernization, 259
Fort Worth Star-Telegram, 542, 543
Fortune, 426, 427, 430, 431, 433, 434
Fourdrinier Paper-Making Process, 144
Fourteenth Amendment, 231, 232, 292
Fourth Estate, 531
Fowle, Zechariah, 72
Fowler, Mark, 543, 548, 549, 555

Index

Fox Studios, 397, 420
Fox Television Network, 544
Frank Leslie's Illustrated Newspaper, 310, 331, 428
Franklin
  Anne Smith, 24
    Benjamin, 19, 23, 32, 33, 35–38, 40, 82, 91, 109, 123, 322
      and *General Magazine*, 33
      and *Pennsylvania Gazette*, 69
      and Plan of Union, 50, 82
      and *Poor Richard's Almanack*, 36
  James, 19, 40
Frederick Douglass' Paper, 196
Freedom's Journal, 195, 196
Freeman, 198
Freeman, Frederick Kemper, 168
Freeman, Legh Richmond, 168
Freeman's Journal
  of Francis Bailey, 69
Freeman's Oath (The), 12
Fremont, John C., 207
French and Indian War, 49, 50, 75, 82, 101
French Revolution, 104, 106
Freneau, Philip, 108, 109
Frequency Modulation, 480, 482
Friendly, Fred, 544, 547, 548
Frontier Index, 168
Frontier newspapers
  and post offices, 164
  development of, 163
  financing of, 164
Fuerbringer, Otto, 515
Fugitive Slave Act of 1793, 188
Fuller, Margaret, 183, 248
Furness, Betty, 486

Gales, Joseph Jr., 117, 118, 121
Gales, Joseph Sr., 117
Galloway, Joseph, 71, 91
Gallup, George, 413, 501
Galveston News, 174
Gannett, Ezra, 161
Gannett Company, 377, 378, 541, 542, 549, 550
Garfield (Ks.) *County Call*, 172
Garrison, William Lloyd, 189, 191, 194, 196–198, 291
Garvey, Marcus, 364
Gazette of the United States, 105–106
General Electric, 390, 391, 504, 544
General Telephone and Electronics Corporation, 507
Genet, Edmond, 104, 109
Geneva Conference on Freedom of Information
  of 1948, 467

Genius of Universal Emancipation, 188, 189
George III
  King of England, 67
Gerry, Elbridge, 84
Gianetti, Louis, 395, 421
Gibbons, Sheila, 183
Gibson, Charles Dana, 355
Gies, Joseph, 434, 436
Gilder, Richard Watson, 313, 314
Gill, John, 52, 55, 75
Glover, Jose, 12
Goddard, Mary Katherine, 88
Goddard, William, 87, 88
Godkin, Edwin, 234, 249–251
Golden Argosy, 329
Goldenson, Leonard, 544
Goldsborough, Laird S., 430
Goodhue, James M., 172
Gordon, Thomas, 42
Gottlieb, Robert, 553
Gould, Jay, 266
Grady, Henry, 229, 231, 246, 247, 251
Graham, Fred, 546
Grapes of Wrath, 421
Gray, Patrick, 536
Greeley, Horace, 170, 180–187, 191, 192, 197, 199, 207, 248
Green
  Bartholomew, 12, 33
  Duff, 122
  Jonas, 40
  Samuel, 12, 33, 40
  Samuel, Jr., 12
  Timothy, 40
  Timothy, Jr., 33
Green Dragon Tavern, 5
Greene, Tom, 521
Greenleaf, Thomas, 89
Greenleaf, William, 56
Gridley, Jeremiah, 123
Griffith, David Wark, 396
Griswold, Roger, 114
Guardian
  of Boston, 297
"Gunsmoke," 479
Gutenberg, Johann, 5

Hadden, Briton, 405, 412, 426
Halberstam, David, 505, 514
Haldeman, H. R., 534–536
Hale, David, 136, 158
Hall, David
  and *Pennsylvania Gazette*, 69
Hall, Joseph, 171
Hallin, Daniel C., 513, 515, 517
Hallock, Gerard, 136, 139, 158
Halstead, Murat, 212

INDEX

Hamilton, Alexander, 84, 101, 105, 106, 115, 118
  and Federalist papers, 84
Hamilton, Andrew, 43
Hamilton, Richard F., 379
Harbour News Association, 139
Harding, Warren G., 391
Hardy, Thomas, 311
Hardy, W. S., 299
Hare, Jimmy, 277
Hargis, Billy James, 506
Harnden, William F., 138
Harper's, 309–313, 316, 534, 551, 552
  and Atlantic Richfield Co., 552
  and MacArthur Foundation, 552
Harper's Weekly, 209, 238, 243, 310, 428
Harris, Benjamin, 18
Harris, Joel Chandler, 247
Harrison, William Henry, 159
Harte-Hanks Communications, 542
Hartford Courant, 541
Harvard College
  printing for, 13
Havas, 206, 418, 458
"Have Gun, Will Travel," 479
Hawthorne, Nathaniel, 248
Hayes, Rutherford B., 234
Hays, Will H., 420
Healy, Jr., George W., 459
Hearst, William Randolph, 149, 256, 258, 262, 268–278, 285, 339, 355, 357, 377, 413, 414, 428, 430, 431, 434, 437
  and *Harvard Lampoon*, 271
  and the *Daily Mirror*, 375
Hell-Fire Club, 22
Hellman, Lillian, 431
Helms, Jesse, 546
Hemingway, Ernest, 318, 430
Hennock, Frieda, 546
Henry VIII, 8, 9
Herald of Freedom (Lawrence, Ks.), 169, 173
Herschel, Sir John, 135, 136
Hertz, Heinrich, 389
Heth, Joyce, 379
Hidden History of the Korean War, 494
Higgins, Marguerite, 446, 447
Higginson, Thomas Wentworth, 171
Hinton, Richard, 171
Hiss, Alger, 430
Hitler, Adolf, 418, 419, 449
Ho Chi Minh, 512, 514
Holland, Josiah Gilbert, 313
Hollywood Production Code, 420
Holmes, Justice Oliver Wendell, 346
Holt, Elizabeth, 87, 88
Holt, John, 58, 69, 87, 88
Homestead Act, 184

Hone, Phillip, 141, 142
Honolulu Advertiser, 511
Honolulu Bulletin, 511
Honor Thy Father, 522
Hoopes, Roy, 431
Hoover, Herbert, 391
Hoover, J. Edgar, 413, 423, 425, 433, 434, 468, 476, 490
House and Home, 313
House of Representatives
  coverage by *Intelligencer*, 117
House Un-American Activities Committee, 430, 489
Howard, Joseph, 215
Howard, Roy, 377
Howard University, 232
Hoyt, E. Palmer, 459
Hughes, Langston, 318
Humphreys, James Jr., 68
Hunt, Howard, 534, 536
Huntley, Chet, 500
Hutchins, Robert, 464, 467
Hutchinson, Governor Thomas, 52
Hynds, Ernest, 501

Idiot's Delight, 459
I. F. Stone's Weekly, 494
Illinois Central railroad, 380
Illinois Public Utility Information Committee, 381
Impartiality
  and Benjamin Franklin, 35
  in colonial press, 30, 40, 50, 75
In Cold Blood, 521
In Fact, 414
In Search of Excellence, 544
"In the News," 547
Independence
  and modernization, 258, 263
Independent (The), 319
Independent Gazetteer
  of Joseph Gales, Sr., 117
  of Oswald, 88
Ingersoll, Ralph, 405, 425, 431, 432
Inland Daily Press Association, 550
Insull, Samuel, 381
Intelsat, 508
International Film Service, 273
International News Photos, 271
International News Service, 271, 446, 510
International Paper Company, 378
International Telephone and Telegraph, 507
International Typographical Union, 240
Interpretation, 405, 409, 411–414, 425, 439, 411
  as synthesis in 1930s, 412
  development of in 1930s, 409

Index

Interstate Commerce Act
  of 1886, 380
Inverted pyramid style, 205
Irwin, Will, 38
"It Happened One Night," 421

Jacksboro Gazette, 302
Jacksboro (Tx.) *Rural Citizen*, 300, 301
Jackson, Andrew, 121, 122, 141
Jacksonian Democracy, 146
James I
  King of England, 9, 12, 14
James II
  King of England, 10
Jay, John, 84, 104
  and Federalist papers, 84
  and Treaty, 104
Jazz age, 376
Jefferson, Thomas, 60, 85, 101, 106, 108, 109, 115, 117, 120, 124
Jennings, Peter, 545
Jensen, Merrill, 68
Jerome, Leonard, 187
Jewett, Ellen
  murder of, 141, 148, 237
Johnson, Andrew, 185, 186
  as president, 231, 232
Johnson, John, 495
Johnson, Lyndon Baines, 503
Johnston, James, 52
Johnston, Stanley, 457
Johnstone, John, 502
Jones, George, 187
Journal
  of Lucy Stone, 292
Journal of Commerce, 215
Journal of Occurrences, 49, 55, 75
Journal of Science, 136, 137
Journalism Bulletin, 411
Journalist (The), 281
Junior Munsey, 329

Kai-Shek, Chiang, 430
Kai-Shek, Madame Chiang, 430
Kaltenborn, Hans von, 447, 449, 486
Kandy Kolored Tangerine Flake Streamline Baby, 521
Kansas City Star, 262, 280, 340, 542, 543
Kansas Farmer, 301
Kansas Workman, 298
Kany, Robert Hurd
  on colonial circulations, 69
Karnow, Stanley, 513, 515
Kaul, Arthur, 144, 148, 149
Kautz, John, 264
KDKA, 391
Keaton, Buster, 396

Keimer, Samuel, 33, 35, 322
Keith, William, 35
Kendall, Amos, 194
Kendall, George, 139
Kennedy, John Fitzgerald, 499, 500, 503, 506, 507, 514, 517, 522
Kennedy, Robert, 518
Kent, Frank, 412
Kentucke Gazette, 172
Kentucky Gazette, 191
Kielbowicz, Richard, 92
Kimball, Frederick J., 380
King Features Service, 271
Kinsley, Michael, 313
Kirchwey, Frieda, 494
Kleindienst, Richard, 536
Knapp, Louisa May, 319
Kneeland, Samuel, 33
Knight Newspapers, 542
Know-Nothing Party, 173
Knox, Thomas, 214
Koenig steam press, 144
Kollock, Sheppard, 69
Kraft Television Theatre, 482
Ku Klux Klan, 232, 233, 246, 460

La Presse of Paris, 241
Labor press, 147
LaCourse, Richard, 165
Ladies' Home Journal, 310, 319, 321
Ladies' Journal and Practical Housekeeper, 319
Lamont, Thomas, 324
Landis, Judge Kennesaw Mountain, 351
Lange, Dorothea, 452, 453
Lanpher, Katherine, 283
Lapham, Lewis, 312
Larson, Cedric, 353
Lasker, Albert, 383
Lawrence, David, 412
Lawrence Herald of Freedom, 169
Lawson, Samuel, 283
Lee, Alfred McClung, 133
Lee, Richard Henry, 60, 72, 85
Lee, Robert E.
  surrender at Appomattox, 231
Legion of Decency, 459
Lehrer, Jim, 545
Leiser, Ernest, 545
Leonard, Thomas, 237, 238, 243
"Letters From a Farmer in Pennsylvania," 49, 54, 55
"Letters from a Federal Farmer," 85
"Letters To A Farmer in Philadelphia," 66
"Letters To Country Girls," 193
Lexington,
  Battle of, 59, 63, 79
Lexington Observer and Reporter, 191

567

INDEX

Libel, 501, 518–520, 526, 527
Liberal Republicans, 184, 185
Liberator, 189, 190, 197, 198, 291, 361, 437
Liberia Herald, 195
Licensing
   broadcast, 416, 480, 482, 487–488
   colonial, 13, 23
   European, 25
   in England, 10, 11
   in Massachusetts, 14
Liddy, G. Gordon, 534, 536
Life, 410, 420, 426, 428–433, 454, 515, 518, 525, 526
   and Black Star Agency, 428
   and instant success, 429
"Life of an American Fireman," 395
Lily, 291
Lincoln, Abraham, 184, 185, 192, 197, 203, 207, 215, 220, 346
Lind, Jenny, 379
Lindbergh, Charles, 278
Lingeman, Richard, 473
Lippmann, Walter, 144, 146, 268, 356–358, 410, 412, 514, 527
Literary Digest, 357, 412, 413, 426
Little-Compton Scourge, 22
Livingston, Robert R., 60
Local Press
   and modernization, 264
Locke, Richard Adams, 135–137
Lodge, Henry Cabot, 312
Lofton, John, 347, 351
London Daily News, 249
Lonely Crowd (The), 549
Long, Huey, 419
Look, 429, 459, 523, 525, 526
Lords of the Press, 414
Lorentz, Pare, 410
Lorimer, George, 322
Los Angeles Star, 163
Los Angeles Times, 502, 541
Loudon, Samuel, 64, 69
Louis XVI, 104
Louisiana Purchase, 102
Louisville Courier-Journal, 234, 245, 246, 341, 539
Louisville Examiner, 192
Louisville Journal, 190
Lovejoy, Elijah, 191
Lowden, Governor Frank O., 365
Loyall Nine, 52
Luce, Henry, 405, 410, 412, 414, 425–431, 433, 434, 436, 444, 464
   and politics, 429
Lumiere, Luis and Auguste, 395
Lundy, Benjamin, 188, 189
Lux Radio Theatre, 418

Lyon, Matthew, 114–115

MacArthur, Douglass, 456
MacDonald, Dwight, 427
MacDougall, Curtis, 411
Macfadden, Bernarr, 375
MacLeish, Archibald, 427
MacNeil, Robert, 545
Mademoiselle, 477
Madison, James, 57, 74, 84, 85, 108, 120, 124
   and constitutional ratification, 80
   and Federalist papers, 84
Madisonian, 143
Magazines, 501, 521, 534, 551, 555
   general interest magazines, 310, 333
   in Colonial America, 123
   in the early republic, 123
   quality monthlies, 309–311, 313, 318, 325, 333, 551
   specialization of, 525–527
Magic Writing Machine, 521–522
Mailer, Norman, 312
"Major Bowes' Original Amateur Hour," 418
Manifest Destiny, 327
Mansfield, Mike, 514
Manzanar Relocation Center, 452
Mao-Tse Tung, 443, 512
"March of Time," 418–420, 430
   as newsreel, 419
Marchand, Roland, 386
Marconi, Guglielmo, 389
Marconi Wireless and Signal Company, 389
Marey, Etienne Jules, 394
Marketing surveys, 383
Marshall Plan, 474
Marx, Karl, 184
Mary
   Queen of England, 9
Maryland Gazette, 38
Maryland Journal, 87
Mason, George, 84
Massachusetts
   assembly in, 14
   Bay Colony, religious freedom in, 14
   radical activity in, 51
Massachusetts Spy, 69, 74
   and circulation, 69
Masses (The), 339, 356, 358, 359, 361, 437
Masters of Deceit, 476
Mather, Cotton, 15, 21
Mather, Increase, 21
Mathews, L. H., 216
Matthews, Herbert, 405
Matthews, T. S., 427
Mauldin, Bill, 450, 451
Maurder, Murrey, 491

Index

Maurin, Peter, 438
Mayer, Ernest, 428, 429
Mayer, Louis B., 460
Mayflower, 291
Mayo, Hamilton, 319
McCarthy, Joseph, 450, 477, 487, 489–494, 496
McClure, Samuel, 316, 323–329, 331
McClure's, 316, 323–329, 331
McCord, James, 534–536
McCormick
  Cyrus, 434
  Joseph Medill, 434
  Medill, 434
  Richard, 204
  Robert, 173, 414, 425, 430, 434, 436, 437
    and the *Daily News*, 375
McElrath, Thomas, 185
McGill, Ralph, 514
McGraw-Hill Publishing Co., 412
McIntyre, Marcus, 423
McKean, Chief Justice Thomas, 88, 89, 116
McKenney, Thomas, 122
McKerns, Joseph P., 144, 148, 149
McKinley, William, 272, 413
McLuhan, Marshall, 508
Mechanics' Press, 147
Media Companies on the Stock Exchange, 541–543
Media Polls, 413
Medill, Joseph, 173, 175, 207, 283, 434
Medill, Samuel, 283
Medina, Harold, 463
Memphis Appeal, 209
Mercantile Advertiser, 139, 140
Meredith, James, 517
Mergenthaler, Otto
  invention of linotype, 243
Metro-Goldwyn-Mayer, 396, 420, 459
Metromedia, 545
Mexican War, 139, 143, 156, 159, 163
  coverage of, 163
Meyer, Philip, 524
Miami Herald, 503, 511
Miami News, 511
Mid-Week Pictorial, 428
Middletown, 429
Midway Islands
  control of 1872, 231
Miller, Henry, 68
Milton, John, 10
  and *Areopagitica*, 10, 36
Milwaukee Advertiser, 172
Milwaukee Journal, 491
Milwaukee Leader, 347, 349, 351
Minneapolis Star and Tribune Co, 312
Minneapolis Star-Journal, 459

Minneapolis Tribune, 459
Minnesota Pioneer, 172
Minow, Newton, 505, 506
Minton, Bruce, 414
Missouri Compromise
  of 1820, 122
Mitchell, Edward, 251
Mitchell, John, 534
Mobile Advertiser and Register, 216
Mock, John, 353
Model Railroader, 525
Modern Bride, 311
Mohr, Charles, 515
Monroe, James, 120, 121
Monroe, Marilyn, 495
Moranda, George
  on colonial circulations, 69
Morgan, J. P., 324
Morris, Esther, 291
Morris, Gouverneur, 40
Morris, Robert, 71
Morris, Willie, 312, 551
Morse, Samuel, 161
Morss, Samuel E., 280
Motion Picture Bureau, 459
Motion Picture Patents Company, 395
Motion Picture Producers and Distributors of America, 420
Mott, Frank Luther, 318
Movable Type, 5
"Mr. Smith Goes to Washington," 421
Muckraking, 310, 311, 317, 322–327, 329, 331, 332
Munchner Illustrierte Presse, 428
Municipal reform
  and modernization, 260
Munsey, Frank, 325, 329, 331
Murdoch, Rupert, 544, 545
Murphy, Carl, 364
Murphy, James, 147
Murrow, Edward R., 447, 449, 450, 500
  and McCarthy, 478, 483, 491–494
Museum, 124
Mussolini, Benito, 459
Mutual Broadcasting Company, 447
Muybridge, Eadweard, 394
My Bondage and My Freedom, 197

Nader, Ralph, 345
Narrative of the Life of Frederick Douglass, 197
Nasaw, David, 341
Nat Turner, 189, 193
Nation, 234, 237, 240, 245, 246, 249, 250, 494
National Association for the Advancement of Colored People, 364

569

National Association of Broadcasters
  and World War II regulation, 454
National Broadcasting Co. v. United States, 488
National Broadcasting Corporation, 417, 418, 430, 446, 449, 459, 478, 479, 482, 483, 488, 489, 504, 507, 533, 544, 545, 548
National Economist, 298
National Farmer, 299
National Gazette, 108, 109
National Intelligencer, 103, 125, 143, 149, 157
  and patronage, 119, 121
  of Gales and Seaton, 116–118
National Journal, 121
National Legion of Decency, 420
National News Council, 532, 539
National Observer, 550
National Recovery Act, 436
National Reform Press Association, 300
National Reformer, 299
National Security Act, 474
National Typographical Union
  organized in 1852, 240
Native American Media, 154, 164, 165, 168
Native Americans, 291
Naturalization Act
  of 1798, 111
Navigation acts, 14
Near vs. Minnesota, 487, 493
Negro Digest, 495
Negro Newspaper Publishers Association, 462
Negro World, 364
Nelson, William Rockhill, 280, 281
Neuharth, Allan, 550
New Deal, 410, 413, 414, 423, 437, 439
New England Courant, 21–25, 522
New England Emigrant Aid Society, 169
New England Journal, 33, 40
New Journalism
  as 1960s reporting style, 520
New Left, 499, 500, 526
New London Gazette, 52
New Nonfiction, 521
New Orleans Courier, 163
New Orleans Picayune, 139, 143, 208
New Orleans Times-Picayune, 459
New Republic, 356, 357, 412, 424, 427, 454, 503
New South, 229, 230, 246, 247
New York: A Serendipiter's Journey, 522
New York American, 431
New York Call, 347
New York City Standard, 197
New York Courier, 140
New York Courier and Enquirer, 135, 137, 139–141, 186, 266

New York Daily Graphic, 243, 428
New York Daily News, 331, 426, 431, 434, 510, 542
New York Evening Post, 94, 134, 183, 204, 250, 327
  of Alexander Hamilton, 117
New York Evening Transcript, 130
New York Express, 138, 139
New York Gazette
  of John Holt, 52
New-York Gazetteer, 62
  Circulation of, 69
New York Globe, 140, 331
New York Graphic, 375
New York Herald, 130, 137, 139–143, 181, 189, 194, 195, 197, 205, 206, 210, 212, 214, 218, 237, 241, 247, 250, 268, 331, 413, 423
  and bankruptcies, 142
  edition of Post, 118
New York Herald Tribune, 412, 430, 446, 447, 453, 522
New York Illustrated Daily News, 212, 375
New York Journal
  under Hearst, 258, 259, 262, 263, 268–271, 273, 276, 277
New York Journal
  of John Holt, 56
New York Journal of Commerce, 133, 136, 139, 141, 158
New-York Magazine: or, Literary Repository, 123
New-York Packet, 64
New York Post, 207, 438, 545
New York Sun, 129, 134, 137, 139–142, 144, 181, 184, 199, 234, 243, 248, 249, 251, 263, 278, 331, 412
  after Civil War, 234
  and Charles Dana, 139
  of Moses Beach, 138–139
New York Times, 171, 180, 181, 184, 186–188, 196, 199, 205, 207, 210, 238, 245, 258, 259, 262, 263, 271, 275, 278, 280, 351, 355, 357, 361, 363, 411, 412, 419, 428, 438, 446, 458, 473, 475, 478, 486, 492, 493, 502, 503, 513–515, 518–520, 522, 527
New York Times vs. Sullivan, 518
New York Tribune, 139, 141, 170, 171, 180–186, 192, 197, 199, 208, 210, 212, 245
New York Weekly Journal, 94
New York World, 215, 256, 258, 259, 262, 263, 265, 266, 268–271, 275, 276, 285, 357, 375, 412
New York World-Telegram, 408
New Yorker, 183, 186, 431, 552, 553
Newburyport Herald, 189

Index

Newhouse Media Chain, 553
Newport Mercury, 25
News correspondents
   during Civil War, 210
   in Civil War, 212
Newsboys, 337, 341, 343
   in 1930s, 436, 437
Newsday, 541
Newsgathering
   in the Civil War, 204
Newsgathering processes
   and modernization, 256
Newspaper Chains, 374, 397
   Gannett, 510
   Hearst Group, 510
   John S. Knight, 508
   Samuel I. Newhouse, 508
   Scripps-Howard, 510
Newspaper Industry
   Women in 1970s, 532
Newspaper Preservation Act, 511, 512, 527
Newspapers
   advertising, 337
   after Civil War, 237–244
   agenda setting, 260
   as common carriers, 94
   beginning dailies, 90–91
   chain ownership, 340
   changes in personnel in 1960s, 502
   circulation in 1970s, 1980s, 540
   colonial, 15, 25
   consolidation, 337
   corporate ownership, 541
   coverage of concentration camps, 453
   dailies in the 1920s, 375–378
   during 1930s, 406
   growth and modernization, 259
   handwritten, 164
   in Civil War, 205–210
   in England, 9–11
   in Richmond, 208
   information, 260
   information and modernization, 278
   labor after Civil War, 238
   management changes in 1960s, 502
   on the frontier, 163, 168
   partisan politics, 104–110
   political independence after Civil War, 238
   reactions to government in 1960s, 502, 503
   Southern, during Civil War, 208–210
   technology after Civil War, 240
   tri-weeklies, 81
   weekly (in early 1900s), 340
   women in industry during 1930s, 406
Newspapers and New Politics, 260
Newsreels, 404, 419, 420, 430
Newsweek, 412, 533, 542

Ngo Dinh Diem, 514
Nineteenth Amendment, 291
Nixon, Richard M., 486, 490, 495, 534–538, 555
Nord, David Paul, 123, 259, 260
North American Review, 309
North Atlantic Treaty Organization, 475
North Star, 196–198, 291
NRA, 436, 437
Nullification crisis, 179
Nye, Gerald B., 460

Oatis, William, 467
Objectivity and the News, 137
Ochs, Adolph, 278
Off Our Backs, 524
Office of Censorship
   see World War II
Oklahoma Press Association, 165
Oliver, Andrew, 52
Oswald, Eleazer, 87–90, 117
Oswald, John, 34
Otis, James, 51, 54
O'Toole, Peter, 522
Outcalt, Richard, 271

Paine, Thomas, 49, 57, 64
   and *Common Sense*, 66–68
Paley, William S., 418, 479, 482, 491
Palmer, Volney, 236
Papal Authority
   in England, 9
Paramount Group, 396, 397
Paramount Newsreels, 446
Paramount Studio, 420, 423
Parker, George, 381
Parks, William, 32, 38, 45
Parliament, 16
   in England, 10, 14
   Reformation, 8
Patterson, Elinor Medill, 434
Patterson, Joseph Medill, 375, 431, 434
Patterson, Robert, 434
Pauly, John, 263
Peck, Henry Thurston, 246
Pember, Don, 463
Penn, William, 41
Pennsylvania Constitution
   of 1776, 91
Pennsylania Evening Post, 90
   of Benjamin Towne, 62
Pennsylvania Gazette
   and Saturday Evening Post, 322
   of David Hall, 62
Pennsylvania Journal, 51, 62
   of Bradford, 71, 72

Pennsylvania Packet, 59, 62, 89, 92
  and *Common Sense*, 67
  and *Daily Advertiser*, 82
  of John Dunlap, 91
Pennsylvania Railroad
  and public relations, 380
Penny Press
  and change, 131
  and content, 133
  and continuity, 131
  and Moon Hoax, 135
  and political independence, 130
  and staffing patterns, 130
  as revolution, 131
  characteristics of, 131–134
  development of, 144
Pensacola Observer, 216
Pentagon Papers, 531, 536
Periodical Publishers Association, 383
Perry, Mert, 515
Personne
  as pseudonym, 212
Peters, Tom, 544
Philadelphia Inquirer, 494, 508
Philadelphia Public Ledger, 130, 133, 139, 144
Philadelphia Times, 331
"Philco Television Playhouse," 479, 482
Phillips, David Graham, 268
Phillips, John, 328, 331, 332
Phillips, Wendell, 196
Photography
  after Civil War, 243–244
  and Japanese Internment, 451, 452
  during Civil War, 217–220
Pickford, Mary, 355, 396
Pilgrim's Progress, 323
Pioneer and Woman's Advocate, 291
Pittsburgh Courier, 364, 365, 460, 462, 495
Pittsburgh Dispatch, 268
Pittsburgh Gazette, 171
PM, 425, 431, 432, 494
Poe, Edgar Allan, 135, 181
Politics, 477
Polk, George, 467
Polk, James, 155
Polk, Leonidas K., 299–302
Polo, Marco, 5
Pope, Daniel, 234, 384
Population
  in colonies, 12
Populists, 298, 305
Porcupine's Gazette, 106
Porter, Edwin S., 395
Portland Oregonian, 459
Post Office, 158, 159
  and World War II, 461
Postal Acts, 102, 344
  of 1792, 92
  of 1794, 92, 124
  of 1798, 1791, 81
  of 1836, 158
  of 1879, 309
  second-class mailing rates, 347
Postal Express, 157–159, 161, 163, 175
Postal rates
  in early Republic, 81, 92
Postal Service
  Boston, 15
  colonial, 11, 15
  New Hampshire, 15
  New York, 15
Power of the Press, 237
Powers, Gary, 503
"Prayer of Twenty Millions," 184
Precision journalism, 521, 524, 525
Press
  and modernization, 255–265
  colonial, 3, 4, 11
  criticism of in 1930s, 414
  critique of during modernization, 265
  England, 4
  freedom of, 10, 116
  in colonial South, 39
  in England, 4
Press and Government
  during 1950s, 487
press and municipal reform, 259–262
Press Association
  in Confederacy, 216, 217
Press Club of Chicago, 283
Press Clubs
  and modernization, 283
Presses
  web-perfecting, 243
Price, Byron, 456
Printer's Ink, 385, 386
Printers' networks, 29, 68
Printing
  colonial, 72
  in England, 8, 9
Printing revolution
  European, 3–8, 25
Prior restraint
  England, 8–10
  in U.S., 487–493, 531, 536
Privy Council
  England, 8
Progress (The), 494
Progressive Farmer, 300, 301
Progressive Party, 310, 323, 331
Prostak, Elaine (Berland), 391
Public broadcasting, 545, 546
Public Broadcasting System, 506, 545
Public Opinion, 410

Index

Public relations
  history of, 374, 379–381, 397
Publick Occurrences, Both Foreign and Domestick, 18
Publishers Associations
  and modernization, 284
Pulitzer, Albert, 271
Pulitzer, Joseph, 256, 258, 260, 262, 265, 266, 268–271, 275, 276, 278, 285, 339
  and editorial platform, 26
  in St. Louis, 238
Puritans, 10, 12
  extending religious influence, 12
  in America, 12
  in England, 9
  persecution in England, 14
Pyle, Ernie, 451

Quakers, 12, 179, 187
Quincy, Josiah, 54

R. Hoe & Company
  and stereotyping, 243
Radio, 373, 374, 387, 389–393, 397, 398, 404, 405, 415–419, 424, 425, 429–431, 439, 474, 504–506, 522
  and Popular Culture in the 1930s, 418
  during the 1950s, 477–480, 482–484, 486, 487, 489, 496
  FM, 480
  Golden Age of, 415
  in the 1950s, 477, 479
Radio Act of 1912, 390
Radio Act of 1927, 393, 416
Radio Corporation of America, 390–392, 398, 480–482, 504, 507, 544
Radio Free Europe, 504
Radio News
  during World War II, 447
  in 1930s, 416, 417
Radio-Television News Directors Association, 506
Raleigh, Sir Walter, 14
Raleigh Register, 117, 118
Ram's Horn, 196, 197
Rand Corporation, 504
Randolph, A. Philip, 462
Randolph, Edmund, 84, 92
Random House, 553
Ray, Charles, 173, 205, 207
Raymond, Henry J., 180, 181, 184, 186, 187, 199, 205
Reader's Digest, 362, 412, 533
Rebel, 245
Reconstruction, 230–234, 240, 245, 246, 251
Red Channels: The Report of Communist Influence in Radio and Television, 489

Red Cross, 381
Red Lion, 506
Reed, John, 358, 359
Reid, Wallace, 420
Reid, Whitelaw, 184, 185, 208, 212
Reisman, David, 549
Religious freedom, 12
Remington, Frederick, 317
Report on Chain Broadcasting, 488
Reporting for Beginners, 411
Republican
  Jeffersonian, 115
  of Calhoun, 122
Republican Banner, 245
Republican Party, 181, 183, 186, 192, 203, 231, 232, 246, 262, 264
  formation of, 181
Resor, Stanley, 383
Respublica v. Oswald, 89
Reston, James, 475, 513
Restoration
  in England, 14
Restrictions on Publishing
  before the Civil War, 193
Reuters, 206, 418, 450
Revere, Paul, 54, 74
Revolution
  of Anthony and Stanton, 293
Rhett, Robert Barnwell, Jr., 199, 209
Rhode-Island Gazette, 24
Richards, Daniel, 172
Richardson, Albert D., 212
Richardson, Elliott, 538
Richmond Dispatch, 208, 209
Richmond Enquirer, 208, 209
Richmond Examiner, 208
Richmond News Leader, 412
Richmond Sentinel, 209
Richmond Whig, 208
Ridder Publications, 542
Rights of All, 196
Riis, Jacob, 263
Riley, Sam, 163
Rise and Fall of the Third Reich (The), 447
Rivers, William, 502
Rivington, James, 62, 64
RKO, 420
Robert, N. L., 144
Robinson, Hubbell Jr., 480
Robinson, Richard P.
  and murder of Jewett, 141
Robinson-Jewett murder, 237
Rocky Mountain Journal, 522
Rocky Mountain News, 159, 355
Rogers, Ginger, 420
Roosevelt, Eleanor, 425

573

INDEX

Roosevelt, Franklin Delano, 278, 454, 456, 460, 473, 474
  and fireside chats, 415
  and press management, 423–425
Roosevelt, Theodore, 246, 317, 320, 344, 362
Roper, Elmo, 413
Rose, Reginald, 483
Rosenthal, A. M., 502
Rosenwald, Lessing, 431
Rosenwald, William, 431
Ross, William P., 168, 553
Rowell, George P., 236
Ruckelshaus, William D., 538
Ruffin, Edmund, 198, 199
Rush, Dr. Benjamin
  and Thomas Paine, 64
Russell, Benjamin, 106
Russell, William Howard, 212
Russo, J. Anthony, 536
Russwurm, John, 195

Sacramento Union, 161
Safer, Morley, 505
Safire, William, 534
Salisbury, Harrison, 515
Salvation Army, 381
Samuel Cornish, 195, 196
San Francisco Bay Guardian, 511, 522
San Francisco Chronicle, 511
San Francisco Examiner, 271, 511
San Francisco News-Call-Bulletin, 511
Sanderson, Katherine Medill, 434
Sanderson, Robert, 434
Sanger, Margaret, 294
Sarnoff, David, 391, 418, 480, 482
Satellites, 507
Saturday Evening Post, 309, 310, 319, 322, 327, 475, 525, 526
Saturday Review, 534, 552
Saturday Visitor, 192
Schell, Jonathan, 552
Schenck vs. United States, 346
Schiller, Daniel, 137, 144, 146–148
Schiller, Herbert, 504
Schlesinger, Arthur
  on revolutionary pamphlets, 64
Schoeffer, Peter, 5, 7
Schudson, Michael, 133, 144, 146, 147, 262, 263, 411, 503, 549
Scott, General Winfield, 163
Scourge of Aristocracy, 115
Screen Actors Guild, 422
Screen Writers Guild, 422
Scribner, Charles, 313
Scribner's, 246, 309, 311, 313, 314, 316–318
Scripps, E. W., 357, 377
Scull, John, 171, 172

Sears, Isaac (King), 62–64
Seaton, W. W., 117, 118, 122
Secession
  in South Carolina, 203
Sectional issues, 180
Sedition Act (See Alien and Sedition Acts)
Seditious libel, 81
  and William Bradford, 41
Seldes, George, 414
Sengstacke, John, 462, 495
Sentinel
  of Fort Wayne, Ind., 280
Sevareid, Eric, 449, 509
Shadow
  as pseudonym, 213
Shafter, General William J., 277
Shaw, Donald, 134
Shawanoe Sun, 165
Shawn, William, 552
Shays, Daniel, 83
Sheehan, Neil, 514
Sheriff, 410
Sherman, General William T., 214
Sherman, Roger, 60
Sherman Anti-Trust Act, 395
Sherwood, Robert, 459
Ship-to-shore communication, 390
Shirer, William, 447, 453, 478
Shuman, Edwin, 281
Sibyl (The), 291
Silence Dogood, 24
Simmons, Azariah H., 139
Sinatra, Frank, 522
Sinclair, Upton, 380
Sirica, John, 536
Six Months in Mexico, 268
Skin Diver, 525
Slavery, 156, 168–170, 173, 179–181, 184, 186–200
Sloan, Hugh, 535
Smalley, George W., 212
Smallpox controversy, 21
Smith, James Morton, 112
Smith, Jeffery A., 31
Smith, Roswell C., 313
Smith, Samuel Harrison, 118
  and *National Intelligencer*, 116
Smith, William
  and *Common Sense*, 67
Smith Act, 462, 463, 468
Smyth, Joseph Hilton, 318
Snyder, Ruth, 375
Social Justice, 438
Socialist Party, 297
Socialist Worker Party, 437
Society of American Artists and Authors, 313

574

Index

Society of Professional Journalists
   Ethics code of 1973, 532
Sons of Liberty, 52
South America
   Aztec communication, 5
South Carolina Gazette, 38
South Carolina Weekly Journal, 38
Southern Christian Leadership Conference, 517
Southern Illustrated News, 209
Southern Improvement Company, 327
Southern Mercury
   of Dallas, 298
Soviet-Nazi Pact
   of 1939, 444
Spanish American War, 270, 274, 285, 312
   and correspondents, 277
Spanish Civil War, 430, 449
Sparkman, John, 486
Spectator, 23
Sperber, A. M., 492
Spirit of Liberty, 192
Spirit of the Times, 196
Springfield (Mass.) Republican, 134
St. Cloud Democrat, 193
St. Cloud Visitor, 193
St. Louis Post-Dispatch, 206, 266, 341
Staats-Zeitung, 266
Stamp Act
   of 1712, 10
   of 1765, 40
   of 1765, 51, 52, 75
   of 1775, 49
"Stand Up and Cheer," 421
Stanley, Henry, 212
Stans, Maurice, 535
Stanton, Elizabeth Cady, 293
Stanton, Frank, 504, 505
Star and Tribune Co., 552
Star Chamber
   court of, 9
"Star Playhouse," 479
Starr, Louis, 212
Stationers Company, 9
Steele, Ian, 4
Stefani, 206
Steffens, Lincoln, 327, 328, 331, 357, 358
Steinbeck, John, 421
Steiner, Melchior, 68
Stereotyping, 144, 241
Steuart, Andrew, 52
Stevenson, Adlai, 486
Stewart, Potter, 531
Stone, Esther, 495
Stone, I. F., 477, 494–496
Stone, Lucy, 292, 294
Stone, Melville, 278, 283

Stott, William, 410
Stout, Harry, 67
Stowe, Harriet Beecher, 188
Stringer, Howard, 546
Stringfellow, J. H., 169, 170
Student Non-Violent Coordinating Committee, 517
Studio One, 483
Suffragist press, 290, 291
Suffragists, 289, 293
Sugar Act
   of 1764, 51
Sullivan, L. B., 519
Sullivan, Mark, 412
Sulzberger, Arthur Ochs, 502, 539
Sunpapers of Baltimore, 139
Supreme Court
   during Reconstruction, 231
Swain, William, 130, 139
Swanberg, W. A., 275
Swanson, Gloria, 396
Sweeney, J. S., 377
Swisshelm, Jane Grey, 192, 193, 293
Swope, Herbert Bayard, 268
Sylvester, Arthur, 503

Tabloids, 373–376, 397
Taft, William Howard, 246
Talese, Gay, 522
Tammany Hall, 238
Tappen, Samuel F., 171
Tarbell, Ida, 324, 326–328, 331
Tariff, 179, 180, 184
Taylor, Charles H., 271
Taylor, James B., 187
Taylor, William Desmond, 420
Technology
   and strikes in 1960s, 510
   linotype, 243
   stereotyping, 241
Telegraph, 154, 157, 161, 163, 175, 204–206, 213–216, 220, 373
   transcontinental, 161
Television, 477, 486, 489, 491, 495, 496, 500, 501, 505, 506, 510, 512, 515, 517, 518, 526
   as vast wasteland, 505
   cable, 533, 542, 544, 545, 548, 555
   development of, 479–484
   elections of 1952, 486
   in 1948 elections, 484
   technology, development, 481–484
Temple, Shirley, 420
tenant farming
   in South after Civil War, 234
Tennessee Valley Authority, 410
Texas Business Press, 174

INDEX

Thackeray, William, 311
Thaumatrope, 394
"The Bridge," 522
"The Great Train Robbery," 395
The Kingdom and the Power, 522
"The Plow That Broke the Plains," 410
"The River," 410
Thomas, Isaiah, 24, 39, 41, 45, 91
   and "Journal of Occurrences," 56
   as historian, 72–75
   on circulations of colonial press, 69
Thompson, Hunter, 523
Thompson, J. Walter, 236, 383, 386
Thoreau, Henry, 248
Thrasher, 216
Three-fifths Compromise, 180
"Thunder on Sycamore Street," 483
Thurlow Weed, 187, 197
Tilden, Samuel J., 234
Time, 405, 426–431, 491, 515
Time, Inc., 414, 418, 426, 427, 429, 464
Times-Mirror Company, 542
Times of London, 212, 241, 545
Timothy
   Elizabeth, 38
   Lewis, 38
   Peter, 38
Tisch, Lawrence, 546
Topeka (Ks.) *Capital*, 301
Towne, Benjamin, 90, 133
   and Declaration of Independence, 62
Trade Routes
   colonial distribution, 32, 49
Trading-with-the-Enemy Act, 346
Trail of Tears, 166
Transportation
   after Civil War, 235
   and communication, 340
   colonial link to communication, 15
Transradio Press, 418
Treason Act, 345
Treaties of Amity and Commerce, 79
Trenchard, John, 42
Tribune
   of Kokomo, Indiana, 264
Tribune and Farmer, 319
Tribune Co., 542
Trotter, William Monroe, 297
True American, 191, 192
True Detective, 311
Truman, Harry S., 413, 451, 473–475, 484, 486, 487, 490
Turner, Cyrus, 192
Turner, Ted, 544–546
Tuttle, William, 366
Twain, Mark, 314

Tweed, William March (Boss), 187, 238, 243, 259
Twenty-One, 483
Tyler, John, 143
Typographical Association of New York organized in 1831, 239

Una, 291
Uncle Tom's Cabin, 188
Underground journalism, 521, 523
Union Labor Party, 297
United Fruit, 390
United Press, 417, 419–421, 428, 431, 434, 438, 443, 446, 447, 449–452, 454, 457, 462, 463, 465, 466, 510
United Press International, 510, 514, 534, 539, 553, 555, 556
United States Information Agency, 474
U.S. News and World Report, 412, 552
"U.S. Steel Hour," 482
Universal Instructor in all Arts and Sciences: and Pennsylvania Magazine
   of Keimer, 35
Universal Negro Improvement Association, 364
Urban journalism
   in late nineteenth century, 258
USA Today, 534, 549–551

Valentino, Rudolph, 396
Van Anda, Carr, 278, 280
Van Dam, Rip, 42
Van Deerlin, Lionel, 548
Van Doren, Charles, 483
Vann, Robert L., 364
Vazquez-Rawa, Mario, 553
Verne, Jules, 268
Vietnam
   coverage of, 512–517
Village Voice, 438, 522
Villard, Henry, 206
Virginia and the Kentucky Resolutions, 1798 and 1799, 113
Virginia Gazette, 39

Wagner Labor Relations Act, 437
Walker, David, 193
Wall Street Journal, 488, 535, 539, 542, 544, 550
Walter, Cornelia, 181
War for Independence, 50, 64, 179
War of 1812, 120
War of the Worlds, 418
War Production Board, 461
Warner, Jack L., 489
Warner Brothers, 459

Index

Washington, Booker T., 295–297
Washington, George, 103, 105, 108–110
 and Constitutional Convention, 82
Washington Globe, 143
Washington Journalism Review, 523
Washington Post, 491, 502, 503, 532–539,
 542, 545, 548, 549, 551, 555
Washington Times, 423
Wasp, 115
Watergate, 531, 534–538
Watterson, Henry, 234, 245–247, 251
WEAF, 392
Weaver, Sylvester L. Jr., 483
Webb, Colonel James Watson, 135, 140,
 141, 187
Weekly Advocate, 196
Welch, John F., Jr., 544
Weller, Leman, 289
Welles, Orson, 418
Wells, H. G., 418
Wells, Robert, 69
Western Pony Express, 159
Western Union, 230, 244, 252
Westinghouse, 390–393
Westliche Post, 265, 266
Westward movement, 154
 across Appalachians, 155
 and transportation, 157
 of penny press, 172
 to Kansas, 156
 to Oregon, 155
 to Texas, 155
Weyler, Commander Valeriano, 274
Wheelman, 325
White, Stanford, 320
White, Theodore, 536
White, William Allen, 258
Whitechapel Club, 283
Wickliffe, Charles, 159
William Lloyd Garrison, 189, 191, 196, 197
Williams, George, 204
Williams, Roger, 12
Wills, Gary, 490
Wilson, Christopher, 319
Wilson, President Woodrow, 344, 345, 351,
 355–357

Winchell, Walter, 478
Wisconsin State Journal, 511
Wisner, George, 135
WJZ, 447
Wolfe, Tom, 521
Wolff, 206, 450
Woman Rebel, 294
Woman's Journal, 294
Women's Christian Temperance Union, 321
Woodhull, Victoria, 294
Woodhull and Claflin's Weekly, 294
Woodward, Bob, 534, 535, 537
Woodward, C. Vann, 229
Woodward, Helen Rosen, 384
Workingman's Advocate, 147
World War II
 censorship, 454, 456
 Code of Wartime Practices, 457
 coverage of concentration camps, 453, 454
 Division of Press Intelligence, 456
 Office of Censorship, 444, 456, 457, 461,
  468
 Office of Facts and Figures, 458, 459, 461
 Office of Government Reports, 458
 Office of the Coordinator of Information,
  458
 Office of War Information, 444, 456, 458,
  459, 461, 468
World's Press of London, 446
Wright, William, 551
Wroth, Lawrence C.
 on colonial circulation, 69
WTBS, 544

Y.M.C.A. Community Chests, 381
Yale Daily News, 426
Yankelovich, Skelly & White, 549
Yates v. United States, 463
Yellow Kid, 271
Young, Owen D., 390
Young America, 319

Zenger, Anna, 43
Zenger, John Peter, 40–46, 94
Zuckerman, Mortimer, 552
Zukor, Adolph, 396
Zworykin, Vladimir, 48